POETRY
for Students

Advisors

POETRY
for Students

**Presenting Analysis, Context, and Criticism
on Commonly Studied Poetry**

VOLUME 37

Sara Constantakis, Project Editor

Foreword by David J. Kelly

GALE
CENGAGE Learning™

Detroit • New York • San Francisco • New Haven, Conn • Waterville, Maine • London

GALE
CENGAGE Learning

Poetry for Students, Volume 37

Project Editor: Sara Constantakis

Rights Acquisition and Management: Jacqueline Flowers, Sari Gordon, Kelly Quin, Robyn Young

Composition: Evi Abou-El-Seoud

Manufacturing: Rhonda Dover

Imaging: John Watkins

Product Design: Pamela A. E. Galbreath, Jennifer Wahi

Content Conversion: Katrina Coach

Product Manager: Meggin Condino

For product information and technology assistance, contact us at
Gale Customer Support, 1-800-877-4253.
For permission to use material from this text or product,
submit all requests online at **www.cengage.com/permissions.**
Further permissions questions can be emailed to
permissionrequest@cengage.com

While every effort has been made to ensure the reliability of the information presented in this publication, Gale, a part of Cengage Learning, does not guarantee the accuracy of the data contained herein. Gale accepts no payment for listing; and inclusion in the publication of any organization, agency, institution, publication, service, or individual does not imply endorsement of the editors or publisher. Errors brought to the attention of the publisher and verified to the satisfaction of the publisher will be corrected in future editions.

Gale
27500 Drake Rd.
Farmington Hills, MI, 48331-3535

ISBN-13: 978-1-4144-6704-7
ISBN-10: 1-4144-6704-4

ISSN 1094-7019

This title is also available as an e-book.
ISBN-13: 978-1-4144-7388-8
ISBN-10: 1-4144-7388-5
Contact your Gale, a part of Cengage Learning sales representative for ordering information.

Printed in Mexico
1 2 3 4 5 6 7 15 14 13 12 11

V

Table of Contents

Just a Few Lines on a Page

I have often thought that poets have the easiest job in the world. A poem, after all, is just a few lines on a page, usually not even extending margin to margin—how long would that take to write, about five minutes? Maybe ten at the most, if you wanted it to rhyme or have a repeating meter. Why, I could start in the morning and produce a book of poetry by dinnertime. But we all know that it isn't that easy. Anyone can come up with enough words, but the poet's job is about writing the *right* ones. The right words will change lives, making people see the world somewhat differently than they saw it just a few minutes earlier. The right words can make a reader who relies on the dictionary for meanings take a greater responsibility for his or her own personal understanding. A poem that is put on the page correctly can bear any amount of analysis, probing, defining, explaining, and interrogating, and something about it will still feel new the next time you read it.

It would be fine with me if I could talk about poetry without using the word "magical," because that word is overused these days to imply "a really good time," often with a certain sweetness about it, and a lot of poetry is neither of these. But if you stop and think about magic—whether it brings to mind sorcery, witchcraft, or bunnies pulled from top hats—it always seems to involve stretching reality to produce a result greater than the sum of its parts and pulling unexpected results out of thin air. This book provides ample cases where a few simple words conjure up whole worlds. We do not actually travel to different times and different cultures, but the poems get into our minds, they find what little we know about the places they are talking about, and then they make that little bit blossom into a bouquet of someone else's life. Poets make us think we are following simple, specific events, but then they leave ideas in our heads that cannot be found on the printed page. Abracadabra.

Sometimes when you finish a poem it doesn't feel as if it has left any supernatural effect on you, like it did not have any more to say beyond the actual words that it used. This happens to everybody, but most often to inexperienced readers: regardless of what is often said about young people's infinite capacity to be amazed, you have to understand what usually does happen, and what could have happened instead, if you are going to be moved by what someone has accomplished. In those cases in which you finish a poem with a "So what?" attitude, the information provided in *Poetry for Students* comes in handy. Readers can feel assured that the poems included here actually are potent magic, not just because a few (or a hundred or ten thousand) professors of literature say they are: they're significant because they can withstand close inspection and still amaze the very same people who have just finished taking them apart and seeing how they work. Turn them inside out, and they will still be able to come alive, again and again. *Poetry for Students* gives readers of any age good practice in feeling the ways poems relate to both the reality of the time and place the poet lived in and the reality of our emotions. Practice is just another word for being a student. The information given here helps you understand the way to read poetry; what to look for, what to expect.

With all of this in mind, I really don't think I would actually like to have a poet's job at all. There are too many skills involved, including precision, honesty, taste, courage, linguistics, passion, compassion, and the ability to keep all sorts of people entertained at once. And that is just what they do with one hand, while the other hand pulls some sort of trick that most of us will never fully understand. I can't even pack all that I need for a weekend into one suitcase, so what would be my chances of stuffing so much life into a few lines? With all that *Poetry for Students* tells us about each poem, I am impressed that any poet can finish three or four poems a year. Read the inside stories of these poems, and you won't be able to approach any poem in the same way you did before.

David J. Kelly
College of Lake County

Introduction

Purpose of the Book

The purpose of *Poetry for Students* (*PfS*) is to provide readers with a guide to understanding, enjoying, and studying poems by giving them easy access to information about the work. Part of Gale's "For Students" Literature line, *PfS* is specifically designed to meet the curricular needs of high school and undergraduate college students and their teachers, as well as the interests of general readers and researchers considering specific poems. While each volume contains entries on "classic" poems frequently studied in classrooms, there are also entries containing hard-to-find information on contemporary poems, including works by multicultural, international, and women poets.

The information covered in each entry includes an introduction to the poem and the poem's author; the actual poem text (if possible); a poem summary, to help readers unravel and understand the meaning of the poem; analysis of important themes in the poem; and an explanation of important literary techniques and movements as they are demonstrated in the poem.

In addition to this material, which helps the readers analyze the poem itself, students are also provided with important information on the literary and historical background informing each work. This includes a historical context essay, a box comparing the time or place the poem was written to modern Western culture, a critical overview essay, and excerpts from critical essays on the poem. A unique feature of *PfS* is a specially commissioned critical essay on each poem, targeted toward the student reader.

To further help today's student in studying and enjoying each poem, information on audio recordings and other media adaptations is provided (if available), as well as reading suggestions for works of fiction and nonfiction on similar themes and topics. Classroom aids include ideas for research papers and lists of critical and reference sources that provide additional material on the poem.

Selection Criteria

The titles for each volume of *PfS* are selected by surveying numerous sources on notable literary works and analyzing course curricula for various schools, school districts, and states. Some of the sources surveyed include: high school and undergraduate literature anthologies and textbooks; lists of award-winners, and recommended titles, including the Young Adult Library Services Association (YALSA) list of best books for young adults.

Input solicited from our expert advisory board—consisting of educators and librarians—guides us to maintain a mix of "classic" and contemporary literary works, a mix of challenging and engaging works (including genre titles that are commonly studied) appropriate for different age levels, and a mix of international, multicultural and women authors. These advisors also consult on each volume's entry list, advising on which titles are most studied, most appropriate, and meet the broadest interests across secondary (grades 7–12) curricula and undergraduate literature studies.

How Each Entry Is Organized

Each entry, or chapter, in *PfS* focuses on one poem. Each entry heading lists the full name of the poem, the author's name, and the date of the poem's publication. The following elements are contained in each entry:

Introduction: a brief overview of the poem which provides information about its first appearance, its literary standing, any controversies surrounding the work, and major conflicts or themes within the work.

Author Biography: this section includes basic facts about the poet's life, and focuses on events and times in the author's life that inspired the poem in question.

Poem Text: when permission has been granted, the poem is reprinted, allowing for quick reference when reading the explication of the following section.

Poem Summary: a description of the major events in the poem. Summaries are broken down with subheads that indicate the lines being discussed.

Themes: a thorough overview of how the major topics, themes, and issues are addressed within the poem. Each theme discussed appears in a separate subhead.

Style: this section addresses important style elements of the poem, such as form, meter, and rhyme scheme; important literary devices used, such as imagery, foreshadowing, and symbolism; and, if applicable, genres to which the work might have belonged, such as Gothicism or Romanticism. Literary terms are explained within the entry, but can also be found in the Glossary.

Historical Context: this section outlines the social, political, and cultural climate in which the author lived and the poem was created. This section may include descriptions of related historical events, pertinent aspects of daily life in the culture, and the artistic and literary sensibilities of the time in which the work was written. If the poem is a historical work, information regarding the time in which the poem is set is also included. Each section is broken down with helpful subheads.

Critical Overview: this section provides background on the critical reputation of the poem, including bannings or any other public controversies surrounding the work. For older works, this section includes a history of how the poem was first received and how perceptions of it may have changed over the years; for more recent poems, direct quotes from early reviews may also be included.

Criticism: an essay commissioned by *PfS* which specifically deals with the poem and is written specifically for the student audience, as well as excerpts from previously published criticism on the work (if available).

Sources: an alphabetical list of critical material quoted in the entry, with full bibliographical information.

Further Reading: an alphabetical list of other critical sources which may prove useful for the student. Includes full bibliographical information and a brief annotation.

Suggested Search Terms: a list of search terms and phrases to jumpstart students' further information seeking. Terms include not just titles and author names but also terms and topics related to the historical and literary context of the works.

In addition, each entry contains the following highlighted sections, set apart from the main text as sidebars:

Media Adaptations: if available, a list of audio recordings as well as any film or television adaptations of the poem, including source information.

Topics for Further Study: a list of potential study questions or research topics dealing with the poem. This section includes questions related to other disciplines the student may be studying, such as American history, world history, science, math, government, business, geography, economics, psychology, etc.

Compare & Contrast: an "at-a-glance" comparison of the cultural and historical differences between the author's time and culture and late twentieth century or early twenty-first century Western culture. This box includes pertinent parallels between the major scientific, political, and cultural movements of the time or place the poem was written, the time or place the poem was set (if a historical work), and modern Western culture. Works written after 1990 may not have this box.

What Do I Read Next?: a list of works that might give a reader points of entry into a classic work (e.g., YA or multicultural titles) and/ or complement the featured poem or serve as a contrast to it. This includes works by the same author and others, works from various genres, YA works, and works from various cultures and eras.

Other Features

PfS includes "Just a Few Lines on a Page," a foreword by David J. Kelly, an adjunct professor of English, College of Lake County, Illinois. This essay provides a straightforward, unpretentious explanation of why poetry should be marveled at and how *PfS* can help teachers show students how to enrich their own reading experiences.

A Cumulative Author/Title Index lists the authors and titles covered in each volume of the *PfS* series.

A Cumulative Nationality/Ethnicity Index breaks down the authors and titles covered in each volume of the *PfS* series by nationality and ethnicity.

A Subject/Theme Index, specific to each volume, provides easy reference for users who may be studying a particular subject or theme rather than a single work. Significant subjects from events to broad themes are included.

A Cumulative Index of First Lines (beginning in Vol. 10) provides easy reference for users who may be familiar with the first line of a poem but may not remember the actual title.

A Cumulative Index of Last Lines (beginning in Vol. 10) provides easy reference for users who may be familiar with the last line of a poem but may not remember the actual title.

Each entry may include illustrations, including photo of the author and other graphics related to the poem.

Citing Poetry for Students

When writing papers, students who quote directly from any volume of *PfS* may use the following general forms. These examples are based on MLA style; teachers may request that students adhere to a different style, so the following examples may be adapted as needed.

When citing text from *PfS* that is not attributed to a particular author (i.e., the Themes, Style,

Historical Context sections, etc.), the following format should be used in the bibliography section:

"Angle of Geese." *Poetry for Students*. Ed. Marie Napierkowski and Mary Ruby. Vol. 2. Detroit: Gale, 1998. 8–9.

When quoting the specially commissioned essay from *PfS* (usually the first piece under the "Criticism" subhead), the following format should be used:

Velie, Alan. Critical Essay on "Angle of Geese." *Poetry for Students*. Ed. Marie Napierkowski and Mary Ruby. Vol. 2. Detroit: Gale, 1998. 7–10.

When quoting a journal or newspaper essay that is reprinted in a volume of *PfS*, the following form may be used:

Luscher, Robert M. "An Emersonian Context of Dickinson's 'The Soul Selects Her Own Society'." *ESQ: A Journal of American Renaissance* 30.2 (1984): 111–16. Excerpted and reprinted in *Poetry for Students*. Ed. Marie Napierkowski and Mary Ruby. Vol. 1. Detroit: Gale, 1998. 266–69.

When quoting material reprinted from a book that appears in a volume of *PfS*, the following form may be used:

Mootry, Maria K. "'Tell It Slant': Disguise and Discovery as Revisionist Poetic Discourse in 'The Bean Eaters'." *A Life Distilled: Gwendolyn Brooks, Her Poetry and Fiction*. Ed. Maria K. Mootry and Gary Smith. Urbana: University of Illinois Press, 1987. 177–80, 191. Excerpted and reprinted in *Poetry for Students*. Ed. Marie Napierkowski and Mary Ruby. Vol. 2. Detroit: Gale, 1998. 22–24.

We Welcome Your Suggestions

The editorial staff of *Poetry for Students* welcomes your comments and ideas. Readers who wish to suggest poems to appear in future volumes, or who have other suggestions, are cordially invited to contact the editor. You may contact the editor via E-mail at: **ForStudentsEditors@cengage.com.** Or write to the editor at:

Editor, *Poetry for Students*
Gale
27500 Drake Road
Farmington Hills, MI 48331-3535

Literary Chronology

1608: John Milton is born on December 9 in London, England.

c. 1652: John Milton's "When I Consider" (Sonnet XIX) is written. It is published in the collection *Poems* in 1673.

1667: Jonathan Swift is born on November 30 in Dublin, Ireland.

1674: Milton dies of gout on November 8 in London, England.

1709: Jonathan Swift's "A Description of the Morning" is published in *Tatler* magazine.

1745: Jonathan Swift dies on October 19 in Dublin, Ireland.

1797: Heinrich Heine is born on December 13 in Düsseldorf (then in France).

1823: Heinrich Heine's "Lorelei" is published.

1849: Emma Lazarus is born on July 22 in New York City.

1856: Heinrich Heine dies on February 17 in Paris.

1868: Edgar Lee Masters is born on August 23 in Garnett, Kansas.

1883: Emma Lazarus's "The New Colossus" is published as an auction item.

1887: Emma Lazarus dies on November 19 in New York.

1889: Gabriela Mistral is born Lucia Goday Alcayaga on April 7 in Vicuna, Chile.

1893: Wilfred Owen is born on March 18 near Oswestry, Shropshire, England.

1915: Edgar Lee Masters's "Lucinda Matlock" is published in the collection *Spoon River Anthology*.

1916: Eve Merriam is born on July 19 in Philadelphia, Pennsylvania.

1918: Wilfred Owen dies of a gunshot wound sustained in battle on November 4 in France.

1920: Wilfred Owen's "Anthem for Doomed Youth" is published in the collection *Poems of Wilfred Owen*.

1924: Gabriela Mistral's "Fear" is published in the collection *Ternura*.

1934: Diana Chang is born in New York, New York.

1934: N. Scott Momaday is born on February 27 in Lawton, Oklahoma.

1939: Margaret Atwood is born on November 18 in Ottawa, Ontario, Canada.

1941: Robert Hass is born on March 1 in San Francisco, California.

1945: Gabriela Mistral is awarded the Nobel Prize for Literature.

1947: Yusef Komunyakaa is born James Willie Brown, Jr. on April 29 in Bogalusa, Louisiana.

1950: Edgar Lee Masters dies of pneumonia on March 5 in Melrose, Pennsylvania.

1952: Judith Ortiz Cofer is born on February 24 in Hormigueros, Puerto Rico.

1952: Rita Frances Dove is born on August 28 in Akron, Ohio.

1957: Gabriela Mistral dies in January in Rosalyn Bay, Long Island, New York.

1957: Li-Young Lee is born on August 19 in Jakarta, Indonesia.

1960: N. Scott Momaday's "A Simile" is published in *Sequoia* magazine and in *Angles of Geese and Other Poems*.

1969: N. Scott Momaday is awarded the Pulitzer Prize for *House Made of Dawn*.

1974: Diana Chang's "Most Satisfied By Snow" is published in *Asian-American Heritage: An Anthology of Prose and Poetry*.

1981: Margaret Atwood's "Mushrooms" is published in the collection *True Stories*.

1983: Eve Merriam's "Two People I Want to Be Like" is published in the collection *If Only I could Tell You: Poems for Young Lovers and Dreamers*.

1983: Rita Frances Dove's "Grape Sherbet" is published in the collection *Museum*.

1986: Li-Young Lee's "The Gift" is published in the collection *Rose*.

1987: Rita Frances Dove is awarded the Pulitzer Prize for Poetry for *Thomas and Beulah*.

1988: Yusef Komunyakaa's "Camouflaging the Chimera" is published in the collection *Dien Cai Dau*.

1992: Eve Merriam dies of complications from cancer on April 11 in New York, New York.

1992: Judith Ortiz Cofer's "The Latin Deli: An Ars Poetica" is published in *Americas Review*.

1994: Yusef Komunyakaa is awarded the Pulitzer Prize for Poetry for *Neon Vernacular: New and Selected Poems*.

2000: Margaret Atwood receives a Booker Prize for *The Blind Assassin*.

2007: Robert Hass is awarded the Pulitzer Prize for Poetry for *Time and Materials: Poems 1997–2005*.

2007: Robert Hass's "World as Will and Representation" is published in *Time and Materials: Poems 1997–2005*.

2009: Diana Chang dies on February 19 in Water Mill, New York.

Acknowledgments

The editors wish to thank the copyright holders of the excerpted criticism included in this volume and the permissions managers of many book and magazine publishing companies for assisting us in securing reproduction rights. We are also grateful to the staffs of the Detroit Public Library, the Library of Congress, the University of Detroit Mercy Library, Wayne State University Purdy/ Kresge Library Complex, and the University of Michigan Libraries for making their resources available to us. Following is a list of the copyright holders who have granted us permission to reproduce material in this volume of *PfS*. Every effort has been made to trace copyright, but if omissions have been made, please let us know.

COPYRIGHTED EXCERPTS IN *PfS*, VOLUME 37, WERE REPRODUCED FROM THE FOLLOWING PERIODICALS:

American Literature, v. 73, 2001. Copyright© 2001, Duke University Press. All rights reserved. Used by permission of the publisher.—*Boundary 2: An International Journal of Literature and Culture*, v. 31, summer, 2004; v. 33, summer, 2006. Copyright © 2004, 2006, Duke University Press. All rights reserved. Both used by permission of the publisher.—*Callaloo: A Journal of African Diaspora Arts and Letters*, winter, 1986; v. 29, summer, 2006. Copyright © 1986, 2006 by The Johns Hopkins University Press. Both reproduced by permission.—*Children's Literature Association Quarterly*, v. 5, winter, 1981. © 1981 Children's Literature Association. Reproduced by permission. —*College Literature*, v. 30, fall, 2003. Copyright © 2003 by West Chester University. Reproduced by permission.—*ELH*, v. 41, spring, 1974. Copyright © 1974 by The Johns Hopkins University Press. Reproduced by permission.—*Essays on Canadian Writing*, summer, 1981. Copyright © 1981 Essays on Canadian Writing Ltd. Reproduced by permission.—*Genre*, v. 39, spring, 2006 for "'Unburying the Dead': Defining a Poetics of Trauma in Yusef Komunyakaa's Poetry of Vietnam and the American South" by Daniel Cross Turner. Copyright © 2006 by the University of Oklahoma. Reproduced by permission of *Genre*, the University of Oklahoma and the author.—*German Quarterly*, v. 53, January, 1980. Copyright © 1980 by the American Association of Teachers of German. Reproduced by permission.—*Harvard Review*, v. 34, June, 2008. Copyright © 2008 *Harvard Review*. Reproduced by permission.—*Iowa Review*, v. 30, winter, 2000-2001 for "Native American Visual Autobiography: Figuring Place, Subjectivity, and History" by Hertha D. Sweet Wong. Reproduced by permission of the author.—*Journal of Negro History*, v. 85, summer, 2000. Copyright © 2000 Association for the Study of African American Life and History, Inc. Reproduced by permission.—*Kenyon Review*, v. 12, fall, 1990 for "An Abundance of Lack: The Fullness of Desire in the Poetry of Robert Hass" by Bruce Bond. Reproduced by permission of the author.—*MELUS*, v. 7, winter, 1980; v. 20, winter, 1995; v. 21, spring, 1996;

v. 22, 1997 Copyright *MELUS: The Society for the Study of Multi-Ethnic Literature of the United States*, 1980, 1995, 1996, 1997. All reproduced by permission.—*Modern Fiction Studies*, v. 38, fall, 1992. Copyright © 1992 by Purdue Research Foundation, West Lafayette, IN 47907. All rights reserved. Reproduced by permission of The Johns Hopkins University. Reproduced by permission.—*Modern Language Review*, v. 87, April, 1992. Copyright © Modern Humanities Research Association 1992. Reproduced by permission of the publisher.—*Mosaic*, v. 37, March, 2004. Copyright © *Mosaic* 2004. Acknowledgment of previous publication is herewith made.—*Notes and Queries*, v. 56, September 1, 2009 for "'A Drawing Down of Blinds': Wilfred Owen's Punning Conclusion to 'Anthem for Doomed Youth'" by Bryan Rivers. Copyright © 2009 Oxford University Press. Reproduced by permission of the publisher and the author.—*Papers on Language & Literature: A Journal for Scholars and Critics of Language and Literature*, v. 8, summer, 1972. Copyright © 1972 by The Board of Trustees, Southern Illinois University at Edwardsville. Reproduced by permission.—*Parnassus: Poetry in Review*, v. 31, 2009 for "Heine and the Composers" by Daniel Albright. Copyright © 2009 Poetry in Review Foundation, NY. Reproduced by permission of the publisher and the author.—*Prooftexts: A Journal of Jewish Literary History*, v. 20, autumn, 2000. Copyright © 2000 Indiana University Press. Reproduced by permission.—*Southern Review*, v. 16, January, 1978 for "The Art and Importance of N. Scott Momaday" by Roger Dickinson-Brown. Reproduced by permission of the author.—*Studies in Short Fiction*, v. 31, summer, 1994. Copyright © 1994 by Studies in Short Fiction. Reproduced by permission.—*Studies in the Literary Imagination*, v. 17, spring, 1984; v. 37, spring, 2004. Copyright © 1984, 2004 Department of English, Georgia State University. Reproduced by permission.—*Studies in the Literary Imagination*, v. 37, spring, 2004. Copyright © 2004 Department of English, Georgia State University. Reproduced by permission.—*UNESCO Courier*, November, 1989. Copyright © 1989 UNESCO. Reproduced by permission.—*Women's Studies*, v. 7, 1980. © 1980 Gordon and Breach, Science Publishers, Inc. Reproduced by permission of Taylor & Francis Group, LLC, http://www.taylorandfrancis.com.—*World Literature Today*, v. 67, summer, 1993. Copyright © 1993 by *World Literature Today*. Reproduced by permission of the publisher.

COPYRIGHTED EXCERPTS IN *PfS*, VOLUME 37, WERE REPRODUCED FROM THE FOLLOWING BOOKS:

Dove, Rita. From *Museum: Poems by Rita Dove*. Carnegie Mellon University Press, 1992. Copyright © 1983 by Rita Dove. All rights reserved. Reproduced by permission of the author.—Heine, Heinrich. From *The Complete Poems of Heinrich Heine: A Modern English Version*. Translated by Hal Draper. Suhrkamp/Insel, 1982. Copyright © 1982 by Hal Draper. All rights reserved. Reproduced by permission.—Honnighausen, Lothar. From "Margaret Atwood's Poetry: 1966-1995," in *Margaret Atwood: Works & Impact*. Edited by Reingard M. Nischik. Camden House, 2000. Copyright © 2000 the Contributors. All rights reserved. Reproduced by permission.—Komunyakaa, Yusef. From *Dien Cai Dau*. Wesleyan University Press, 1988. Copyright © 1988. All rights reserved. Reproduced by permission.—Lazarus, Emma. From "The New Colossus," in *Emma Lazarus: Selected Poems*. Edited by John Hollander. The Library of America, 2005. Introduction, volume compilation, and notes copyright © 2005 by Literary Classics of the United States, Inc. All rights reserved. Reproduced by permission.—Masters, Edgar Lee. From *Spoon River Anthology*. Dover Publications, Inc., 1992. Copyright © 1992 by Dover Publications, Inc. Reproduced by permission.—Merriam, Eve. From "Eve Merriam," in *The Ageless Spirit: Reflections on Living Life to the Fullest in Midlife and the Years Beyond*. Second Edition. Edited by Connie Goldman. Fairview Press, 2004. First edition © 1992 by Phillip L. Berman and Connie Goldman. Reproduced by permission.—Mistral, Gabriela. From *Selected Poems of Gabriela Mistral*. Translated by Ursula K. Le Guin. University of New Mexico Press, 2003. Introduction and English translation © 2003 by Ursula K. Le Guin. Foreword © 2003 by The University of New Mexico Press. Reproduced by permission.—Owen, Wilfred. From "Anthem for Doomed Youth," in *The Collected Poems of Wilfred Owen*. Edited by C. Day Lewis. New Direction Books, 1963. Copyright © 1963 Chatto & Windus Ltd, 1963. Reproduced by permission of New Directions Publishing Corp.—Righelato, Pat. From *Understanding Rita Dove*. University of South Carolina Press, 2006. Copyright © 2006 University of South Carolina. Reproduced by permission.—Swift, Jonathan. From "A Description of the Morning," in *Swift: Poetical Works*.

Edited by Herbert Davis. Oxford University Press, 1967. Copyright © Oxford University Press 1967. Reproduced by permission of Oxford University Press.—Young, Bette Roth. From *Emma Lazarus in Her World: Life and Letters*. Jewish Publication Society, 1995. Copyright © 1995 Bette Roth Young. All rights reserved. Reproduced by permission.

Contributors

Bryan Aubrey: Aubrey holds a Ph.D. in English. Entries on "A Description of the Morning" and "A Simile." Original essays on "A Description of the Morning" and "A Simile."

Jennifer Bussey: Bussey is an independent writer specializing in literature. Entry on "Grape Sherbet." Original essay on "Grape Sherbet."

Catherine Dominic: Dominic is a novelist and a freelance writer and editor. Entries on "Most Satisfied by Snow" and "Two People I Want to Be Like." Original essays on "Most Satisfied by Snow" and "Two People I Want to Be Like."

Charlotte Freeman: Freeman is a freelance writer and former academic who lives in Montana. Entry on "The World as Will and Representation." Original essay on "The World as Will and Representation."

Joyce Hart: Hart is a published author and teacher of creative writing. Entry on "The New Colossus." Original essay on "The New Colossus."

Michael Allen Holmes: Holmes is a writer and editor. Entry on "Camouflaging the Chimera." Original essay on "Camouflaging the Chimera."

Sheri Karmiol: Karmiol teaches literature and drama at the University of New Mexico, where she is a lecturer in the University Honors Program. Entry on "When I Consider (Sonnet XIX)." Original essay on "When I Consider (Sonnet XIX)."

David Kelly: Kelly is a writer who teaches creative writing and literature at several community colleges in Illinois. Entries on "Fear," "The Gift," and "Lucinda Matlock." Original essays on "Fear," "The Gift," and "Lucinda Matlock."

Carl Mowery: Mowery has a doctorate in literature and composition from Southern Illinois University. Original essay on "Fear."

Michael J. O'Neal: O'Neal holds a Ph.D. in English. Entry on "Anthem for Doomed Youth." Original essay on "Anthem for Doomed Youth."

Wendy Perkins: Perkins is an associate professor of English at Prince George's Community College in Maryland. Entry on "The Latin Deli." Original essay on "The Latin Deli."

Rachel Porter: Porter is a freelance writer and editor who holds a bachelor of arts in English literature. Entry on "Mushrooms." Original essay on "Mushrooms."

Chris Semansky: Semansky teaches literature and writing at Portland Community College and is a widely published poet, fiction writer, and critic. Original essay on "The Latin Deli."

Bradley A. Skeen: Skeen is a classicist. Entry on "The Lorelei." Original essay on "The Lorelei."

Anthem for Doomed Youth

"Anthem for Doomed Youth" is a poem by the British poet Wilfred Owen, generally regarded as one of Great Britain's finest World War I poets. The poem was first published in 1920 in the collection *Poems of Wilfred Owen*, edited by Siegfried Sassoon, another World War I poet whose work and personal guidance greatly influenced Owen. The poem was written in 1917 while Owen was a patient at the Craiglockhart War Hospital near Edinburgh, Scotland. Owen was a soldier during World War I (1914–1918), and in 1917 he was hospitalized for "shell shock," a common psychological affliction during the war; today shell shock is called combat stress reaction and is marked by fatigue, disorientation, confusion, loss of memory, and similar symptoms.

Many writers of Owen's generation went off to war with high ideals, believing that they were playing their part in protecting their nation from Germany. The war, however, dragged on, with little progress. New, more destructive weapons were being used, and both sides were mired down in trench warfare on the western front. The number of casualties was high, and soldiers had to fight not only the enemy but dirt, rats, disease, flooded trenches, mud, and the ongoing psychological trauma caused by incessant shelling. Many artists came away from the experience highly disillusioned by the war's carnage and futility. The poetry they wrote in response to their war experiences

WILFRED OWEN

1920

Wilfred Owen with a young boy, possibly his son
(© Hulton-Deutsch Collection / Corbis)

captured that sense of futility and disillusionment. "Anthem for Doomed Youth," written in the form of a sonnet, is generally regarded as being among Owen's best poems.

AUTHOR BIOGRAPHY

Owen was born on March 18, 1893, near the town of Oswestry in Shropshire, England, the oldest of Thomas and Susan Owen's four children. His early life was comfortable, for he and his family lived in a home owned by Owen's grandfather. In 1897, however, the grandfather died, forcing the family to move to lodgings in the town of Birkenhead on England's western coast. He attended the Birkenhead Institute and the Shrewsbury Technical School, but when he was about ten years old, during a vacation in Cheshire, he concluded that his true vocation was writing poetry. He read many poets of the romantic period, including William Wordsworth, Samuel Taylor Coleridge, and particularly Percy Bysshe Shelley and John Keats. He was raised as a devout Anglican, and the Christian Bible was also a major literary influence.

Owen left school in 1911. He passed the entrance examination for the University of London, but he did not score high enough to earn a scholarship, which was the only way he could have attended. Accordingly, he took a position as a lay assistant for the vicar of Dunsden near the city of Reading. He also worked as a teacher at the Wyle Cop School. He was able to attend some classes at University College, Reading (now the University of Reading), where he studied botany and took lessons in Old English. During this period he became disillusioned with the Anglican Church, growing to believe that it placed too much emphasis on ceremony and not enough on helping people in need. Just before World War I began, he taught English and French at the Berlitz School of Languages in Bordeaux, France.

The war began in 1914. On October 21, 1915, Owen enlisted in the Artists' Rifles Officers' Training Corps, and for several months he trained at the Hare Hall Camp in Essex, England. On June 4, 1916, he was commissioned as a second lieutenant in the Manchester Regiment, and in December 1916, he was posted to France with the Lancaster Fusiliers. Like many members of his generation, he marched off to war with much optimism, but soon his attitude about the war would change. In one incident he was blown into the air by a mortar and landed on the remains of a fellow officer. In another incident he was trapped for several days in a German dugout. He was diagnosed with shell shock and in June 1917 was admitted to the Craiglockhart War Hospital in Edinburgh. At Craiglockhart he edited a literary magazine called the *Hydra* and met Sassoon, an encounter that would change the remainder of his short life. Sassoon, along with Owen's doctor, encouraged him to translate his wartime experiences into poetry. Owen's verses became grimmer and more realistic, and they began to reflect the influence of Freudian psychology rather than the romantic themes of poets such as Shelley and Keats.

After his release from the hospital, Owen returned to military service in November 1917. During his stay in the hospital and in the months that followed, he wrote many of the poems for which he is famous. Sassoon introduced him to a literary circle that included such writers as Robert Graves and C. K. Scott-Moncrieff. Owen could have remained on duty in England but, after Sassoon was injured in a friendly fire incident, felt that it was his duty return to the front, take his hero's place, and continue to write poetry about the war.

He returned to the front in the summer of 1918 and led an assault on a number of enemy entrenchments near the French village of Joncourt. On November 4, 1918, just one week before the war ended (almost to the hour), he was shot and killed while attempting to cross the Sambre-Oise Canal in northern France during one of the last Allied victories of the war. Ironically, his mother was given the telegram informing her of her son's death on Armistice Day, November 11, 1918, while listening to celebratory bells ringing throughout the city. On July 30, 1919, he was posthumously awarded the Military Cross for his bravery at Joncourt.

POEM TEXT

What passing-bells for these who die as cattle?
Only the monstrous anger of the guns.
Only the stuttering rifles' rapid rattle
Can patter out their hasty orisons.
No mockeries now for them; no prayers nor
    bells,   5
Nor any voice of mourning save the choirs,—
The shrill, demented choirs of wailing shells;
And bugles calling for them from sad shires.

What candles may be held to speed them all?
Not in the hands of boys, but in their eyes   10
Shall shine the holy glimmers of good-byes.
The pallor of girls' brows shall be their pall;
Their flowers the tenderness of patient minds,
And each slow dusk a drawing-down of blinds.

POEM SUMMARY

Lines 1–4
The title of the poem announces its principal theme. The poem is an *anthem*, which is a hymn or sacred song, typically written in praise of someone or something. The poem's title does not say *a* doomed youth but simply doomed youth. The poem, then, is not an anthem to a particular person but to youth in general. The word *youth* can be taken in two ways. One is to refer to young people, in this case young men who have gone off to war. The other is to refer to the quality of youthfulness. Thus, not only are young men doomed; their youthfulness, innocence, idealism, and perhaps naïveté is seen as doomed as well.

"Anthem for Doomed Youth" is written in the form of a sonnet. Like all sonnets it consists of fourteen lines. Different varieties of the sonnet form have different structures and employ

MEDIA ADAPTATIONS

- In 1962 composer Benjamin Britten included nine of Owen's poems in *War Requiem*, a choral/orchestral work that was commissioned for the reconsecration of Coventry Cathedral in England.

- In 1988 Derek Jaman produced a screen adaptation of *War Requiem* for Anglo International Films and the British Broadcasting Corporation.

- In 1982 Owen's poem "Futility" was set to music by the Ravishing Beauties and can be downloaded at http://www.divshare.com/download/2700503-8ca.

- In 1982 "Anthem for Doomed Youth" was set to music by 10,000 Maniacs. It was included in the album *Human Conflict Number Five* and later in the compilation *Hope Chest*. It can be downloaded at http://www.last.fm/music/10%2C000+Maniacs/Human+Conflict+Number+Five/Anthem+for+Doomed+Youth.

- Owen was the subject of a 2007 British Broadcasting Corporation docudrama titled *Wilfred Owen: A Remembrance Tale*. Owen is played by Samuel Barnett.

different rhyme schemes, but one form begins with eight lines called an octave. The octave in turn consists of two four-line units called quatrains. The poem begins with a question: in a deliberately incomplete sentence the poet asks about the bells that ring for the young men who die as cattle. The reference to passing-bells suggests the ringing of bells during a procession as mourners walk to the cemetery during a funeral. The use of the word *cattle* suggests that the casualties of war are not individuals with homes, families, hopes, and a future but rather indistinguishable animals sent off to slaughter. Continuing with the theme of a funeral, the poet states that the only prayers, or orisons, being said for the young men are the anger of the guns and the rattle of rifles. The noise of battle—the stuttering of rifles, the sound of gunfire, the rattling of weapon fire—replaces the solemn prayers and bell ringing of a funeral. This language makes it clear that the poet is setting his anthem not after the deaths of the soldiers, perhaps in a church, but on the battlefield itself.

Lines 5–8

The second quatrain continues the religious imagery of the first quatrain, although by using the word *mockeries*, the poet suggests that the usual religious observances surrounding the death of young men in war are insincere, inappropriate, or false. There are no prayers or bells. Nor is there any voice of mourning. On the battlefield, the only observance of death is the choirs of shells that wail, just as a mourner might wail in grief at a funeral. The choirs are described as shrill, thus continuing the imagery of sound begun in the first quatrain. Furthermore, the choirs are described as demented or insane. In this way the poet suggests the insanity of the war as he experienced it.

In the final line of the second quatrain, Owen makes reference to bugles, instruments that historically were used to send commands up and down military lines but also to establish a martial theme at a military funeral. The poet says that these bugles call to the men in battle from sad shires. This phrase has a dual meaning. On the one hand it can suggest home; the implication is that young men from the shires of England are being called to their homes. On the other hand, the sad shires can be read as the place to which the young men are being called through their deaths. The reference to shires, with their farms and grazing land, ties the lines back to the first line of the poem with its reference to cattle.

Lines 9–12

If the first eight lines of the poem rely primarily on the imagery of sound, the final six lines of the poem, called the sestet, rely on visual imagery. Again, the poet begins with a question, asking about the candles that may be held to lead the dead on their way. The reference to candles again suggests a funeral procession or perhaps the candles that would be lit in a church during a funeral, but the horror of the war and its carnage do not allow for light. Rather, the emphasis is on darkness. The candles are not held in the hands of mere boys who have gone to war but rather will exist in the eyes of the dead, where the glimmer of good-byes will be seen. The glimmer is described as holy, continuing the theme of a religious observance.

The quatrain concludes with a further visual image: that of the paleness of girls' brows, which is described as a pall. The word *pall* can be read in two ways. Sometimes the word is used to refer to anything that produces an effect of gloom, such as smoke. The reader is then invited to imagine the smoke that covers a battlefield. The primary meaning, though, is that of a cloth that is draped over a coffin or a body, but the battlefield dead will not be covered with palls as they would at a conventional church funeral. Only the pallor of death covers them.

Lines 13 and 14

The poem concludes with a couplet (two rhymed lines). The previous quatrain, though, ends with a semicolon, so the final two lines are to be read as a continuation of the thought begun in the preceding lines. At a conventional funeral there would be flowers. However, just as the battlefield dead will not be covered with a pall, there will not be flowers for them. The only flowers will be the tenderness shown by patient minds, likely a reference to the dead soldiers' loved ones back home, who will endure the deaths of sons, brothers, and husbands with patience.

Alternatively, the reference to patient minds could be to the young men themselves, who quietly and heroically endure their fates. The poem's final line refers to dusk, that is, the time when the day darkens and fades away. The dusk is said to be slow, and although certainly many men die abruptly on a battlefield, Owen envisions them leaving this world slowly, perhaps suggesting that being a soldier in wartime constitutes a kind of slow death. The poem concludes with a final visual image, that of the blinds being pulled down over the windows in a home. Just as there are no candles lighting the way to death but rather only the glimmer of good-byes, so death is seen as a drawing down of blinds as the night approaches. The blinds in this case would be the soldiers' eyelids, which close as the men die. The poet benefits from the dual meaning of the word *blinds*. On the one hand the word denotes the shades that cover a window. On the other it suggests blindness, seen here as an indicator of death.

THEMES

Disillusionment

Clearly, the major theme of "Anthem for Doomed Youth" is disillusionment, specifically with war. When war was declared in August 1914, the Allied

TOPICS FOR FURTHER STUDY

- Conduct research on World War I—its causes, the combatant nations, and the conduct of the war, with emphasis on the trench warfare along the western front. Prepare an animated timeline of the key events of World War I that indicates how those events might have affected the life of Wilfred Owen and other poets and artists of the era. Use poetry readings, sound, and visuals to enhance the impact of the events.

- What steps did the nations of the world try to take to prevent another war after World War I? Investigate such developments as the Treaty of Versailles, the establishment of the League of Nations (the precursor of today's United Nations), and various disarmament agreements such as the Kellogg-Briand Pact of 1928. Prepare a table of these developments that includes their aims and whether or not they were effective.

- Scott Westerfeld's *Leviathan* is a young-adult novel that imagines an alternative World War I reality. In the novel, the two central characters, who are enemies, encounter one another. Compare this novel with Owen's vision of the war. Prepare a brief essay in which you imagine how Owen might have reacted to Westerfeld's novel.

- World War I is often described as the first modern war. Conduct research into how this war differed from earlier wars. In particular, what role did technology play in the conduct of the war? What new weapons were used? From your investigations, prepare a slide show or similar computerized presentation with visuals of the war and the way it was conducted. Post your slide show on your blog, social networking site, or other appropriate place.

- Investigate the life and work of another World War I poet or writer. Possibilities include Siegfried Sassoon, Rupert Brooke, W. H. Auden, and Robert Graves. Prepare an oral and visual report about the writer and how his work reflects themes similar to those found in "Anthem for Doomed Youth."

- During World War I, roughly 380,000 African Americans served in the U.S. military. Some 200,000 of those were sent to Europe. Conduct research on African American participation in the war, including the heroic efforts of the 369th Infantry Division in France. Write a brief essay on the exploits of this division and how African Americans contributed to the war effort. Post your essay on your Web log and invite comments about the service of minority groups in various wars.

nations, consisting principally of England, France, and Russia, took up arms against the Central Powers, consisting primarily of Germany, the Ottoman Empire, and Austria-Hungary. Among the Allied powers, Germany and its allies were regarded as the clear aggressors in the war, for Germany's ruler, Kaiser Wilhelm, coveted an empire that would rival the empires of France and England. Although few people wanted to see war break out, when it did, the people of England supported the war with enthusiasm. In an atmosphere of patriotism, flags, parades, and marching bands, young men throughout the nation enlisted to fight. Those who chose not to enlist were often criticized publicly as cowards. Thus, young men such as Wilfred Owen faced an enormous amount of pressure to enlist in the armed forces.

The war, though, was conducted badly. All along the western front in France, trenches were dug by both sides. These trenches were the staging points for assaults on the enemy. Companies of soldiers would go "over the top" into muddy, devastated areas referred to as "no-man's land." Machine gunners from the other side would mow

World War I soldier *(Losevsky Pavel / Shutterstock.com)*

the assaulting troops down. Canisters of poison gas, usually mustard gas or chlorine gas, were launched at enemy troops. Shelling and bombardment were a constant. In the face of mud, disease, rats, and heavy casualties, many soldiers became disillusioned with the war. What began as adventure and patriotic duty quickly turned into horror.

Innocence

Closely related to the theme of disillusionment with the war is the theme of loss of innocence. The poem's title calls attention to the fact that the war was fought by primarily young men. These men had been motivated by a sense of patriotic duty and perhaps a sense of adventure. Many of the men from England who fought in the war were born and raised in rural areas, the shires referred to in the poem. Many of these men had never traveled anywhere, even within their native country. Suddenly, the war presented the opportunity for them to see another part of the world and to interact with people from all over the nation and the world. Given England's military successes in

the past, the size of its navy, and the extent of its empire, men enlisted in the military believing that England would easily prevail on the battlefield. This naïve view was quickly dispelled.

It is often argued that prior to World War I, Great Britain was perhaps smug and self-satisfied. The people of Great Britain and its rulers believed that England was the world's greatest, most benevolent, most prosperous nation, one obligated to export its way of life and Christian values to other peoples. World War I created a seismic shift in attitude. Although Great Britain was on the side of the victorious Allies, the devastation of the war created a new, more sober attitude, one reflected in "Anthem for Doomed Youth."

STYLE

Alliteration and Assonance

Owen frequently relies on alliteration (the repetition of initial consonants) in his poetry. "Anthem for Doomed Youth" is no exception. Examples include the repeated *r* sound and the repeated *p* sound. The *d* and *g* sounds are also repeated. In addition to alliteration, Owen frequently employs assonance (the repetition of vowel sounds). The most noteworthy example of assonance in "Anthem for Doomed Youth" is the repeated use of the long *i* sound.

Sonnet

"Anthem for Doomed Youth" is written in the form of a sonnet, a word that comes from the Italian word for tune or song. The sonnet form originated in Italy in about the fourteenth century. One of its most prominent early practitioners was the Italian poet Petrarch. Later, in the sixteenth century, the form was imported to England, where William Shakespeare used the form in a sequence of sonnets.

All sonnets consist of fourteen lines. However, two different types of sonnets emerged. The first, called the Petrarchan sonnet, consists of two parts: an octave (eight lines), followed by a sestet (six lines). The octave, usually with a rhyme scheme *abbaabba*, asks a question, poses a problem, or creates an emotional tension. The sestet answers the question, solves the problem, or resolves the emotional tension. Various rhyme schemes are used in the sestet, but a common one is *cdecde*.

The English sonnet, sometimes called the Shakespearean sonnet, is structured differently. Instead of an octave and a sestet, it consists of three quatrains (four-line stanzas). Typically, the rhyme scheme of the Shakespearean sonnet is *abab cdcd efef*. The poem concludes with a couplet (a pair of lines) with the rhyme *gg*. The first twelve lines develop a theme, which is resolved in some way in the final couplet.

"Anthem for Doomed Youth" combines the Petrarchan and Shakespearean forms. Like the Petrarchan sonnet, it is divided into an octave and a sestet, but like the Shakespearean form, the first four lines of the sestet continue the rhyme pattern of the octave, and the final two lines are a rhymed couplet. While Owen combines the two forms, the overall structure is more Petrarchan than Shakespearean, for the octave develops an emotional situation that is resolved in the sestet.

Imagery

"Anthem for Doomed Youth" relies on two types of images. In the octave, the principal images are those of sound. Numerous words contribute to this imagery, including the sounds of guns, bells, choirs, and bugles. In the sestet, the principal images are those of sight. This pattern is reinforced by references to candles, glimmering, shining, pallor, and dusk.

Elegy

While "Anthem for Doomed Youth" is in the form of a sonnet, in type the poem is an elegy. An elegy is a poem that expresses sorrow for one who has died. Usually, elegies are suffused with melancholy and lament. The elegy dates back to classical Greece and Rome. Sometimes elegies are written to mourn the passing of a particular person. Other elegies are written to lament death in general and include reflections on what has been lost to the world. One particular type of elegy is the pastoral elegy. This is a highly conventional form that represents its subject in an idealized country setting. Typically, it includes a description of a funeral procession, a description of the mourning of those left behind, and general reflections on death. Although "Anthem for Doomed Youth" is not strictly speaking a pastoral elegy, it contains elements of the pastoral form through its use of references to the countryside (cattle and shires), allusions to funeral processions and the trappings of funerals, and its general atmosphere of melancholy.

HISTORICAL CONTEXT

World War I

The roots of World War I extended back to at least 1908 and a series of crises in the Balkan region of eastern Europe. That year Austria annexed Bosnia, a move that angered Serbia, which since the nineteenth century had tried to create a unified, independent Slavic nation made up of Serbians, Bosnians, Croats, and Slovenes in the Balkan Peninsula. This state would be independent of Russia, which dominated the Serbs and the Bosnians, and of the Austro-Hungarian Empire, which dominated the Slovenes and the Croats. Austria saw Serbia as an enemy that was trying to claim parts of Austria's already crumbling empire. Although the Serbs were allies of Russia, Russia had been weakened by war with Japan in 1905 and could do little more than protest the annexation of Bosnia. A second crisis occurred in 1912–1913, when war broke out in the Balkans. When the war ended, Austria-Hungary, together with other European powers, backed the formation of an independent Albania that would prevent the Serbs from gaining access to the Adriatic Sea—again frustrating Serbian nationalism. Once more, Russia could do little more than protest.

By 1914 Europe was a powder keg of secretive alliances, fears, and suspicions. The match that ignited the powder keg that would become World War I was lit on June 28, 1914, when Gavrilo Princip, a young Bosnian Serb revolutionary and a member of a secret society called Union or Death, or the Black Hand, assassinated Archduke Francis Ferdinand, heir to the throne of Austria-Hungary, on the streets of the Bosnian capital city of Sarajevo. Due to the entangling alliance system, by August, all of Europe was at war.

Austria wanted to put an end to Slavic agitation on its southern border, and with the support of its major ally, Germany, Austria issued an ultimatum to Serbia, demanding that it investigate the assassination and punish those responsible. Serbia counted on support from Russia. Russia, in turn, counted on the support of France, which had strong ties with Russia because it had long feared having to fight a war against the larger and more heavily industrialized Germany. France, desperate to keep Russia as an ally, supported Russia in its response to the crisis.

Serbia rejected Austrian demands, so Austria declared war on Serbia. Russia prepared to defend Serbia and expected that Germany would

COMPARE
&
CONTRAST

- **1917:** Warfare is conducted in a conventional fashion, with large armies and navies, battle fronts, and heavy use of artillery, hand grenades, machine guns, and rifles.

  Today: Warfare tends to be unconventional with reliance on small, mobile, quick-strike forces, computerized self-guided weapons, satellite imagery, and air cover to locate, disrupt, and attack the enemy.

- **1917:** European nations are engaged in the process of empire building, with colonies in Africa, the Middle East, and Asia. Alliances and military forces are used to protect those colonies and the sea routes that connected them to the European countries and to extend the nation's influence in other parts of the world.

  Today: For the most part, the nations of Europe have relinquished their colonies, and nations they formerly controlled in Africa, the Middle East, and Asia have gained their independence.

- **1917:** Combatants in World War I use biological and chemical weapons, particularly poison gases such as mustard gas and chlorine gas. Germany first uses poison gas in 1915, and the Allies follows suit soon after. As many as one hundred thousand deaths result from gas attacks throughout the war, and many soldiers who survive gas attacks are blinded or horribly disfigured.

  Today: Largely in response to World War I, most of the world's nations have signed treaties banning the use of chemical and biological weapons, although many advanced nations continue to conduct research in such weapons, largely to find treatments and antidotes in case another nation uses them.

- **1917:** Although some poetry is experimental, much poetry continues to rely on traditional forms such as the sonnet, with lines of regular length, stanzas, rhyme, and similar traditional poetic devices.

  Today: Poets rely less on traditional forms, rhyme schemes, stanzaic arrangements, and the like; although some poets occasionally use traditional forms, most of their work is free verse.

---

join the fight, so Russia massed troops on the German border. On August 1, 1914, Germany declared war on Russia. Because Germany believed that France would support Russia, it also declared war on France two days later. Meanwhile, Great Britain, like France, feared a growing and increasingly militarized Germany. Germany believed that Great Britain would remain neutral, but when Germany invaded Belgium on its way into France, England had no choice but to declare war on Germany on August 4.

World War I lasted for just over four years, at a terrible cost. Ten million men were killed, and another twenty million were wounded. The stalemate ended after Russia withdrew from the war and the United States declared war on Germany in April 1917. American troops fought for only about four months in 1918, but they were enough to tip the balance in favor of the Allies against Germany and Austria-Hungary. On November 12, 1918, the day after the war ended, the last Austrian emperor, Charles I, abdicated. On November 13 Austria proclaimed itself a republic, and a week later Hungary did the same. The Treaty of Versailles, signed in 1919 to formally end the war, imposed ruinous financial reparations on Germany, devastating its economy. The result was political instability in Germany, which sowed the seeds that led to Nazism, Adolf Hitler's rise to power, and the outbreak of World War II a mere twenty years later.

Imperialism and Colonialism
Closely related to the conditions that fomented World War I was the issue of imperialism and

World War I cemetery *(Chrislofoto / Shutterstock.com)*

colonialism. During the nineteenth and early-twentieth centuries, the nations of Europe vied for supremacy in other parts of the world. In many instances their motives were economic: colonies provided cheap and reliable sources of raw materials and labor, as well as markets for goods made in the home countries. In some instances, the colonial powers were motivated by the belief that it was their obligation to civilize and bring Christianity to the peoples of Africa, the Middle East, and Asia. Whatever the motivations, the fact is that the Europeans formed and maintained empires, and this desire for territorial expansion played a role in the outbreak of World War I.

One of the major colonial powers was Great Britain. For a century preceding World War I, Britain had expanded its empire and controlled some ten million square miles of territory and some four hundred million people. Its chief colony was India. At the same time, Germany, France, and Belgium joined in the so-called "Scramble for Africa," forming colonies on that continent. To the east, the Russian and Ottoman (Turkish) empires expanded with the acquisition of neighboring territories. These empires, along with those

maintained by Great Britain, attempted to fill the power vacuum created by the collapse of the Persian Empire and the weakening of China. In sum, a state of intense competition existed among the European nations. This competition led to the formation of armies and the development of weapons of war, particularly navies. In such an atmosphere of suspicion and distrust, World War I was almost inevitable.

CRITICAL OVERVIEW

Enthusiasm for Owen's poetry grew slowly. Owen published only a handful of his poems during his lifetime, and they were published in outlets that few people were likely to see. World War I was so horrifying that many people wanted to simply forget it, so Owen's poetry, as well as that of other war poets, was in some sense forgotten in the years after the war. One of Owen's earliest supporters was Siegfried Sassoon, a poet who advised Owen during their time together at the Craiglockhart War Hospital and who edited and published an edition of Owen's poems in 1920.

In *Wilfred Owen*, Jon Stallworthy quotes Sassoon's praise for Owen's "sumptuous epithets and large-scale imagery, its noble naturalness and the depth of meaning." Writing specifically about "Anthem for Doomed Youth," Sassoon adds, "This new sonnet was a revelation.... It confronted me with classic and imaginative serenity." Another early critic, Edmund Blunden, in "Memoir," reprinted in C. Day Lewis's *The Collected Poems of Wilfred Owen*, calls Owen "an unwearied worker in the laboratory of word, rhythm, and music of language." Blunden also refers to Owen's "innate, unconventional command over language, and [his] rich and living vocabulary," concluding that Owen had a "genius for poetry." Lewis, who edited the collection of poems, says that Owen's "imaginative sympathy was high and constant" and concludes that Owen's poems were the "finest written by any English poet of the World War I and probably the greatest poems about war in our literature."

It was not until the 1960s and 1970s that critics more generally began to revisit Owen's poetry and come to recognize him as one of the great war poets. Dennis Welland, in *Wilfred Owen: A Critical Study*, praises Owen's poems for the "vividness of their presentation of the actuality of trench warfare" and finds the poems "deeply moving in the eloquent directness of their sincerity of feeling and honesty of expression." Owen's growing reputation has allowed critics such as Andrew Himes, in *Voices in Wartime Anthology*, to state: "Now [Owen is] regarded, by far and away, as the greatest of the First World War poets."

While many critics have had high praise for Owen's poetry, some have been ambivalent. For example, in *Taking It like a Man*, Adrian Caesar states that "Owen was comforted by the thought that his poems were speaking for the inarticulate soldiery." Caesar also comments that Owen

> has a love-hate relationship with the war and this ambivalence extends to every facet of his response. On the one hand he wished to "educate" the home-front as to the horrors of trench warfare, but on the other he consistently portrayed the home-front as incapable of learning. And the horrors of trench warfare had an undeniable fascination for him.

The implication of Caesar's remarks is that Owen's purpose and poetic vision are slightly muddled and inconsistent. Dominic Hibberd, in *Wilfred Owen*, finds a similar lack of clarity, explaining that

> "Anthem" is one of Owen's most famous war poems but it does not represent his final thoughts about war. As for the sonnet form, it was too strict and conventional a frame for his swiftly developing ideas; it had long been his favourite, but after "Anthem" it was largely abandoned in favour of more varied and flexible shapes.

Although Owen is widely regarded as among the leading World War I poets, some prominent critics have dismissed his work. In *Out of Battle: The Poetry of the Great War*, Jon Silkin, in reference to "Anthem for Doomed Youth," refers to the "weakness of the poem" and quotes Peter Dale, who said that the poem "sets up memory as an equalizer of the suffering on the field and in the home and makes some sort of compensation out of it." A harsher critic was Craig Raine, quoted in Tim Kendall's *Modern English War Poetry*, who wrote: "Wilfred Owen's tiny corpus is perhaps the most overrated poetry in the twentieth century." Kendall also quotes poet Philip Larkin, who wrote that "the temporal accidents of [Owen's] lifetime ... make independent critical assessment so difficult." Larkin's point is that readers feel sympathy for the suffering that Owen underwent, but that suffering does not necessarily result in good poetry. Finally, Kendall quotes Donald Davie, who dismissed Owen's poetry as "incompetent." Davie, like Larkin, was examining the poetry as poetry, and while he acknowledged that readers can sympathize with the ordeals of war that Owen examined, from a strictly technical and aesthetic perspective, the poems, in Davie's view, are a failure.

CRITICISM

Michael J. O'Neal

O'Neal holds a Ph.D. in English. In the following essay, he examines how Owen's revisions of "Anthem for Doomed Youth" improved the poem.

Readers who pick up the text of a literary work assume they are reading the final version of the work as the author intended it. A published literary work generally goes through a lengthy process of writing and rewriting, editing by the publisher, copyediting, and proofreading. At each stage of the process, the author is at hand to make and approve changes, leading to the final form of the work. While this assumption is likely true for

WHAT DO I READ NEXT?

- The classic novel about the horrors and futility of World War I is Erich Maria Remarque's *All Quiet on the Western Front*. Remarque was a German veteran who first published the novel in a newspaper in 1928. The novel was published in book form in 1929 and sold more than two and a half million copies in eighteen months.

- *The Guns of August* by Barbara W. Tuchman stands as one of the finest histories of the conflict that became World War I. It is widely available, including in a 2004 Presidio Press illustrated, paperback edition.

- An important incident in the history of World War I is the genocide committed against Christian Armenians in Turkey in 1915. Adam Bagdasarian's *Forgotten Fire* (2000) tells the story of the genocide from the perspective of a twelve-year-old Armenian boy.

- The classic American novel about World War I is Ernest Hemingway's *A Farewell to Arms*, published in 1929. On the surface the novel is a love story, told from the perspec-

tive of a young lieutenant who falls in love with a nurse. More fundamentally, the novel is about the tragedy of war and the cynicism of soldiers.

- Modern-day reflections on warfare can be found in *Voices from Wartime Anthology*, published by Andrew Himes in 2005. Items in the anthology include poems by Iraqi poets Ali Habash ("Rockets Destroying a Happy Family") and Sinan Antoon ("Wrinkles on the Wind's Forehead"). A perspective on the war in Vietnam is provided by Nguyen Duy in "The Honey Comes from Within."

- Siegfried Sassoon was a mentor to and influence on Owen. Some of his poems have been gathered in the *The War Poems of Siegfried Sassoon* in a 2010 paperback edition.

- Margaret Rostkowski's *After the Dancing Days* (1986) is a young-adult novel that tells the story of a young girl in Kansas who befriends a wounded World War I veteran to help mourn the loss of her favorite uncle who was killed in France.

---

modern, published literature, it is a dubious assumption for literature from a former era, particularly if the work was not published during the author's lifetime. Shakespeare, for example, creates numerous problems for modern textual editors. None of Shakespeare's manuscripts survive, and Shakespeare himself did not supervise the publication of any of his plays. Among the versions that do exist, passages are often garbled; words seem to be left out, and so on. Thus, publishing an edition of a play by Shakespeare involves some educated guesswork on the part of the editor. A considerable amount of scholarly publication is devoted to discussion about what the text of the play should actually say.

Editors face similar problems when confronted with the work of Wilfred Owen. Owen published only a handful of poems during his

lifetime, and they were published in outlets that few readers were likely to see. The rest remain in manuscript form, complete with cross-outs and changes. Some of the poems contain alterations made by Siegfried Sassoon. Making matters more difficult for the textual editor is that many of the poems exist in several versions, each version different from the others in major and minor ways.

"Anthem for Doomed Youth" is no exception. It is known that Owen began writing the poem in 1917, probably in about September. At this time he was a patient at the Craiglockhart War Hospital. There he met the poet Siegfried Sassoon, and Sassoon edited some of his poetry, including "Anthem for Doomed Youth." The poem went through several revisions with the result that four drafts of it are today housed at the British Museum, two drafts were in the

> BECAUSE OWEN NEVER PUBLISHED THE
> POEM HIMSELF, IT IS DIFFICULT TO KNOW WHICH, IF
> ANY, OF THESE VERSIONS HE PREFERRED, WHICH
> CHANGES HE MIGHT HAVE UNDONE, AND WHETHER
> HE CONSIDERED THE POEM TO BE FINISHED."

possession of Owen's brother Harold, and one draft was in the possession of his cousin Leslie Gunston. The version of the poem most often reprinted is the one arrived at by Edmund Blunden in a 1931 edition of the poems. Blunden was faced with the need to gather all the known versions of the poem, compare them, and make judgments about a version of the poem that Owen would likely have approved. Because Owen never published the poem himself, it is difficult to know which, if any, of these versions he preferred, which changes he might have undone, and whether he considered the poem to be finished. The modern reader is left to speculate.

One result of these numerous drafts is that the reader can compare them to gain a sense of the poet's processes and the development of his artistry. Presumably, the changes Owen made to the poem in successive drafts improved it, at least in his estimation. In making these changes, Owen was able to sharpen the poem's imagery, reinforce his theme, improve the poem's imagery of sound, and in general impose greater unity on what started out as a mere draft. By tracing the nature of the changes Owen made, readers can better appreciate the poem's artistry and gain insight into the kinds of effects that Owen wanted to achieve.

One example is the poem's title. In its final form, the title of the poem refers to doomed youth. In earlier drafts of the poem, though, Owen used the phrase "dead youth," but Sassoon suggested the change in the title. The revision makes the title more effective for two reasons. One is that it suggests that the men killed in the war had no choice; their fate was sealed from the moment they left England. The revision further suggests that the war was a futile exercise, that the men were not fighting for a noble ideal but were being thrown onto killing fields with no real hope of survival and no real hope of achieving some worthwhile end. In this way the theme of the poem is strengthened. The other way in which the revised title is more effective is that the two words together employ assonance (repeated vowels sounds). Thus, "doomed" is more poetic than the simple "dead."

In a similar vein, in the first line Owen uses the pronoun "these," but in earlier drafts he used the word "you." He made a similar change in line 4, changing "your" to the word "their." These changes seem minor, but in making them Owen made the poem in some sense less personal and therefore more general. The use of words like "you" suggest that the poem is addressed to a particular youth or group of youths. By making the change, Owen is not addressing particular soldiers but soldiers in general, and again, this underlines the theme of the poem, that all of the men who fought in the war were doomed to take part in an exercise in futility.

Other revisions contribute to the poem's artistry. In line 8 Owen originally had the flat phrase "across the shires." By changing the line to its current form, he emphasized the melancholy of the poem and its theme while at the same time introducing an alliterative element through the repeated *s* sound. He also experimented with the phrasing involving cattle in line 1. In one earlier draft he used the expression "those who die in herds," which he later revised to "dumb-dying cattle." The first is flat; it has a prosaic quality. The second version seems labored, as though the poet was trying to hard to introduce an alliterative phrase. Through continued tinkering he arrived at the best expression, one that successfully compares soldiers to cattle going off to slaughter.

Similarly, in line 7, with its reference to the shrillness of demented choirs, he originally had the phrase "long-drawn sighs." Again, the original was flat and not particularly original. A long-drawn sigh could refer to any type of passing emotion that prompts a person to sigh. The revision sharpens the theme of the poem by emphasizing the insanity of the war while strengthening the auditory imagery of the poem's octave. The octave is now more unified with its pattern of references to sound: bells, rattle, patter, choirs, bugles, and shrillness. This type of auditory imagery is particularly appropriate in a poem that is called an anthem, itself a reference to sound.

One expression that was troublesome to Owen was the epithet concerning patient minds in line 13. In early drafts he tried numerous

The last line of the poem mentions "a drawing-down of blinds." *(djgis | Shutterstock.com)*

expressions, including "martial minds," "silent minds," and "rough men's minds." The earlier versions were weak; he seemed to have tried the words simply because they had the right number of syllables, although it should be noted that some versions of the poem preserve "silent minds," probably because the expression was Owen's rather than the revision suggested by Sassoon. The alternate version of the phrase, though, sharpens the sense of the line by suggesting that the only possible response to the futility and death of the war is quiet endurance. Further, the change continues the alliteration of the "p" sound from line 12, which in turn provides a poetic link with the "p" sound found in lines 1, 4, and 5. The result is to give the poem greater unity.

These are some of the major revisions Owen made to "Anthem for Doomed Youth." They show the poet in the process of artistic creation, kneading and molding his words to clarify his

theme and increase the artistry of his poem. They also show the artist in collaboration with another artist, for some of the changes Owen made were suggested by Sassoon. The result is a poem that evolved from a first, rather inartistic and vague draft into one of the great poems of the World War I era.

Source: Michael O'Neal, Critical Essay on "Anthem for Doomed Youth," in *Poetry for Students*, Gale, Cengage Learning, 2011.

Bryan Rivers

In the following essay, Rivers examines Owen's motives behind the last lines of "Anthem for Doomed Youth."

Wilfred Owen's poem, 'Anthem for Doomed Youth,' ends with the poignant lines:

> The pallor of girls' brows shall be their pall;
> Their flowers the tenderness of patient minds,
> And each slow dusk a drawing-down of blinds.

OWEN, IT APPEARS, STRUCK JUST THE
RIGHT BALANCE BETWEEN POIGNANCY AND
SOCIAL REALISM IN THE LAST LINE OF
HIS FAMOUS POEM."

When the poem was first published, in 1920, its concluding image of dusk as a 'drawing-down of blinds' was particularly evocative as it alluded to the common British practice of drawing window blinds to indicate that a household was in mourning. During the First World War, because British regiments were recruited locally, this custom often had a strong visual impact when a regiment suffered severe casualties and entire communities were consequently affected. In London, for example, after a major battle in France, almost all the houses on some streets had the blinds drawn; there was little traffic, none of the habitual conversing on street corners and, out of respect for grieving families, no loud or unnecessary noise. A reverential silence would fall over localized areas of the normally bustling metropolis. Owen, it appears, struck just the right balance between poignancy and social realism in the last line of his famous poem.

The measured, elegiac tone of 'Anthem for Doomed Youth' seems, initially, to distinguish the poem from Owen's more sardonic pieces; a perfect illustration of his statement, found in the draft Preface to his unpublished verses, that: 'The Poetry is in the pity.' However, there are strong secondary meanings to the poem's last line, derived from alternative meanings of the word 'blind,' which link 'Anthem for Doomed Youth' more closely with Owen's opposition to the war and European militarism.

The *Oxford English Dictionary (OED)* gives an alternative meaning of 'blind,' derived from specialized military terminology, as: 'a screen or other structure used in fortification, sieges, etc., to protect from the enemy's firing.' Although the *OED* gives 1802 as the latest known usage, from *James' Military Dictionary*, the term was still current at the end of the nineteenth century. For example, the 1895 edition of *Farrow's Military Encyclopedia* explains the term 'Blindage' as follows: 'When a trench has to be pushed forward in a position where the command of the dangerous

point is so great that it cannot be sheltered from the plunging fire by traverses, it is covered on the top and on the sides by fascines and earth supported by a framework, and is termed a *blindage*.' A generation later, the term was still current in British military textbooks used during the First World War. Thus, in *Notes for Infantry Officers on Trench Warfare. Compiled by the General Staff*, which Owen received as standard issue, one finds an illustration indicating how a 'shell trench' may be 'blinded if material is available.'

A related but more specialized military application of 'blind,' as a verb, in the sense of to conceal and to protect artillery pieces from enemy fire, is also found in the *OED*; thus: 'to provide with blindages' is cited in connection with 'guns blinded with iron mantelets.' In 1895 Farrow defined 'blinds' as: 'Shutters of an embrasure; they are musket-proof, and at a siege, at the discretion of the Officer Commanding the Artillery, are made up by the Engineer Department from materials available on the spot.' The same entry describes how, during the Crimean War, coils of rope were used 'in addition to the ordinary blind, to protect the gunners from the fire of riflemen when laying the gun.' By the First World War, high-velocity sniping rifles, aerial photography, bombs and long range artillery made the use of concealing, protective 'blinds' even more imperative.

At some point, in military parlance, the sense of 'blind' as concealment was combined with the popular, general usage of the word 'blind,' defined by the *OED* as: 'a corner or other feature where the road or course ahead is concealed from view.' For example, the Introduction to *Diagrams of Field Defenses*, another handbook issued to officers by the General Staff during the First World War, stipulates that: 'The *trace*, or pattern on the ground, of trenches may be laid out in various ways, but the general line must not be too straight . . . in order to prevent the enemy from enfilading the trenches should he get into them.' For this reason it was stipulated that 'communication,' 'fire,' and 'traffic' trenches should never intersect at right angles, or proceed for more than thirty feet in a straight line. Thus, to 'blind' a trench meant to construct it with an irregular, zigzag or continuously curving trace, or to intersect with another trench in such a way as to prevent enemy troops from firing directly along, or easily occupying, long stretches of the trench. This usage is found in *Notes for Infantry Officers*, where a section devoted to the protection of machine gun emplacements states that: 'In order to insure invisibility, all communication trenches leading to the emplacements must be constructed as blinded saps.' The same publication includes illustrations indicating how the zigzag trace of a communication trench allows it to be 'blinded continuously' to prevent enfilading enemy fire. There are also two captions, accompanying illustrations on how to construct trenches to defend the raised edges of mine craters, which call for a 'blinded entrance when possible.' Farrow provides yet another military meaning of 'blind' in the term 'blind shells' which are: 'shells which do not explode on impact, or at the time it is intended they should.'

One should not be surprised to find echoes of military terminology in Owen's war poems since, as Douglas Kerr has ably demonstrated, 'the army's language challenged, changed and became part of the language of the poet.' These alternative meanings of 'blind,' all derived from specialized military vocabulary current during the First World War, cleverly enable the last line of the poem to be read, in a secondary sense, as expressing a hope that a collective national mourning will result in a 'drawing down,' or physical dismantling, of the extensive system of 'blinds' or trench fortifications, concealed artillery and unexploded munitions which had caused the deaths of so many young men. For Owen, it is the grief of the nation, not military victory on foreign soil, which will lead to genuine, lasting demilitarization.

A further meaning of 'blind' is derived from the more common figurative sense of: 'any thing or action intended to conceal one's real design; a pretence, a pretext.' In this regard, one can potentially trace the influence of Siegfried Sassoon on Owen's thoughts regarding the continued prosecution of the war. The two met at Craiglockhart hospital, in August 1917, and Owen wrote 'Anthem for Doomed Youth' between September and October of that year. Sassoon later described how, in October 1917, the two men met in his private room 'almost every evening' to discuss poetry and the conduct of the war and how, during that period: 'we vowed our confederacy to unmask the ugly face of Mars and—in the words of Thomas Hardy—"war's apology wholly stultify."'

In Sassoon's famous letter protesting the continuation of the war, which was read in the House of Commons on 30 July 1917, and reported in the *Times* the next day, Sassoon wrote: '*I am not protesting against the conduct of the War, but against the political errors and insincerities for which the fighting men are being sacrificed. On behalf of those who are suffering now I make this protest against the deception which is being practised on them.*' In his 'rough notes' for the first draft of the letter he was more blunt, claiming that '*Fighting men are victims of conspiracy among (a) politicians; (b) military caste; (c) people who are making money out of the War,*' and that he wishes to '*destroy the system of deception, etc., which prevents people from facing the truth.*' Sassoon's references to '*insincerities,*' '*the deception which is being practiced*' on British troops, '*conspiracy*' and '*the system of deception,*' anticipated by just a few weeks Owen's punning protest against the 'blinds,' or deceptions, which will hopefully suffer a figurative demolition or 'drawing-down' at the hands of those who survive the carnage of the war. For Owen, collective national grief over the casualties suffered during the conflict will produce a more sceptical, questioning, and informed populace no longer easily manipulated by the lies and deceptions, or 'blinds,' perpetrated by government and military authorities.

Sassoon's letter, and Owen's poem, were written for different audiences, and intended for different arenas, but their goals were identical: to protest against the continuation of the war. Owen's punning on the word 'blinds' infused the conclusion of 'Anthem for Doomed Youth' with a rich interplay of complementary meanings, reinforcing the poem's innate poignancy with a strong vein of political protest which would not have been lost on its original audience, many of whom would have been familiar with the military jargon of the trenches, when his poems were posthumously published, with Sassoon's help, in 1920.

Source: Bryan Rivers, "A Drawing Down of Blinds: Wilfred Owen's Punning Conclusion to 'Anthem for Doomed Youth,'" in *Notes and Queries*, Vol. 56, No. 3, September 1, 2009, pp. 409–11.

Douglas Kerr

In the following excerpt, Kerr explains how Owen's war experience influenced his poetry.

...After his enlistment the bodily consciousness of Owen's poems becomes more substantial. In his early work the human body had been largely constituted of pale skin, lips, cheeks, hands, hair, and eyes. But with his changed way of life (and perhaps, too, the example of the heartier Georgian poets) the represented body evolves, developing muscles, teeth, back and thighs, and a tanned skin. It is not at all a paradox that the disciplines of army life, as John Brophy remembered, gave soldiers 'a renewed zest in animal pleasures,' and Brophy finds this physicality

"THE POET, LIKE THE SOLDIER, KNEW WHAT
HE WAS DOING IN ACCEPTING THE DISCIPLINES
OF THE WARS."

inscribed in army slang itself, for 'the exhilaration which most men felt in the hardening of their bodies and the sharpening of their physical faculties is clearly to be traced in the imagery, the onomatopoeia and the sensuous fidelity of many of these words [of soldiers' slang].' Owen greatly enjoyed the circumstances of physical activity shared with large numbers of fit young men, and the homo-eroticism already present in his pre-war poetry looked for and found worthy (and as it were legitimate) subjects in the army. In June 1918 at Scarborough he cast a veteran's eye on a new draft of conscripts, 'awful specimens, almost green-pale, another Race altogether from the mahogany swashbucklers who have finished their training' (*CL*). It could be added that the well-trained body was the dearer for the danger that awaited it. 'Training,' a strange poem written in the same month (June 1918) apparently after a cross-country run (*CL*), seems narcissistically enthralled by the beauty of the body preparing for sacrifice.

... The army sought to discipline speech as it disciplined the body, and in the event these constraints which the army imposed on language were much to the benefit of Owen's writing. His experience of the army does seem to have coincided with a tightening-up of style. Discipline and precision, the army virtues, had never been among Owen's desiderata for poetry: he did not even much like to find these things in discourse where they might more commonly be supposed to belong, confessing in 1914 that 'I am only conscious of any satisfaction in Scientific Reading or Thinking when it rounds off into a poetical generality and vagueness' (*CL*). Music and feeling are what the early poems are after—'De la musique avant toute chose'—and these were commodities which writers of an aesthetic tendency liked to wrap in the tasteful or suggestive blur that enraged Ezra Pound. When the army became available to Owen as a literary subject it gave his writing a field

of material observation and at the same time a new quality of terseness, where before he had tended to luxuriance. The effect is not so much a metamorphosis as a widening of stylistic range.

> One dawn, our wire patrol
> Carried him. This time, Death had not missed.
> We could do nothing but wipe his bleeding cough.
> Could it be accident?—Rifles go off . . .
> Not sniped? No. (Later they found the English ball.)
> ('S.I.W.')

Subject-matter aside, this kind of movement would have been inconceivable in a pre-1916 Owen poem. This is a new accent, economical of feeling and not concerned with music, the voice of that military pronoun. (And you may search for hours through the manuals for a first-person singular.) Owen learned to vary pace and accent by moving between this spare and functional language and the foliate romanticism he had from his earlier reading. 'Insensibility' refuses music and feeling through five increasingly tense stanzas, to release them in a great wash at the end of the sixth. The interlocutor in 'Strange Meeting' moves in the other direction, when the romantic autobiography ('I went hunting wild / After the wildest beauty in the world') reaches an unadorned conclusion in the matter-of-fact 'I am the enemy you killed, my friend.'

The army had little time for personal difference: much of its special language is encoded in speech genres in fixed ritual form, the least favourable conditions for reflecting individuality in language. There was no room for variation or elaboration, for example, in the standard military command, an entirely automated utterance. 'All the activity of the disciplined individual,' says Foucault, 'must be punctuated and sustained by injunctions whose efficacy rests on brevity and clarity; the order does not need to be explained or formulated; it must trigger off the required behaviour and that is enough.' Individual variation among a very severely restricted range of parameters was possible in the Field Service Postcard (Army Form A2042), on which nothing could be written except the date and the signature of the sender, whose message was composed by deleting options appropriately.

> I am quite well.
> I have been admitted into hospital.
> Sick and am going on well.
> {
> Wounded and hope to be discharged soon.
> I am being sent down to the base.

And so on. It was an interesting challenge, and there were others. The army's bureaucracy produced an endless supply of forms for officers to complete. With the Reserve Battalion in Scarborough in 1918, Owen was familiar with the duties of the Subaltern of the Day, illustrated (in Captain Hood's *Duties for All Ranks*) in a specimen report.

> *Form of Report*
> I inspected rations yesterday, and saw them weighed and issued. They were of . . . quality.
> I visited the breakfasts and found them . . .
> The men were . . . properly dressed. There were . . . complaints.
> I inspected all the guards coming off duty and found them . . .
> I visited the soldiers-in-arrest in the Detention Room and found them . . .

And so on. The *pro forma* accountability of bureaucratic utterances like this could be brought face to face with the language of a quite different code, with a different idea of what responsibility might mean. It is one of Owen's most studied discursive confrontations.

> For 14 hours yesterday I was at work—teaching Christ to lift his cross by numbers, and how to adjust his crown; and not to imagine he thirst till after the last halt; I attended his supper to see that there were no complaints; and inspected his feet to see that they should be worthy of the nails. I see to it that he is dumb and stands to attention before his accusers. With a piece of silver I buy him every day, and with maps I make him familiar with the topography of Golgotha. (*CL*)

. . . Owen's lyrical compassion has power because he can command this brisk and dispassionate voice too. It can be the voice of the villains of his war poetry, satirized and condemned for their callousness, but it is also the voice of the soldier at work, for without the disciplines the work could not be done, and, so long as the work was to be done, personal feeling might have to be deferred, the only allowable elegy an automatic gesture. In October 1918 he told Sassoon that his battalion had been in the fighting and suffered serious losses, including 'the boy by my side, shot through the head, [who] lay on top of me, soaking my shoulder, for half an hour,' and he continued: 'I shall feel again as soon as I dare, but now I must not. I don't take the cigarette out of my mouth when I write Deceased over their letters' (*CL*).

'Insensibility,' a concourse where so many of Owen's concerns meet, explores these matters of the mental discipline of the wars. It invokes for its own grim purposes the classic formula of beatitude and pastoral idyll.

. . . Vigny's ambiguous advice had borne a strange fruit. The war did not make Owen a poet, but it made him a particular kind of poet. In giving him a subject, it also decisively formed his style by making available to his repertoire a discourse—disciplined, concrete, masculine, impersonal—at odds with the qualities he had previously thought of and cultivated as poetic, qualities of the upper-case Poetry with which, he said, he was not concerned now. Army language did enrich Owen's poetry (as army experience widened its range) by interrupting it with an unfamiliar and unromantic way of speaking, seeing, and judging. This new voice, the voice of his working life in his last three years, challenged the softer and more lyrical voice in Owen though it did not drown it: they speak to each other.

The army made Owen a modern poet. In an eerie way, the army itself was a modernist in its language, and belongs in company or relationship with contemporary modernizers: Yeats who wanted his writing to be more masculine, Pound cultivating an exact spareness, Lewis and T. E. Hulme variously dismantling individualism to expose the inhuman, Eliot setting a rigorous training programme in tradition and disciplined impersonality for the recruit to poetry, and all these perhaps in their distance from what might be called the civilian public or nation at home. But while the army taught Owen the uses (the necessity, sometimes) of a new toughness, an 'insensibility,' a curb on personal feelings, it also showed him how (as some modernist writing was soon to demonstrate) these things could breed monsters of indifference and authoritarian brutality; these perils, too, became his subjects. The poet, like the soldier, knew what he was doing in accepting the disciplines of the wars.

Source: Douglas Kerr, "The Disciplines of the Wars: Army Training and the Language of Wilfred Owen," in *Modern Language Review*, Vol. 87, No. 2, April 1992, pp. 286–99.

SOURCES

Blunden, Edmund, "Introduction," in *The Collected Poems of Wilfred Owen*, edited by C. Day Lewis, New Directions, 1963, pp. 11, 169.

Caesar, Adrian, *Taking It like a Man: Suffering, Sexuality and the War Poets*, Manchester University Press, 1993, pp. 150, 160.

Hibberd, Dominic, *Wilfred Owen*, Longman Group, 1975, p. 25.

————, *Wilfred Owen: A New Biography*, Ivan R. Dee, 2003, p. 270.

Himes, Andrew, *Voices in Wartime Anthology*, Whit Press, 2005, p. 170.

Kendall, Tim, *Modern English War Poetry*, Oxford University Press, 2006, pp. 46, 47.

Lewis, C. Day, ed., *The Collected Poems of Wilfred Owen*, New Directions, 1963, p. 28.

Owen, Wilfred, "Anthem for Doomed Youth," in *The Collected Poems of Wilfred Owen*, edited by C. Day Lewis, New Directions, 1963, p. 44.

Silkin, Jon, *Out of Battle: The Poetry of the Great War*, Oxford University Press, 1972, p. 211.

Stallworthy, John, *Wilfred Owen*, Oxford University Press, 1974, pp. 221, 222.

Welland, Dennis, *Wilfred Owen: A Critical Study*, rev. ed., Chatto & Windus, 1978, p. 73.

The volume contains personal letters, song lyrics, poems, posters, and similar documents from World War I. Introductory essays define each primary source document and its context and suggest strategies for analyzing and evaluating it.

Reilly, Catherine, ed., *Scars upon My Heart: Women's Poetry and Verse of the First World War*, Virago UK, 2006.

This collection of poetry reminds readers of the suffering of women as well as men during the World War I. It shows that women were writing antiwar poetry before Wilfred Owen and Siegfried Sassoon did and that the common view that women at home were idealistic and ignorant of war's realities was false. These poems grow out of the direct experiences of nursing the victims of trench warfare or losing sons, brothers, and lovers.

Stokesbury, James L., *A Short History of World War I*, Harper Paperbacks, 1981.

This history of World War I is written for young adults. It examines the international context of the war, the major battles, and the role of modern technology in the conflict in an easy-to-understand format.

FURTHER READING

Carlisle, Rodney P., *World War I*, Facts on File, 2007.

This volume from the "Eyewitness History" series was written for young adults. It explores the social, cultural, military, and political impacts of World War I on American society. It discusses the war as a catalyst for World War II, the cold war, and current events. It highlights the war's historical connections to such topics as terrorism, the influence of technology on warfare, and weapons of mass destruction. It provides numerous firsthand accounts from diaries, letters, speeches, and newspaper accounts.

Coetzee, Frans, and Marilyn Shevin-Coetzee, *World War I: A History in Documents*, Oxford University Press, 2002.

SUGGESTED SEARCH TERMS

Anthem for Doomed Youth

World War I poetry

western front AND World War I

Wilfred Owen

World War I

World War I poetry

World War I poetry AND disillusionment

war poets

Wilfred Owen AND Siegfried Sassoon

Camouflaging the Chimera

YUSEF KOMUNYAKAA

1988

Some fourteen years after serving as an information specialist—that is, a military journalist—for the U.S. Army in the Vietnam War, Yusef Komunyakaa found himself inspired to write poems based on his wartime experiences. Circumstances seemed to conspire to first bring this verse to the poet's mind: he was renovating a house in New Orleans in the summer of 1984, climbing up and down a ladder while working on the twelve-foot-high ceilings, when he found himself recording in his notebook images from the war. As he would later note in an interview with William Baer for the *Kenyon Review*, "there was a kind of familiar tropic heat that day. So it was the heat, and the dust, and the dismantling of things—and that's how it happened."

Dien Cai Dau (1988), Komunyakaa's second and more significant volume of poetry about the Vietnam War, takes its title from a Vietnamese expression meaning "crazy in the head" that was used to refer to the American soldiers who fought there. In contrast to much of the Vietnam War verse penned during or soon after the war, *Dien Cai Dau* is notable for largely foregoing the raw power of graphic shock in favor of the more enduring virtues of illuminative reflection. The volume opens fittingly with "Camouflaging the Chimera," a poem that delves into the mortal tension of soldiers engulfed in nature while poised to spring an ambush. The ambush has not yet been sprung by the poem's end, such that the life-or-death tension stays with the

Yusef Komunyakaa (AP Images)

reader long after the last line has been read. This poem can also be found in the author's *Pleasure Dome: New and Collected Poems* (2001).

AUTHOR BIOGRAPHY

Komunyakaa was born as James Willie Brown, Jr., in Bogalusa, Louisiana, on April 29, 1947, the first of six children to his working-class parents. Later in life, he would change his name to adopt the surname his grandfather originally brought to America when immigrating, as a stowaway, on a ship from Trinidad. Louisiana was in the throes of segregation during Komunyakaa's youth, and he recalls the racial tension that characterized daily life, with the Ku Klux Klan a significant regional presence. Fortunately, this did not prevent him from appreciating and learning from the bucolic rural landscape that surrounded him; he later considered becoming a photographer or a painter. His father was a carpenter who made his eldest child an apprentice, and Komunyakaa learned something of artistic precision from his father's meticulous approach to carpentry. He read the Bible twice in its entirety, absorbing the import of its unique cadence, and then moved on to Edgar Allan Poe, William Shakespeare, and the Harlem Renaissance writers. After composing a hundred-line rhyming poem to commemorate his class's high school graduation in 1965, he enrolled in the U.S. Army.

Initially training to be an infantry officer, Komunyakaa sought an unlikely transfer to the information field upon realizing the great degree of danger faced by platoon leaders. He was assigned work as a journalist—he would edit the military newspaper *Southern Cross*—and found himself flown into combat situations by helicopter daily to provide coverage of operations in the field. He also wrote a column on the culture of the Vietnamese, "Viet Style," which led him to develop greater compassion for the Vietnamese people—a perspective reflected in some of his war poems. Komunyakaa earned a Bronze Star for his service. Upon returning to the United States, he enrolled at the University of Colorado, where he first studied creative writing, graduating with a bachelor of arts degree in 1975. He earned a master of arts from Colorado State University and a master of fine arts in creative writing from the University of California, Irvine, in 1980.

Komunyakaa's writing career developed quickly; he professed a habit of working on three collections at once. After two early chapbooks, he received a pair of fellowships, including one from the National Endowment for the Arts. He earned critical praise for *Copacetic* (1984), a collection with jazz stylings about his childhood, and *I Apologize for the Eyes in My Head* (1986), covering race relations, mortality, and the mysteries of life. After *Toys in a Field* (1987), a brief chapbook addressing the Vietnam War, Komunyakaa delved further into those experiences with *Dien Cai Dau* (1988). He has since published over half a dozen collections, including the Pulitzer Prize-winning *Neon Vernacular* (1993), and edited a number of anthologies. Meanwhile, he has taught at various universities, including Indiana University at Bloomington for a dozen years. As of 2010 he was teaching at New York University.

POEM TEXT

We tied branches to our helmets.
We painted our faces & rifles
with mud from a riverbank,

blades of grass hung from the pockets
of our tiger suits. We wove   5
ourselves into the terrain,
content to be a hummingbird's target.

We hugged bamboo & leaned
against a breeze off the river,
slow-dragging with ghosts   10

from Saigon to Bangkok,
with women left in doorways
reaching in from America.
We aimed at dark-hearted songbirds.

In our way station of shadows   15
rock apes tried to blow our cover,
throwing stones at the sunset. Chameleons

crawled our spines, changing from day
to night: green to gold,
gold to black. But we waited   20
till the moon touched metal,

till something almost broke
inside us. VC struggled
with the hillside, like black silk

wrestling iron through grass.   25
We weren't there. The river ran
through our bones. Small animals took refuge
against our bodies; we held our breath,

ready to spring the L-shaped
ambush, as a world revolved   30
under each man's eyelid.

POEM SUMMARY

The *chimera* of the title can be understood to refer not just to the camouflaged troops of the poem but more broadly to the entire U.S. military presence in Southeast Asia through the Vietnam War. The word has two distinct definitions that are relevant to this context. The original meaning is founded in Greek mythology, being the name of a female creature with the head of a lion, the body of a goat, and the tail of a serpent; accordingly, as defined in *Merriam-Webster's 11th Collegiate Dictionary*, the word can refer to any "imaginary monster compounded of incongruous parts," a fitting description for the sprawling, politically ambiguous, internally conflicted American military effort in Vietnam.

MEDIA ADAPTATIONS

- Komunyakaa can be heard reciting "Camouflaging the Chimera" in a recording found online at http://www.ibiblio.org/ipa/poems/komunyakaa/camouflaging_the_chimera.php in the *Internet Poetry Archive*.

In relation to the first meaning, *chimera* can also refer to "an illusion or fabrication of the mind," especially "an unrealizable dream." This connotation may align with a Vietnamese perspective on the American troops, who were mostly Caucasian, making their complexion fairly otherworldly to rural Vietnamese eyes, and who were thrust into a war that had nothing to do with them personally, as if they were merely the fabrication of U.S. politicians' minds—a dream of military success that would never be realized.

Stanzas 1–2

While lyrically deft in its presentation of imagery, "Camouflaging the Chimera" mostly presents pictures to the reader in a straightforward manner. Beyond the instances of wordplay, objects and actions are described clearly, and the reader is unlikely to be confused about the circumstances. In the first stanza, the poet at once refers to the common tools of war, linking the soldiers' headgear and firearms with the elements of nature used to disguise them. The narrator, using first-person plural pronouns, is understood to be among the soldiers who camouflaged themselves.

The second stanza completes the image of the troops by noting the grass hanging from their uniforms, which are patterned with camouflage stripes. Line 5 then leads the reader to imagine the troops weaving something, perhaps out of grass, but line 6 reveals the metaphorical use of the verb, as the camouflaged soldiers have, rather, woven themselves into the setting. They are perhaps disguised well enough to lead even hummingbirds to mistake them for plants or flowers.

Stanzas 3–4

The ensuing stanzas, throughout the poem, contribute to the reader's sense of both the soldiers' excruciating stillness and the tranquil pace of the natural world. In line 8 the soldiers embrace bamboo, vegetation characteristic of Asian locales, and are said to lean—perhaps, the reader may imagine, leaning their guns against something in a moment of respite, but line 9 has the soldiers themselves leaning against a gentle wind, as if in their fatigue, lazily swaying with the bamboo, they are held up by that wind. The *slow drag* is an informal dance step done to ragtime music (as featured in the Broadway play *Harlem*) that typically involves a couple dancing close together. Thus, the poet imagines the soldiers swaying in dance not only with ghosts from Vietnam to Thailand—perhaps the ghosts of civilian women killed through the war—but also with the images or ideas of the women they have left behind in America, who can reach the soldiers only through letters. In their idleness, the men point their weapons at birds, whose songs can perhaps only be heard as sorrowful by the homesick soldier. The birds' songs might also be heard as laments for those soon to be dead when the ambush is sprung.

Stanzas 5–6

Lines 15–17 describe how a breed of ape would threaten the soldiers' position by hurling rocks, ostensibly toward the setting sun but presumably in the vicinity of, if not directly at, the concealed regiment. The senselessness of the apes' tossing rocks at the sun suggests that there was no way the soldiers could have stopped them, especially given that their priority was concealment.

Ending stanza 5, the mention of the chameleons presents beings analogous to the soldiers in the natural world. In an image that can be characterized as surrealist, the chameleons are portrayed as crawling along the soldiers' backs while changing color in accord with the hour, turning golden at dusk and black at night. Still, the soldiers wait, until moonlight is reflected off their metallic weapons. While each of the first two pairs of stanzas ends in a period, this third pair of stanzas ends in a comma, signaling a slight increase in the flow of the text leading into the close of the poem.

Stanzas 7–9

The soldiers wait so long that an internal something—perhaps their resolve, or their confidence, or even their sanity—almost breaks. The

Vietcong (as abbreviated), the enemy, first appear in line 23, grappling with the terrain; the concealed American soldiers presumably have a view of the Vietcong's crawling approach to the point of intended ambush. Half-concealed in the grass as they would be, the Vietcong appear as little more than black garments tangling with glinting weapons. The sight of the Vietcong prompts the narrator's comment that the American troops were not there—a comment that could be the mantra of the camouflaged soldier or a reference to the Vietcong's ignorance of the Americans' concealed position.

Meanwhile, nature yet engulfs the soldiers. Some or all of them must be concealed within a river, which courses not just over their skin but through their bones, in an image that likely leaves the reader feeling chilled. Little creatures huddle against the soldiers, but still they wait, hardly daring to breathe. The clause that ends line 28 continues to the poem's end; recalling that breathless moment, the narrator's thoughts resolve first around what was surely the most essential notion then in his mind, the shape of the ambush about to be sprung, and second around the expansive notion that each silent soldier, like the narrator, was the sole witness to his own universe of thoughts, sentiments, and daydreamed images.

THEMES

Nature

The most prominent theme in "Camouflaging the Chimera" is the juxtaposition of the soldiers and their war-related objects and thoughts with the lush nature that surrounds them. Komunyakaa has noted that while growing up in rural Louisiana, he appreciated and became attuned to the pace of nature. In an interview with Toi Derricotte for *Callaloo*, he described spending time in the woods and engaging in "a kind of meditation on that landscape" that led him to see the rituals of animals and insects as reflecting the rituals of humankind. Upon arriving in Vietnam, then, as he told William Baer, he "was especially struck by the land itself, the terrain. It was such a vibrant landscape," with "vegetation everywhere." It thus comes as little surprise that nature plays such a primary role in this poem, the vanguard of his Vietnam War collection *Dien Cai Dau*.

TOPICS FOR FURTHER STUDY

- Think of a time when, whether because of or despite the environment and circumstances in which you found yourself, your body was very still and your senses were highly attuned to what was happening around you. Write a poem in the style of Komunyakaa's "Camouflaging the Chimera" that portrays the circumstances, your state of mind, and the images of this time. Record your poem using a computer presentation tool and set it to images and background music.

- Pick two other poems from *Dien Cai Dau* and write a paper comparing and contrasting them with each other and with "Camouflaging the Chimera," addressing the structures, tones, and themes of the poems. Since Komunyakaa uses recurring images in this volume, be sure to analyze similarities and differences in the poems' images and their symbolic meanings.

- Conduct online research on tourism in modern-day Vietnam, collect several attractive images of the landscape, and then create a fold-up brochure advertising travel in Vietnam, geared toward a modern American audience. Include a sensitively written

section addressing veterans of the Vietnam War who may be interested in revisiting the country, mentioning any specific accommodations for veterans that you find in your research. Compile a list of your Internet sources on the last page of the brochure.

- Read three poems about three different wars from *War and the Pity of War*, an anthology of poetry for young adults edited by Neil Philip. Write a paper comparing and contrasting these poets and poems, considering the differences between the wars and the motivations for those wars, the nationalities of the poets, and the themes and styles of the poems. Post your essay on a teacher-created blog site and encourage your classmates to comment on your poems as you comment on their poems.

- Create a multimedia presentation on the anti-Vietnam War movement, discussing resistance to the draft, demonstrations, antiwar pop music, and major events in the course of the movement, such as the infamous shootings that occurred at Kent State University in 1970.

Indeed, every stanza but the last features at least one significant image from nature: the river in stanza 1, the grass and hummingbird in stanza 2, the bamboo and breeze in stanza 3, the birds in stanza 4, the apes and sunset in stanza 5, the chameleons and moon in stanza 6, the hillside in stanza 7, and the animals in stanza 8. Only stanza 9, which zeroes in on the precise thoughts of the individual soldiers in the moments leading up to the awaited ambush, forgoes any natural image. These images provide a setting that, beyond being a background, induces constant interaction with the soldiers in a variety of ways. After smearing themselves and their weapons with the earth and grass,

the soldiers hug the bamboo and lean on the breeze, all while standing or crouching in the river water. The animals alternately oppose the soldiers, as do the apes hurling rocks, and unite with them, as do the chameleons and small creatures. Meanwhile, the soldiers and birds take turns aiming at each other. Komunyakaa effectively carries images such as these from poem to poem; the critic Thomas F. Marvin has noted in his essay "Komunyakaa's 'Facing It,'" in the *Explicator* that, beginning with this poem, "throughout *Dien Cai Dau* images of birds represent both lovers left behind and the enemy soldiers who interrupt erotic reveries with sudden violence."

Throughout the poem, and especially at the close, the proceedings of war intrude on nature. Though surrounded by wildlife, the soldiers are highly conscious of both the ghosts of Vietnam—especially, one would guess, the ghosts of those who have died in the war—and the loved ones they have left behind in America. Their rifles, ever held in their hands, become a sort of moon dial in measuring the time by reflecting the moonlight. When the Vietcong appear, the defining image intertwines their black uniforms, their iron weapons, and the grass of the hillside. By the poem's end, thoughts of nature have all but disappeared as the moment of ambush approaches.

Surrealism

The experiences of soldiers who fought in the Vietnam War, in the foreign jungles filled with unfamiliar flora and fauna and populated by an enemy whose guerilla tactics allowed them to disappear into the landscape, are often considered and portrayed in a surrealist mode (using the element of surprise or what is not expected ordinarily). Indeed, the wartime experiences were so strange—and often shocking and horrifying—that it can be very difficult for the reader who has only known peace to imagine them in a realist mindset. Komunyakaa himself noted, in speaking with Baer, that his poetry "was informed by classical surrealism" and the "surrealist/dadaist poets." Furthermore, when asked by Baer about the "hallucinatory imagery" of his Vietnam War poems, Komunyakaa confirmed that "surrealism informed the psychological and emotional underpinnings of that experience."

Though not a dominant aspect of this poem, surrealism is present in the images of circumstances that take place within the bounds of reality but that strike the reader as so unnatural or unlikely as to be unreal. Though primarily metaphorical, the description of soldiers leaning against the breeze may produce a surrealist image of just that action in the reader's mind. Similarly, the images of chameleons taking day and night to crawl along the soldiers' backs and of small animals treating the soldiers' bodies as places of refuge may strike the reader as surreal. The poem may be most surreal in its overall effect. As Derricotte notes, "the tone of the poem is dreamlike," perhaps leading the reader to wonder, "Is the war a dream? Is the poem itself a dream?" The open nature of these

Jungle in Vietnam (Narcis Parfenti | Shutterstock.com)

questions endows the poem with a degree of open-endedness with respect to perspectives on reality.

STYLE

Structured Free Verse

"Camouflaging the Chimera" is written in free verse, with neither meter nor rhyme. Furthermore, there are few, if any, conspicuous instances of internal rhyme, consonance, or assonance; occasionally pairs of nearby words share a sound, but these similar sounds do not appear to be conscious attempts on the part of the poet. Komunyakaa seems to have instead focused on the images being presented, choosing words for their contributions to the images rather than for their linguistic appeal. Though written in free verse, the poem does have a definite structure. The stanzas alternate between three and four lines in length, and the lines are also all of similar length, with between four and seven words. This gives the poem a steadiness that perhaps reflects the steady passage of time experienced by the waiting soldiers.

Sustained Tension

A significant aspect of the poem is the manner in which tension is sustained throughout. Thematically this tension derives from the scene being described: soldiers awaiting the enemy in ambush, inherently a very tense situation. The tension can be seen as sustained beyond the end of the poem since the moment of the ambush is never reached; the reader is left to bear the accumulated tension indefinitely.

Stylistically, the poet's use of enjambment—ending lines in the middle of phrases—can be seen to lend the poem a rhythmic and logical unpredictability that also contributes to the enduring tension. The reader is left wondering in line 5 what is being woven, in line 8 what is leaning, in line 23 with what or whom the Vietcong are struggling, and in line 26 where the river is running. A number of other images are similarly left incomplete across lines and across stanzas, sometimes turning out as might be expected, sometimes not. The reader may not be surprised to learn in line 3 that mud is being used to paint the soldiers and their firearms, but the reader probably does not expect the chameleons, mentioned at the end of stanza 5, to be crawling across the soldiers' bodies or the small animals, mentioned in line 27, to be huddled against the soldiers.

Komunyakaa attributed profound significance to the poetic strategy of enjambment in an interview with Vicente F. Gotera for *Callaloo*, saying that it engenders "what I like to call 'extended possibilities.' The line grows. It's not a linguistic labyrinth; it's in logical segments, and yet it grows. It's the whole process of becoming; that's how we are as humans." As used in this poem, the logical unpredictability of enjambment indeed reflects the unpredictability, even in utter stillness, of the human experience.

HISTORICAL CONTEXT

The Vietnam War and the Poetic Response

The Vietnam War was the defining event in the lives of hundreds of thousands of young Americans from Komunyakaa's generation. The war originally erupted between democratic South Vietnam and communist North Vietnam, which was supported by the guerilla tactics of the Vietcong, a group of communist sympathizers based in South Vietnam. With cold war antagonism between the United States and the Soviet Union dominating international relations, the United States steadily increased its commitment of troops in the early years in the name of democracy—or in fear of communism. President Lyndon Johnson and Congress escalated American involvement under ambiguous circumstances—largely in response to a marine attack that may have never happened—passing the Gulf of Tonkin Resolution to allow military operations to be conducted without any formal declaration of war. As the United States became mired ever deeper in the conflict, more antiwar demonstrations at home called the ethics of U.S. involvement into question.

Beyond the politics, the reality on the ground for American troops was a nightmare. The terrain, mostly jungle, was extremely unfamiliar, and the Vietcong took full advantage of their intricate knowledge of their homeland, building networks of tunnels and using guerrilla tactics that often made it difficult for U.S. troops not only to engage the enemy but also simply to identify them. Surprise attacks were common, and among the U.S. soldiers who survived, many found their nerves fraying over time. In American culture, the surreal experience of the war later became the subject of a wide variety of artistic treatments, the most prominent being films like *Platoon* and *Apocalypse Now*, which captivated millions of viscerally astounded theatergoers. As for literature, memoirs, fiction, and poetry all abounded.

Critics have attributed much of the impetus for artistic responses to the Vietnam War to a documentary urge—a need to establish a record of the senseless situations and actions that marked the war from the soldiers' perspective. Some Vietnam War poetry, especially that produced in the heat of the conflict, is marked by graphic depictions of the mutilated bodies of fellow soldiers. Most of the war's poets have made concerted efforts to portray the environment in which it was fought.

Gotera, in his *Radical Visions: Poetry by Vietnam Veterans*, has identified three modes, which often overlap, employed by the war's literary witnesses. The antipoetic mode is marked by indifference, if not antipathy, to poetic conventions, out of the belief that stiffly structured verse

COMPARE
&
CONTRAST

- **Late 1960s:** North Vietnam, a Communist nation, and South Vietnam, a democratic one, wage war, with the United States supporting South Vietnam in hopes of preventing a Communist takeover, while the Soviet Union and Communist China support the Vietcong and North Vietnam.

  Late 1980s: Following North Vietnam's capture of Saigon and the defeat of South Vietnam, the Socialist Republic of Vietnam, established in 1976, operates the country under Communist principles.

  Today: Following the government's Renovation of 1986, Vietnamese markets are partly opened, private businesses and competition are encouraged, and foreign investment is allowed, such that the nation's economic situation is much improved compared with two decades earlier.

- **Late 1960s:** The number of U.S. troops in Vietnam steadily increases under President Lyndon Johnson, until over half a million troops are fighting by the end of 1968.

  Late 1980s: Following the Vietnamese government's Renovation of 1986 and subsequent opening of financial markets to foreign investment, Americans traveling to Vietnam are likely to be tourists, veterans revisiting their past, or investors.

  Today: With its years of peace and increased participation in capitalist markets, Vietnam sees steady increases in tourism, with over a quarter million Americans visiting annually.

- **Late 1960s:** Being a largely agricultural and rural nation, Vietnam has only 15 to 18 percent of its population living in urban areas.

  Late 1980s: In response to high unemployment in urban areas in the early 1980s, some people are relocated to rural areas, such that only 18 percent of the population still live in urban areas.

  Today: In accord with global trends of population increase and urbanization, Vietnam has 30 percent of its people living in urban areas.

---

cannot best convey the surrealism of the Vietnam experience, as well as in opposition to war generally, denying it the glorifying treatment of metered, rhyming verse. The aesthetic mode, to the contrary, features attention to poetic stylings; Basil Paquet, for one, used the technically demanding sonnet form to treat the war. A third mode is the cathartic, which is characterized by attempts to either confess one's own acts in the war, to purge memories of the war, or to reconcile one's past as a soldier with one's ensuing life as a survivor and peaceable citizen. Gotera singles out Komunyakaa as a poet who transcends these classifications in balancing

> the psychological needs which underlie the three modes: the need for *truth* coded as journalistic documentation, the need for *beauty* as potentially upheld by poetic innovation, and the need

for *sanity* . . . , not only of the mind, but of the full person, through ritual purification.

Blurring of the Color Line

While the Vietnam War raged overseas, the most critical domestic issue in the United States was the ongoing civil rights movement. Racial concerns were also relevant among those serving in Vietnam, where black soldiers were far outnumbered by white soldiers and were made the target of morale-breaking campaigns waged by the Vietcong, who used a radio personality known as "Hanoi Hannah" to ask African Americans why they should die in the name of a racist country.

Komunyakaa wrote a poem titled "Hanoi Hannah," included in *Dien Cai Dau*, in which the woman's disembodied voice, broadcast from

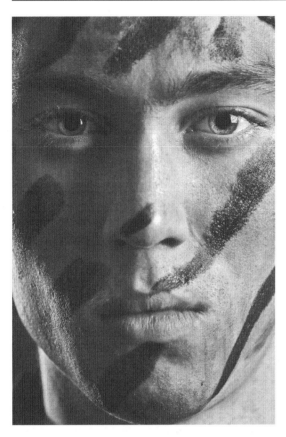

Portrait of a young soldier with black facepaint
(konstantynov | Shutterstock.com)

behind enemy lines, plays Tina Turner for the homesick soldiers before unceremoniously announcing the death of Martin Luther King, Jr., in Memphis, Tennessee—and indeed, some soldiers first heard of King's assassination precisely in this manner.

In many of his poems, Komunyakaa does not overtly focus on any perceived or actual divisions among the white and black soldiers serving alongside each other. "Camouflaging the Chimera," the opening poem of *Dien Cai Dau*, pointedly uses only first-person plural pronouns to refer to the soldiers; they are certainly to be understood as a unified group. In the interview with Baer, Komunyakaa acknowledged that race was a subject of discourse among black soldiers, but he also stressed that the circumstances were "extremely overwhelming," such that "you were keenly sensitive to surviving, and you knew that you had to connect to the other American soldiers."

In the thick of combat, then, racial concerns all but disappeared—and Komunyakaa's poems

can be seen as drawing on and endorsing this blurring of the color line among the soldiers. "Tu Do Street" is one of the poems in *Dien Cai Dau* that does focus on racial differences, describing the informally segregated bars frequented by off-duty soldiers. Marvin notes in his essay "Komunyakaa's 'Facing It'" in the *Explicator* that Komunyakaa concludes this poem with a note of solidarity, stressing that "underneath the superficial distinctions that divide us into separate races and nations, our common humanity links us in profound and mysterious ways."

CRITICAL OVERVIEW

Critical responses to Komunyakaa's collections have been generally favorable. Reviewing *Dien Cai Dau* for the *New York Times*, Wayne Koestenbaum praises aspects of the volume but also finds it lacking in respects. He ambivalently remarks, "Though his tersely-phrased chronicles, like documentary photographs, give us the illusion that we are facing unmediated reality, they rely on a predictable though powerful set of literary conventions." Koestenbaum's issues with the work stem from his conviction that Komunyakaa's use of images is somehow duplicitous—as if the poet may be deceiving the reader; Koestenbaum notes, "Imagery may pose as reasonably accurate reportage, but it also subtly editorializes. . . . Mr. Komunyakaa thus maintains a double relationship to his material—using images that raise and beg questions." He acknowledges that Komunyakaa's frequently foreshortened scenes are "powerful" but complains that the approach "distorts or disguises point of view, and mystifies the events it seems to describe so lucidly." Koestenbaum concludes, "Though I regret the absence of a poem in this volume that exceeds in form, length or ambition the scope of individual, atomized narratives, the book's implications are richer than the poems separately betray."

Kevin Stein, to the contrary, in his essay "Vietnam and the 'Voice Within': Public and Private History in Yusef Komunyakaa's *Dien Cai Dau*," recognizes that the poet's representative intentions are deliberate and complex. He remarks, "While the actual events of history possess a real presence, the speaker nearly always subordinates them to a more intuited, felt, and existential sense of what it meant . . . to experience the Vietnam War." Stein perceives that Komunyakaa's "quest is inward and subjective," a "private search for meaning" that allows for artistic flexibility in the presentation of images and in fluctuation between past, present, and future tense.

Similarly, Owen W. Gilman, Jr., introducing *America Rediscovered: Critical Essays on Literature and Film of the Vietnam War*, admiringly observes that "Komunyakaa's particular lyric and surrealistic talents create a poetry of consolation, self-renewal, and transformation that moves beyond the documentary and polemical urge of most veterans' poetic texts."

Characterizing the verse of *Dien Cai Dau* in the *Dictionary of Literary Biography*, Kirkland C. Jones observes that through Komunyakaa's liberal use of comparative devices like metaphors and similes, "the personas in the poems remain simultaneously inside and outside the experience. These poems, all in the present tense, fix the fleeting images like mountings in a zoology lab—under glass." Jones positively asserts that Komunyakaa "has come of age, not only as a Southern American or African American bard, but as a world-class poet who is careful to restrain the emotions and moods he creates." Jones at last declares, "His poetry is as rhythmic and fluid as his speaking voice, and just as mellow and introspective."

As the moving but straightforward opening poem in *Dien Cai Dau*, "Camouflaging the Chimera" has received less critical attention than others from the volume. Jones calls the poem "powerful." Gotera, in *Radical Visions: Poetry by Vietnam Veterans*, stresses the role of the opening poem in establishing the surrealist tone of the volume: "Through surrealism, Komunyakaa *discovers*—or perhaps more appropriately, *reveals*—Vietnam and does not only document its *apparent* surrealism for an incredulous audience. . . . 'Camouflaging the Chimera' enacts this process of revelation." Focusing on the poem's contents in his essay "Working in the Space of Disaster: Yusef Komunyakaa's Dialogues with America," Michael C. Dowdy says it suggests that "community is possible when everyone works together for a common cause; the process must be one in which all community members work together with their eyes open to the emergent world and its dangers."

CRITICISM

Michael Allen Holmes

Holmes is a writer and editor. In the following essay, he considers how "Camouflaging the Chimera" traces progress toward a moment of awakening in the Zen Buddhist tradition.

"Camouflaging the Chimera" serves as an effective opening poem for Komunyakaa's Vietnam War verse collection *Dien Cai Dau*, which offers the poet's reflections on his experiences as an African American soldier-journalist, recorded some fourteen years later. The poem plunges the reader into wartime circumstances by conjuring the tension of soldiers waiting to spring an ambush. Engulfed in nature, the soldiers must remain supremely focused on remaining still, since a snapped twig or even a cough or sneeze could expose their position and lead to the failure of their mission—and perhaps even to their deaths. The poem ends in the moments before the ambush, when the enemy has come within sight but has not yet reached the camouflaged soldiers, allowing the terrific tension to be sustained through the volume's subsequent poems. Curiously, the poem's concluding lines, which zero in on the thoughts of the individual soldiers, can be read as relating that in those very tense of moments before the ambush, the soldiers happen to find themselves in a state of awakening in the Zen Buddhist sense.

In *Zen Keys*, the Vietnamese Zen master Thich Nhat Hanh discusses the essential aspects of Zen Buddhist modes of thought and the Zen approach to bringing the mind to a state of awakening. Nhat Hanh discusses how the Buddha—originally named Siddhartha Gautama, a man living in India in the sixth and fifth centuries BCE who achieved awakening while sitting under a fig tree and established the precepts of Buddhism—developed the notion of *anatman*, or not-self. The concept of the not-self holds that no thing or person has a fixed identity but rather is always in flux, always changing as the world and everything within it continuously evolves. This concept was first posited in opposition to the rigid caste system of Brahmanism, which leaves some members of society forever branded as Untouchables. If the self is not fixed, as in Buddhism, then no person can be considered inherently inferior to others. Nhat Hanh notes that "the notion of not-self is the point of departure of Buddhism."

" THROUGH ALL THE ABANDONMENT OF SELF, THE COMMUNING WITH NATURE, AND THE IMMERSION IN THE WORLD OF SENSORY PERCEPTION, BOTH THE SOLDIERS AND THE READER MAY BE LEFT IN A LINGERING STATE OF ZEN-LIKE AWAKENING."

With respect to perceptions of the self, Komunyakaa has spoken much about the fluctuations in identity that may be experienced by a soldier, such as he experienced while serving in the Vietnam War. A soldier, of course, must wholly subordinate his own interests to the interests of his commanders and his army. A soldier may not refuse an order for fear of death, no matter how certain his death may seem. In a politically ambiguous war, if the soldier does not believe the cause is worth fighting for, he is doubly removed from his own interests—physically as well as ethically.

In an interview with Muna Asali in *Blue Notes: Essays, Interviews, and Commentaries,* Komunyakaa described the African American soldier of *Dien Cai Dau* as "rather uncomfortable with his role. Maybe the agent of freewill lurks like a specter in his psyche." Or maybe "he knows that he's merely a cog in the whole contradictory machinery some might call democracy or even manifest destiny." Indeed, in a sense, the soldier is by nature and necessity forced into an acceptance of the negation of his own self—he is but a single integral part of the whole of reality around him. In "Camouflaging the Chimera," this acceptance of the notion of not-self can be understood from the poet's exclusive use of the first-person plural pronouns *we, us,* and *our.* The narrating soldier does not speak of himself as independent from the other soldiers; he exists only in a collective sense.

Nhat Hanh relates that one of the most basic Zen concepts is that of *mindfulness,* whereby one keeps one's mind focused on precisely what one is doing, whether walking, sitting, reading, washing, or anything else. Nhat Hanh notes, "In the monastery, the practitioner does everything in mindfulness: carries water, looks for firewood,

prepares food, plants lettuce...." He further assures the reader that "if we are mindful of each thing we do, even if we do the exact same things as others, we can enter directly into the world of Zen." Komunyakaa, in an interview with Toi Derricotte for *Callaloo,* reported learning something of mindfulness from his father, a meticulous carpenter who instilled in his son a belief in the importance of work. The poet genially remarked that his father "thought that physical labor would lead to freedom and salvation. So I learned a whole lot about the rituals of work." The poet concluded that "there is a kind of confrontation and celebration within our everyday lives." Thus, Nhat Hanh and Komunyakaa alike speak of appreciating and celebrating one's everyday acts through mindfulness.

Mindfulness, then, is in opposition to a focus on the gathering and wielding of knowledge and concepts, which do not exist in living reality. As Nhat Hanh states, "according to Buddhism, knowledge is the greatest obstacle to awakening. If we are trapped by our knowledge, we will not have the possibility of going beyond it and realizing awakening." Zen practice entails going from "being lost in the world of concepts" to "bringing light to each act of our existence, living in a way that mindfulness is present all of the time. When walking past the cypress tree in the courtyard, we really see it." Nhat Hanh stresses that one must be ever present in the reality of the physical world:

> The world of reality is that of lemon and maple trees, of mountains and rivers. If you *see* it, it is present in its complete reality. If you do not it is a world of ghosts and concepts, of birth and death.

Again, then, the circumstances of "Camouflaging the Chimera" demonstrate that the soldier may be forced into a Zen-like approach to existence. Trained to be acutely aware of everything around him, since his survival will surely depend on his presence of mind, the soldier is ever deliberately acting and consciously observing his environment. Komunyakaa's simple declarative statements relating the soldiers' actions reflect a high degree of mindfulness on their part. In camouflaging themselves, they consciously tie branches to their helmets and paint their faces, and they gain a tactile sense of both the bamboo, which they are said to embrace, and the breeze, which they are said to lean against. The "world of ghosts and concepts, of birth and death" does

WHAT DO I READ NEXT?

- *Neon Vernacular: New and Collected Poems* (1993), which won the Pulitzer Prize for Poetry in 1994, is Komunyakaa's most renowned volume, covering a variety of topics related to his experiences.

- The renowned North Vietnamese author Nguyen Quang Thieu penned a volume of verse that was translated into English as *The Insomnia of Fire* (1995) by Komunyakaa and Martha Collins. This volume won the Vietnam Writers' Association National Award for poetry.

- In interviews Komunyakaa has praised a variety of poets and novelists who have influenced him, including Melvin Tolson, whose verse adroitly unifies street and literary language. Tolson's first collection, *Rendezvous with America* (1944), contains what is thought his best poem, "Dark Symphony" (1941), which considers the intersection of European American and African American history.

- Langston Hughes is another black poet who inspired Komunyakaa, especially for his celebration of ordinary people and his poetic roots in folk tradition. *Selected Poems of Langston Hughes* was published in 1958.

- Komunyakaa characterizes Robert Hayden, who wrote for the Depression-era Federal Writers' Project on African American folk culture and history, as a strong American voice. *Selected Poems by Robert Hayden*

(1966) includes "Middle Passage," one of his most famous works, about the transatlantic voyage made by Africans seized to become slaves.

- Komunyakaa also professes to admire the work of James Baldwin, including both his novels and his essays; he has reported reading Baldwin's essay collection *Nobody Knows My Name* (1961) about twenty-five times.

- *Winning Hearts and Minds*, edited by Larry Rottmann, Jan Barry, and Basil T. Paquet, published in 1972, claims to be the first anthology of Vietnam War poetry written by veterans, giving voice to their experiences.

- Tim O'Brien is one of the most famous authors of fiction about the Vietnam War. His short-story collection *The Things They Carried* (1990) focuses on the experiences of a single platoon and shifting versions of the truth.

- In *Mare's War* (2009), by Tanita Davis, a novel for young adults, a grandmother tells her grandchildren about her experiences as an African American serving in the Women's Army Corps during World War II.

- André Breton was a French poet who influenced Komunyakaa as a founder of surrealism. The volume *André Breton: Selected Works* (2003) includes translations of some of his most famous poetry.

---

intrude on their thoughts, as they imagine themselves dancing with the ghosts of Vietnam and the memories of loved ones back home.

However, the soldiers then take aim at the singing birds—a physical act, performed perhaps in preparation for the coming ambush—and for the next four stanzas, virtually nothing exists beyond physical reality. The soldiers are confronted by apes hurling rocks, but they are

not distracted from their mission. The soldiers feel the chameleons crawling across their backs and see them changing colors, but they remain undisturbed, doing nothing to prevent the lizards' advances. The only intangible object presented through this section is the undefined something that, owing to the excruciating wait, almost breaks inside them; but whatever this thing is, it goes unidentified and it does not break. The soldiers, then, can be understood to outlast and even overcome this threat to their mindfulness. As Nhat Hanh asserts, "The world of Zen is the world of pure experience without concepts," and the soldiers can be understood to have reached just such a purely experiential state of mind.

The penultimate stanza recalls the Zen concept of not-self several times. Foremost is the statement that the soldiers were somehow not there or not present. While this is most readily understood as a statement of their camouflage, it can also be read as a direct statement of the negation of the soldiers' selves; in that their individualized selves are not there, they have become one with the reality around them. Furthermore, the boundaries between the soldiers and both the environment and its creatures are described as blurred: the river is said to flow through their bones, and little animals use their bodies for refuge. Thus, the soldiers' selves merge with or become indistinguishable from the surrounding nature and the selves of the animals.

The final stanza presents the reader with what can be understood as a moment of awakening. After the stanza's first line notes the soldiers' acute consciousness of the shape of the coming ambush—the shape of the collective action they are about to take—the final two lines speak of a world revolving beneath the eyelid of each man. The precise concept intended by the poet here is unclear owing to the conciseness of the description. The phrasing can be likened to the idiom about "one's life passing before one's eyes" when threatened with impending death, a moment that can be understood as a sort of epiphany, yet the difference between a *life*, as in the idiom, and a *world*, as in the poem, is so significant that the poem's words cannot be read as equivalent to the idiom.

Instead, a description of the experience of awakening offered by Nhat Hanh seems most relevant: "To reach truth is not to accumulate knowledge, but to awaken to the *heart of reality*. Reality reveals itself complete and whole at the moment of awakening." The soldiers, indeed, seem to experience a moment in which the whole of reality—an entire world—is revealed to them; notably, this world is different for each soldier, as for the first time in the poem the narrator differentiates between the individuals.

Nhat Hanh again offers insight when he points out that an essential aspect of awakening is seeing into one's own true nature. He quotes an eleventh-century Vietnamese monk named Cuu Chi as saying, "All methods aiming at the realization of awakening have their origin in your true nature. The true nature of everything is in your mind." Thus, each person can be understood to have a different perspective on the heart of reality based on his or her own nature and mind. The words of Cuu Chi further approximate the soldiers' state of mind at the poem's close:

> The free person sees all, because he knows that there is nothing to be seen. He perceives all, not being deceived by concepts. When he looks at things, he sees their true nature.... This is the only way to arrive at awakening.

Komunyakaa would perhaps reject the notion that in the moments before springing an ambush, soldiers might have the mental freedom to reach a state of awakening. However, with their senses heightened to the greatest degree, with their individual pasts utterly irrelevant to their immediate circumstances, and with potential futures likely banished from their minds, since the future could very well bring their death, the soldiers can be said, ideally, to inhabit a state of perfect mindfulness in the present. Nhat Hanh does characterize the awakened person as being "free, serene, and happy," and obviously the primally tensed soldiers are far from being awakened as such, but Nhat Hanh also states that "in the light of awakening...emotions based on concepts no longer affect us." Again, then, ideally, the single-minded soldier exists in just such an emotionless state. A final concession would be that this momentary state of awakening would certainly be disrupted as soon as the ambush is sprung, but in this poem, the ambush is never sprung. Through all the abandonment of self, the communing with nature, and the immersion in the world of sensory perception, both the soldiers and the reader may be left in a lingering state of Zen-like awakening.

Source: Michael Allen Holmes, Critical Essay on "Camouflaging the Chimera," in *Poetry for Students*, Gale, Cengage Learning, 2011.

Kyle G. Dargan

In the following excerpted interview, Dargan questions Komunyakaa about his feelings toward rap music, jazz, and poetry.

Vietnam Veterans Memorial Wall in Washington, DC (Caitlin Mirra | Shutterstock.com)

This conversation took place August 24, 2005 during the Bread Loaf Writers' Conference, Ripton, VT.

> *Back in the days when I was a teenager*
> *Before I had status and before I had a pager*
> *You could find the Abstract listening to hip-hop*
> *My pops used to say it reminded him of be-bop*
> *I said, "Well daddy don't you know that things go in cycles"*
> *The way that Bobby Brown is just amping like Michael*
> *It's all expected, things are for the looking*
> *If you got the money, Quest is for the booking*

DARGAN: I was talking to Jericho Brown yesterday and he told me you two had already gotten started on this conversation.

KOMUNYAKAA: [*laughing*] Oh really?

DARGAN: He was telling me about how you saw hip-hop, and the negative effects it has, as linked to a larger structure—what seemed like possibly a larger plan, which was implemented on black communities. I am wondering if you could

recount that for me or just give me a sense of how you see that web being woven.

KOMUNYAKAA: Well, I hate to attempt to align hip-hop with something that has been planned, a conspiracy theory or anything like that, but the effects seem so negative. Of course, most likely, a conspiracy happens within the heart and soul of the community itself. Our entire critical apparatus has been undermined. One reason is because we were always, or rather I have always, seen black Americans as caretakers of positive vision and a kind of music which linked us to the past, present, future. The music produced prior to hip-hop I see as the music of inclusion. It was a music that beckoned for people to come together and that's why the music has functioned as a choice of weapon against the larger problems of black existence.

DARGAN: I agree with you; and one thing I see is that the slave spiritual was negro in the sense

"FOR THE MOST PART, JAZZ LOST THE BLACK COMMUNITY IN THE U.S. WHEN IT WAS DIVORCED FROM DANCE, WHEN ONE HAD TO LISTEN AND NOT COMPETE. I DO THINK, WITH THE AFRICAN AMERICAN CULTURE, WE DO POSSESS THE CAPACITY TO EMBRACE THAT WHICH INVOLVES REFLECTION."

that it took a Christian, European religious concept and infused it with an African musical sensibility and created something new that ultimately was used to subvert the system. In a lot of ways, I see hip-hop as the same in the sense you had these urban communities where resources were being taken away from the people—you weren't getting music instruction, you weren't getting any introduction to the arts. What the kids did is say, "Alright, if you are not going to give me the opportunity to do this, then I am going to make my own instruments. I'm going to take a turntable and make that an instrument, I'm going to take a sampling machine and create some new music from it . . ."

> *Come on everybody, let's get with the fly modes*
> *Still got room on the truck, load the back, boom*
> *Listen to the rhyme to get a mental picture*
> *Of this black man through black woman victim*
> *Why do I say that, 'cause I gotta speak the truth man*
> *Doing what we feel for the music is the proof and*
> *Planted on the ground, the act is so together*
> *Bona fide strong, you need leverage to sever*
> *The unit, yes, the unit, yes, the unit called the jazz is*
> *Deliberately cheered—LP filled with street goods*
> *You can find it on the rack in your record store*
> *If you get the record, then your thoughts are adored*
> *And appreciated, cause we're ever so glad we made it*
> *We work hard, so we gotta thank God*
> *Dishing out the plastic, do the dance till you're spastic*
> *If you dis, it gets drastic*

KOMUNYAKAA: But at the same time, if we want to speak of the "us" / "them" syndrome, it still uses *their* technology to underscore *our* shortcomings. What I mean is that black Americans were playing music long before it was institutionalized in schools. Before the drums were banned in the Congo Square in New Orleans. Even when we

couldn't buy instruments we made them—we were very vibrant in our imagination. It does take a certain lifelong commitment to play an instrument. It's not easy. Sometimes, Charlie Parker of Coltrane practiced ten or twelve hours a day. To play one's mouth [*laughs*], it can happen over night. This illusion of shortcuts can undermine us. A good example of this—I was talking to someone who said, "You know, there's money available for young people to play music in Trenton." I said, "What do you mean there's money?" He said, "Well, it's there and we can't find anybody to play instruments." That is one of the problems, you know.

DARGAN: But what age group were they talking about?

KOMUNYAKAA: They're talking about elementary students and teenagers.

DARGAN: That's the thing, though. Because if you're not getting kids when they're little and they have no introduction to arts at all, to give them a trumpet at age sixteen . . .

KOMUNYAKAA: No. At one time, the music happened within the community, regardless. Within the family. The passion to excel was woven into the fabric of the community. There were always instruments—people instructing each other. If the instrument is there, one finds a way to play it, to perfect that instrument. But if that precision is de-emphasized, the music isn't going to happen. Instead, our allegiance to that which appears easy is perfected. We can get over. We can do it over night, you know? We'll write it—not even write—we will *say* a few rhymes and get over. I think that's the attitude. I don't think this is what Lee Morgan's sister was thinking when she gave him a trumpet when he was fourteen.

> *Listen to the rhymes, 'cause its time to make gravy*
> *If it moves your booty, then shake, shake it baby*
> *All the way to Africa, a.k.a. The Motherland*
> *Stick out the left, then I'll ask for the other hand*
> *That's the right hand, Black Man*
> *Only if you was noted as my man*
> *If I get the credit, then I'll think I deserve it*
> *If you fake moves, don't fix your mouth to word it*
> *Get in the zone of positivity, not negativity*
> *'Cause we gotta strive for longevity*
> *If you botch up, what's in that ass?*
> *What? A pair of Nikes, size ten-and-a-half*

KOMUNYAKAA: And the misogyny is very problematic. Rap is a music of put downs . . .

DARGAN: Generally?

KOMUNYAKAA: Yes, generally. If we consider folklore, African American Folklore was so damn inventive. I don't care if it's "The Signifying Monkey" or some of the jailhouse toasts. These rhymes were relentless. They were rhymes of insinuation, innuendo. When you heard one, you had to participate. It was an act of inclusion. So there's a simple meaning, a surface meaning, but there's also a larger, deeper meaning and I don't think that's the case with hip-hop or rap.

DARGAN: I agree that right now that may be the case, but I feel like, in terms of black music, every genre of black music at some point hits that place where it gets absorbed into popular culture in a way that those types of demands that were initially put on it by the community, to have that creativity, to have that brio, get lost. I remember when I was growing up, most of what I got in relationship to jazz was smooth jazz. And I know, now that I've gone back and listened to what was closer to the inception of jazz, that that music and smooth jazz are nowhere close and I don't even think should be considered in the same vein.

KOMUNYAKAA: Right, I agree.

DARGAN: In the same way, I'm not sure that the hip-hop produced now is much different. I feel like the hip-hop being produced is the equivalent of smooth jazz. It's something that's easy to be reproduced, it's something that's commercial and that you can sit back and listen to without having any investment in at all.

KOMUNYAKAA: Well, true listeners of jazz never listen to smooth jazz. They know the tradition. Of course, that became the question, "Where can jazz go?" I think that jazz has always been an international music—now we have to become aware of what Cuban musicians are doing, what's happening in Japan, and what's happening with Polish players such as Tomasz Stanko or Jannsz Muniak. For the most part, jazz lost the black community in the U.S. when it was divorced from dance, when one had to listen and not compete. I do think, with the African American culture, we do possess the capacity to embrace that which involves reflection. This is what I believe and feel, maybe some will disagree, but the listener does not have to compete with the musician. I feel our emphasis has been primarily on interactive entertainment. Modern jazz requires one's attention. One can get booted out of the village vanguard for talking. Rappers

and hip-hoppers need to exist within a zone of noise.

You gotta be a winner all the time
Can't fall prey to a hip-hop crime
With the dope raps and dope tracks for your for
*   blocks*
From the fly girlies to the hardest of the rocks
Musically the Quest is on the rise
We're on these excursions so you must realize
That continually I pop my Zulu
If you don't like it, get off the Zulu tip

... DARGAN: It's funny for me—well not funny, but interesting—just in the sense of how seeing something as part of the past affects the appreciation for it. I mean, I feel like, right now, I'm in the middle of hip-hop. I was born at the beginning and I grew up through its maturation, so I know the good stuff. I'm here now for the stuff that I know most of which is detrimental. It is hard for me to make any general claim about hip-hop because I say, "Well, I know it was this and I know what it is now." So I can't say, straight up, hip-hop is a terrible thing, but I can recognize what it is now.

KOMUNYAKAA: What was good and what was bad about it, yes.

DARGAN: And the one thing I always question is whether we will ever get back to that point where hip-hop was something that was generating dialogues and being creative or will there have to be a new black music and what will the new black music be.

KOMUNYAKAA: Well I'll tell you one thing, it will never be the same after having hip-hop inserted in there. At one time, we produced music without being overtaken with concerns about money, fame, and all those things that come or don't come. The music was being produced because there was a need for it. There was a function, but also a kind of personal need, you know? One could be made to feel a certain kind of power, but one could also be to made feel like a whole person by what he or she was singing, playing on the piano—trying to get every note right, playing way deep into the night without worrying about if it was going to make a dollar. I would love to embrace the music and I've tried. I've listened to it, but even going back and listening to The Last Poets...I couldn't believe I had ever listened to The Last Poets, but I did in the 1970s, you know, but I was listening with a different ear. A lot of the concerns were different. I didn't necessarily want the entertainment because there were so many other things to entertain me. Just being alive [*laughing*] is entertainment enough.

Even with someone such as Miles Davis— I'm writing this essay now called "The Birth of the Uncool" playing off Miles Davis' *The Birth of the Cool*. Miles makes a statement. He says the reason he stopped playing ballads was that he loved them too much. When *Bitches Brew*, the first LP of the fusion records, came out I said "Gosh, this is different," but by the time the third one came out I said, "Wait. I want to hear the lyricism, the lyrical bravado behind Miles' trumpet." I didn't want these little screams and squotes and relying on the wa-wa of the electronics to accelerate, to produce the music. I wanted his genius behind it, not some programmer, some engineer, sitting in a room over there somewhere.

> Beats that are hard, beats that are funky
> It could get you hooked like a crackhead junkie
> What you gotta do is know that the Tribe is in the
>   sphere
> The Abstract Poet, prominent like Shakespeare
> (Or Edgar Allan Poe, it don't stop)

Source: Kyle G. Dargan, "'Excursions': A Conversation with Yusef Komunyakaa," in *Callaloo: A Journal of African Diaspora Arts and Letters*, Vol. 29, No. 3, Summer 2006, pp. 741–50.

Daniel Cross Turner

In the following excerpt, Turner, through an examination of Komunyakaa's poetry, argues that lyric poetry is better able to capture scenes of trauma than prose.

In "What We Don't Talk about When We Talk about Poetry" (1998), Marjorie Perloff calls for studies that will investigate intersections between poetry and critical theory, and read current poetics according to historical contexts: "a sense of history and a sense of theory: these are the twin poles of criticism missing from most poetry discourse today." Perloff rightly asserts, *contra* Bakhtin's famous dictum against the supposedly monologic quality of lyric poetry, that "poetic language is never simply unique, natural, and universal; it is the product, in large part, of particular social, historical, and cultural formations. And these formations demand study." Perloff's call has not yet been wholly answered. There is currently in the academy a bias against poetry in favor of genres that seem to reflect historical conditions more "transparently." Working within the context of postcolonial studies, Jahan Ramazani describes this prejudice against poetry's capacity to signify social and political history: "since

> THROUGHOUT HIS VIETNAM POETRY,
> KOMUNYAKAA AVOIDS THE CLICHÉD RHETORIC OF
> PERSONAL AND NATIONAL HEALING, OR ELSE POINTS
> UP ITS VERY OVERTRANSPARENCY."

poetry mediates experience through a language of exceptional figural and formal density, it is a less transparent medium by which to recuperate the history, politics, and sociology of postcolonial societies." Although the poetic medium is thus "harder to annex as textual synecdoche for the social world," poetry is deeply connected to the circumstances of its cultural production, precisely because of its intensive focus on the form of the message, and by extension, on the shaping forms of our lives. In order to elaborate on Ramazani's observations on the historicity of poetic forms, I will establish an interrelation between the power of poetic rhythm and the historical force of trauma in the poetry of Yusef Komunyakaa (1947-).

This essay argues that lyric poetry registers trauma in a manner distinct from prose: namely, that poetic rhythm, through its pattern of repression and return, is capable of approximating the nature of the traumatic experience, though this always takes place at a remove, since meter itself is not traumatizing, but provides an apt vehicle for representing the unrepresentable quality of trauma. Komunyakaa creates haunting figures of traumatic memory by fusing these with the inassimilable, repetitive force of poetic rhythm, which serves in his verse as a persistent nonverbal analogy for the inarticulateness of traumatic history. His poems about trauma experienced both as an African American growing up in the South and as a U.S. soldier in Vietnam represent a poetics of trauma based in two of the most compelling sites for "the reconfiguration of lyric as speaking, once again, not for the hypothetical 'sensitive' and 'authentic' individual . . . but for the larger cultural and philosophical moment" (Perloff 185). The unrecuperable aspect of rhythm in his verse presents a knowing double-bind. On the one hand, it coincides neatly with the traumatic subject matter of many of his poems of Vietnam and the American South, thus merging form and content and marking trauma as a crucial lens for understanding much of his poetry. On the other hand, the play of poetic meter in his work aestheticizes the traumatic moments being described: in exposing to view the process through which violent memories are made pleasurable, Komunyakaa's use of rhythm becomes a vehicle for challenging the pathos-laden quality of the current conceptualization of trauma.

Komunyakaa's poetics of trauma engenders an account not merely of trauma as a subject of poetry, but of poetry as a distinct means of recording trauma, thereby moving beyond a rhetorical formulation of trauma and into a poetical theorization by focusing on what distinguishes poetry from prose: the physical experience of rhythm. By pressing words against meter, sense against sound, poetry typically exhibits a heightened formal density based on its rhythmic play. My reading of Komunyakaa's poetry is symptomatic—if in ways at once universal and specific—of how poetry can help both to reassess the ethos of a nonteleological culture that has been stripped of redemptive metanarratives and, more specifically, to engage with the culturally located traumatic episodes of southern lynch law and Vietnam combat. His poetic representations of traumatic memory not only exhibit a sustained capacity for metahistorical challenge to the linearity of traditional historiography, but also unveil poetry as an especially apt vehicle for commenting on the workings of a period of metaphysical deadness, where the past cannot be fully recuperated by narrative means. In addition to images of violent fissure, the post-traumatic quality of poetry takes place at the zero level of form, with an understanding of rhythm as an inassimilable repetitive force. The rhythmic structure of poems underscores the materiality of words in themselves, evoking an experience of language as pure physical sensation separated from the conditions of meaning. Reveling in the driving momentum of language as meaningless impression, we paradoxically experience a momentary stay against confusion—we avoid confusion not by outthinking it (a matter of a poem's content, its sense), but by unthinking it (the negating effect of a poem's form, its sound). Since the percussive quality of verse only takes on value *ex post facto*, we are called to allegorize the visceral power of these

rhythms. Like traumatic recurrences, rhythmical poetry is founded on repetitions that carry no inherent valence, for "sound, like poetry 'itself,' can never be completely recuperated as ideas, as content, as narrative, as extralexical meaning" (Bernstein 21). In both cases, the returns are literally *embodied* and can be translated into narrative structures only incompletely.

Trauma is this condition of unknowing *in extremis*: what we should know because we lived through it, witnessed it with our own eyes, is precisely what is unknown and unknowable to us, and the repetitions only serve to exacerbate this irreconcilable gap—the pain of *never knowing* is most deeply impressed on us through trauma. The traumatic content of many of Komunyakaa's poems about Vietnam and the South elucidates a context for interpreting rhythm's resistance to meaning, signaling traumatic repetition as the primary and most intensive elaboration of the rhythm's inexhaustible power. His traumatic poetics thus countermands Adorno's famous aphorism that "after Auschwitz, it is no longer possible to write poems" (362), instead demonstrating the productive capacity of writing poetry as a particularly commensurate method for confronting trauma.

1. DEFINING A POETICS OF TRAUMA

On a philosophical level, critics have argued that the contemporary moment is distinctively post-traumatic, marked by an ethos of metaphysical emptiness, where repetitions of the past, no longer guaranteed by any larger *teleos*, threaten to become meaningless. Per current theoretical explanations, trauma is inflicted when ruptures in consciousness become inassimilable as a consequence of the untimely arrival of danger. Trauma theory holds that those who cannot remember the past are condemned literally, viscerally, to repeat it, without the illusion of narrative mastery and cathartic working-through. Traumatic ruptures can occur on cultural as well as individual levels, as Vietnam and, more recently, 9/11 have demonstrated. The vision of the contemporary age as a post-traumatic world of teleological dead-ends is reflected in Komunyakaa's poems against the all too real trauma of the South and Vietnam, his memories as a Black southerner living under Jim Crow and his experiences of combat terror as a soldier in the War in Vietnam. His verse explores connections between the ubiquitous threat of lynching in the American South and the pressures of combat in Vietnam, where African American soldiers who were denied full citizenship at home were enlisted to fight a war to determine the freedoms of the North and South Vietnamese. The intersections of Vietnam with the racially divided South imbue Komunyakaa's poetry with more than regional significance, shifting his work to a transregional, even transnational level. In the next section of this essay, I will define fully what is meant by a poetics of trauma, and then in the succeeding segments I will trace this concept through the culturally situated sites of trauma constructed in Komunyakaa's verse, from the American South to Vietnam and back again.

What has often been described as Komunyakaa's surrealistic technique—his process of "serendipitous yoking" which creates "a fiercely imagined and stylized world of charged, almost vortexlike, imagery and sensation" (Gotera 307)—functions as a photographic double exposure, where two conflicting realities become superimposed, thereby undercutting facile attempts at catharsis via narrative reconstructions of the disintegrated moment. His terse, two- to three-beat lines are imbued with a frenetic energy through breakneck tonal shifts that commingle vernacular phrasings with images of the surreal. In contrast to the spatialized "visual" rhythms of current concrete and nonlinear poetries, Komunyakaa practices a type of free verse that is still very much bound to aural repetitions. The rhythmical density and unbalanced metrical turns of his verse put words and meaning out of sync, as his rhythms present a broken sequence. The irruptive, start-and-stop pull of his poems—their uneven, halting drive and violently enjambed lineation—suggests the insistence of traumatic recurrence and rupture, especially when contiguous with traumatic subject matter. His lopsided meters and truncated lines make the rhythm palpable, unavoidable, producing highly resistant material, while his splintered lyrics disrupt facile narrativization....

2. TELLING THE WOUNDS OF SOUTHERN HISTORY: THE SOUTH AS SITE OF RACIAL TRAUMA

One of the most compelling voices in contemporary American poetry, Komunyakaa is perhaps most famous for poems filtering trauma through the memory of Vietnam published in *Toys in a Field* (1986), *Dien Cai Dau* (1988), and *Thieves of Paradise* (1998). Yet the traumatic memory of the killing fields of Southeast Asia must share space with the South in his poetry. As the poet himself has noted, "like the word made flesh, the South has been woven through my bones... Coming of age there, I was fully aware of both the natural beauty and the social terror surrounding me. The challenge became to acknowledge and resist this terror" ("More Than a State of Mind"). His southern poems included in volumes such as *Copacetic* (1984), *I Apologize for the Eyes in My Head* (1986), and *Magic City* (1992) depict poor, Black, rural Louisiana as a third-world state hidden within American national boundaries, where the pressures of poverty and racial victimage place African Americans in a condition that Orlando Patterson has described as social death: to make southern Blacks live in fear of actual death by deprivation and violence is to hollow out their existence of social value, to mark them as socially dead. Komunyakaa's poetry is informed by an engagement with the blood-stained history of the South—its particular legacy of chattel slavery, spectacle lynching, the threat of the Ku Klux Klan, white resistance to the Civil Rights Movement, and the bureaucratized violence of the prison system. His verse reflects the South's enduring function as the nation's shadow of racist ideology, exposing southern culture as a primary site of race- and class-based conflict. He serves as a collector of the shards of the traumatically broken past, searching for an art commensurate with the racial horrors of southern history. To invoke "Family Tree" (1984), Komunyakaa's poems turn Dixie's "cotton fields" into "ghost fields," raising the specter of racial turmoil and substandard economic conditions afflicting the Black South. He expands his critique of southern culture to include an indictment of American nationalist ideology through his Vietnam poems, which bear witness not only to how the southern cultural institution of racism haunts the Black soldier's experience in Vietnam, but also to the ways in which the remains of the war continue to unsettle American and southern collective memory. His significance as a national poet is enhanced precisely because of his importance as a southern poet, as the entanglements of southern history reveal deeply set political and social tensions disrupting America at large. In his poetry, the South becomes "an emblem of America writ locally" (Baker 97).

In "Landscape for the Disappeared" (1986), Komunyakaa locates the ghostly remains of African American southerners in a vision of the Louisiana landscape that is haunted by the present absence of lost Blacks, "the hás-béen mén / & wómen" who emerge from peat bogs and "come báck to ús álmost héaled." His darkly surreal landscape of broken bodies with "fáces / wáter-lógged ínto their ówn / púre expréssion, unánsweráble / quéstions ón their líps" provides no space for mourning: his dead have already been disappeared. The landscape is a figure of memory so scarred by racial trauma that it can not be fully healed through narrative repetition, for nothing out of nothing comes: "Sáy it agáin—we are / spáred nóthing." Forced to live under the conditions of social death in life, the disappeared Black underclass is kept inarticulate in literal death: "We cáll báck the ónes / we've néver knówn, with stóries / more óurs than théirs." The eerie returns of the unhealed dead allegorize the function of the poem's rhythm as a deadness that is alive, an absorbing nothingness that is full of physical reality. Read within the context of this grotesquely other Louisiana, the concentrated heavy stresses—in some lines nearly every syllable is accented—suggest rhythm's status as an abjectly unrecuperable force.

Komunyakaa's "Family Tree" further demonstrates the South's particular status as intensive site of racial trauma as he subverts the white southern tradition of ancestor worship by detailing the broken heritage of a Black family tree blasted apart by racial violence, which ranges from slavery to the lynch mob to the institutional prejudice of the prison system. For a Black family surviving Jim Crow, the shift from family tree to lynching tree is more than metonymic, showing that, unlike their white counterparts, African American southerners have no access to a grounding sense of coherent southernness. The interspersion of tightly controlled lines lends an overlay of deadpan restraint to the speaker's protest, though ultimately the form does not absorb, but heightens the driving sense of racial outrage

> When my fáther spéaks
> of hánging trées
> I knów
> áll the óld próphets
> tíed dówn in the eléctric cháir.

Prison has become a new version of slavery, the electric chair substituting for the whipping post. Komunyakaa exposes the power dynamics behind a prison system that is doubly biased against the working class and African Americans, suggesting that moving the procedure indoors and giving it legal sanction do not erase the resemblance between official executions and lynchings. The aura of humaneness projected around executions is an enabling fiction that permits a diffusion of the state's powers of surveillance and discipline, which falls particularly heavy on those already marginalized by race and class. That this disciplinary strategy is exercised against lower-class southern Black men outside the confines of the legal system is evident in the father's remembrance of the "hanging trees" which have become perversely naturalized into the landscape. The shift from "cotton fields" to "ghost fields" in the final lines reveals a deeply imprinted traumatic relation between the conditions of slavery and the poverty as well as racial brutality that is the double inheritance of the descendents of slavery's victims. The ghosts of slavery are literally reborn in the broken figures of the socially dead:

> We've séen shádows
> like wórkhórses
> límp acróss ghóst fields
> & hérd the rifle cráck.
> Bláckbírds
> blóod flówered
> in the héart
> of the sóuthern sún.
> Bráss támbourínes,
> óctave of páin
> cléar as blóod on a sílent mírror.
> Sómeone clóse to ús
> drágged awáy in dáwnlíght
> hére in these íron yéars.

The southern landscape is stained by the blood of Blacks who count as mere "shadows," an underclass of "workhorses" for white interests. Nature itself suffers a traumatic wound as blackbirds become "blood flowered / in the heart / of the southern sun." Komunyakaa's ambivalence over the poetic process of aestheticizing trauma is suggested by this metaphor—when blood becomes flower, trauma is in danger of being sugared over by pathos. His probing into the dangerous space in which haunting is made beautiful is further evident in the poem's closing image, which effects a poetic synesthesia, where sound evokes vision, as the "octave of pain" is translated into the visual register, becoming "clear as blood on a silent mirror." This image reflects a movement from the piercing, kinetic force of sound to the still life of the silent mirror, a figure of empty mimesis that threatens to permit the traumatic image to die away. By placing us between the dead reflection of a silent mirror and the shooting pain of sound and blood, the echo of the rifle crack and the octave of pain, Komunyakaa challenges us to be mindful of the real political aftershocks of racial trauma, to hear the dead's cry as a living protest. The poem's recourse to an appalling, penetrating sound—underscored by the lines' recurrent spondees—points up the interconnection of rhythm and the traumatic operation of memory. The image thematizes "the tension between sound and logic" that "reflects the physical resistance in the medium of poetry" (Bernstein 21) through a terrifying resounding of the abject, one that emphatically echoes the South's particular history as a site of racial trauma.

3. TRANSCULTURAL CROSSINGS AND UNHOMECOMINGS

The post-traumatic force of Komunyakaa's rhythmic returns equally gives form to the violent history of Vietnam as he invokes a traumatic poetics to explore how American racism has been exported to Southeast Asia on two interrelated levels: (1) the violently enforced racist codes of the American South were still in place for African American servicemen in Vietnam and (2) as a global form of manifest destiny, the war was an extension of American cultural chauvinism and our willful misreading of the political and ethnic distinctiveness of the other. In exposing the persistent repetitions of racist ideology at home and abroad, his poetic transitioning between southern and Vietnamese settings calls into question the very definition of "southernness," relocating southern racism to a global context. Regional identification still matters—indeed, it is violently imprinted on his own southern past—but it is placed in conflict with other codes of identification, including race, class, and nation, which take on transregional qualities. His abject spaces traumatically rupture a stabilizing sense of place-bound identity, which was never fully available to a Black southerner born into Jim Crow. His poetry invokes the traumatically delineated boundaries of the South at the same time that it points to violent recurrences beyond the South in a Southeast Asian cultural landscape equally burdened with traumatic memory, both for American soldiers and for the native Vietnamese. Komunyakaa exploits the powers of the uncanny in an

effort to record the violent alienation of southern Blacks as well as Vietnam soldiers and veterans, subjects connected by their traumatic disconnectedness through the pressures of racism and combat. In the words of "Monsoon Season" (1986), his poetry is an exercise in "unburying the dead," making the dead into ghosts that tell, if obliquely, the stories of their lives in order to point the way to surviving—if not fully surmounting—trauma, for "to be a survivor is to be bound to the dead" (Tal 120).

In *Dien Cai Dau*, a phrase meaning "crazy" in Vietnamese, he records the trauma—personal, regional, national, and international—of the Vietnam era. The characters in these poems seem forever "nailed to the moment" of trauma, searching for the right language to bridge the tautological gaps of conflicted memory. As they move among surreal landscapes, they are caught in continual expectation of the Freudian uncanny in its most literal sense as the internally divergent experience of an "unhomelike" feeling, a moment of extreme psychic displacement. The open field of the Vietnamese terrain produces a discontinuous feed of traumatic memories, particularly for the African American soldier in Vietnam, who suffers a doubled sense of self-estrangement. In the words of "Jungle Surrender," he carries us to the unhomely space "between / central Georgia & Tay Ninh Province." Transferring his critique to the combat zones of Vietnam further exposes the condition of social death as African American GIs are exploited for American political and military gain—a condition made all the more painful for southern Blacks who survived Jim Crow only to be exposed to further racism and trauma overseas. These poems share an awareness of the incapacity of the American national narrative of progress to integrate the political and military failure of Vietnam; the redemptive mythos of manifest destiny has withered in its attempted reincarnation on Southeast Asian soil.

Komunyakaa's traumatic poetics thus takes us out of the South and establishes Vietnam as a further, intersecting space of historical trauma. The conjunction between the South and Southeast Asia is dramatized in repressed memories of racial turmoil that return to haunt African American soldiers in Vietnam, such as in "Hanoi Hannah" (whose eerily disembodied voice invokes Ray Charles and Tina Turner and coos to Black servicemen, "You're dead as King today in

Memphis," "Re-Creating the Scene" (which connects the racial chauvinism that permits the rape and probable murder of a Vietnamese woman by U.S. soldiers to the image of a Confederate flag flapping from an Army jeep's antenna), "One-Legged Stool" (in which a Black POW resolves to survive, although survival means that he will return to the threat of violence back "home" in the South), "Camouflaging the Chimera" (where soldiers put on an ironic form of blackface: "We painted our faces & rifles / with mud from a riverbank"), and "Commmuniqué" (which describes a U.S.O. show with an all-white cast of performers—save Lola Falana who "looks awful white"—that reminds Black soldiers of their roots in the racially splintered South: "We want our hearts wrung out like rags & ground down / to Georgia dust"). Against nostalgic tales that posit Vietnam battlefields as real-life melting pots where interracial bonding occurs under the pressures of combat, Komunyakaa's poems record the frustrations of a Black GI who confronts continued segregation on account of white soldiers. The figure of cross-racial bonding is a momentary illusion, for, as the Black speaker of "Tu Do Street" remarks, "We have played Judas where / only machine-gun fire brings us / together." Off the battlefield, he is met with blunt racism, as "Music divides the evening" between Black and white and he returns in memory to Bogalusa with its "White Only / signs & Hank Snow."

Throughout his Vietnam poetry, Komunyakaa avoids the clichéd rhetoric of personal and national healing, or else points up its very over-transparency. "Facing It" continues this critique by revealing the potential for the Wall to be converted too readily from a place of mourning for the veteran into a site of cultural tourism for those less deeply connected to the traumatic aftereffects of the conflict. If the trauma reflected in "Facing It" is made to seem illusionistic from the vantage of those not directly affected by tragic memories of the war (thematized in the illusion of the white vet's lost arm—perhaps a phantom phantom pain), then the contrary mode of emotional detachment seems equally so. The woman brushing the boy's hair may really be only erasing names—a cheap pasting over of the psychic wounds of the war. This gesture may be less a sign of her maternal connectedness than of her sheer disconnectedness from the Wall and the violent past it reflects as through a glass darkly. The poem therefore admits detachment as one of the range of meanings produced by the war and the Wall, as the woman and her son may represent not mourners, but simply tourists on a visit to the National Mall. The idea that the Vietnam Veterans Memorial reflects for some little more than a tourist stop or else is translated too easily into a reassuring form of cultural pathos and healing is set against the poem's painstaking description of the shared, yet inarticulate trauma of the two veterans, Black and white, who remain inextricably bound to the dead. The depiction of the two survivors struggling to confront the Wall reveals the intersubjective power of poetry to make us see, at least momentarily, from the vantage of the other, however difficult this exchange may be. The truncated lines, telling enjambments, and concentrated stresses condition our experience of the poem's rhythms, causing us to share, for the time being, the language of the Black veteran. We literally conspire (from the Latin meaning "to breathe together") with the rhythm of his words and are made to see the past through his eyes: our pale eyes look through his, and the speaker indeed becomes "a window" for us. The Wall, like the war itself, raises more questions than it answers, as does Komunyakaa's closing poem, which provides only an ironic sense of closure for *Dien Cai Dau*, leaving us unsure of precisely what we're left to face. The poem suggests that government-sponsored memorials are meant to exorcise as much as commemorate the dead, and the balm of public pathos may not cleanse the wounds of the individual soldier or of the nation.

Thieves of Paradise denotes a further transnational shift by reexamining the war from *outside* the frame of American collective memory. These poems return to the geopolitical territory of Southeast Asia, asking us to consider "Vietnam" not merely as a name for the American war and its effects on the U.S. military and homefront, but as a people and a culture unto itself. In "Buried Light," the trauma of the war threatens to irrupt once more, as the dead past literally resurfaces, embodied in the fragmented bodies that emerge in a modern Vietnamese rice paddy:

> Múd rises, árcing acróss the sún. Some mónolíthic gód has fállen to his knées. Déad stárs shówer dówn. It was thére wáiting more than twénty yéars, some demónic égg spéared by the plówshare. Mángled légs and árms dánce in the múddy wáter till a sílence rólls óver the páddie like a móuntain of white gáuze.

There is confusion between the mutilated bodies of the past and the present. The uncovered land mine unearths a land still entrenched in the war, a nation that cannot so easily turn swords into plowshares. Vietnamese history is still traumatized: the silence that "rolls over the paddle like a mountain of white gauze" provides a figure of the possibility of healing (medical gauze wrapping up the wounds of the nation) counterbalanced by the impossibility of healing (the white gauze as a death shroud, where the future of Vietnam is bound to its violent past). The poem darkly works back against the flood of American global capitalism into Southeast Asia, recalling the existence of an agrarian-based Vietnamese culture, stifled by U.S. political, economic, and military interference. The prose-like structure maintains Komunyakaa's distinctive two- to three-beat, stress-heavy pattern, with its insistent double accents and trochaic starts, yet this base is submerged within the extended lineation. The buried rhythm emerges, producing another post-traumatic dance of death that ends in ineffable silence, underscored by the repetition of "l" sounds that (dis)connects mangled legs with the rolling silence. Through the inexhaustible force of its rhythm, "Buried Light" exposes a vision of history that is no longer progressive, but recursive and digressive, a vision of history that has no end. The poem serves as a haunting repetition of the earlier "Landscape for the Disappeared," producing one further connection between Vietnam and the South, one more in the sequence of uncanny returns that remind us how history is marked by the loss at the center of commemorative rituals. It is this embedded sense of loss—paralleled by the abject returns of the lines' embedded meter—that persists despite narrative distortions that attempt to bury the deadness of the past. "Buried Light" fulfills the cycle of Komunyakaa's traumatic poetics that reenacts memories of both Vietnam and the American South.

The geographic and historical particularity of Yusef Komunyakaa's traumatic subjects in conjunction with his attention to the unassimilated, repetitive quality of rhythm provide a critique not only of southern and American racism but also of the definition of trauma itself. Overriding essentialist definitions of place-bound identity by exposing the multiple identifications engendered by arbitrary yet powerful regional histories, his verse reveals how the conflicts of southern culture were exported to Vietnam, and how the international politics of Southeast Asia have overshadowed the inner turmoil of the American South. His poetics of trauma demonstrates why these transcultural connections are so powerful, specifically through his poems' disruption of narrative continuity and the compulsion to repeat. His poetry merges the excessive materiality of rhythmic repetition with the inassimilable quality of traumatic recurrence, thereby exposing the dying words of redemptive cultural narratives—words promising a transcendence of death that die themselves in the making. And yet his poetics also offers a sustained challenge to standard-issue trauma theory by demonstrating a productive responsibility to the past without merely reiterating the facile psychiatric and political rhetoric of healing. His poems remain to bring the buried into the light, manifesting a need to make trauma meaningful for the survivors and for others through poetry's intersubjective potential. In doing so, his poetry both records and challenges, reflects and refracts, the political and philosophical limitations of the current theorization of trauma. His poetics invokes a pointed sense of history, but refuses, in post-traumatic fashion, to assimilate accepted tropes of historiography. Instead, the uncanny returns most forcefully through the recalcitrant repetitions of his poetic form, which provides resistant cultural material by producing one of the most compelling—because traumatically imprinted—instances of what Bernstein defines in *A Poetics* (1992) as the "non-absorbability" of poetic discourse. By commingling the sublime power of poetic rhythm with the abject force of traumatic memory in the cross-cultural landscapes of Vietnam and the American South, Komunyakaa's poetry forces us to reassess the claims of trauma theory by challenging it as a potential mode of political solipsism, questioning the endgame that drops us into a fatalistic cycle of repetition without hope of amelioration—if the past is nontranscendable, resistance is futile. Rejecting such a fatalistic and quietist position, his work shows us that poetry is necessarily a historicized form, one that can foster responsible engagement with the traumatic past. His poetics of trauma frees us momentarily by leaving us to unbury the dead.

Source: Daniel Cross Turner, "'Unburying the Dead': Defining a Poetics of Trauma in Yusef Komunyakaa's Poetry of Vietnam and the American South," in *Genre*, Vol. 39, No. 1, Spring 2006, pp. 115–39.

THE *SPECIALNESS* OF HIS EXPERIENCES AS
AN AFRICAN AMERICAN MAN IN THE UNITED STATES
HAS WHETTED KOMUNYAKAA'S APPRECIATION FOR
THE CONCRETE REALITIES OF PEOPLE WE SELDOM
HEAR ABOUT IN POETRY, INCLUDING VIETNAMESE
WOMEN, FACTORY WORKERS, ABUSIVE HUSBANDS,
AND MUTILATED CIVILIANS."

Angela M. Salas

In the following excerpt, Salas explores how Komunyakaa's life experience has affected his poetic aesthetic.

...One author who has neither despaired nor denied his heritage is the poet Yusef Komunyakaa, who has addressed war, race, guilt, redemption, and world mythologies in eleven volumes of poetry. Komunyakaa, born in 1947, is one of the most respected, influential, and anthologized poets of his generation. His opinions matter as he serves as a juror for poetry contests, thereby institutionalizing his own aesthetic ideals, and as he works with writing students at Princeton University. That Komunyakaa is the subject of numerous published interviews touching, variously, upon his life, his views of art, and his many goals as a poet, suggests that authors and interviewers have found him an articulate and interesting contemplator of his craft. As such, Yusef Komunyakaa's determined arc towards an all-encompassing vision, with his simultaneous and stubborn honoring of the particularity of the sources of his vision, will be instructive to readers who are interested in the ways race can be read onto an author's work, and the manner in which Komunyakaa complicates reductive, race-obsessed readings. As Radiclani Clytus asserts in his introduction to *Blue Notes: Essays, Interviews, and Commentaries*, "much of what [Komunyakaa] writes reflects his inextricable link to a sentiment seldom acknowledged in African American poetics—the idea that a 'black' experience should not particularize the presentation of art" (2000, vii).

Indeed, commenting upon the "ghettoization" which Baldwin and Hayden both lamented, Komunyakaa has maintained:

I think the idea of ghettoization is imposed upon certain people, and that it is a pigeonhole the artist attempts to traverse by all means. But we cannot crawl out of our skin, even when we try to lie to ourselves or say that race doesn't matter, that art and artists are color-blind, which is no more than an empty, delinquent illusion. (Asali 2000, 76)

Much of the critical acclaim Komunyakaa has received in his career can be attributed to readers' and critics' sense that his is an "authentic" voice, the voice of a man who has been to the places and experienced the things of which he writes. *Dien Cai Dau* (1988), in which "Facing It," Komunyakaa's frequently reprinted meditation upon the Vietnam Veterans Memorial, most famously appears, takes as its subject the poet's observations and experiences as a military correspondent during the war in Vietnam. Indeed, one reviewer has described "Facing It" as "the most poignant elegy that has been written about the Vietnam War" (Gwinn 1994, 744), an opinion clearly shared by the many editors who have included the poem in volumes of war poetry, Vietnam War poetry, and anthologies of contemporary American poetry.

Magic City (1992), which presents another of Komunyakaa's most celebrated poems, "My Father's Love Letters," explores the poet's childhood in Bogalusa, Louisiana, during the days of Jim Crow. Bogalusa had an active, intimidating Klan presence, but was also the birthplace of the Deacons for Defense and Justice, a group of African American men who exercised armed resistance to white racist oppression. Indeed, in the poem "Knights of the White Camellia & the Deacons of Defense," which appears in *Magic City*, Komunyakaa reanimates a confrontation between hooded white supremacists and stalwart, undisguised, African American citizens of Bogalusa. The poems of *Magic City*, like those of *Dien Cai Dau*, have been praised for their artistry, but also for their authenticity. This combination of artistry and lived experienced earned *Neon Vernacular: New and Selected Poems* (1993) the Pulitzer Prize for Poetry in 1994. Readers and critics note and applaud the extreme erudition of the poems in these volumes, which are informed by Komunyakaa's knowledge of such things as surrealism, the Negritude poets, William Blake, William Shakespeare, war poetry, language poetry, the Black Arts Movement, the New Black Aesthetic, the King James Bible, and the writings of Hayden, Brooks, and the classical Roman poet Catallus. In Komunyakaa's case, the searing nature of lived experience has not resulted in cathartic poetry but in rigorous, learned, and demanding art.

Yusef Komunyakaa's literary career reveals a specific aesthetic attempt to achieve an unmediated connection with his readers: a connection informed, but not determined, by his life and experiences as an African American man. These attempts are in some way akin to those of James Baldwin. As a teenager, Komunyakaa read Baldwin's *Nobody Knows My Name* (1961) from which the first epigraph of this article was taken, in the segregated public library of his home town; he has cited Baldwin's work as instrumental in the formation of his consciousness (Gotera 2000, 59–60). Komunyakaa has traveled widely, to such places as Mexico, Vietnam, Japan, and Australia; it is notable, however, that he has not needed to become an expatriate, as did Baldwin, to become a successful writer. Perhaps Baldwin's account of his own dilemmas gave Komunyakaa the mental space to map out his human journey; more likely, the phenomenal, if uncompleted, changes in the social and racial *status quo* in the United States have given the younger writer an emotional and psychological liberation Baldwin lacked.

While drawing strength from the particularity of his experience as an African American southerner, and as a veteran of the American war in Vietnam, Komunyakaa nonetheless insists that he can function imaginatively from many different positions, not all of which derive from autobiography. In his career, Komunyakaa has taken on the personae of a female Vietnamese rape victim, of tricksters, of a white member of a lynch mob, of combat veterans, and of his remembered childhood self, a feat he accomplishes in *Magic City*. Indeed, Komunyakaa maintains that a poet must have a capacity for human empathy, saying that "the world is so large, and we are so small. How dare an artist *not* imagine the world from the perspective of someone other than himself? It's all part of the ongoing dialogue we must have between ourselves and the world" (Salas 1999, interview). Race, gender, age, experience, and upbringing all inform our perceptions of the world, but they needn't contain our imaginations and sympathies. Thus, while tough mindedly rendering

racial intimidation in "History Lessons" from *Magic City*, Komunyakaa also imagines the dreams of Vietnamese refugees, in "Boat People," from *Dien Cai Dau*. Komunyakaa enlarges our imaginations to encompass both a frightened grandmother whispering "*Son, you ain't gonna live long*" to the youth who faces down a bullying white deliveryman, and the Vietnamese refugees who "cling to each other, / faces like yellow sea grapes, / wounded by doubt & salt."

… Komunyakaa deploys a painter's eye in seeing and animating this scene of loss and suspended animation. In less precise hands "Shrines" might be simply another poem deploring the misfit between the remains of Vietnam's traditional values, such as ancestor worship, and pervasive Western influence. In this case, the erosion of Vietnamese tradition results, at least in part, from advanced video technologies that both capture people's images and render other, fantasy images to them. There is "no serpent to guard these new shrines," but what, indeed, are these shrines, except televisions sets? The ghosts of past generations are lost and neglected, unable to nurture Vietnam's future, because those with electricity, like people everywhere else, have fallen in love with the fantasies that flicker on television screens, and now consume images and packaged stories, from "Hong Kong, Thailand, and America."

The Vietnamese fought and won against China's, France's, and the United States' colonizing efforts in turn, seeking to preserve their autonomy, their language, their culture, and their world vision. In "Shrines," Komunyakaa offers the intriguing possibility that the Vietnamese struggle for autonomy has been defeated by television, which paralyzes everything in the evening, except for the "ghostly jitter-bug flicker" of videos. The same technology "tries to make an amputee whole again," to create a consumable image, a palatable story, about the Vietnam War. That story will be transmitted around the world and, perhaps, back to these people who sit "wherever electricity goes." Television watchers will see this amputee, who sits among them, with new eyes once he has been defined and interpreted by the television's narrative. It is a singular irony few poets could render so succinctly: a nation of people who fought so hard and so successfully to maintain independence and retain their language and ways of thought, now "fall[s] asleep inside someone else's dream," "as if losing the gift of speech." Vietnam is an independent political entity, but it has still been colonized by other countries. The nation has lost much of what it battled to protect, and a constant diet of television has seduced the population away from resistance to outside forces, effectively distracting, if not winning, their hearts and minds. Readers can take some relief in getting this observation from Komunyakaa, as it is uncorrupted by distracting cynicism, even though the observation itself might breed a feeling of cynicism.

In *Talking Dirty to the Gods* (2000), his most recent volume of entirely original work (*Pleasure Dome: New and Collected Poems* was published in 2001, and generously includes Komunyakaa's earliest, out of print, chapbooks), Komunyakaa has stunned critics and readers with yet another bravura performance. *Talking Dirty to the Gods* consists of 132 poems of four quatrains each, and the poet's meditations range widely, as usual, but stay far from the autobiographical elements that have for so long intrigued his readers. Poet and critic April Bernard refers to this volume as "a series of meditations on Gods and the Things They Do" (2000, 36), while Durriel E. Harris notes that "From maggot to dirt dauber to various manifestations of devil, demigod, beast and divinity, Komunyakaa explores the majesty of the worlds human beings inhabit, worrying the lines between modern and ancient Greek and Hindu mythologies in a celebration of imagination" (2001, 36).

Like its predecessors, *Talking Dirty to the Gods* takes into consideration the matters of war, betrayal, music, myth, and love, and thus cannot be said to be a total departure from what readers expect of Komunyakaa. Still, this volume has stunned many readers and reviewers, who approvingly note Komunyakaa's wit and his extensive learning, traits that have always been in evidence. Beyond this, however, they often have little else to say about a volume that ranges from meditations on the statue of the Etruscan She-Wolf in the Capitoline Museum in Rome, to the "Cadavere di Donna," the famous cast of a woman killed in Vesuvius' eruption in 79 AD. Most of the months of the year are given poems in this volume, while all seven of the deadly sins, mentioned tangentially in *Thieves of Paradise*, appear. These poems require time, attention, and recourse to either a first rate classical education or an excellent set of reference books, populated as they are with obscure, surprising, and frequently delightful allusions. While sometimes emotionally wrenching, the poems of this volume are also intensely cerebral, as if Komunyakaa has decided that it is about time his readers think as hard as he does, and has set about making us do so.

In *Talking Dirty to the Gods*, Komunyakaa's narrative voice is disembodied and makes few overt references to race or to the author's personal experiences. Komunyakaa has long demonstrated the ability to attend to matters outside of race, while acknowledging that his view of these matters is inflected by his color, a fact which isn't changed in *Talking Dirty*. Indeed, the rapier-sharp poem "Venus of Willendorf" would be much different, were it not written by an African American man with insights into how theories of physiognomy have perpetuated and do perpetuate racist ideologies. However, in "Remus & Romulus" Komunyakaa's race seems irrelevant. And, while he addresses slavery in a number of the poems in *Talking Dirty*, Komunyakaa does so in the context of the ancient world, rather than in more familiar North American contexts. Indeed, Yusef Komunyakaa's associations of ancient artifacts and crimes with the contemporary world are both startling and apt, placing the horror of the Middle Passage in a context that makes it all the more chilling for its very ordinariness in world history. Komunyakaa has done his homework, using a lifetime of observation, thought, and reading as his resources, and this volume is at least as original and artful as its predecessors, despite being well outside the terrain with which Komunyakaa's readers are most comfortable.

The first line of "Unnatural State of the Unicorn," the first poem in *I Apologize For the Eyes in My Head* is the injunction to "Introduce me first as a man." Each volume that Komunyakaa has produced since 1986 has pushed this point home. Without any attempt at Anatole Broyard's racial recusal, Yusef Komunyakaa has built a body of work in which his personal experience as an African American, southern, working class, Vietnam War veteran has broadened, not limited, his compassion and imagination. No attentive reader could accuse Yusef Komunyakaa of being "merely a Negro; or even, merely a Negro writer" in the way Baldwin feared. And yet Komunyakaa has never attempted to deny or efface his race. He has rendered the subjectivities of "others," whether female rape victims or overworked fathers, with insight, restraint, grace, and humanity. The *specialness* of his experiences as an African American man in the United States has whetted Komunyakaa's appreciation for the concrete realities of people we seldom hear about in poetry, including Vietnamese women, factory workers, abusive husbands, and mutilated civilians. What readers receive from Komunyakaa is a determined balance and precision, as well as an even-handed view of lives in progress. The lives Komunyakaa examines are bounded by war, by violence, and by the atrocity we humans are so able to visit on each other. However, Komunyakaa's empathy invests his subjects with terrible beauty.

In the end, the choice is up to readers as much as writers. Do readers continue to make whiteness the "default position" for individuality, thus reading authors such as Yusef Komunyakaa as either raceless scribes or as lyrical sociologists? Or do readers really sit tight and pay attention, learning to empathize in the same ways our finest writers have trained themselves to do? Readers' preoccupation with race, to the exclusion of all other things, caused Baldwin and Broyard untold anguish, and also robbed readers of the gifts these authors could have provided, had they not been so hamstrung by the world's race-based expectations of their abilities and their interests. Still, denial of race, and of its centrality in American life, is a convenient and amoral fiction, as Komunyakaa himself has asserted, and will, too, impoverish readers and writers. Between these two unsatisfactory extremes stands Yusef Komunyakaa, who seeks to expand his and his readers' understanding of humanity, inhumanity, and the ways our individual *specialness* (to return to James Baldwin) can connect us to each other.

Source: Angela M. Salas, "Race, Human Empathy, and Negative Capability: The Poetry of Yusef Komunyakaa," in *College Literature*, Vol. 30, No. 4, Fall 2003, pp. 32–53.

SOURCES

Asali, Muna, "An Interview with Yusef Komunyakaa," in *Blue Notes: Essays, Interviews, and Commentaries*, edited by Radiclani Clytus, University of Michigan Press, 2000, pp. 76–84.

Aubert, Alvin, "Yusef Komunyakaa: The Unified Vision—Canonization and Humanity," in *African American Review*, Vol. 27, No. 1, Spring 1993, pp. 119–23.

Baer, William, "Still Negotiating with the Images: An Interview with Yusef Komunyakaa," in *Kenyon Review*, New Series, Vol. 20, Nos. 3/4, Summer/Fall 1998, pp. 5–20.

Chattarji, Subarno, *Memories of a Lost War: American Poetic Responses to the Vietnam War*, Clarendon Press, 2001, pp. 131–34.

Cima, Ronald J., *Vietnam: A Country Study*, Government Publication Office, 1987, http://countrystudies.us/vietnam/ (accessed April 20, 2010).

Conley, Susan, "About Yusef Komunyakaa," in *Ploughshares*, Vol. 23, No. 1, Spring 1997, pp. 202–07.

Derricotte, Toi, "Seeing and Re-seeing: An Exchange between Yusef Komunyakaa and Toi Derricotte," in *Callaloo*, Vol. 28, No. 3, Summer 2005, pp. 513–18.

Dowdy, Michael C., "Working in the Space of Disaster: Yusef Komunyakaa's Dialogues with America," in *Callaloo*, Vol. 28, No. 3, Summer 2005, pp. 812–23.

DuBois, W. E. B., *The Souls of Black Folk*, 1903, reprint, Bantam Books, 1989, p. 5.

Gilman, Owen W., Jr., *America Rediscovered: Critical Essays on Literature and Film of the Vietnam War*, edited by Owen W. Gilman, Jr., and Lorrie Smith, Garland Publishing, 1990, p. xviii.

Gotera, Vicente F., "'Lines of Tempered Steel': An Interview with Yusef Komunyakaa," in *Callaloo*, Vol. 13, No. 2, Spring 1990, pp. 213–29.

———, *Radical Visions: Poetry by Vietnam Veterans*, University of Georgia Press, 1994, pp. 25–29, 302–16.

Jones, Kirkland C., "Yusef Komunyakaa," in *Dictionary of Literary Biography*, Vol. 120: *American Poets since World War II, Third Series*, edited by R. S. Gwynn, The Gale Group, 1992, pp. 176–79.

Koestenbaum, Wayne, "University Presses: Distortions in the Glass," in *New York Times*, September 24, 1989.

Komunyakaa, Yusef, "American Voices and the Cakewalk of Language: Yusef Komunyakaa in Conversation with Terrance Hayes," in *Black Renaissance/Renaissance Noire*, Vol. 5, No. 1, Spring 2003, pp. 113–24.

———, "Camouflaging the Chimera," in *Dien Cai Dau*, Wesleyan University Press, 1988, pp. 3–4.

———, *Pleasure Dome: New and Collected Poems*, Wesleyan University Press, 2001.

Marvin, Thomas F., "Komunyakaa's 'Facing It,'" in *Explicator*, Vol. 61, No. 4, Summer 2003, pp. 242–45.

———, "Komunyakaa's 'Tu Do Street,'" in *Explicator*, Vol. 64, No. 4, Summer 2006, pp. 248–51.

Nhat Hanh, Thich, *Zen Keys*, Doubleday, 1995, pp. 28, 38, 44, 52–54, 84–85, 88, 94–95.

Stein, Kevin, "Vietnam and the 'Voice Within'": Public and Private History in Yusef Komunyakaa's *Dien Cai*

Dau," in *Massachusetts Review*, Vol. 36, No. 4, Winter 1995/1996, pp. 541–61.

FURTHER READING

Ehrhart, W. D., *Unaccustomed Mercy: Soldier-Poets of the Vietnam War*, Texas Tech University Press, 1989.
    In this anthology, Ehrhart has collected the work of twelve poets, including Komunyakaa, whom he considers the best among veteran writers of the Vietnam War.

Kovic, Ron, *Born on the Fourth of July*, McGraw-Hill, 1976.
    This is the autobiography of Kovic, who was paralyzed while serving in the Vietnam War and became an antiwar activist. A film version of the book, starring Tom Cruise and directed by Oliver Stone, was produced in 1989.

Mahony, Philip, *From Both Sides Now: The Poetry of the Vietnam War and Its Aftermath*, Scribner, 1998.
    Mahony offers a collection of poetry about the Vietnam War and the ensuing years that includes works by Vietnamese authors.

Van Huy, Nguyen, and Laurel Kendall, eds., *Vietnam: Journeys of Body, Mind, and Spirit*, University of California Press, 2003.
    This book offers many full-color photographs in its exploration of contemporary Vietnamese traditions, culture, and spiritualism.

SUGGESTED SEARCH TERMS

Yusef Komunyakaa

Camouflaging the Chimera

Dien Cai Dau

Vietnam War AND Komunyakaa

veteran poetry AND Vietnam

war poetry AND Vietnam

African American AND Komunyakaa

surrealism AND Komunyakaa

surrealism AND war poetry

A Description of the Morning

"A Description of the Morning" is a poem by the eighteenth-century English satirist Jonathan Swift. It was first published in the *Tatler* magazine on April 30, 1709. The forty-two-year-old Swift had been living in London for about seventeen months at the time, and his friend, the Irish writer Sir Richard Steele (1672–1729) had just started publishing, with Swift's help, this satirical magazine. Swift's poem appeared in the ninth issue, just two weeks after the very first one. Steele recognized that the poem was based on the area in London where Swift lived and commended it for its realistic portrayal of city life. Swift was at the time already well known for his work as a prose satirist and as a man of wit.

Today Swift is known primarily for his two prose works, *A Tale of a Tub* and *Gulliver's Travels*. His poetry may have, on the whole, proved less enduring, but the poem "A Description of the Morning" has always attracted admiration and commentary as an example of the characteristic way Swift perceived the world around him. It can be found in *Jonathan Swift: Major Works* (2008), edited by Angus Ross and David Woolley in the Oxford World's Classics series, and *The Tale of a Tub: And Other Works* (Forgotten Books, 2010).

AUTHOR BIOGRAPHY

Swift was born on November 30, 1667, in Dublin, Ireland, to Protestant Anglo-Irish parents. His father died before he was born, and his

JONATHAN SWIFT

1709

Jonathan Swift *(The Library of Congress)*

superiority of ancient literature over modern, date from this period. They were both published in 1704.

In 1701, Swift received a D.D. from Dublin University and published his first political pamphlet, supporting the Whigs against the Tories. During this first decade of the eighteenth century he visited England on a number of occasions, moving in the highest social, literary, and political circles. In 1707, he was sent to London to appeal for the repeal of taxes on the Irish clergy, but he was unsuccessful. While in London he wrote "A Description of the Morning" and another poem about city life, "A Description of a City Shower." Both poems were published in the *Tatler* magazine in 1709 and 1710, respectively.

Swift returned to Ireland in 1709, although he continued to make visits to England. In 1713, he was appointed dean of Saint Patrick's Cathedral in Dublin. Swift began writing his most famous work *Gulliver's Travels*, in 1720 and completed it in 1725. A satire on English society in the form a travel journal made by a ship's physician about his visits to several imaginary and fantastic societies, it was published in England the following year.

Swift made his last visit to England in 1727. Two years later he published what became one of his best-known works, the satirical *A Modest Proposal*, which advocated that to prevent poor Irish children being a burden on their parents and their country, they should be eaten by rich English people. The pamphlet reveals Swift's fierce sympathy with the Irish poor, and his anger at the way they were exploited by the English.

In his later years, Swift's mental health deteriorated. He lost his memory and became senile. He died in Dublin on October 19, 1745.

mother returned to England, leaving Swift in the care of relatives. Swift began his schooling at the Kilkenny Grammar School and then attended Trinity College in Dublin, from which he graduated in 1686.

After a bloodless revolution put the Protestant William of Orange on the English throne in 1688, Swift moved to England the following year and became secretary to Sir William Temple, a retired diplomat. While in Temple's employ he befriended young Esther Johnson, and this was to become a lifelong relationship. They may even have been secretly married in 1716. In 1692, Swift received an M.A. from Oxford University and published his first poem, "Ode to the Athenian Society."

In 1694, Swift left Temple's employment and returned to Ireland, where he was ordained as a deacon, and a year later as a priest, in the Anglican Church. During the latter half of this decade, Swift wrote two of the several works for which he is best remembered. His prose satire on religion, *A Tale of a Tub*, and *The Battle of the Books*, a satire in which he argued for the

POEM TEXT

Now hardly here and there a Hackney-Coach
Appearing, show'd the Ruddy Morns Approach.
Now *Betty* from her Masters Bed had flown,
And softly stole to discompose her own.
The Slipshod Prentice from his Masters Door,   5
Had par'd the Dirt, and Sprinkled round the Floor.
Now *Moll* had whirl'd her Mop with dext'rous Airs,
Prepar'd to Scrub the Entry and the Stairs.
The Youth with Broomy Stumps began to trace

The Kennel-Edge, where Wheels had worn
    the Place.   10
The Smallcoal-Man was heard with Cadence
    deep,
'Till drown'd in Shriller Notes of *Chimney-*
    Sweep.
Duns at his Lordships Gate began to meet,
And Brickdust *Moll* had Scream'd through
    half a Street.
The Turnkey now his Flock returning sees,   15
Duly let out a Nights to Steal for Fees.
The watchful Bailiffs take their silent Stands,
And School-Boys lag with Satchels in their
    Hands.

POEM SUMMARY

Lines 1–4

"A Description of the Morning" is an eighteen-line poem written in couplets that depict, in realistic, down-to-earth rather than romantic or idealized fashion, an early morning in early eighteenth-century London. In the first couplet, the signs of morning, rather than being the sight of the sun god Apollo, who ancient Greeks thought was drawn by chariots across the sky, come instead by a hackney coach or two. A hackney coach was a horse-drawn carriage that could be hired by anyone who needed to get around the city. First introduced in London in the seventeenth century, sometimes they were referred to as chariots. The next couplet (lines 3–4) describes a servant girl named Betty. She has spent the night with her master but now she quickly returns to her own quarters, mussing up her own bed so that no one will know she did not sleep there.

Lines 5–8

In lines 5 and 6, an apprentice begins to work. He appears not to be very conscientious, but his job is to keep his master's house clean. He peels away dirt and sprinkles water on the floor. This was a common method of cleaning in those days. The water solidified the dust and made it easier to remove. In the next couplet, a woman named Moll is preparing to scrub the stairs and the entryway. Like the apprentice, she appears to be less than committed to her task. She twirls her mop around nicely without actually doing any real work.

Lines 9–12

In line 9, the narrator's observing eye has moved from inside buildings to the outside, where a boy is starting to sweep the gutter clean, where the wheels of the coaches have worn down the surface and left old nails. He is searching for those old nails (according to a note by Swift or an early editor that appeared with the poem). He appears to be ill-equipped for his purpose, however, because the broom he uses is worn out from too much use. In line 11, the narrator's description moves from the sights of the early morning to the sounds that can be heard. A man who sells coal calls out his wares in a deep voice, followed and drowned out by the higher-pitched voice of the boy chimney sweep.

Lines 13–16

In line 13, some men assemble outside the house of a member of the upper class to demand payment of a debt. (A "dun" is a person who collects debt; the verb "to dun" means to ask repeatedly for payment of a debt.) In line 14, a woman shouts loudly, so that half the street can hear her. She is advertising for sale powdered brick that can be used for cleaning. The next couplet (lines 15–16) shows the jailer who watches as his prisoners return. He lets them out at night so they can rob people and then give some of the money to the jailer in exchange for favors.

Lines 17–18

In the final couplet, bailiffs stand at the ready. Bailiffs are court officials who have power to make arrests or to reclaim property in payment of a debt. The final line describes boys who reluctantly set off for school carrying their satchels. It appears that they walk as slowly as they can, not wanting to arrive.

THEMES

Urban Life

"A Description of the Morning" presents a series of snapshots, colored by the poet's own attitude, of daybreak in a street in London. The people who inhabit the poem are from the lower social orders, and the picture is a gritty, down-to-earth one, not glamorous at all, as England's largest city commences yet another day. The poem presents the ugly underside of London's finery. These are the people who in order to survive

TOPICS FOR FURTHER STUDY

- Get up at dawn or early morning one day and observe what is going on in your house and on your street. What kinds of human activities are being performed, and by whom? Make some notes and then write a rhymed poem of couplets that presents "a description of the morning" as you see it.

- Read T. S. Eliot's poem "Morning at the Window" (found in *The Wasteland and other Poems*) and write an essay in which you compare it to "A Description of the Morning." How are the two poems similar and how do they differ? Post your essay on your Web log and invite your classmates to comment on the two poems.

- Go to http://www.glogster.com and create a glog (a kind of poster) that presents different images of a city you are familiar with. Using words and pictures, you can present the city in a positive or a negative light, or in ambiguous ways that make people think about what the city really is like. Your poster can make a satirical point about the city if you wish. You might take a look at the city's Web site, or at travel brochures, and note how different these presentations are from the way the city is in actuality—if that is the case.

- Go to http://www.helium.com/items/1235431-funny-stuff-if-youre-a-sadist and read the satirical essay about high school by Andy Frakes. Then write your own satirical essay about your high school. You can get tips about how to write a satirical essay from Carl Hose's article at http://www.ehow.com/how_5653646_write-satire-essay.html/. You can find a useful definition of satire at http://www.gale.cengage.com/free_resources/glossary/glossary_s.htm#s.

have to serve their social "betters" and make life easier for them. They are the ones who help make the city work at its most basic level,

cleaning houses and streets and carrying on small trade. However, at least in the first part of the poem, no one appears to be doing a very good job, which may indicate that the poet wishes to draw attention in a satirical manner to some of London's social ills or injustices. Although he does not directly criticize or condemn anything, his picture of contemporary London is less than ideal. The servant Betty, for example, is not behaving as society's moral code suggests that she might—but then neither is her master, who might be thought of as taking advantage of her low status and dependence on him as her employer. The adjective *slipshod* applied to the apprentice in line 5 undercuts the work of cleaning he is engaged in. (The word can refer to shoes that are worn down at the heel, but also means careless or slovenly.) It may also be that the poet intends the reader to draw a similar conclusion regarding the activity of the cleaning woman Moll in the next couplet; she skillfully twirls her mop with an emphasis on show rather than actual work.

The third and fourth couplets emphasize dirt, and that emphasis is continued when the poem moves from inside to outside the house. The boy (probably very young) who sweeps the gutters has to manage with an old, worn-down broom, and the mention of the young chimney sweep up so early is a reminder of the long and dangerous workdays put in by the chimney sweeps in London at the time. Both the boy and the man selling coal—which creates the fires that blacken the chimneys that the sweeps must then clean—show how hard it is for people such as these to make a living in London. At the other end of the social scale, a glimpse is presented of the extravagancy of the privileged classes, as the debt collectors gather outside the house of one of London's aristocrats. When the narrator adds the screaming woman in line 14, the corrupt jailer in the final couplet, and the fact, made clear in the last line, that criminals walk the street at night intent on theft, it appears that this corner of London is not all that it could be in terms of social order and harmony.

Irony

The poem is intended as a kind of ironic reversal of traditional pastoral poetry, which presents an idealized portrait of country life (often by poets who did not actually live in the country). Instead, Swift presents a realistic portrait of

A country sunrise *(MC_PP | Shutterstock.com)*

urban life that offers a number of hints that reveal how he is satirizing the pastoral tradition. It was common in classical poetry, for example, to present a glorious image of dawn as the sun god Apollo moves across the sky in a chariot drawn by immortal horses. But the chariots in "A Description of the Morning" are hackney coaches and the horses mortal ones. Instead of dawn in a natural setting, presided over by a god, this is dawn in a commercial setting, as people start to travel and go about their business.

Further elements of the satire on the pastoral ideal occur in lines 11–14, which describe the early morning sounds in London: the man selling coal, who makes people aware of his presence with his deep voice, and the higher notes made by the boy chimney sweep. Those sounds are then augmented by the screaming of the woman in line 14. All this is a parody of the dawn chorus of birds that can be heard in a country setting. The urban reality shown in the poem is quite different. Another parody of the pastoral poem, which may often depict a shepherd with his flock, is the couplet that makes up lines 15 and 16. The

shepherd in Swift's poem is the jailer, and his flock are the returning prisoners whom he has sent out to steal at night so they can pay him for any favors he bestows on them. Instead of a country shepherd who tends to his flock, this urban "shepherd" exploits them.

STYLE

Heroic Couplets

The poem is written in heroic couplets. A couplet is two successive lines of poetry that are rhymed. A poem written in couplets will therefore rhyme *aa bb cc* and so on. The term heroic was applied to couplets in seventeenth- and eighteenth-century English verse because many epic (that is, heroic) poems were written in this form. Swift's contemporary, Alexander Pope, was the acknowledged master of the heroic couplet. These couplets are usually referred to as closed. This means that each couplet is a self-contained syntactical unit. The clue to spotting this is that often the couplet ends with a period, thus making it one complete sentence. All nine couplets in "A Description of the Morning" end with periods.

Heroic couplets are written in iambic pentameter. An iamb is a poetic foot consisting of two syllables, the first unstressed and the second stressed. It is the most common foot in English poetry. A pentameter consists of five feet. This poem is quite regular in maintaining the iambic pentameter with few variations. Variations do appear in the first feet of lines 13 and 16, in which the stresses are inverted, a strong stress preceding a weak one. This is called a trochaic foot. Writers of heroic couplets often vary the rhythm by frequent use of a caesura, or pause (usually indicated by a comma or semicolon) within the line, but Swift in this poem makes little use of this device, which appears only in lines, 2, 5, and 10.

Use of Tenses

The poet's use of verb tense in this poem is quite complicated. One might expect "A Description of the Morning" to be written in the present or past tense throughout, but, in fact, the tense is varied. The poem begins with the word "Now," which suggests present tense, but it slips into the past tense in the second line of the first couplet. The same pattern is discernible in the second couplet, which also starts with "now" but then moves into the pluperfect tense (sometimes called past perfect and referring to actions that have been completed in the past before another event or action), which continues into line 8. The fifth couplet (lines 9–10) is in the simple past tense, and the pluperfect tense reappears before the final four lines, which are all in present tense. It is as if in this rather odd manipulation of tenses, the poet is waking up his sleepy reader at dawn, not only leading him or her from inside the house and then outside to the street but also alternating between describing what has just happened before finally showing what is happening right now in the present.

HISTORICAL CONTEXT

London in the Eighteenth Century

In the eighteenth century, London was the biggest city in England by a large margin, with a population fifteen times that of Bristol and Norwich, the two next largest cities. More than one person in ten in England lived in London at the time. London was the center of the country's trade, receiving raw materials from all over, which were turned into manufactured goods for export throughout the world. London was a shipbuilding and financial center, and crafts such as clock making and glassblowing flourished. Many skilled tradesmen made a reasonably good living, while the nobility and the wealthy built lavish town houses from which they could enjoy all the pleasures and amenities the city offered.

Life for the lower classes (the kind of people described in Swift's "A Description of the Morning"), however, was not as pleasant. People, including women and children, worked long hours for low wages in bad conditions. The plight of the chimney sweeps, some of them as young as age four, was particularly shocking. Many were killed or maimed while performing their difficult, dirty, and dangerous jobs. They began their work before dawn and labored until midday. As Peter Ackroyd explains in his book *Blake: A Biography*:

> There was a great need for their services in London, where the flues were characteristically narrow or twisted so that they easily became constricted. The average size of these vents was something like seven inches square, and the small child was prodded or pushed into the even small spaces within; sometimes they were encouraged with poles, or pricked with pins, or scorched with fire to make them climb with more enthusiasm.

Thousands of the poor lived in crowded, poorly constructed buildings that were often in danger of collapse. According to G. M. Trevelyan, in *Illustrated English Social History*, "the lower strata of the population...lived under the most filthy conditions of overcrowding, without sanitation, police, or doctors, and far beyond the range of philanthropy, education, and religion." Contributing to the ill health of the populace was air pollution from coal burning. The coal was transported to London from Newcastle in northeast England or Swansea in south Wales, and almost every house in the city burned coal for heating. When combined with similar pollution from factories, Londoners would have endured dense fog on many days of the year. In her book *Eighteenth-Century London Life*, Rosamond Bayne-Powell quotes a traveler to London who reported that "the smoke gains ground every day.... This smoke being loaded with terrestrial particles... forms a cloud which the sun penetrates but

COMPARE & CONTRAST

- **Eighteenth Century:** London is the biggest city in England. In 1715, it has a population of about 630,000. The population steadily rises, reaching 740,000 by 1760. The city occupies only one-tenth of the area that it would cover by the twentieth century.

  Today: London is the capital city of the United Kingdom, and it is the most populous city in the European Union. In 2007, the city has over 7.5 million residents. One in twelve people in the United Kingdom lives in London. London is one of the world's great financial centers and is also a popular destination for tourists.

- **Eighteenth Century:** One of the principal means of getting around London is by hackney coach. There are hundreds of such coaches, although people complain that they are noisy, and tradesmen grumble that they are deprived of business because passengers in the coaches are unable to see into their shop windows. Many people get around London by boat on the River Thames. Until 1738, there is only one bridge over the river (London Bridge), so the Thames is crowded with traffic, and there are thirty landing places within a short distance.

  Today: London is a crowded city with many means of public transportation. The famous double-decker red buses carry workers and tourists alike around the city, and there are thousands of licensed taxis. London also has a subway system, known as the Underground or the Tube, which carries people efficiently and safely to all corners of London.

- **Eighteenth Century:** The first part of the century, up until the death of Alexander Pope in 1744, is known as the Augustan Age in English literature. The leading writers are Pope, Swift, Joseph Addison, and Sir Richard Steele. These writers value order, good taste, and reason rather than the imagination. They write with a moral purpose in mind. Poetry is written in heroic couplets, and satire flourishes, including the mock-epic.

  Today: Poets write in a great variety of forms. Rhymed verse is no longer the dominant form, and poets seldom write heroic couplets. The most popular type of poetry is free verse, unrhymed poetry in which poets have the license to create whatever form and structure best fits their purpose, and to use whatever language they choose.

---

rarely." Not surprisingly, given the conditions in which so many lived, the death rate in London was high, even higher than the birth rate. According to Derek Jarrett, in *Britain: 1688–1815*, in the early eighteenth century "most London parishes buried three people for every two that they baptized. Typhus, smallpox, influenza and other diseases ran continually through the squalid and insanitary tenements into which the London poor crowded." The population was replenished by immigration from Ireland and many other countries, including Jews from Poland, as well as by the movement from the English countryside of people who had heard of opportunities to be had and riches to be made in the great city.

Violence, Crime, and Prisons

In the early eighteenth century, London was governed by magistrates and possessed a militia, but it was still a violent, unruly place. "Few prudent men ventured out alone after dark.... Friends made up parties for mutual protection when they returned from the coffee house or the tavern," wrote Bayne-Powell. Londoners had good reason to fear thieves and cutthroats, and they also had to deal with a fearsome collection of artisans and apprentices known as the London mob, who could band together and create havoc on the flimsiest of excuses. According to Trevelyan, the London mob was "the largest and least manageable mob in the island."

An illustration of a hackney-coach (*Andjelka Simic | Shutterstock.com*)

Crime in London was widespread and there were severe punishments for those who were caught. There were two hundred crimes punishable by the death penalty, and hundreds of people were hanged in public every year. Other punishments included whipping, branding, and the stocks and the pillory.

London also possessed fourteen prisons, including the most famous, Newgate, which had been in existence since the twelfth century. Conditions in Newgate were very bad. According to Bayne-Powell, prisoners lived on bread, often in short supply, and inadequate supplies of water. Each person received only three pints or a quart of water per day for all their needs. If the prisoners were poor, all they had for bedding was some straw on a stone or earthen floor. If they had money, they could hire some bedding from the jailer (one of the favors perhaps that the jailer in "A Description of the Morning" will do for the criminals he lets out at night to steal so they can afford to enrich him in this manner).

Bayne-Powell quotes the report of a visitor to Newgate named Maitland in 1754:

> It is a dismal place within. The prisoners are sometimes packed so close together and the air so corrupted by their stench and nastiness that it occasions a disease called the Jail Distemper of which they die by dozens, and cartloads of them are carried out, and thrown into a pit in the churchyard of Christchurch without ceremony....

Maitland also observed that many innocent people were sent to jail and put in irons so that the jailer could extort money from them.

There were also debtors' prisons, the largest of which was the Fleet. Those who were unable to pay their debts would languish in these jails, which were also run so that the jailers made money from any of the prisoners who could pay for some meager luxury. (The lord in "A Description of the Morning" who has the debt collectors waiting outside his house may well end up in a debtors's prison if he cannot pay them.)

CRITICAL OVERVIEW

"A Description of the Morning" has attracted quite a bit of critical attention over the years. Some critics such as F. W. Bateson have seen it as Swift's satirical indictment of bad social conditions in London. Others, however, deny that the descriptions of various aspects of London life at dawn amount to a clear statement of a moral theme. The latter is the approach taken by A. B. England in *Energy and Order in the Poetry of Swift*, who sees in the poem simply an "aggregation of miscellaneous and irreducible particulars," evidence of Swift's depiction of "a reality that is sufficiently miscellaneous to defy ordering attempts at classification and systemization." J. A. Downie, however, in *Jonathan Swift: Political Writer*, takes a different view. He describes the poem as a "town-eclogue," and argues that "the most remarkable feature of a poem such as this is the manner in which it relates to a coherent satiric vision." He adds that the poem is a "gentle satire . . . employing none of the harshness of which Swift is capable." Rather, it is a "detached, passive observation of the movements and sounds that herald the dawn in London." For W. B. Carnochan, in *Confinement and Flight: An Essay on English Literature of the Eighteenth Century*, the poem is notable for "the way it suspends motion and falls away into silence. It has little of the movement and bustle and coming alive expected of the morning." Carnochan identifies Swift's "tricks with tenses" as the technique by which the poet creates this sense of stillness and concludes that the poem is "a study in arrested motion." Nora Crow Jaffe, in an essay on Swift in *Dictionary of Literary Biography*, comments that the poem "has as its governing principle the interplay of order and disorder." She points out that "the figures who appear in the poem have duties that should contribute to the ordering of their world." However, "[m]ost of these figures charged with preserving order are actively engaged in disrupting it." Jaffe concludes:

> Swift seems to be suggesting that radical disorder is the state of this world, and the best that can ever be attained is a frail and unstable impression of order. He emphasizes the sense of disorderly flux by catching all his characters at a transitional moment, when the reality is just coming into contact with the respectable illusion.

CRITICISM

Bryan Aubrey

Aubrey holds a Ph.D. in English. In the following essay, he discusses Jonathan Swift's intentions in writing "A Description of the Morning" in light of various ways in which readers and critics have interpreted the poem.

When Swift wrote "A Description of the Morning" he was living in lodgings on the Strand, one of London's great streets, with a history going back six hundred years or more. About three-quarters of a mile long, it is situated just north of the river Thames and runs parallel to it. In Swift's time and before, it was the principal route from the city of London to the palace of Westminster. In 1660, seven years before Swift's birth, it had witnessed a spectacular royal procession as the monarchy was restored, and Charles II returned to London following his exile. By the time Swift took up his residence on the Strand, however, the nobility had long left their palaces there, and as "A Description of the Morning" shows, at least the portion of the Strand where Swift was lodging was the domain of more humble folk.

What Swift's intention was when he wrote this poem has long been debated. Was he just collecting a few miscellaneous details about an early morning in London and presenting them realistically, like a disinterested journalist might? Or was he shaping his presentation in a certain way, with a certain theme in mind? Was he trying to draw attention to the squalor of London, the bad social conditions, as a form of protest? Was the poem intended as a satire or a parody, but if so, of what? Many of the literary critics who write about Swift have offered their opinions about this short poem, which is usually considered one of the best of Swift's relatively early work in the genre. For A. B. England, in "World without Order: Some Thoughts on the Poetry of Swift," the poem uses realism to make a thematic point; it possesses the "fragmentary, confused effect of realism" but also "attain[s] a kind of thematic pattern. For the picture is so near to being an undifferentiated reflection of disorder that it makes a satiric point without seeming tailored to a didactic end." England's point is that the poem does portray both social evils that should be addressed and activities that are, from a moral point of view, neutral, and does so in a manner that suggests that society

WHAT DO I READ NEXT?

- Swift's poem "Stella's Birthday, 1721," is the second of seven birthday poems Swift wrote for his close friend, Esther Johnson. Like "A Description of the Morning," it is written in couplets, but the meter is different. This poem is written in tetrameter rather than pentameter, which means that each line consists of four feet rather than five. The poem is a tribute to Stella's attractiveness, which, the poet, says, will endure even as she grows old. (Stella was forty years old at the time, although for the purposes of the poem, Swift refers to her as thirty-six.) The poem can be found in *The Writings of Jonathan Swift*, a Norton Critical Edition (1973), edited by Robert A. Greenberg and William Bowman Piper.

- Swift's most popular and celebrated work is *Gulliver's Travels*. This journey into imaginative fictional worlds is available in an abridged, Classic Starts edition aimed at young-adult readers. Published in 2006, the book is edited by Martin Woodside and illustrated by Jamel Akib.

- *London: The Biography* (2000) by novelist and biographer Peter Ackroyd, is a very engaging history, full of interesting anecdotes, of London from prehistory to modern times. In nearly eight hundred pages, Ackroyd surveys the city in times of trouble and plenty, building and destruction. He discusses contrasts of wealth and poverty, the city's massive growth over the centuries, its neighborhoods and churches, its plagues and fires, as well as crime, violence, and punishment; politics; the river Thames; and many other topics.

- Modernist poet T. S. Eliot's "Preludes" were published in 1917 in Eliot's *Prufrock and Other Observations*. There are four preludes, each describing a certain time of day in the city. Preludes II and III describe the coming of morning in a city in which people live spiritually impoverished lives. Unlike Swift's poem, Eliot concentrates on inner rather than outer life. The "Preludes" are available in Eliot's *Collected Poems, 1909–1962*, published in 1991.

- The English romantic poet William Wordsworth, although he is closely associated with England's Lake District, also wrote a sonnet about London, "Composed upon Westminster Bridge, September 3, 1802." This was nearly a hundred years after Swift's poem, and Westminster Bridge did not exist in Swift's time (it was completed in 1750). The poem is also set at dawn, but Wordsworth sees the dawn in London as a beautiful event in a splendid city. The contrast with Swift's satiric view could not be greater. The poem can be found in *William Wordsworth: The Major Works* (2008), edited by Stephen Gill, or any other edition of Wordsworth's work and many anthologies.

- Claude McKay (1889–1948), was a Jamaican poet who moved to the United States in 1912 and became involved in the Harlem Renaissance, a period of significant literary output by African American writers during the 1920s. His poem "The White City," first published in 1921, presents a view of a city that would not have occurred to Swift (or Eliot or Wordsworth, although Blake would have understood it). It is a poem about how he embraces his hatred of the mighty "white city" (because as a black man he is an alien in it). This hatred fuels his life, and he cherishes it for that reason. The poem can be found in McKay's *Selected Poems* (1999) and also online at the Web site maintained by the Poetry Foundation, http://www.poetryfoundation.org.

> CERTAINLY SWIFT, AS A SATIRIST WHO WAS
> ALWAYS ALERT TO THE DISCREPANCY BETWEEN THE
> IDEAL AND THE ACTUAL (THE WAY THINGS 'REALLY
> ARE'), APPLIED A STRONG DOSE OF REALISM TO HIS
> LONDON DAWN SCENE, WHETHER OR NOT A
> CONDEMNATORY PURPOSE WAS STRONG IN HIS
> MIND."

does not differentiate between these two things, but regards both with a "uniform indifference."

Of the realistic element in the poem there can be no doubt. By realism is meant the representation of things the way that they actually are, sometimes referred to as verisimilitude, the appearance of being true. Many critics remark on the presence of dirt and disorder in the poem, and London in the early eighteenth century had plenty of both. There were no city services for cleaning streets. People were responsible for cleaning the section of the street in front of their own door. Not until 1762 did the city of London take on the responsibility of keeping the streets clean. Swift's own poem, "A Description of a City Shower," a kind of companion piece to "A Description of the Morning," published in the *Tatler* in 1710, provides ample evidence of what happened to London's streets during a downpour. In the poem, the gutters overflow with mud and filth of all kinds, including drowned cats and puppies, and offal (internal organs) from butchers' stalls. In 1741, Dr. Samuel Johnson, the renowned man of letters and great lover of London, observed that the city "abounds with such heaps of filth, as a savage would look on in amazement" (quoted by David Daiches and John Flower in their book, *Literary Landscapes of the British Isles: A Narrative Atlas*).

David Vieth, in his reading of the poem in his essay "Metaphors and Metamorphoses: Basic Techniques in the Middle Period of Swift's Poetry, 1698–1719" in *Contemporary Studies of Swift's Poetry*, finds the theme of disorder and sees the poem as a parody of a "Christian miracle," the miracle being "the divine fiat 'Let there be light,'

which created the garden of Eden," thus imposing order on chaos. Vieth argues that Swift intended his depiction of "the shabby, dimly lit, dirty (in both physical and moral senses) milieu of early eighteenth-century London, striving halfheartedly to restore order and cleanliness" to represent a failure of that divine ordering principle in the contemporary city. London is therefore a "fallen city," and the poet presents the disorder in a way that suggests and invites moral disapproval. This is a sophisticated reading that has not convinced all readers or critics of the poem. Although no single interpretation can be considered the definitive view, it might perhaps be said that if Swift is writing in a way that invites moral condemnation of the little scenes he presents, he is being more than a little oblique about it. The poem is rather gentle in its depiction of the people who emerge at dawn in London; it has, for example, none of the unequivocal condemnation of social conditions that is apparent in William Blake's poem "London," written near the end of the eighteenth century. Much of the detail in the poem, as England suggests, does not imply moral indignation. If the maid Betty (lines 3–4) is to be censured for her lack of morals, such judgment should not be made of Moll (lines 7–8) as she prepares to clean the entry and the stairs; the boy searching for old nails in the gutter (line 10); nor the coal man who is merely selling his wares (line 11); and surely least of all the schoolboys going to school as slowly as they possibly can (line 18). (If Rosamond Bayne-Powell's account in *Eighteenth-Century London Life* of the poor state of schools in London is anything to go by, the schoolboys can hardly be blamed for their tardiness. There were many schools in the city, but "the dirt and brutality of eighteenth-century England were exemplified in the schools.")

The first readers of this poem, those who picked up their copy of the ninth issue of the satirical magazine the *Tatler*, in which the poem was first published, were given some help in how to read it. The poem was introduced by a note, written by the publisher and friend of Swift, Sir Richard Steele. Steele, in a note reproduced on the *Representative Poetry Online* Web site maintained by the University of Toronto, observed:

> [T]he town has, this half age, been tormented with insects called *easy writers*. ... Such jaunty scribblers are so justly laughed at for their sonnets on *Phillis* and *Chloris*, and fantastical descriptions in 'em, that an ingenious kinsman of mine ... [Swift] has, to avoid their strain,

run into a way perfectly new, and described things exactly as they happen: he never forms trees, or nymphs, or groves, where they are not, but makes the incidents just as they really appear. For an example of it: I stole out of his manuscript the following lines: they are a description of the morning, but of the morning in town; nay, of the morning at this end of the town, where my kinsman at present lodges.

This is probably as good a guide on how to read the poem as any that has appeared since. Steele gives a clue to Swift's intent, which was to parody the flowery pastoral poems that were popular during the Augustan Age and followed classical models. Such poems presented rosy pictures of dawn coming to a perfect rustic setting in which humble but happy shepherds abound without a care in the world, shady groves are plentiful, and—if the poet has a mythological bent—the odd nymph or two will make a beguiling appearance. In a very detailed reading of the poem, which he describes as a "comic imitation of the classical ideal," Roger Savage, in his essay, "Swift's Fallen City: 'A Description of the Morning'" in *Essential Articles for the Study of Jonathan Swift's Poetry*, has given a number of examples of the kind of poems Swift was parodying, including one from Edward Bysshe's book, *British Parnassus*, although that title did not appear until 1714, five years after Swift's "A Description of the Morning."

Once the parody is pointed out, it becomes very easy to see: instead of a mythological scenario in which the goddess of the dawn, Aurora, awakes and creates a beautiful background for the sun god Apollo to rise in the sky, Swift's dawn is marked by the gritty realism of the noisy hackney coaches, the sounds of people shouting (unlike the singing birds of the traditional pastoral), and a "shepherd," the jailer, whose "flock" consists of the returning convicts whom he exploits for money. Savage differs from Steele, however, in seeing more of a didactic purpose behind the poem. For Steele, Swift makes the incidents "just as they really appear." In other words, his approach is objective, but for Savage, Swift "looks for the sordid," and his purpose is to present an "*exposé* of the corruption, triviality and untidiness of what passes for day-to-day reality in 1709." Savage's point is a reminder that presenting things "just as they really appear," in an objective fashion, is harder than it sounds (even if that is the poet's intention), because what a person chooses to see, and

A chimney sweeper (© *Mary Evans Picture Library | Alamy*)

how he or she presents it to others, is inevitably influenced by the person's subjective perceptions and attitudes of mind. Certainly Swift, as a satirist who was always alert to the discrepancy between the ideal and the actual (the way things "really are"), applied a strong dose of realism to his London dawn scene, whether or not a condemnatory purpose was strong in his mind. It is as if he is saying: this is real life rather than an imaginative invention; accept it or reject it if you will, but this is the way it appears.

Source: Bryan Aubrey, Critical Essay on "A Description of the Morning," in *Poetry for Students*, Gale, Cengage Learning, 2011.

A. B. England

In the following excerpt, England examines critical responses to "A Description of the Morning," as well as possible interpretive errors within those responses.

BUT THIS DOES SUGGEST THE POSSIBILITY
THAT SWIFT REGARDED THE POEM AS INNOVATIVE,
EXPERIMENTAL, CAPABLE OF DISORIENTING
READERS WHO LOOK FOR ORTHODOX MODES OF
LITERARY ORGANIZATION."

In an elegantly argued review of Stanley Fish's *Is There a Text in This Class?*, Denis Donoghue points to a problem that many people are troubled by when they confront that kind of literary analysis which focuses attention on the experience of the reader. "Who is the reader?" Donoghue asks, and he says some valuable things about the difficulty of describing the experience created by a literary artifact when we cannot get inside the heads of the many different individual readers of it, and when, even if we could, we would probably find a baffling variety of responses. We can try to answer his question, as Fish has done, by imagining hypothetical types of reader, and by thinking about the "interpretive communities" to which they might belong. Or, alternatively, we can locate actual readers by looking at writings about literature that have been published and are thus available to us. Such writings appear to provide evidence of how certain informed minds have experienced particular texts: it would seem that we do know who the reader is in such cases, and we can see his mind at work in the process of reading the text. This kind of evidence will be particularly useful if there are any similarities in the critical writings we examine, and if any tendency seems to prevail. For we may then be able to recognize signs of some fundamental or universal reader-experience that has been stimulated by the text in question, and the individual readers we examine may take on representative significance.

We might hesitate to pursue such a course of inquiry, though, if we consider some arguments that Fish put forward several years ago when he was beginning to explore the subject of reader-experience. These arguments form part of a theory that has developed and changed considerably since they were first advanced, but they make a point about literary-critical essays that

concerns the whole question of the value such essays have for the study of reader-experience, and that still needs to be considered. Because of this, and for other reasons that will soon become clear, his discussion is a useful means by which to approach some central issues. Fish was interested in a "primary or basic level" of experience which he identified "more or less with perception itself." It was this experience which, for him, brought into being and defined the literary text that was being read. And he argued that a typical literary-critical publication does not in fact provide access to such an experience because in writing his analysis the critic will inevitably depart from it. What is defined in the work of a critic is a "secondary or after-the-fact level" of experience, at which the reader engages in "an act of intellection, more or less equivalent with what we usually call interpretation." This act of interpretation represents a "subsequent and distorting activity" that is often "so removed from the act of reading that the latter ... is hardly remembered." And finally, " ... a reader who is also a critic will feel compelled to translate his experience into the vocabulary of the critical principles he self-consciously holds"; "he will ... be reporting not on his immediate or basic response to a work but on his response (as dictated by his theoretical persuasion) to that response." This line of argument seems to discredit from the start any attempt to discover in the works of literary critics the kind of reader-experience that will help us to understand a particular text. But, as Fish himself has come to recognize, there are certain problems in the argument, some of which are important to the subject of this essay. For example, it is dangerous to suggest that processes of intellection subsequent to the initial reading are necessarily separate from the crucial, text-defining experience. Such will certainly be the case if one believes that the only significant form of experience is that "primary or basic" level that Fish sought to re-create and that, for him, really constituted the identity of the text. But it seems possible that certain features of a text's identity may not be defined by that immediate experience, and that "subsequent intellection" may operate in ways that are not necessarily "distorting" but further developments of a complex experience stimulated by the text; in other words, that the "experience" generated by a text may be a continuing and developing thing. If one accepts these possibilities, then works of literary criticism may be seen as potentially significant respositories of reader-experiences that help us to understand literary texts. And in the following essay, I shall look at certain critical responses to Swift's poem, "A Description of the Morning," in exactly this way. As we look at these critical essays, however, we shall see that the above remarks by Fish are extremely pertinent to a pattern that appears in them all. For in each essay there is a distinction between an initial experience of the work and a subsequent experience which is essentially determined by processes of "intellection." Moreover, although I believe that this secondary process of intellection is a crucial part of the "experience" generated by the poem and thus helps us to understand the nature of the text in question, it does also happen to be, in the case of this poem, "distorting." What it distorts, however, is not the "true" experience generated by the text, but the very structure of the text itself. And in saying this, I am expressing a belief that the text of "Morning" has an existence independent of the minds and reading-experiences of the critics I shall discuss, and that it is possible for the acts of description and interpretation practised upon it to be inaccurate. It seems to me that one feature of this text's identity is that it has stimulated certain critics into a significant kind of interpretive error, and that the actions into which they have been drawn are sufficiently compromising to suggest that the effect of Swift's poem has been somewhat like a process of entrapment.

. . . In 1972 David Vieth published an essay which advanced a different interpretation of the poem, but in which certain features of what I think may be an archetypal pattern of reader-experience again appeared. To begin with, Vieth recognized that initial sensation of discontinuity which tends to be created by the poem, and seemed to regard it as a feature of his own reading-experience; he wrote, "At the most literal level, nearly every reader of the poem has been struck by the drably realistic effect it achieves by cataloguing, in a flat, even tone, an apparently random selection of details from an urban dawn." This comment refers to two of the distinctive qualities which are, as Vieth says, so often felt on a first reading of the poem; first, the lack of connection between the several items, and second, the absence of words that express attitudes or feelings towards the items described. However, Vieth takes a noticeably dismissive attitude towards the perception of these

characteristics; he describes it as characteristic of a reading that does not go further than "the most literal level." In seeking to pass beyond this level, and to achieve what he calls a "more comprehensive" act of interpretation, Vieth says, "In 'A Description of the Morning' . . . meaningful order is so little evident that a full aesthetic response requires the reader to search for it. He is challenged, in the words of 'The Lady's Dressing Room,' to find 'Such Order from Confusion sprung.'" Thus, it is the apparent absence of meaningful order which stimulates the reader to seek that order, the evident lack of a thematic statement which challenges him to engage in a quest for such a statement. And as Vieth builds his interpretation, the primary justification for creating it appears to lie in its power to bring order to the miscellaneous surface of the poem; as he puts it, "The reading of 'A Description of the Morning' as a parody of Creation, as depicting a postlapsarian world of disorder and imperfection, is best supported by its consistent ability to explain the seemingly miscellaneous details in Swift's poem." There is no suggestion here that the poem's details themselves exert any pressure towards interpretation on the mind of the reader. But the essential value of the thematic reading is felt to lie in its power and in the power of the reader's mind to counteract the impression of disorder initially given by the poem. And once again, the act of interpretation leads to certain moments that demonstrate the fundamental recalcitrance of the text. Vieth argues that the words of the poem do express certain quite strong attitudes towards the items they describe and that these attitudes cohere to form a vision of "imperfection" and "disorder" in a fallen world. But in order to establish this he is forced, for example, to claim that when the speaker refers to Moll as whirling her mop with "dext'rous Airs" he is communicating the critical implication that she may not be intending to work with "genuine dexterity and diligence," and later on, that the oldness of the nails which have fallen from passing vehicles and the "worn" condition of the road-edges where they lie are symptoms of a postlapsarian imperfection which the poem consistently, and with moral disapproval, defines. It seems to me that at these moments a noticeably forceful and assertive interpretive pressure is being brought to bear on the text, and that as a consequence a considerable degree of strain appears in the analysis.

... The poem appears to be extremely open in that it exerts so little overt thematic pressure on the reader's mind; and one consequence of this is that it has seemed to invite us, as educated readers, to take particularly active initiatives in the pursuit of meaning. A poem constructed in this way may very well be a greater temptation to interpretive acts than one with definite thematic imperatives that clearly limit the possibilities of speculation. It may seem that it is possible to read almost anything into such a poem; one critic can claim that the speaker feels as much hatred of human society as does the deranged Gulliver at the end of his travels, another can refer to the "positive pleasure" Swift feels in observing the details of the city. But since the form of the poem is genuinely and radically open, and since each interpretive effort is an effort towards the achievement of a kind of closure, the poem ultimately has the effect of compromising or discrediting these efforts as some part or other insists on remaining less than completely accessible, and thus reveals the attempt at interpretive closure to be inadequate. And by "inadequate" I do not mean simply incapable of accounting for the full richness of the poem's texture, which is no doubt the case with all interpretations of literature, but fundamentally inappropriate to the real nature of the poem.

In order to understand the kind of poem that "Morning" really is, we need to pay close attention to the apparatus with which it was first presented to public view in Richard Steele's *Tatler*. Jaffe points out that Swift's relationship with Steele was very close at the time the poem was published, and she recognizes the possibility that he may have written the introduction himself (76). At any rate, given Swift's interest in this kind of introductory editorial apparatus, it is almost impossible to believe that he was unaware of it prior to publication. In a very deliberate way, the writer of this introduction seeks to divest the poem of general or representative significance; he says that the morning described in the poem is not only "in town," but in a certain part of town where the author lives "at present," thus suggesting that the details of the poem are determined by the particular aggregation of objects occurring in a particular place at a particular moment. The writer goes on to forestall potential imitators, and gives an example of the kind of sequence that might appear in a poem imitative of this one. He says, "... I bar all descriptions of the evenings; as, a medley of verses signifying, grey peas are now cried warm: that wenches now begin to amble round the passages of the playhouse." Now although it might be possible with a little ingenuity to imagine a relationship between the grey peas and the wenches, it is clear that in this case such a relationship would be accidental, and that it is not the intention of the writer to move our minds towards a consideration of it. Rather, he seeks to move us towards an experience of random collocation "signifying" nothing. His whole point is that the kind of poem Swift has written does not work by means of logical or meaningful juxtapositions, but by the juxtaposition of items which may be adjacent to each other on the street but do not connect with each other in the manner of coherent discourse. That, it would appear, is intended to be crucial to the fun of this kind of poem, its studied departure from consecutiveness and logical order. The writer of the introduction further defines the poet's manner as a "way perfectly new," quite different from the predictable structures of what he calls "easy writing," and therefore likely to be disconcerting to readers who expect to encounter traditional and orthodox connections.

Swift was well aware of the human mind's impulse to find order in apparently random sequences, and he created an extreme and ludicrous image of it in his account of the academy of Lagado. But I do not wish to suggest that his purpose in this poem was to trick readers into inappropriate responses and thus make fools of them, or to turn interpreting readers into objects of satire. The poem simply does not seem to have designs on us in that way. And after all, Swift would no doubt feel that most of the interpretations that have been offered do their authors some moral, intellectual, or scholarly credit; there are obvious differences between these interpreters and the academicians of Lagado. We may, however, quite legitimately note certain effects that the poem has had on its readers, and that a fundamental pattern of experience appears in several of the writings about it that have been published in the last twenty years. It is probably futile, in the absence of clear evidence, to speculate about what Swift's intentions with regard to his audience may have been. All we really have to go on is the *Tatler* introduction. But this does suggest the possibility that Swift regarded the poem as innovative, experimental, capable of disorienting readers who look for orthodox modes of literary organization. And this suggests the further possibility that he would not have been entirely surprised by a pattern of reader-experience that involves an insistent pursuit of clarifying and ordering lines of direction.

... The desire for an ordering and unifying interpretation continues to express itself in various ways. In my own most recent attempt to describe the poem, I tried, as I have tried here, to argue against some interpretations that I did not find convincing. A reviewer of the book in which this attempt appeared then took me to task for failing to propose a "substantial" interpretation of my own. She quoted the following statement from my account: "If it is true that the Augustan poet was preoccupied with 'the task of imposing unity on the multitudinous world, of finding some approximation to the order and meaning intended by the Divine Mind itself,' then 'A Description of the Morning' seems carefully designed to suggest the difficulty of his task." This interpretative statement was found by the reviewer to be too "modest" and "inconclusive." And yet it draws attention to the difficulty of the poet's task in creating areas of order out of the fragmented universe he contemplates, and thus defines the poem as a comment on the disconnectedness and discreteness of that universe. It seems to me now that this interpretation, rather than being modest, is probably too assertive. For although it is faithful to the truly miscellaneous quality of Swift's sequence, it does suggest that the poem in the end makes a thematic statement about the nature of reality. Such a response to the poem is certainly tempting. It provides a means of adapting Vieth's and Jaffe's interpretations by removing the element of moral blame. It is also consistent with the approach taken by a recent theorist to the subject of "discontinuous form" in modern literature: "The form of an open work is properly seen by its reader as consisting of disconnected and unconnectable fragments that represent reality as it is interpreted by modern science and epistemology." But this poem really maintains a studied silence on the question of how "reality" is to be interpreted. And since the silence is one which we feel is awkward, we find it difficult to restrain ourselves from attempting to fill it.

Thus, the effect which the poem has had upon several readers has been in some ways like a process of entrapment. The readers who have experienced this effect have not always been aware of its nature. But obviously we are not always aware that we are being drawn into compromising situations; that is sometimes evident only to outside observers. To recognize and understand the experience should eventually cause us to return with renewed attention to that way of perceiving the details of the poem which so many readers agree is a feature of their first or immediate response. And if we do this, it seems to me that the process of entrapment may ultimately become liberating. For that original reading experience may be seen as having considerable value, especially when it is compared to the predictable and rigidly patterned experience that had come to be associated with poems on this subject, and that we know Swift was seeking to counteract. The central principle of Swift's highly experimental poem is a mode of perception by which each successively presented object is seen in its separate individuality, rather than in its relationship to other objects or to general ideas, and without being placed in a context that causes it to serve an overriding moral or philosophical purpose. Swift celebrates such a mode of perception throughout the early stages of the *Journal to Stella*, and it was clearly a matter of great interest to him. At the same time, the *Tatler* introduction suggests that he knew it would be disconcerting to readers of literature. And because the experience is disconcerting, or at least not the kind of experience we readily associate with eighteenth-century literature, we will probably continue to resist it in our reading of this poem. The evidence suggests that we will continue to seek connections that we think may lead to a unifying interpretation. And what will draw us into such quests will be the highly stimulating absence of those characteristics which would enable the quests to be successful.

Source: A. B. England, "The Perils of Discontinuous Form: 'A Description of the Morning' and Some of Its Readers," in *Studies in the Literary Imagination*, Vol. 17, No. 1, Spring 1984, pp. 3–15.

David M. Vieth

In the following essay, Vieth explains his reading of "A Description of the Morning" as a parody of creation.

As one of Jonathan Swift's most popular poems, "A Description of the Morning" has deservedly enjoyed much critical discussion. A major dimension of its meaning seems, however, to have escaped notice.

IN 'A DESCRIPTION OF THE MORNING,' ON
THE OTHER HAND, MEANINGFUL ORDER IS SO LITTLE
EVIDENT THAT A FULL AESTHETIC RESPONSE
REQUIRES THE READER TO SEARCH FOR IT."

Now hardly here and there an Hackney-Coach
Appearing, show'd the Ruddy Morns Approach.
Now *Betty* from her Masters Bed had flown,
And softly stole to discompose her own.
The Slipshod Prentice from his Masters Door,
Had par'd the Dirt, and Sprinkled round the
    Floor.
Now *Moll* had whirl'd her Mop with dext'rous Airs,
Prepar'd to Scrub the Entry and the Stairs.
The Youth with Broomy Stumps began to trace
The Kennel-Edge, where Wheels had worn the
    Place.
The Smallcoal-Man was heard with Cadence deep,
'Till drown'd in Shriller Notes of Chimney-Sweep,
Duns at his Lordships Gate began to meet,
And Brickdust *Moll* had Scream'd through half the
    Street.
The Turnkey now his Flock returning sees,
Duly let out a Nights to Steal for Fees.
The watchful Bailiffs take their silent Stands,
And School-Boys lag with Satchels in their Hands.

A review of previous criticism points to the
need for a more comprehensive interpretation. At
the most literal level, nearly every reader of the
poem has been struck by the drably realistic effect
it achieves by cataloguing, in a flat, even tone, an
apparently random selection of details from an
urban dawn. Like so much of Swift's verse, it is
rooted in the here and now, growing out of
actual, particular, concrete circumstances. In the
often-quoted words of the *Tatler* when the poem
was first published in 1709, the poet has
"describ'd Things exactly as they happen: He
never forms Fields, or Nymphs, or Groves,
where they are not, but makes the Incidents just
as they really appear." His lines are not only "a
Description of the Morning, but of the Morning
in Town; nay, of the Morning at this End of the
Town, where [the poet] at present lodges."

Backhandedly recognized in the *Tatler's*
reference to "Fields, or Nymphs, or Groves" is
a second level of the poem's meaning, its implicit
ironic contrast between the sordid nature of

a modern urban environment and the ideal, country nature of classical pastoral, especially as
portrayed in a conventional "dawn-scene." Most
obviously, Betty the chambermaid stealing from
her master's bed parallels Aurora "flown" from
the bed of aged Tithonus to usher in the day
(3–4), while the turnkey overseeing his returning
"Flock" of thieves corresponds to a shepherd caring for his sheep (15–16). Recently, A. B. England
and Roger Savage have pushed interpretation further by characterizing Swift's scene as, respectively, a "world without order" and a "fallen city."

These lines of interpretation converge
toward a single conclusion: "A Description of
the Morning" is a parody of the divine fiat of
Creation, "Let there be light," by which God
imposed Logos upon Chaos. In a postlapsarian
world, such a diurnal reenactment of Creation is
inescapably parodic; the light generated is dim at
best, and the degree of order is minimal. This
interpretation lends special relevance to Swift's
use of mock-pastoral, for according to prevailing
neoclassic theory, derived from Rapin, "pastoral
is an image of what they call the Golden age." In
theme and technique, "A Description of the
Morning" resembles other poems by Swift,
including several he composed close to the same
date. As mock-pastoral and a parody of Creation, it anticipates "A Description of a City
Shower," which is both mock-georgic and a
reenactment of the biblical Deluge that produces
merely a temporary physical cleansing and no
discernible moral purification. Similarly, in "Baucis and Philemon" the combination of Ovidian
metamorphosis and Christian miracle results in
no significant moral improvement and only a
superficial rearrangement of physical circumstances. In "Vanbrug's House" a phoenix rises from
its ashes a fraction of its former size, and in "The
Day of Judgement" the entire human race, like
the denizens of T. S. Eliot's Waste Land, proves
lacking in the moral stature needed for damna-
tion in the traditional Christian sense.

The reading of "A Description of the Morning" as a parody of Creation, as depicting a
postlapsarian world of disorder and imperfection, is best supported by its consistent ability
to explain the seemingly miscellaneous details in
Swift's poem. Thus, in the initial four lines,
Betty's mussing of her bed to hide her affair
with her employer amusingly exploits a physical

disorder to cover up a moral disorder—as well as, secondarily, confusing social and domestic hierarchies. Disorder is connoted by the word *stole*. Incidentally, the lack of connection between Betty and the "Hackney-Coach" of line 1 suggests that the coach corresponds, not to Aurora's chariot, but to that of Apollo, the pagan god of light and the sun, who would here stand for the Christian God as Jove does in "The Day of Judgement"; elsewhere Swift refers to Apollo's chariot as a "coach." ("Hackney-Coach" is grammatically singular although it signifies a plural in the poem's surface meaning.) Besides the disjunction between the mock-Aurora and the hackney-coach, the latter is for hire and perhaps empty. Imperfection is further emphasized in line 1 by the syntactical displacement of "hardly," which in this context could mean either "with difficulty" or "just barely."

The next three couplets continue, mainly in the physical world, the halfhearted campaign of order against disorder and imperfection. The apprentice, cleaning away dirt and sprinkling the floor, is nevertheless "Slipshod" (5–6). Moll the charwoman makes a show of beginning to scrub with "dext'rous Airs," not necessarily with genuine dexterity and diligence (7–8). The young scavenger has only "Stumps" of brooms for tools, he looks for old nails rather than new, his search is along the kennel (gutter), and the kennel-edge itself is "worn" (9–10).

Lines 11–14 offer an anarchy of sounds that parodies the harmonious bird songs of a conventional pastoral "dawn-scene." Not only are some of these sounds, the "Shriller Notes" of the chimney sweep and the screaming of "Brickdust *Moll*," individually unmusical, but they clash with each other, the "Cadence deep" of the coal vendor being "drown'd" (a distant allusion to the Deluge?) by the chimney sweep's cry. Framed by this dissonance is the disarray of the nobleman's finances (13); the contrast in social levels merely underlines the common element of disorder. Further, all four examples in lines 11–14 may have to do with finances and commerce.

Lines 15–16 are a nest of Chinese boxes involving physical, social, legal, financial, moral, and even literary order. The criminal inmates (disorder), ostensibly confined by the prison (order), are let out to "Steal" (disorder) according

to a scheme of "Fees" levied by the turnkey (order). The speciousness of this mock-order, which limits licensed stealing to nighttime, is underscored by the sarcasm of "Duly" in addition to the pastoral implications of "Flock." In the final couplet, order is embodied in the "watchful Bailiffs" and the school discipline, while disorder is incipient both in the conditions that require bailiffs and in the loitering of the schoolboy.

Paradoxically, and typically Swiftian, "A Description of the Morning" intimates a greater degree of order and a more positive significance than appears on its rather bland surface. Merely describing the details of a disorder in a repetitive pattern implies some sort of underlying order. Indeed, order is implied simply by casting the description in poetic form. Moreover, Swift imputes meaning to his urban scene by linking it, ironically or otherwise, to established literary traditions: generally to classical pastoral and the "dawn-scene"; more specifically, in his superficially anticlimactic but actually strategic last line, to the *topos* of the dilatory schoolboy with his satchel, which was already familiar in such works as Charles Cotton's "Morning Quatrains" and Shakespeare's *As You Like It*. This and similar details, for instance the whirling of Moll's mop (7), hint at a fundamental vitality in Swift's city like the fecundity of the Chaos that is celebrated ironically in Rochester's *Upon Nothing*.

Swift's heroic couplets reverse the relationship of order and disorder that he uses in the more familiar tetrameter couplet style he inherited from *Hudibras*. There, the polysyllabic rhymes, short lines, and sometimes strained syntax express an order so obtrusive that its validity is constantly called in question. In "A Description of the Morning," on the other hand, meaningful order is so little evident that a full aesthetic response requires the reader to search for it. He is challenged, in the words of "The Lady's Dressing Room," to find "Such Order from Confusion sprung."

Source: David M. Vieth, "*Fiat Lux*: Logos versus Chaos in Swift's 'A Description of the Morning,'" in *Papers on Language & Literature: A Journal for Scholars and Critics of Language and Literature*, Vol. 8, No. 3, Summer 1972, pp . 302–07.

Herbert Davis

In the following excerpt, Davis examines the place of Swift's work in the canon of great poetry.

" BUT IT MUST BE ADMITTED THAT SWIFT IS RATHER THE MORALIST, CONCERNED NOT SO MUCH WITH HIS OWN EMOTIONAL CONDITION AS WITH THE EFFECT HE AIMS TO HAVE ON HIS READERS."

It has become a fashion of these days to attempt revaluations—a pleasant enough game but too likely to lead merely to a reversal of the values of the previous generation. The critic and the literary historian are of course obliged as a result of fresh knowledge or of a new point of view constantly to rearrange their material; and it is tempting to bring forward some writers whose work is less commonly noted and to eliminate altogether the stock figures who have been given a central place in the textbooks. Take Milton away from the seventeenth century, for example—immediately Donne and Dryden look different, and we are better prepared perhaps for the greatness of Pope. There would be no great harm done—indeed, it would be rather fun in a lecture to imitate this method, and to startle you by a fresh challenge. Forget the "line of wit"—as it has been called—from Donne to Pope, change the focus, take a longer view up and down the centuries, and who will be left as the most fascinating and the most dominating figure between Milton and Blake—who but Jonathan Swift? Yes, you would probably reply, we know that he was generally acknowledged by the Augustans as the greatest wit and satirist, the greatest genius even of that age, and he is often spoken of still as the most perfect writer of English prose. But nobody has ever claimed that he was a great poet. He can be witty in verse, and he can be satirical; but his poems are all occasional pieces, bagatelles; he never even attempted to write a serious, a great, poem.

...It is not easy to decide how best to approach Swift's poetry; it is so occasional, so varied in form and in mood. For my purpose there is perhaps an advantage in looking at it in the order in which it was published—to see it as Swift authorized its publication from time to time. The first publication of which we can be certain was an "Ode to the Athenian Society," with a prefatory letter dated Moor Park, February 4, 1691, and signed Jonathan Swift, which was printed in the *Supplement to the Fifth Volume of the Athenian Gazette* in 1692. It is the only one of his Pindaric odes which he printed himself, and it was reprinted three times during his life, though he probably would have preferred it to be forgotten like the rest of his early work. But it is worth looking at carefully. It is wholly in the manner of the time, reminding us in its form of that most popular poet Abraham Cowley and in its subject of that amateur scientist Sir Thomas Browne. Here indeed are "the wild excursions of a youthful pen, full of enthusiasm, quitting the 'narrow Path of Sense For a dear Ramble thro' Impertinence,' attacking the Wits, Epicureans, and atheists—'those who've made Railing a Rule of Wit and Obloquy a Trade.'" It is common to speak of the turgid eloquence of these Pindarics; but it must be admitted too that a certain rough force is there and in the midst of compliment and enthusiasm for things which Swift was soon to regard as misguided and absurd, there is already a touch of scepticism, an awareness "how fleeting and how vain our Learning and our Wit, how subject to the attacks of Censure and Pedantry and Pride."

It was not till 1711—twenty years later—that Swift authorized the publication, in a *Miscellany* also containing some of his early prose, of fifteen poems, some of which had already been attributed to him in unauthorized collections put out by Curll in 1709 and 1710. The contrast between these poems and the Pindarics is complete. The new poems are all humorous or satirical, and the language used is emptied of all rhetoric; the vocabulary and the order is the same as that of everyday speech or, as Swift himself puts it, "Something in Verse as True as Prose." Their character is most easily indicated by describing them as by the author of *A Tale of a Tub*. And the change that had come over Swift while he lived with Sir William Temple and had driven him from poetry to satire is told in some lines written in 1693, occasioned by Sir William Temple's late illness and recovery, which were not printed till 1789.

> Ah, should I tell a secret yet unknown,
> That thou ne'er hadst a being of thy own,
> But a wild form dependent on the brain,
> Scatt'ring loose features o'er the optic vein;
> Troubling the chrystal fountain of the sight,
> Which darts on poets eyes a trembling light;
> Kindled while reason sleeps, but quickly flies,

Like antic shapes in dreams, from waking eyes:
In sum, a glitt'ring voice, a painted name,
A walking vapor, like thy sister fame.

. . .

There thy enchantment broke, and from this hour
I here renounce thy visionary pow'r;
And since thy essence on my breath depends,
Thus with a puff the whole delusion ends.

I don't know whether among the many papers that Swift wrote and destroyed there were any attempts at a comedy; it was a way, as his friend Congreve had shown, to quick fame and preferment. But a poem like "Mrs. Francis Harris' Petition" makes one think that Swift might well have developed a vein of superb comic dialogue. He shows here an astonishing power—such as Wordsworth, for instance, never had—of taking the very phrases of ordinary common speech and tossing them without any awkward inversions into simple rhyming verse.

So the *Chaplain* came in; now the Servants say, he is
    my Sweet-heart,
Because he's always in my Chamber, and I always
    take his Part;
So, as the *Devil* would have it, before I was aware,
    out I blunder'd,
Parson, said I, can you cast a *Nativity*, when a
    Body's plunder'd?
(Now you must know, he hates to be call'd *Parson*,
    like the *Devil*.)
Truly, says he, Mrs. *Nab*, it might become you to be
    more civil:
If your Money be gone, as a Learned *Divine* says,
    d'ye see,
You are no *Text* for my Handling, so take that from
    me:
I was never taken for a *Conjurer* before, I'd have you
    to know.
Lord, said I, don't be angry, I'm sure I never
    thought you so;
You know, I honour the Cloth, I design to be a
    Parson's Wife,
I never took one in *Your Coat* for a *Conjurer* in all
    my Life.
With that, he twisted his Girdle at me like a Rope, as
    who should say,
Now you may go hang your self for me, and so went
    away.

You may say this is doggerel, not verse; but there is the same power in the excellent narrative of "Baucis and Philemon," in which the tone is carefully adapted to the burlesque form, if you read it as Swift first wrote it before the revision made under the influence of Addison. This is, of course, in the manner of Hudibras, whose vigor

and roughness Swift always admired. But in his own handling of the octosyllabic couplet he adds variety and range and, without losing any of the spontaneity and ease of movement, achieves an economy which reminds us of his prose.

We are too often reminded in Butler of that method of writing verse which he himself glances at in this passage:

But those that write in Rhime, still make
The one verse for the others sake:
For, one for sense, and one for Rhime,
I think's sufficient at one time.

Swift is never content with one verse for sense and one for rhyme. Even when he uses the heroic couplet, which he instinctively avoided for the most part as unnecessarily long, he fills the line without the use of recurring epithets, which so often make it monotonous. And when they do appear in the usual places, they carry their full weight of meaning:

The Turnkey now his Flock returning sees,
Duly let out a Nights to Steal for Fees.
The watchful Bailiffs take their silent Stands
And School-Boys lag with Satchels in their Hands.

Those are the last lines of a "Description of the Morning," which had appeared in the *Tatler*. But Swift was prouder of his later contribution—"A City Shower"—of which he writes to Stella: "They say 'tis the best thing I ever writ, and I think so too." Here we find already two elements so often present in his verse, which give his satire a double edge—a criticism of life put into a form which is at the same time a parody of current fashions in literature. While Addison and Pope were politely and urbanely making fun of the extravagances of sophisticated society, being at the same time charmed and attracted by it and accepting the foundations upon which it was built, Swift was to become a ruthless exposer of its shams and pretenses and injustices, a sceptical and critical observer of its glories and its boasted Augustan grandeurs. It was a joke to write a poem about the smells from the sink, the washing on the line, and the contents of the open drains at the side of the London streets, just as it was a joke later on to write about the intimacies of the lady's dressing-room or the marriage bed. And his readers for the most part accepted it as the humor of this eccentric and witty Dean, who could write about anything from a broomstick to the lord treasurer's staff of office. But some of his jokes had a wry flavor, and they suspected that he was a dangerous person, very different from the kindly Mr. Addison, or even Mr. Pope, who had unfortunately come too much under his influence and turned wholly to satire instead of writing pretty pastorals, translations, and soothing moral pieces.

… It is interesting to compare such work with the satirical portraits of Dryden and Pope. I should be inclined to say that Swift is more emotional and personal. Dryden—the master of contempt, as he has so well been called—is comparatively aloof and distant in his manner, Pope triumphantly gay as he flicks his victims round the ring like a circus master. In Swift's fiercest attacks there is no room left for any sense of play, for any of the tricks of the virtuoso—a fierce indignation burns within him, fed by his outraged sense of justice, his bitterness at the hollow mockery of so much human greatness. In the best of these pieces of invective his emotion is mastered, his words are clear and simple:

> His Grace! impossible! what dead!
> Of old age too, and in his bed!
> And could that Mighty Warrior Fall?
> And so inglorious, after all!
> Well, since he's gone, no matter how,
> The last loud trump must wake him now:
> And, trust me, as the noise grows stronger,
> He'd wish to sleep a little longer.
> And could he be indeed so old
> As by the news-papers we're told?
> Threescore, I think, is pretty high;
> 'Twas time in conscience he should die.
> This world he cumber'd long enough;
> He burnt his candle to the snuff;
> And that's the reason, some folks think,
> He left behind *so great a s—k.*
> Behold his funeral appears,
> Nor widow's sighs, nor orphan's tears,
> Wont at such times each heart to pierce,
> Attend the progress of his herse.
> But what of that, his friends may say,
> He had those honours in his day.
> True to his profit and his pride,
> He made them weep before he dy'd.
>
> Come hither, all ye empty things,
> Ye bubbles rais'd by breath of Kings;
> Who float upon the tide of state,
> Come hither, and behold your fate.
> Let pride be taught by this rebuke,
> How very mean a thing's a Duke;
> From all his ill-got honours flung,
> Turn'd to that dirt from whence he sprung.

It begins so quietly, with a sneer that is hardly perceptible, proceeds with a few crude jokes, as though the subject were worth no serious consideration, and ends with a sort of dismissal as complete as it is devastating:

> From all his ill-got honours flung,
> Turn'd to that dirt from whence he sprung

Notice that if you change two words in those lines you would have an almost conventional epitaph:

> From all his earthly honours flung,
> Turn'd to that dust from whence he sprung.

A great deal of Swift's verse if examined carefully would, I think, prove to be a sort of verbal parody of this kind. The worst of the verses written against the Hon. Richard Tighe, called "Clad All in Brown," is actually a parody on the tenth poem of Cowley's *Mistress.* They are a good example of the kind of thing D. H. Lawrence came to indulge in, which he called "Nettles" and described as bursts of anger, flung out spontaneously and providing the writer with a vent for his feelings—the sort of feelings it is good to get rid of. But it must be admitted that Swift is rather the moralist, concerned not so much with his own emotional condition as with the effect he aims to have on his readers. Even after the death of Chief Justice Whitshed, he still feels it to be his duty to pursue such a villain, and so he puts out all sort of squibs, which can be hawked about the streets in such form as to stick in the minds of the populace.

Source: Herbert Davis, "The Poetry of Jonathan Swift," in *College English,* Vol. 2, No. 2, November 1940, pp. 102–15.

SOURCES

Ackroyd, Peter, *Blake: A Biography,* Knopf, 1996, p. 124.

Bateson, F. W., *English Poetry: A Critical Introduction,* 2nd ed., Longmans Green, 1966, pp. 124–25.

Bayne-Powell, Rosamond, *Eighteenth-Century London Life,* E. P. Dutton, 1938, pp. 199, 209, 271–72, 379.

Carnochan, W. B., *Confinement and Flight: An Essay on English Literature of the Eighteenth Century,* University of California Press, 1977, pp. 67–69.

Daiches, David, and John Flower, *Literary Landscapes of the British Isles: A Narrative Atlas,* Paddington Press, 1979, p. 50.

Downie, J. A., *Jonathan Swift: Political Writer,* Routledge & Kegan Paul, 1984, p. 125.

England, A. B., *Energy and Order in the Poetry of Swift,* Associated University Presses, 1980, p. 100.

———, "World without Order: Some Thoughts on the Poetry of Swift," in *Essential Articles for the Study of*

Jonathan Swift's Poetry, edited by David M. Vieth, Archon Books, 1984, p. 43.

Jaffe, Nora Crow, "Jonathan Swift," in *Dictionary of Literary Biography*, Vol. 95, *Eighteenth-Century British Poets, First Series*, edited by John E. Sitter, Gale Research, 1990, pp. 275–301.

Jarrett, Derek, *Britain: 1688–1815*, Longman, 1970, p. 37.

"Largest EU City," in *Office for National Statistics*, http://www.statistics.gov.uk/cci/nugget.asp?id = 384 (accessed May 7, 2010).

Manlove, C. N., "Swift's Structures: 'A Description of the Morning' and Some Others," in *Studies in English Literature, 1500–1900*, Vol. 29, Summer 1989, pp. 463–72.

"A Population History of London," in *The Proceedings of the Old Bailey*, http://www.oldbaileyonline.org/static/Population-history-of-london.jsp#a1760-1815 (accessed May 7, 2010).

Savage, Roger, "Swift's Fallen City: 'A Description of the Morning,'" in *Essential Articles for the Study of Jonathan Swift's Poetry*, edited by David M. Vieth, Archon Books, 1984, pp. 130, 138, 140.

Swift, Jonathan, "A Description of the Morning," in *Swift: Poetical Works*, edited by Herbert Davis, Oxford University Press, 1967, p. 86.

———, "A Description of the Morning," in *Representative Poetry Online*, University of Toronto Libraries, http://rpo.library.utoronto.ca/poem/2062.html (accessed May 20, 2010).

Trevelyan, G. M., *Illustrated English Social History*, Vol. 3, *The Eighteenth Century*, Penguin, 1968, pp. 70–71.

Vieth, David M., "Metaphors and Metamorphoses: Basic Techniques in the Middle Period of Swift's Poetry, 1698–1719," in *Contemporary Studies of Swift's Poetry*, edited by John Irwin Fisher and Donald C. Mell, Jr., Associated University Presses, 1981, p. 57.

FURTHER READING

Bloom, Harold, and Daniel Cook, eds., *Jonathan Swift*, Bloom's Classic Critical Views, Chelsea House, 2009.

This collection of critical articles on Swift from a variety of historical periods is intended as an aid to young student researchers.

Fox, Christopher, ed., *The Cambridge Companion to Jonathan Swift*, Cambridge University Press, 2003.

A collection of thirteen essays on all aspects of Swift's work, as well as an introduction by Fox, this work makes an excellent introduction for anyone who is just becoming acquainted with Swift.

Hitchcock, Tim, *Down and Out in Eighteenth-Century London*, Hambledon and London, 2004.

This is a study of those who eked out a living on the margins of society in eighteenth-century London, sweeping roads, selling matches, doing whatever they could to survive, including begging.

Scott, James, *Satire: From Horace to Yesterday's Comic Strips*, Prestwick House, 2005.

This is a concise, lively introduction to satire through the ages. The author first defines satire, and then examines it as it appears in poetry, fiction, and essays, as well as cartoons, television, and movies. Authors discussed include Horace, Swift, Geoffrey Chaucer, Voltaire, Mark Twain, and H. L. Mencken.

SUGGESTED SEARCH TERMS

Jonathan Swift

Jonathan Swift AND A Description of the Morning

satire AND eighteenth century

London AND history

heroic couplets

Augustan Age AND English literature

satire AND Swift

poetry AND Swift

London AND Swift

Fear

GABRIELA MISTRAL

1924

"From her maternal hand this poet offers us her potion, which has the savor of earth and which quenches the thirst of the heart." These are the words of the Nobel Committee when Gabriela Mistral was awarded the Nobel Prize for Literature in 1945. In the same speech, it was also noted that "Gabriela Mistral shared her maternal love with the children whom she taught." "Fear" was published in Mistral's second collection of poetry, *Ternura* (Tenderness). The poems in this book are referred to as children's poems, even though they have decidedly mature themes, and they have, in the years since the collection was first published in 1924, become standards of elementary-school education in Chile and throughout Latin America.

In a section at the end of the book called "Colophon by Way of Explaining," Mistral discussed why she chose to write a book about mothers and children. She wrote, "The woman who has never nursed, who does not feel the weight of her child against her body, who never puts anyone to sleep day or night, how can she possibly hum a *berceuse* [lullaby]?" Ironically, although she dedicated her life to children through her profession as an educator, Mistral herself never married and never had a child. Her ideas about the bond between mothers and children, which have come to mean so much to generations of mothers who are thrilled to find at last their feelings expressed in print, came to the author second-hand, through observation of

Gabriela Mistral (© *Mary Evans Picture Library / Alamy*)

the hundreds of children that she worked with as a teacher and her experience in growing up in a household of teachers. As is apparent from the popular and critical acclaim lavished upon her work about motherhood, Mistral was able to touch upon the very real emotions of the experience even though she did not live the experience herself.

AUTHOR BIOGRAPHY

Mistral was one of the most famous poets to come out of Chile and the first poet from a Latin American nation to win the Nobel Prize for Literature. She lived a colorful and active life, visiting foreign cities as a representative of Chile, and was recognized as an expert in education throughout the Americas. Her father, a teacher, married a widow who already had a fifteen-year-old daughter. On April 7, 1889, Mistral was born Lucia Goday Alcayaga in Vicuna, in the Elqui valley in northern Chile. When she was three, her father abandoned the family, and

she was raised and educated by her mother and her half-sister Emilina, who were both teachers. She spent her childhood in the natural, rural setting of the Elqui valley.

By the time she was fifteen, she was already a teaching assistant. At eighteen she met Romello Ureta, a railroad engineer, and fell in love, but their relationship did not work out; not long after they broke up, for reasons unrelated to his relationship with Mistral, he committed suicide. His death affected her the rest of her life. In 1910, she received her official teaching certificate, and by 1912 she was recognized across Chile for her work in teaching poor people.

In 1914, Mistral won a national poetry competition with three sonnets that she titled *Los Sonetos de la Muerte* (Sonnets of Death). This was the first time she used the pen name "Gabriela Mistral," which she would be known by for the rest of her life—Gabriela after the angel Gabriel, and Mistral after the fierce, cold wind that blows over the south of France.

In 1922, Mexico's Secretary of Education invited Mistral to collaborate with him on reforming that country's education system, and she moved to Mexico City for two years. In 1921, a professor at Columbia University in New York gave a lecture about her poetry, and when interested members of the audience tried to look up her work they found that no books of her work had ever been published; this led to the publication of *Desolación* (Desolation) in 1922. *Ternura*, the book in which "Fear" appears, followed in 1924. It is a book about children and motherhood, with poems familiar to generations of children who grew up in Latin America.

Mistral continued to publish influential prose pieces and to travel the world as a consultant in affairs of education. Her only other two books of poetry, published at wide intervals of time, were *Tala* (Felling, as in felling trees) in 1938 and *Lager* in 1954. She received the Nobel Prize for Literature in 1945. Starting in 1933 and for the next twenty years, Mistral was Chile's consul to several cities throughout the world, including Lisbon, Los Angeles, and Madrid. She also served as the Chilean delegate to the United Nations, retiring in 1954 to Rosalyn Bay, Long Island, New York, where she died in January 1957. On her tomb is the inscription, "What the soul does for the body so does the poet for her people."

POEM TEXT

I don't want my daughter
to get turned into a swallow.
She'd dive straight up to heaven
and never come down to our mattress,
she'd make a nest up in the eaves   5
and I couldn't comb her hair.
I don't want my daughter
turned into a swallow.

I don't want my daughter
to get made into a princess.   10
If she wears golden slippers
how can she play in the fields?
And when the night comes
she wouldn't lie beside me.
I don't want my daughter   15
turned into a princess.

And most of all I don't want them
to go and make her queen!
They'd set her on a throne
so high I couldn't reach it,   20
and when the night came
I couldn't rock her.
I don't want my daughter
to become a queen!

MEDIA ADAPTATIONS

- Babbitt Instructional Resources produced a videocassette with accompanying teacher's guidebook and script called *Gabriela Mistral: Poems of Chile* in 1999.

- Mistral's poem "El Ruego" is read in Spanish on the 1960 album *Antologia Oral: Poesia Hispanoamerican del Siglo XX* (Oral Anthology: Spanish-American Poetry of the 20th Century). It is available as an MP3 download on Amazon.com.

- Dina Rot sings Mistral's poem "Cosas" on her album *Yo Canto a Los Poetas-Cartas* (1998). It is available as an MP3 download on Amazon.com.

- Catalina Levinton recites Mistral's poem "Dios Lo Quiere" on her album *Catalina Levinton-Recital Poetico* (1958). It is available as an MP3 download on Amazon.com.

POEM SUMMARY

Stanza 1

This poem opens with a seemingly nonsensical fear: the speaker does not want her young daughter to be transformed into a swallow. Swallows are small, fast birds known for socializing with other birds of their kind and forming large colonies. They also are known for the long distances of their migrations. When the speaker of this poem infers that some unidentified people or force could turn her little girl into a bird, she is speaking metaphorically, referring to aspects of the swallow that the girl would have if she went through such a transformation. In this case, the fear expressed is that the girl will, as she grows up, start socializing with others of her kind and fly away, traveling with them rather than staying near her home. At this point in the poem, the reader does not know how such a transformation could occur, but it seems that it would be something done *to* the girl, not something she does herself. Even at the end of the poem, we are offered no clear idea of the cause behind the potential changes. There may be some particular mysterious group that wants control of the daughter, but, with no other evidence offered,

the best answer seems to be that the mysterious "them" are simply the people with whom a young girl will come into contact while growing up: the world of school, teachers, and classmates that directs a child's attention outside the home.

A parent's fear of losing his or her child is so powerful that it is natural to associate it with watching the child disappear off into the vast unknown, as mentioned in the third line. Mistral was certainly familiar with air travel, but she spent her childhood in a rural, provincial area of Chile during the end of the nineteenth century, with neither the automobiles nor the air travel that would later conquer great distances. She was well aware of the intimidating vastness of the open sky, of the ways that a simple rural person could feel that someone was hopelessly gone once he or she had disappeared beyond the field of vision. It would be the same way that a parent would feel upon losing sight of his or her child. The reference in line 4 to a shared bed means that the child would not return home each night as children do when they are dependent upon their parents for support, just as birds leave to make their own nests, as referenced in line 5.

While the opening lines of the poem indicate that the speaker's fear is caused by the thought that her daughter will fly far away, this section indicates that she does not want her going even a short distance. It would seem, in the natural progression of life, that a parent would be glad to have her child attached to the same house where she grew up, with a stable home that is easily in her mother's sight. Rejecting this distance from her daughter means that this speaker is not willing to tolerate even the normal distances that will come between a mother and her growing child. The act of combing the child's hair, mentioned in line 6, symbolizes taking care of the child in ways that involve the very personal act of touching.

The stanza closes with a repetition of the first two lines. This gives the poem a song-like quality, with a refrain that emphasizes the most important facts. In this case, readers are reminded first of the cause of the speaker's fear, the possible transformation of her daughter into a bird. Another key element is the unknown nature of the force that would cause this change; the phrasing emphasizes the daughter's helplessness and the threat to the girl that comes from mysterious outside forces.

Stanza 2

The diction here is just slightly different from the first two lines of stanza 1. Then, the mother expressed the fear that the girl would be turned into a swallow; this second stanza expresses the fear that she will be made into a princess. The word choice shows less aggression this time, though, indicating that it would take less force on the part of the mysterious outsiders to perform this transformation. This is, in fact, quite likely; many little girls would welcome a transformation into a princess. This slight change in verb subtly indicates that the daughter might be open to change, even though the mother does not want it. Just as the first stanza surprises the reader with the idea that someone might be able to change a child into a bird, this stanza draws attention by stating the mother's opposition to the world glorifying her daughter. Often, parents refer to girl children as "princess," indicating that they are privileged by birth, that they should have no duties other than being themselves, and that the wealth of the world will be handed to them. When

this speaker wishes that her daughter not be given such easy privilege, readers sit up and take notice.

There is an implicit love of nature here that the poem just presents, without supporting. The speaker of the poem wishes against her daughter's social success because she does not want the girl to lose touch with nature, to become unable to play in the meadow. The way that this is presented emphasizes the idea that pampering the girl would separate her from nature. The poem assumes that she would, as a princess, wear golden slippers: small, dainty, and impractical for romping across uncultivated ground.

Like lines 5 and 6 in stanza 1, lines 13 and 14 contain a direct statement of the speaker's personal desire to keep her daughter to herself, away from the outside world. This time, however, there is less reason to believe that the fear of losing her daughter has to do with the girl's welfare and more reason to see it as a fear of being alone. While the earlier statement emphasized the selflessness of the act by stating the speaker's wish to serve her daughter, by combing her hair, this stanza states her wish as being directly for the speaker's, not the daughter's, benefit. It expresses the fear that the mother could no longer sleep at her daughter's side, which indicates that the speaker is concerned with her own loneliness.

Once again, repeating the first lines of the stanza has the effect of a refrain from a song, emphasizing the main idea to make it easier for a listener or reader to remember. This time, however, there is an added measure of desperation on the part of the speaker, whose own self-interest is more plainly on display. The repetition now seems like a way of reminding and assuring herself that what she fears cannot hurt her.

Stanza 3

One would expect that nothing but good would come to the daughter from becoming a queen, attaining the ultimate in power in the human social world. Being a queen would certainly be better than being a princess, because a queen holds true power while a princess only has potential. Once again, however, this poem challenges expectations by presenting a mother's wish for her daughter *not* to be made into a queen. She would like that even less than she would like her to be a princess. An element of reality is implied in the fact that the mysterious "they" (finally identified, though still left unnamed) are assumed to have the power to make all of the transformations in this poem take place.

In these lines, the speaker's fear reaches its emotional height. She fears that her daughter's social ascendancy would create an insurmountable division between them. In the scenario that she suggests here, the daughter may have the ability (through the power of "them") to rise up to the level of royalty, but the speaker is so humble that she could never even be in the presence of royalty, not even if the queen is her daughter. Psychologically, it makes sense that a mother would worry that her daughter might transcend her own humble roots and find herself in company that would keep her own mother away. The odd psychological element throughout this poem is the projection of the unnamed "them," used to represent social forces that would take the daughter away from her mother. Her fear of losing her daughter, which is a natural by-product of a parent's love, is personified, though incompletely, by characters that are not given names or identities.

These lines indicate the selfless concern for the child that is missing from the parallel lines in the previous stanza. Lines 13 and 14 in stanza 2 indicate the speaker's wish for comfort when she says that she does not want to lose the feeling of having the daughter in her bed; here, the mother wants to be able to rock her daughter in the night, to give comfort to her. The use of the night as the time of fear, when either of them would need comfort, is fairly standard in poetry, based on a normal fear of the dark and the discomfort and mystery of being unable to see. Repeating this fear in the final stanza emphasizes the idea that this poem is not just about a mother's natural concern that her daughter will grow up and leave her but that it has its roots in deeper, more powerful, psychological mysteries.

The same pattern that ended the other two stanzas—the repetition of the first two lines—is played out again here, with one slight difference, the addition of an exclamation mark at the end. Since this is another repetition of a thought that has already been expressed at the beginning of the stanza, the effect of the exclamation point is not to add any new information, just emotion. This speaker *really* does not want her little girl made into a queen. Repetition and the exclamation mark push the speaker's fear even higher, almost to a degree of terror, making it difficult to read this as a normal case of discomfort about

her little girl growing up. Mistral presents this speaker as a complex character who has a right to be concerned but who has let her maternal fear, especially her fear of what might be done to her daughter by unidentified forces, take control of her mind.

THEMES

Nature

From the details provided, it is clear that the speaker lives in a rural setting: she sleeps on a straw bed and she knows enough about birds to imagine which type of bird her daughter would become if she were to become one. She knows that swallows travel with large flocks of other swallows and that they cover vast distances in their migrations, which means that they leave for long periods of time. The transformation to a swallow in the first stanza is not presented as a return to nature but as a corruption of nature, forcing a little girl to separate from her mother. One of the primary fears worrying the speaker of this poem is that her little girl might no longer be able to play in the meadow if she becomes too deeply a part of society, symbolized here by golden slippers, valuable and fragile. She would prefer her daughter to not be pampered by the excessive delicacy of culture, to instead keep in touch with her surroundings (as long as her surroundings are the rural area that the speaker knows as home). The image of playing in the meadow is an idealized way of imagining that the child can remain one with nature, presenting childhood play as part of nature and little golden slippers as the opposite of it.

Natural Cycles

This poem presents a parent fearing the changes that will happen to a little girl. Change is inevitable, and it is natural that a parent would fear that change might cause her daughter to drift away, a fear that reflects the intensity of the parent's current involvement in the child's life. The likelihood of change is treated creatively here, described in terms of transformations that have less to do with reality than with the parent's emotional state. Of course a child cannot be transformed from a human into a bird, but the parent might feel as if the child is a bird when she leaves, like a bird flying from its nest. Children from humble backgrounds are not spontaneously

TOPICS FOR FURTHER STUDY

- Find a fairy tale in which a person is turned into a bird or an animal, and use its situation to illuminate the situation described in "Fear." Create a PowerPoint or other multimedia presentation that uses scenes from the fairy tale to illustrate your points.

- A modern-day equivalent of turning a little girl into a princess might be turning her into a pop- or rock-music star. Create a poem that describes the concerns a mother might have over such a turn of events. Post your poem to a Web page and invite comments from your teacher and classmates on the themes and style of your poem.

- Pick a famous person from history and create a report on the relationship between this person and his or her mother. Use Internet and library research, especially biographies and autobiographies to find information and remember to cite all sources.

- Read the young-adult novel *The Unwritten Rule* (2010) by Elizabeth Scott. It contains several very realistic conversations between a mother and daughter. Choose one of those conversations and write a free verse poem that mimics "Fear" in the way the mother addresses her concerns for the daughter in the conversation you chose.

turned into princesses either, but to a parent, looking on as society gives the girl the adoration she used to get from her mother, it might feel as if she becomes a princess. She also does not need to fear the girl being turned into a queen, but if the girl were to become someday a woman of power and influence, it would feel to her mother as if she were a queen. The poem speculates that all of these changes and transformations would be brought about by some power, referenced in only the vaguest terms as some group of people who would want to make the girl into a sparrow, a princess, or a queen for unexplained reasons.

The most reasonable understanding of this group is that they are the people whom a growing child would meet throughout her life, and that her transformation would then be just the normal result of the influence of other people.

Society

The speaker of this poem has, like all parents, a special bond with her daughter: it is a small, private society with just two members, shared when the speaker rocks her child and combs her hair. Beyond their small world is a larger one inhabited by people who want to change the daughter in ways that would take her away. If they were to succeed in turning the daughter into a swallow, a princess, or a queen, she would be a successful part of their world, but she would not be part of the mother's any more. The poem's title refers to a mother's fear of losing her daughter—not to death, not to disagreement, but to the world of other people. This fear is expressed most directly and most poignantly in the poem's third stanza, in which the mother hopes against her daughter's social success by visualizing a scenario in which her daughter would be made queen, with all of the command over society that a queen has, but when she is placed on the throne her mother would not be able to see her any more. This reflects the social responsibilities of a queen, who would not be allowed to associate with a commoner even if it was her parent. Social allegiances would, in such a case, become more important than private bonds.

As much as readers can sympathize with the poem's speaker for her fear of losing the intimate relationship she shares with her daughter, it is based on her fear of society in general. She fears that a public life will give her daughter the freedom that a bird has, that it will offer the honors due a princess or, even worse, the power due a queen. By imagining that society could or would bestow such honors, the narrator proves herself to be unfamiliar with the ways of public life, uncertain of what it might do. She is a woman who sleeps on a straw bed, who rocks her child to sleep and combs her child's hair—she understands a small world, not society at large. Not understanding the larger social world, she fears it, and her fear makes her imagine the public world coming to take away the thing she values most.

The speaker of the poem says she does not want her daughter " to get made into a princess." *(Svetlana Turilov/ Shutterstock.com)*

STYLE

Free Verse

Even in its original Spanish, "Fear" follows no strict rhyming or rhythmic pattern. This is appropriate because the speaker of the poem, sleeping on a straw mattress and worrying that her daughter will one day be too good to associate with her, is a simple woman and would not have a voice that is very polished or refined. Still, there are sections that follow rhythmic structures. This structure has more to do with displaying the poet's skill than the character's personality. There are definite rhythmic patterns in "Fear," but they do not contribute to an overall rhythmic design.

Other elements help to give readers a sense that the author has a firm control on the ideas expressed here. Each stanza has eight lines, and each begins and ends with a variation on the same two lines. There is no set length for the individual lines. They do not all have the same number of syllables, but there is not any great degree of variance, either. For instance, there are no very short or very long lines. This speaker is a person of moderation—the whole poem is about fear of change—but she is too simple to have her ideas presented in an elaborate, ornamental, or complex pattern.

Modernism

When Mistral wrote "Fear" in the 1920s, the modernism movement that influenced artistic theory across the world was settling into maturity. Literary theorists use the term "modernism" to describe a wide variety of changes that came about at the beginning of the twentieth century. It is generally used to explain the backlash against literary tradition, a reaction caused by the way psychoanalysis (a way of studying the human mind) changed the understanding of personal behavior and Marxism (a theory of economics and government) changed the understanding of social behavior. In poetry, modernism involved casting away traditional forms and concepts of beauty and using words that evoked an emotional impression instead of primarily those that had a beautiful sound together. Many forms of modernism, such as surrealism, imagism, and dadaism, were more concerned with striking readers with a powerful feeling than with overall logic.

In Latin American countries, literary trends generally followed the European trends of the time. A unique literary theory had not been developed, and much of the literature that was read and discussed was from Europe or the United States. For instance, when Mistral's collection *Ternura* was published, there was no body of children's literature in Latin America. She had to make what she could out of the modernist sense of using direct language and out of the folktales of her native country.

In many ways, her poems in *Ternura* anticipate what may be Latin America's greatest contribution to world literature, which is the magical realism movement that started in the 1960s and continues today. Magical realism, usually associated with fiction, is a joining of a serious, realistic tone with supernatural occurrences that readers know do not really happen in this world. Some of the earliest and most widely read examples of this genre are Colombian author Gabriel García Márquez's 1967 novel *One Hundred Years of Solitude* and Argentine writer Julio Cortazar's *Hopscotch*, from 1966. Both of these works contain elements that would be called fantasy in other books, treating them with a realist's seriousness. As Márquez, who won the Nobel Prize for Literature in 1982, explains it, the tone he was trying to achieve "was based on the way grandmother used to tell stories. She told things that sounded supernatural and fantastic, but she told them with complete naturalness."

HISTORICAL CONTEXT

Chile is a long, narrow country that runs along the western coast of South America. The Andes mountain range runs the length of the inland border. Chile was originally inhabited by Araucanian natives, but it was colonized by the Spanish in 1550. Unlike many South American countries, Chile does not have abundant deposits of gold or silver ore, and for this reason its growth as a colony was slow. It does, however, have great stores of iron, copper, and nitrates. During the Industrial Revolution that swept the world in the nineteenth century, as factories and machines

became more important everywhere, these elements became crucial for manufacturing. Especially influential were Chile's nitrates, which were essential in the fertilizers that became increasingly valuable as countries all over the world moved from farm economies to urban industrial societies, and also for the manufacture of explosives. By the dawn of the twentieth century, Chile became a rich country thanks to nitrate production.

The country's greatest problem was that its nitrate wealth was not evenly distributed. The country's wealth was in the hands of a small proportion of people. As the economy grew, cities grew at a tremendous rate, too fast to control, and they ended up breeding slums. The government looked after the interests of the wealthy: starting in 1891, Chile was a parliamentary republic, with the parliament appointing the president and his cabinet. The parliament was elected, but the elections were controlled by wealthy business people.

Labor organizations started to gain in popularity at the beginning of the twentieth century, advocating socialist and anarchist policies that would take wealth from the rich and put it in the hands of the common people. In cities and in the nitrate and copper mines in the north, where Mistral grew up, unions encouraged workers to fight against their employers to increase their financial positions and working conditions. Because the government was, essentially, an arm of the owners of industry, government forces were used to fight the workers. One particularly stirring episode in the struggle for labor reform was a massacre at the miners' camp at Iquique in 1907, where government troops killed striking workers. Economic tensions became even more strained during the following decade when, during World War I from 1914 to 1918, the world's usage of nitrates dwindled. Even worse was the fact that during the war, Germany developed synthetic nitrates for its explosives; the reduced demand for naturally occurring nitrates devastated the Chilean economy.

In the 1920s, when "Fear" was written, the government of Chile was changing. In 1920, Arturo Alessandri was made president in an attempt to keep the people from rebelling and taking over the government. Although the parliament had appointed Alessandri to be a moderate and to look after the interests of the parliament members, he turned out to be a true

COMPARE
&
CONTRAST

- **1924:** The interest of the United States in Chile and other South American countries is limited to their production of rich ores. In Chile, the Chuquicamata copper mine and the Tofo iron mines produce metals of greater purity than those found in North America.

  Today: Chile still produces about 35 percent of the world's copper, which accounts for 45 percent of Chilean exports.

- **1924:** In 1920, a long term drop in the birth rate began as primary education became free, compulsory, and nonsectarian for boys and girls, providing opportunities other than motherhood for women.

  Today: On April 29, 2010, the Chilean Women, Work and Maternity Commission was created and mandated to update the labor and maternity policies for the nation because the fertility rate had dropped to just 1.9 children per woman, not enough for population replacement.

- **1924:** A right-wing military coup ousts Arturo Alessandri, who had been president of Chile since 1920. Supporters of Alessandri help him gain back the presidency the following year.

  Today: Sebastián Piñera becomes the first president from the political right to be elected since the ouster of dictatorial president General Augusto Pinochet in 1989.

reformer once in office. He was popular with the people, but he had trouble getting any measures passed by Parliament, and therefore the country sank into deeper financial trouble during his presidency. In 1924, Alessandri bypassed the legislators and went straight to the people who elected them, and with the people's support he was able to have his reform legislation passed. This incited a coup by military right-wingers, who took control of the government in September of 1924. The reformists had enough power by then to perform a second coup in January of 1925, and a new constitution was drawn up that gave more power to the common people but that also made compromises with the wealthy landowners to ensure their cooperation. This constitution served the country until the early 1970s, when Salvador Allende became the first president elected with a Marxist agenda in a non-Communist country. Three years into Allende's administration, he was ousted by a coup led by General Augusto Pinochet, with American support. Pinochet ruled the country for almost twenty years and had himself declared a senator for life. By the late 1980s, the government began to allow more

social and economic freedoms. In 1989, Pinochet was voted out of office, and the parliament received a new majority of members. Since then, Chile has had five presidents representing both sides of the political spectrum.

CRITICAL OVERVIEW

Through the decades, Mistral has remained continuously popular in South America, especially her native Chile, but in North America her reputation has been kept alive mainly by the good word of critics. It was, in fact, good critical response that led to the publication of her first book, *Desolación*. It was not until a professor at Columbia University in New York, Federico de Onis, talked about Mistral's poetry in a lecture that interested readers created a demand that a publisher filled. Margaret Bates points out, in her introduction to *Selected Poems of Gabriela Mistral*, why it has been so difficult to capture the flavor of Mistral's poetry for North American readers. They are especially difficult to translate,

Europe and North America has been unimpeachable. In South America and among Chileans, she is a sentimental favorite, a source of pride and a symbol of the culture. "She carried within her a fusion of Basque and Indian heritage," writes Margot Arce de Vázquez, formerly the chair of the Department of Spanish Studies at the University of Puerto Rico. "Spanish in her rebellious individualistic spirit; very Indian in her long, deep silences and that priestly aura of stone idol. To this representative cultural value must be added the great value of her literary work, an incomparable document for what it reveals of her person and for its unique American accent."

The poem is about a mother and her child. (Studio 1 One | Shutterstock.com)

she writes, because "the effect of utter simplicity is backed up by a subtle, complex, hidden machine that extracts from each word, from each sound and accent, its maximum challenge." Bates quoted Marcel Bataillon, author of *Erasme et L'Esoagne*, saying that he had "found even more reason to love the Spanish language after reading Gabriela."

Critics examining Mistral's poetry, especially the poems from *Ternura*, try to separate the attitude of rural simplicity in her work from the actual simplicity of her humble origins. In an essay called "Gabriela Mistral, the Restless Soul," Majorie Agosin notes, "The Elqui Valley, Chilean women and children, created Gabriela Mistral's voice; it sprang from her depths, and was destined for the exterior world." It was the combination of this rural, home-bound persona and her worldliness as an international traveler that gave Mistral her distinct voice, according to Agosin.

Since winning the Nobel Prize for Literature in 1945, Mistral's reputation with critics in

CRITICISM

David Kelly

Kelly is an instructor of creative writing and composition at two colleges in Illinois. In the following essay, he looks at several of the poems from Mistral's book Ternura *and how they successfully capture the idea of motherhood.*

The poems in Gabriela Mistral's second collection, *Ternura*, are supposed to be about mothers and their relationships with their children. The author calls them "colloquies the mother holds with her own soul, with her child, and with the Earth Spirit around her, visible by day and audible by night." Addressing the wide, emotion-laden subject of motherhood is an ambitious thing to try, particularly because Mistral was not a mother herself. Like New England poet Emily Dickinson, she was confident in what she knew about her subject and did not feel the need to justify herself with the weak excuse of experience, which proves nothing (you cannot, for instance, expect everyone who has a spleen to be qualified by that intimate experience to explain what it does or where in the body it is located). Unlike Dickinson, who published hardly anything in her lifetime, Mistral put her theoretical works out in the open for all who had actually experienced motherhood to see and criticize, and she traveled the world, living in different countries as an emissary of her government, while Dickinson only left her hometown a few times in her lifetime. What are readers to learn from this? For one thing, it is clear that Gabriela Mistral, living among mothers and children as an educator

WHAT DO I READ NEXT?

- *Madwomen: The "Locas mujeres" Poems of Gabriela Mistral* (2008) is a bilingual edition of some of her most important poems translated by Randall Couch. These are poems of catastrophe and mourning that explore the meaning of self.

- Isabel Allende is the niece of slain Chilean president Salvador Allende. Her 1986 novel *The House of the Spirits* tells the story of one powerful family that captures the spirit of the country. It became an international best seller.

- Short stories by Chilean women from 1920 to the present are compiled in the 1995 anthology *What Is Secret: Short Stories by Chilean Women*, edited by Marjorie Agosin.

- Alfonsina Storni was an Argentine author who wrote poetry at about the same time as Mistral. Her poems are available in English translation in *Alfonsina Storni: Selected Poems*, a 1995 White Pines Press paperback.

- Pablo Neruda is another poet from Chile; in 1971, he won the Nobel Prize for Literature. His first book of poetry was published a year before "Fear" was published in *Ternura*. Neruda's best works are available in English and Spanish in *Pablo Neruda: Selected Poems/Bilingual Edition*, published in 1990 by Houghton Mifflin.

- An American poet who, like Mistral, wrote more from understanding than experience was Emily Dickinson, the famous Belle of Amherst. After years of various Dickinson poems showing up in various places, they were collected in 1960 in a definitive edition, edited by Thomas H. Johnson, called *The Complete Poems of Emily Dickinson*.

- *Heart by Heart: Mothers and Daughters Listening to Each Other: An Anthology of Stories by and about Mothers and Daughters with Commentary* (published in 2004 by iUniverse) is a collection of poems and stories from all stages of the relationships between mothers and daughters—from birth to death, edited by Marianne Preger-Simon, MD, a psychologist who has led workshops that explore the mother-daughter relationship. It would be a great resource for mothers and teen daughters to read together.

- Award-winning Native American poet Joy Harjo's 2002 collection, *How We Became Human: New and Selected Poems 1975–2001*, includes poems on what constitutes family and the quest for love.

- *Political Bodies: Gender, History, and the Struggle for Narrative Power in Recent Chilean Literature* (2002) is part of the Bucknell Studies in Latin American Literature and Theory series. This volume, by Alice A. Nelson, seeks to trace the new social movements in Chile to changes in Latin American literature, especially the feminist element.

since age fourteen (and as a child before that), did more research on the subject she was theorizing about than Emily Dickinson did. Mistral was also more confident about her conclusions. She was successful in capturing the bonds of motherhood, and Dickinson was successful in capturing the complexities of romantic love. Neither case gives any conclusive evidence about experience, observation, or popular sentiment.

It is, in fact, its bold departure from popular sentiment that marks Gabriela Mistral's greatness. The aspects of the maternal state of mind that she captures in *Ternura* are not ones that readers are accustomed to seeing on paper, and yet readers know, as she did, that they are right. Much of the public face of motherhood is about selflessness, about extending beyond oneself, about giving up all one has that is good, if necessary, and taking on another's troubles.

> THE ASPECTS OF THE MATERNAL STATE OF
> MIND THAT SHE CAPTURES IN *TERNURA* ARE NOT
> ONES THAT READERS ARE ACCUSTOMED TO SEEING
> ON PAPER, AND YET READERS KNOW, AS SHE DID,
> THAT THEY ARE RIGHT."

Motherhood, in short, is the drama of life's most noble moments.

The problem, as even those of us who are not mothers can realize, is that this view of nobleness is incomplete. That which has life's greatest moments must logically be balanced with some rough spots as well. Art seldom probes the deeply troublesome things about being a mother. It is commonplace to hear that it is a lot of work with little thanks, but these apparent negatives actually add to the positive side of the equation, pointing out the superior character of one who can put up with such trouble. Sometimes macabre stories are circulated about negligent mothers abandoning or abusing their children, but these stories are news precisely because they are so unusual. In societies where men dominate the economies, mothers are "paid" for their labors with honor; this is referred to as "the cult of the mother," in which society assigns special privileges, as well as special responsibilities, to motherhood. Unfortunately, honor is too often taken too far, blotting out the dishonorable instead of recognizing it.

What Mistral brought to the discussion with *Ternura* was a piercing examination of the subject, putting it into a quiet place, beyond all of the surrounding cultural noise and clutter in the atmosphere. She did not have to emphasize negative examples of motherhood because the truth is deeper and more profound than could ever be conveyed through specific examples. At the heart of the beauty of motherhood she found the psychological truths of sadness, loneliness, and fear.

The titles of the poems in *Ternura* are not the kinds of titles that usually appear in the upbeat version that literature—not just popular literature, but the most intellectual, too—often

presents. They include "The Sad Mother," "Bitter Song," and "Fear." The poems with titles that are less disturbing are no less forlorn in the stories that they tell about women who look at their children and see their own continuance (for whatever that is worth) and at the same time their own vulnerability. These women measure their own lives by how close or far their infants are to them.

"Bitter Song," for instance, starts with the mother/speaker suggesting that her son play a game with her, imagining that they are a king and a queen, and it states as obvious that the bounties of nature are his. The son's birthright—granted to him because, well, because he is her beloved—includes detailed descriptions of the lands that are his. A common glorification of motherhood would be content to list the wondrous things that this mother wishes for her child, but Mistral includes a stanza in parentheses about the child shivering and the non-nourishing breasts of the mother, and later in the poem she repeats the entire stanza. The sense of motherhood is conveyed by the abundance she can see around her while watching her child do without, while the bitterness of the title comes from the repeated question that makes us think about who really does own this land, and how that owner could possibly deserve such wealth more than a son who is loved so much. The reason Mistral is able to introduce the darkness that is left out of so much other literature about motherhood is that there is a scapegoat, someone to blame for the suffering in this poem: the landowners.

And what of "The Sad Mother"? If there is one thing that the traditional uplifting ideal of motherhood does not have room for, it is sadness, except for the momentary sadness that occurs with a glimpse of life's difficulties. In the ideal of the selfless mother that popular culture promotes, it is the woman's place to keep quiet about her own suffering while tending to her child's; here, the mother openly discusses her existential terror and admits that her child is a way of blocking out what is frightening in her life. There are three four-line stanzas, culminating in a stanza that is unsettling not because it admits that a mother can be sad—as mentioned before, a mother's suffering often serves to make her seem more noble—but because she so blatantly uses her child as a tool. Mistral broke new ground on the concept of motherhood in *Ternura*

The speaker of the poem says she does not want her daughter "turned into a swallow." (Jim Nelson / Shutterstock.com)

by allowing selfishness into the same poem as maternal love, not claiming that one leads to or causes the other, only admitting that a respectable person may have both at once.

"Fear" is all about selfishness. The title refers to the fear that the child will one day go off and leave the mother alone. This in itself is a natural fear—no one wants to be alone, and the whole point of being a loving mother is that she wants to be with her child. The courageous thing that Mistral does in "Fear" is having the poem's speaker admit that she would not want to be separated from her child even if it meant that the child would have a better life. She does not want her child turned into a queen, the speaker says, because she would not be able to see her daughter each night. The poem does not look at the situation of the queen on the throne, which, presumably, would be pretty good: the mother, for once in literature, is lamenting her own loss at the child's gain. Like "Bitter Song," "Fear" presents an external society that is the cause of the problem between the mother and child. The three stanzas are about resistance to "them"

turning the child into a sparrow, a princess, and a queen, respectively—but this time the offensive intruders pose no threat to the child, only to the mother's self-interest.

Motherhood is not a fragile thing. There is no reason for literature to view only a narrow range of what it involves, ignoring the fear and the sorrow, as if to talk about them would somehow be disrespectful to mothers (accusing them of not being able to transcend or suppress these aspects, perhaps, or accusing them of not being perfect). It is understandable that one would want to focus on motherhood's brighter aspects as a sign of respect, but there is a greater respect in truth. Even those of us who are not mothers can tell that Gabriela Mistral had the truth in hand in her collection *Ternura*.

Source: David Kelly, Critical Essay on "Fear," in *Poetry for Students*, Gale, Cengage Learning, 2011.

Carl Mowery

Mowery has a doctorate in literature and composition from Southern Illinois University. In this

THIS POEM EMPHATICALLY PRESENTS THE IMPORTANCE OF THE ROLE OF THE LATIN AMERICAN MOTHER TO HOLD HER CHILDREN CLOSE."

essay, he examines the themes of loss and separation and the bond between a mother and her daughter in "Fear."

In *Lecturas para mujeres* (Readings for Women) (1923), Mistral reflects on the role of women and mothers in society. She believes that mothers and motherhood represent the means to national formation in both the physical sense and the figurative sense. However, she is in constant fear that mothers and women will be victimized and abandoned by the nation and their men. The conflicts between the expectations of women creating life and then being abandoned by their offspring, are at the root of much of Mistral's writing, including her poetry. In "Fear," she examines the conflict between traditional family values and family structures and the loss of those traditions.

Mistral illuminates her deeply held belief in maintaining strong family bonds in *Lecturas*. In this work, she expresses a concern and uncertainty about what she sees as the dissolution of the family unit. She raises questions about the loss of the bonds between husband and wife as a result of the increase of outside activity by the wife, even though these were not the most important bonds. As Elizabeth A. Marchant notes in her essay "The Professional Outsider: Gabriela Mistral on Motherhood and Nation" in *Latin American Literary Review*, "the bonds between mother and child lie at the core of Mistral's" concerns. "Fear," published in 1924, addresses a specific issue: the loss of the maternal bond between mother and daughter.

In Latin cultures, there is a strong family bond built on affection between the same-sex members of the family, fathers for their sons, mothers for their daughters. Fathers develop a relationship with their sons that involves instructing the son in the ways of *machismo*, a typical Latin attitude that does not allow boys and men to show emotion, pain, or weakness of any kind.

Mothers develop a relationship with their daughters and try to keep their daughters close, to instruct them in the ways of the household and how to be nurturing mothers themselves in the future. For mothers, it is important to keep their daughters free from outside influences as long as possible and to help them cultivate the sense of what is or is not important.

One important cultural aspect of the mothers' attempts to control their daughters' interactions with boys has traditionally been through the role of a chaperone. When young people became attracted to one another or when the families of young people decided on mates for their sons and daughters, the mother of the girl often took the role of chaperone for the couple during social engagements. Some of these practices have since been forgotten, but Latin American mothers still have great care and concern for the welfare of their daughters. For the mother, anyone or anything that comes between her and her daughter is an intruder and must be kept at bay.

There are three characters in the poem: a mother, who is the narrator; the daughter, who is the object of the mother's fears; and "them," an unnamed entity that has an effect on the other two. In "Fear," the intruders are different in each stanza, but they accomplish the same disturbing result: separation of the mother and daughter. In the first stanza the intruder is symbolized by the image of the swallow, a bird that seemingly flits to and fro without purpose or direction. The loss of the sense of direction is contrary to the mother's wishes. Mistral's statements about this sense of direction are found in *Lecturas* when she urges her contemporaries to follow the ancient and eternal roles and models of the past. Her position was rooted in her belief that "gender roles were stable and bonds between women and children were privileged," according to Marchant. Therefore, any violation of these privileged roles was unacceptable. Such a violation was an interruption of traditional family roles and contributed to a loss of the opportunity for affection between the mother and her daughter, which constitutes her fear in this stanza.

The intruder in the second stanza is more sinister because it adds materialism to the distractions which interfere with the maternal bonds. The slippers are symbolic of the increasing materialism of society (even in the 1920s). The mother fears that the daughter will become so interested in material things that the mother will be neglected or forgotten. Mistral also addresses this issue in a prose poem, "To the Children." (A prose poem is one in which the poetic wording is presented in paragraph form, not in the typical stanza form.) In this poem, the mother encourages her children to take the dust of her body after she has died and to use the dust for play and as a vehicle for remembering her after she is gone. She warns the children against letting her dust become part of a brick (a symbol of materialism) but rather to let her dust be a part of the road where the children play. In this way the mother will still be a part of the children's lives. In "Fear," the mother wonders how the daughter can play when encumbered by materialistic objects. The loss of play then becomes the loss of the maternal bond when the daughter will no longer be sleeping beside her.

For the mother the worst kind of departure is found in the last stanza. She warns her daughter against allowing someone else to make the decisions for her. Leaving under such circumstances will create an insurmountable barrier between the two. Here the mother fears that her daughter will take on airs and postures; she fears that her daughter will assume that she is better than the mother and reject the mother's comfort.

In the third stanza, the mother fears the most significant loss of all: the alienation of affection from her daughter. The simple pleasures of giving comfort, for example by combing her hair (symbolically maintaining the maternal bond with the daughter), will be lost forever. In her poem "Nio Mexicano" (Mexican Boy), the act of combing a child's hair is mentioned four times and is the major symbol of maintaining the bond between mother and child.

The theme of the poem is loss and separation; this concern lies at the heart of Mistral's beliefs. Despite never having married or borne children, Mistral had "a deep but never satisfied maternal longing" which left "sadness on [her] life and work," in the words of Herman E. Hespelt in the essay "Gabriela Mistral" in *An Anthology of Spanish American Literature*. Examination of many of her poems will reveal a great affection for children and for the role of the mother in tending to her children. In the *Lecturas*, Mistral urges her contemporaries to follow the patterns of the mothers of the past. In this publication, she presses for a cohesive family unit with an educated mother as the central figure, according to Marchant. "Fear" makes the same point, as the mother cajoles, urges, and finally warns about the difficulties ahead if the daughter were to leave the mother under dubious circumstances.

In the poem "Close to Me," Mistral is even more graphic and passionate in her beliefs that the mother-child bond ought not be broken. In addition, the last line in the poem "Close to Me" is even more dramatic. These are the sentiments she expresses in "Fear," although not as directly. This poem emphatically presents the importance of the role of the Latin American mother to hold her children close. The plea for the child to sleep near the mother is strong and falls within the normal structure of Latin American families. Mistral uses this image of the closely bonded pair to lend artistic power to the point she is making.

Source: Carl Mowery, Critical Essay on "Fear," in *Poetry for Students*, Gale, Cengage Learning, 2011.

UNESCO Courier

In the following essay, an UNESCO Courier *reviewer characterizes Mistral's work as "harsh," philosophical, and ultimately universal, as she united poetry and humanism in one powerful voice.*

The life of Gabriela Mistral, who was born on 7 April 1889 in a village in northern Chile and died in New York in 1957, was devoted to an intellectual and spiritual quest. From her early days in Chile's Elqui valley to her European travels on cultural and diplomatic assignments, the story of her career reads almost like a myth. The needy peasant girl becomes the doyenne of Latin American literature. The humble rural schoolteacher is awarded some of the world's highest honours, including the Nobel Prize for Literature in 1945.

Gabriela Mistral's poetry, from her 1922 collection *Desolación* (Desolation) to *Lagar* (The Wine Press) of 1954, was written in harsh, powerful and colloquial language. Like her massive output of prose, it is informed by a visionary, prophetic sense of the destiny of Latin America. But readers in Europe and countries as culturally diverse as Israel, China and Japan, also found a meaning in the humanism and poetry of her work.

In many books, theses, poetic and philosophical reflections, it is possible to trace the influence of this Latin American writer from a country which, within a mere half century, produced three writers of world stature: Gabriela Mistral, Vicente Huidobro, and Pablo Neruda.

Why has Gabriela Mistral's work had a universal impact? As in the case of all true creative artists, attachment to her own familiar world did not exclude a strong feeling for other languages and cultures. She acknowledged her debt not only to Saint Theresa and to the Spanish poet Luis de Gongora y Argote but to Dante, Rabindranath Tagore, and the great Russian writers, and, Christian though she was, to the great sages of Buddhism.

Closely identified with her country and with her people ("I am and will remain," she said, "a daughter of my land"), Gabriela Mistral described her personal experience with a voice which all humanity could recognize, drawing from a tragic love affair a song of love and tenderness which speaks to people everywhere. In her sympathy for the downtrodden and her readiness to defend their cause, poetry and humanism become one: "We must give expression to the soul in all its intensity, and boldly utter the message which springs from the heart before it ceases to beat."

Source: Review of the works of Gabriela Mistral, *UNESCO Courier*, November 1989, p. 49.

SOURCES

Arce de Vázquez, Margot, *Gabriela Mistral: The Poet and Her Work*, New York University Press, 1964.

Agosin, Marjorie, "Gabriela Mistral, the Restless Soul," in *Gabriela Mistral: A Reader*, White Pine Press, 1993, pp. 17–24.

Bates, Margaret, "Introduction," in *Selected Poems of Gabriela Mistral*, translated and edited by Doris Dana, Johns Hopkins University Press, 1973, pp. xv–xxvi.

"Chile—Education," in *Encyclopedia of the Nations*, http://www.nationsencyclopedia.com/Americas/Chile-EDUCATION.html (accessed September 22, 2010).

"Copper Mining in Chile: Overview," in *MBendi Information Services*, http://www.mbendi.com/indy/ming/cppr/sa/cl/p0005.htm (accessed August 2, 2010).

Estrada, Daniela, "Maternity Leave—Longer, or for All Working Mothers?" in *IPS*, http://ipsnews.net/news.asp?idnews=51812 (accessed September 22, 2010).

Hespelt, E. Herman, "Gabriela Mistral," in *An Anthology of Spanish American Literature*, F. S. Crofts, 1946, p. 730.

Marchant, Elizabeth A., "The Professional Outsider: Gabriela Mistral on Motherhood and Nation," in *Latin American Literary Review*, Vol. 27, No. 53, January/June 1999, pp. 49–66.

Mistral, Gabriela, "Fear," in *Selected Poems of Gabriela Mistral*, introduction and translation by Ursula Le Guin, University of New Mexico Press, p. 86.

FURTHER READING

Castro-Klaren, Sara, Sylvia Molloy, and Beatriz Sarlo, eds., *Women's Writing in Latin America: An Anthology*, Westview Press, 1991.

The introduction to this book is interesting but complex for students; however, the examples of writing that are included offer a good variety of styles and themes.

Fiol-Matta, Licia, *Queer Mother for the Nation: The State and Gabriela Mistral*, University of Minnesota Press, 2002.

Fiol-Matta tells the story of Mistral's rise as a poet idol who was considered the mother figure of Latin America for generations. Fiol-Matta uses Mistral's own primary source documents to reconstruct her relationship with the Chilean government authorities that allowed her popularity.

Hughes, Brenda, *Folk Tales from Chile*, Hippocrene Books, 1998.

Intended primarily for children, this book retells some fascinating traditional tales that capture the flavor of the transformations in "Fear."

Rodriguez, Ileana, *House/Garden/Nation: Space, Gender, and Ethnicity in Post-colonial Latin American Literatures by Women*, translated by Robert Carr and Ileana Rodriguez, Duke University Press, 1994.

This book is an academic exploration of issues of gender and ethnicity in Latin America after the colonial period. It does not specifically examine Mistral, but it does give a good background to the period in which she worked.

SUGGESTED SEARCH TERMS

Gabriela Mistral AND Latin American literature

Mistral AND Fear

Mistral AND Ternura

Mistral AND motherhood

Mistral AND poetry

Mistral AND Chile

Mistral AND Chilean poet

Mistral AND Isabel Allende

Mistral AND feminism

Mistral AND diplomat

The Gift

LI-YOUNG LEE
1986

"The Gift" is an early poem by Chinese American poet Li-Young Lee. It is characteristic of Lee's style: understated in its use of free verse and common, almost simple language, it plumbs the depths of human emotion by taking a careful look at a small moment in the poet's life. The poem recounts a time when Lee was a boy and had a metal sliver in his palm. His father, to distract him from the pain of having it removed, told him a story. His father's demeanor inspired so much love in the boy that years later, when removing a sliver from his wife's hand, he finds himself striving be as gentle as he remembers his father having been.

Lee frequently writes about relationships with his family, and particularly his father, who suffered political persecution in Communist China before escaping with his family while Lee was still a child. His father was the most common subject in *Rose*, the 1986 collection in which "The Gift" was published. Since its publication, Lee has published several more poetry collections and won numerous awards. He is considered one of the most talented, powerful American writers of the early twenty-first century, as well as being one of the foremost Asian American poets of his generation.

AUTHOR BIOGRAPHY

Lee was born in Jakarta, Indonesia, on August 19, 1957. He is descended from Yuan Shikai,

China's first republican president, on his mother's side, while on his father's side his ancestors were businessmen and criminals. His father was a doctor who worked for a while as the personal physician to Mao Zedong in China. In Jakarta, his father helped found Gamaliel University. Soon after Lee was born, his father was arrested for sedition (political speech against the government) against Indonesian President Achmed Sukarno, and he spent a year in a prison camp. The family underwent a long trek after his escape, through Hong Kong, Macau, and Japan, before finally settling in the United States in 1964.

Lee attended the University of Pittsburgh, where he received a bachelor of arts degree in 1979. It was at Pittsburgh that he began writing and found his love for poetry. It was also there that he met his wife, Donna, with whom he later had two sons. He attended the University of Arizona in 1979–1980 and the State University of New York at Brockport in 1980–1981.

Lee's first poetry collection, *Rose*, the 1986 volume that contains the poem "The Gift," earned him national recognition by winning the Delmore Schwartz Memorial Poetry Award. He has authored three more collections of poetry: *The City in Which I Love You*, published in 1991; *Book of My Nights*, published in 2001; and *Behind My Eyes*, published in 2008. He has also published an acclaimed autobiography titled *The Winged Seed: A Remembrance*, which won a 1996 American Book Award from the Before Columbus Foundation. Lee has won numerous poetry accolades, including a Whiting Writer's Award in 1988 and a Lannan Literary Award in 1995. His book *The City in Which I Love You* was a Lamont Poetry Selection in 1990, and *Book of My Nights* won the 2002 William Carlos Williams Award. He has received Guggenheim and National Endowment for the Arts Fellowships and grants from the Illinois Arts Council and the Pennsylvania Council on the Arts.

POEM SUMMARY

Stanza 1

"The Gift" tells a story, beginning with Lee as a seven-year-old boy who has somehow gotten a piece of metal lodged under the skin in his palm. His father is there to help him, but the poem implies without explicitly saying that the boy was resistant to his father's help. He shrinks away from the momentary pain of having the splinter removed and needs to be distracted, even though he states later in the stanza that he thought the splinter was something that might kill him.

The father's distraction is a story that he tells his son. Lee captures the moment, rendering specific details that the grown man remembers of the father talking to him, such as the tone of his voice and the beauty of his face. The boy's pain is implied by the fact that the father had to use a knife blade to extract the splinter, but he never mentions the pain directly: what he does recall, instead, is the fact that the story his father was telling was still going on by the time the splinter was removed. The story was so engrossing, and the bond being formed as his father told it so strong, that the boy wanted the experience that he had at first dreaded to keep going on.

Stanza 2

One of the most important aspects of this story is mentioned without any emphasis in the beginning of stanza 2. After explaining that the story his father told was so engrossing that it made him forget his fear and pain, Lee admits that as an adult he does not remember the story itself. The father's point was clearly to distract his son by telling him something amazing, but what lingers in the son's memory after he has grown up is the fact that the father looked him in the eye and talked to him in a close, intimate way.

Lee devotes most of the stanza 2 to details about the father that were left out the quick version of the story given at first. The father's voice is described, first by using a nature metaphor: it is, like water from deep underground. His vocal quality is then compared to the tone one would use while praying. His hands are also described, using the unusual verbal strategy of making a noun of the word "measure" in the metaphor. By reducing his father's presence to these two elements, voice and hand, Lee captures the feeling of being a child, looking up to someone who is large and imposing. By the time stanza 2 comes to an end, readers are focused on the interaction between the father and his son, just as the poet is in his own memory. The splinter is successfully swept away from the reader's attention.

MEDIA ADAPTATIONS

- The Lannan Foundation released a video interview with Lee and Michael Silverblatt discussing Lee's work and political views in March 2000. This was soon after the publication of his second poetry collection and his memoir, *The Winged Seed*, and he reads from all three of his works. The video is available at libraries and at the Lannan Foundation's Web site (http://podcast.lannan.org/2010/06/01/li-young-lee-with-michael-silverblatt-conversation-29-march-2000-video).

- On the Shout Factory's 2006 compact disc collection *Poetry on Record: 98 Poets Read Their Work, 1888–2006*, Lee reads his poem "My Father, in Heaven, Is Reading out Loud."

- Lee, along with other influential poets of his generation, was profiled and interviewed by Bill Moyers for the PBS series *The Power of the Word*. This 1989 series is available on video and DVD from PBS Home Video.

- *Li-Young Lee: Always a Rose* is the title of a 1990 video profile of the poet, part of the "Profiles of Contemporary American Authors" series hosted by Tom Vitale. The video of the program is available from Atlas Video.

Stanza 3

The poem shifts its narrative position in stanza 3, addressing directly the reader. Lee suggests that the reader could go back in time with him to that scene. Instead of saying that the reader might view the scene, however, he proposes that someone could "enter" it, becoming wholly immersed in the event. He knows that a person coming into the event would have an incorrect impression of what was going on: rather than seeing the man take the sliver out of the boy's hand, the observer would think that he was putting something into him. Lee uses images of a tear to suggest that the father might be planting sorrow in the boy, and a flame, which might suggest courage or life.

In the second half of the stanza, Lee grows up to be the speaker of this poem. He is bent over his wife's hand. The stanza closes without explaining what he is doing with his wife's hand, though readers can already see the parallel between this gesture his father's, decades earlier.

Stanza 4

The last stanza of the poem is by far the longest, twice the length of the next longest stanza. It starts by describing a scene in which Lee takes a splinter out of his wife's thumb with the same tender concern that his father used on his hand years earlier. He describes this with the same second-person voice established in stanza 3, speaking directly to the reader and giving the reader directions.

In line 24, Lee returns to the scene of his childhood, recalling how he felt in the aftermath of the splinter removal. He shows his feelings by giving a few possible reactions that he might have had, calling the splinter names that reflect its potentially lethal nature. He states directly that he did not, at the time, think of the metal shaving going through his system, ending up in his heart, and killing him. The thoughts that he did not come up with as a boy indicate that he did think them later in the process of growing up. He eventually learned to think about abstract consequences, but such things did not bother him on that afternoon, showing that his father's calm demeanor spared him that traumatic experience at the time. His awareness of death came later.

At the end of this stanza, Lee does not return the scene to the present action, with him removing a splinter from his wife's thumb. Instead, he stays in the past. The last few lines have Lee kissing his father. Earlier, he said that it might seem to an observer that the father was putting something into his son instead of taking something out of him, and this is echoed in line 34, which says that he did get something from his father that day. The poem never explicitly says what it is that Lee's father gave him, leaving readers to draw their own conclusions about this from the way that he uses his father's calm approach to control the situation that might possibly cause pain to his wife. The kiss in the last line leaves readers with the clear impression that he appreciated, and still appreciates, how his father handled the situation.

TOPICS FOR FURTHER STUDY

- Any foreign element introduced into the body might interfere with the circulatory system or introduce bacteria that cause infections. Research the worst, most extreme results the speaker of the poem might have gotten from leaving his splinter untreated. Put images together to create a short, instructive video that cautions your classmates about the worst dangers of splinters and explains the proper medical procedures for splinter removal and care.

- Put out a call on your preferred social networking system for stories about the kindest thing people's fathers ever did for them—their own "gift." Group the results into categories, from most like the story told in the poem to least. Explain the results in a blog on your social network.

- Find a Web site of poetry written by poets your age or younger. Choose one of the poems there and rewrite it in the way that you think Lee would have written it. Explain your rewrite to members of your small group or class, pointing out the choices you made, and have them give you other suggestions about how to make the style of your rewritten poem more like Lee's.

- Lee describes himself as having been afraid of death at the age of seven. Read the theories of two psychologists about children's awareness of death—those of Sigmund Freud and Elisabeth Kübler-Ross, for instance—and write a dialogue where the two psychologists debate what to say to the child in the poem.

- Find a traditional Asian folk story that you think Lee's father might have used to distract him when he was young and make an animation or live video of it and post it online. Aim to make your video one that could be used to distract young people.

- Find a poem about marriage. Write a short story that illustrates a scene from the childhood of one of the couple, showing where they learned specific behaviors that are presented in the original poem.

THEMES

Father-Child Relations

Although it is not explicit in this poem, there is a clear implication that the son is surprised at how gentle his father can be. Before his father starts removing the splinter, which is before the story of the poem begins, he is afraid of what will happen, indicating a fear that his father will not be able to solve the problem. He even mentions having worried about death. But soon he finds himself calmed by his father's presence. What puts the boy at ease is not the story he is told, but the way the man moves his hands; the low, even tone of his voice; and even the handsomeness of his face. He is intrigued by his father like a hypnotized person is put in a trance. In the end, he learns a lesson from the event, taking away from it a new understanding of how respect can help calm pain.

This learning process is central to parent-child relationships. Lee does not claim that the father handled the situation the way he did in order to teach his son a lesson, but only to keep him quiet during the process of splinter removal. Still, Lee treats the event as having been given a gift, something that he can take with him as he grows up, to be used when he needs it to calm his wife. Parental relations are full of such moments when children learn both good and bad behaviors from their parents. Though fathers are generally portrayed as being more cold and unemotional than mothers, it is the surprising emotional contact with his father that makes this son capable of being a good husband.

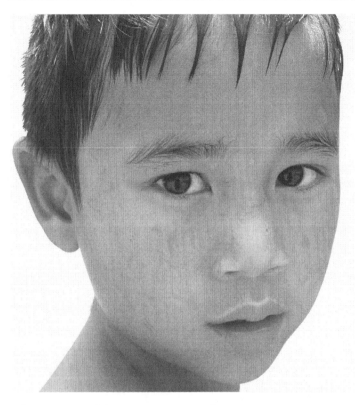

The narrator of the poem is a young boy. *(paulaphoto | Shutterstock.com)*

Husband-Wife Relationships

The speaker of this poem applies the same approach to taking a splinter from his wife's hand that his father with him. This does not mean that Lee finds the two relationships to be equal. The comparison only works because a husband and wife need to have trust in their relationship, and the experience with his father has taught Lee how trust can be earned in a circumstance like this. Nothing is said about the wife cowering in fear, as the boy once did. The speaker is not trying to calm his wife, only to handle her so gently that her splinter can be extracted without pain.

Death

Because the boy is afraid to have the metal sliver taken from his palm, he needs his father's reassurance. He could be afraid of a new, painful experience, and there are legitimate reasons to worry about a metal splinter: it could lead to an infection, or he could contract tetanus. But Lee explains the boy's fear as having a more specific, more powerful cause. He is afraid of death. In the poem's fifth line, he says that the fear of

death had been in his mind before his father started comforting him.

Awareness of one's own mortality is not as common in children as it is in adults, who have had time to see more deaths and who understand human limitations more thoroughly. This marks the boy in the poem as unusual. What is even more unusual is that he overcomes his fear of death, instead of allowing it to distract to him. In the last stanza, the poem explains that witnessing his father's calm, decisive actions allowed the boy to stop thinking of the errant sliver as an assassin, and to quit dwelling on the unlikelihood that the sliver could enter his blood stream and then his heart. He no longer thinks of the presence of death, only of his love for his father.

Storytelling

Although it eventually proves to be unnecessary, the father in this poem relies upon the power of the story that he tells to distract his son from his pain and worries. He trusts that the spoken word can capture his son's imagination so thoroughly that it will work like an anesthetic. Lee does not tell readers what the story was, but there is never any question that the right story could make the boy forget what he is about to endure.

The story is not related in this poem because the focus quickly shifts from the tale to his father's gentle demeanor. In explaining the situation this way, Lee goes beyond the strengths of a well-told story. A good story may indeed be powerful, this poem implies, but even more powerful is close human interaction.

STYLE

In Media Res

The phrase *in media res* means "in the middle of things" in Latin. This poem starts in the middle of the situation it describes. A metal splinter has already become lodged in the boy's hand; he has already gone to his father with it; and the father has already assessed the situation and made his decision about how to handle it. At the end of the first stanza, the narrator takes readers back in time a bit to show that he had previously thought that the sliver might kill him. Starting in the middle of the action this way allows Lee to engage readers' imaginations by cutting to the moment that is most emotionally important, while also making readers curious about what led up to this moment.

Imagery

Imagery is the use of description of physical detail by a writer to evoke a sensation or emotion. Unlike a metaphor, an image might not have a one-to-one correspondence with something else, but might instead be used just to convey what the situation felt like. In stanza 2 of "The Gift," for example, Lee describes his father's hands with great detail. That description is not meant to be a code for something hidden, but every detail is important to let readers feel what it must have been like to be a boy under his father's control in a time of need. The way he later shaves his wife's thumbnail down provides readers with another image, showing his own tenderness without actually talking about it. The kiss he gives his father is also an image: to read it as a metaphor and say that it *means* any one particular thing would be a disservice to the rest of the poem, making it almost pointless. Lee gives his readers these images, and others, because the situation he describes is a relatively minor one in a child's life, almost irrelevant

unless readers connect to the unstated emotions it evokes.

Point of View

The point of view of this poem is first person. The speaker consistently refers to himself throughout the poem, using first-person pronouns and adjectives such as "I" and "my." In the third stanza, the point of view shifts slightly. It is still told by a first-person narrator, but a second character, a "you," is introduced. This "you" is not a specific person, such as a character in the story told in the poem or a person in the speaker's life. It is, instead, a more casual, general use of the word "you" to indicate a reader that the poet does not know, an unidentified audience. In a more formal piece, Lee might have used the generic "one" as a substitute for "you," but that would detract from the intimate tone of the poem as it stands.

HISTORICAL CONTEXT

The Public Face of Poetry

At the time that "The Gift" was first published in 1986, American poetry was at the depth of public obscurity. Its height was decades earlier, in the 1920s, when the modernist movement created a resurgence in public interest in new works by poets: writers like e. e. cummings, Robert Frost, and T. S. Eliot became household names because poets took themselves seriously as artists, and magazines were the most common form of mass media. Interest in poetry cooled during the difficult economic times of the Great Depression, during the 1930s, and in the war years of the 1940s. In the post-war years, however, starting at the end of the 1940s and through the 1950s, poetry entered a new era of public attention.

Although the 1950s, like any era, had writers working in a range of styles, there were two major strands that came to dominate public perception. First were the avant-garde writers, who sought to follow the modernist principles of constant experimentation. In popular culture, the most prominent of these were the Beat Generation writers: Alan Ginsburg, Gary Snyder, Lawrence Ferlinghetti, Gregory Corso, and others. Though mimicked and often parodied as "Beatniks," the Beat style was highly visible.

The other main thread was intellectual poetry. Of this category, the most influential sub-category was confessional poetry, associated with writers

COMPARE
&
CONTRAST

- **1986:** China, the country that Lee and his family emigrated from, is a closed society. Little is known about the Chinese people or the lives that they lead.

  Today: China is a vital leader in the world economy. Although trade considerations have made China more involved with other cultures, the communist government has done much to maintain control over social life.

- **1986:** Poetry is an academic pursuit, considered mysterious by average citizens. Poets such as Donald Justice, Galway Kinnell, Mary Oliver, and William Meredith are well known in literary circles but are seldom known by the general public.

  Today: Spoken word music forms like hip-hop and audience-friendly poetry slams have made a new generation of audiences familiar with poetry. Fans of hip hop artists like Kanye West and Lil Wayne cross over to the works of performance poets like Patricia Smith and Saul Williams, often becoming involved in the slam poetry movement.

- **1986:** Medical programs popular on American television, such as *St. Elsewhere* and *Trapper John, MD*, focus on social situations, giving just a very general sense of the science that drives them.

  Today: Medical programs are more technically advanced: common television shows such as *House* or the members of the *CSI* series explain medical conditions in realistic and graphic terms. A child like the one in the poem could watch such shows and develop a realistic fear that a splinter could kill him.

- **1986:** The field of psychology called "cultural psychology" becomes prominent in the 1980s and 90s. The theory driving cultural psychology is that mind of a child, like the one in the poem who fears death from a splinter, is heavily influenced by the culture he comes from.

  Today: Because of advances made with psychotropic drugs in treating phobias and cognitive disorders, psychology has taken a strong tilt toward treating physical causes of psychological disorders.

- **1986:** A writer of Asian background, like Lee, is rare on the American literary scene. Critics look for evidence of how his cultural background affects the family relationships he describes.

  Today: Multicultural literature is increasingly more common. Although books and magazines are still published featuring one culture or another, modern readers are familiar with seeing similarities, rather than only differences, among cultures.

---

like John Berryman, Robert Lowell, Sylvia Plath, and Theodore Roethke. The term *confessional* came from the fact that these writers sought to delve deeper and deeper into their own personal lives for poetic material, regardless of how embarrassing the details might seem to readers. Lee, writing in the 1980s about his close relationship with family members in a personal tone, is considered a descendant of this school of poetry.

The 1950s saw a huge increase in college registration, as millions of young American men and women who would not have been able to afford college before the war were given free tuition under the government's G.I. Bill. Liberal arts programs prospered: writers who made their fame fighting the establishment, like Ginsburg, Snyder, and John Ashbery, took teaching positions. These programs turned out thousands of young writers each year. Through the 1970s and 1980s, poetry increasingly became a purely intellectual pursuit, considered to be written by and understood by those who were trained in it.

A father and son (Elena Kouptsova-Vasic / Shutterstock.com)

Though large in academic terms, the overall audience for poetry dwindled. In his 1985 study *American Poetry and Culture, 1945–1980*, Robert von Hallberg includes a quote from Charles Molesworth that captures the situation: "Though there are over seven hundred manuscripts submitted each year to the Yale Younger Poets competition, scarcely any first book by an American poet will sell that many copies." The fact that Lee was able to find a publisher for his first collection, *Rose*, have it reviewed in publications of national stature, and keep it in print to this day is a testimony to the book and the writer.

CRITICAL OVERVIEW

Lee was twenty nine years old when he published his first collection of poetry, *Rose*, which includes the poem "The Gift." From the start, the book was recognized for its excellence. Well-known poet Gerald Stern, who had been Lee's professor and mentor at the University of Pittsburgh, introduced the world to Lee with a stirring foreword to *Rose*. He writes that from the start:

> I was amazed by the large vision, the deep seriousness and the almost heroic ideal, reminiscent more of John Keats, Rainer Maria Rilke and perhaps Theodore Roethke than William Carlos Williams on the one hand or T. S. Eliot on the other.

The book won the Delmore Schwartz Memorial Poetry Award upon its publication and then earned the praise of critics in small literary periodicals, followed by similar praise in large national publications.

In the *Kenyon Review*, for instance, Martin McGovern includes a review of the book in an overview called "Recent Poetry from Independent Presses." McGovern mentions "The Gift," though he incorrectly identifies the woman in the poem as the speaker's mother—the wife of his father—and not the wife of the speaker himself. McGovern expresses his surprise that Lee is able to avoid predictability while writing poems about his father and commends him for being able to control his poems by giving them all slight differences: "although the observer remains constant," he notes, "the observer's state of mind varies, from naïveté to understanding, from fear to love." McGovern also reports that Lee "often writes with a directness both simple and lyrical," praise often repeated by reviewers.

A contributor to *Library Journal* reviewed Lee's initial poetry collection in November 1986, soon after it was published. "In this outstanding first book of poems, Lee is unafraid to show emotion," reviewer Rochelle Ratner notes, "especially when writing about his father or his wife." In the *New York Times* in 1987, Matthew Flamm observes the narrative tone by noting that Lee's first book "has a disarming modesty about it that turns out to be the foot in the door of a whole range of sad, strange and even monumental experiences." He finds Lee to be "so convincingly sincere that he gets away with all sorts of things," and notes that in his poetry, Lee is willing to display suffering, joy, and mortality in tandem, which Flamm considers a great strength.

In 1991, after Lee published his second book *The City In Which I Love You* to great acclaim, Jessica Greenbaum of the *Nation* devoted a column, "Memory's Citizen," to analyzing the two collections together. Like other reviewers, she notes the similarity of his work to that of American poet Walt Whitman, observing that another reviewer for the *Georgia Review* "has said Lee might sound too much like him." Greenbaum, like other reviewers, focuses on Lee's voice: "Sometimes a poet's voice distinguishes itself by carrying authority and by addressing a singular authority," she says. "That has been my experience reading Li-Young Lee's poems."

In the decades since *Rose* was first published, Lee's stature among American poets has grown, and he is now considered one of the country's treasured writers.

CRITICISM

David Kelly

Kelly is a writer who teaches creative writing and literature at several community colleges in Illinois. In the following essay, he examines the apparent lack of style in "The Gift" and how the poem is helped by what is missing.

Lee is a poet known for his ability to transcend style. The images and observations in

> GENERALLY, LEE USES COMMON, SIMPLE WORDS, AND HE USES THEM IN THE WAYS THAT THEY ARE CUSTOMARILY USED. JUST AS HIS POETRY LACKS STRUCTURAL ARTIFICE, IT ALSO HAS LITTLE USE FOR VERBAL CLEVERNESS."

Lee's poems speak for themselves, conveying the poet's message to readers without any support from the sublime tweaks of form that help other writers convey their thoughts. For some poets, style can be the point of a poem—readers are asked to care little about what the writer has to say less than how they say it. For others, the majority, style works as an amplifier, a tool to give readers deeper understanding of the poem's message. In Lee's work, style is usually a distraction to be avoided: readers need to keep their attention on the events being described and not be thinking about the author or about the poem's very existence.

"The Gift" offers a good example of this. It is an emotional poem about Lee's father that has no identifiable form, but that is written with such intensity that the common phrase *free verse* does not seem to capture its style. Many of Lee's early poems were about his father, Lee Kuo Yuan, a physician and political refugee. In "The Gift," the father displays a personal magnetism that has to be shown because it too singular to describe. Lee shows the father bending down to remove a splinter from his son's hand, telling the boy a story to keep his mind off of the pain of digging under his skin with a knife. The child focuses on his father so intensely that, as an adult, the poet says he does not recall the story his father told, but only his father's handsome face and reassuring hands. Later, that past event is linked to a present-tense story about a similar situation, in which the poet extracts a sliver from the hand of his wife. The process of being kept confident and hopeful is described as a gift the poet's father gave to him, in contrast to the threat that his father removed from him.

There are infinite ways for a poet to handle the telling of such a tale. Rhyming would not be a poor choice in this particular case: the poem is

WHAT DO I READ NEXT?

- Critics have compared the father-son relationship in this poem to the one portrayed in Theodore Roethke's classic poem "My Papa's Waltz." That poem, about a frightening and abusive father, approaches its subject with a similar tone. It is often reprinted in literature anthologies and can be found in *The Collected Poems of Theodore Roethke*, published by Anchor Books in 1974.

- Gene Luen Yang's graphic novel *American Born Chinese* blends stories of ordinary people, gods, and television characters to capture the feel of being a young first generation Chinese American. It was published in 2006 by Roaring Brook Press and won the National Book Award for Young People's Literature.

- Arthur Sze is a second-generation Chinese American writer born in New York in 1950. He has also written a poem called "The Gift." It is a more mysterious, elusive poem about the unknowable things in life. It was published in the *Georgia Review* in the Spring 2006 issue and is also available online at the *Poetry International* Web site.

- In his poem "The Cleaving," Lee takes another look at his father, from an adult perspective that is more critical, not as full of admiration as he is in this poem. "The Cleaving" tells of a trip to the market with his father, with detailed images of the old man's frailties. This long poem is one of Lee's best known. It is in his 1990 collection

The City In Which I Love You, published by BOA Editions.

- Lee talks extensively about his father and the man's effect on his life as an artist in his 1995 memoir *The Winged Seed: A Remembrance*, published by Hungry Mind Press.

- Readers interested in Lee's thoughts can read a dozen interviews with him, compiled in the collection *Breaking the Alabaster Jar: Conversations with Li-Young Lee*, tracking his maturation from a young poet to a seasoned professional. It was published in 2006 by BOA Editions.

- William Carlos Williams's short story "The Use of Force" is about a doctor who is forced to take an aggressive approach toward a little girl who might be hiding a dangerous illness. It is included in *The Doctor Stories*, a collection compiled by Robert Coles and published in 1984 by New Directions.

- Nikki Giovanni's poem "The World Is Not a Pleasant Place" offers a more sentimental look at the same ideas Lee examines here, touching on the idea of childhood fears and the ways that adults can help calm them. This poem is included in *The Invisible Ladder: An Anthology of Contemporary American Poems for Young Readers*, a collection edited by Liz Rosenberg. It was published by Henry Holt in 1996.

---

about a lesson learned in childhood, one that has been absorbed as an integral part of the speaker's personality. One of the best uses of the constant repetition of a rhyme is to show how an idea is drilled into memory. And if Lee had used a steady rhythm, or had followed a formal stanzaic structure, it would make sense because he would be mirroring the father's calming nature, the sense of order used to dampen the boy's

worries. If Lee had given readers the story in its straightforward chronological sequence, starting with the splinter in the boy's hand and ending when the wife's splinter is removed, the poem would have given emphasis to the learning process, playing up the effect of the cause.

Lee uses none of these techniques in "The Gift." Though light and precise, the words he uses do not relate to one another with the use

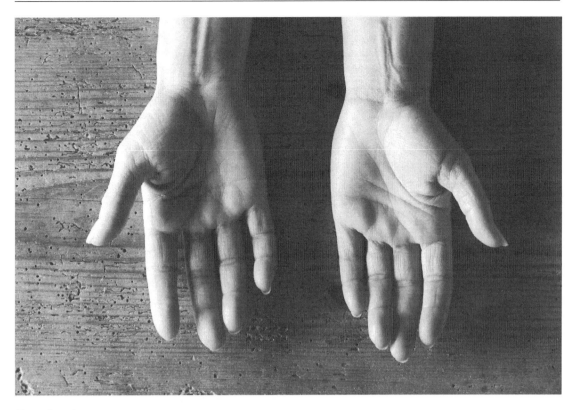

Open hands *(Rene Jansa | Shutterstock.com)*

of similar sounds. The lines do not scan; the stanzas follow no particular structure. The story itself is divided, going from the father and son as they deal with the splinter to the son remembering that moment, years later. Then he discusses the wife's modern-day splinter, but by the middle of the fourth stanza he is back to where his mind was before his father came to his rescue. By stanza's end the boy is kissing his father, grateful that the situation with the splinter ended well. Lee gives himself license to change direction at any time in the poem, to follow emotions in the same way that the mind tends to.

It would be wrong to look at poems like "The Gift" as being devoid of any form. Even without a traditional form, a line is a line and a stanza is a stanza, and so a pattern is bound to occur, even if it is not a recognizable one. As mentioned before, the lack of a rhyme scheme, or even occasional rhyme, and the absence of a continuous rhythm all serve to make their own statement. They tell readers to turn their attention away from the sound of the poem's words.

By default, the heart of the poem becomes the story's overall meaning.

Lee is not a poet who chooses words that jump off the page, stunning readers with their just-rightness, any more than he is very concerned with their sounds. There are a few words in "The Gift" that draw attention because of their oddness, forcing readers to pause and think about them for a moment before accepting their perfection. Recalling his father's "lovely" face might give readers pause, especially in the absence of any specific details about what makes that face lovely; so could using the word "measure" as a noun, as a synonym for his father's hands. Such choices are rare, however. Generally, Lee uses common, simple words, and he uses them in the ways that they are customarily used. Just as his poetry lacks structural artifice, it also has little use for verbal cleverness. The overall effect is that readers listen more closely to what the poem has to say. By not placing his words where they are in order to entertain, Lee encourages his readers to feel, consciously or not, that the message he has to give them must be very important indeed.

While a poet is allowed to reject rhythm and rhyme, it is not possible to present a poem with no shape. "The Gift" is divided into stanzas, and the stanzas follow no recurring pattern. No two are the same length, and they do not grow in length, diminish in length, alternate long-short-long-short or long-short-short-long or any variation on these. The stanzas are five lines, eight lines, seven lines, and fifteen lines. The first stanza is just too short to be grouped with the two that follow, but not short enough to counterbalance the fourth stanza, which is much more lengthy.

Once again, the message that comes from this is the poet's disregard for structure. By not running the poem straight down the page, the poet has created a work of stanzas, and there is some meaning to the way they stand in relation to one another. If readers are not supposed to think about the balance of one stanza against another, then the reason that stanzas exist at all must lie in the places that Lee decided to break the flow of his poem.

The first stanza ends with the young boy's thoughts of death, a concept the poem explains later. The second stanza ends with the father asserting his comforting presence—again, this is not the last word on the subject, as this theme reappears at the end of the poem. The third stanza ends with readers being brought into the present, the *here*, and introduces them to the wife and the splinter in her hand. This situation is continued after the stanza break, then completed in three lines and not discussed again.

Everything that is set up earlier in the poem is reprised in the fourth stanza—the boy, the wife, the emotional bond between father and son. Instead of analyzing one aspect of the situation after another, Lee opens one thread, then another, then another, before tying them all together at the end. Although doing it this way makes sense, a reader does not have to be aware of this design in order for the poem to work. It is a unique structure that would have no place in another poem, that fits this poem only because it is part of the identity of "The Gift," which is what makes it an example of art in its most basic and effective sense.

Though poets generally make use of the traditional tools of their trade, there is no rule that says they are obliged to do so. With writing that is so rich in meaning that readers cannot take a moment's distraction to think about his style, Lee manages to raise the standards with his poetry. His accomplishment should not be considered a judgment on other writers, who arrange words on the page like images on a canvas and who combine the sounds of their words the way a composer combines musical textures. Lee has a style that works for his subject matter. This is every artist's goal.

Source: David Kelly, Critical Essay on "The Gift," in *Poetry for Students*, Gale, Cengage Learning, 2011.

Wenying Xu

In the following excerpt, Xu postulates that Lee has adopted a transcendental outlook in his poetry that is neither exclusively Chinese nor American.

Li-Young Lee is an ethnic Chinese without the birthright to an ancestral culture, without a grounding knowledge of the Chinese language, and without the community of a Chinatown or a suburban Asian American community. His condition of exile, however, has proved to be immensely productive of emotional intensity and imagination, and his poetics derives largely from his ontological condition as an exile, driven by the desire to transcend time and space by appealing to the metaphysical, to the exclusion of the cultural and material. As if no material or cultural location were sufficient for his poetics and identity, Lee formulates a transcendentalism—one that has a strong affinity with the ideas of its American father, Ralph Waldo Emerson—in which the poet's true self becomes God or the "universe mind," unfettered by cultural/ethnic allegiances. As such, the poet has no dialogue, as Lee claims, with his sociocultural composition. His polemical disavowals of ethnic identification on the ground of transcendentalism, however, are in dialectic tension with his frequent usage of ethnic signifiers in his poetry.

This tension in Lee begs the question that Stuart Hall asks of a Caribbean filmmaker: "From where does he/she speak?" Quite different from the popular idea of an intuitive knowledge of the self, Hall proposes that one's cultural identity is constructed through his or her semantic practices, and semantic practices are never stable and finished. The tension lying between Lee's quest for the Absolute and the necessity to speak from a material place constitutes a dynamic realm in which he operates as an Asian diasporic American transcendentalist poet, multiple selves that Lee attempts to unify with the lexicon of

> HIS DISAVOWAL OF HIS ETHNIC IDENTIFICATION IN ORDER TO BE REGARDED AS A TRANSCENDENTALIST POET, A SOUL SPEAKING FROM NOWHERE AS VENDLER INSISTS, CREATES A DYNAMIC TENSION IN HIS POETRY."

American transcendentalism. He would disagree with Hall, who argues, "We all write and speak from a particular place and time, from a history and a culture which is specific." It goes without saying that Lee cannot escape relying on cultural, material places from which to speak, but it is not easy to locate *the place* that is central to his poetics. In this essay, I will argue that it is Asian food that serves as a central place from which he speaks, a locus that constructs and defines his sense of reality. It is the references to food/eating that enable his articulation of the universe mind and his self-representation as an exilic/transcendent poet. By centering on alimentary imageries and motifs, I will also show that his ethnic self and the transcendental self are not mutually exclusive, as he tries to argue.

Most critics classify Lee as an Asian American poet and choose to focus on his experience as an émigré and his double identity as a Chinese in exile and an American in citizenship. For example, Judith Kitchen, in the *Georgia Review*, attributes Lee's poetry in *The City in Which I Love You* to his unique subject position as "a Chinese American trying to make sense of both his heritage and his inheritance." Yibing Huang, writing for *Amerasia Journal*, assesses Lee's book of prose poetry, *The Winged Seed*, to be "a typical fable of Asian American experience, of how tradition and the parents' generation are always, in consciousness or the unconscious, linked with pain and burden." Lee expresses his strong objection to this classification in an interview with Tod Marshall: "I have no dialogue with cultural existence. Culture made that up— Asian American, African-American, whatever. I have no interest in that. I have an interest in spiritual lineage to poetry—through Eliot, Donne, Lorca, Tu Fu, Neruda, David the Psalmist. ... Somehow an artist has to discover a dialogue that is so essential to his being, to his self, that it is no longer cultural ... but a dialogue with his truest self. His most naked spirit" (Marshall, 132). Lee believes that poetry in dialogue with the cultural is a "lower form of art" (Marshall, 131). It is like poetry "built on sand; it looks solid, but it isn't because it speaks from a self that is grounded in things" (Marshall, 133), and things disappear. True poetry, he claims, sheds the poet's false/cultural identity. In the same vein, Helen Vendler proposes that the "lyric desires for a stripping-away of the details associated with a socially specified self in order to reach its desired all-purpose abstraction." "If the normal home of selfhood is the novel," she asserts in valorizing poetry, " ... then the home of 'soul' is the lyric, where the human being becomes a set of warring passions independent of time and space."

In such polemical appeal to the naked self, Lee demonstrates his ambivalence toward his own ethnicity. This ambivalence, however, has little to do with culturally enforced self-loathing. For him, cultural identities are works of the rational mind, and true poetry works against it. He remarks in an interview, "I've noticed that we can't be free of stereotypes as long as we're thinking with our rational mind. So it was important for me to take a breath and then go under ... to try to escape all stereotypical views of what an Asian is in America, what an immigrant is. ... The only way I could escape those stereotypes was to defy my own rational thinking." Rejecting his Asian American identity, for Lee, does not purport a willing surrender to assimilation. Rather than becoming an American, he desires the "state of nobodyhood." His response to his ontological condition as an exile taking the form of cultural transcendence aims to counter the stereotypes of Asians in the U.S. popular culture. He explains in the same interview, "The culture we live in offers or imposes versions of 'somebodyhoods' that are really shallow and false. ... If I can attain a state of 'nobodyhood,' which is the same thing as the state of 'everybodyhood,' that's much richer and more full of potential than some false, made up, Hollywood magazine, university, or cultural version of 'somebodyhood.'" The seeming paradox of nobody being everybody is central to his transcendentalism, which strives to achieve the state of the naked self in relationship to God.

Diaspora, for Lee, is not a uniquely ethnic condition; rather, it is a human condition, a view derived from Genesis in which human history begins in dual exile from the Garden of Eden and the presence of God. "It is arrogant of the dominant culture," he comments, "to think it's not part of a diaspora." He regards himself exilic in this sense: "The difficulty is that the earth is not my home." Consequently, his affinity with the universalistic concept of mankind overrides his affinity with Asia. In his memoir, the recurrent conceit of "the winged seed" serves as his self-representation. Interestingly, *diaspora* is composed of *dia* ("through," "throughout") and *spora* ("spores," "sperm"), a notion with a strong connection with this conceit. Contrary to its connotation of ungroundedness, however, the winged seed as a trope turns out to be deeply grounded in Asian history. He has taken the seed trope from "the garden of nutmeg" in the Song of Songs, which his father evoked in a Thanksgiving message.

> East of you or me, he [his father] claimed, east of even the last man from China, lived a sentient perfume, an inbreathing and uttering seed, our original agent. ... it is the mother of spices; the song of songs ... both the late wine and our original milk, it is a fecund nard. And there go forth from this vital seed figures distilled a day, or a year, or a century. ... An ark, all fragrance, is our trove, the Seed, stringent past jasmine. "We are embalmed in a shabby human closet," he said. "Get out! Get to the garden of nutmeg."

In the West, spices became vital to medicine, cosmetics, cuisine, and religious and official ceremonials ever since the conquest of Alexander forced the East into contact with the Hellenic world. But not until the 1500s did spices become one of the most coveted commodities in Europe, so coveted that they were compared to gold. The Spice Islands, part of today's Indonesia, became irresistible to the Occidental as early as the beginning of the 1500s. One can say that the dangerous voyages from Europe to the Spice Islands were the precursor to the Western colonization of Asia. Giles Milton writes, "Nutmeg ... was the most coveted luxury in seventeenth-century Europe, a spice held to have such powerful medicinal properties that men would risk their lives to acquire it." At the beginning of the spice trade, "ten pounds of nutmeg cost less than one English penny. In London, it was sold at "a mark-up of a staggering 60,000 per cent." The ruthless, sometimes bloody, competition among the European traders escalated the price of spices and resulted in rampant violence against each other as well as the islanders. In the context of British history, it is the spice trade that called for the formation of the East India Company, which played an essential role in the opium trade and in the process of colonizing Asia, particularly South Asia.

The seed trope represents his father's as well as Lee's own wandering in the postcolonial world—the seed is "born flying," "to begin its longest journey to find its birthplace, that place of eternal unrest. From unrest to unrest it [is] moving. And without so much as a map to guide it, and without so much as a light" (*Seed*). Having been transported to unknown places, the only destination the seed knows is journey itself. Lee adopts the seed as a traveling and protean identity for himself. "I was one of those seeds," he writes, "my father kept in the pocket of his suit. ... " (*Seed*). To be a winged seed entails movement, possibility, and hybridization, all of which paradoxically create in Lee both the sense of free floating and the inevitability of rooting, for despite its destiny of constant movement, it carries hope, promises new flowering, and secures regeneration in a distant land. His journey to God, allegorized by the seed trope, therefore, takes both spiritual and cultural paths.

Few of Lee's critics take into account his transcendental yearnings as part and parcel of his social living. They either want to rescue him from ethnic determinism or to fault him for not being sufficiently ethnic. Xiaojing Zhou argues against the tendency of some critics to interpret Lee's poetry by emphasizing his Chineseness. By reducing his art to expressions of his ethnicity, Zhou points out, critics minimize "the rich cross-cultural sources of influence on Lee's work and of the creative experiment in his poetry." On the strength of Hans-Georg Gadamer's notion of fusions of horizons, she theorizes that "one's heritage is not possessed once for all, nor is it necessarily inherited through ethnic lineage. Rather, it is changed and renewed with the changing conditions of human life and human consciousness." In his essay on Lee's "Persimmons," Steven Yao remarks that many of Lee's critics (including Zhou) "have relied on an overly simplistic model for cross-cultural literary production." In a close reading of Lee's most anthologized poem, Yao makes the case that "Lee achieves only a superficial integration, or 'hybridization,' of Chinese and American culture," and "'grafting' offers a more exact term than hybridity for understanding Lee's accomplishment in 'Persimmons'" (Yao, 19–20). To him, Lee is more American than Asian American because Lee's knowledge of China is so meager that the Chinese culture he represents offers only a "voyeuristic appeal" (Yao, 6).

Both Zhou's and Yao's efforts to free Lee from interpretive limitations, however, only partially meet his own self-portrait as a poet on a quest for the Absolute. To be Asian, American, or Asian American occupies little space in his polemical self-representation. His metaphysical schema aims to rid him of such labels: "My true self is universe or God. I assume that my true nature is God. I assume that I am God in my true nature" (Marshall, 134). What Lee claims to be true of himself he attributes to all true poets. "When I read poetry, I feel I'm in the presence of universe mind; that is, a mind I would describe as a 360-degree seeing; it is manifold in consciousness" (Marshall, 130).

Lee's transcendentalism bears a strong resemblance to Emerson's, whose famous declaration goes, "[A]ll mean egotism vanishes, I become a transparent eyeball; I am nothing; I see all." Lee's "360-degree seeing" and Emerson's "transparent eyeball" offer a political liberal license to all "true" poets, as Lee deems them, and "true" poets possess the naked self that is the universe mind or God, free from cultural and social constraints and therefore free from the blind spots that all people have, constituted as they are by race, class, gender, religion, language, and so forth. In his statement, "I am born into the great, the universal mind. I, the imperfect, adore my own Perfect," Emerson anticipates Lee's self-anointment as God in his true nature, a god that is twin to Emerson's "Oversoul, within which every man's particular being is contained and made one with all others." The concept of "self" in both men's articulations of the transcendent, therefore, is seated in essentialism. Harold Bloom, in his usual abstruse eloquence, describes Emersonism as the American Religion, "*Self*-reliance, in Emerson ... is the religion that celebrates and reveres what in the self is before the Creation, a whatness which from the perspective of religious orthodoxy can only be the primal Abyss."

As an American transcendentalist, Lee is situated within the American poetic tradition of the sublime. His appeal to that which is *other* of the social is an appeal to what Vendler calls "the grand, the sublime, and the unnameable." Departing from European Romanticism, the object of the sublime in American poetry is much more than nature itself; it is nation, technology, and power that have been elevated to sublimity. Many of the major interpreters of American poetry, such as Bloom and Vendler, regard the American sublime as a sensibility that defines American poetry as much as the American spirit. Nativist in sentiment, their assessment of American poetry would probably annoy Lee, if not affront him, for he refuses to be a grateful guest in this country by critiquing it and by considering it "a country / wholly unfound to himself." In his poem "The City in Which I Love You," he presents a picture of the American street, as chaotic and dangerous as any in Jakarta, from where his family escaped.

> Past the guarded schoolyards, the boarded-up
> churches,
> swastikaed
> synagogues, defended houses of worship, past
> newspapered windows of tenements, among the
> violated,
> the prosecuted citizenry, throughout this
> storied, buttressed, scavenged, policed
> city I call home, in which I am a guest ...

Compact in this sharp imagery are stories of crime, racism, poverty, and inhumanity that are commonplace in urban America.

... As soon as the ethnic self is constructed, Lee proceeds to empty it out by moving his motif of eating to that of death and by meditating on the nothingness of this material world in order to "witness the spirit, the invisible, the law" (Marshall, 141). The poem's metaphysical moment, therefore, is made possible only through the extravagant display of food, its killing, cutting, cleaning, cooking, and its eating, much of which is culturally specific. Continuing the trope of eating, he writes,

> Bodies eating bodies, heads eating heads,
> we are nothing eating nothing,
> and though we feast,
> are filled, overfilled,
> we go famished.
> We gang the doors of death.
> That is, our deaths are fed
> that we may continue our daily dying,
> our bodies going
> down, while the plates-soon-empty
> are passed around, that true
> direction of our true prayers ...
> . . . .
> As we eat we're eaten. (*City*)

The references of eating, being eaten, and dying configure to voice his metaphysics that materials fade away and only the pure consciousness of the universe mind lasts. Only after he establishes the trope of eating is he able to cancel out materiality and cultural/ethnic identification in favor of transcendentalism.

In the poem's conclusion, Lee returns to the theme of ethnicity. This time, it becomes expanded by his metaphysical meditation to include a diverse cluster of ethnic markers that may or may not be Asian, only to be rid of them all. Urged on by his reflection on death/change, Lee releases the rein on his utopian impulse to de-ethnicize, de-gender the butcher by exploding his ethnicity to such an extent that its overflowing labels come to mean nothing. What remains after such an explosion of ethnic signifiers is the singularity of his face:

> the sorrow of his Shang
> dynasty face,
> African face with slit eyes. He is
> my sister, this
> beautiful Bedouin, this Shulamite,
> keeper of Sabbaths, diviner
> of holy texts, this dark
> dancer, this Jew, this Asian, this one
> with the Cambodian face, Vietnamese face, this
>   Chinese
> I daily face,
> this immigrant,
> this man with my own face. (*City*)

The butcher, after passing through these conventional ethnic markers, in the last line becomes simply "this man with my own face," embodying all, therefore emptied out of all ethnicities. Simultaneously, Lee also purges the butcher's gender by referring to him as "my sister" and "this dark dancer." The butcher thus becomes the transcendent self embodying all ethnicities and genders, and therefore is tied down by none.

In settling for the final identification of the butcher to be "this man with my own face," Lee also postulates that the specificity of an individual cannot be reduced to his or her socially constituted identities. Although this ethical specificity is other than any of the social masks people wear, still they always wear social masks. The I-Thou encounter (which Gadamer regards to be the necessary presupposition of all discourse) must transcend socially constructed categories. Emmanuel Levinas argues that interpersonal ethical relationships have priority over each individual's social identity. We are different because of a singularity

that, in such encounters, calls for a responsibility to the other which cannot be passed off to anyone else. The other to whom one is responsible always remains an embodied, socially constituted person. Lee's poem's last word—"face"—captures this ethical relationship best. It is the face-to-face encounter that is central to our relationship with others, and in such an encounter, uniqueness overwhelms sameness, and the universality of uniqueness overwhelms difference.

Lee's interpersonal ethics originates from his transcendentalist impulse that aspires to render cultural differentiation meaningless. Yet, it is precisely his cultural difference that makes him a fascinating poet. His disavowal of his ethnic identification in order to be regarded as a transcendentalist poet, a soul speaking from nowhere as Vendler insists, creates a dynamic tension in his poetry. On the one hand, Lee's poetry works its way exactly through Asian diasporic signifiers, and on the other, his wish to be stripped of all cultural identifications and politics ironically places him squarely within American transcendentalist and sublimic tradition, a culture irrevocably tied to the U.S history of imperialism, as Wilson explicates convincingly. Lee's poetic journey toward the transcendent turns out to be a cornucopia of cultural particularities, such as Asian food. His wonderful poetry reveals profoundly his strong affiliations with both Asian and American cultures, neither of which is free from political implications. It is his poetry that best argues against his own polemical position and demonstrates that in order not to reify the social it is not necessary to postulate a universe mind.

Source: Wenying Xu, "Transcendentalism, Ethnicity, and Food in the Work of Li-Young Lee," in *Boundary 2: An International Journal of Literature and Culture*, Vol. 33, No. 2, Summer 2006, pp. 129–57.

Jeffrey F. L. Partridge

In the following excerpt, Partridge interrogates the politics of authorial identity, and examines the difference between approaching a writer's work as Asian American or simply American.

In one of his longest and best-known poems, "The Cleaving," Li-Young Lee announces his desire to devour Ralph Waldo Emerson like a steamed fish in a Chinese meal. The reader forgives this breach of table etiquette because, as Lee informs us, Emerson said the whole Chinese race was ugly—he deserves to be eaten. But Lee's poem is more sophisticated and more philosophical than this tit-for-tat scenario suggests. In

IN LI-YOUNG LEE'S POETRY, EATING IS A
CULTURAL ACTIVITY THAT ENACTS FAMILIAL AND
ETHNIC COMMUNITY."

"The Cleaving," eating is assault, but it is also digestion and assimilation.

Lee brings the butcher's shop close to the banquet table by deliberately playing on the two senses of the verb "cleave" to suggest both chopping up and clinging to, and thus the poem vacillates between the act of rejection and the process of assimilation. Eating in this poem may begin with the butcher's chopping block, but it is ultimately about communion.

The dialectics of Lee's poem reveal a blind spot in contemporary critical theory's discussion of the ethnic author. In valorizing the so-called marginal element in ways that reproduce it as "central" to our cultural concerns, contemporary criticism, in spite of itself, insists upon the segregation of the "ethnic writer" from the "mainstream." As such, we are in danger of patronizingly valuing ethnic writing as a "dynamic" and "colorful" literature of outsiders that brings new "life" to America's tired literary traditions. By insisting on marginality for ethnic authors, we also ignore the dialectical relationship that exists between these writers and the various traditions of American literature to which they, like any other American author, belong. Li-Young Lee's dinner/communion with Ralph Waldo Emerson and Walt Whitman in "The Cleaving" illustrates what is at stake when we approach a given writer as either "Asian American" or "American." Lee's poem shrewdly questions the either/or between these authorial identities. . . .

II. DEVOURING RACISM

In Li-Young Lee's poetry, eating is a cultural activity that enacts familial and ethnic community. The Chinese meal of rice and steamed fish in "Eating Together" is a metaphor that combines generational continuity with a sense of familial belonging after the death of the poet's father, and this metaphor is juxtaposed with the loneliness of the meal described in "Eating Alone."

These poems from Lee's first book of poetry, *Rose*, contextualize eating as a familial activity fraught with personal (though not just private) significance. In a much longer poem, "The Cleaving" (from his second book of poetry, *The City in Which I Love You*), eating becomes both a sign of cultural communion with other Chinese immigrants (i.e. the larger cultural community) as well as an aggressive weapon against racism in American society and American literature. The poet "transforms words into things capable of competing with food" (Deleuze and Guattari 20) when, in order to speak as a poet for his community, he "eats" that community and he "eats" Ralph Waldo Emerson and his insulting and reductive remark that the Chinese "managed to preserve to a hair . . . the ugliest features in the world."

"The Cleaving" forcefully asserts the place of the Chinese American poet in the American literary tradition by simultaneously attacking and embracing that tradition through the Asian American literary trope of what Sau-ling Cynthia Wong calls "the big eating hero." Regardless of cultural contexts, eating is an image of both domination and acquiescence. As Wong reminds us, "ingestion is the physical act that mediates between self and non-self, native essence and foreign matter, the inside and the outside." Deleuze and Guattari similarly argue that eating, like speaking, is a fundamental act of deterritorialization of the Other that ultimately reterritorializes the space of the Other through the activity of "the mouth, the tongue, and the teeth." The difference between writing and eating for Deleuze and Guattari is that writing reterritorializes language as something more "capable of competing with food," whereas eating merely deterritorializes.

Eating, in any case, allows the speaker in "The Cleaving" to mediate between his own voice and the American literary tradition. The poet expresses the seemingly divergent actions of attacking (or hacking) and embracing through his use of the verb "cleave." The verb "to cleave" encompasses opposing possibilities: to "split" or "divide by force" (here a transitive verb), and to "adhere closely," "hold fast," or "cling" (here an intransitive verb). In the poem, Lee writes that

> change
> resides in the embrace
> of the effaced and the effacer,
> in the covenant of the opened and the opener.

Like the sharp-edged cleaver wielded by the Chinese butcher, the poem "coaxes, cleaves, brings change" through violent images of eating and devouring; the teeth also functioning as a kind of cleaver.

Writing within the Chinese tradition of the conquering hero, the poet in "The Cleaving" is the "big eater": like Brave Orchid in *The Woman Warrior*, who vanquishes life-threatening ghosts through eating, the poet is driven by "necessity" to ingest all forms of nutrition, no matter how unpalatable they may seem to the reader. The speaker ingests the brain of the duck and the head of the carp. He also expresses a desire to eat the butcher, the Chinese race, Ralph Waldo Emerson, and even death itself. As these descriptions attest, becoming a big eater is not simply a matter of eating what one must to survive but actually learning to enjoy as delicacies the parts that others may simply discard as inedible. According to Wong, big eaters in Asian American literature are defined by "an ability to eat unpromising substances and to extract sustenance, even a sort of willed enjoyment, from them; to put it symbolically, it is the ability to cope with the constraints and persecutions Asian Americans have had to endure as immigrants and racial minorities."

The sixth stanza of the poem launches into a frenzy of big eating that speaks of both the poem's response to racism as well as its function as poetic utterance. The poem's pace is driven by the quick transition from one "food-item" to another: fish, butcher, bodies, features, hairs, Emerson, and the carp's/Emerson's head. Although the poet expresses his desire to eat in the conditional voice ("I would eat"), the steady repetition of the monosyllabic and aggressive "eat" hurls the reader from one image to another:

What is it in me will not let
the world be, would eat
not just this fish,
but the one who killed it,
the butcher who cleaned it.
I would eat the way he
squats, the way he reaches into the plastic tubs
and pulls out a fish, clubs it, takes it
to the sink, guts it, drops it on the weighing pan.
I would eat that thrash
and plunge of the watery body
in the water, that liquid violence
between the man's hands,
I would eat
the gutless twitching on the scales,
three pounds of dumb

nerve and pulse, I would eat it all
to utter it.

This segment describes more than simply eating a fish: the fish is not sitting idly on a plate, cooked and ready for consumption. The fish is alive and vigorous, and it is that vigor, that "violence," that the speaker wishes to absorb: "I would eat that thrash / and plunge, that liquid violence." There is something vital in the fish that the speaker seeks to obtain, in much the same way that traditional Chinese eating relates the properties of the eaten to the properties of the eater. This traditional concept brings Lee's poem into conversation with that tradition but also, again, with other Asian American texts. In Lee's poem, however, the "thrash," "plunge," and "liquid violence" relate to vitality (as does the image of the "liquid violence / between the man's hands," which may also suggest sexual potency); but they also relate to death: the fish, after all, is in its dying throes. As the stanza develops, the presence of death and the speaker's reaction to it become central.

The speaker's attraction to the fish's "twitching" death under the butcher's club is burdened with meaning. Eating the struggles of the fish (the "thrash" and the "plunge") in its dying throes is like eating the struggles of the immigrant community.

... I would eat it all
to utter it.
The deaths at the sinks, those bodies prepared
for eating, I would eat,
and the standing deaths
at the counters, in the aisles,
the walking deaths in the streets,
the death-far-from-home, the death-
in-a-strange-land, these Chinatown
deaths, these American deaths.
I would devour this race to sing it. ...

The death of the fish ("the deaths at the sinks") leads the speaker to consider other deaths around him: "the standing deaths / at the counters" are the butchers and fishmongers of the Hon Kee Grocery; the deaths "in the aisles" are the customers; "the walking deaths in the streets" are connected to the "Chinatown deaths," that is, the streets of Chinatown surrounding the grocery; and "Chinatown deaths" are immigrant deaths ("far-from-home" and "in-a-strange-land"). Finally, these deaths of immigrants from Asia are "American deaths": they occur in America, but more importantly, the line suggests that leaving one's country to live and die in America is an American experience. The next line confirms that these are Asian immigrants whom the speaker wishes to ingest: "I would devour *this race* to sing it" (emphasis added).

The struggles, the thrashing and plunging, of the immigrant Chinese are the result of anti-Chinese sentiment, as the next segment suggests:

> I would devour this race to sing it,
> this race that according to Emerson
> *managed to preserve to a hair*
> *for three or four thousand years*
> *the ugliest features in the world.*
> I would eat these features, eat
> the last three or four thousand years, every hair.
> And I would eat Emerson, his transparent soul, his
> soporific transcendence.

The quotation from Emerson's journals is the point at which Lee most explicitly enters into a conversation with the American literary tradition. For now, however, I will discuss Lee's emphasis on the quotation's racism, thus bracketing for the moment the literary and poetic tradition Emerson represents as well as the context of Emerson's journal entry. The speaker's response to Emerson's racist remarks is central to the entire poem. The poet contrasts his own poetic utterance, the speaker's ability to speak, with the muteness of the fish, which as we have seen above stands for the Chinese immigrant:

> the gutless twitching on the scales,
> three pounds of *dumb*
> nerve and pulse, I would eat it all
> to utter it. (italics added)

The response of the Chinese immigrant to racism has been a "dumb" (i.e., mute) struggle: the immigrant thrashes and plunges but remains unable to articulate a response to the discursive power behind popular, literary, and institutional racism. The speaker responds with a discursive feast modeled after the big-eating heroes of Chinese legends: "I would eat this head, / glazed in pepper-speckled sauce."

The fish's head comes to represent both the immigrant community (whose "features" and "hairs" the speaker says he would eat) as well as Emerson's racist comments, the "opaque" eyes of the fish head reminding us of the "transparent eyeball" of Emerson's philosophy. Perhaps the idea of eating these negative comments would strike some American readers as an odd gesture. Swallowing hardship for some might be a

courageous act that reveals one's mental toughness, but it also carries connotations of acquiescence, of giving in. Yet, in Chinese American literary tradition, swallowing hardship, or "eating bitter," is often represented as a heroic act. According to Wong,

> disagreeable food puts to the test one's capacity to consolidate one's self by appropriating resources from the external environment, to convert the seemingly useless into the useful, refuse into nutrition. Physical survival is incompatible with a finicky palate; psychological survival hinges on the wresting of meaning from arbitrary infliction of humiliation and pain; survival of family and the ethnic group not only presupposes individually successful eating but may demand unusually difficult "swallowing" to ensure a continued supply of nourishment for the next generation.

The speaker in "The Cleaving" turns the "seemingly useless into the useful" when he eats Emerson's racist remarks. Rather than cringing and retreating from them, he "devours" them, much the way that he devours the fish's head ("with a stiff tongue lick out / the cheek-meat"). The speaker openly relishes the fish head, describing his experience as "sensual." This ravishing enjoyment is an act of defiance in Bakhtin's sense of the carnivalesque—an overturning of hegemonic and hierarchical order, a response to the age-old argument that Chinese eating habits mark them as barbaric and inhumane. As with his response to Emerson's racist statement, the speaker embraces the notion of the champion eater; he does not adopt white American eating habits but makes his pride in his own culture's customs his weapon. That the speaker's eating is more than an individual response is suggested by the manner in which he consumes the fish's cheeks: "the way I was taught, the way I've watched / others before me do." The speaker eats in a cultural way; he has learned this eating from his community. Thus, while those who came before him may have been able to devour only a literal fish in this way, the speaker meshes "ethnic eating" with linguistic skill and poetic discourse to devour racist discourse.

In Lee's poetry, cultural eating is not always expressed in violent terms, despite the carnivalesque and grotesque imagery described above. In his first book of poetry, *Rose*, Lee exalts the communal and relational significance of eating in a Chinese family, a significance that he expands to the immigrant community in "The

Cleaving." His poem "Eating Alone" describes his loneliness as he tends his garden and thinks of his recently deceased father. The loss of his father is so poignant for the young poet that he imagines his father waving to him in the garden, only to realize, he says, that it was "the shovel, leaning where I had / left it." The poem then concludes with a stanza describing a Chinese meal that he prepares and consumes alone:

> White rice steaming, almost done. Sweet green peas
> fried in onions. Shrimp braised in sesame
> oil and garlic. And my own loneliness.
> What more could I, a young man, want.

The final line's sardonic tone is achieved through the juxtaposing of the poet's father's absence from the garden and his implicit absence from the table. There is no joy in the "bare," "cold, / brown and old" garden without his father's presence. The illusion of his presence merely increases the loneliness the poet describes at the table.

The title of another poem in *Rose*, "Eating Together," provides an intertextual juxtaposition with "Eating Alone." In "Eating Together," the father is still absent, but the community of family around their Chinese meal remembers the father as the conveyor of tradition and, significantly, as no longer alone. In the community of family, the poet is not lonely, and neither is his father. The family continues the tradition of eating together. Moreover, the mother has taken the father's place, as signified by her eating the sweetest meat nestled in the trout's head. In "The Cleaving," this same love of community through the communion of cultural eating is contrasted with the violent eating required in devouring racism. In his paean to the Chinese immigrant in stanza five, the poet says of his fellow Chinese immigrants that they are

> happy, talkative, voracious
> at day's end,
> eager to eat
> four kinds of meat
> prepared four different ways,
> numerous plates and bowls of rice and vegetables,
> each made by distinct affections
> and brought to table by many hands.

Significantly, the cultural eating of the family in "Eating Together" opens to the cultural eating of the immigrant community in "The Cleaving." Cultural eating is as much an image of revolt against racism as it is a statement of community and, as we will see below, of transcendence.

Source: Jeffrey F. L. Partridge, "The Politics of Ethnic Authorship: Li-Young Lee, Emerson, and Whitman at the Banquet Table," in *Studies in the Literary Imagination*, Vol. 37, No. 1, Spring 2004, pp. 103–26.

Xiaojing Zhou

In the following excerpt, Zhou points to the problem of critics explaining Lee's poetry with an emphasis on his Chinese identity. In close detail, Zhou examines other ways in which Lee re-creates his self-image.

Li-Young Lee's two prize-winning books of poetry, *Rose* (1986) and *The City in Which I Love You* (1990), contain processes of self-exploration and self-invention through memories of life in exile and experiences of disconnection, dispossession, and alienation. While providing him with a frame of reference to explore the self, autobiographical materials in his poems also serve as a point of departure for Lee to re-define and re-create the self as an immigrant in America and as a poet. At the same time, the process of Lee's construction and invention of identity is accompanied by his development of a set of poetic strategies through which the acquired knowledge and identity are forcefully articulated and expressed.

However, both Lee's identity re-creation and his poetic innovation are overlooked by critics who attempt to explain his poetry by emphasizing his Chinese ethnicity. In his complimentary foreword to *Rose*, Gerald Stern writes that what "characterizes Lee's poetry," among other things, is "a pursuit of certain Chinese ideas, or Chinese memories. ..." For Stern, Lee's father and his Chinese cultural heritage are fundamental components to his poetry: "Maybe Lee—as a poet—is lucky to have had the father he had and the culture he had. Maybe they combine in such a way as to make his own poetry possible. Even unique." Stern's attribution of the making of Lee's poetry and its characteristics to his Chinese heritage is reiterated by L. Ling-chi Wang and Henry Yiheng Zhao, editors of *Chinese American Poetry: An Anthology* (1991), who claim that the unique "quality" of Lee's poetry "boils down to 'a pursuit of certain Chinese ideas, or Chinese memories.'" To illustrate what they mean by the Chineseness in Lee's poetry, Wang and Zhao cite Lee's poem "My Indigo" as an example. Lee's method of expressing his feelings and state of mind by describing a

"I CAN'T TELL IF MY BEING CHINESE IS AN
ADVANTAGE OR NOT, BUT I CAN'T IMAGINE
ANYTHING ELSE EXCEPT WRITING AS AN OUTSIDER.'"

phenomenon in nature in this poem may be borrowed from Chinese classical poetry. But rather than showing any particular "Chinese ideas," the directness of erotic feelings and the celebration of sexual love in "My Indigo" bear some affinity to *The Song of Songs* which is one of Lee's favorite books of poetry. And the speaker's comment on the indigo flower's condition of isolation and living "a while in two worlds / at once" (*Rose*), expresses Lee's own feelings resulting from his experience of life in exile, wandering from country to country within a short period of time, rather than illustrating any ideas or memories which can be defined as typically Chinese.

Ethnocentric readings of Lee's poems by Stern, Wang, and Zhao are not only misleading, but also reductive of the rich cross-cultural sources of influence on Lee's work and of the creative experiment in his poetry. Their readings presuppose a misconception that a pure and fixed Chinese culture has been inherited and maintained by Chinese immigrants and their descendants in America. As Sau-ling Cynthia Wong has pointed out, "Asian American writers, however rooted on this land they or their families may have been, tend to be regarded as direct transplants from Asia or as custodians of an esoteric subculture." This tendency in reading Asian American writers risks relegating their works to a marginalized niche. As a corrective to ethnocentric misreading of Asian American poetry, Shirley Lim proposes "an ethnocentered reading" based on "an ethnopoetics" which will function on three levels—stylistic, linguistic, and contextual. In my view, the contextual level is more important than the other two, for the context of the creative subject and act, to a large extent, determines the stylistic and linguistic aspects of the work Ethnocentric readings of Asian American writers such as Li-Young Lee result from a narrow focus on the poet's heritage of Chinese culture which, by implication, is enclosed.

Without contextualizing the heritage of Lee's poetry beyond his ethnicity, interpretations of his style or use of diction exclusively in terms of his ethnicity still cannot escape an ethnocentric misreading, as shown in Wang and Zhao's comments on Lee's "My Indigo."

By contextualizing the heritage of Lee's poetry, I mean examining Lee's poems within their "horizon" in the sense of Hans-Georg Gadamer's hermeneutics. For Gadamer, the concept of "horizon" suggests "possibility of expansion," of "opening up of new horizons." The limits of horizon are never fixed; "the closed horizon that is supposed to enclose a culture," Gadamer contends, "is an abstraction." He argues that

> The historical movement of human life consists in the fact that it is never absolutely bound to any one standpoint, and hence can never have a truly closed horizon. The horizon is, rather, something into which we move and that moves with us. Horizons change for a person who is moving.

This concept of horizon is shaped by history, by the particular situations of people's lived lives, and by their consciousness. Gadamer notes that "Our own past and that other past toward which our historical consciousness is directed help to shape this moving horizon out of which human life always lives and which determines it as heritage and tradition." In other words, one's heritage is not possessed once for all, nor is it necessarily inherited through ethnic lineage. Rather, it is changed and renewed with the changing conditions of human life and human consciousness.

In this sense, Li-Young Lee's poems cannot be fully understood or appreciated by tracing his heritage, which is mistakenly categorized as exclusively Chinese. Lee learned to love poetry from his exposure to Chinese classical poems and the Psalms. As a child, Lee learned to recite classical Chinese poems from his father, who had a classical Chinese education and used to recite poems from the Tang Dynasty to his children. His father also used to read to his family constantly from the King James Bible, which became one of Lee's favorite books. Lee's poems and poetics are largely shaped by his experience as a refugee and immigrant and by his readings in English, being educated from grade school through college in the United States. He was born in 1957 in Indonesia of Chinese parents. His mother is the granddaughter of China's provisional president, Yuan Shikai, elected in 1912 during the country's transition from monarchy to republic. Lee's paternal grandfather was a gangster and an entrepreneur. Thus his parents' marriage in communist China was much frowned upon, and his parents eventually fled to Indonesia, where Lee's father taught medicine and philosophy at Gamliel University in Jakarta. In 1958, Lee's father was incarcerated by Sukarno because of his interest in Western culture and ideas; he loved Shakespeare, opera, Kierkegaard, and the Bible. After nineteen months imprisonment, he escaped, and the family fled Indonesia with him. For several years, they traveled throughout Indochina and Southeast Asia before finally settling down, first in Hong Kong and then in the United States. In the U.S., his father studied theology at a seminary in Pittsburgh and later became a Presbyterian minister in a small town in Pennsylvania.

Because of this background, Lee finds that "the wandering of the children of Israel" in the Book of Exodus "has profound resonance for [him]" (Moyers). And his consequent feelings of loss, disconnection and dislocation are often reflected in his poems. One of his early poems, "I Ask My Mother to Sing," deals with the emotional reality of his family as refugees and immigrants:

> She begins, and my grandmother joins her.
> Mother and daughter sing like young girls.
> If my father were alive, he would play
> his accordion and sway like a boat.
>
> I've never been in Peking, or the Summer Palace,
> nor stood on the great Stone Boat to watch
> the rain begin on Kuen Ming Lake, the picnickers
> running away in the grass.
>
> But I love to hear it sung;
> how the waterlilies fill with rain until
> they overturn, spilling water into water,
> then rock back, and fill with more.
>
> Both women have begun to cry.
> But neither stops her song. (*Rose*)

This poem marks several losses: the death of the father, a vanished world within the Forbidden City in Peking and its way of life in the royal palace, and the speaker's inability to connect himself to that world and its culture of his Chinese heritage. As Lee observes in an interview, seeing his father's name in Chinese characters on his tomb stone with all these American flags on the other graves makes him feel strange rather than nostalgic. "I don't know what to feel nostalgic *for*," says Lee. "It's simply a feeling of disconnection and dislocation" (Moyers). Here

in the poem, the speaker does not share his mother's and grandmother's memories, nor their nostalgia. But that lost world and its culture, in whatever fragmentary fashion, has been passed on to the speaker through the song.

The difference between the speaker's feeling of disconnectedness and his mother's and grandmother's feeling of dislocation and nostalgia shows a generational disparity which is characteristic of immigrants' experiences. This difference indicates discontinuity and fragmentation in the speaker's inherited Chinese history, culture, and identity, which at the same time are opened to "new horizons," to use Gadamer's words again. The speaker's, or rather Lee's, position of straddling different cultures and histories leads to an expansion of his conceptual and perceptual horizon. This position, according to Mikhail Bakhtin, can be creatively productive. Bakhtin emphasizes that "the most intense and productive life of culture takes place on the boundaries of its individual areas and not in places where these areas have become enclosed in their own specificity" (*Speech Genres*). This productiveness, Bakhtin indicates, is the result of interactions of different points of view:

> In the realm of culture, outsidedness is a most powerful factor in understanding. It is only in the eyes of *another* culture that foreign culture reveals itself fully and profoundly. ... A meaning only reveals its depths once it has encountered and come into contact with another, foreign meaning: they engage in a kind of dialogue, which surmounts the closedness and one-sidedness of these particular meanings, these cultures. We raise new questions for a foreign culture, ones that it did not raise itself; we seek answers to our own questions in it; and the foreign culture responds to us by revealing to us its new aspects and new semantic depths.

Li-Young Lee's bi-cultural heritage enables him to escape "closedness and one-sidedness" in his perception and views. His cross-cultural experience helps generate and enrich his poems.

... Li-Young Lee's poems, like the poems of Marilyn Chin and others, illustrate that Chinese-Americans can remake themselves in images of their own invention. However, rather than rejecting the broken image of the "great-grandfather" who helped build America's railroads, the invention of new Chinese-American images in Lee's poems is rooted in the reality of Chinese-Americans' lives. As Lee articulates passionately in "The Cleaving," his singing of the world and his people must be proceeded by embracing and understanding both. His singing is made possible by transformations of the self and experience; the renewal of the self is accompanied by a renewal of the traditional poetic form and language.

As a poet, Lee must wrestle with the limits of poetic form, and search for new possibilities of language, in order to tell his "human tale." Lee wrote in a letter, "I can't tell if my being Chinese is an advantage or not, but I can't imagine anything else except writing as an outsider." He added: "It's bracing to be reminded [that] we're *all* guests in the language, any language." In another letter, Lee expressed his hope that the reader of "The Cleaving" will note the "richness" and "earthiness" of its language. Li-Young Lee's poems enact and embody the processes of poetic innovation and identity invention beyond the boundaries of any single cultural heritage or ethnic identity.

Source: Xiaojing Zhou, "Inheritance and Invention in Li-Young Lee's Poetry," in *MELUS*, Vol. 21, No. 1, Spring 1996, pp. 112–32.

SOURCES

Flamm, Matthew, "Facing Up to the Deadly Ordinary," in *New York Times*, October 4, 1987, http://www.nytimes.com/1987/10/04/books/facing-up-to-the-deadly-ordinary.html (accessed June 10, 2010).

Greenbaum, Jessica, "Memory's Citizen," in *Nation*, October 7, 1991, pp. 416–18.

Lee, Li-Young, "The Gift," in *Rose*, BOA Editions, 1986, pp. 15–16.

McGovern, Martin, "Recent Poetry from Independent Presses," in *Kenyon Review*, Vol. 9, No. 4, Fall 1987, pp. 131–37.

Ratner, Rochelle, review of *Rose*, in *Library Journal*, Vol. 111, No. 18, November 1, 1986, p. 100.

Stern, Gerald, "Foreword," in *Rose*, BOA Editions, 1986, p. 8.

Von Hallberg, Robert, *American Poetry and Culture, 1945–1980*, Harvard University Press, 1885, p. 11.

FURTHER READING

Hongo, Garrett, "Introduction: Culture Wars in Asian America," in *Under Western Eyes: Personal Essays from Asian Americans*, edited by Garrett Hongo, Anchor Books, 1995, pp. 1–33.

    Hongo, himself a famed Asian American poet, provides a good overview of the culture in which Lee is writing. This book also includes a lengthy excerpt from Lee's autobiography.

Lorenz, Johnny, "The Way a Calendar Divides: A Refugee's Sense of Time in the Work of Li-Young Lee," in *Asian-American Literature in the International Context*, edited by Rocine G. Davis and Sami Ludwig, Transaction Publishers, 2002, pp. 157–69.

    In this study of Lee's poetry, Lorenz uses Lee's childhood, spent wandering for years to escape Indonesia, as the focus.

Neff, David, "The Politics of Ethnic Authorship: Li-Young Lee, Emerson, and Whitman," in *Beyond Literary Chinatown*, University of Washington Press, 2007, pp. 77–98.

    This essay uses Lee to examine the current trend toward multiculturalism in literature, exploring how much the author's ethnic background is relevant in studying his writing.

Partridge, Jeffrey, "Remembering the Man Who Forgot Nothing," in *Christianity Today*, Vol. 32, No. 12, September 2, 1988, p. 63.

    Partridge details how Lee's readings of his father's journals led him to convert to Christianity.

Xiaojing, Zhou, "Inheritance and Invention in Li-Young Lee's Poetry," in *MELUS*, Vol. 21, No. 1, Spring 1996, pp. 113–32.

    This extensive literary study of Lee's work up to the mid-1990s focuses on the role of his ethnic heritage in his work and the relationship of ethnicity to his family life.

SUGGESTED SEARCH TERMS

Li-Young Lee

father AND Li-Young Lee

Chinese American poetry

father AND poetry

splinter AND death

young-adult poetry AND Li-Young Lee

Li-Young Lee AND The Gift

Li-Young Lee AND Asian poetry

Li-Young Lee AND Chinese American poetry

Grape Sherbet

RITA DOVE

1983

Former Poet Laureate of the United States and Pulitzer Prize-winning poet Rita Frances Dove is known for her confident, multidimensional verse that reflects her insight into what it means to be a woman, an African American, an American, and a person. Her poetry is not about advancing an agenda but sharing something personal and meaningful with the reader. Much of her poetry is set in the past, giving the speaker the advantage of perspective and wisdom. Although some of it is emotionally charged, it can also be nostalgic without veering into idealism. Published in 1983 in the collection *Museum*, "Grape Sherbet" is such a poem. The speaker shares a specific childhood memory, part of a tradition in which her father took the children to play in the cemetery on Memorial Day. The speaker has fond feelings as she looks back. She remembers feeling carefree at the time, and now the benefit of maturity leaves her feeling grateful to and appreciative of her father.

"Grape Sherbet" is not a poem whose meaning is clear on first glance, it requires the reader to do some work to uncover the significance of the memory. The process forces the reader deeper into the speaker's memory, slowly arriving at the meaning of the event. It is likely the same process the speaker herself went through to understand why her father held such a tradition. The poem's themes include impermanence, memory, and family.

Rita Dove *(© Tim Wright / Corbis)*

AUTHOR BIOGRAPHY

Dove was born in Akron, Ohio, on August 28, 1952. Her parents were Elvira and Ray Dove. Her father was a research chemist who was successful in the tire industry despite the challenges that African Americans faced. As a child, Dove was encouraged to read the many books around her home. Her love of reading and natural creativity led to the writing and production of plays. Dove attended Miami University in Oxford, Ohio, on a National Merit scholarship, graduating in 1973. She then attended the University of Tubingen in West Germany from 1974 to 1975 on a Fulbright fellowship before receiving her master of fine arts degree at the University of Iowa in 1977. That was the year she published her first chapbook, *Ten Poems*. On March 23, 1979, Dove married writer Fred Viebahn; the couple has one daughter, Aviva Chantal Tamu Dove-Viebahn.

In the time since then, Dove has grown as a poet, seeing seventeen volumes of poetry published, in addition to a novel, a short story collection, and a play. *Museum*, in which "Grape Sherbet" appears, was her fifth collection, published in 1983. That year she was awarded a Guggenheim fellowship, and only three years later, she received a Pulitzer Prize for *Thomas and Beulah*, a work inspired by the lives of her maternal grandparents. Dove is only the second African American poet to have won the Pulitzer, following Gwendolyn Brooks.

Dove's writing reflects the rich heritage of her African American roots. However, she does not set out to write exclusively about the black experience in America. She has a global view, and her poetry expresses her sensitivity to women's issues, music, and universal human experience. When those things rise out of her African American perspective, the resulting work is natural, not forced. Critics and readers appreciate Dove as a writer who knows her own mind and voice, and her admirers were not surprised when in 1993, at age forty, she became the youngest poet ever named poet laureate of the United States.

Dove has taught at various universities across the country. Before becoming a Commonwealth Professor of English at the University of Virginia, she taught at Arizona State University and Tuskegee Institute. Her contributions to poetry are not limited to writing and teaching; she has also been appointed as judge and jury member in such esteemed settings as Pulitzer Prize committees, National Book Award panels, and for the Amy Lowell Fellowship. Her achievements reflect her work's accomplishment and longevity. She also received a Great American Artist Award by the National Association for the Advancement of Colored People in 1993; in 1996, the National Humanities Medal and the Heinz Award in arts and humanities in 1996; and she was named a chancellor of the Academy of American Poets in 2006.

POEM TEXT

> The day? Memorial.
> After the grill
> Dad appears with his masterpiece—
> swirled snow, gelled light.
> We cheer. The recipe's   5
> a secret and he fights
> a smile, his cap turned up
> so that bib resembles a duck.

That morning we galloped
through the grassed-over mounds   10
and named each stone
for a lost milk tooth. Each dollop
of sherbet, later,
is a miracle,
like salt on a melon that makes it sweeter.   15

Everyone agrees—it's wonderful!
It's just how we imagined lavender
would taste. The diabetic grandmother
stares from the porch,
a torch   20
of pure refusal.

We thought no one was lying
there under our feet,
we thought it
was a joke. I've been trying   25
to remember the taste,
but it doesn't exist.
Now I see why
you bothered,
father.   30

POEM SUMMARY

Stanza 1

The speaker opens the poem by letting the reader know that the setting is Memorial Day, the U.S. holiday that honors war veterans and takes place near the beginning of summer. Dove introduces the setting in the form of a question and its answer, which immediately gives the poem a relaxed, conversational feel. It also lets the reader know that the setting is significant; the poem will be a memory about Memorial Day. The first person the poem introduces is the speaker's father. He has grilled a meal for everyone, and then he appears with his masterpiece, the grape sherbet of the poem's title. It is described in glowing, sensory terms; it seems snowy and light. The image of a father, after presiding over the grill, handing out a frozen treat on a hot day is evocative of summertime, and it is a familiar memory for many readers.

The sherbet is greeted with cheers, providing a brief image of simple pleasures. The reader then learns that the sherbet recipe is a secret, which is another common experience. Many family recipes are closely guarded secrets, saved for special gatherings and traditions. The description of the father fighting back a smile indicates his utter satisfaction at the cheering and at everyone's delight in enjoying his secret recipe sherbet. The speaker describes her father

as wearing a cap with the bill turned upward instead of going out straight. She thinks he looks like a duck. It is a fun, light-hearted image.

Stanza 2

The second stanza opens with a somewhat confusing time reference to the morning. The speaker seems to be continuing the action of the first stanza, but she is actually explaining what the group did before the other festivities of the day (grilling, eating sherbet, and so on). The second stanza describes a group of people running through a grassy area where there are mounds and stones. The reader understands that the speaker means a cemetery, although this is not made explicit. The children are running happily through it, disregarding the words on the stones and instead naming each headstone for a lost baby tooth.

The second part of stanza 2 flashes forward again, to when the children are enjoying their melting sherbet. The speaker equates each spoonful of sherbet with a miracle, similar to the way salt paradoxically makes melon taste sweeter. By contrasting these two images in the second stanza, the speaker is drawing contrasts to show how one thing unexpectedly makes another thing more intensely itself. The innocence of the children playing in a cemetery makes the sacrifice of Memorial Day more poignant, just as a sprinkle of salt on a piece of fruit can make the fruit sweeter instead of salty.

Stanza 3

The third stanza brings the poem's focus sharply back to the children's enjoyment of the sherbet. Everyone in attendance at the gathering—which presumably includes other adults besides the father—reaches a consensus that the sherbet is wonderful. They share in the carefree delight of a simple treat and agree that the sherbet tastes exactly how lavender should taste. They are wrapped up in the experience and their senses are fully engaged. In a bout of synaesthesia (a technique in which one sense is used to describe the manifestation of another), they can taste color! To counterbalance the total surrender to fun, the speaker describes a diabetic grandmother who seems to be looking on with disapproval. She stares at them with their sherbet, from a distance, refusing to participate. She is described as a torch, which draws a sharp and destructive contrast to the sherbet, and her refusal is staunch. Her health condition prevents her from being part of the group, so she refuses to get anywhere near everyone else.

Stanza 4

In stanza 4, the speaker brings the poem into the present. The reader meets the adult, mature person who is remembering the frivolous delights of childhood. The memory is sweet and nostalgic, but looking back, the speaker sees something much deeper. Dove ties the meaning of the poem to her first line, where she let the reader know that the Memorial Day setting would be important.

She says that when they were running and playing among the mounds and naming the stones all those years ago, they did not think about people being buried there. Right under their playful little feet, real people were lying beneath their headstones. She recalls that they thought it was a joke, which lets the reader know that the father had tried to tell them the significance of the cemetery, but it seems the children were too innocent and playful to grasp it at all. Now, however, the speaker understands it fully.

She comments that she has been trying to remember the taste, but she cannot. When she was a child, the experience of the sherbet was the central part of the day. Now, she cannot even remember how it tasted, only that they had it. What she does draw from the memory as an adult is what her father was trying to do with the children.

The poem can be read as describing either one particular Memorial Day, and thus a single event, or a composite of this group's Memorial Day tradition. There is no mention of such a tradition or yearly trips to the cemetery, and there are specific details that would not likely be present every year (such as the grandmother). On the other hand, the speaker sets the poem on Memorial Day, not Memorial Day of a particular year. This is a matter of interpretation by the reader, but what is clear is that at the end of the poem, the speaker remembers it vividly. In adulthood, she now understands why her father went to the trouble of taking the kids to the cemetery on Memorial Day and telling them that people were buried there. The poem ends on a note of encouragement: the father's lesson was not wasted after all.

THEMES

Impermanence

"Grape Sherbet" is full of examples of things that are not permanent. Although the tone is light, sentimental, and grateful, the message is fundamentally about the fleeting nature of life. Dove drives this point home in the minor details, beginning in the second line, where the reader is informed that the grilling is over. Already, the reader is met with something that has come and gone, but it is replaced with the masterpiece of the sherbet, which the reader also knows will melt quickly in warm weather. In the second stanza, the children are galloping through a cemetery, acknowledging the headstones just enough to name each one for a lost baby tooth. This is a strong image of impermanence and how it affects everyone, regardless of life experience or maturity. The headstones are stark reminders of the impermanence of life itself, including the relationships, activities, hopes, and plans it entails. This is what the father understands. On the other hand, the children's baby teeth (which the poet calls milk teeth) are not their permanent teeth. The children are far more aware of the fleeting nature of their baby teeth than they are aware of the fleeting nature of life, yet both realities are encompassed in the single image of headstones, which look like teeth to the children.

More subtly, Dove demonstrates the impermanence of innocence. She was one of the children playing and thinking about baby teeth, but now she is an adult thinking about the graves—perhaps the graves of fallen soldiers, since the gathering took place on Memorial Day. Her childlike innocence is so distant that she cannot even remember the taste of the sherbet. That sensory experience was also temporary.

What keeps the poem from being morose is the tone and the way the poet replaces one thing with another. Without lapsing into an outright meditation on the cycles of life, she shows that they exist in the telling of the memory. The grilled meal is gone, but it is replaced with a creamy dessert. The baby teeth are replaced by adult teeth. The innocence of the speaker is replaced by wisdom. The reader can easily conclude that the fallen soldiers are replaced by something else. The light tone of the poem suggests that they are not merely replaced by more soldiers who will die, but rather that their lives

TOPICS FOR FURTHER STUDY

- How does your family or community celebrate Memorial Day? Using digital photography or videography, capture the essence of this day as it relates to your own family, neighborhood, or city. This may require you to conduct some interviews to find out what observances are held, so be willing to do the work to make your presentation accurate. Feel free to make your project strictly informational or more editorial in nature. You may choose to focus on military ceremony, community honor, display of flags, and similar observations, or you may choose to focus on barbecues, shopping, or other ways that people celebrate—or fail to celebrate—fallen veterans.

- Explore the many ways the art world has depicted cemeteries over the years. Select five works of art (in any medium) that collectively say something about the human response to death and remembrance. Create an online video or slide show of these works, along with selections of music, quotations, speeches, or any other audio components that support your point of view.

- Memorial Day has become a nationwide holiday in the United States. What is the economic impact of the holiday? Research the effects of employee days off, retail sales, consumer behavior, and other economic factors. Assemble a presentation for Congress about why we should or should not continue to observe Memorial Day from a strictly economic point of view.

- Do other countries have a national holiday similar to Memorial Day? Conduct research to find other countries that observe a similar holiday (being careful not to confuse it with other patriotic holidays such as Independence Day or Veterans Day) and how they celebrate. Once you have enough information, put together digital charts, graphs, and diagrams to show the similarities and differences. If it makes your work more understandable, include a brief summary of how each country began its holiday.

- Read about the family customs in several different cultures in the young-adult book *Our Human Family: Ties That Bind* by Rebecca Clay and edited by Beth Steinhorn. Write an essay in which you compare the role that family plays in the Memorial Day celebration in "Grape Sherbet" and in one or more of the cultures you chose.

---

make way for and support this American summer celebration.

Memory

Dove develops the theme of memory in "Grape Sherbet" at both a personal level and a collective level. The speaker is sharing a memory; the first three stanzas are all recollection. Why a poem's speaker shares a memory with the reader is always important. In this case, the speaker realizes something new about her experience when she remembers it as an adult. She sees how she experienced it at the time, but she now appreciates what her father was trying to do. Before

launching the festivities of the day, he wanted the children to understand why they were celebrating Memorial Day. He was trying to teach them something that they did not really comprehend. He was also doing his part to honor the fallen soldiers on the day set apart to do just that. Only in the speaker's memory does she learn the lesson and love her father a little more for it.

There is an element of collective memory in the poem, too. The nation sets aside Memorial Day specifically to remember the sacrifices made by the men and women of the armed forces. Dove's poem is set on Memorial Day, so she is bringing the reader's attention to the fact that

Grape sherbet *(Gregory Gerber / Shutterstock.com)*

adult, has a deeper appreciation for her father through this memory of him, the depiction of the father demonstrates his love for his family. He has a day off from work, and he is giving it to his family. He cooks for them, makes sherbet for them, takes them on a trip to the cemetery, and tries to pass something meaningful along to them. His interest is not just in spending time with the children, though. Stanza 3 describes the disapproving grandmother, whose diabetes is keeping her from enjoying the sherbet. The speaker's father is including multiple generations of his family in the celebration of the holiday. In the end, the poem suggests that the father passed his love of family onto the speaker. By showing the importance of getting family together to enjoy one another, he has given the speaker a love for her family that has carried into her adulthood.

STYLE

Setting

Dove creates a strong sense of setting in this poem, placing the reader's attention squarely on when and where the memory she is describing takes place. The time, as she states outright in the very first line, is Memorial Day. This setting is reinforced by the visit to the cemetery, where the father pays his respect to fallen servicemen and women, while instilling his values in his children by bringing them with him to the cemetery. Even the activities of the day are traditional Memorial Day weekend activities to which many readers can relate. The family setting thus becomes important. The family is gathered together for a barbecue followed by a what seems to be a homemade treat. (The recipe is secret; if the sherbet is not homemade, then the father's hidden smile suggests he bought it and is presenting it as his own.) The holiday setting and the family setting are both important, as indicated by how inseparable they are in the speaker's memory.

Free Verse

In typical Dove style, "Grape Sherbet" is written in free verse. That means that the poem does not have a set meter or rhyme scheme, with the result being freer and more conversational than a highly structured poem. Poets who write in free verse rely on the patterns of the language and movement of the poem to determine its pace and

groups of people, indeed entire nations, have shared memories. In both cases, Dove expresses the importance of taking the time to honor the memories that are so much a part of her.

Family

"Grape Sherbet" is presented within a framework of family, and Dove carries the theme subtly through the poem from start to finish. Broadly, the poem is about Memorial Day remembrance, but specifically, the speaker's sentiment about the holiday stems from her father's efforts to bring the reality of the day to his family. The poem is entirely about the speaker's father; he grills, he brings the grape sherbet, he takes the children to the cemetery, and it is he whom the speaker honors in the poem. The poem is set on Memorial Day, but it is not really about remembering American history and its wars; the poem is about the speaker's memory of her father and her appreciation for him now.

The family theme encompasses several generations in the poem. While the speaker, now an rhythm, generally rejecting what can seem artificial about conventional poetic structures. In "Grape Sherbet," the choice of free verse suits the reflective nature of the poem. The sequence of images and words seems natural and spontaneous. For many readers, this style makes the speaker easier to identify with, which is consistent with Dove's idea of poetry as an expression of real human experience and the universal connections among people.

Wordplay

Although "Grape Sherbet" is written in free verse, Dove introduces a bit of wordplay in the poem. For example, in line 4, she repeats the *s* and *l* sounds. The effect is auditory; reading aloud, the line sounds like people enjoying slurping their slippery sherbet. The last line of the first stanza introduces a simile, comparing the father's upturned cap brim to a duck. It is a whimsical image that reinforces the fun, carefree spirit of the family's time together. Near the beginning of the second stanza, the suggestion of a pun on *morning* and its homophone *mourning* brings a slight shift to the tone of the poem. The note of sadness is subtle, but then, the second stanza describes the children's utter obliviousness to the significance of their surroundings. Another case of alliteration is present in the first two lines of the second stanza, in which the poet repeats the *g* sound, tying the lines together even more tightly with assonance as she repeats the *a* vowel sound in the same words.

The third stanza shifts the scene back to the moment in which everyone except the grandmother is enjoying the sherbet. Synaesthesia is when one sense is used to describe another; in this case, the taste of the sherbet is just like they imagined the color lavender would taste. It is fanciful and shows how the people there have given themselves completely over to the experience.

The last two lines of the poem are the only ones that rhyme. After the rest of the poem has flowed in free verse, this sudden rhyme at the end catches the reader's attention in a powerful way. Dove does this to drive home the central message of the poem and to draw attention to the fact that she is no longer addressing the reader. She finishes the poem by directly addressing her father.

HISTORICAL CONTEXT

Memorial Day

After the Civil War (1861–1865), Americans felt a deep need to remember formally the many soldiers who died. Because this need arose so naturally, it is impossible to know for sure where the very first memorial occurred. In 1866, the South saw its first Memorial Day–type expressions. Ladies' groups formed to honor the fallen soldiers, setting aside specific days in their towns to visit and decorate the graves of Confederate soldiers. In 1868, the North had its first Memorial Day remembrance. Congressman John Logan, who was also a general and the commander-in-chief of the Grand Army of the Republic (a Union veteran organization), chose May 30 as Memorial Day and had his posts visit and decorate the graves of fallen Union soldiers.

In the southern and northern states, the memorial events gained momentum until Congress, in 1876, established an official national Memorial Day to be recognized every May 30. Because the southern states did not have an agreed-upon date, Congress chose the date used by the northern states. For those honoring the Confederacy or the Union, the day was solemn and usually began with a church service. Many events included time in the actual cemeteries, where speeches were made, graves were decorated, gun salutes were performed, and "Taps" was played. The United States, however, was still not fully united. In the North, Memorial Day was only for Union soldiers, and the day focused as much on the preservation of the Union and the end of slavery as it did on the sacrifice made by those who gave their lives. Members of the Grand Army of the Republic were obligated to attend, and soldiers were on duty to ensure that no Confederate graves were honored. In the South, the ladies' groups continued to visit and decorate graves, but only those of Confederate soldiers.

The pain and toil of Reconstruction eventually brought the two sides together. Veterans on both sides struggled to keep the patriotic spirit alive, and they found that their shared experiences were a strong bond. As a counterpoint to the trend toward recreation on Memorial Day, veterans organized military parades to bring the public's attention back to the profound courage of the men who fought and died in the Civil War. Surprisingly, veterans of the South and veterans of the North reconciled.

COMPARE & CONTRAST

- **1980s:** In 1987, Dove's *Thomas and Beulah* is awarded the Pulitzer Prize for Poetry. Dove is the second African American recipient of this prize; Gwendolyn Brooks's *Annie Allen* won the award in 1950.

  Today: In 2007, Natasha Tretheway's *Native Guard* wins the Pulitzer Prize for Poetry. Tretheway's father, also a poet, is white, and her late mother was African American.

- **1980s:** Although the Equal Rights Amendment is not ratified in 1982, opportunities and visibility for women continue to open up. President Ronald Reagan swears in the first woman on the Supreme Court, Justice Sandra Day O'Connor. In 1983, the first American woman travels into space when Sally Ride spends six days in orbit as part of the crew of the shuttle *Challenger*.

  Today: Although there are still obstacles for women in some careers and industries, women are valued and respected members of virtually every field. In 2007, Nancy Pelosi becomes the first female Speaker of the U.S. House of Representatives, and when the 111th Congress convenes in 2009, ninety-one women hold seats.

- **1980s:** For eight years, beginning in 1980, a war rages between Iran and Iraq, threatening the already shaky stability of the Middle East. America's involvement is limited: the country provides supplies and applies political pressure as a superpower and negotiates the release of U.S. citizens held hostage by the Iranian government for more than a year. The United States becomes more involved in 1987, but the war ends the following year.

  Today: In 2003, the United States leads a multinational invasion of Iraq with the intention of overthrowing Saddam Hussein. The United States is successful in overthrowing Hussein's government, and he is executed in Iraq in 2006. As of summer 2010, American troops are still in Iraq.

As the turn of the century neared, more Americans found meaning in Memorial Day (sometimes called Decoration Day). The holiday also picked up political steam, with a tradition arising of the president speaking at Arlington National Cemetery. In the midst of the Vietnam War, many Americans lost interest in the patriotism and honoring of sacrifice associated with Memorial Day. In 1968, Congress changed the observance of Memorial Day to the last Monday of May. Being a national holiday and therefore a long weekend for many Americans, the holiday is now often focused on gatherings of friends and families, resting, or shopping.

The Postmodern Period in American Literature

Dove wrote and taught during the American postmodern period, also called the period of the confessional self in American literature (1960 to the present). Taking shape in the 1960s, postmodern literature has been influenced by individualism, rebellion, and cynicism. The Vietnam War, arguably the most unpopular war in American history, stirred young Americans to make their voices heard. Passion, emotion, and possibility proved to be strong drivers of an unprecedented youth movement. The civil rights movement of the 1960s, energy shortages in the 1970s, an increasingly global perspective, and a university culture influenced by the highs and lows of the 1960s led to more widespread (and more outspoken) doubt about authority and capitalism.

The artistic response to these factors was introspective. Artists, musicians, and writers explored a sense of self that did not rely as much on imagination and unrealistic fiction as in the past. Instead, they sought meaning in the real world, and where

The speaker of the poem is at a picnic with her father. (Glenda M. Powers / Shutterstock.com)

they saw flaws, they set out to make change. Postmodernist writing can be political, intensely personal, or experimental. Ethnic subgenres have flourished as writers explore and embrace their unique cultural roots. As a result, the diverse experiences of different peoples in America have been added to the nation's literature. Prominent postmodern poets include Sylvia Plath, Theodore Roethke, Robert Lowell, Kathleen Norris, and James Tate, as well as Dove herself. Some of the notable novelists in this style are William Styron, Saul Bellow, Norman Mailer, John Updike, Thomas Pynchon, and Philip Roth. Prominent postmodern playwrights include Tennessee Williams and Edward Albee.

CRITICAL OVERVIEW

Before her Pulitzer Prize-winning *Thomas and Beulah* was published, Dove's reputation as a serious poet had already been established by the poetry collection *Museum*, in which "Grape Sherbet" first appeared. In fact, in an interview with Grace Cavalieri for the *American Poetry Review*, Dove remarks that *Museum* paved the way for *Thomas and Beulah* because it brought attention to important historical figures, but "we see the side that no one sees when the lights are on. Moving from there to the underside of history, looking at history through two 'ordinary people,' was a natural step."

Critics were impressed by Dove's polished yet natural voice and her skillful use of imagery in *Museum*, in which she draws from her travels in Europe and from her own family life. Although she writes in free verse, reviewers did not charge her with carelessness or disregard for poetic convention. Kirkland C. Jones remarks in a *Dictionary of Literary Biography* entry, "This book presents a mature Dove, expert in the use of recurrent images of light and darkness. Most critics noticed these poems' polish and their author's growth since the late 1970s." Jones adds that he was impressed by the wide variety in subject matter. Although reviewers appreciated the universal nature of many of the poems, some of them were left wanting more insight into the poet as a person, as a woman, and as an African American.

Museum is divided into sections; "Grape Sherbet" is included in the third section, titled "My Father's Telescope." Critics were drawn to her depiction of her father and the way she expresses her feelings about him in the past and in the present. She evokes memories, as she does in "Grape Sherbet." Dove explains to Judith Kitchen and Stan Sanvel Rubin in the *Black American Literature Forum* that her objective in *Museum* was to capture artifacts of life, not the kind people find in a museum, but artifacts such as memories and family history. In describing the book's section about her father, she explains: "In a way that's the memory, childhood focusing on a father, what he seemed like to me then." Larry Smith, in the *Reference Guide to American Literature*, comments on Dove's approach to this volume of poetry:

> The poems in her collection *Museum* are almost too diverse and diffuse as she travels around the globe picking up pieces of life like stones which she polishes with her ample craft. It is not until part three of that book, 'My Father's Telescope,' that she finds her subject in the love and humor of her father's life. Through her

intensely felt family portraits she is able to achieve a larger sense of human family.

As Dove has continued to build her career as a writer of poetry and other genres, critics have generally applauded her contributions to American literature. Whereas many writers peak and then disappear, Dove has demonstrated longevity in a demanding field. In 2005, Sharmaine Small of *Footsteps* reviewed Dove's life and career. Reflecting on her poetry as a whole, Small observes, "Her subjects for poetry are varied, but Dove is known for giving voices to people and characters who are often not heard." This is certainly true of the two main characters in "Grape Sherbet." Small adds, "Her themes often explore relationships and she is noted for her musicality in her lines in addition to the words."

CRITICISM

Jennifer Bussey

Bussey is an independent writer specializing in literature. In the following essay, she considers "Grape Sherbet" in light of three classic cemetery poems: John McCrae's "In Flanders Fields," Emily Dickinson's "Because I Could Not Stop for Death," and Thomas Gray's "Elegy Written in a Country Churchyard."

"Grape Sherbet" was first published in *Museum* (1983), placed in the section about Dove's father. The poem recounts a childhood memory of the speaker's father taking the children to visit a cemetery on Memorial Day and then enjoying a day of family time, grilling a meal and eating grape sherbet. Dove is intentional and forthright in her poem's setting of Memorial Day, and she fashions memorable images of children running and playing through the headstones, so oblivious that they name the grave markers after their own lost baby teeth. Dove's playful graveyard scene is one of many in American and English literature depicting a graveyard, and the poems treating the subject are nearly as diverse as human emotion itself. To see how Dove's poem stands up within the tradition, it is important to compare and contrast it with classic poems set in cemeteries. A good cross-section of such poems includes John McCrae's "In Flanders Fields," Emily Dickinson's "Because I Could Not Stop for Death," and Thomas Gray's "Elegy Written in a Country

Churchyard." These poems are discussed here in reverse chronological order, going from the most recent (after Dove's poem) to the oldest.

"In Flanders Fields" (1915) was written by Canadian physician and lieutenant colonel John McCrae in response to World War I. The poem describes a cemetery where soldiers are buried and where poppies now blow gently in the wind. The poem, written from the perspective of the collective dead, contrasts the lively activities of the men only a few days before they died. In the final stanza, they ask the reader to take up their cause and not let their lives be lost for nothing. Like "Grape Sherbet," this poem is set in a cemetery where veterans are buried. McCrae also uses vivid imagery and contrasts the solemn setting with carefree elements, as Dove does. Where Dove contrasts children playing and remembering something as inconsequential as lost baby teeth, McCrae turns his attention to nature to provide the counterpoint to the otherwise morose setting. "In Flanders Fields" describes poppies and larks, along with the memory of a recent sunset and the universal experience of love. Unlike the children in "Grape Sherbet," however, McCrae's larks participate in the patriotic swell of the poem. According to the speakers, the larks continue to sing bravely despite gunfire on the ground.

Although the two poems have a similar setting and shared themes, there are significant differences between them. Dove's speaker is an adult remembering her childish innocence or mortality, concluding with a special appreciation for her father. McCrae's poem, however, is spoken by the dead, who are acutely and devastatingly aware of the realities of war and death. Perhaps this is why McCrae's poem ends with a passionate plea for the cause of the fallen to be carried on by the living. Dove's poem ends on a quiet, sentimental note; McCrae's poem ends with a mandate.

WHAT DO I READ NEXT?

- *Cool Salsa: Bilingual Poems on Growing up Latino in the United States* (1995), edited by Lori Carlson, is a favorite collection in many school libraries. Its many poets (some well known, such as Sandra Cisneros, but many not) bring their styles, perspectives, and experiences into a single volume to show the reader how the Latino experience in America is unique but also to show what young adults have in common despite culture or ethnicity.

- Dove's *Thomas and Beulah* (1986) won the 1987 Pulitzer Prize for Poetry. Inspired by and loosely based on the lives of Dove's grandparents, this volume contains poems from the perspectives of both characters. Read in order, they tell the story of the couple's marriage and life together.

- Edited by Lorrie Goldensohn, *American War Poetry: An Anthology* (2006) brings together poetry about war throughout American history. Organized by war, the poems present a wide range of feelings, experiences, and points of view.

- *Postmodern American Poetry: A Norton Anthology* (1994), edited by Paul Hoover, contains the work of more than one hundred poets who collectively ushered in a new era of poetry in American literature. The poets and their styles are diverse, representing such movements as the Beats, the Black Mountain poets, and the Deep Imagists.

- The Winter 1993–1994 issue of *Belles Lettres* contains an article titled "Rita Dove: Judith Pierce Rosenberg Interviews Our New Poet Laureate." In this interview, Rosenberg asks Dove about her prestigious status among American poets and talks with her about the other important areas of her life, namely, her family and her students.

- Writing poetry is not easy, so Margaret Ryan wrote *How to Write a Poem (Speak Out! Write On!)* (1996), which teaches adolescents and teenagers how to find their unique voices and work through a process that enables them to write poetry. In an encouraging tone, Ryan makes poetry less intimidating so that young writers can express themselves in this genre.

- Therese Steffen's 2001 *Crossing Color: Transcultural Space and Place in Rita Dove's Poetry, Fiction, and Drama* is the first comprehensive biography and critical overview of the poet's career.

Interestingly, both poems include a torch. Dove's poem features a diabetic grandmother who is metaphorically a torch in her refusal to participate in enjoying the sherbet. McCrae's torch is also a metaphor, but a very serious one. The dead soldiers throw a torch to the living so it can be held high and serve as a call to arms and a remembrance. The poppies of "In Flanders Fields" are another evocative symbol. Used in this poem because of their striking presence in Flanders, Belgium, the site of great bloodshed in World War I, the poppies came to signify Remembrance Day in Great Britain. McCrae's poem led to poppies being the recognized way to commemorate the British equivalent of Memorial Day.

Emily Dickinson lived from 1830 to 1886, writing books of poetry that she barely saw published before her death. Among her most well known poems is "Because I Could Not Stop for Death," a poem describing the speaker going through the process of passing from this world into the next. Dickinson chooses an elaborate metaphor of death as a suitor who arrives in his carriage to pick up the speaker as she goes about her busy life. It is a comforting depiction of death, with nothing threatening at all. The carriage takes the woman past schoolchildren playing (an image that is paralleled in Dove's poem), a field and a sunset, and then her own grave. Dickinson's speaker describes this sight in metaphorical terms: the fresh grave is a house swelling in the ground with a scant roof and cornice. At the end of the poem, the speaker reflects on the passage of time and her gradual realization that day that the carriage was headed into eternity.

Here is another example of the poem's speaker being the one who has died, as in the McCrae poem. Dickinson's speaker has a very different perspective than Dove's speaker. At the moment of seeing the grave, neither speaker absorbs the impact of what she sees. In Dove's poem, the children barely notice the graves, so caught up are they in their own games. In Dickinson's, the speaker never even acknowledges that she is seeing a grave; she carries the house metaphor through to the end. In both works, most of the poem is a memory, with the speaker creating distance at the end.

Dickinson's poem has nothing to do with the cause of death, and it certainly is not about war, courage, or patriotism. Her poem is singularly about the process of dying and moving into eternity with ease. Dove's poem makes no mention of eternity or the afterlife because its focus is appreciating the speaker's father. Despite the cemetery setting, these poems are not frightening, even though they deal with death as it intrudes on an otherwise average day.

Thomas Gray's "Elegy Written in a Country Churchyard" may be the most famous poem in English literature set in a cemetery. Gray's poem is written in lofty language with a formal tone; its speaker is reflecting on the loss felt when someone dies. Although the tone and central message of this poem are quite different from those of "Grape Sherbet," the two works share important features. Both have an opening line that tips the reader off as to where the poet is headed in the poem. Dove's poem begins by establishing that it is Memorial Day, letting the reader know that memory and honoring the past will be important to the poem. Gray's poem begins with an ominous bell announcing the end of the day. This lets the reader know that the poem will be a serious, traditional reflection on death's finality. After the first line, both poems describe the pace and activity of daily life. In Dove's poem, it is the Memorial Day food and family togetherness. In Gray's poem, it is a herd, a farmer, a sunset, and

the insects and animals of nighttime. Like Dove, Gray does not tell the reader explicitly when the poem turns to the cemetery. Gray uses images of turf, hollowed out areas, and sleep.

Although they are very different in language, tone, and substance, "Grape Sherbet" and "Elegy Written in a Country Churchyard" both emphasize the importance of family and memory. Despite the different responses shown in them, these poems are tied together by a focus on universal human experience. Dove's poem focuses on the importance of family first to her father and later to her, but the poem says nothing of the families of the deceased. In Gray's poem, however, the speaker is much more of an observer, and his feelings are not for himself or his own family, but solely for the families and loved ones who must face their lives again without the person who is now buried in the churchyard. Whereas Dove explores a memory of her father's life, Gray explores the impact of losing a loved one to death. Interestingly, "In Flanders Fields" echoes Gray's poem in that there is a responsibility for the living to remember the dead. Coming into the cemetery, the speakers are struck with the need to do more than feel sad. The best way to honor a memory, these poets say, is to do something. Dickinson's poem is silent on this, and Dove's poem honors the memory by simply remembering fondly.

Here are four poems by four different poets in different historical times and places, all addressing the topic of death. An exhaustive study of the tradition of this theme in literature would be an enormous undertaking. These four poems, however, offer a fair cross-section of poets, themes, emotions, and purposes. There is a lot of bad poetry about death, but Dove, McCrae, Dickinson, and Gray offer authentic, thoughtful poetry about death and remembrance. Naturally, there are parallels as well as contrasts among them. As the newcomer to this particular group, Dove proves that she has a place among the great poets in literature.

Source: Jennifer Bussey, Critical Essay on "Grape Sherbet," in *Poetry for Students*, Gale, Cengage Learning, 2011.

Pat Righelato

In the following excerpt, Righelato contextualizes and explains poems included in the third segment of Dove's collection, Museum, *called "My Father's Telescope."*

Memorial Day grill (*BlueOrange Studio / Shutterstock.com*)

If *The Yellow House on the Corner* ends on an upbeat note, Dove's next volume, *Museum*, is an altogether flintier artifact, the product of a dig into cultural origins that is, at times, discomforting. *Museum* is less buoyant than *The Yellow House on the Corner*, more ruthless in its inspections. It would be an exaggeration to say that in the first part of *Museum* the past is a rubbish dump submitted to the American imperial gaze, but it is certainly passed under a candid review, and not without mordant humor. There are, of course, continuities with the first volume, most notably in the delight in fable and legend. If the past is a collection of artifacts, it is also the stories about them that succeeding generations reshape. Dove is very conscious of the paradox of the historicist imagination that seeks to recover the otherness of the past yet also looks for, or unexpectedly finds, its own reflection. . . .

Writing the Father

. . . The vantage point of the third part of *Museum*, "My Father's Telescope," is, as the epigraph from a Bessie Smith blues suggests, the "hill" from which a different perspective of one's roots can be taken. The sequence of poems that follows are rooted in Dove's Akron, Ohio, childhood: "All my beginning memories come out of my experiences in Akron. . . . It's not true to write about some place that doesn't have that emotional resonance for you. . . . Akron is my own." The poems have a specificity of sensory detail, an anecdotal pleasure that evoke belonging, place in the sense of a secure identity, a *familiar* location. Within so much that is known, the poet recognizes the unknown elements of her father in the title of the section and the lead poem, "My Father's Telescope": "My father is someone that I've had a hard time understanding. Sometimes

"THE POEM ITSELF IS A KIND A FORMAL
MEMORIALIZING IN ART, AN INCONGRUOUS FIXING
OF THAT WHICH, LIKE THE SHERBET, IS EVANESCENT,
WITH A COMIC TOUCH IN SUGGESTING THE
PATERNAL EGO."

he seemed like another planet, very far away. And to draw him closer was also part of the sense of that title." The idea of the telescope therefore combines studying him as a feature of her childhood topography, bringing a distant object close, but also trying to understand his viewpoint, as if looking out from his, at times, frustrated perspective. The title also connects with the final part of the volume, which expands from the personal to the global. Dove was writing the poems during the period in which satellite images of Saturn and Jupiter were beamed back to Earth, so the whole section is informed by the sense that near and far are contiguous, capable of being connected.

The first poem, "Grape Sherbet," is threaded by a Proustian joke, a memory of a childhood occasion in which the poet's father made grape sherbet; the taste to the children was like "lavender" or "salt on a melon," but to the adult trying to remember, the taste "doesn't exist." It is not the taste that brings back the memory. Instead, this is a deliberate effort to exhibit her father's character. The word "Memorial" in the first line is appropriate to the fact that the day was a special one, a visit to the family graves. The poem itself is a kind a formal memorializing in art, an incongruous fixing of that which, like the sherbet, is evanescent, with a comic touch in suggesting the paternal ego. There are no confessional hatreds here, just a touch of good-humored rivalry as if to say, Daddy, producer of the "masterpiece" of sherbet, this poem is *my* emperor of ice cream. What lasts, though, is the idea of family continuity, the belief that it matters:

Now I see why
you bothered,
father.

Existence is perpetuated in caring memory and memory is formally carried in art. The care with which the sherbet was constructed in all its fragility is the same kind of caring that ensures important things are not forgotten. The poem plays lightly on its Stevensian themes of sensory delight, transience, and death, as if Wallace Stevens's idealist austerity had been touched with family exuberance. For Dove, as for Stevens, the poem is the paradoxical memorial of that which melts away yet is also the renewal of its occasion.

An autobiographical series of poems by a female poet in search of a father stimulates comparison with Sylvia Plath's more agonized but equally crafted endeavor to "put together" her father. Plath's poem "The Colossus" evokes a ruin, yet a building site in which the poet, "scaling little ladders," reconstructs her father and inserts herself into the literary canon. Plath's linking of the personal and the political was more savage, of course, in "Daddy," her dramatization of the paternal as hateful tyrant, figured in terms of the Nazi jack-boot, violence generating violence. In her more imagistic poem "Ariel," the personal was melted down into the mythical. Dove's enterprise is closer to Plath's emotional range and scale in her mythic series *Mother Love* (1995), yet the crafting of the father poems in *Museum* owes much to the achievement of Plath's generation. The artificial barrier between formalism and a confessional or autobiographical mode had been dismantled, as Dove has commented:

These battles have already been fought. And these are not easy battles—between confessionalism and beat poetry and formalism, or whether poetry adheres to gender or not, or whether it adheres to whatever black aesthetics. These discussions have been on the table. We haven't had to clear the path first before writing.

The poems about Dove's father, for all their intertextual resonance and awareness of the literary traditions of autobiography and memory, also depict a father with a definite character: his passion for rose growing is referred to again in the 1993 poem "In the Old Neighborhood," which prefaces *Selected Poems*, in which he is described as a man who "each summer . . . brandishes color / over the neighborhood." In "Roses," the savagery of his obsession in combating predators and in hungrily shaping the destiny of his prize cultivars is comically expressed in his pruning shears as a "mammoth claw resting between meals." Both "Roses" and "Grape Sherbet" portray a man of intense, even rigid, standards of attainment, as if the frustrations of his professional life are partially vented in the intensity of these domestic activities.

Dove's father trained as an industrial chemist, the first black chemist to qualify in the Goodyear Tire Company in Akron, but the company barred him for a considerable time from working in that professional capacity. Instead, he had to work as an elevator man. These biographical details are not mentioned in the poems; they express a child's perspective in a domestic context. "Roses," in particular, represents Dove as a child, bewildered by the "flat dark fury" of the father's face, as she is forced to participate in the slaughter of the beetles infesting his beloved roses. The color scheme of the poem delivers a Blakean antithesis, a clash between the "pinkish eyelids of the roses" and the "dark fury" of their preserver. Blakean, too, is the fact that the disease-carrying beetles come from Japan (the episode is dated 1961), as if another vengeful twist to the war and blight between the two countries. The savagery with which the father destroys the beetles in order to produce a perfect "inculpable" rose is a metaphor for global combat yet also a personal displacement of frustrated energy that terrifies the uncomprehending child. The group of poems about her father captures how the harshness in his character is part of a scientific determination to explore and know. Paternal protector or ruthless educator, a father is a metamorphic being.

Source: Pat Righelato, "*Museum*: Bringing Dark Wood to Life," in *Understanding Rita Dove*, University of South Carolina Press, 2006, pp. 35–68.

Jennifer Walters

In the following excerpt, Walters illustrates how, despite different styles, Rita Dove and Nikki Giovanni's poems carry out the same themes.

Throughout the centuries, African-American women have acted as agents in their own history, and in doing so defined themselves, for themselves, their communities, and the larger society. Nowhere has this been more apparent than in literature, where experiences, analyses, and understandings are put on paper. And through these stories, African-American women continue the tradition of recording history and the changing times with perspectives that reflect the struggles and survival of African-Americans. Their unique contribution to American poetry brought black women power and a voice—a voice that

> DOVE MAKES ONE WONDER WHAT HISTORICAL TRUTH IS IF EVERYONE POSSESSES A DIFFERENT PERSPECTIVE OF THE SAME EVENT. THIS SORT OF HISTORICAL MANIPULATION SERVES AS THE REASON FOR THE EXCLUSION OF ACCURATE AFRICAN-AMERICAN HISTORY IN TEXTBOOKS AND CLASSROOMS ACROSS THE NATION."

began with such poets as Phillis Wheatley and thrives today.

Nikki Giovanni and Rita Dove, two contemporary poets of great distinction, are examples of self-defined African-American women who found a voice through writing. Their poems are written in very different styles but involve similar themes. Giovanni's and Dove's successes are comparable and their paths similar, although they worked at different periods in contemporary literature. Both poets clearly possess a true passion and voice for writing, making their lives and works worthy of attention and discussion. This essay will compare the backgrounds of Nikki Giovanni and Rita Dove and their contributions to literature and, in doing so, reveal how they as poets help to reshape African-American history.

. . . Rita Dove's childhood, although perhaps more sheltered than Giovanni's, provided a basis for education and inspiration much like Giovanni's. Born nine years later, in 1952, she and her family also lived in Ohio, in Akron, where her parents were the first in their family to succeed in the professional world. Her father was a chemist, and her mother was a housewife, and Dove grew up in a middle-class neighborhood, with two younger sisters and an older brother. Dove describes herself as growing up "protected, in a loving, supportive, but stern environment." Although she never held any aspirations to be a writer, she was a voracious reader and began writing short stories as a little girl. Much like Giovanni, Dove was inspired by a teacher, Miss Oeschsner, who took her to a book signing while in high school. This event, and Miss Oeschsner's encouragement, helped

Dove realize that writing was a viable profession.

Like Giovanni, Dove excelled in school, graduating as one of the highest nationally ranked high school students in 1970. Although she planned to become a lawyer, in response to her parents' expectations, she was increasingly drawn to creative writing classes and eventually graduated from Miami University of Ohio with a bachelor's degree in English." While Giovanni was involved with the Black Arts Movement and the Black Power Movement, Dove excelled in the world of academia. She studied in Germany, helping to perfect her own German, and then enrolled at the Iowa Writer's Workshop, one of the most acclaimed writing programs in America. Dove went on to publish her first volume, entitled *Ten Poems*, in 1977, followed by several other works, including the short story collection in *Fifth Sunday* (1985) and a 1992 novel, *Through the Ivory Gate*.

Throughout the publication of all ten of her books, Dove continued to attend competitive writers' conferences around the world. She soon gained international attention with *Thomas and Beulah*, a collection of poems to be read in sequence that traced the lives of her grandparents in the industrial Midwest. This collection, in fact, served as a collective account of the lives of African-Americans and the great migration from the South to Northern industrial cities. The impressive volume earned her the Pulitzer Prize in poetry in 1987, making her the second African-American to hold the honor, following Gwendolyn Brooks in 1950.

Dove attained one of the highest honors awarded to poets when she was named the United States Poet Laureate in May 1993. She is the first African-American to hold the position and, at age 40, also the youngest. Besides her duties as Poet Laureate, she is Commonwealth Professor of English at the University of Virginia and also a wife and mother.

. . . Like Giovanni, Dove resists ideology in all its guises, preferring that the individual mind *discover* truth and meaning within poetry, instead of trying to shape it. Dove took a dramatic turn away from what she saw as the loose form and domineering intentions of the revolutionary poets that came a half-generation before her. Dove, much like Giovanni after her departure from the movements, views poetry as a function of the writer, and she has

a profound respect for the future and place of poetry in the everday lives of ordinary people. Although Dove's poetry is reflective of the African-American experience, she is more accepted by the literary establishment than Giovanni, perhaps due to her rejection of the loose style of the revolutionary poets that came before her.

Where Giovanni is more subjective in her highly personal poems, Dove is a historical poet, writing of black experience through the lives of "ordinary" people in a very objective way. In her volume *The Yellow House*, one group of poems is devoted to themes of slavery and freedom. In the poem "The Abduction" Dove accounts with simple and poignant clarity Solomon Northrup's recapture after his escape to freedom:

> "I floated on water I could not drink. Though the pillow
> was stone, I climbed no ladder in that sleep.
> I woke and found myself alone, in darkness and in chains."

By distancing herself, Dove gives voice to the people she writes about, and when dealing with the psychological terrors of slavery, she is lending a voice to people who often did not have one.

Dove lends her voice to her maternal grandparents in *Thomas and Beulah*, and both tell their stories of being African-American in the twentieth century. Though both characters are deeply involved with one another, their perceptions and reactions to events on their lives are very different. Not only does this narrative serve as a voice for African-Americans in history, it also tells of the manipulation of history. The story twice-told depends on the *reactions* rather than actions of the characters involved. However, it is clear that even two characters deeply involved with one another tell very different stories. This speaks to a larger picture of our own interpretations of history presented to future generations. Dove makes one wonder what historical truth is if everyone possesses a different perspective of the same event. This sort of historical manipulation serves as the reason for the exclusion of accurate African-American history in textbooks and classrooms across the nation.

Dove tackles issues of racism in contemporary society, as well as in the past, through autobiographical poems such as "Genetic Expedition." She writes of her own interracial marriage, and the curious, often veiled nature of racism in today's society. Dove writes:

> "... My child has
> her father's hips, his hair
> like the miller's daughter, combed gold.
> Though her lips are mine, housewives
> stare when we cross the parking lot
> because of that ghostly profusion."

Her poems that deal with racism are written in a highly personal yet probing manner, in a way which explores the issue uniquely.

Whether writing about the contemporary or Historical Black Experience, Dove sends a clear message: there are many kinds of American traditions. As an African-American woman, her poetry exists in the context of those facts in the history that she understands, but she hopes to break new ground for African-American writers in a literary tradition that tends to label and pigeon-hole black poetry into one genre. As Arnold Rampersad, an African-American educator and critic, said in reference to Dove's poetry, "... one finds an eagerness [in her poetry], perhaps even an anxiety, to transcend—if not actually repudiate—black cultural nationalism in the name of a more inclusive sensibility."

In escaping the "confining image of [a] long-suffering commitment to Black people," and writing about her international relationship. Dove has joined the ranks of many contemporary African-American women writers, such as Audre Lorde and June Jordan, who have violated several taboos, and in doing so created "another safe space where Black women can articulate a self-defined standpoint." Giovanni also participated in creating this "safe space" using her words as a "form of activism." Both Giovanni and Dove succeeded in breaking new ground as African-American poets but both maintained a decidedly rich style of verse, thick with the voices and styles of African-American heritage, including music and dialects.

In a very literal way Giovanni has used music to enhance her poetry. Her 1971 recording of *Truth Is On Its Way* placed her recitation of poems against the back drop of gospel music—a combination she found perfectly logical, and the public found remarkably powerful. Giovanni also refers to music quite often in her work, whether in homage to such musical giants as Aretha Franklin in "Revolutionary Dreams" where she "dreams of being a natural woman," or in poems where she intentionally styles the words in the blues and soul tradition. Her poetry often mimics a free jazz style as in,

> "I wish I could be a melody...like a
> damp...gray...feline
> fog...staccatoing...stealthily...over the city..."

Dove also creates musical textures and believes rhythm within a poem to be an extremely important element. This rhythm, she insists, is "the way our entire body gets involved in the language being spoken. And even if we are reading the poem silently, those rhythms exist." It is not surprising that Dove filters her poetry through melody and rhythm, considering her love of music and her skills as a cellist. Some poems are so melodic they seem to become music, as in "Summit Beach, 1921" where she writes,

> "She could wait, she was gold.
> When the right man smiled it would be
> music skittering up her calf
> like a chuckle."

Furthermore, Dove's use of southern black dialect successfully adds personality to the historical characters she shapes poetry around. Giovanni effectively used black forms during the 1960's, in ways that added to the poem, whereas other poets use of slang and dialect often tended to detract from the point of the poem. In controlling the language within her verse. Giovanni's own personality emerged on the page, purely individualistic and at times even humorous.

Both Nikki Giovanni and Rita Dove are true individuals with clearly different poetic styles. Nonetheless, both have created poems that have touched a multitude of people and in doing so they have helped re-define African-Americans and particularly African-American women's identity in history. They are political in their messages but hold true to their own ideologies and are artistic in the beauty they create with words. Perhaps most important, however, is the invaluable contribution they have made to literature with voices that are telling and true.

Source: Jennifer Walters, "Nikki Giovanni and Rita Dove: Poets Redefining," in *Journal of Negro History*, Vol. 85, No. 3, Summer 2000, pp. 210–17.

Arnold Rampersad

In the following excerpt, Rampersad examines Dove's work within the context of African American poetry.

"

CEREBRAL, SKEPTICAL, AND YET AT THE
SAME TIME INTENSELY HUMAN, SHE LOOKS ON THE
WIDE WORLD AND THE FALLEN CENTURIES WITH
THE SAME ESSENTIALLY IRONIC CONSCIOUSNESS,
THE SAME SHREWD INTELLIGENCE THAT DOES NOT
ABSOLUTELY FORBID LOVE, BUT CONDITIONS IT,
THAT MARKS THE RECREATION OF HER OWN
PRIVATE PAST."

... Now, on the other hand, with the consistently accomplished work of thirty-three year old Rita Dove, there is at least one clear sign if not of a coming renaissance of poetry, then at least of the emergence of an unusually strong new figure who might provide leadership by brilliant example. Thus far, Rita Dove has produced a remarkable record of publications in a wide range of respected poetry and other literary journals. Two books of verse, *The Yellow House on the Corner* (1980) and *Museum* (1983), have appeared from Carnegie-Mellon University Press. A third book-length manuscript of poetry, "Thomas and Beulah," is scheduled to be published early in 1986 by the same house. Clearly Rita Dove has both the energy and the sense of professionalism required to lead other writers. Most importantly—even a first reading of her two books makes it clear that she also possesses the talent to do so. Dove is surely one of the three or four most gifted young black American poets to appear since LeRoi Jones ambled with deceptive nonchalance onto the scene in the late nineteen fifties, and perhaps the most disciplined and technically accomplished black poet to arrive since Gwendolyn Brooks began her remarkable career in the nineteen forties.

These references to the sixties and early seventies are pointed. Rita Dove's work shows a keen awareness of this period—but mainly as a point of radical departure for her in the development of her own aesthetic. In many ways, her poems are exactly the opposite of those that have come to be considered quintessentially black verse in recent years. Instead of looseness of

structure, one finds in her poems remarkably tight control; instead of a reliance on reckless inspiration, one recognizes discipline and practice, and long, taxing hours in competitive university poetry workshops and in her study; instead of a range of reference limited to personal confession, one finds personal reference disciplined by a measuring of distance and a prizing of objectivity; instead of an obsession with the theme of race, one finds an eagerness, perhaps even an anxiety, to transcend—if not actually to repudiate—black cultural nationalism in the name of a more inclusive sensibility. Hers is a brilliant mind, reinforced by what appears to be very wide reading, that seeks for itself the widest possible play, an ever expanding range of reference, the most acute distinctions, and the most subtle shadings of meaning.

... As a poet, Dove loathes sentimentality; she is so hypersensitive to false sweetness that her work will sometimes seem far too demanding to the reader who takes honey with his poetry. Perhaps this general principle, as much as anything else, also explains her tough-minded attitude to race. Certainly she is only modestly sentimental about her own past; she insists on looking back with dancing irony and a disciplined will to understand, and not simply evoke or indulge. Dove's aim in her evocations of her past, her "roots," is a glistening but really scrubbed and unvarnished remembrance of lost time. "Grape Sherbet," from "My Father's Telescope":

> The day? Memorial.
> After the grill
> Dad appears with his masterpiece—
> swirled snow, gelled light.
> We cheer. The recipe's
> a secret and he fights
> a smile, his cap turned up
> so the bib resembles a duck.
> . . .
> Everyone agrees—it's wonderful!
> It's just how we imagined lavender
> would taste. The diabetic grandmother
> stares from the porch,
> a torch of pure refusal . . .

Dove insists on a more austere governance of intimacy than many poets, and most people, are willing to concede. Even when she looks back with affection on the memory of growing up with her father, her manner is one of mock chastisement. The stars are *not* far apart, as he had taught her. No; with passing time

> . . . houses
> shrivel, un-lost,

and porches sag;
neighbors phone

to report cracks
in the cellar floor,

roots of the willow
coming up. Stars

speak to a child.
The past

is silent . . .

Between father and daughter, now man and grown woman, "Outer space is / inconceivably / intimate."

As much as she values home, Dove ranges widely as writer; it is an essential part of her commission to herself as a poet. Europe, as the prime example, is a neighboring field to be mastered like the field of home. The composer Robert Schumann, a German woman who has lost her man in war and lives thereafter crazed by grief ("She went inside, / fed the parakeet, / broke its neck"), the age-old science and mystery and ritual of making champagne—Rita Dove sees everywhere a continuity of human experience. Africa and Asia come more lightly within her frame of reference, but nowhere is she a perfect stranger. The past, too, for her is everything in human history of which she can be made aware, not least of all in the antiquity of Europe and Asia, or the Middle Ages. Dove's approach is neither panoramic nor political; still less is it for cultural genuflection. Cerebral, skeptical, and yet at the same time intensely human, she looks on the wide world and the fallen centuries with the same essentially ironic consciousness, the same shrewd intelligence that does not absolutely forbid love, but conditions it, that marks the recreation of her own private past. "Catherine of Alexandria" memorializes a celebrated would-be martyr of the early Christian church:

Deprived of learning and
the chance to travel,
No wonder sainthood
came as a voice

in your bed—
and what went on
each night was fit
for nobody's ears

but Jesus'. His
breath of a lily.
His spiraling
pain. Each morning

the nightshirt bunched
above your waist—
a kept promise,
a ring of milk.

Dove's imaginative flights are tacked down again and gain by homey details: "the woolens stacked on cedar / shelves back home in your / father's shop," in "Catherine of Siena"; the "two bronze jugs, worth more / than a family pays in taxes / for the privilege to stay / alive, a year, together," in "Tou Wan Speaks To Her Husband, Liu Sheng." On the patina of dust obscuring the humanity of the past from our eyes Rita Dove quietly traces a finger. She writes in a colloquial, familiar idiom that subdues the glittering exotic and makes the ultimate effect of most of these "foreign" poems to be nothing less than a documentation of her claim to the whole world as her home.

The absence of strain in her voice, and the almost uncanny sense of peace and grace that infuses this wide-ranging poetry, suggest that Dove has already reached her mature, natural stride as a poet. I suspect that this judgment might be premature in itself. Both volumes are so tightly controlled, so guarded against excess, that some readers may find them in certain places—perhaps even as a totality—too closely crafted, too reserved, for unqualified appreciation. I think that what we may have in these two books—although they already outclass the complete works of many other poets, and virtually all black poets of Dove's generation—is in fact only the beginning of a major career. In which direction will Dove's great talent take her? I believe that, paradoxically for someone so determined to be a world citizen, she may yet gain her greatest strength by returning to some place closer to her old neighborhood.

Very carefully, I do not say her "home"—much less her "real home" or her "true home." Such terms, made shabby by the huckster, are millstones to a poet like Dove; for her, a house is not necessarily a home. In the end, she may yet as a poet redefine for all of us what "home" means. Dove herself would probably benefit in her own way as an artist from this active redefinition. Then one should perhaps see in her work a loosening of rhythms and a greater willingness to surrender to improvisational and other gifts that she has kept in check but certainly earned the right to indulge. I would expect a vision growing more and more—again paradoxically—into narrower focus and consistency, with the emphasis shifting from irony and learning and calm intelligence towards the celebrations of the more wayward energy that springs naturally out of human circumstance.

Source: Arnold Rampersad, "The Poems of Rita Dove," in *Callaloo: A Journal of African Diaspora Arts and Letters*, No. 26, Winter 1986, pp. 52–60.

SOURCES

Cavalieri, Grace, "Rita Dove: An Interview," in *American Poetry Review*, Vol. 24, No. 2, March-April 1995, pp. 11–15.

Dove, Rita, "Grape Sherbet," in *Museum*, Carnegie Mellon University Press, 1983, p. 47.

Harmon, William, and Hugh Holman, "Period of the Confession and Postmodernism in American Literature, 1960—," in *A Handbook to Literature*, Pearson Prentice Hall, 2009, pp. 408–09.

Jones, Kirkland C., "Rita Dove," in *Dictionary of Literary Biography*, Vol. 120, *American Poets Since World War II*, Gale Research, 1992, pp. 47–51.

Kitchen, Judith, and Stan Sanvel Rubin, "A Conversation with Rita Dove," in *Black American Literature Forum*, Vol. 20, No. 3, Fall 1986, pp. 227–40.

Santino, Jack, "Toward Midsummer: Celebrating the Season of the Sun," in *All around the Year: Holidays and Celebrations in American Life*, University of Illinois Press, 1995, pp. 112–41.

Small, Sharmaine, "The Oscar Goes to . . . (Rita Dove First African American 'Poet of the Nation')," in *Footsteps*, Vol. 7, No. 2, March/April 2005, pp. 42–43.

Smith, Larry, "Rita Dove: Overview," in *Reference Guide to American Literature*, 3rd ed., edited by Jim Kamp, St. James Press, 1994.

FURTHER READING

Bloom, Harold, *Bloom's Biocritiques: Gwendolyn Brooks*, Chelsea House, 2004.

> Renowned literary critic and historian Bloom takes a close look at the life of Gwendolyn Brooks and how the historical context shaped her poetry. Brooks won the distinction of being the first African American to win the Pulitzer Prize for Poetry and the second African American Poet Laureate of the United States.

Mountjoy, Shane, *The Women's Rights Movement: Moving toward Equality*, Chelsea House, 2007.

> Dove has had an ongoing interest in women's rights and opportunities for women in every aspect of American culture. Mountjoy's young-adult review of the history of the women's rights movement gives readers the background to better appreciate the accomplishments of Dove's career.

Pareira, Malin, *Rita Dove's Cosmopolitanism*, University of Illinois Press, 2003.

> Pareira examines Dove's body of work, exploring issues such as ethnicity and universality and delving into the dark and painful themes, as well as those that are easier to manage. In addition to reviewing Dove's poetry, Pareira includes an interview with the poet and comments about such extraordinary life experiences as the Poet Laureate.

Ratiner, Steven, "Rita Dove: In an Interview," *Christian Science Monitor*, May 26, 1993, pp. 16–17.

> Ratiner asks Dove a series of questions about her view of the importance of history and her role in preserving it as a poet. Dove also discusses topics as wide-ranging as her upbringing, music, and censorship.

SUGGESTED SEARCH TERMS

Rita Dove

Rita Frances Dove

Rita Dove AND Grape Sherbet

Museum AND Grape Sherbet

African American AND Pulitzer Prize for poetry

African American AND poet laureate

Memorial Day AND poetry

postmodern poetry AND free verse AND Rita Dove

Rita Dove AND musicality

Rita Dove AND family AND traditions

The Latin Deli: An Ars Poetica

JUDITH ORTIZ COFER

1992

Judith Ortiz Cofer first published "The Latin Deli: An Ars Poetica" in *Americas Review* in 1992. The poem also appears in a 1993 collection of poems, short stories, and personal essays titled *The Latin Deli: Prose and Poetry*. The collection received much critical acclaim. The title poem focuses on a place where Latino immigrants meet to talk to each other in their native language and to buy food from their homelands. The deli and its owner offer a respite from the culture clash that immigrants experience in the United States. As they walk down the aisles reciting the names of their native foods like poetry, they are able to hang on to the traditions of the past in order to maintain a clear sense of their cultural heritage. Ortiz Cofer transfers her own experience as an immigrant to art and so establishes a link between herself and the deli owner. Ortiz Cofer suggests that through her poems and stories that focus on the lives of Latino immigrants, she, like the owner of the deli, offers comfort and a sense of identity to others who share her heritage.

AUTHOR BIOGRAPHY

Ortiz Cofer was born Judith Ortiz on February 24, 1952, in Hormigueros, Puerto Rico, to J. M. and Fanny Ortiz. Her family immigrated to the United States in 1956 when her father joined the U.S. Navy. The family made frequent trips back to

Puerto Rico from their home in Paterson, New Jersey, during her childhood. This travel between the two cultures would have an important effect on her writing. When Cofer was fifteen, the family moved to Augusta, Georgia. She was one of three minority students, and the only Puerto Rican, in her high school graduating class of 2000 students.

In 1971, she married Charles Cofer and they had one daughter. Ortiz Cofer received a bachelor's degree from Georgia's Augusta College (again as the only Puerto Rican graduate) in 1974 and a master of arts degree from Florida Atlantic University in 1977. She also studied at Oxford University in 1977. She held several teaching positions in Florida and Georgia before she began teaching at the University of Georgia in 1984, where she was honored with a Regents and Franklin professorship of English and creative writing in 1999.

Ortiz Cofer began writing while she was a graduate student. She first wrote poems about Latina women and then broadened her literary endeavors to the novel, short story, essay, and autobiography. She has written a dozen books since the publication of her first poetry chapbook, *Latin Women Pray*, in 1980. Her work has also been included in numerous collections and anthologies, and demand for her work in Spanish-speaking countries has resulted in translations of many of her works in Latin America.

Her work has been widely recognized both in Georgia and nationally. Her autobiographical essay collection *Woman in Front of the Sun: On Becoming a Writer* won the Georgia Writers Association 2001 Georgia Author of the Year Award in creative nonfiction. Both *The Latin Deli* and her novel *The Meaning of Consuelo* were named on the Georgia Center for the Book lists of "25 Books All Georgians Should Read" in 2005 and 2008, respectively.

Ortiz Cofer has received many awards, including Scholar of the English-Speaking Union at Oxford University, 1977; fellow of the Fine Arts Council of Florida, 1980; Bread Loaf Writers' Conference scholar, 1981; John Atherton Scholar in Poetry, 1982; a grant from Witter Bynner Foundation for Poetry, 1988, for *Letters from a Caribbean Island* (poetry); a National Endowment for the Arts fellowship in poetry, 1989; a Pulitzer Prize nomination, 1989, for the novel *The Line of the Sun*; the Pushcart Prize for nonfiction, 1990;

the O. Henry Prize for short story, 1994; and the Anisfield Wolf Award in Race Relations, 1994, for *The Latin Deli*.

POEM SUMMARY

Title

The full title of the poem is "The Latin Deli: An Ars Poetica." "Ars poetica" is Latin for "the art of poetry," and it is the title of a poetical treatise by the Roman poet Horace (65–68 BCE) and a poem by Archibald MacLeish written in 1926. In Ortiz Cofer's poem, the "art of poetry" can be interpreted in different ways. The deli itself can be like a poem to the customers, as it provides them with meaning in their lives. Since "The Latin Deli" is the first poem in the collection in which it appears, Cofer could also be suggesting that through her poems and stories that center on the lives of Hispanic or Latino immigrants, she offers comfort and a sense of identity to others who share her heritage.

Lines 1–7

In lines 1–7 Ortiz Cofer introduces the poem's main character, whom she describes as a protector or supporter of immigrants—which Ortiz Cofer can also be considered, because of her art. She delays mentioning her subject until line 7, after she has given a partial description of the deli. First she describes the Formica counter on which sits an old cash register with a Madonna and child religious icon on top of it. This mixture of imagery reflects the reality of life for the Spanish-speaking immigrants who come into the store. These items reflect the lower economic status of the neighborhood and take on a double meaning. The customers of the deli come there to connect with their heritage, and so these objects would comfort them. The antiquated cash register keeps them in touch with the past. When Ortiz Cofer capitalizes the words describing the religious statue, she suggests that these figures represent Mary and Jesus. They symbolize the customers' strong religious beliefs that they have carried with them to the United States. Since these beliefs often clash with the more secular American culture, the statue helps them reinforce their sense of identity. In lines 4–6, Ortiz Cofer describes the intoxicating, exciting smells of dried codfish and green plantains—food that reflects the immigrants' culture. Food and religion are intertwined when she describes the

MEDIA ADAPTATIONS

- A video podcast of Ortiz Cofer speaking at the 2003 National Book Festival is available for viewing at the Library of Congress Web site.

- Ortiz Cofer reads from her book *The Latin Deli* on the Web site *Developing Writers: A Workshop for High School Teachers.*

plantain stalks hanging like offerings dedicated to the religious icons.

Line 7 finally returns to the owner, who in the first line had been described as occupying a place of authority in the deli. Ortiz Cofer gives the owner a type of sacred status as she opens her food bins for her customers, providing them with a much-needed cultural link. The owner watches over her customers like a sacred mother, offering them comfort and a strong sense of self.

Lines 8–10

These three lines briefly describe the deli owner and touch on her interaction with her customers. Ortiz Cofer introduces her in a nondescript way as a woman of no distinct age, suggesting that rather than being one specific person, she is an amalgam of all the women who run delis in ethnic neighborhoods. Her role in the neighborhood is to spend her days retelling old, tired stories while listening to the inhabitants express dissatisfaction about their life in America and reminisce fondly about their past.

Lines 11–17

These lines describe both the laments and hopes of the immigrants for their lives in America, as well as a nostalgia for their home. These lines also identify the different groups that come together in the deli. Puerto Ricans dislike the deli's high prices, and Cubans boast of a wonderful reunion with Havana, the capital of Cuba. In their determination to hold onto the past, they refuse to admit that life has continued in their homeland without them. Mexicans who shop at the deli are looking to make their fortune in the United States.

Lines 18–23

Lines 18–23 return the focus to the deli owner, noting that her customers gain comfort from being able to speak Spanish to her. The image of maternal comfort is reinforced by her physical description. She is described as soft and round, with an open, loving face. These physical details help provide them with a sense of identity, because when they look at her, they can see their own mothers, aunts, and grandmothers to whom they can tell all their problems.

Lines 24–28

Ortiz Cofer continues the maternal image with the owner's smiles of satisfaction at the customers as they lovingly read the Spanish labels of the food in the deli's aisles. These names read aloud stir memories of their childhoods in their homelands. Ortiz Cofer reinforces this emotion when she uses alliteration in this passage with the soothing sounds of a repetitive *l*.

Lines 29–38

In these lines, Ortiz Cofer returns the focus first to the owner, who personally wraps her customers' orders, and then to the customers themselves, whose shopping there becomes an integral part in their struggle to maintain their cultural identity. The food is more expensive in the deli, but the customers do not really mind the extra cost. The food they would get from an American supermarket chain would not satisfy their desire for a place where they can connect with each other and with their heritage. The Spanish-speaking people who come to this store have lost a clear vision of themselves in the difficult process of assimilation, as symbolized by an elderly, frail man in his warm winter clothing. His love of his homeland emerges in the sounds of his language as he brings a shopping list. The final lines return the focus to the owner and her almost supernatural powers as she anticipates her customers' needs. In line 36, the owner's abilities to connect with her customers seem to be not just magical but religious, linking her again with the statue of Mary on the cash register. The poem closes with a focus on the difficult task of providing comfort to these transplanted people. At the end of the poem, a maritime metaphor of trade and commerce explains how the owner enables her customers to reestablish a clear vision of self through the products from their homelands.

THEMES

Cultural Conflict

The clash between American and Hispanic/Latino culture becomes the impetus for immigrants to come to the deli. In an interview in *MELUS*, Ortiz Cofer notes that this theme predominates in all the stories and poems in *The Latin Deli*. Her work reflects her own experience trying to reconcile the contradictions in her cultural identity. She explains,

> I write in English, yet I write obsessively about my Puerto Rican experience.... That is how my psyche works. I am a composite of two worlds.... I lived with these conflictive expectations: the pressures from my father to become very well versed in the English language and the Anglo customs, and from my mother not to forget where we came from. That is something that I deal with in my work all the time.

In the same interview, she explains more about her cultural background:

> One of the things that is so dissonant about the lives of children in my situation is that I would go to school in Paterson and mix and mingle with the Anglos and Blacks, where the system of values and rules were so much different than those inside our apartment, which my mother kept sacred. In our apartment we spoke only Spanish, we listened only to Spanish music, we talked about *la casa* [the house] (back home in Puerto Rico) all the time. We practiced a very intense Catholic religion, with candles in the bathtub, pictures of the Virgin and Jesus everywhere.

The customers in the deli, like Ortiz Cofer's parents, struggled to hang on to the traditions of the past, in order to maintain a clear sense of who they are and where they came from. There they see the symbols of their culture: the religious statue and the food. They also can hear and speak their native tongue.

Identity

In an interview with Rafael Ocasio in *Callaloo*, Ortiz Cofer explains how places like the deli helped Spanish immigrants reestablish their cultural identity. She writes,

> The book is called *The Latin Deli* because the centers, the hearts of the barrios in New Jersey were the bodegas.... Food is important in its nur-

TOPICS FOR FURTHER STUDY

- Read another selection from Ortiz Cofer's *The Latin Deli: Prose and Poetry*. What are the themes in it that are also addressed in "The Latin Deli"? Create a Venn diagram that illustrates your comparisons.

- With a group of students, research the sociological, educational, economic, and psychological effects of cultural assimilation on a group of immigrants to the United States from a different continent. Create a Wikispace with those content divisions and post the information that you find in the appropriate division. When the Wiki is completed, write an essay that summarizes the effects that most groups have in common.

- Write a free verse poem that describes what you would miss about your culture if you moved to another country that did not have English as its dominant language. Post your poem to your Web page and invite your classmates to comment on what they would miss most.

- Read the young-adult novel *Behind the Mountains: The Diary of Celiane Esperance* (2002) by Edwidge Danticat. Write an essay that compares the feelings that Celiane has with those expressed in "The Latin Deli."

- Through interviews, library research, or Internet research, find out about the experiences of some people of different ages (children, teens, parents, and the elderly) who have immigrated to the United States. Find out what the biggest obstacles to overcome were and the most difficult parts of the assimilation process for each age group. Which groups had an easier time, which groups struggled the most to fit in? Create a multimedia presentation that uses music, art, and interviews (if possible) to describe the struggles of different age groups.

turing of the barrio. To my parents their idea of paradise was eating *pasteles* [pork meat turnovers].

The deli owner in "The Latin Deli" is similar to a woman in one of the collection's short stories, "Corazon's Café." Ortiz Cofer explains:

Fruits at the Latin deli *(Dallas Events Inc / Shutterstock.com)*

[This woman is] fully committed to nurturing the barrio, to bringing life to it, not by standing on a soap box, not by becoming a great philosopher, but by keeping this bodega open. So that the people of 'el building' could have their *pasteles*, could have their café [coffee], could have a taste of what they needed to nurture them spiritually.

Art and Life

The customers in the deli elevate the status of the items there to art as they lovingly read the labels of the boxes and cans of food. The store items become poetry, reminding the customers of their culture and so reaffirming their sense of themselves.

This connection between art and everyday life also emerges in the relationship that Ortiz Cofer establishes between herself and the deli owner. Ortiz Cofer suggests that through her poems and stories that center on the lives of Hispanic or Latino immigrants, she, like the owner of the deli, offers comfort and a sense of identity to others who share her heritage. In the *Callaloo* interview with Ocasio, she notes:

The idea of staying alive by telling stories is something that has always fascinated me. . . . I like the idea of the never-ending story that feeds one generation and then another. It's my own literary heritage; I am nourished by the stories that I heard and then I feed others, I hope. All my women—Corazon, Mama, all of them—rely on their imaginations to make their lives richer and to teach their daughters.

STYLE

Free Verse

Ortiz Cofer wrote "The Latin Deli" in free verse, which varies line length and does not have an established meter, rhythm, or rhyme scheme. The poetic line becomes its basic rhythmic unit. Line breaks highlight important words in the poem. In "The Latin Deli," Ortiz Cofer frequently ends her lines with words that help convey the poem's themes. For example she ends lines 4–7 with words that reinforce the importance for the immigrants of the deli's Spanish food and the deli owner's position as supporter, providing solace through food. Lines 18 and 19 end with words that illustrate how the deli helps the customers reestablish comforting connections with their heritage.

Repetition of sounds in a poem can also emphasize key words and images and so create poetic structure, as well as providing pleasure. This poem uses alliteration, the repetition of initial consonant sounds, to mark significant themes. For instance, the alliteration in lines 26 and 27 emphasizes the joy the customers feel when they speak in their native language.

Spiritual Elements

Many of Ortiz Cofer's works show various forms of religion or spiritual beliefs incorporated into daily life. In this poem, for example, a Christian icon of the Madonna and Child sits atop the cash register, and the deli owner is seen as similar to a saint or the Madonna. Other works have characters who believe in *espiritismo* (spiritism, a belief in spirits that can affect many aspects of human life) or *santería* (a West African and Caribbean religion). These beliefs have a unique importance, for Ortiz Cofer, in the lives of her immigrant characters. In the *Callaloo* interview, she writes,

> The migrant Puerto Rican brought espiritismo to the United States in order to feel some connection with and some control over a world that was extremely confusing. And so it took on a different role than on the island.

The connection to the supernatural or the divine, she writes, provides "an outlet for their emotions, a way to feel that they are in control of their world." In *The Latin Deli*, it is part of a connection to their homelands.

The importance of the spiritual world bears some similarity to the literary technique of magical realism, a style that incorporates fantastic or bizarre elements into an otherwise realistic setting. However, in the same interview, Ortiz Cofer notes that while magical realism requires the reader "to accept supernatural phenomena and to practice suspension of disbelief," her work is about people's beliefs, not fantastical events. "I am writing about an ordinary, everyday thing that most Puerto Ricans live with," she says. She writes about the lives of people who believe in miracles, but not about miracles themselves.

HISTORICAL CONTEXT

Puerto Rican Literature

Puerto Rican literature began to flourish in the nineteenth century, when the first printing press arrived in South America. The illiteracy rate was very high, and the only people with access to libraries were plantation families and colonial government officials. The earliest writings were protest pieces about Spanish colonial rule by journalists who were influenced by the romantic movement to write about the injustices of slavery and poverty. Their writings were punishable by prison terms or banishment. The officially sanctioned literature commissioned by the Spanish government, on the other hand, consisted only of histories of the island; even fiction and poetry had historical themes.

The early protest writings helped promote ideas of independence that followed the independence movements in Haiti and then the countries of Central and South America. Many Puerto Rican writers welcomed the Spanish-American War in 1898, hoping incorrectly that the island would be granted independence. When it was instead ceded to the United States, the writers changed course and began to write about the injustice of American rule; they frequently expressed patriotism in their writings.

By the 1940s, the Puerto Rican diaspora (a scattering of emigrants to other regions) had begun, resulting in the immigration of millions to the United States, many to New York City and Chicago. Puerto Ricans now began to write about new subjects: the hardships associated with assimilation and discrimination, and a longing for the old way of life. A new movement began in New York City with the writing of Jesús Colón, the Nuyorican movement (the term means "New York Rican"). The writers of the movement promoted the idea of maintaining the cultural identity of the Puerto Rican people by expressing their feelings and thoughts in all forms of writing. The Nuyorican Poets Café, which opened in 1973, has become a high respected literary organization that promotes all types of innovative poetry.

Ortiz Cofer is not technically a Nuyorican, but she often participates in conferences and workshops with their writers. When Ocasio, in an interview in *Kenyon Review*, asked Ortiz Cofer about the influence of the movement on her writing, she responded,

COMPARE
&
CONTRAST

- **1990s:** In 1990, 22.4 million Hispanics make up 9 percent of the population of the United States. Only eight states have counties in which Hispanics make up more than 25 percent of the population.

  Today: 47.8 million Hispanics make up 14.8 percent of the population of the United States. Fourteen states have counties in which Hispanics are more than 25 percent of the population.

  1990s: According to Maribel Ortiz-Márquez, despite funding cuts for Puerto Rican studies and ethnic studies in general, and less publication in the United States, there is an upsurge of critical attention in Spanish about Puerto Rican literature. With more than two hundred participants from Puerto Rico and the United States, the September 1996 Puerto Rican Studies Association conference in Puerto Rico attests to that vitality.

  Today: The Puerto Rican Studies Association continues to meet each year and in 2010 presents the first Puerto Rican Studies Association Book Award. The award is given in recognition of the book that best addresses issues and concerns of Puerto Ricans and their communities and represents a preeminent contribution to the field of Puerto Rican studies.

  1990s: Urban gentrification in ethnic neighborhoods invites the opening of large chain supermarkets in many parts of large cities formerly underserved except by ethnic delicatessens and grocery stores.

  Today: Ethnic delis and markets dwindle in number as large chain supermarkets embrace the value of selling ethnic food items and marketing to their ethnic customers. The supermarkets make ethnic items less expensive and more easily accessible than the traditional ethnic delis.

The Nuyorican writers have nourished me in the sense that it is good to know that they are completing the mosaic of Puerto Rican literature in the United States. There is not just one reality to being a Puerto Rican writer. I am putting together a different view.

Demise of the Puerto Rican Influence in New York City

In 1950, 79 percent of all Latinos in New York City were Puerto Rican, but by 2000, only 37 percent of New York City Latinos were Puerto Rican despite the overall increase of Puerto Ricans residing in the United States. The question of why the population has changed in this way was addressed by Mireya Navarro in a 2000 *New York Times* article reprinted in the *Puerto Rico Herald.* For those who remain, according to Navarro, this decline has "provided them with a moment to look back on, and assess, the Puerto Rican experience in New York."

According to the article, in 2000, Puerto Ricans were much poorer than other immigrants and minority groups. About 40 percent in New York City qualified as living in poverty, a greater percentage than for African Americans or for Hispanics in general. It was difficult to study the economic situation of Puerto Ricans, Navarro writes, because there was a tendency to move frequently back and forth between the city and the island. Even more interesting, of those leaving New York City permanently for the island, 40 percent were now native-born U.S. citizens.

Even more distressing was the educational situation. Navarro found that only 10 percent of New York Puerto Ricans older than twenty-five had a college degree. The educational crisis is enhanced by residential segregation, neglected schools, and lack of family involvement in education. Language barriers were often pointed to as an educational issue, but most Puerto Ricans in New

A couple shops at the Latin deli *(iofoto / Shutterstock.com)*

York City were second- or third-generation and speak English.

Economically, the arrival of many Puerto Ricans between 1940 and 1970 coincided with the beginning of the end of the manufacturing supremacy of the northeast region of the United States. According to Navarro's findings, this was just part of a greater trend of movement to suburbs or other regions of the country for economic reasons.

Welfare reform has also been a factor. Since Puerto Ricans are U.S. citizens, they were immediately entitled to social benefits upon their arrival in the United States. According to Navarro, sociologists say that "among single mothers with young children, who often found welfare more attractive than a low-paying job with no benefits," a cycle of poverty that relied on public assistance emerged. This cycle was cut short by the 1996 Welfare Reform Act.

Finally, Navarro points out the complicating factors of resistance to acculturation in favor of a Puerto Rican nationalism. She quotes a New York City councilwoman, Margarita Lopez, who told Navarro that despite living in the city for over twenty years, she had to make a

conscious decision "to embrace this country." There is a similarity to the characters in the poem "The Latin Deli," who seek out familiar cultural products from their homelands.

CRITICAL OVERVIEW

Ortiz Cofer first published "The Latin Deli: An Ars Poetica" in *Americas Review* in 1992; she reprinted it in 1993 in a collection of poems, short stories, and personal essays titled *The Latin Deli*. The work received overwhelmingly positive critical reviews despite the fears of Michael J. O'Shea, who states in a review of the book for *Studies in Short Fiction* that "readers and reviewers might overlook the volume because of its eclecticism . . . or because they incorrectly assume that its appeal is specifically 'ethnic.'"

Booklist contributor Whitney Scott writes that Ortiz Cofer's collection of her stories, essays, and poems is a "delicious smorgasbord of the sights, smells, tastes, and sounds recalled from a cross–cultural girlhood." Scott adds, "Whether delineating the yearnings for an island homeland or the frustrations of a first-generation immigrant's struggles to grow up in 'el building' in a New Jersey barrio, Ortiz Cofer's work is rich in evocative detail and universal concerns."

A reviewer for *Kirkus Reviews* finds the book "a remarkably cohesive, moving collection—a tribute both to Cofer's considerable talent and her heritage." A *Publishers Weekly* reviewer states that "the book is full of strong female figures and explores the complexities of Latina identity."

Kenneth Wishnia, in a *MELUS* article, focuses on themes present in the poem. He notes that Ortiz Cofer "works with many themes that are common to ethnic–American literature, for example, the feeling of being in exile in a strange land, where the sound of Spoken Spanish is so comforting that even a grocery list reads 'like poetry.'"

CRITICISM

Wendy Perkins

Perkins is an associate professor of English at Prince George's Community College in Maryland. In the following essay, she examines one of the dominant themes in "The Latin Deli: An Ars Poetica"—the relationship between art and experience.

In his poetical treatise "Ars Poetica," which is Latin for "the art of poetry," the Roman poet Horace writes of the importance of "decorum" in poetry, by which he means the appropriate connection between the parts of the poem and its whole. His principle of decorum emphasizes a concern with the relationship of a poem to the reader—how the writer shapes the work to produce a pleasing experience for the reader. Ortiz Cofer's "The Latin Deli: An Ars Poetica" also focuses on this relationship between reader and author. In the poem's description of the interaction between the Latina deli owner and her customers, Ortiz Cofer establishes two connections: between herself and the deli owner and between herself and her readers. Ortiz Cofer suggests that through this poem that centers on the reality of Latino immigrant life, she, like the owner of the deli, can offer comfort and a sense of identity to others who share her heritage. This effect, then, results from the art of her poetry.

In an interview in *MELUS*, Ortiz Cofer tells Edna Acosta-Belen about her personal vision of the relationship between art and experience:

WHAT DO I READ NEXT?

- In *Boricuas: Influential Puerto Rican Writings—An Anthology* (1995), editor Roberto Santiago includes more than fifty selections of poetry, fiction, plays, essays, monologues, screenplays, and speeches from some of the most creative and lively Puerto Rican writers.

- Ortiz Cofer's 1995 collection of short stories for young adults, *An Island Like You: Stories of the Barrio*, is set in a New Jersey barrio; the stories focus on Puerto Rican teenagers.

- "The Latin Deli" was published in 1993 in the collection *The Latin Deli: Prose and Poetry*. This collection of poems, short stories, and essays by Judith Ortiz Cofer depicts the experiences of Puerto Rican immigrants.

- *Raining Backwards* (1997) by Roberto G. Fernandez looks at the lives of multiple generations of a family in Cuba and Miami. Like Ortiz Cofer, Fernandez focuses on the problems of assimilation in America.

- *Woman in Front of the Sun: On Becoming a Writer* (2000) is a collection of Ortiz Cofer's essays and poems that tell the story of how she became a writer.

- *Commons* (2002) is the fourth collection of poetry by the Korean poet Myung Mi Kim. This collection, like Ortiz Cofer's work, deals with the cultural and linguistic displacement that results from immigration.

As I was growing up, I learned from [my female relatives'] very strong sense of imagination. For them storytelling played a purpose. When my *abuela* sat us down to tell a story, we learned something from it, even though we always laughed. That was her way of teaching. So early on, I instinctively knew storytelling was a form of empowerment, that the women in my family were passing on power from one generation to another through fables and stories. They were teaching each other how to cope with life.

In an interview with Ocasio in *Callaloo*, Ortiz Cofer adds that these women were "powerful

THE SPANISH-SPEAKING PEOPLE WHO COME TO HER STORE HAVE LOST A CLEAR VISION OF THEMSELVES IN THE DIFFICULT PROCESS OF ASSIMILATION."

matriarchs" for her: "In my developing consciousness as a story-teller I saw that there was power there, power to influence." Commenting on her transfer of that oral tradition into literature, she explains, "I like the idea of the never-ending story that feeds one generation and then another. It's my own literary heritage; I am nourished by the stories that I heard and then I feed others."

The poem "The Latin Deli" opens her 1993 collection of stories, poems, and personal narratives, *The Latin Deli: Prose and Poetry*, which focuses on the daily struggles of Latino immigrants as they cope with the difficult process of assimilation. Her works, like the offerings in the deli, help sustain those who read them. Ortiz Cofer's careful shaping of "The Latin Deli" sets the tone of the collection and establishes the crucial relationship between art and reader. In the *MELUS* interview, Ortiz Cofer discusses her own assimilation experiences after she immigrated from her native Puerto Rico to Paterson, New Jersey:

> I write in English, yet I write obsessively about my Puerto Rican experience.... That is how my psyche works. I am a composite of two worlds.... I lived with ... conflictive expectations: the pressures from my father to become very well versed in the English language and the Anglo customs, and from my mother not to forget where we came from. That is something that I deal with in my work all the time.

"The Latin Deli" exemplifies her maternal relatives' earnest desire to maintain a sense of cultural identity. The deli's customers respond to the challenge of living between two cultures by returning to the deli to experience the world of their homeland as they speak to each other and the owner in Spanish and as they sample the sights, aromas, and tastes of the offerings there. In the first few lines of the poem, Ortiz Cofer describes the deli, including the items that have a positive effect on the customers. First she notes the old cash register and religious statue

on the counter. The customers of the deli come there to connect with their heritage, and so these objects comfort them. The antiquity of the cash register keeps them in touch with the past. The capitalization of the words describing the religious icon suggests that these figures are Mary and Jesus and highlights the spiritual nature of the deli. The statue symbolizes the customers' strong religious beliefs that they have carried with them to the United States. Since these beliefs often clashed with the more secular American culture and their children's active assimilation efforts, the statue helps them reinforce their sense of identity. In lines 4–6, food also becomes an important item in the deli. Ortiz Cofer describes the aroma of dried codfish and green plantains—food that reflects the immigrants' culture. She reinforces the religious theme when she describes the plantain stalks hanging like dedicated gifts.

Later in the poem, the customers read aloud the names of the foods on the shelves, which stir memories of their lost childhood. Ortiz Cofer reinforces their sense of emotion with alliteration of soothing sounds. Their shopping there becomes an integral part in their struggle to maintain their cultural identity. Ortiz Cofer notes that the food is more expensive in the deli, but the customers really do not mind the extra cost. The food they would get from an American supermarket chain would not satisfy their need for a place where they can connect with each other and with their heritage. The Spanish-speaking people who come to her store have lost a clear vision of themselves in the difficult process of assimilation. The old man in winter garb shows his love of his homeland in the sounds of his language as he brings a shopping list filled with words that bring back a flood of memories. In her *MELUS* interview, Ortiz Cofer notes her own connection to her native language and its influence on her art: "I use Spanish words and phrases almost as an incantation to lead me back to the images I need."

In the interview in *Callaloo*, Ortiz Cofer describes her own experience with the Latin delis in her neighborhood: "The hearts of the barrios in New Jersey were the bodegas, which were called delis by some of us. There were Jewish and Italian delis. So if you sold sandwiches, well, it was a deli and that was part of our language.... Food is important in its nurturing of the barrio. To my parents their idea of paradise was eating *pasteles* (pork meat turnovers)." The deli owner in the poem commits herself to nurturing her customers by offering them the products of their homeland. Ortiz Cofer reveals the deli owner's vital connection to the Latino immigrants as she alternates her focus in the poem back and forth between them. She calls the owner a protector of immigrants, who rules over the deli. Ortiz Cofer gives the owner a sacred status as she offers her food bins to her customers, providing them with a sorely needed cultural link. The owner watches over her customers like a Madonna, offering them comfort and a strong sense of self. This ageless woman becomes an amalgam of all the women who run delis in ethnic neighborhoods. Her role there is to spend her days helping her customers assimilate—fit into their life in America—while also reminiscing fondly about their past. Ortiz Cofer's physical description of her reinforces her nurturing image. These physical details help provide her customers with a sense of identity, since when they look at her, they see their maternal family figures.

In the poem's closing section, Ortiz Cofer reinforces her ties to the deli owner and her customers/readers. She uses a style reminiscent of magical realism—the incorporation of supernatural elements into everyday life—when she describes the owner's ability to provide just the right foods to provide the customers with comfort and a sense of belonging. In the final lines of the poem, she notes the difficulties that both she and the deli owner face in their attempts to provide solace to these transplanted people whose hearts have become closed to all but the happy memories of the past. The mission for both Ortiz Cofer and the deli owner is to open these hearts in order to enable their readers and customers to reestablish a clear vision of self. Thus, the deli and the poem become a haven for Latino immigrants, like Ortiz Cofer, to reconnect with their cultural heritage and so find a respite for a time from the difficult process of acculturation.

Source: Wendy Perkins, Critical Essay on "The Latin Deli: An Ars Poetica," in *Poetry for Students*, Gale, Cengage Learning, 2011.

Chris Semansky

Semansky teaches literature and writing at Portland Community College and is a widely published poet, fiction writer, and critic. In the following essay, he explores the relationship between nostalgia and poetry in "The Latin Deli: An Ars Poetica."

In terms of population, the fastest growing segment of the United States is Hispanic.

Fish counter at the Latin deli (Jane Rix | Shutterstock.com)

Hispanics constitute the largest minority population in the country, and Spanish is the most frequently spoken language, after English. Mexicans, Cubans, and Puerto Ricans make up the bulk of the Hispanic population. The Mexican population is largely concentrated in the West and Southwest, with California and Texas boasting the largest numbers. Cubans have a large presence in South Florida, and Puerto Ricans are heavily concentrated in New York City and northern New Jersey. The United States, or the "mainland," as it is known to Puerto Ricans, is considered a place of economic opportunity and freedom, and the rate of immigration to the states from Hispanic countries is very high. However, with opportunity also comes sacrifice. Those who leave home and come to America miss their homeland and a sense of belonging to a more homogeneous culture where family, neighborhood, and town often form the backbone of one's identity. Many immigrants become exiles of a sort, caught between cultures, not wholly belonging to either their new home or their old. "The Latin Deli: An Ars Poetica" explores the nature of yearning for a place and a way of life that has been lost, linking it to the "stuff" of poetry itself.

The most profound feature of romantic poetry and, arguably, modern poetry is the sense of loss: loss of love, loss of life, loss of identity. This loss is often couched in terms of nostalgia, a profound and insatiable desire for

THE PROMISE THAT THE PATRONESS OFFERS
IS THE PROMISE OF POETRY. POETRY, LIKE THE
PATRONESS, IS ABLE TO BRING TO MIND THINGS
THAT EXIST ONLY IN THE HUMAN HEART."

the past. Ortiz Cofer evokes this nostalgia in the opening lines of the poem.

When Ortiz Cofer later describes the things the immigrants remember as "canned," she is using a figure of speech that plays on the fact that delicatessens sell canned goods as well as produce and other items. Because this yearning and the attendant memories on which the yearning is based are repeated in almost ritualistic fashion, "canned" is used in its sense of prepackaged, something that can be used time and time again with exactly the same effects. Canned laughter, or laugh tracks, a staple of television situation comedies, is one example of this effect. Nostalgia by its nature is always the same, a melancholic yearning for the past that can never be appeased. It repeats itself precisely because it cannot be appeased. The deli lends itself to feelings of nostalgia because its features and products are similar to those of the immigrants' homelands.

The delicatessen is described as a cross between a church and a museum. Ortiz Cofer's description suggests that this is not one Latin deli, but *all* Latin delis. The food here and the Catholic icon, a Mary and Jesus statue, are staples of many Latin countries, most of which are heavily Roman Catholic (Puerto Rico is 85 percent Catholic). Rather than satisfy the exiles' longing, however, the deli catalyzes it. These people are emotional exiles as well as physical ones. Though they have left their countries for a better life, they still long for the comfort of their homeland, as represented by foodstuffs such as plantains, a variety of banana that cannot be eaten raw, and Bustelo coffee, a particularly strong blend especially popular in Puerto Rico. The smells and sights of these items remind customers of their past and encourages them to act in particular ways. They become caricatures of exiles from their respective countries: the Puerto Ricans exaggerate and complain about how expensive goods are in the states; the Cubans beat their chests and brag of the day when they will

overthrow Castro; the Mexicans are obsessed with making money to escape their impoverished lives. Stuck in the past, these cultural "interlopers" nonetheless must deal with the present. Their inability to do so forces them to live in a kind of purgatory, where their homeland is dangled in front of them like a lure only to be pulled away when they get closer to it.

The proprietor of the deli is herself a combination of Mother Mary, museum curator, and muse. Like the exiles and the deli itself, she is a type, a representative of many people and not an individual. Sexless and smiling, she embodies all of the characteristics of the stereotypical Latina mother with her soft, wide body and open, smiling face. She symbolizes their heritage, the values of Latin culture, and stands for all that is good about the places they have left. In this way, she anchors the exiles in the past even though their hopes and dreams are also in the present and for the future.

Ortiz Cofer underscores the exiles' desire by focusing on language; the visitors to the deli want to hear the sounds of Spanish being spoken. Verbalizing the names of goods (for example, candy) takes the exiles deeper into their purgatory. The past is now like some unattainable lover, whose name they call but who will never answer. Ortiz Cofer once again highlights the frozen nature of the exiles' desire by describing these confections in a way that revives memories of childhood in the old country. Though the candies promise to be sweet, they are stale, as they have always been. They symbolize the static quality of impossible want.

The final images of the poem describe the extreme pathos of the exiles' situation. An old man, symbolizing all old men who are exiles, must have the ham and cheese sandwich from *this* deli, even though he could buy a less expensive sandwich elsewhere. The proprietor, in her role as patron saint of the exiles, attempts to satisfy this need by making the sandwich in the way that the man remembers it being made in his own country. The man's hunger is an appropriate metaphor, and the physical nourishment with which the deli supplies him only keeps his real hunger for his homeland alive. That she perceives the needs of these exiles and supplies items from their past suggests that she has powers, magical and religious. Her real trade is in desire. No doubt caught between cultures herself, the owner presumably also keeps her own dreams of her homeland alive by dealing in the hopes of others.

How can this description of a Latin delicatessen be called an "Ars Poetica," or art of poetry? If readers consider the patroness a muse as well and consider the customers as poets, this title can be better understood. Historically, patrons, both individuals and organizations, have materially and through encouragement supported poets. A good current example is the National Endowment of the Arts, which gives money every year to poets and artists to help them begin or complete projects. In return, poets acknowledge the support, sometimes in their verse itself. The owner of the Latin deli offers customers emotional support and confirmation that their desires are legitimate even though it is just old memories that she sells. As muse, she inspires the exiles. In her store they find Spanish being spoken in the mournful reciting of the names of deli products, finding solace (and misery) in the act of naming itself. The promise that the patroness offers is the promise of poetry. Poetry, like the patroness, is able to bring to mind things that exist only in the human heart. Poetry makes something out of nothing, and it often originates in the imagination, the same place that gives birth to nostalgia and dreams. But there is something ironic in Ortiz Cofer's calling her poem an ars poetica, for if we understand the deli as a sad place, a stagnant place where heartbroken exiles are sold the same illusions over and over again, we must understand poetry, by extension, as something akin to the act of lying. This is similar to how Plato saw poetry in *The Republic*, when he argued for it to be banned from his utopian community because it represented no truth of its own but rather provoked the emotions and kept humanity from knowing real truth. In evoking the exiles' feelings of hopelessness and despair, Ortiz Cofer is not making anything up; rather, she is mining reality itself for the lies that we tell ourselves. The art of poetry for Ortiz Cofer, then, is the art of unmasking the readers' own self-deceptions.

Source: Chris Semansky, Critical Essay on "The Latin Deli: An Ars Poetica," in *Poetry for Students*, Gale, Cengage Learning, 2011.

Kenneth Wishnia

In the following review of The Latin Deli: Prose and Poetry, *Wishnia states that the work of Ortiz Cofer "defies convenient classification," although she addresses many common themes of ethnic American writing, including the various subthemes of culture clash, such as sexuality, mores, and belief systems.*

Judith Ortiz Cofer's writing defies convenient classification, although she works with many themes that are common to ethnic–American literature, for example, the feeling of being in exile in a strange land, where the sound of Spoken Spanish is so comforting that even a grocery list reads "like poetry." The daily struggle to consolidate opposing identities is perhaps most clearly exemplified by the tradition which determines that a latina becomes a "woman" at age 15, which means, paradoxically, not more freedom but more restrictions, since womanhood is defined as sexual maturity, which must then be contained at all costs. This leaves one of her characters feeling "like an exile in the foreign country of my parents' house" because of "absurd" rules that do not apply to her present reality in Paterson, New Jersey.

Another striking example of such cultural clash occurs in the story, "Advanced Biology," in which a ninth grade Jewish boy tells the eighth-grade narrator about both the Holocaust and reproductive biology. This leads her to doubt both God's "Mysterious Ways" and the Virgin Birth (and to have a screaming match with her mother on the topic), but concludes with her asking:

> Why not allow Evolution and Eve, Biology, and the Virgin Birth? Why not take a vacation from logic? I will not be away for too long, I will not let myself be tempted to remain in the sealed garden of blind faith; I'll stay just long enough to rest myself from the exhausting enterprise of leading the examined life.

Indeed, Ortiz Cofer invites us to do the same when she presents the story of a young Puerto Rican girl's first disappointing attempt to date a non-latino Catholic. In "American History," we get a fictionalized account of the girl living in a tenement in Paterson, who takes a liking to a "white" boy from Georgia named Eugene, only to have her mother warn her, "You are heading for humiliation and pain." Soon Eugene's mother tells her in a "honey-drenched voice" that it's "nothing personal," but she should "run back home now" and never try to speak to the boy again. In "The Story of My Body," a similar situation occurs, and her mother tells her, "You better be ready for disappointment." The warning is followed by the boy's father saying, "Ortiz? That's Spanish, isn't it?" as he looks at her picture in the yearbook and shakes his head No. In the poem "To a Daughter I Cannot Console," the narrator telephones her mother for advice on how to console her own lovesick sixteen-year-old daughter, and when her mother asks her "to remember the boy I had cried over for days. / I could not for several minutes / recall that face." The reader is left with the impression that such an event must have happened to Ortiz Cofer, or else why would she describe it three different ways in the same book? But it is precisely these "three different ways" that ask us—perhaps even compel us—to withdraw from "the exhausting enterprise" of examining too closely. Such events are common ethnic-American experiences, and thus all versions are in some way equally "true."

Other familiar themes treated in colorful and moving ways include the preparation of food (one character derives some fragment of solace after the death of her husband by entering her apartment building at dinnertime, and inhaling deeply "the aromas of her country," and there is a hilarious episode in which some furious adolescent petting is abruptly ended because the narrator has to go stir the red kidney beans before they get ruined), the untranslatability of certain culturally-bound concepts into English (nada can mean so much more than "nothing"), disappointment with fathers, men, and God, and the different standards of beauty between cultures. The essay "The Paterson Public Library" should be required reading in all high schools and colleges.

One especially provocative issue will have to serve for discussion: "The Story of My Body" begins, "I was born a white girl in Puerto Rico but became a brown girl when I came to live in the United States." This essay, about how our identities are often dependent upon how others define us, is followed by a poem appropriately called, "The Chameleon," and another essay, "The Myth of the Latin Woman: I Just Met a Girl Named Maria," in which Ortiz Cofer exposes and rejects common stereotypes of latinas as "hot," "sizzling," etc., explaining that in Puerto Rico, women felt freer to dress and move "provocatively" because the climate demanded it, and they were more-or-less protected by "the traditions, mores, and laws of a Spanish/Catholic system of morality and machismo whose main rule was You may look at my sister, but if you touch her I will kill you."

Yet, at the opening of "The Myth of the Latin Woman," Ortiz Cofer writes about how she coveted "that British [self-]control," and in the poem, "Who Will Not Be Vanquished?" she writes:

Morning suits us Spanish women.
Tragedy turns us into Antigone—maybe we
are bred for the part.

Perhaps an "insider" can write this, but does it not also suggest that we all have our own preferred stereotypes? (In a related issue, three of the reviewers who are cited on the back of the book don't seem to be familiar with the traditional Spanish system of naming, referring to the author as "Cofer," when she clearly identifies herself as "Ortiz Cofer.")

In "5:00 A.M.: Writing as Ritual," Ortiz Cofer describes a period in her life when motherhood and adjunct-teaching freshman composition at three different campuses somehow failed to fulfill her completely, and she writes that "There was something missing in my life that I came close to only when I turned to my writing." There is a bit of this sentiment in all of us.

Source: Kenneth Wishnia, Review of *The Latin Deli: Prose and Poetry*, in *MELUS*, Vol. 22, No. 3, 1997, p. 206.

Michael J. O'Shea

In the following review of The Latin Deli: Prose and Poetry, *O'Shea praises Ortiz Cofer's eclecticism, calling her writings "profound, poignant, funny, universal, and moving."*

Judith Ortiz Cofer, author of fiction, poetry collections and essays, presents all three in her latest book, *The Latin Deli*. Some readers and reviewers might overlook the volume because of its eclecticism. (It might have escaped editorial notice in this journal, for instance, because about 60 percent of the volume is devoted to poetry and essays.) Others might ignore it because they incorrectly assume that its appeal is specifically "ethnic." The latter premise reminds me of a mid–Atlantic university administrator I knew whose office would not subscribe to the *New York Times* because "we don't care what's going on in New York." For the record, then, don't buy this book solely for the poems, solely for the stories, or solely for the essays; moreover, don't buy this book solely to read about the experiences of Puerto Rican characters in the continental US. Instead, buy this book for the profound, poignant, funny, universal and moving epiphanies between its covers.

Cofer's combination of essays and poems produces a sustained embroidery on the short stories (and vice versa). Indeed, the essays and personal poems (especially the poems "Absolution in the

New Year," "Who Will Not Be Vanquished?," and "Anniversary," and the essays "Advanced Biology," "The Story of My Body," and "The Myth of the Latin Woman: I Just Met a Girl Named Maria") reveal some of the autobiographical materials that Cofer uses in her stories. Her characters include young Puerto Rican girls who, like her, grow up in Paterson, New Jersey, in or around a tenement known as "El Building." In "American History," the teenaged protagonist is so focused on her impending study "date" with the blond–haired Eugene that she is unable to respond to the other events of 22 November 1963. Her mother, offended by the daughter's failure to grieve over the Kennedy assassination, predicts that her infatuation with an Anglo boy will bring only "humiliation and pain." The prediction comes true immediately when Eugene's mother refuses to let the girl in the house. In a bitter epiphany recalling Joyce's "Araby" and "The Dead," the girl "went to my window and pressed my face to the cool glass. Looking up at the light I could see the white snow falling like a lace veil over its face. I did not look down to see it turning gray as it touched the ground below."

There are other echoes of Joyce, from the explicit allusions to *Ulysses* in the epistolary narrative "Letter from a Caribbean Island" to the homely character in "Nada" whose "long nose nearly touched the tip of his chin" (like Maria's in Joyce's "Clay"). On a more sustained level, Cofer's stories recall Joyce's *Dubliners* in their cumulative portrait of El Building's characters in different stages of maturity, from young Eva, who is baffled by the evidence of her father's marital infidelity in "By Love Betrayed," through the emotional powerhouse of "Corazon's Cafe," encapsulating two lives in the narrative frame of the hours following a young husband's sudden death. As the childless widow is surrounded in the embrace of her community, Cofer sketches that community's members with extraordinary economy and force.

Cofer's essays and poems are highly personal and as powerful as her stories. The interplay between her non-fictional commentary on the power of writing ("5:00 A.M.: Writing as Ritual") and the poems and stories that demonstrate that power constitute an implicit narrative structure tying the volume together. Several poems (among them "Saint Rose of Lima" and "Counting") evoke the power of Catholic symbol and mysticism recalled through some secular distance, yet

retaining not only the power of vivid recollection but also that conferred by artistic transformation. The emotional range of the volume is impressive, from the moving posthumous reconciliation with a father in "Absolution in the New Year" (with its disarmingly witty yet powerful coda, "There is more where this came from") to the funny adolescent pangs of "The Story of My Body" ("Wonder Woman was stacked. She had a cleavage framed by the spread wings of a golden eagle and a muscular body that has become fashionable with women only recently.").

Cofer's writing is not "about" being a Latina woman in America, nor is it "about" what critics call "marginality" or "Otherness," except to the extent that we are all marginal or Other to some degree. Who could be less "Other" in U.S. society, for instance, than George [H. W.] Bush; but who has been more marginalized than he was in and since the last U.S. presidential election? Judith Ortiz Cofer's work touches on human concerns that speak to none Other than all of us. She is an author worth knowing.

Source: Michael J. O'Shea, Review of *The Latin Deli: Prose and Poetry*, in *Studies in Short Fiction*, Vol. 31, No. 3, Summer 1994, p. 502.

SOURCES

Acosta-Belén, Edna, "A *MELUS* Interview: Judith Ortiz Cofer," in *MELUS*, Vol. 18, No. 3, Fall 1993, pp. 83–97.

"Hispanics in the United States," in *U.S. Census Bureau*, http://www.census.gov/population/www/socdemo/hispanic/files/Internet_Hispanic_in_US_2006.pdf (accessed July 4, 2010).

"History" in *Nuyorican Poets Café*, http://www.nuyorican.org/history.php (accessed July 4, 2010).

"Judith Ortiz Cofer," in *Scholastic.com*, http://www2.scholastic.com/browse/contributor.jsp?id=2945 (accessed July 4, 2010).

"Judith Ortiz Cofer," in *Voices from the Gap*, University of Minnesota Web site, http://voices.cla.umn.edu/artistpages/coferJudith.php (accessed July 4, 2010).

Navarro, Mireya, "Puerto Rican Presence Wanes in New York," in *Puerto Rico Herald*, reprinted from *New York Times*, February 28, 2000, http://www.puertorico-herald.org/issues/vol4n09/PRPresenceWanes-en.html (accessed July 4, 2010).

"New—PRSA Awards—New," in *Puerto Rican Studies Association*, http://www.puertorican-studies.org/ (accessed July 4, 2010).

Ocasio, Rafael, "The Infinite Variety of the Puerto Rican Reality: An Interview with Judith Ortiz Cofer," in *Callaloo*, Vol. 17, No. 3, Summer 1994, p. 730.

———, "Puerto Rican Literature in Georgia? An Interview with Judith Ortiz Cofer," in *Kenyon Review*, Vol. 14, No. 4, Fall 1992, pp. 43–50.

Ortiz Cofer, Judith, "The Latin Deli: An Ars Poetica," in *The Latin Deli: Prose and Poetry*, University of Georgia Press, 1993, pp. 3–4.

Ortiz-Márquez, Maribel, "Puerto Rican Literature, 1988–96: An Annotated Bibliography," in *ADFL Bulletin*, Vol. 28, No. 2, Winter 1997, pp. 49–54, http://web2.adfl.org/adfl/bulletin/v28n2/282049.htm (accessed July 4, 2010).

O'Shea, Michael J., Review of *The Latin Deli: Prose and Poetry*, in *Studies in Short Fiction*, Vol. 31, No. 3, Summer 1994, pp. 502–04.

"The Poetry-Poets of the Chicano/a Movement, Nuyorican Poetry, Transition to Academia, Other Voices," http://www.jrank.org/cultures/pages/4323/Poetry.html#ixzz0sl6PdDHY (accessed July 4, 2010).

Review of *The Latin Deli*, in *Kirkus Reviews*, Vol. 61, October 1, 1993, p. 1218.

———, in *Publishers Weekly*, Vol. 240, No. 45, November 8, 1993, p. 60.

Scott, Whitney, Review of *The Latin Deli*, in *Booklist*, November 15, 1993.

Wishnia, Kenneth, Review of *The Latin Deli: Prose and Poetry*, in *MELUS*, Vol. 22, No. 3, Fall 1997, p. 206.

FURTHER READING

Christie, John, and Jose Gonzalez, *Latino Boom: An Anthology of U.S. Latino Literature*, Longman, 2004.
This thematically organized anthology of Latino literature provides resources for class discussion and analysis. It offers both complete works and excerpts written originally in English, by a variety of authors, ranging from the established Latino/a writers to newcomers in a wide range of styles.

Dalleo, Raphael, and Elena Machado Saez, *The Latino/a Canon and the Emergence of Post-sixties Literature*, Palgrave Macmillan, 2007.
This study of Latino and Latina literature challenges the idea that literature after the 1960s was written for political reasons rather than for the literature market, as is the claim about modern Latino/a literature.

Lee, A. Robert, *Multicultural American Literature: Comparative Black, Native, Latino/a, and Asian American Fictions*, University Press of Mississippi, 2003.
Lee is a British scholar who analyzes each type of fiction within its cultural setting. He looks at the way each group's literature has been influenced by culture and politics in terms of both subject and style.

Olmes, Margarite Fernandez, and Harold Augenbraum, eds., *The Latino Reader: An American Literary Tradition from 1542 to the Present*, Mariner Books, 1997.
Augenbraum and Olmes trace the roots of Latino/a literature back to the mid-sixteenth century in their selection of both primary sources and essays, poetry, drama, and fiction, including texts translated into English for the first time. The resulting anthology is an effective compilation of a wide range of literature.

SUGGESTED SEARCH TERMS

Ortiz Cofer AND The Latin Deli

Ortiz Cofer AND magical realism

Ortiz Cofer AND Latino/a literature

Judith Ortiz Cofer

Ortiz Cofer AND Puerto Rican literature

Ortiz Cofer AND poetry

Ortiz Cofer AND young-adult literature

Ortiz Cofer AND Hispanic literature

Ortiz Cofer AND Nuyorican

The Lorelei

HEINRICH HEINE

1823

Alongside Goethe, Schiller, and Novlais, Heinrich Heine is considered to be among the greatest German romantic poets. Although his body of writing includes dramas, journalism, and entire verse novels, the rest of his work is overshadowed in popularity by a single lyric poem of twenty-four lines: "The Lorelei." Especially in its musical setting by Friedrich Silcher, "The Lorelei" is considered a national treasure of German literature and culture. Even during the Nazi period, the poem could not be suppressed and was not burned like the rest of Heine's works because of his Jewish origin. Instead, "The Lorelei" was frequently republished by attributing it to an anonymous author. The poem was also embraced as a symbol of cultural identity by the German American community, as embodied in the Lorelei monument by Ernst Herter erected in the Bronx in 1899. Today, "The Lorelei" is the most frequently reprinted of Heine's poems, although often outside of its place in the *Homecoming* cycle. A good source for the poem is Hal Draper's 1982 translation of Heine's complete poetry, *The Complete Poems of Heinrich Heine: A Modern English Version*.

"The Lorelei" is often assumed to reflect German folk tradition. In fact, it is based on a fairy tale invented by German novelist Clemens Brentano in 1801, taking its name from the Lorelei Rock, one of the most beautiful spots in the Rhone valley. The poem's story of a water nymph whose song causes sailors to crash into the Lorelei Rock incorporates many typical elements of Indo-European

Heinrich Heine (German Information Center)

and Germanic tradition. Heine uses the subject matter of the poem to explore larger ideas about identity and poetry itself. Heine's work in turn has inspired dozens of other poets to write on the Lorelei theme, notably Guillaume Apollonaire and Sylvia Plath.

AUTHOR BIOGRAPHY

Heine was born into a Jewish family on December 13, 1797, in Düsseldorf, Germany, a city on the lower Rhine River. The city was, at the time, occupied by France, but was soon incorporated into Napoleon's client state of the Grand Duchy of Berg. After 1815, Düsseldorf became part of the Kingdom of Prussia. In this way Heine's home passed from the furor of the French Revolution to the center of German nationalism. Heine studied at the University of Berlin (where he worked closely with the philosopher Georg Wilhelm Friedrich Hegel), and after earning a law degree in 1825 he converted to Lutheranism to escape institutional anti-Semitism in Germany. His immediate plan was to find employment as a university professor, a profession legally closed to Jews

under Prussian law. He never obtained an official position and supported himself as a writer, not only as a poet, but more profitably as a playwright and journalist. In 1823, he published his most famous work, the lyric poem, "The Lorelei."

In 1831, Heine moved to Paris where he lived the rest of his life. The move was partly motivated by his conception of Napoleon as a liberator and enlightener from past barbaric ages of superstition, and partly because in Germany he still faced anti-Semitism and state censorship of his publications despite his formal conversion. In his outlook, Heine was thoroughly secular and modern, and well-integrated into the leading edge of German progressive intellectualism then known as Young Germany. His teacher Hegel had been of the most important philosophers of his generation and a leading figure of German romanticism. Heine's ideals were freedom, progress, human brotherhood, and liberalism. In exile, his orientation always remained German; he frequently used his fatherland as an object of tragic loss in his poetic work. While becoming increasingly interested in Jewish culture late in life, Heine never resumed the practice of Judaism. He was not religious but sought a personal spiritual enlightenment. In Paris, Heine was a frequent contributor to Karl Marx's journal *Vorwärts* (*Forward*), which was aimed at German liberals despite having to be smuggled into the country illegally. While Heine believed communist revolution was inevitable because of inequalities in the new industrial economy, he lamented that it would also mean a break with cultural traditions. Heine developed a debilitating illness that kept him bedridden for the last eight years of his life but did not decrease his literary output. He died at home in Paris on February, 17, 1856.

POEM TEXT

I do not know what it means that
I am so sadly inclined;
There is an old tale and its scenes that
Will not depart from my mind.

The air is cool and darkling,   5
And peaceful flows the Rhine;
The mountain top is sparkling,
The setting sunbeams shine.

The fairest maid is reclining
In wondrous beauty there,   10
Her golden jewels are shining,
She combs her golden hair.

With a golden comb she is combing,
And sings a song so free,
It casts a spell on the gloaming,   15
A magical melody.

The boatman listens, and o'er him
Wild-aching passions roll;
He sees but the maiden before him,
He sees not reef or shoal.   20

I think, at last the wave swallows
The boat and the boatman's cry;
And this is the fate that follows
The song of the Lorelei.

POEM SUMMARY

Stanza 1

The poem begins with a speaker referring to himself in the first person. This authorial voice is not to be confused with Heine's own authentic identity as a person separate from his work: it is a character created by Heine in just the same way as the other characters in the poem. This narrative voice says that he is in a reverie or state of mental reflection that has left him melancholy. He is not able to understand the cause of this sadness. But, in any case, it leads him to remember an old fairy tale. Its episodes and locations form unbidden in his imagination.

Stanza 2

The narrative voice begins to recall the details of the fairy tale that has intruded into his consciousness from memory. He describes the physical setting of the story in highly evocative language. The scene takes place at sunset over the Rhine River. There is also a mountain over the river. This is the Lorelei Rock, a high, sheer basalt cliff that rises above the Rhine. The narrative voice emphasizes the coolness of the end of the day and the effects on the sunlight that come only at dusk: the mixture of shadow and light, the play of the light on the waters of the Rhine, and the rays of the setting sun coming over the horizon. The manner evokes German romantic paintings, as in the landscapes of Caspar David Friederich. The overall effect is to display the beauty of the natural, as opposed to the man-made, world, a key theme of romanticism.

Stanza 3

In the third stanza, the narrator's recollection conjures up the image of a beautiful young woman (revealed to be the Lorelei in the last line of the poem). She is lying down, presumably supporting

MEDIA ADAPTATIONS

herself on one arm since she is also combing her blonde hair. She is wearing golden jewelry set with gems that are shining, presumably with reflected sun light. This raises an irresolvable question: where is this figure located in the scene? The fact that the sunset is glinting off of her jewelry would suggest that she is on top of the Lorelei Rock where she would be best positioned to catch the light in this way. But other evidence, later in the poem, will suggest, but not demand, that she is lower down, at the level of the river. The statue of the Lorelei at the tourist site in modern St. Goar, Germany, which is intended to depict this moment of the poem, is located on a low mole (large stone used as a pier or breakwater) jutting out into the river.

Stanza 4

The narrative voice renews his description of the Lorelei combing her hair. This emphasis suggests that it is a characteristic action and indicative of vanity. This would seem to be confirmed by the display of the gold jewelry. More importantly, the Lorelei is also singing a song, described as free, and yet at the same time, it casts a magical spell over the landscape. The fact that the song is also a spell reflects something fundamental about the nature of poetry. In the post-Enlightenment, scientific, modern age, spells are not often relevant, and stereotypes of spells in contemporary mass-market literature and films usually depict them as spoken in verse. But linguistically, ancient words with Indo-European origins like *enchant, incantation,* or *ode* refer to song, poetry, and spells as a single, undifferentiated entity. The Lorelei's singing and spell casting are one in the same thing.

Stanza 5

A new character arrives onto the scene: a boatman sailing on the Rhine. He is the object of the Lorelei's spell. Like the voice of the sirens in Greek mythology, the Lorelei's song excites the passions of the boatman. His senses are blinded to the dangers of the river and he can see nothing but the object of his desire, the figure of the Lorelei. If the Lorelei's song is free, the passions it excites in the boatman are enslaved to it: he is bound into such a state of excitation that he cannot control or temper his will or actions. Since the vision of her is distracting the boatman from the dangers of the river (the channel by the Lorelei Rock is the narrowest, swiftest, most dangerous part of the Rhine), it would make sense that the Lorelei is on the river bank where she could most easily be seen by anyone sailing on the river. But the boatman is under a spell that affects his perception. She could just as easily be on top of the rock and cause the boatman to see some magical image of her. For this reason, there is no way to decide the issue of her location; Heine gives too few clues.

Stanza 6

The narrative voice now returns to speaking in the first person and qualifies this stanza by claiming that the recollection being recounted is uncertain. In any case, what is represented is that the boatman's ship is wrecked and that he answers the song of the Lorelei with his own final cry as he drowns. This disaster is said to be the inevitable consequence of the Lorelei singing. As beautiful and as enchanting as the song of the Lorelei is, it is a force for destruction and disorder. This is an unresolved paradox. At the same time that the song is free, how can it impose on its audience the ultimate cost of death? Seemingly it must be this

tragedy, and the unresolved contradiction that underlies it, that disturbed the peace of the narrator at the beginning of the poem. The cause is brought to light, but nothing is accomplished to raise his spirits by doing so.

THEMES

Failure of Romanticism

Since the earliest times, authority in Western culture, whether political, intellectual, or spiritual, was based on tradition. In the seventeenth and eighteenth centuries, this changed with the Scientific Revolution and the Enlightenment. Reason became the basis of authority, attacking aristocratic privilege and dogmatic theological and philosophical beliefs (most famously in Galileo's discovery that the earth orbits the sun, rather than the sun moving around a fixed earth). The romantic generation in the 1790s and the early decades of the nineteenth century had to come to grips with this disconnect between tradition and modernity. Life in Germany was disrupted in a particularly acute way as the radical consequence of the Enlightenment, the French Revolution, and the Napoleonic Wars of the early 1800s.

The romantic response to these dislocations, by German poets like Friederich Schiller and philosophers like Heine's teacher Hegel, was to view the progress of history as well as the components of human experience as a dialectical process: in Aristotle's system of syllogistic logic, a known thesis and antithesis could be reconciled to produce a previously unknown synthesis. They hoped tradition and the Enlightenment could react in the same way and produce a synthesis of romanticism as a new ideal. Hegel began with an explanation of Christian salvation history: the creation and the fall were resolved into redemption. It seemed that the disconnect between feeling and reason, between authority and freedom, nature and culture, ancient and modern, and even between knower and known, subject and object, or God and man, could be resolved to discover something new and superior to either term in the syllogism. Heine's friend and publisher Karl Marx adopted the same idea to the economic and political sphere in his dialectical materialism, reading history as a series of revolutions and reactions leading ineluctably, in his view, to a communist utopia. The German romantics came to believe that the ultimate resolution of history, of self and the

TOPICS FOR FURTHER STUDY

- Listen to different sound recordings of "The Lorelei," especially those by Silcher, Schumann, and Liszt (performances can be found by searching Internet sites such as YouTube). Compare them to the third movement of Shostakovich's Symphony no. 14, which is a setting (composed music) of the French poet Guillaume Apollinaire's version of the original Lorelei poem by Brentano. What moods and feelings are provoked by the various pieces? How do they illustrate or contextualize the original poem? Write an appreciation of these pieces in the form of an essay.

- Re-envision Lorelei as the Afro-Caribbean goddess Mami Wata. Research her history and attributes using online and library resources. Then rewrite "The Lorelei" (or transpose the tale into a short story) using a Caribbean setting.

- Read *A Tramp Abroad*, in which Mark Twain satirized the use of "The Lorelei" in tourist literature, both in guide books and travel writing. Today "The Lorelei" is widely used on tourist sites on the Internet to promote tourism to the middle Rhine, and is frequently mentioned in blogs kept by tourists. Make a record of these sites using Delicious.com or other online bookmarking program. How has the use of the poem and the site in tourist information changed over the past 150 years? Create a twenty-first century Web site that invites tourists to visit the site of the Lorelei Rock. Use the words of the poem, pictures, and music to enhance your site. Alternately, make your site satiric, in the style of Twain's piece.

- Rosalie K. Fry's young-adult novel, *The Secret of Ron Mor Skerry*, as well as its film adaptation, *The Secret of Roan Inish* (rated PG), concern the encounter of a young woman with a selkie, a traditional water spirit similar to the Lorelei. Read the novel or watch the film and research the background of the selkie in Celtic myth. Then research the Germanic mythology of the nixie on which the Lorelei was based. Give a class presentation (perhaps illustrated by brief scenes from the film and other visuals), discussing how the two mythological traditions are adapted into modern works of art.

- Although the Lorelei is a modern invention, she is based on traditional Indo-European figures such as the sirens, the melusine, the selkie, or the rusulka. Research these figures on the Internet. Write a poem or short story about such a mythical being living in a body of water near your house. Post your poem on your blog and invite your classmates to comment on the form, style, and theme of your poem.

---

world, and of so many other opposites, could not be found directly, but could be more successfully suggested through art. They suggested that philosophy may point out that the world is fragmented, but only art can heal that break. Thus the beauty that had fallen away with tradition and that no longer existed in the modern could be restored by the creation of a new mythology.

At first glance, it may appear that "The Lorelei" is exactly that kind of romantic response since it is the creation of a new myth, the tying of traditional mythology to a novel place (the Lorelei Rock) to create a new work of art. The phenomenal success of the poem as an expression of a German sense of place and of German nationalism might seem to suggest the same. But "The Lorelei" can only be viewed as a simple folk tale when it is detached from its context. "The Lorelei" is the second piece in a cycle of Heine's poetry he called *The Homecoming*. The first poem describes the poems in the collection, including "The Lorelei," as the songs that a child sings to himself to distract himself from the fear of the dark. That alone casts "The Lorelei" in an entirely different light.

And the poem itself is not so simple. It begins with the poet's self-awareness of some lack or conflict in himself expressed in melancholy. This leads him to recall the Lorelei myth. There is certainly an encounter with tradition as one might expect to begin the romantic dialectic. But instead there is a failure of dialectical progression: the boat, an instrument of the ordered human world, is destroyed by its encounter with tradition in the form of the Germanic nixie mythology. This seeming failure might be explicable in terms of romantic aesthetics, since many romantic works were often purposefully crafted as fragments that only tell part of the story. But another poem in *The Homecoming* cycle, "Twilight of the Gods" suggests otherwise. This poem, which in many respects is the climax of the book, begins with a celebration of peasant culture expressed through the Mayday festival—that is, the traditional part of the romantic dialectic. But the modern poet rejects this and instead sees a vision of a war in heaven, with the gods and spirits of Germanic and Greek myth driving out the monotheistic god of modern Christianity. This is indeed a representation of the romantic dialectic, but there is no creative resolution. Instead, the poet sees his own guardian angel destroyed and the whole universe extinguished in endless night: Heine has begun to despair of the possibility of romanticism achieving its aims in renewal of culture and the regeneration of man. It is this fear of darkness he is trying to sing away.

The same failure of the romantic process is seen in miniature in "The Lorelei." The encounter of the modern poet with tradition fails to make a romantic synthesis and instead results in his destruction. In the same way, while Heine originally had great faith in the political philosophy of Marx, he eventually came to believe that although political and economic revolution was inevitable, it would not be creative of anything new, but only destructive. The same ultimate rejection of romantic idealism can be seen in other late romantic poets such as the Englishman John Keats in his 1819 epic fragment "The Fall of Hyperion."

Poetry

Since antiquity, poetry itself has been one of the most important subjects examined by poets. At one level "The Lorelei" can be read as allegory of poetry, that is, as a symbolic expression of Heine's thoughts on the nature of his own work. The Lorelei herself is beautiful and shining like poetry. More particularly, she sings. It is only in modern times that poetry and song can be seen as different

A wood engraving of a painting by Otto Lingner, depicting the mythical figure of the Lorelei
(© INTERFOTO / Alamy)

categories of expression. For the traditional poet, his work is always song. The Lorelei can be seen as a type of muse singing to the poet's imagination. In particular, her song is said to be free, like the uncontrolled impulse of inspiration.

But the Lorelei's song brings death to its audience: it enchants (meaning both *sings to* and *puts under a spell*) the passing boatman so that he does not pay attention to where he is, causing him to crash his boat and drown in the river. The boatman, then is the poet, mesmerized by the beauty of his inspiration, but unable to control it with his craft of creating ordered, controlled poetic form as a boatman must control the helm of his craft. The last stanza of the poem drives home the point that destruction inevitably follows the Lorelei's song. This is a surprisingly negative evaluation of the power of poetry by a poet. It is the poet himself who is destroyed in the conflict between the inspiring, muse-like song of the Lorelei and the rigid, helmsman-like control of the poet as he attempts to give form to inspiration. For the romantic, any resolution between opposites like inspiration and control ought to result in the creation of something new. But here there is no hint of such creation, but rather destruction that undercuts the romantic vision.

STYLE

Poetics

"The Lorelei" is written in traditional lyric form, in stanzas of four lines. The lines alternate between iambic quadrameter and iambic trimeter. The rhyme is in the pattern *ABAB*.

Heine achieves two particular poetic effects. When the Lorelei initially appears in the first line of the third stanza in his original German, he calls her "Jungfrau," which often and quite correctly is translated as "girl" or "maiden." However, the German term is also the ordinary way of referring to the Virgin Mary. This use establishes an impression in the reader's mind that is slowly reversed when the poem reveals that this "Jungfrau" does not save but rather destroys. If an English translation were made using "virgin" it could not have the same effect, since the greater specificity of that word in English would make the device seem heavy-handed and contrived.

Heine's other notable poetic device is deployed in the fourth and fifth stanzas. He models in his language the famous echo of the Lorelei Rock. He uses word pairs that fall either at the start and end of a given line or at the start of two successive lines. Within each pair, the first is nearly repeated by the second but only with some small change of sound. This effect has been better imitated by more sensitive translators.

Travel Writing

"The Lorelei" has remarkable connections with travel writing and tourist handbooks in several different areas. The Lorelei is not a traditional myth or folktale, but rather the 1801 literary creation of Brentano. In 1812, however, Aloys Schreiber, a professor at the University of Heidelberg, published a guidebook for tourists boating on the Rhine (*Handbook for Traveling the Rhine from Scahffhausen to Holland*). In the section dealing with the Lorelei Rock he presents his own version of Brentano's fairy tale that is markedly different from the original. As far as its plot and outward events are concerned, Heine gives poetic form to part of Schreiber's narrative rather than to Brentano's (or any of the other poetic versions that had been published before Heine wrote). The motif of hair-combing, the blond color of the Lorelei's hair, her location in the Rhine as opposed to on top of the rock where Brentano placed her, as well as other details, all come from Schreiber. So Heine's

poem in one sense, in its outward form, has its origin in tourist literature. Tourist handbooks and memoirs of travels were far more widely and more seriously read in the nineteenth century than today because travel was considered an essential part of aristocratic education. Heine wrote his own travel book, *Travel Pictures*, in four parts from 1826–1831.

"The Lorelei" was soon included in guidebooks, especially after it became a popular song in the setting by Silcher. In fact, Mark Twain, in his 1879 satire of travel writing, *A Tramp Abroad*, devotes an entire chapter to the Lorelei in mockery of tourist handbooks. Twain transcribes a translation typically offered in those days in tourist handbooks that is so bad he undoubtedly rewrote it for comic effect. He points out that the bad meter of the translation would have made it impossible to sing to the score of Silcher's setting usually provided in the handbooks. Twain also offers his own quite good (and entirely metrical) translation of the poem. Significantly, Twain embeds "The Lorelei" in Schrieber's larger narrative (or rather a satirical but recognizable version of it), associating Heine's poem still more closely with travel literature. Twain's point is that for his typical American reader, "The Lorelei" had been reduced to kitsch, becoming a sort of grand advertising slogan for the tourist industry. Even today, Internet searches for Heine and Lorelei turn up many sites that use the poem to promote tourism on the middle Rhine. The Lorelei Rock itself has been developed as a tourist site, with a visitor's center, parking lot, statue of the Lorelei, and hiking trails. Tour boats on the Rhine below the rock are also common.

Translation

Most American readers encounter "The Lorelei" detached from its original context, and even its original language, reading it only in translation from the German. In *A Tramp Abroad*, Twain points out the difficulties this imposes on the reader by making two translations of the poem, one only slightly more horrible, tedious, and misguided than those commonly available in popular literature in the nineteenth century, and one that represents a genuine version of the original. But even in this Twain is not able to convey both the sense of Heine's words and echo his poetic form and achievement. Something is inevitably lost in translation.

COMPARE & CONTRAST

- **1820s:** Western European states like Prussia and Great Britain routinely censor political speech, even when offered by poets such as Heine or Percy Bysshe Shelley.

  Today: Freedom of speech is recognized as the heart of the Western tradition, although some recent trends, such as the Irish blasphemy law, the use of British Libel law to quash scientific controversy, and the prosecution of politicians in the Netherlands and Austria for hate speech due to criticism of Islam, may reveal cracks in this foundation of Western liberty.

- **1820s:** Poetry is generally recognized as the most important form of literature and is widely appreciated at every level of society.

  Today: New poetry is increasingly limited to an academic elite and is disappearing from the consciousness of popular culture. New poetry is, for instance, no long published in daily newspapers as it was as late as the 1930s, and most Americans cannot name the poet laureate of the United States, or name a poem that has been written in the last decade.

- **1820s:** Because Germany is fragmented into dozens of large and small states, German national identity rests shared cultural achievements such as "The Lorelei."

  Today: Germany was first unified in 1870, but was then partitioned into two countries, East and West Germany, after World War II. West Germany is one of the founding nations of the original European Union (EU) in 1951, and when Germany reunifies in 1989, Germany becomes a single member state of the new EU in 1993.

- **1820s:** If one shouted from a boat on the Rhine while passing the Lorelei Rock, a complex pattern of echoes resulted, sometimes said to be five or seven in number.

  Today: Traffic noise from passing cars and power boats masks the echo at the Lorelei Rock.

HISTORICAL CONTEXT

National Revival

One goal of German romanticism was national revival in a spiritual identity, rather than in a necessarily limited political sense. Given the disunity of the German Empire, divided among dozens of small sovereign states until 1870, there was tension between the celebration of local tradition and ideas of national unification. One reason the romantics were so interested in fairy tales was because of their local character. Such stories were viewed as more authentic or naïve because they originated in peasant, rather than learned, culture. They symbolized the German love of the land and the nation. Of course, "The Lorelei" is not an authentic fairy tale. It grew from the longing to create a literature of special importance for the middle Rhine, one of the most beautiful areas of Germany, and one dearly loved by the Lorelei's originator Brentano. In later times, above all in its musical settings, this distinction was disregarded, and "The Lorelei" was celebrated as a national treasure precisely because it was mistakenly viewed as a fusion of authentic tradition and high art. Indeed, the highly nationalistic character of the popular appreciation of the song is what limited the efforts of the Nazis to censor it.

Natural History of the Lorelei Rock

The Lure Ley or Lorelei Rock is a massive cliff on the east bank of the middle Rhine River, opposite the town of St. Goar in Germany, about thirty miles north of Koblenz. Even today the area is relatively undeveloped. The Lorelei Rock is part of the vineyards the Counts of Katzenelnbogen

The Rhine River *(Fernando Cortes / Shutterstock.com)*

originally planted in the fourteenth century. The rock itself is made of slate, which in medieval German is called *Lei* or *Ley*. The meaning of the first part of the name is not clear, but probably comes from the German verb *luren*, which means to see or spy, and in this case would refer to the vantage overlooking the Rhine from the top of the rock.

The rock itself and other cliffs in the area create a very strong echo that can reflect a loud shout back and forth five to seven times. Through the late nineteenth century, a small spring fed a waterfall about halfway up the rock (it can be seen in old tourist postcards), whose noise was amplified by the echo into a general murmuring throughout the valley. This strange soundscape gave rise to the local dialectal word *lurlein*, which means murmuring or echoing. (In some sources the word is mistakenly said to give rise to the name of the rock.)

While not truly rapids, the channel below the Lorelei Rock is the narrowest on the German part of the Rhine and has a very swift current. In addition, there are dangerous underwater rocks in the area, so throughout history the Lorelei has been the site of an unusual number of boating accidents. This undoubtedly suggested the siren theme of Heine's poem, though it did not give rise to local legend.

CRITICAL OVERVIEW

The first and by far the most notable response to Heine's whole body of work, including the "The Lorelei," was censorship. Less than ten years after its composition, the whole of Heine's work was banned in Germany. Despite his obvious love for the German nation, Heine was viewed as threatening to Germany because he was of Jewish origin (despite his conversion); because he believed drastic change, even revolution (as occurred in 1848), was inevitable in Germany; and because he believed that German society ought to be reformed to spread equality and to lessen traditional aristocratic privilege. But censorship rarely has its intended effect, and Heine's works (printed in France) circulated widely in Germany anyway. "The Lorelei" in particular could not be suppressed, but quickly became a national favorite in Germany as an embodiment of the national symbol of the Rhine River. Even when censorship was renewed in the twentieth century by the Nazis, the work could not be erased, as Hugo Bieber points out in his anthology of Heine's biographical writings:

> The Nazi regime burned Heine's books. But at least one poem of Heinrich Heine even the most ruthless rule of violence could never banish from the memory of the German people. The grossest brutality... could not prevent Heine's "The Lorelei" from being read, sung and printed in popular song books as before. Authorities had to content themselves with omitting the name of the poet and tolerating the poem as "a popular song of unknown authorship."

Inasmuch as Heine's books were indeed burned by the Nazis, his famous line from his drama *Almansor*—"Where men burn books, they will burn people also in the end"—is sometimes taken in an almost prophetic sense.

Be that as it may, Heine's works have received relatively little attention from American and British scholars. The foundational study in English on "The Lorelei" is the piece by Allen Wilson Porterfield in the October 1915 issue of *Modern Philology*. He clears up the issues of Heine's source material. The Lorelei figure was invented by Brentano in a poem embedded in his 1801 novel *Godwi*. In 1812, Joseph von Eichendorff wrote his own Lorelei poem, as did the Graf von Loeben in 1821. Heine, writing in 1823, probably knew all three poems, but, Porterfield explains, Heine's most important sources were the tourist handbooks for the Rhine valley that had quickly taken up the Lorelei legend and made their own expansions and transformations of it. The German scholar Laura Hofrichter in her *Heinrich Heine* expresses a common psychological interpretation of the poem, that the boatman's journey is Heine's own life, in danger of shipwreck because of the seductions of poetry in 1822 when he was working on his law degree. Erika Tunner, in her essay in the *European Romanticism* anthology, relates Lorelei to other romantic destructive seductresses, such as Keats's La belle dame sans merci or Coleridge's Geraldine. She also makes a definitive refutation of the idea current in popular culture in Germany, and even among some scholars, that "The Lorelei" was based on a traditional fairy tale linked to the Lorelei Rock.

CRITICISM

Bradley A. Skeen

Skeen is a classicist. In the following essay, he explores the "Lorelei" theme in folklore and art.

Erika Tunner, in her article in *European Romanticism*, notes a prevalent stereotype about "The Lorelei": "Ever since Heinrich Heine... wrote his celebrated poem, the Lore Lay has for many people become a fairy tale from earlier, indeed ancient times that refuses to be dismissed from the mind." In fact, however, there is no traditional Fairdale of the sort described by Heine associated with the Lorelei Rock (an actual place on the Middle Rhine). But Heine did not invent his story out of whole cloth either. Heine was a link in a chain of artistic creation that began twenty years before the "The Lorelei" and continued for half a century longer to the opera of Richard Wagner, and whose metal was indeed forged from many veins of myth.

The romantic period was an era of intense interest in myths and fairy tales and saw the publications of many fairy tale collections drawn from traditional folk stories. By far the best known of these is the 1812 volume *German Folk Tales* of Jakob and Wilhelm Grimm, informally known as Grimm's Fairy Tales. Brentano, a close friend of the Grimms, first suggested to them that they begin to research folk tales. While both Clemens Brentano and the Grimms mixed scholarship and literary creativity in their work, Brentano favored the latter. In his 1801 novel, *Godwi*, Brentano went beyond collecting tales from traditional story tellers and, like many other romantics, composed his own original fairy tale, inserting it into the text of the novel. Brentano rendered his story in verse, although genuine fairy tales usually circulated among the peasant population in prose.

In Brentano's poem, a witch named Lorelei lives on the Lorelei Rock and has perfected the art of using her magical powers to seduce men. Because she can no longer bear to use her enchantments against the only man that she loves, she begs the local bishop to execute her for witchcraft. When he, too, becomes smitten with her on sight, the bishop refuses and sentences her only to be imprisoned in a convent. As an armed escort of knights is conducting her there across the top of the Lorelei Rock, she sees her lover coming to rescue her in a boat crossing the Rhine. Unable to set him free of her spell in any other way, Lorelei kills herself by leaping over the cliff.

WHAT DO I READ NEXT?

- Matthew Arnold's *Heinrich Heine* (1863) offers an appreciation of the German poet as a political and social activist by a near contemporary. It can be found digitized in its entirety at Google Books.

- Christine E. Schluze's two volume 2010 young-adult fantasy novel, *The Last Musician and the Pool of Lorelei*, while it does not follow the Lorelei legend particularly closely, does take up Heine's use of song/poetry as symbol of spiritually destructive power.

- *Mami Wata: Arts for Water Spirits in Africa and Its Diasporas* by Henry John Drewal is the catalog of a 2008 exhibition at the Fowler Museum at University of California, Los Angeles. It consists of images used in the cult of Mami Wata, a Lorelei-like goddess widely worshipped in West African and Afro-Caribbean religions.

- The essays in the 2006 anthology *Music of the Sirens*, edited by Linda Phyllis Austern and Inna Nardoditskaya, comparatively analyze siren and water nymph legends from around the world, including the Lorelei, the Afro-Caribbean Mami Wata, and indigenous legends about captivating nymphs in the Andes.

- Johan Wolfgang von Goethe's 1773 novel *The Sorrows of Young Werther* is perhaps the single best known work of German romanticism in the English-speaking world. It has been translated many times, but the earliest anonymous rendering from 1784 is available in a digitized version at Google Books.

- A number of Heine's longer essays, including the main examples of his travel writing, are collected and translated by Ritchie Robinson in his 1993 Penguin anthology, *Selected Prose*.

- Wieland Schmied's 1995 book, *Caspar David Friedrich*, provides a survey of the life and work of the most important German romantic painter, whose work is comparable in spirit to Heine's poetry.

- "The Lorelei" has qualities of a traditional German fairy tale. Many fairy and folk tales were collected and published by Jakob and Wilhelm Grimm in the early 1800s. A recent edition of their complete stories can be found in *Grimms' Fairy Tales*, brought out by Collector's Library in 2009.

The story immediately became so popular that in 1812 Aloys Schreiber, in his *Handbook for traveling the Rhine from Scahffhausen to Holland*, expanded on Brentano's poem, giving the Lorelei a sort of afterlife as a water spirit living in the Rhine that delights in causing ships passing her rock to crash, as the rapids in that area are the most dangerous natural hazard on the river. It is this story that Heine used as the basis for his own his "The Lorelei."

It is hardly surprising that a story about a water spirit in the form of a beautiful woman causing ships to crash should be so arresting and seem somehow so familiar. It is a story, repeated again and again in Western literature, that goes back to the earliest Indo-European traditions at the beginning of Western culture. The most famous version of the tale occurs in ancient Greek literature in book twelve of Homer's *The Odyssey*, where Odysseus must guide his ship past an island infested with sirens: birds of prey with the faces of beautiful women whose song is so beautiful its draws sailors to crash and die upon the rocks. The cunning Odysseus stops his sailors' ears with wax so they cannot hear the song, but has himself tied to the mast of his ship so that he can hear its beauty and yet not be drawn to his death.

Given the classical education enjoyed by the aristocratic class of Germans for whom Heine's writings were intended, that story was probably

ROMANTIC ART, RATHER THAN ANCIENT TRADITION, BOUND THE MYTHOLOGY OF THE WATER SPRITE, SIREN, OR NIXIE TO THE LORELEI ROCK."

Schreiber and Heine's primary referent. However, the same kinds of stories are common in German folklore. They are vividly described by Jakob Grimm in his *Teutonic Mythology*, both as they occur in eighteenth century folklore and in the oldest sources of Germanic language and culture. Creatures called a neck or nixie were commonly believed to inhabit any body of water (including rivers, especially the Elbe and the Danube, but curiously not the Rhine). While they could take many forms, they typically appeared as a beautiful young woman. According to Grimm, a common story holds that the "*nixe* ... is to be seen sitting in the sun, *combing* her long hair ... or emerging from the waves with the upper half of her body, which is exceedingly beautiful." They are unusually bloodthirsty for spirits of Germanic folklore and are said to have demanded human sacrifice in pre-Christian times. Grimm is able to summarize one type of the nixie mythology in this way: "Like the sirens, the nixe by her song draws listening youth to herself, and into the deep."

All of the structural elements of the Lorelei myth are present here in German folk tradition, but they had to be transposed to the Lorelei Rock in the Rhine. Travel writer Schreiber was the first to link the nixie mythology to the Lorelei Rock. Only after he made the connection did poets write on the same theme. In 1821 von Loeben composed a Lorelei poem quite simply describing a Lorelei-Nixie. He was followed by Heine whose 1823 "The Lorelei" took up that theme using it for a far deeper work of art that has become a classic of both German and world literature.

Romantic art, rather than ancient tradition, bound the mythology of the water sprite, siren, or nixie to the Lorelei Rock. One legend, however, though not a very widely known one, was native to that place. One of the Germanic tribes that invaded the Roman Empire in late antiquity (the sixth century CE) and caused the collapse of the western province were the Burgundians. In the chaos of that era, traditionally called the dark ages in English but the national migration in modern Germany, the Burgundians briefly established a kingdom on the middle Rhine that was soon destroyed by the Huns. The end of the Burgundian kingdom (about which there is little historical knowledge) gave rise to a cycle of epic poetry in medieval Germany known collectively as the *Nibelungenlied* or Song of the Nibelung.

The Nibelungen of the title were supposedly a race of mythical dwarves who lived underground and worked as miners and smiths. They produced a magical golden treasure, the Nibelungen hoard that according to the legend was the secret source of the power of Burgundy (in some versions it was won for them by the hero Siegfried). According to one quite obscure local legend on the middle Rhine, after the collapse of Burgundy, the dwarves took back their treasure and hid it inside the Lorelei Rock. This was perhaps suggested by the fact that *Lur* is a German word for dwarf, making a pun with Lorelei, and more particularly with the older form of the name Lure Ley. None other than the antiquarian Brentano ferreted out this forgotten tale and included it in his 1846 book, *Legends of the Rhine*. But he could not resist again elaborating on it with his own invention. In Brentano's new version the treasure is not buried in the mountain, but rather at the bottom of the Rhine river, and he makes its guardian none other than Heine's singing nixie, the Lorelei. Nixies do appear in the *Nibelungenlied*, but they live in the Danube, not the Rhine (and, interestingly, they claim to be able to foretell the future, like the sirens of Homer, but they indifferently lie or tell the truth, like the Muses of Hesiod). But it is Brentano that makes a nixie the guardian of the Nibelungen hoard. So in this way the Lorelei legend comes full circle from Brentano, to Shreiber, to Heine, and then back to Brentano.

The last link in the chain is the composer Richard Wagner. His work, too, was based on adapting traditional German myths in his many operas. Between 1848 and 1874 he composed a cycle of four operas adapting the *Nibelungenlied*, *Der Ring des Nibelungen*, generally known as the Ring cycle. In this work, he follows Brentano's creation wholeheartedly, and placed the Nibelungen hoard at the bottom of the Rhine, where it is guarded by not one, but three Rhine Maidens. There can be no question that Brentano was Wagner's source, since the details he uses are Brentano's invention and, like the Lorelei herself, do not appear

A shipwreck (© *Lebrecht Music and Arts Photo Library / Alamy*)

in any traditional material. Wagner himself never uses the term 'Lorelei' however, since by his time it would have been too closely associated with Heine and would have seemed excessively derivative, and no doubt also because of Wagner's well-known antipathy to Heine owning to his own pronounced anti-Semitism.

The German romantics believed that the highest truths could only be obtained through art, that the process of artistic creation alone could produce something new and grander through the reconciliation of opposites such as the naive and the sentimental, the natural and the created. The history of the Lorelei motif is the history of creation through the reconciliation of received folk tradition and artistic craft. At every step Brentano, Heine, and Wagner created something new by reshaping something old. In "The Lorelei," Heine used his created myth to communicate profound aesthetic and philosophical truths, no more suspected by an audience that appreciates the poem as an old German fairy tale than are the rocks lurking under the swift flowing surface waters of the Rhine suspected by the boatmen on the river. Wagner likewise created a new kind

of opera whose mythic allegories of philosophy and history go almost unrecognized by his audience today. Ironically, of the three, Brentano is completely unknown today in the English speaking world (very few of his works have even been translated); yet it was his work most of all that forged the links between myth and art, even if his own achievements lack the sparkling luster of Heine's and Wagner's.

Source: Bradley Skeen, Critical Essay on "The Lorelei," in *Poetry for Students*, Gale, Cengage Learning, 2011.

Daniel Albright

In the following excerpt, Albright examines several musical arrangements of Heine's poetry by famous composers such as Schubert.

1. SELF-SCRUTINY I

We're in a cozy salon, soft in focus, lit with warm red, full of upholstered leather furniture in the best modern taste. The soprano, sober in a fur-collared jacket, gazes at us as the pianist plays the gentle prelude. There's something odd about the windows: The left one shows a somewhat jittery

> FOR SCHUBERT, HEINE'S TEXTS INVITE DECLAMATORY GESTURE OF A SPECIAL KIND THAT HOVERS ANXIOUSLY IN THE FORBIDDEN SPACES NEAR THE TONIC: A MINOR OR MAJOR SECOND BELOW AND ABOVE."

scene, as if a minor earthquake were taking place unnoticed; the right, an eye and part of the mouth of the soprano's huge face.

2. SELF-SCRUTINY II

Heinrich Heine and Franz Schubert were born in the same year, 1797. If Heine had died when Schubert died, in 1828, it would have been an enormous loss to German letters and German music alike—for one thing, Wagner might never have written *The Flying Dutchman*, based on a brief satirical episode in one of Heine's novels. But the history of the German Lied might not have been drastically changed, because most of the lyric poems that inflamed the imagination of countless composers, not just in Germany, had already been published—many of them in the "Lyrisches Intermezzo" section (first published 1823) of the *Buch der Lieder* (1827).

Schubert had only a little time to take note of Heine's work, but six of the fourteen songs in *Schwanengesang* (a song cycle compiled, not without skill, by a publisher after Schubert's death) are to texts by Heine. One of these songs is "Der Doppelgänger":

> The night is quiet, the small streets still,
> Here, in this house, a girl lived once.
> She left the city long ago,
> But the house still stands, just as it was.
>
> And a man stands there, and cranes his neck,
> His knuckles white, mouth agape,
> I shudder as I come to look:
> The moon shows me my own shape.
>
> My double—pale companion-ghost!
> Why do you ape my inner pain,
> The torture of the love I lost,
> The hurt I need to feel again?

This poem succinctly states Heine's whole lyric agon. The poet is drawn to revisit some scene of havoc and desolation, to relive rejection, loss, pain, vain yearning. But he stands aloof from his own feeling, takes a restrained delight in cultivating a persona of ruin. Yeats once said that the traditional masks of the lyric poet are those of "lover or saint, sage or sensualist, or mere mocker of all life." Heine evolved a new and compelling mask, that of lover as ironist, at once rendered immune by his ironic distance and excoriated by his inability to take full part in his own feeling. (Heine described his art as "malicious-sentimental.") In "Der Doppelgänger" it's far from clear which is the ghost and which the real man: The poet himself may be the revenant haunting the place where he once felt authentic emotion, where some fragment of an authentic being still lingers to feel it.

Schubert's setting is based on a four-note figure: scale-degrees 1-#7-3-2 in B minor, in slow, steady dotted-half-notes: B-A#-D-C#. This is the sort of figure less common in songs than in instrumental music, where it might be the head of a fugue or the basis of a *passacaglia*. Leopold Godowsky wrote a *passacaglia* on a striking, somewhat similar figure from Schubert's unfinished symphony (speaking of B minor!); Beethoven's piano sonata Op. 110 isolates a four-note figure only slightly different in shape from that of "Der Doppelgänger"; and the famous B-A-C-H figure (in English note-spelling, B$-A-C-B), which haunts compositions by Schumann, Liszt, Rimsky-Korsakov, and many others, is not far away either. In the song, the figure is an obsessive presence: first, in that the piano keeps repeating it in a simple harmonization (i-V-III-V, sometimes deforming to i-v-III-V^7, with a corresponding drop of the figure's #^{7} to ♮^{7}); second, in that almost every chord in the song contains an F#, a dominant pedal, until the great *fff* chord on the second syllable of "Gestalt" ("The moon shows me my own shape"). The song's vocal line also begins on a monotone F#, and shows a strong tendency to return to the note again, until the word "Gestalt," when it rises a semitone to G. The Doppelgänger and the poet are right next to one another, only a semitone apart, and yet belong to different harmonic universes: The *fff* chord is, in effect, a simple C^7, but Schubert pushes it to an extremity of pallid horror.

This is the pattern for some of his other Heine settings. They tend not to have tuneful vocal lines—of course Schubert could write catchy melodies, such as "Heidenröslein," almost a folk song by now, but a surprising number of his finest songs don't invite humming in the shower. For

Schubert, Heine's texts invite declamatory gesture of a special kind that hovers anxiously in the forbidden spaces near the tonic: a minor or major second below and above. For example, "Der Atlas," a far more desperate and urgent song, sounds nothing like "Der Doppelgänger" but is confected to the same recipe:

> I am the luckless Atlas! A world,
> I have to bear the whole world of sorrows,
> I bear the unbearable, and the heart
> In my body wants to break.
>
> Arrogant heart, you, you wanted this!
> You wanted to be happy, forever happy,
> Or forever wretched, arrogant heart.
> It happened: you are wretched.

Here Heine uses an unrhymed verse form derived from Horace (and therefore suitable for his classical theme). But unlike Hölderlin or (at times) Goethe, he doesn't try to make German sound like Latin by using dispersed syntax held together only by the case-endings of the nouns and adjectives; instead all is tidy, iambic, and chaste in Heine's normal manner. This Atlas of pain can't escape from his burden, nor the poem from its tight-lipped, grim formality, although the loss of rhyme may solace it a bit.

Schubert, in finding a tone-equivalent, once again constructed the song from a four-note figure: scale degrees 1-3-#7-1 in G minor, harmonized i-i-V-i. This is the most ordinary harmonization possible, just a regular tonic-dominant movement, but Schubert puts extraordinary stress on the F# in the dominant chord, heightening its dissonance with G, the tonic note; it's as if Atlas sags a semitone below pitch under the overwhelming weight, then with a weight-lifter's grunt heaves the world back to its original position. Indeed, in the vocal line the singer sings only the first three notes of the figure—he needs to take a breath before resuming the tonic note. The song proceeds just like "Der Doppelgänger": There's an episode based on rising chromatics ("brechen Will das Herz"—the comparable moment in "Der Doppelgänger"—occurs at "Du Doppelgänger, du bleicher Geselle!"), and a climactic wail that takes the singer a semitone too high. He repeats the line "Die ganze Welt der Schmerzen muß ich tragen" in an emphatic tonic arpeggio, rising through an octave, but then pushes past the G to A♭, harmonized to an *fff* B♭7 chord—which isn't particularly strange in itself (just a seventh chord in the relative major), but Schubert wrings the maximum dissonance out of

that A♭ abutted brutally against the preceding G. As at the climax of "Der Doppelgänger," the startling glare of a major chord represents a spasm of pain after the habitual minor of the rest of the song: In a gasp of strength, Atlas lifts the world a little higher than it's supposed to be, before he sinks back into his usual dejection. But "Der Atlas" differs from "Der Doppelgänger" in one important way: "Der Atlas" is a highly rhythmic song, almost a sort of dance of sheer misery. Both the rhythm and the melodic contour of the four-note figure have a certain resemblance to the old tune called "La folia," or "Les folies d'Espagne," popularized by Corelli, C. P. E. Bach, and others. It sometimes serves (as the title suggests) as a badge of madness: For example, in Vivaldi's opera *Orlando furioso* (1727) the crazed Orlando sings "la, la, la" to the tune of "La folia." I don't know if Schubert was conscious of the similarity, but the music may hint that the world's weight has driven Atlas mad. Susan Youens has argued, in *Heine and the Lied*, that the song is "a resonant prison for all eternity," but maybe the hopeless madness of the situation, like the loss of rhyme-fetters, offers an escape, even if only the escape of psychosis.

Perhaps the most sophisticated of the six Heine settings in *Schwanengesang* is "Die Stadt." The poem is quite similar to "Der Doppelgänger," a visit to a significant extinct place. In this case, however, it's not the poet but the city that's its own phantom double:

> On the far horizon
> Appears, like shapes in a cloud,
> The city with its towers;
> The twilight's like a shroud.
>
> A damp gust makes ripples
> In the gray canal;
> The oarsman rows my skiff
> With *tempo mesto* pull.
>
> From the world's edge rises
> Once again the sun
> And shines upon the place
> Where I lost someone.

The song begins in a state of sheer rhythmlessness. The piano shivers with faint arpeggios of a diminished chord. (The score adds the marking *diminuendo*, as if harmony and tempo alike were an exercise in diminishment.) As the voice enters, rhythm suddenly becomes quite pronounced, double-dotted chords in the tonic, C minor; the vocal line begins as little more than a monotone on G, occasionally rising a semitone to A♭. The song offers little in the way of melody or figuration, only the light finger-ripples of the diminished chord and a declamatory voice, singing mostly on the tonic or the dominant note, lifting itself a half-step when stabbed by insight. "My heart aches, and a drowsy numbness pains / My sense" runs the first line of "Ode to a Nightingale," and "Die Stadt" is about drowsy numbness interspersed with small tightenings and clenches. The paralysis is almost complete: The singer, having taken a boat into non-existence, illustrates his limbo with non-melodies, forms of talking-to-oneself carried out by other means. Of course it's only a fluke that Schubert happened to die soon after writing these songs, but they can appear to be at once a climax of his song-art and a repudiation of singing itself. If "Die Stadt" were much sparer, it would be little more than a recitation of the poem; perhaps only Othmar Schoeck, in "Lebendig begraben" (1927), made the Lied even closer to speech. In "Die Stadt," song is little more than speech's Doppelgänger.

4. THE SELF-CANCELING-OUT OF ART

. . . In a notebook, Kafka jotted the phrase "the self-canceling-out of art"—a procedure that Heine, a century before, had understood well. If "Ich grolle nicht" is a self-canceling song in that it's a complaining non-complaint, other Heine poems extend the principle of self-excoriation to his own poetry.

Both of Schumann's song-cycles based on Heine's poetry, the *Liederkreis*, Op. 24, and *Dichterliebe*, Op. 48, conclude with poems in which the poet builds a sarcophagus for his own songs. In the first of these, it's interesting to note the absence of myrtles in the first line—Schumann, a great lover of myrtles, simply crammed them into the song:

> Make my book a black wood box,
> Adorn with rose and golden flecks.
> It shall be coffin large enough
> For the songs inspired by my love.
>
> I want to bury Love in that chest!
> For on Love's grave there blossoms Rest,
> A flower I would gladly have—
> But it blooms, I know, on my own grave.
>
> Here are the songs I once belched up
> Like lava spewed from Etna's top,
> With blinding sparks and rumbles vast
> From my heart's own pyroclast.
>
> On these pages lie corpse-cold,
> Dumb, cloud-pale, the words I told;

> But they might kindle once again
> If Love herself would enter in.
>
> I feel my songs will soon renew
> When Love upon them sheds her dew—
> This book once opened by your hand,
> My darling, in a distant land.
>
> If Love will chant her magic there
> The letters of the text will stare
> Imploringly on your fair face
> And breathe a whisper of Love's grace.

This gentle poem is a model of reader-response theory: The song moulders in the book until the reader, the One Right Reader, ensorcels it, ensouls it. Its sequel, at the end of *Dichterliebe*, is far more ambiguous:

> The putrid, evil songs,
> Bad dreams that will not stop—
> It's time to dig a hole,
> Time to coffin them up.
>
> I won't say what they are,
> But lots are going in;
> The coffin must be larger
> Than the Heidelberg Tun.
>
> And for this coffin, fetch
> Planks of the stoutest kinds;
> It has to be as long,
> Long as the bridge at Mainz.
>
> And fetch twelve giants, oh,
> Strong to lift huge stones,
> Strong as that Christopher
> Cathedraled at Cologne.
>
> The giants have the coffin,
> Toss it into the deep,
> For such an enormous thing
> Only the sea can keep.
>
> It has to be heavy, huge—
> Shall I tell you why?
> My pains have all to fit,
> In it my love must lie.

Not so gentle. Schumann's setting (in the key of C♯ minor) begins with a huge gesture, a thrusting down the whole diapason by means of a figure prominent in both the piano and the vocal line: C♯-G♯-C♯. When the singer mentions the Heidelberg Tun, and the great bridge at Mainz, and the Köln Cathedral, the piano utters a little figure of glee, similar to the figure that Wagner would use ten years later in *Das Rheingold*, to represent the arrogance of the dwarf-king Alberich, when he exercises the power of the Ring. It's a laughing figure, but, as elsewhere in Schumann's Heine settings, it cuts both ways: Even as the poet's vile poems are buried, the size of the coffin confirms his stature. The mood of the song softens toward the end: The emphatic gestures peter out into hesitant syncopations, as if the singer were regretting his hasty decision, in this loud palinode, to unsing his songs. (When Dante Rossetti, a few years later, buried the manuscripts of his poems in his wife's coffin, he was forced to exhume her body in order to publish them.) The song terminates in a long postlude for the piano in the tonic major, *andante espressivo*, which might be regarded either as an example of the defunct sad-sentimental lyric stuff that will trouble the world no longer, or as a warm requiem-hymn over the poems' grave, or as the song's refusal to remain buried, its assertion of its merit against the poet's own wishes—the song wriggles out of its marine casket and floats to the surface. Myself, I incline to the last interpretation: Great art has often been made out of art's confessions of impotence and inadequacy.

Source: Daniel Albright, "Heine and the Composers," in *Parnassus: Poetry in Review*, Vol. 31, No. 1/2, 2009, pp. 176–201.

Willi Goetschel

In the following essay, Goetschel argues that Heine had an attitude toward secularism that was unique among his contemporaries, and that he viewed it as a problem instead of merely a solution.

Heinrich Heine's secularism is of a particular kind. Occupying a prominent, if not dominant, place in his writing, the secularist impulse plays a central role in his poetry and prose. But rather than taking secularization as a universal yardstick to measure success or failure of the project of Enlightenment and historical progress, his poetic project reflects the problem of secularism in a critical fashion. Heine resists the temptation of unreservedly subscribing to the imperatives of secularization, as if they would not warrant careful examination of their hidden assumptions and implications. Rather, and more critically, he inscribes and rewrites secularization in a manner that offers a self-consciously creative reinscription of the past and present. As a consequence, Heine's critical secularism presents an alternative approach that prompts us to take a fresh look at current discussions on secularism.

In resolutely critical response to the exigencies of his time, Heine engages in the cause of secularization with a different sense of urgency than his contemporaries. Yet, in doing so, he never loses sight of the profound ambivalence of the

> THIS MUTUAL DEPENDENCE OF RELIGION AND SECULARISM IS WHAT, AT TIMES, GIVES THE WORLD OF HEINE'S POETRY ITS HAUNTED OUTLOOK."

implications of secularization for the meaning of modernity. Heine's writing addresses secularization as the formidable problem and challenge of modernity rather than simply as the solution. Liberating, yet, at the same time, profoundly challenging, secularism is for Heine a constitutive moment in the experience of modernity. As a result, modernity emerges in Heine's work as a project deeply steeped in the problems of secularization.

But Heine's project sets itself apart from other discourses of secularism. Against the impasse of the alternative of either forsaking all religious intentions for a modern atheism or invoking some religious authenticity that would acknowledge secularization simply as validation of its own deeper truth, he takes a different approach. Born and raised as a member of the generation of the grandchildren of Moses Mendelssohn, the great champion of German Jewish emancipation, Heine responds to the predicament of the precarious legal, social, political, and cultural status of German Jews with a keen sense of the problem of secularization in modern society. From the point of view of Heine and his Jewish contemporaries, secularization never would nor could present an unproblematic final answer to theology's long anachronistic hold. In their eyes, even the most advanced forms of secularism at hand betrayed too much of a Christian particularism to justify any claim to universalism. In a way, their Jewish particularity served as a critical test case for gauging exactly how nineteenth-century variants of European secularisms would work out.

For Heine, who once quipped that the entry ticket to European culture came in the form of baptism, secularism presented a project that called for a critical grasp of the problem of religion. After all, he soon was to learn that instead of gaining acceptance and respectability, his baptism stamped him once more as a stereotypical Jew, only this time without the possibility to wash off his Jewishness by holy water. Reducing religion to either universal theological truth or socially acceptable form of superstition was no longer a viable option for him.

As early nineteenth-century forms of European secularism showed their theological underpinnings, it became increasingly clear that no gesture of radically cutting off the theological and religious roots would ever lead to complete secularization that would no longer privilege one form of religion over others. Rather, it became increasingly clear that secularization meant an ongoing process whose success would depend on the continuing recognition and critique of its theological and religious underpinnings.

Heine's signal contribution to the genealogy of a critical notion of secularism consists in the creative recovery and working through of this problematic. While other critics posit the process of secularization as narrative following a simple, straightforward trajectory from religion to its disenchantment, demise, and dissolution, Heine presents a theory and practice of secularization that engages religious difference as a critical force that highlights secularization in both its enabling and disabling aspects. Whimsically, but with a critical purpose, moving back and forth between Judaism and Christianity, and free of any anxieties of denominational allegiance and fixation, Heine presents secularism as a force not outside but within, or more precisely, between, religions. He stages secularization through the shifting of perspectives, presenting Catholicism, Protestantism, and Judaism from the ever-changing point of view of an observer whose loyalties remain strategic but are, at the same time, guided by a knowing appreciation of the redeeming function of the critical force of religion in whatever guise it might manifest itself.

What on the surface seems for many critics of Heine like a shifty and supposedly shaky outlook reveals itself, upon closer examination, as a thoughtful and artfully mounted appreciation of the fundamental significance of the legacy of religion for modernity. Not unlike the Marrano experience of the Sephardic Jews of the seventeenth century and of their philosophical exponent Spinoza—Heine's declared hero—Heine finds himself caught between the conflicting claims of Judaism, Christianity, and the challenge of modernity. For Heine, just as for the Marranos, an exclusionary privileging of one over the other religious tradition does not seem to be a viable option, because, according to their experience, Judaism, Christianity, and modernity present too much of an intertwined complex to isolate one from the other as the singularly universal truth. But in contrast to Marrano culture, whose profound skepticism separates them from their Jewish legacy in ways too radical for Judaism to provide any possibility for positive identification, Heine considers Jewish tradition a fundamental but ignored, if not repressed, part of Christian tradition and modernity. This allows him to take a sovereign stand toward religious traditions, which provides the groundwork for a critical platform for theorizing secularism.

Heine, the baptized Jew, does not need to return to Judaism, which he never left in the first place. Stubbornly resistant against any urge for religious or cultural supremacy, the double exposure to both Judaism and Christian culture allows him to understand secularization to be a matter of perspective. What Nietzsche will later develop into a full-fledged theory of perspectivism is already prefigured in Heine. Heine launches his secularism as a contrastive perspectivism that views secularization as an ever-changing differential movement addressing one particular religion in critical difference to the religious and theological theory and practice of its other. In switching positions between Christian and Jewish points of view, the critical force of Heine's lyric and narrative trajectories emerges in its unique poetic voice. This continuing religious code switching opens the horizon that throws secularization into sharp profile as it provides a critical space for expressing the undiminished complexity of the process of secularization. This oscillating movement at the heart of Heine's secularism makes for a distinctly post-Romantic notion of religion. His provocative blend of post-Enlightenment and historico-philosophical tenets provides the framework for a critical recognition of religion as a modern phenomenon.

Heine thus understands secularization as a critical concept in the Kantian sense. For him, secularization does not denote a doctrinary project whose truth claims simply erase or overwrite tradition. Rather, he casts secularization as a process that sheds light on the complicities and hidden affinities between a fully emancipated rationalism and its other, that is, religion, tradition, even superstition. This mutual dependence of religion and secularism is what, at times, gives the world of Heine's poetry its haunted outlook.

But far from simply presenting a self-obsessed anxiety of the uncanny, the staging of this haunting interdependence signals the moment of the critical in Heine's work, for such haunting does not derive from the return of religion but from secularism's zealous rigor, eager to deny and suppress the claims of religion. In critical distinction, Heine's poetry and prose propose that only a consistently self-reflective critique of religion, one that poetically imagines its own blind spots as constitutively connected to what it critiques, will succeed in the release of the emancipatory power that secularization promises.

What appears in his early poetry to be subtly interwoven with a heightened post-Romantic sensitivity articulates itself over the course of Heine's writing career in ever-sharper and more palpable terms, as his critical secularism becomes ever-more outspoken and distinct. But the pulsating energy of this critical secularism, responsible for the pointed irony for which Heine is so notorious, registers already in his earliest and seemingly romanticizing texts.

BOOK OF SONGS

Secularizing the canon of metaphors in a cheerfully playful but consistent manner, Heine's early poetry represents a coherently executed project of the secularization of German classic and Romantic poetry. His poetry removes the theme of love and longing, of lost love, desire, and lust, from its traditional context, in which the world was presented as metaphysically secured by the safety net of the decor of a Christian worldview, which was either implicitly present or explicitly invoked. While paganizing poetry, like Goethe's early poems, or Schiller's classicizing ones, would propose an alternative to Christian worldviews, their poetry would not reflect, address, or engage in the kind of radical secularization project typical for Heine. For in his love poetry, the ironic turn that leads to the dismantling of both the expectations of the reader and the longings of the lyrical I directly challenges and undermines the mind/body dichotomy underpinning Christian worldviews. The recurrent theme of excess sensualism that runs through Heine's poetry like a leitmotif carries a secularizing force no other German poet would express with such persistent determination before Heine. The love poems, which have become widely known through Robert Schumann's lieder cycle *Dichterliebe*, express this tendency in a remarkably subliminal yet distinct fashion. While the

romanticizing compositions often seek to cover up this tension or domesticate it into a Romantic mood, the poetry's breaks and disillusionments create a unique secularization effect. Much of the sting of Heine's poignant irony derives from this shocklike repetition of the moment of secularization. His poetry rejects the traditional canon of love. Loss of love, rejection, and disappointment are no longer transcended or "sublimated." Instead, the sting of the pangs of love is given unmitigated expression. Nothing exists in this poetic universe that can soften the pain of love and existence; nothing can redeem it. The melancholy and woe are set free from any metaphysical or religious meaning. Running counter to both classic and Romantic poetic conventions, Heine's lyrical subject stands abandoned and in defiant rejection of any metaphysical consolation.

Heine's most famous and popular poem, "Lorelei," exemplifies this kind of secularism in a paradigmatic manner. A careful reading of the poem, whose notoriously longing voice has been given prominent status as an expression of heightened German national sentiment, reveals a dimension of critical reflection that calls for attention. Beneath the powerfully suggestive but, at the same time, precariously thin surface of Romantic veneer, the poem performs an intriguing poetic act of secularization. The pretended ignorance and loss of cultural memory is given its interminable resolution in what follows the enchanting, singsong-like opening lines: "I don't know the reason why / I should be feeling so sad." What seems irretrievably lost and unfathomable to the rational subject is retrieved—through the poem's act of remembrance—through the figure of loss. As the poem recalls the fatally bewitching powers of Lorelei, it expresses a mourning that laments, beyond the recovery of memory, what escapes the grasp of the secular mind. The poem's stirringly soothing style gives voice to the powerful hold of the mythical, whose spell transfixes the gaze of the secular the more it desires to break that spell. But rather than an expression of anxiety or fear, the poem articulates a critical comment on the predicament of secularism: as it figures secularization as disenchantment, whose loss remains incommensurable with the promise of secular hope, it reminds the reader of secularization's loss as its curse. Secularization is, then, not an unproblematic process but fraught with uneasy difficulties that haunt the secular: "A tale of times gone by / Keeps running through my head" (Heine/Pollak, 9). The suggestive tension between the unknowing melancholy of forgetting and the obsessive memory of an old-time tale brings out the aporia that defines the project of disenchantment as ambivalent in nature. The poem stages this ambivalence in programmatic manner: its melancholy sadness is not only prompted by the forgetting and the anxiety that results from such forgetting. More critically, melancholy figures in this poem also as remembering, a remembering that remains melancholy as long as it remains unable to recognize the source of its sadness as the problem of secularism.

As the poem begins to speak of olden times, it appears to move seamlessly into the past, a past that the poem, however, stages in the present. It is not until the final line that the poem changes to the past perfect, but not without another curious twist added. While Lorelei's seductive powers bewitch the boatman, evoking his deadly desire and longing, the text performs a curious move that both enforces and undermines the illusion of the quasi-mythological image the poem conjures. If we are told that the lyrical I believes now that both boatman and boat sink, the issue of the status of this story emerges with underhanded virulence. What is a reader, who stumbles over this "Ich glaube" (I fancy), to think of the story, then, as a whole? This "Ich glaube" both makes and unmakes the narrative fundament on which the narrative seems to stand: the tradition of a tale that is at the same time both remembered and not quite remembered. Signaling indecision, the past becomes transparent as mediated through a present that is linked to the past it does and does not remember, a past that breaks into the present in fragmented form to light up, if only for an instance, to disappear again. Instead of a continuous narrative that links past and present in uninterrupted form, "Lorelei" reminds the reader that continuity remains a precarious and fragile specter, and that connection with the past is an ever-new challenge to the present it haunts:

> Ich glaube, die Wellen verschlingen
> Am Ende Schiffer und Kahn;
> Und das hat mit ihrem Singen
> Die Lore-Ley getan.

> [I fancy the waves will cover
> Both boatman and boat before long;
> And that was done to her lover
> By the Lorelei and her song.] (Heine/Pollak, 8–9)

While the rhythm seems to suggest a smooth transition into the final stanza, the lyrics undermine

this appearance. In ironic suspense, as belief rather than knowledge, the words *Ich glaube* (I believe) highlight the problematic character of this production of the past as one that becomes legible as a fiction of the present. The semblance of simplicity is subverted here and the fictional character of the past exposed. The melancholy sense of loss gives voice to the mourning of a past figured as present. What gives this poem its uncanny force is not its mythological or fairy-tale dimension but the way the narrative is inscribed in the lyrical I's own present.

Beyond a nostalgic return to the past and a celebration of the present, the text expresses a heightened sense for the precarious fragility of the present that defines modernity. In this poem, the contemporary and the noncontemporary can no longer be neatly kept apart. They cannot be contained as two distinctly separate entities. Instead, their interdependence emerges as an uneasy, conflicted condition. The Lorelei's singing reaches into the present and haunts it as the vanishing trace of the past. But the poem does not allow the reader to settle comfortably in nostalgic sentimentalism. Nor can the haunting impulse of the poem be explained away as the trace of the Romantic uncanny. Instead, the poem presents an irresistible enactment of the feeling and the recognition of the noncontemporary as the constitutive moment of the present: the simultaneity of a past invoked that remains elusive but just strong enough to operate the powerful call of the past for those who wish to live exclusively in the present:

> Er schaut nicht die Felsenriffe,
> Er schaut nur in die Höh.

> [He sees not the cliffs approaching,
> His eyes are fastened above.] (Heine/Pollak, 9)

The one who does not look down but only up, who only looks ahead but fails to look back, is doomed, the poem reminds us. But, then, a particular kind of doubt underlies this poem:

> Ich glaube, die Wellen verschlingen
> Am Ende Schiffer und Kahn.

> [I fancy the waves will cover
> Both boatman and boat before long.] (Heine/Pollak, 9)

This is not an absolute doubt but rather a qualifying doubt, a doubt that hesitates to pass for history, or fact. It is a legend, a tale. But while the lyrical I cannot forget it, remembering it does not cure it of melancholy. Part of the poem's potent melancholy stems from its insight that the past can be addressed only head-on, as the present, and that the present can be grasped only as the past.

Read as a tale of modernity and the problem of secularization, "Lorelei" reminds us that emancipation and liberation from the irrational forces come with the cost of a loss whose mourning may produce the enticing beauty of poetic magic. But this loss will always leave the mourner with the recognition that reason rests on the precariously fluid grounds of the irrational it "fancies" to have secularized.

To highlight the moment of secularization, let me, on a lighter note, compare Heine's poem with a later version of the Lorelei song by two other Jewish authors/composers. If the Gershwin brothers' "Loreley" takes the myth of Lorelei to the extremes of secularization, reducing her to a lascivious seducer in the age of bimboism, where the inexplicable is reduced to sexiness, their version highlights, by contrast, Heine's concern to comprehend secularization as an open-ended affair that provides the ground for emancipation only as long as this process is understood as an ongoing project in progress. In the age of the early-twentieth-century mass culture industry, one could say, this process had to come to an end if it was not to jeopardize the self-congratulatory assuredness of the man of the "free world."

Source: Willi Goetschel, "Heine's Critical Secularism," in *Boundary 2: An International Journal of Literature and Culture*, Vol. 31, No. 2, Summer 2004, pp. 149–71.

Ignace Feuerlicht

In the following excerpt, Feurlicht considers the legends surrounding Heine's poem "The Lorelei."

The "Lorelei" is one of the most popular poems, a must for German schools and choirs, and a help for commercial advertising in some countries and for tourism in Germany. The strange nymph has become part of everyday life, but 150 years after its origin, Heine's poem still poses questions about its connections with legends and with other poets, about its artistic means and merits, and about its meaning or message. There is plenty of controversy and in some cases the poem's first line may become the interpreter's last word: "Ich weiss nicht, was soll es bedeuten."

Sometimes the view is voiced that Heine, unlike his romantic predecessors, restored the original legend. However, there is no old tradition calling an oread or a water nymph Lore-Ley, and there is no ancient legend about a maiden singing on top of the Lurley rock who has no

> WHAT DISTINGUISHES HEINE'S LORE-LEY MOST SHARPLY FROM THE LORELEYS IN OTHER POEMS AND FROM THE GREEK SIRENS IS HER ABSOLUTE LACK OF COMMUNICATION."

communication with passing men. For centuries, the beautiful and multiple echo of the Lurley aroused, of course, great interest and seems to have spawned some local legends.

Around the year 1500, the poet and humanist Konrad Celtes mentions the ancient belief in forest deities (gnomes?) living in the caves of the Lurley and causing the echo. In his *Origines Palatinae* of 1612, Freher speaks of forest nymphs and oreads who were thought to voice the echo. In those ancient times, the echo was not ascribed to a single being, who would probably have received a proper name. Therefore, the opinion that in the original legend the echo was the voice of a "Bergfrau" is unfounded. Nor was one single gnome thought to be the source of the echo.

There are no legends about the Lurley dating from the eighteenth century. The first decade of the nineteenth century saw Brentano's poetic creation of the Lore Lay. Before Brentano, the name Lurley was apparently also used for the echo itself. But Brentano was the first, and Eichendorff the second, to call a beautiful and dangerous woman by the name of the dangerous rock with the beautiful echo.

In the second decade, two university professors were engaged less in exploring than in enlarging, fictionalizing, and popularizing the story or stories about the Lurley. In 1811 the historian Niklas Vogt explained the echo as the voice of a beautiful woman who had enchanted all men except the one she loved, and who therefore threw herself into the Rhine. Vogt referred to Brentano's ballad as his source. Only a few years later, obviously realizing that Brentano had invented the story, Vogt discarded most of it.

. . . The women in the "Lorelei" poems are all *femmes fatales*, but there are essential differences among them. In Brentano and Eichendorff there is a psychological background, a "reason" for the destructiveness of the woman. She takes vengeance on all men for having been jilted by her lover. In Heine's nymph there is no motive to be discovered. Brentano's Lore Lay is an unhappy sorceress living in Bacharach. Eichendorff's Lorelei is a wealthy witch, who at night rides on horseback in the forest. Heine's Lore-Ley is apparently a nymph, who whiles an evening away on a rock combing her hair and singing.

The Lurley legends were about an echo, and there is a triple echo at the end of Brentano's ballad. The stage in Eichendorff's poem is not near the Lurley rock; the woman has only a castle high on a rock overlooking the Rhine. But like an oread in the legend she echoes the man, repeating his "line" ("Es ist schon spät, es wird schon kalt"). There is no echo in Loeben's "Lurleyfels," but in Heine's poem there is not just the lack of an echo, there is the uncanny feeling of an anti-echo. The man does not say a word, while the maiden is singing neither in a reaction to the man's voice or presence, nor in anticipation of his words or action or death. This nymph does not echo the man's words or feelings; she ignores him completely.

One is not even sure that she notices him. The feelings about the man attributed to her, the "heartlessness," the "evil or . . . stupidly malignant soul," the "delight in destroying others," are gratuitous additions of interpreters. Even "indifference" goes perhaps too far, since it implies that the Lore-Ley at least sees or knows the man.

What distinguishes Heine's Lore-Ley most sharply from the Loreleys in other poems and from the Greek sirens is her absolute lack of communication. In Brentano's poem the sorceress talks quite a bit to other persons. In Eichendorff's "Waldgespräch" the witch is engaged in a dialogue with her victim. In Loeben's poem the "Zauberfräulein" looks for the men and at them and sings to them. The sirens sing to the passing sailors. They address Odysseus, whose name and history they know.

What also sets Heine's Lore-Ley manifestly apart from similar legendary or pseudolegendary figures is the fact that she is shown in "action" on one man only. It is *the* boatsman who is in the fairy tale and in Heine's mind. The uncertainty about the victim's fate, expressed in the last stanza, would carry no weight if the "fairy tale" related the shipwrecks of many men, if it were about a frequent evening happening on the Rhine, a routine shipwreck accompanied by music. The "I" sees only one man in the picture, and makes no generalization.

The first stanza and the last one, which constitute the frame of the story or of the painting, are introduced and dominated by the "I." They both are about reality, but (or is it therefore?) present perhaps more difficulties to the understanding than the fairy tale. In the beginning, the "I" professes not to know the "meaning" of his sadness, which apparently has some connection with an obsessive fairy tale but is never explained. Interpreters have explained it as caused by the fairy tale. It is also possible to see the obsession with the sad fairy tale as a result of the melancholy mood. At any rate, it is left to the imagination of the reader to sense a connection between the catastrophe of the boatsman and a tragic love, past or present, of the "I." Some critics speak of "Angst," obviously taking the cue from the first poem of the "Heimkehr" cycle, of which the "Lorelei" is the second, where Heine states that his poems are attempts at exorcising his "Angst." Specifically, Heine's fear of exams or of his life being wrecked are said to be the reasons of his sadness.

If the last stanza were only added to convey the boatsman's fate, it would be superfluous, since there cannot be any doubt about it. Yet the poet seems to have some doubts. The "I" of the first stanza is back, so is the uncertainty. But how can he be uncertain about the end of a fairy tale which has a very meager plot? Is this just a strange lapse of memory? Or is he only softening the terrible thought, because his own emotional or social shipwreck is involved? What makes this uncertainty even stranger is that it is followed by the (in more than one way) flat statement that the Lore-Ley has "done" it. There is no doubt here. Thus, as the first stanza consists of two negative statements, the last stanza consists of two not entirely consistent affirmative statements.

Not only the return to the reality and to the "I" of the first stanza makes the last stanza indispensable, but seemingly also the naming of the strange and guilty being. It is curious and, some would say, ironical that the enigmatic and melodious name is revealed in an otherwise pedestrian sentence. Actually Heine's disclosing the name of the beautiful maiden in the nearly climactic position of the next to the last word does not explain anything, it leaves many questions unanswered. The poem starts with a puzzling sadness and ends with a puzzling name.

The maiden is obviously not identical with Brentano's sorceress, who was the first being to bear that name, nor with Eichendorff's witch. Then who is she? And what is she thinking, if anything, or feeling, if anything? Is she only concerned with her beauty? What are the words of her "Lied"? Is she singing although a man drowns, or so that a man should drown, or only while a man drowns? There cannot be generally accepted answers to these questions.

Even such a simple question, whether she is a mountain nymph or a water nymph, has the scholars divided. In Schreiber's book, Heine's main source, she is an undine, although she lives in a rock. In Loeben's version, a possible source, she is a sea nymph. In "Schnabelewopski" Heine mentions sea nymphs who sit on cliffs, comb their hair and sing. While some scholars, therefore, call the Lore-Ley a water nymph, others insist that in the sixteenth and seventeenth centuries there was no mention of water spirits in connection with the Lurley and that, therefore, the Lore-Ley is a rock nymph.

One avoids this controversy and other dilemmas concerning the Lore-Ley by rationally explaining the beautiful maiden as a mere dream vision of the lovesick boatsman, or as a hallucination produced by the magic mood of the evening. But this explication dismisses not only the difficulties but the legend itself and the mystery and charm of the Lore-Ley. Whoever solves the enigma dissolves the poem.

There is no mystery in the formal aspect of Heine's "Lied," although opinions about it differ too. One may praise the "aptness" of the language, but its "simplicity" is deceiving.

Stylistically there is a marked contrast between the frame and the painting. Only the frame has subordinate clauses. The sad mood of the "I" and the sad fate of the boatsman are mentioned in these subordinate clauses. The language in the first and last stanzas is simple, prosaic, while the old fairy tale has poetic, unusual, and archaic expressions. Some critics wince at the poetic style, the superlative "schönste," and the three "golden." They probably would prefer the understating style of the first stanza to continue through the poem, disregarding the contrast between reality and fairy tale.

There has been particularly some criticism of certain phrases in the fourth and fifth stanzas. "Wundersam" was branded as the word of a critic rather than a poet, although other poets have used it too. "Gewaltig" has been found to be inconsistent with the nature of the Lore-Ley and with "wundersam" and compared to the sudden blast of a trombone which tears apart the harmony in an alienation effect. But the word refers to the melody, not to the sound. It is not a synonym of "loud" or "deafening" but of "irresistible" or "magic." Contrary to a scholar's view, there is no conscious "disfigurement" and irony whatever in "Melodei," the old form of "Melodie." It has been used by Heine and by others before without any ironical intentions and is appropriate for a tale of "olden times."

"Wildes Weh" is accused of being dangerously close to the pitfalls of bombast and sentimentality, and of being an obtrusive alliteration. But the man's reaction to an unusual phenomenon can only be expressed in an unusual phrase. His frenzied fit of passion for the strange and unreachable beauty cannot be simply called "love" or "yearning."

While the style of the six quatrains displays some uncommon features, the rhythmic structure is quite common, especially in folk-songs. It is about the same as in Brentano's and Loeben's Loreley poems. Each line has three stresses, while the number and position of the unstressed syllables is not fixed. The first and third lines have feminine, the second and fourth lines masculine rhymes. There is a pause in the middle of each stanza, marked by a semicolon. Although the metrical structure is not original, critics praise its "incomparable suppleness," which makes the lines appear "alternately short and long in spite of the fixed number of feet." The "slightly dactylic rhythm" is even said to "suggest the motion of the waves."

The language of the poem has been called melodious. One French critic speaks of the prodigious and sweet song of the vowels, another French critic of the "lulling melody" and the "magic of the vowels, alternately soft and sonorous." A German scholar feels that Heine's art to suggest the darkening landscape and the brilliant vision by acoustically differing sounds and rhymes amounts to incantation. He even hears a melancholy cello accompanying the first stanza. Others extol the beautiful sounds of the lines about the "wondrous melody."

Somebody who lacks the aesthetic sensitivity of these learned listeners finds the poem about the magic of music, which has acquired its great popularity as a song, rather wanting in musical appeal.

It does not compare with "Leise zieht durch mein Gemüt." For a truly "wondrous and powerful" song of the Loreley one has to listen to Frau Lureley in Brentano's "Rheinmärchen": "Singer leise, leise, leise,/ Singt ein flüsternd Wiegenlied."

Friedrich Silcher's music has given Heine's poem its "ultimate and definitive form," some think. One biased observer not only credits the music with the great success of the poem, but even claims to hear in it the flowing of the Rhine. But one rather agrees with those who call it a "third-rate piece of music," which "blurs, even destroys essential beauties of the poem," and almost completely eliminates its magic by its dragging mediocrity. The music sounds as if written for a barrel organ and does not even attempt to do justice to the restlessness, the mysterious spell of beauty, and the catastrophe the poem is about. It is not its "ultimate form," but its ultimate irony. The fascination it has exercised over millions of people is worlds apart from the magic of the Lore-Ley's melody. It is its travesty.

It has been widely accepted that Heine keeps a "distance" between himself and the "fairy tale" as well as the maiden and the boatsman, to the extent that he evinces irony, and that at the end he feels relief, even smiles or scoffs at the poor victim of a misguided imagination. But Heine has no more distance than one has to one's own feelings, thoughts, or memories. He cannot get rid of the fairy tale; it is now an important part of him. There is no distance between his inner life and the external plot and therefore there is no transition between the first and the second stanzas.

The fairy tale, although of "old times," is not shown as happening "once upon a time," but as happening in the present; it is happening to the "I," and it is told in the present tense. The "fantasy" is not unmasked as an illusion. There is no "disillusionment" at the end, as one routinely expects in a Heine poem.

On the contrary. The narrator is still obsessed by the fairy tale and blames the Lore-Ley for the boatsman's death in a manner that has been called "naive and popular," in a tone that sounds perhaps even "bitter and accusatory," at any rate, in a way one would blame somebody in reality for a misdeed, as if the Lore-Ley really existed. This simple statement about the Lore-Ley's fault is the last sentence, the last word of the poem, not any remark about the reason and the end of the

sadness, about the personal life of the "I," or about the "real" reality, or the true present. There is no "relief" here, no smile, no irony, and no distance.

Based very shakily on the assumption of a "distance," some interpretations assign to the little poem a peculiar position in Heine's artistic development, or in the history of literary movements, or even the history of civilization. It is said to represent a personal farewell to romanticism or a generational farewell to poetry. An influential analysis finds it to be not a romantic work of art but an expression of nostalgia for romanticism, for the time when people believed in the blue flower. It is not located in the wondrous world of romanticism but at a certain distance from it, and the reader is painfully aware of the end of romanticism, as another critic avers. Such observations are in contrast to the view or feeling of generations that the poem is a romantic, indeed *the* romantic song.

The exclusion of the "Lorelei" from genuinely romantic poetry stems partly from the wrong assumption that the Lore-Ley at the end is revealed as an illusion, disastrous at that. This revelation is taken by one critic to be poetry's self-revelation as deceit and lie, as announcing its imminent end. That such self-condemnation is expressed in an eminently successful poem where a "wondrous melody" is shown as exerting an irresistible charm is hardly believable. This view is based on the strange supposition that the siren's singing is nothing but an accidental accompaniment of her combing her hair, and that she actually is silent. Yet the melody is characterized by two strong and long adjectives, and at the end the poet accuses the siren of having "done" it not with combing her hair, nor with her unsurpassed beauty, but with her singing. The "Lorelei" is an expression of art's great vitality rather than of a foreboding or even announcement of poetry's death.

Another, half biographical, half philosophical interpretation sees in Heine's poem a depiction of the "inevitable punishment" for "hedonism and the unfettered cult of beauty." But even if Heine could be defined as a hedonist, and his "ultimate goal" in life had been "hedonistic enjoyment," which is at least debatable, the lonely boatsman in the little boat, of whose life and thoughts we know nothing, is hardly a prototype of a hedonist, even if he had sought out the sight and sounds of the siren.

Most critics do not find in the "Lorelei" any abstract message but think that it depicts Heine's unhappy love for his rich and beautiful cousin Amalie, the "human Lorelei," who was "remote from him" because of her marriage and because she spoke a different language, and who "became the archetype of the eternally unreachable" woman. The "fairy tale" then is the story of Heine's personal experience and the allegedly unexplainable sad mood is that of his unrequited love.

The Lore-Ley appears as a mythological stylization of a woman who because of her position, her wealth (even her comb is of gold), and her beauty towers above the man, who can only look up at her but does not get her attention, and who is ruined by his hopeless passion. But the Lore-Ley is also a siren. It almost looks like private irony that Heine endows her with the gift of magical music, while Amalie had no understanding for his poetry and for art in general.

The biographical and erotic view of the poem can be supplemented by a wider view. It appears not only as an expression of Heine's feelings for a *femme fatale* and of his erotic despair, but also as a symbol of the contrast between beauty (of nature, woman, and art) and everyday drabness, between illusion (imagination, dream, fairy tale) and reality, between the permanence and power of art and the fleetingness and weakness of life, between an upper, mysterious world of greatness, harmony, serenity, vigor, and clarity and a lower, all-too-familiar world of smallness, unrest, uncertainty, pain, helplessness, and death. Whoever has eyes only for the dazzling images of beauty and art, founders in the world of hard and dark reality. Or, in Platen's often quoted words: "Wer die Schönheit angeschaut mit Augen, ist dem Tode schon anheimgegeben."

Source: Ignace Feuerlicht, "Heine's 'Lorelei': Legend, Literature, Life," in *German Quarterly*, Vol. 53, No. 1, January 1980, pp. 82–94.

SOURCES

Bieber, Hugo, ed., *Heinrich Heine: A Biographical Anthology*, translated by Moses Hadas, Jewish Publication Society of America, 1956.

Brentano, Clemens, "The Lorelei," in *Lays and Legends of the Rhine*, Charles Jugel, 1847, pp. 54–55.

Eichendorff, Joseph von, "Lorelei," in *The World's Great Masterpieces*, Vol. 9, American Literary Society, 1899, pp. 4120–21.

Gray, Christopher, "Sturm und Drang over a Memorial to Heinrich Heine," in *New York Times*, May 27, 2007, http://www.nytimes.com/2007/05/27/realestate/27scap.html?_r=1 (accessed April 14, 2010).

Grimm, Jakob, *Teutonic Mythology*, translated from the fourth edition by James Steven Stallybrass, 4 vols., George Bell & Sons, 1882–88, pp. 487–99.

———, and Wilhelm Grimm, *German Folk Tales*, translated by Francis P. Magoun and Alexander H. Krappe, 1812, reprinted, Southern Illinois University Press, 1960.

Heine, Heinrich, "The Lorelei," in *The Complete Poems of Heinrich Heine: A Modern English Verse Translation*, translated by Hal Draper, Shurkamp/Insel, 1982, pp. 76–77.

Hofrichter, Laura, *Heinrich Heine*, translated by Barker Fairley, Clarendon, 1963.

Loeben, Ferdinand Graf von, "The Lorelei," in *Literary Magnet*, Vol. 1, 1826, p. 296.

Porterfield, Allen Wilson, "Graf von Loeben and the Legend of Lorelei," in *Modern Philology*, Vol. 13, No. 6, October 1915, pp. 306–32.

Sandor, A. I., *The Exile of Gods: Interpretation of a Theme, a Theory and a Technique in the Work of Heinrich Heine*, Mouton, 1967.

Seyhan, Azade, "What is Romanticism and Where did it Come from?" in *The Cambridge Companion to German Romanticism*, edited by Nicholas Saul, Cambridge University Press, 2009, pp. 1–20.

Tunner, Erika, "The Lore Lay—a Fairy Tale from Ancient Times?" in *European Romanticism: Literary Cross-Currents, Modes, and Models*, edited by Gerhart Hoffmeister, Wayne State University Press, 1990, 269–86.

Twain, Mark, *A Tramp Abroad*, Vol. 1, Harper and Brothers, 1879, pp. 119–29.

FURTHER READING

Brod, Max, *Heinrich Heine: The Artist in Revolt*, translated by Joseph Witriol, New York University Press, 1957.
> Although originally written in German in 1934, this largely political assessment of Heine's career was, like much of Heine's own work, censored and not allowed to be published in Germany until after World War II, due to anti-Semitism.

Durrani, Osman, ed., *German Poetry of the Romantic Era: An Anthology*, St. Martin's Press, 1986.

This collection of poetry by Heine's contemporaries provides a framework for understanding his poetic achievement.

Heine, Heinrich, *Heinrich Heine: His Wit, Wisdom, Poetry*, J. G Cupples, 1892.
    Available as a public domain digitized volume, this anthology provides an extensive selection of Heine's verse and prose arranged by topic.

Von Emden, Ludwig, ed., *The Family Life of Heinrich Heine: One Hundred and Twenty-two Family Letters of the Poet Hitherto Unpublished from His College Days to His Death*, translated by Charles de Kay, Haskell House, 1970.
    These family letters provide insight into Heine's spiritual and artistic development.

SUGGESTED SEARCH TERMS

Heinrich Heine

Lorelei

Lorelei AND Heine

romanticism

nixie

fairytale AND allegory

fairytale AND Heine

Middle Rhine AND Heine

German AND folklore

Lieder AND Lorelei

Lucinda Matlock

EDGAR LEE MASTERS

1915

"Lucinda Matlock" is one of the most famous poems written by Edgar Lee Masters. Based on the poet's grandmother, it is written in the voice of a woman who, having lived to the age of ninety-six, addresses readers from beyond the grave about the pain and beauty in her life in the rural American heartland. Having outlived eight of the twelve children born to her, readers might expect Lucinda to wallow in the difficulty of the homesteader life she led, but she ends the poem admonishing those who let their sorrows get the best of them.

This poem comes from *Spoon River Anthology*, which many critics consider one of the greatest poetry collections in American literature. Published in 1915, the book presents a series of monologues representing 214 residents who lived and died in the mythical Spoon River, Illinois, a small prairie town. For inspiration, Masters read the tombstones in the small towns that he grew up in, near the banks of the actual river that inspired his book's title. *Spoon River Anthology* made Masters, who was a practicing lawyer at the time, a literary sensation and a household name. Unfortunately, he was never able to replicate the book's success. The other biographies, plays, and poetry collections he wrote, including a 1924 sequel called *The New Spoon River*, never gained him the critical or popular acclaim he received for *Spoon River Anthology*, which remained his life's great literary achievement. *Spoon River Anthology*, including "Lucinda

Edgar Lee Masters (The Library of Congress)

Matlock," is still in print in several editions, including a Penguin Classics edition published in 2008.

AUTHOR BIOGRAPHY

Masters was born in Garnett, Kansas, on August 23, 1868, where his parents lived for just a little over a year. His father, Hardin Wallace Masters, was a lawyer, which is the occupation that Masters himself was to follow. The poet's childhood was spent in small Illinois towns: first in Petersburg, near the farm owned by his father's parents, Squire Davis and Lucinda Masters; and later, from 1880 on, in Lewistown, along the Spoon River. After high school, he attended a preparatory program at Knox College in Galesburg, Illinois, for a year in 1889. Instead of enrolling in college at Knox the following year, Masters went to work in his father's law firm. By 1891 he had learned enough about the law to pass the bar exam. After a brief partnership with his father, Masters moved to Chicago in 1892. There he

practiced law with Clarence Darrow, the lawyer best known for defending the theory of evolution in the 1925 Scopes Trial.

Masters married Helen Jenkins, the daughter of a Chicago lawyer, in 1898. He worked with Darrow from 1903 to 1911, after which he left to form his own firm due to a volatile personal relationship with Darrow. By that time Masters had published several books of poetry, using pseudonyms including Dexter Wallace. In 1914, a visit from his mother stirred in him a wave of nostalgia about life in Petersburg and Lewistown. Between May and December of that year, while still working full time as a lawyer, he composed over two hundred poems about life in small-town Illinois, including "Lucinda Matlock." They were published under the name Webster Ford in a St. Louis journal. The popularity of these poems led to the collection *Spoon River Anthology* in 1915.

The critical and popular success of *Spoon River Anthology* established a high standard for writing that Masters was never to repeat. His subsequent poetry, including the collections *The Great Valley* in 1916, *Starved Rock* in 1919, and *The New Spoon River* in 1924, was not well regarded in academic circles, though the Masters name was popular enough to keep him employed as a writer. He was not a literary success with the six novels he wrote or the biographies of Abraham Lincoln, Walt Whitman, and Mark Twain, among others, that he published during the 1930s.

Masters's personal life was affected by his literary success. Never a faithful husband, he left his wife and children in 1923 in what became a protracted, bitter divorce. He eventually married Ellen Coyne in 1926. He and Coyne lived in New York at first, far from Masters's Midwestern roots. Later they moved to North Carolina and Pennsylvania, where she taught school. Masters was in poor health throughout the 1940s, suffering from chronic bouts of pneumonia and other ailments. On March 5, 1950, he died in a nursing home in Melrose Park, Pennsylvania. He is buried in Petersburg, Illinois.

POEM TEXT

I went to the dances at Chandlerville,
And played snap-out at Winchester.
One time we changed partners,
Driving home in the moonlight of middle June,

And then I found Davis.   5
We were married and lived together for seventy
    years,
Enjoying, working, raising the twelve children,
Eight of whom we lost
Ere I had reached the age of sixty.
I spun, I wove, I kept the house, I nursed the
    sick,   10
I made the garden, and for holiday
Rambled over the fields where sang the larks,
And by Spoon River gathering many a shell,
And many a flower and medicinal weed—
Shouting to the wooded hills, singing to the
    green valleys.   15
At ninety-six I had lived enough, that is all,
And passed to a sweet repose.
What is this I hear of sorrow and weariness,
Anger, discontent and drooping hopes?
Degenerate sons and daughters,   20
Life is too strong for you—
It takes life to love Life.

POEM SUMMARY

Lines 1–4

The first four lines of the poem describe Lucinda Matlock's life before she met Davis Matlock, the man who was to be her husband. As a young woman, she went to other towns to socialize. Although Spoon River, the setting of the poems in this collection, is a fictional place, other towns mentioned in this poem actually existed and could have been visited by the author.

In line 1, Lucinda mentions going to dances at Chandlerville, which is located in western Illinois, in Cass County. Winchester, mentioned in line 2, is about thirty-five miles south of Chandlerville, in Scott County. Both are within ten miles of the actual Spoon River.

The poem reflects a sense of innocence as it looks back more than seventy years, possibly to the 1840s. Lucinda recalls going to dances, and she also recalls playing snap-out, which various sources describe as a card game (sometimes just referred to as "snap") or a party game akin to "musical chairs." In line 3 the speaker refers to changing partners, which sounds like it refers to either dancing or card playing, though in line 4 she continues that thought to show that the change of partners occurred during the ride home in the moonlight, in a carriage or wagon. The implication is that Lucinda was romantically adventurous in her younger years.

MEDIA ADAPTATIONS

- Masters reads "Lucinda Matlock" on the four-disc box set *Poetry On Record: 98 Poets Read Their Work (1888-2006)*, released by Shout Factory in 2006.

- *Spoon River Anthology* was adapted for the Broadway stage by Joseph Cates and the Spoon River Anthology Company. It opened at the Booth Theater in New York City on September 29, 1963. Charles Aidman composed the songs for the adaptation. The stars of the original production were Betty Garrett, Joyce Van Patten, Robert Elston, and Charles Aidman. The original cast recording of the 1963 Broadway musical was released on vinyl by Columbia in 1963, but has not been reissued on compact disc.

- Parts of Masters's book are acted out, with background information, in *Spoon River Anthology & A Poetic Portrait Gallery*, originally part of the PBS television series *Anyone for Tennyson?* It was released on DVD by Monterrey Home Video in 1997. The program features performances by William Shatner and the First Poetry Quartet.

- "Lucinda Matlock" is one of several poems included in a ten-part cycle of classical compositions composed by Lita Grier and released on *Songs From Spoon River: Reflections of a Peacemaker and Other Vocal Music*. This song and several from the Spoon River set are sung by Elizabeth Norman. The CD was released in 2009 on the Cedille label.

Line 5

The poem's fifth line represents a transitional moment in the life of the speaker. Grammatically, this line continues the thought that was begun in line 3 concerning Lucinda's days as an eligible, young woman. The arbitrary switch of partners on the ride home one night leads her to meet Davis, her future husband. The period at the end of line 5 represents not only the end of the thought, but the end of her life as a young single woman.

Lines 6–9

In four lines, Lucinda summarizes seventy years of her life. The facts are clear: she was married to her husband Davis for seventy years; they had twelve children; she outlived all but four of them. Lucinda considered this to be a good, enjoyable life, though a strenuous one, centered around work.

The tone of these four lines is significant in its lack of emotion. While describing the births and deaths of her children and the seventy years of her life with Davis, Lucinda maintains a voice that is sincere but could not be characterized as passionate. This aspect is important for conveying the typical midwestern farm woman in the nineteenth century, showing the stoicism that makes it possible for her to survive a harsh life.

Lines 10–15

This section of the poem describes how Lucinda spends most of the days of her life. Line 10 focuses on the domestic chores associated with keeping a household, ranging from making clothes to seeing her husband and children through their various illnesses. In line 11, the poem's focus shifts to her life outdoors, as Lucinda describes working in her garden. The nature setting carries over in line 12, where she reminisces about wandering across fields and listening to the birds sing as a form of recreation and pleasure. Domestic life is implied in line 13, where she talks about gathering shells along the banks of the Spoon River, and is reintroduced into the poem fully in line 14, where she mentions herbs that can be used for medicine, taking readers back to her home life and her job of nursing the sick in her family, as mentioned in line 10.

This long run of ruminations, combining the pleasures of wandering through the countryside and the responsibilities of being a mother and wife out on the prairie, ends with an affirmation by Lucinda, expressed in line 15. She describes raising her voice, shouting and singing out loud, with no other purpose than just the sheer exuberance of enjoying being where she is.

Lines 16–17

Lucinda describes her death at age ninety-six with no recriminations. She feels that her life has been complete, and she likens death to lying down to rest.

Lines 18–19

After summarizing her long life and death, Lucinda expresses her dismay about the people who tend to focus their attention on the negative things in life. Her question about negativity is posed in the present tense, indicating that she is listening, from beyond death, to the voices of those still alive. The fact that it is a question implies Lucinda's incredulity: she is not really questioning whether or not she has heard such dour perspectives on life, she is only trying to express her disbelief that such despair actually exists.

Lines 20–22

At the end of the poem, Lucinda speaks directly to those who dwell on the negative aspects of their lives. She starts by describing those with such attitudes as "degenerate." While this is a term commonly used as an insult, to imply that someone is corrupt or inferior, its most basic definition, of something that has altered or weakened over time, could just be her non-judgmental way of describing people who have less strength to face the world than their ancestors had.

The poem's final lines identify the core problem for those who find life too burdensome. Life is not as horrible as complainers try to make it seem, the speaker implies. If they are overwhelmed, it is because they are weak. They do not have enough life in them to stand up and accept the challenges that Life—a philosophical concept, as opposed to simple existence—presents to everyone. Lucinda's philosophy, which enables her to survive and love her existence while living a long life full of sorrow, watching death claim those she loves all around her, is that Life is not a cause of despair. She turns the responsibility for a happy life back onto the person, not the universe, identifying it as a matter of attitude. She uses this poem to speak her lesson directly to those who she thinks are viewing things wrongly.

THEMES

Aging

This poem covers the life span of a woman who lived to be ninety-six years old, a long life in almost any culture. This was especially true in the rural United States of the nineteenth century, where the unavailability of health care held the

TOPICS FOR FURTHER STUDY

- Read Christiana Holmes Tilson's autobiography about being a pioneer woman in southern Illinois in the early 1800s, *A Woman's Story of Pioneer Illinois*, which has appealed to young adults since its first publication in 1919. Write a dialogue for two students to portray Tilson and Lucinda Matlock, discussing their lives on the prairie. Use a digital camera to create a presentation and post it on YouTube for your class to view.

- The poet's grandfather Squire Davis Masters, who was married to the woman who inspired "Lucinda Matlock," fought in the Black Hawk War in 1832 as a captain of the militia. Read some background about the Black Hawk War and design a Web page from the perspective of the Native American tribe who fought it, outlining their political position about the southern Illinois territory and incorporating maps and documents. Include a section for comments by members of the Kickapoo, Sauk, and Fox tribes.

- Use a Web site such as Mindomo to create a mind map for Lucinda on a summer day when she is in her forties, charting her responsibilities and priorities. Do some research to find as many responsibilities as you can for a woman of her time in her position.

- Research parents whose children have died before them, to find out how they cope. Create an annotated bibliography: a list of books or Web sites with brief descriptions of each, explaining why they would be useful for Lucinda.

- Use a family tree/genealogy Web site to find the name and some details about an ancestor that you did not know. Write a poem in that person's voice and submit it to your class along with the researched information. Explain why you think your ancestor would feel the way presented him or her in your poem.

---

average life span to under fifty years of age. The poem covers three eras in Lucinda's life, beginning in young adulthood and following her through middle age and finally, to the end of her life. As a young woman, she embraced life by keeping socially active, traveling the countryside to attend dances and parties. Her middle years were fraught with struggle, as she worked to keep up with domestic chores, tended to the health of her husband and children, and coped with the heartache of watching her children die while she lived on. At the end of her life she was content, so that as she looks back from the afterlife she still feels that her life was worthwhile.

Lucinda's attitude remains consistent throughout the years presented in this poem. Though her changing circumstances present her with increasing challenges that no one could rightly prepare for, Masters shows her to be the same person from one age to the next. Age, as it is presented in this poem,

does not affect an individual's core personality, if one's character is strong, as Lucinda' is. Aging is shown as a series of events to be met and accepted.

Marriage

From the very first time that Lucinda mentions Davis, who she will later wed, readers can tell that their marriage will be a happy one. In line 5 she introduces him as someone she "found," not as someone she "met." The following line presents the telling detail that their marriage stayed intact and close for an impressive seventy years, and it is followed by the observation that enjoyment was more prominent than work in their lives.

Davis is not specifically mentioned in the rest of the poem. Instead, he is referred to with the other family members his wife cares for. In the perspective of this poem, marriage is a group

In love for seventy years *(Robert Crum | Shutterstock.com)*

project, its pleasures found in the united effort of the family.

Hope

The strongest theme of Lucinda's story is her undying belief in enduring hope. The poem provides readers with solid reasons that Lucinda might have lost hope along her life's journey. As the poem explains, she and her husband have withstood the deaths of the majority of their children, and it is implied that several of these deaths happened when the children were adults. Lucinda says that she greeted her own death when its time arrived, not because she had turned bitter with life, but because she was tired and ready for rest. She also expresses dismay and frustration with those who give up hope, saying so directly in lines 18 and 19.

In the last three lines of the poem, Lucinda addresses those whose hope is failing them as her sons and daughters, though she could be talking about anyone who lives on after her. Although they may be willing to give in to their sorrow and weariness, she has not lost her hope for them. By addressing the despondent people directly,

Lucinda is affirming her hope that they will listen to her and possibly learn from her experience, so that they might be able to make the corrections to their outlook while there is still time to enjoy the life they have.

Nature

One of the best reasons for Lucinda to keep her hope is her strong connection to the natural world. Masters establishes this bond directly in five lines in the middle of the poem. He starts in line 11 with a mention of her garden, tying her relationship with nature to her ongoing sense of responsibility for feeding her large family. He also introduces an image of Lucinda wandering across the countryside, listening to the songs of birds and following the river along its bank to find shells. Her wanderings are said to yield plants with healing properties for her to use to nurse her family's illnesses.

Line 15 presents readers with a joyous image, a graphic depiction of the love of Life that will be asserted in the final line of the poem. By this point in the poem, Lucinda is a grown woman with serious responsibilities. Given the high rate of infant mortality in the pre-industrial areas of the nation, it is likely that some, if not most, of the deceased children she discusses in line 8 were already dead, lost in childhood. Still, line 15 shows her giving voice to her delight with being in nature. The feelings she has about nature make her sing out loud and shout for no other reason than pure glee. The delight expressed in this line is undeniable.

STYLE

Colloquial Diction

Masters writes in the direct, plain-speaking voice of a woman who lived in the country for all of her ninety-five years. In line 2 Lucinda mentions the game snap-out, which is listed in Paul G. Brewster's *Children's Games and Rhymes* as a version of the game "Clap in and Clap Out," a game for pairing boys and girls at parties. If this is indeed the game she is talking about, Lucinda's variation on the title could well reflect the local name for it, a colloquial name specific to her geographic region.

In line 9 she uses the word "ere" to mean "before," which is a reflection of how unschooled country people in the past picked up elevated language from the most familiar reading sources available to them: the Bible and copies of Shakespeare's works. Line 17 includes the colloquialism "passed," a shortened form of "passed on" to refer to death. These touches give readers a sense of what sort of person Lucinda is. Most of her diction is refined, if not formal, the kind that would normally be used by an educated person.

Dramatic Monologue

"Lucinda Matlock" is presented as a dramatic monologue. In the poem, Lucinda is explaining herself and talking about her life. The words she uses imply that she is introducing herself to someone, though the identity of her audience is not clear. Some readers may interpret her reference to "sons and daughters" in line 20 to mean that she is literally talking to her offspring, and maybe future descendants, but the words can also be interpreted to mean that she looks upon all of humanity as her responsibility.

The dramatic monologue is a traditional form in poetry and was particularly popular in the Victorian era, throughout the last half of the nineteenth century. Two famous examples of it are Alfred, Lord Tennyson's poem "Ulysses" and Robert Browning's "My Last Duchess." Writing in the dramatic monologue form that had been most frequently associated with the century before his gave Masters's poetry an antiquated feel, even when his work was brand new.

Imagery

At the beginning of the poem, Masters uses few concrete images. The most specific detail given in the first nine lines is the moonlight over the carriage ride home in June, mentioned in line 4. When she talks about the countryside where she lived, however, Lucinda offers ample sensory impressions. She talks about her garden, flowers and weeds, and hills and valleys adorned with flowers and trees. Besides evoking the sense of sight, she also uses aural images, from the songs of the larks to the voice of the narrator herself as she shouts and sings. While the beginning of the poem focuses on establishing a situation, and the last lines are directed toward Lucinda's philosophy of life, the middle of the poem offers readers sensory details that briefly allow them to feel what life was like for this woman.

HISTORICAL CONTEXT

Rural Illinois

Much of the power of *Spoon River Anthology* comes from Masters's ability to evoke a specific sense of place. The region these poems are set in has a specific history that is unique in creating the effect that the poems convey.

Thirty years after its admission into the Union as a state in 1818, Illinois already showed a dual personality. In the north was Chicago, one of the fastest growing metropolises in the country, and across the Mississippi River in the south was St. Louis, Missouri, a main departure point for the western territories. In between these large, influential urban areas, however, lay several hundred miles of open land. The settlers of this land often migrated from states that later joined the Confederacy during the Civil War, most notably Tennessee and Kentucky. A burgeoning coal mining industry in the central and southern parts of the state attracted a large percent of settlers from Virginia, also a future Confederate state. After the Civil War, the nation and the urban areas of the state tended to follow the policies of the industrialized north, but the lower two-thirds of Illinois

COMPARE
&
CONTRAST

- **1915:** Almost 55 percent of the United States population, which is approximately 100 million people, lives in rural areas.

  Today: The nation's population has tripled, but the percent of the population living in rural areas drops to just over 20 percent by 2000.

- **1915:** Giving birth to children is dangerous. For every 100,000 births in the United States, nearly 800 women die. In addition, approximately one of every ten infants die within the first year of life.

  Today: The infant mortality rate has dropped to about 7 deaths per 1000 births. In addition, the mortality rate for mothers has fallen to less than 14 deaths per 100,000 births.

- **1915:** People in small rural towns have little exposure to life outside of their own communities and have to travel across the countryside if they want to meet people outside of their home towns.

  Today: Social networking sites on the Internet make it possible to communicate with like-minded people and make new friends across the globe.

- **1915:** A person raising her family out in the open country might rely on medicinal herbs to treat their illnesses.

  Today: Advances in medicine have created tested treatments for most diseases. Social programs like Medicaid help to make these medicines available to families that cannot afford them.

- **1915:** Divorce is rare. Meeting people who married young and stayed together for their entire lives is not uncommon.

  Today: Almost 40 percent of all marriages in the United States end in divorce. This is lower than the all-time high, hit in the early 1980s, but the number of people marrying is also lower.

---

still identified with the Confederate states that had surrounded it.

The Industrial Revolution of the later nineteenth century had little effect on the rural counties that Masters wrote about. The greatest change during that time was the state's growing population. According to "Illinois Population by Race, Sex, Age, Nativity, and Urban-rural Residence: 1800–1990," in *Historical Statistics of the United States, Earliest Times to the Present: Millennial Edition*, population density went from 0.99 persons per square mile in 1820 to 100.61 persons per square mile in 1910, roughly the life span of Masters's grandmother, who was the inspiration for Lucinda Matlock. This population expansion was concentrated in the cities, but it also meant that the open fields that Masters explored growing up in the 1870s were increasingly given over to cultivation. Although the southern counties of Illinois retained their

agrarian identity, Masters still imbued his poems with a sense of nostalgia for the loss of nature, a sense that was common throughout the growing country at the beginning of the twentieth century.

Modernism

Spoon River Anthology was published at a time when poetry was undergoing a dramatic transformation: the modernist movement, which most literary critics agree began in the mid-1910s. Masters's work does not show all of the characteristics associated with modernism, but it clearly gleaned some of its popularity by being associated with the new artistic spirit in the air.

Modernism was a shift in artistic attitudes that took place simultaneously among all art forms, including poetry and fiction, art, music, architecture, and more. It represented a desire to find new ways of looking at old problems, to

Working in the garden (*Ladushka | Shutterstock.com*)

rhythm or rhyme. The styles that Masters uses for his poems in *Spoon River Anthology* are not exotic, but neither do they follow the familiar patterns of rhythm and rhyme that audiences expected of poetry. They are well suited for the plain-spoken farmland people who narrate them: one often-quoted axiom of modernist writing, attributed to poet Ezra Pound, is "form serves function," which applies perfectly to Masters's style. Though modernism was not to receive its most widespread recognition until the 1920s, with works like Eliot's *The Waste Land* and Woolf's *Mrs. Dalloway*, the utter uniqueness of the *Spoon River Anthology* poems show them to be drawn from the same social explosion.

CRITICAL OVERVIEW

By 1914, Masters was a sporadic poet who had published two books of verse, as well as essays and plays, under the pseudonym Dexter Wallace. In May 1914, he began publishing poems from his Spoon River series in *Reedy's Mirror*, a St. Louis literary journal, using the pen name Webster Ford. His poems were an immediate success. Early reviews were positive. In *Poetry* magazine, Alice Corbin Henderson praises Masters, noting that "*Spoon River Anthology* reflects American life not in a superficial, but in a deeper, sense." When *Spoon River Anthology* was published as a book in May 1915, it became a literary sensation. "Masters was the poet of the year, with the *Anthology* proclaimed by *Publishers Weekly* the year's 'outstanding book—not only the outstanding book of poetry,'" John H. Wrenn and Margaret M. Wrenn state in their study *Edgar Lee Masters*. The Wrenns also quote Ezra Pound, one of the most influential literary figures of the time, demanding in a letter to Harriet Monroe, the publisher of *Poetry*, that she publish more of Masters's poems. They also quote a later review in the *Egoist*, in which Pound enthusiastically declares, "At last! At last America has discovered a poet."

redefine what art means to life. Throughout the nineteenth century, literature and art had been stagnant in their views, with writers in the United States copying the styles that were set by artists in Great Britain during the reign of Queen Victoria, whose personality set the tone for the empire for more than sixty years. Her death, soon after the dawn of a new century, left artists curious for new ways of self-expression. The dawn of World War I in 1914 caused an even greater need for change, as the traditional outlooks seemed irrelevant in a time when one war could engage most of the world, and when new military tools, such as airplanes and chemical weapons, brought unheard of methods of spreading misery.

Modernist writers such as James Joyce, Virginia Woolf, Ezra Pound, and T. S. Eliot sought to reimagine the ways in which stories and poems communicated with readers. As a result, modernist writing came to be associated with new, experimental styles, such as the stream-of-consciousness novel or poetry based on images instead of on

Unfortunately, Masters was never able to expand on his success. He lived another thirty-five years and published several more volumes of poems, along with novels and biographies, but critics never gave them the acclaim they gave *Spoon River Anthology*. His most critically accepted book was the sequel to *Spoon River*, published in 1924, called *The New Spoon River*.

"Reviews were mixed when the book was published . . . ," writes Herbert K. Russell, Masters's biographer, "a few people finding *The New Spoon River* superior but most preferring the old." Russell also notes that "*The New Spoon River* was far more successful than many literary sequels, and it is usually considered Masters's second-most important volume of verse, preceding his own favorite, *Domesday Book*." According to John E. Hallwas, *Spoon River Anthology* was Masters's most successful book because it showed his struggle to find his poetic voice. "The many books and poems that followed it—including *The New Spoon River*—tended to be merely assertive and simplistic because they were not forged in the fire of self-examination," Hallwas writes. Although Masters struggled unsuccessfully to reproduce its success, this single volume is considered enough to assure his place in the annals of American poetry.

CRITICISM

David Kelly

Kelly is a writer who teaches creative writing and literature at several community colleges in Illinois. In the following essay, he describes the way that Masters has completely linked the concept of nature to Lucinda's personality.

In his autobiography, *Across Spoon River: A Biography*, Masters discusses a period in his life when he was fortunate enough to spend time with his father's mother, Lucinda Masters. Eager to find out all he could about her childhood, her family connections, and how she came to be the good-natured person she was, Masters interviewed her for hours, writing down her remembrances. Somewhere along the way, he noticed a discrepancy: her father, she told him, was named Lawrence Young, but his records from previous conversations showed that her maiden name was Lucinda Wasson. When he asked why her name was not Lucinda Young, she explained that her father had courted her mother and then had abandoned her when she was pregnant, without marrying her. "I never told my father that his mother was a natural child; and I believe he did not know it," Masters wrote.

The phrase "natural child" is seldom used anymore to describe a child who is born out of wedlock, but it is perfectly appropriate for Masters's feelings about his grandmother, whom he

used as his model for "Lucinda Matlock," one his best-known *Spoon River Anthology* poems. After describing his grandmother as a dancer in her youth, which is a trait she shares with the fictional Lucinda Matlock, Masters notes, "In her vitality and good humor she bore every evidence of being a love child." Clearly, Masters believed that the circumstances of his grandmother's birth were at least somewhat responsible for the woman's disposition. He talked about her as if, by lacking the bond of marriage between her parents, she was born with a deeper connection to nature than most.

From a twenty-first century perspective, such a bond might seem nothing more than obvious. Lucinda Masters grew up in the early 1800s, dying in 1910 at the age of ninety-five. She predated automobiles, airplanes, and electricity; she was in her mid-fifties when the transcontinental railroad was completed. Her world was the prairie and all of its trappings, the birds and flowers and riverbeds, the hills and valleys that Masters describes in his poetry. One would not have to be born a "natural child" to live with a deep appreciation of nature back when there were so few man-made distractions to absorb her time. Still, there were other options for shaping her world view. She could have grown up to view nature as an emblem of religion, for instance, instead of as an end unto itself. But that was not the personality Masters saw in his version of young Lucinda Wasson, and so it was not the personality type he gave her fictionalized self.

At the end of the poem, Lucinda Matlock refers to life with a capital "L," an honor that is usually applied to pronouns like "He" or "His" when speaking of God. Masters uses the capitalization to draw the connection between what his character refers to as "Life" and what others think of as the one supreme and eternal Ruler. For her, it is Life itself, without the intercession of another being, that gives her existence meaning. Her travels across the countryside are not just diversions, then; they are her way of getting in touch with the heart and soul of existence, a way of worshipping what is most important.

The connection between humanity and nature is drawn in the poem when Masters calls attention to his character's use of medicinal herbs. It was likely a common practice, at a time when much medicine was undiscovered and medical practitioners were rare, but the very commonness of herbal medicine is what makes it strange

WHAT DO I READ NEXT?

- The poem that follows this one in *Spoon River Anthology* (Dover edition published in 1992) is "Davis Matlock," featuring the voice of the man that Lucinda was married to for seventy years. It is based on Masters's grandfather Squire Davis Masters ("Matlock" was the poet's grandfather's mother's maiden name).

- Critics often comment that Sherwood Anderson's book *Winesburg, Ohio* comes very close to being a prose fiction version of *Spoon River Anthology*. Like Masters's collection, Anderson's novel is a patchwork of stories taking place in an imaginary small town in America's heartland. Constantly in print since its first edition in 1919, the book was published in a new edition by Signet Classics in 2005.

- The dark side of small-town America at the time Masters was writing comes out in Sinclair Lewis's 1920 novel *Main Street*. Lewis's satiric look at a fictionalized country town, Gopher Prairie, exposes the gossip and narrow-mindedness that Masters ignores in his portrait of Spoon River. *Main Street* is available in the Library of America's compilation *Lewis: Main Street and Babbitt*, which was published in 1992.

- One of the most significant books published during the Harlem Renaissance was Jean Toomer's novel *Cane*. Instead of idealizing one fictional town, Toomer spreads his exploration of African American life in the early 1920s across rural and urban settings, giving a very different look at life in the United States than the one Masters offers. *Cane* was first published in 1923, and is currently available in a 1993 edition from Livewright publishers.

- In 1977, Masters's son Hardin Wallace Masters published a book about his life with the poet. *Edgar Lee Masters: A Biographical Sketchbook About a Famous American Author*, published by Associated University Press, is no longer in print but is available in many libraries.

- The old woman in Erin Khue Ninh's memoir, "Grandma," lived her long life in Vietnam, but she has a relationship to the countryside and to healing herbs that give her a direct relationship to Lucinda. This piece can be found in *Grand Mothers: Poems, Reminiscences, and Short Stories About The Keepers Of Our Traditions*, a collection for young adults edited by Nikki Giovanni, published in 1996 by Henry Holt.

---

that Masters would draw attention to it. The combination of herbs and medicine, along with the knowledge of how they can be used, is important for understanding Lucinda Matlock and her relationship to nature.

Another clue to who she is can be found in Masters's use of the word "holiday" to describe her rambles by field and river bank, listening to the birds sing. Holiday can be used to describe a vacation, but that sense of the word has little application here: what would Lucinda need a vacation for? Work is synonymous to enjoyment to her, and her beliefs are anchored in her responsibilities. The other sense of holiday—that of religious

observance, derived from "holy day"— better fits her approach to life. Everything described or not described in this poem, from dancing to rambling to her understated acceptance of the many deaths of children she gave life to, suggests a transcendental view of the physical world.

This point is made even clearer in the context of *Spoon River Anthology*. Masters follows "Lucinda Matlock" with "Davis Matlock," giving a voice to the man Lucinda was married to her for more than seventy years. If their worldviews were too similar, then giving a poem in *Spoon River Anthology* to each of them would be redundant. If they were too far apart, however, the significance

Hills and valleys (shalunts | Shutterstock.com)

of their long marriage would be lost. Their views of life have to complement each other in order to make their poems worthwhile. Masters is not required to say that every long marriage is made of pieces that work together in harmony, and it is unlikely, given his tumultuous personal life, that he would take such a position. He does, though, have to acknowledge that seventy years together would create some sort of combination of views.

Davis Matlock is the theologian in the family. His poem is structured as an intellectual query about the complexities of the natural world, of social interaction, and the question of how much self-assertion a person should have. Overall, he wants to know God's will. Masters structures Davis's poem as something like a logical proof—the word "suppose" begins the first line and recurs throughout, stating assumptions that lead to a conclusion. Lucinda's poem, on the other hand, is presented as a narrative, telling the story of her long life. In the end, Davis shakily claims two possible readings of God's will: that assertion will make God proud, or that there is only eternal

nothingness waiting beyond the grave anyway. Lucinda merely asserts what she feels to be true, without wondering if she has gotten it right or wrong. Davis is too aware of himself, plagued with human self-consciousness; Lucinda, as a child of nature, is at peace with herself, viewing those who give in to anger or hopelessness as degenerates.

Masters was not a simple man—not simple enough, at least, to feel that his grandmother's basic essence was different from most people's simply because her parents were not married. It is possible that he could have called her a "natural child" with a smirk, well aware of the way its double meaning would apply to his grandmother's case. More likely would be the idea that he saw the lack of a marriage bond as a circumstance that freed Lucinda Wasson, allowing her to explore her world and find the meaning of virtue on her own terms. In the Mississippi River valley of the 1800s, this freedom would, of course, lead her toward nature. Masters apparently loved both of his grandparents equally, and their fictional representatives in *Spoon River Anthology* are both presented with respect. While the poem "Davis Matlock" shows a man struggling with uncertainty, however, "Lucinda Matlock" presents a child of nature who lives in nature, relaxed in a state of grace.

Source: David Kelly, Critical Essay on "Lucinda Matlock," in *Poetry for Students*, Gale, Cengage Learning, 2011.

Hester L. Furey

In the following excerpt, Furey uses "Carl Hamblin" from Spoon River Anthology *as an example of turn-of-the-century Chicago poetry.*

ACROSS SPOON RIVER

In our common sense, poetry and journalism speak distinct and separate kinds of truth. This belief helps underwrite the most widely accepted narrative of the rise of modernism—in which expatriate experimental writers figure as brilliant, adventurous risk-takers, rightly seeking in Europe a more sophisticated and worthy environment for their work, rejecting a nineteenth-century American culture which is coded as dull, tasteless, formulaic, and confining. The related conclusion—here quoted from an official history of the state of Illinois—that "about 1912 poetry rose suddenly as a more vivid factor in American life" found its way into common sense by the 1930s (Bogart and Mathews 53). Yet the configuration of arguments surround the "place" of poetry in turn-of-the-century Chicago demonstrates that the redefined domain exemplified by *Poetry* magazine depends for its legitimacy upon an altogether formulaic depiction of the American public sphere: it is demonized as a low, threatening, and unworthy setting from which a romanticized poetry must be rescued. In this scenario "true" poets are those who identify themselves primarily with their literary work. This definition constructs the artist as necessarily a person of leisure—contingent in Harriet Monroe's case entirely upon the patronage of wealthy Chicago industrialists—who is above politics, outside history, "transcendent." Through a series of (un)critical relays, we have come to take for granted the truth value of Monroe's narrative about the state of poetry in her time. This essay subjects that account to extended criticism, treating it not as fact but as rhetoric. I propose that we consider turn-of-the-century Chicago poetry, constructed as "lack" for so long, on its own terms. We know that this body of work does not reflect the aesthetic

> MASTERS' COMPLAINTS IN HIS AUTOBIOGRAPHY, *ACROSS SPOON RIVER*, ARE DIRECTED PRIMARILY AT THE SNOBBERY OF VARIOUS SALONS AND CLUBS IN CHICAGO THAT HE ENCOUNTERED NOT ONLY BECAUSE OF HIS RURAL BACKGROUND BUT ALSO BECAUSE AS A LIBERAL LAWYER HE DEFENDED THE RIGHTS OF WORKING-CLASS IMMIGRANTS AND STRIKERS."

imperatives of Monroe or Pound: the question then is what aesthetics it does reflect or create.

"Carl Hamblin," a poem in Edgar Lee Masters' 1915 bestseller *Spoon River Anthology*, provides information about those incompletely erased aesthetics and the conditions of their erasure. Counterpointing the allegorical language of dream-revelation with the grotesque imagery of Midwestern popular justice, the poem links the publication of poetry to the free speech agendas of late nineteenth-century newspapers and thus to the censorship of the press surrounding the 1886 Haymarket incident.

> The press of the Spoon River *Clarion* was wrecked,
> And I was tarred and feathered,
> For publishing this on the day the Anarchists were hanged in Chicago:
> "I saw a beautiful woman with bandaged eyes
> Standing on the steps of a marble temple.
> Great multitudes passed in front of her,
> Lifting their faces to her imploringly.
> In her left hand she held a sword.
> She was brandishing the sword,
> Sometimes striking a child, again a laborer,
> Again a slinking woman, again a lunatic.
> In her right hand she held a scale;
> Into the scale pieces of gold were tossed
> By those who dodged the strokes of the sword.
> A man in a black gown read from a manuscript:
> 'She is no respecter of persons.'
> Then a youth wearing a red cap
> Leaped to her side and snatched away the bandage.
> And lo, the lashes had been eaten away
> From the oozy eye-lids;
> The eye-balls were seared with a milky mucus;
> The madness of a dying soul
> Was written on her face—
> But the multitude saw why she wore the bandage."

In accordance with other poems in *Spoon River*, Hamblin's epitaph delves beneath the surface of small town appearances and exposes a hidden, complicated, and often sordid inner life. In this respect the book is a modernist project, combining lyric dramatic monologues and tones of romantic nostalgia with the harsher elements of naturalism and Gilded Age yellow journalism, not only undermining commonly held beliefs but also disturbing our perspectives on the town so many times that, in the end, generalization itself becomes a suspect activity. Bearing this in mind, I want to trace in this essay one of the many socio-aesthetic relationships whose presence helps shape *Spoon River*.

The speaker of "Carl Hamblin" embodies to some degree our preconceptions of Gilded Age journalists—his zealous enthusiasm for the work of exposing civic corruption, for example, extends into the afterlife. Part of his ongoing work in that role, I propose, is that he serves as a marker for a cultural moment since edited from popular memory: such characters may seem unlikely to us as publishers of poetry or as the guardians of culture in any sense, yet here is a journalist whose signature act is to publish a poem. If we set these prejudices aside, however, and think about the psychic and linguistic work that poetry does, Hamblin's apparent investment in establishing a connection between poetry and his work as a journalist begins to make sense.

"Carl Hamblin" suggests that poetry's presence in a journalistic setting serves an integral purpose: namely, poetry can interpret the news with more freedom than journalists are usually permitted. In this case, the use of poetry allows Hamblin to reframe the Haymarket episode, and thus the work of the Anarchists, in narratives larger than the struggle between McCormick Harvester and the Eight-Hour-Day Movement. The image of a youth in red changing forever the appearance of national icons evokes the (then freshly disturbing) history of the Paris Commune and subsequent changes in that city's structure, which had already inspired the construction of armories and the enlistment of National Guards in American cities (Painter 18–24). From a pro-labor perspective, the incident signifies a change in working-class consciousness, an epistemological break. The youth sabotages America's image

as a classless society and discredits the judicial system as a fair and impartial producer of truth. Foregrounding the interwoven mechanisms of our truth-producing systems (poetry, journalism, the judicial system, and "community standards"), the poem thus reproduces many of the rhetorical gestures of the Haymarket Anarchists. Further, the genre of poetry allows the newspaper to incorporate a voice with a much higher level of authority than journalists usually enjoy. Reading the historic event in terms of more widely accepted mythic systems, the poem's voice imitates the style of Biblical dream-prophecy, issuing a double message of indictment (of the dominant culture, the captors) and promise (to the chosen ones, of a way out of captivity). The judgment on the Anarchists (reinscribed by the attack on Carl Hamblin's press) turns out to be a judgment on the dominant culture.

By implicating small-town or rural America in Carl Hamblin's demise, the testimonies in Masters' book suggest that despite perennial proclamations about First Amendment rights, there is something quintessentially American about "Judge Lynch." The event seems completely in keeping with the Southern Illinoisian tradition of lynch mobs—one thinks here of the 1835 death of the Alton abolitionist, Reverend Elijah P. Lovejoy, shot and killed while attempting to repair his press after its fourth wrecking. Further, *Spoon River Anthology*'s appearance in 1915, in *Poetry*'s Chicago, almost twenty years after the Haymarket incident and in a literary environment where Ezra Pound's influence was already beginning to be felt, means that this part of the book was very likely to be read as an attack upon American provincialism and upon the limited space open in this cultural backwater to "true" poets.

Yet the surface potential in "Carl Hamblin" for appropriation into a literary-historical narrative of rural America's "backwardness" contrasts sharply with Masters' account of his own relationships to Chicago and the newspaper industry as a poet. Masters' complaints in his autobiography, *Across Spoon River*, are directed primarily at the snobbery of various salons and clubs in Chicago that he encountered not only because of his rural background but also because as a liberal lawyer he defended the rights of working-class immigrants and strikers. *Across Spoon River* provides evidence of support for poets from the newspaper community in the Midwest. For example, Masters wrote *Spoon River* at the urging of William M. Reedy, who published many of Masters' poems, including early parts of *Spoon River*, in the St. Louis *Mirror*.

Although "Carl Hamblin" allegorizes the multi-level suppression of the Radical Left's voice in America, indicting American society for its hypocritical and murderous pretense of "classlessness," at the same time it testifies to the presence, even in Spoon River, of critical thinking, political dissent, journalistic integrity, poetic visions, and social idealism. Marking what Paul Avrich refers to as "the first 'Red Scare' in American History" (xii), the poem records a moment when poems could be published in newspapers and function significantly alongside material more familiar to us as journalism, and when poetry's implication in newspaper commitments to explicit political agendas, presumably including the practices of free speech and social criticism, was taken for granted.

The cultural indictment of the poem should be turned in another direction, then, if we are to explore the connection of "American" and "Judge Lynch" without consenting to the premises of an Eliot/Pound-inspired version of American literary history. Since a significant portion of the Radical Left's discursive efforts during the period 1880–1940 took the form of poetry and song, literary historians' collaboration in representing America as a cultural wasteland worked together with other discourses to function, even if inadvertently (and Pound's well-known broadcast career makes this an unlikely possibility), as political censorship . . . .

Source: Hester L. Furey, "Poetry and Rhetoric of Dissent in Turn-of-the-Century Chicago," in *Modern Fiction Studies*, Vol. 38, No. 3, Fall 1992, pp. 671–86.

Carl Van Doren

In the following excerpt, Van Doren characterizes Spoon River Anthology *as the first example of "the newest style" in American fiction and as an example of "revolt from the village" literature.*

The newest style in American fiction dates from the appearance, in 1915, of *Spoon River Anthology*, though it required five years for the influence of that book to pass thoroughly over

> AN ADMIRABLE SCHEME OCCURRED TO HIM: HE WOULD IMAGINE A GRAVEYARD SUCH AS EVERY AMERICAN VILLAGE HAS AND WOULD EQUIP IT WITH EPITAPHS OF A RUTHLESS VERACITY SUCH AS NO VILLAGE EVER SAW PUT INTO WORDS."

from poetry to prose. For nearly half a century native literature had been faithful to the cult of the village, celebrating its delicate merits with sentimental affection and with unwearied interest digging into odd corners of the country for persons and incidents illustrative of the essential goodness and heroism which, so the doctrine ran, lie beneath unexciting surfaces. Certain critical dispositions, aware of agrarian discontent or given to a preference for cities, might now and then lay disrespectful hands upon the life of the farm; but even these generally hesitated to touch the village, sacred since Goldsmith in spite of Crabbe, sacred since Washington Irving in spite of E. W. Howe.

The village seemed too cosy a microcosm to be disturbed. There it lay in the mind's eye, neat, compact, organized, traditional. . . . Mr. Howe in *The Story of a Country Town* had long ago made it cynically clear—to the few who mad him—that villages which prided themselves upon their pioneer energy might in fact be stagnant backwaters or dusty centers of futility, where existence went round and round while elsewhere the broad current moved away from them. Mark Twain in "The Man that Corrupted Hadleyburg" had more recently put it bitterly on record that villages which prided themselves upon their simple virtues might from lack of temptation have become a hospitable soil for meanness and falsehood, merely waiting for the proper seed. And Clarence Darrow in his elegiac "Farmington" had insisted that one village at least had been the seat of as much restless longing as of simple bliss. *Spoon River Anthology* in its different dialect did little more than to confirm these mordant, neglected testimonies.

That Mr. Masters was not neglected must be explained in part, of course, by his different dialect. The Greek anthology had suggested to him something which was, he said, "if less than verse, yet more than prose"; and he went, with the step of genius, beyond any "formal resuscitation of the Greek epigrams, ironical and tender, satirical and sympathetic, as casual experiments in unrelated themes," to an "epic rendition of modern life" which suggests the novel in its largest aspects. An admirable scheme occurred to him: he would imagine a graveyard such as every American village has and would equip it with epitaphs of a ruthless veracity such as no village ever saw put into words. The effect was as if all the few honest epitaphs in the world had suddenly come together in one place and sent up a shout of revelation.

Conventional readers had the thrill of being shocked and of finding an opportunity to defend the customary reticences; ironical readers had the delight of coming upon a host of witnesses to the contrast which irony perpetually observes between appearance and reality; readers militant for the "truth" discovered an occasion to demand that pious fictions should be done away with and the naked facts exposed to the sanative glare of noon. And all these readers, most of them unconsciously no doubt, shared the fearful joy of sitting down at an almost incomparably abundant feast of scandal. Where now were the mild decencies of Tiverton, of Old Chester, of Friendship Village? The roofs and walls of Spoon River were gone and the passers-by saw into every bedroom; the closets were open and all the skeletons rattled undenied; brains and breasts had unlocked themselves and set their most private treasures out for the most public gaze.

It was the scandal and not the poetry of *Spoon River*, criticism may suspect, which particularly spread its fame. Mr. Masters used an especial candor in affairs of sex, an instinct which, secretive everywhere, has rarely ever been so much so as in the American villages of fiction, where love ordinarily exhibited itself in none but the chastest phases, as if it knew no savage vagaries, transgressed no ordinances, shook no souls out of the approved routines. Reaction from too much sweet drove Mr. Masters naturally to too much sour; sex in Spoon River slinks and festers, as if it were an instinct which had not been schooled—however imperfectly—by thousands of years of human society to some modification of its rages and some civil direction of its restless

power. But here, as with the other aspects of behavior in his village, he showed himself impatient, indeed violent, toward all subterfuges. There is filth, he said in effect, behind whited sepulchers; drag it into the light and such illusions will no longer trick the uninstructed into paying honor where no honor appertains and will no longer beckon the deluded to an imitation of careers which are actually unworthy.

Spoon River has not even the outward comeliness which the village of tradition would possess: it is slack and shabby. Nor is its decay chronicled in any mood of tender pathos. What strikes its chronicler most is the general demoralization of the town. Except for a few saints and poets, whom he acclaims with a lyric ardor, the population is sunk in greed and hypocrisy and—as if this were actually the worst of all—complacent apathy. Spiritually it dwindles and rots; externally it clings to a pitiless decorum which veils its faults and almost makes it overlook them, so great has the breach come to be between its practices and its professions. Again and again its poet goes back to the heroic founders of Spoon River, back to the days which nurtured Lincoln, whose shadow lies mighty, beneficent, too often unheeded, over the degenerate sons and daughters of a smaller day; and from an older, robuster integrity Mr. Masters takes a standard by which he morosely measures the purposelessness and furtiveness and supineness and dulness of the village which has forgotten its true ancestors.

Anger like his springs from a poetic elevation of spirit; toward the end *Spoon River Anthology* rises to a mystical vision of human life by comparison with which the scavenging epitaphs of the first half seem, though witty, yet insolent and trivial. It is perhaps not necessary to point out that the numerous poets and novelists who have learned a lesson from the book have learned it less powerfully from the difficult later pages than from those in which the text is easiest.

Mr. Masters himself has not always remembered the harder and better lesson. During a half dozen years he has published more than a half dozen books which have all inherited the credit of the *Anthology* but which all betray the turbulent, nervous habit of experimentation which makes up a large share of his literary character. There comes to mind the figure of a blindfolded Apollo, eager and lusty, who continually runs forward on the trail of poetry and truth but who, because of his blindfoldedness, only now and then strikes the central track. Five of Mr.

Masters's later books are collections of miscellaneous verse; during the fruitful year 1920 he undertook two longer flights of fiction. In *Mitch Miller* he attempted in prose to write a new *Tom Sawyer* for the Spoon River district; in *Domesday Book* be applied the method of *The Ring and the Book* to the material of Starved Rock. The impulse of the first must have been much the same as Mark Twain's: a desire to catch in a stouter net than memory itself the recollections of boyhood which haunt disillusioned men. But as Mr. Masters is immensely less boylike than Mark Twain, elegy and argument thrust themselves into the chronicle of Mitch and Skeet, with an occasional tincture of a fierce hatred felt toward the politics and theology of Spoon River. A story of boyhood, that lithe, muscular age, cannot carry such a burden of doctrine. The narrative is tangled in a snarl of moods. Its movement is often thick, its wings often gummed and heavy.

The same qualities may be noted in *Domesday Book*. Its scheme and machinery are promising: a philosophical coroner, holding his inquest over the body of a girl found mysteriously dead, undertakes to trace the mystery not only to its immediate cause but up to its primary source and out to its remotest consequences. At times the tale means to be an allegory of America during the troubled, rolled, destroying years of the war; at times it means to be a "census spiritual" of American society. Elenor Murray, in her birth and love and sufferings and desperate end, is represented as pure nature, "essential genius," acting out its fated processes in a world of futile or corrupting inhibitions. But Mr. Masters has less skill at portraying the sheer genius of an individual than at arraigning the inhibitions of the individual's society. When he steps down from his watchtower of irony he can hate as no other American poet does. His hates, however, do not always pass into poetry; they too frequently remain hard, sullen masses of animosity not fused with his narrative but standing out from it and adding an unmistakable personal rhythm to the rough beat of his verse. So, too, do his heaps of turgid learning and his scientific speculations often remain undigested. A good many of his characters are cut to fit the narrative plan, not chosen from reality to make up the narrative. The total effect is often crude and heavy; and yet beneath these uncompleted surfaces are the sinews of enormous power: a greedy gusto for life, a wide imaginative experience, tumultuous uprushes of emotion and expression, an acute if undisciplined intelligence,

great masses of the veritable stuff of existence out of which great novels are made.

Source: Carl Van Doren, "New Style: The Revolt from the Village," in *Contemporary American Novelist: 1900–1920*, Macmillan, 1922, pp. 132–76.

Conrad Aiken

In the following essay, Aiken argues that Masters is a positive realist writer.

Mr. Masters is a welcome, though perplexing, figure in contemporary American poetry. Welcome, because along with Mr. Frost, and perhaps Mr. Robinson and Mr. Sandburg, he is a realist, and because a vigorous strain of realism is so profoundly needed in our literature today—as indeed it has always been needed. Perplexing, because his relative importance, as posterity will see it, is so extraordinarily difficult to gauge. Of his welcome there can be no question. There has been a disposition among poets and critics of poetry during the last three years to assume that the most important changes, or revolutions, taking place in American poetry at present are those that regard form. The Imagists and other free verse writers have found their encomiasts, and to them the renewed vitality of American poetry has in consequence been a little too freely ascribed. No one will deny that the current changes in poetic form—the earlier blind revolt, the later effort to mint new forms which shall be organic—have their value. But we should not forget that of equal and possibly greater importance has been the attempt of our realists to alter not merely the form of poetry but also its content. What Mr. [John] Masefield and Mr. [Wilfrid Wilson] Gibson did in England, it remained for Mr. Masters and Mr. Frost to do in America. The influence of *Spoon River Anthology* and *North of Boston* can hardly yet be estimated.

Mr. Masters is [a realistic artist], though there are traces in him of the [lyric artist] as well. The curious thing is that while he frequently manifests a vivid desire to employ the lyric kind of magic, he nearly always fails at it; his average of success with the realistic magic is consistently very much higher. He is essentially a digger-out of facts, particularly of those facts which regard the mechanism of human character. In the presence of richly human material—the sufferings, the despairs, the foolish illusions, the amazing overweenings of the individual man or woman—he has the cold hunger of the microscope. Curiosity is his compelling motive, not the desire for beauty. He is insatiable for facts and events, for the secrets of human behaviour.

Consequently it is as a narrator that he does his best work. He is essentially a psychological story-teller, one who has chosen for his medium not prose but verse, a tumbling and jostling and over-crowded sort of verse, which, to be sure, frequently becomes prose. Was Mr. Masters wise in making this choice? He is by nature extremely loquacious and discursive—it appears to be painful for him to cut down to mere essentials—and prose would seem to be a more natural medium for such a mind. But while he almost always fails to compress his material to the point where it becomes singly powerful, it is only the fact that he uses a verse form which compels him to compress at all; and it is also clear that at his moments of keenest pleasure in dissective narration he can only experience satis-faction in a verse of sharply accentuated ictus. It is at these moments that his work takes on the quality of realistic magic, the magic of vivid action, dra-matic truthfulness, muscular reality. We are made to feel powerfully the thrust and fecundity of human life, particularly its animalism, we are also made to feel its struggle to be, or to believe itself; something more. It is in the perception and expres-sion of this something more that Mr. Masters chiefly fails, not because he is not aware of it (he repeatedly makes it clear that he is, though not of course in the guise of sentimentality) but because at this point his power and felicity of expression aban-don him.

There is no poet in America today whose work is so amazingly uneven, whose sense of values is so disconcertingly uncertain. While in some respects Mr. Masters's intellectual equipment is richer than that of any of his rivals, it has about it also some-thing of the *nouveau riche*. Much of his erudition seems only half digested, much of it is inaccurate, much of it smells of quackery or the woman's page of the morning paper. Much of it too is dragged in by the heels and is very dull reading. Moreover, this uncertainty—one might almost say unripe-ness—besets Mr. Masters on the aesthetic plane quite as clearly as on the intellectual. To put it synaesthetically, he appears not to know a yellow word from a purple one. He goes from a passage of great power to a passage of bathos, from the viv-idly true to the blatantly false, from the incisive to the dull, without the least awareness. *In Songs and Satires* one passes, in bewilderment, from "Ara-bel," remarkably sustained in atmosphere, vivid in its portraiture, skilful in its use of suspense, to the ludicrous ineffectuality of the Launcelot poem, in which many solemn events are unintentionally comic.... This means of course that Mr. Masters

is not in the thorough sense an artist. He does not know the effect of what he is doing. He is indeed, as an artist, careless to the point of recklessness. It is as if a steam dredge should become pearl diver: he occasionally finds an oyster, sometimes a pearl; but he drags up also an amazing amount of mud. His felicities and monstrosities are alike the acci-dents of temperament, not the designs of art. Hasty composition is repeatedly manifest.

And yet on the whole one is more optimistic as to the future of Mr. Masters after reading [*Songs and Satires*] than at any time since the appearance of *Spoon River Anthology*. Bad and good are still confounded, but in more encouraging propor-tions. From "Widow LaRue," "Front the Ages with a Smile," "Tomorrow is my Birthday," "Saint Deseret" one gets an almost unmixed pleasure. In these one feels the magic of reality. These poems, like "Arabel" and "In the Cage," are synthesized; and it is in this vein that one would like to see Mr. Masters continue, avoiding the pitfalls of the historical, the philosophical, the pseudo-scientific.... His influence has been widespread and wholesome. We are badly in need of poets who are unafraid to call a spade a damned shovel. And a good many of us are too ready to forget that realistic magic is quite as legitimate in poetry as lyric magic, and quite as clearly in the English tradition. If art is the effort of man to understand himself by means of self-expression, then surely it should not be all ghosts and cobwebs and soul-stuff.... Mr. Mas-ters reminds us that we are both complex and physical.

Source: Conrad Aiken, "The Two Magics: Edgar Lee Masters," in *Scepticisms: Notes on Contemporary Poetry*, Knopf, 1919, pp. 65–75.

Carl Sandburg

In the following excerpt, Sandburg, himself a famous poet, praises the highly personal nature of the poems in the Spoon River Anthology.

I saw Masters write this book [the *Spoon River Anthology*]. He wrote it in snatched mome-nts between fighting injunctions against a wait-resses' union striving for the right to picket and gain one day's rest a week, battling from court to court for compensation to a railroad engineer rendered a loathsome cripple by the defective machinery of a locomotive, having his life amid affairs as intense as those he writes of.

At The Book and Play Club one night Mas-ters tried to tell how he came to write the

Anthology. Of course, he couldn't tell. There are no writers of great books able to tell the how and why of a dominating spirit that seizes them and wrenches the flashing pages from them. But there are a few forces known that play a part. And among these Masters said he wanted emphasis placed on *Poetry,* voices calling "Unhand me," verses and lines from all manner and schools of writers welcomed in Harriet Monroe's magazine.

Once in a while a man comes along who writes a book that has his own heart-beats in it. The people whose faces took out from the pages of the book are the people of life itself, each trait of them as plain or as mysterious as in the old home valley where the writer came from. Such a writer and book are realized here.

Masters' home town is Lewiston, Illinois, on the banks of the Spoon River. There actually is such a river where Masters waded bare-foot as a boy, and where the dead and the living folk of his book have fished or swam, or thrown pebbles and watched the widening circles. It is not far, less than a few hours' drive, from where Abraham Lincoln was raised. People who knew Lincoln are living there today.

Well, some two hundred and twenty portraits in free verse have been etched by Masters from this valley. They are Illinois people. Also they are the people of anywhere and everywhere in so-called civilization.

Aner Clute is the immortal girl of the streets. Chase Henry is the town drunkard of all time. The railroad lawyer, the corrupt judge, the prohibitionist, the various adulterers and adulteresses, the Sunday School superintendent, the mothers and fathers who lived for sacrifice in gratitude, joy—all these people look out from this book with haunting eyes, and there are baffled mouths and brows calm in the facing of their destinies.

In the year 1914 Masters not only handled all of his regular law practice, heavy and grilling. Besides, he wrote the *Spoon River Anthology.* There were times when he was clean fagged with the day's work. But a spell was on him to throw into written form a picture gallery, a series of short movies of individuals he had seen back home. Each page in the anthology is a locked-up portrait now freed....

There is vitality, drops of heart blood, poured into Lee Masters' book. He has other books in him as vivid and poignant. Let us hope luck holds

him by the hand and takes him along where he can write out these other ones.

Source: Carl Sandburg, "Notes for a Review of *The Spoon River Anthology,*" in *Little Review,* Vol. 2, No. 3, May 1915, pp. 42–43.

Floyd Dell

In the following excerpt, Dell commends Spoon River Anthology *for the inclusiveness with which it treats small-town life and inhabitants.*

It is laid up as a charming fault against many if not most poets that they are chiefly interested in themselves. . . .

But when the poet appears who cannot but see in the faces of men and women the half-confessed secrets of pride and passion, who cannot but observe and reflect upon the course of their loves and hatreds, and who if he searches his own heart does so to discover what these other people are like—when such a poet appears, we mix our affectionate admiration with a deeper respect. For if we seek in his pictures, as we are said to seek instinctively in all literature, for our own likeness, we find it mirrored against a more significant background, moving to sterner and more ironic destinies. It is for that reason that we concede to such poetry, almost against our preferences, the title "great."

And it is for that reason that we are likely to find a strange impressiveness, akin to greatness, in the *Spoon River Anthology* of Edgar Lee Masters. It is the work of a man who has seen much of life with curious eyes, brooded much upon its subtle and ironic patterns, and traced those patterns for us with grave candor. It is a book which, whether one likes it or not, one must respect.

There are excellent reasons for disliking the *Spoon River Anthology.* For one thing, it is couched in free verse which many will find harsh and unmelodious. For another, its language is curt and factual often to the point of baldness, and is almost entirely lacking not merely in rhetorical adornments but in the imaginative and atmospheric use of words. It is indeed almost wanting in the ordinary properties of verse—though here and there a beautiful cadence, a striking simile, or a richly imaginative phrase appears, like a rose suddenly flowering out of one of those stone-fences that shoulder their way between raw-furroughed New England fields.

But in this curt, undemonstrative language there is set forth the history of an Illinois town, its lives, its passions, its aspirations, its failures. Sordid and splendid, pathetic and obscene, the life of Spoon River reveals itself. The way in which Mr. Masters has put this life before us is in a series of epitaphs—such epitaphs as were never carved on any gravestone. Sometimes it is as though the dead, with the clear light of perfect understanding flooding in upon their still warm passions, spoke for the first time truly of their lives. But for the most part these speaking shades still keep their old illusions, and are what they were in life save in one thing only: they look back and not forward. Quietly or with a shadowy anger, tenderly or ironically, but always briefly, they tell of themselves, adding their tag of ghostly wisdom, or some message to the living, or some comment on the world that still wags on.

We are presently to hear the story of Old Bill Piersol, and of the judge who sentenced Hod Putt; of the judge's son and daughter, and of those they loved; of the village puritan, who is indignant that lovers' kisses should be exchanged over his grave; of the saloonkeeper that was put out of business by the puritan; of the men who found happiness in drink, and their wives; of the preacher, and the village atheist; of the girl who ran away from home, and the one who came back to her father's house to nurse an old grief; of those who loved books, and had visions; of those who beat life at her game, and those whom life cheated.

Gradually the story of Spoon River takes shape in one's mind. Figures pass and repass, seen from the angle of this man or that woman. Secrets are revealed. The whole life of the community in thought and action, high intention and tawdry accident, is unrolled. The feeling that we are in touch with actuality comes to compensate for the intensity and beauty which we are accustomed to expect as the knock to which we open our sympathies. Against these emotions, so bluntly and yet so truly represented, we feel that we have no right to shut our hearts. . . .

And at the end one has not only been made to respond to the varying passions of these people of Spoon River, but has been cast under the spell of the author's own attitude toward life, which is deeply ironic. If we share, as most of us do, the cheerful American romanticism about life, a romanticism in which the disturbing fact of death cannot be said to have any place, it is something of a triumph for the author's art to have made us feel, even if only for a little while, that it is toward death that life leads, and that this is the final secret of life.

Whether the art of this book has any relation to the art of poetry is a delicate question. The theory of free verse has been expounded of late with obscure precision by the professors of unacademic art, and its rules laid down with enthusiastic severity. One would not like to contradict them, and still less would one desire to repudiate, even in the interest of such a work as this one, the honorable tradition of verbal beauty and intensity in poetry. It is perhaps more profitable to consider whether the author's point of view is not in one respect a serious limitation. Every artist is entitled to his own philosophy. But in reading the *Spoon River Anthology* one feels that its author's high ironic attitude toward life cuts him off from appreciation of what is perhaps the most fundamental and characteristic thing in America—a humorous faith, a comedic courage, a gay and religious confidence in the goodness of things. A poet immersed in this American romanticism would give a more complete account of American life; and would be perhaps the better philosopher.

Source: Floyd Dell, "*Spoon River* People," in *New Republic*, Vol. 2, No. 24, April 17, 1915, pp. 14–15.

SOURCES

"Achievements in Public Health, 1900—1990: Healthier Mothers and Babies," in *Morbidity and Mortality Weekly Report*, Centers for Disease Control, Vol. 48, No. 38, October 1, 1999, pp. 849–58.

Brewster, Paul G., *Children's Games and Rhymes*, Arno Press, 1976, p. 123.

"Census 2000 Population Statistics," in *U. S. Department of Transportation: Federal Highway Administration*, http://www.fhwa.dot.gov/planning/census/cps2k.htm (accessed June 16, 2010).

Haines, Michael R., "Illinois Population by Race, Sex, Age, Nativity, and Urban-rural Residence: 1800–1990," Table Aa3300-3396, in *Historical Statistics of the United States, Earliest Times to the Present: Millennial Edition*, Cambridge University Press, 2006.

Henderson, Alice Corbin, Review of *Spoon River Anthology*, in *Poetry*, June 1915, pp. 146–47, reprinted in *Twentieth-Century Literary Criticism*, Vol. 2, edited by Dedria Bryfonski, Gale Research, 1979.

Hallwas, John E., "Introduction," in *Spoon River Anthology: An Annotated Edition*, University of Illinois Press, 1992, pp. 67–68.

Masters, Edgar Lee, *Across Spoon River: An Autobiography*, University of Illinois Press, 1991, p. 7.

———, "Lucinda Matlock," in *Spoon River Anthology*, Dover Publications, 1992, pp. 106–107.

Russell, Herbert K., *Edgar Lee Masters: A Biography*, University of Illinois Press, 2001, p. 223.

Wrenn, John H., and Margaret M. Wrenn, *Edgar Lee Masters*, Twayne Publishers, 1983, pp. 58–61.

FURTHER READING

Hollander, John, "Voice of America," in *New Republic*, July 27, 1992, pp. 47–53.
> In reviewing the release of *Spoon River Anthology: An Annotated Edition*, Hollander gives a comprehensive overview of Masters's career and literary reputation.

Lowell, Amy, "Edgar Lee Masters and Carl Sandburg," in *Tendencies in Modern American Poetry*, Houghton Mifflin, 1921, 129–235.
> Lowell, one of America's great poets, draws connections between two of the most famous poets of her time while they were both at the peak of their careers.

Primeau, Ronald, *Beyond Spoon River: The Legacy of Edgar Lee Masters*, University of Texas Press, 1981.
> This book provides an analysis of Masters's life and his works by one of the premier Masters scholars.

Riney-Kehrberg, Pamela, "The Limits of Community: Martha Friesen of Hamilton County, Kansas," in *Midwestern Women Work, Community, and Leadership at the Crossroads*, edited by Lucy Eldersveld Murphy and Wendy Hamand Venet, Indiana University Press, 1998, pp. 48–60.
> This scholarly study of women's roles in pioneer life in the Midwest looks at one specific example to show the effects of isolation.

SUGGESTED SEARCH TERMS

Lucinda Matlock AND Edgar Lee Masters

Edgar Lee Masters AND Spoon River

Lucinda Matlock AND age

Spoon River Anthology AND modernism

Edgar Lee Masters AND T. S. Eliot

Edgar Lee Masters AND nature

Spoon River Anthology AND aging

Edgar Lee Masters AND Illinois

Illinois AND natural remedies

Edgar Lee Masters AND Squire Davis Masters

Most Satisfied by Snow

DIANA CHANG

1974

Although best known as a novelist of works dealing with themes of ethnicity and identity, the Chinese American writer Diana Chang is also an acclaimed poet. Chang's poetry deals occasionally with themes similar to those found in her novels, but her poems also take inspiration from the world of nature. These poems often have a meditative feel in their brevity and in their quiet, contemplative voice. In this short free-verse poem (a poem without metrical or rhyme patterns), her contemplation of the natural world serves as a springboard for larger philosophical explorations. She touches on the notions of personal growth and the significance of an individual in relation to his or her environment. Using only twenty-five words, Chang captures details that form more expansive images in the reader's mind that in turn are transformed by Chang's spare language about substance and matter into musings about personal identity, transformation, and relevance.

Originally published by Washington Square Press in 1974 in *Asian-American Heritage: An Anthology of Prose and Poetry*, edited by David Hsin-Fu Wand, "Most Satisfied by Snow" later appeared in Chang's 1984 poetry collection *What Matisse is After*, published by Contact II Publications. The poem can also be found in the textbook *Prentice Hall Literature: Timeless Voices, Timeless Themes: The American Experience*, published by Prentice Hall in 2002.

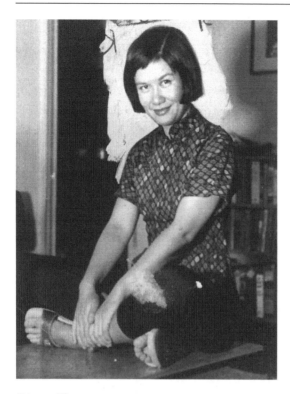

Diana Chang (The Library of Congress)

AUTHOR BIOGRAPHY

Born in New York in 1934, Chang moved with her parents to China when she was an infant. Her father, K. C. Chang, was a Chinese architect, and her mother, Eva Lee, was an American of Eurasian (a mixture of European and Asian backgrounds) descent. Chang was raised in Beijing and Shanghai, among other Chinese cities, and she attended school in the international sector of Shanghai. After World War II ended in 1945, Chang completed high school before returning to the United States, where she entered Barnard College. She graduated in 1949, having studied philosophy, English, and creative writing. Living in New York City, Chang worked as an editor for a book publishing firm and began writing her first novel *The Frontiers of Love*, which was published in 1956.

Between 1959 and 1978, Chang wrote five more novels. In 1979, Chang once again became affiliated with Barnard College, serving as an adjunct associate professor of creative writing. She also worked as a literary editor. While editing the literary journal, the *American Pen*, Chang published her first volume of poetry, *The Horizon*

Is Definitely Speaking, in 1982. This collection was followed by *What Matisse Is After* (1984), the volume that contains "Most Satisfied by Snow." Chang published other poetry collections, as well as several short stories, during the 1980s and 1990s and has won a number of prestigious literary awards, including a John Hay Whitney Opportunity fellowship and a Fulbright scholarship. She published short stories and poetry regularly in several literary journals and was actively involved in sharing her talents through the Asian American Writer's Workshop in New York City, and in the East End Poetry Workshop on Long Island. As an artist, Chang displayed her work in showings in New York. Chang died on February 19, 2009.

POEM SUMMARY

Stanza 1

"Most Satisfied by Snow" is divided into five short units, or stanzas. A stanza is a division of poetry in which lines are grouped in such a way as to emphasize particular themes, ideas, or images. Stanzas are used to divide poetry in the same way that paragraphs divide prose. The first stanza of Chang's poem is the longest of the five, containing three lines, while the others contain only two. In the first stanza, Chang describes fog pressing against the windows. Chang employs the technique of personification in this stanza, when she states that the fog understands what it needs to do. (Personification is the attribution of human characteristics to nonhuman things.) The poet also suggests that the fog is not alone in knowing what to do. One can read the line as an implication either that the poet, like the fog, knows what it should be doing or that the fog and something or someone else also knows. The meaning is unclear at this point in the poem, but it is elaborated on as the poem progresses.

Stanza 2

In the next brief stanza, Chang describes the way spaces become a part of us also. She links the second stanza with the first, suggesting that the spaces are like the fog in their ability to do their job. Her imagery, as well as her use of a comma in the second line, keeps the pace of the poem slow, forcing the reader to contemplate the idea at hand. Specifically, the reader must wonder how spaces are something that can be spread throughout a person, perceived in every part of one's being. The linkage of fog and spaces suggests similarities between the two apparently opposite notions. Fog fills up the space outside, and spaces fill up an individual. What Chang does not address is the nature of the spaces she mentions. It is possible she refers to pockets of emptiness, empty spaces that people carry around inside of them. On the other hand, she might be using the idea of spaces to denote the more specific concept of place, perhaps suggesting that people are shaped by the places that have influenced them.

Stanza 3

The third stanza incorporates the use of a first-person speaker. While a speaker or narrator is often implied in poetry, poets sometimes use the first-person voice (where the narrator is referred to as "I") to convey thoughts in the poem. Often this speaker may be associated with the poet, although it is not always safe to make such an assumption. In the case of "Most Satisfied by Snow," there are few discernable clues that would suggest the "I" of the poem is not Chang herself, as it is primarily a meditation inspired by nature. In the third stanza, Chang states that when she is contemplating snow, a particular understanding overcomes her, a revelation she does not explore further until next stanza. This narrator is also implied in the earlier stanzas through the use of personal pronouns.

Stanza 4

In this tiny stanza, consisting of two one-word lines, Chang insists that physical substance has significance. Using variants of words that have the same sound and spelling but different meanings—matter as substance and matter as significance—Chang playfully incorporates science and philosophy into a contemplative nature poem apparently about fog and snow. Only on the surface is the poem concerned with weather, as these natural elements inspire grander thoughts. Contemplating the snow, Chang realizes how everything—natural elements like fog and snow and more metaphysical notions like the spaces inside people—has weight and significance and meaning. (Metaphysics is a branch of philosophy that explores the nature of concepts that transcend the physical world and the relationship between the mind and its perception of reality.)

Stanza 5

The last stanza is almost as brief as the preceding stanza, consisting of only three words. Once again using the first-person voice, Chang observes

the way she blossoms, just as her ideas regarding the significance of matter have flowered, or unfolded into being, in the previous stanza. The use of natural imagery has progressed from the fog of the initial stanza, to the snow of the third, to the flowers suggested in the final stanza. This temporal movement, almost from season to season, highlights the sense of gradual development, related not only to the passage of time but also to the formation of ideas. Again, this slow pace bolsters the sense of the meditative nature of the poem. Additionally, the image of the poet herself blossoming implies personal transformation or an evolution of ideas and of identity.

THEMES

Nature

Much of Chang's poetry is inspired by nature, and in many ways, "Most Satisfied by Snow" is a nature poem. As is common in nature poetry, the observed features or elements are described and wondered at, but are also examined within the context of the poet's relationship with the natural world. This is the case in "Most Satisfied by Snow." In the poem, the emphasis is placed upon the association or interaction between the poet and the natural world, while the elements themselves are discussed with a minimal amount of description. The natural elements of fog and snow are central features of the poem, and other word choices are suggestive of the natural world as well, as when Chang describes the way she blooms and flourishes. In the poem, the elements of fog and snow create connections in the poet's mind to other ideas. Fog hangs in the air, filling up the empty spaces, pressing against the windows. The snow observed by the poet is able to fully occupy the poet's focus, yet she describes the snow in even sparer terms than the fog.

It is while studying the snow, however, that Chang realizes the importance of physical substances in the world, the relevance of things like snow and fog. Chang does not make any sort of distinction or explanation regarding to whom such things matter or why they matter. She simply recognizes that snow and fog as elements have a specific function. Chang contemplates the significance of this idea that even things—such as fog and snow—do what they are supposed to do. These types of matter, she muses, have both

TOPICS FOR FURTHER STUDY

- Chang's work is deeply philosophical. Using resources such as Sharon M. Kaye and Paul Thompson's 2007 *More Philosophy for Teens: Examining Reality and Knowledge*, explore some of the philosophical issues Chang touches on in her work. Select a topic, such as the nature of identity or the perception of reality, and write a report in which you research and discuss the various philosophical arguments concerning your topic. Your report should present a basic overview of the topic and should include a summary of the viewpoints of noted philosophers. For example, a report on existentialism would necessarily discuss the viewpoint of Søren Kierkegaard, a philosopher who is regarded as the father of existentialism. Likewise, an examination of nihilism would present the arguments of Friedrich Nietzsche. Present your findings in either a written paper, a Power Point presentation, or a Web page accessible by your classmates.

- In "Most Satisfied by Snow," Chang expresses her insights on the evolutionary nature of identity. Write your own free-verse poem in which you explore your views on personal identity. Is your conception of who you are shaped by your ethnic background? Are you, like Chang, inspired by nature? Consider the way the language you employ and the structure of the poem (such as the stanzaic divisions and the line length) all contribute to its tone. Recite your poem to the class or create a visual presentation in which the text of the poem is accompanied by your artwork.

- Chang's work, including her novels and poems, often focuses on the topic of identity and occasionally on the specific notion of ethnic identity. The Hispanic American poet Juan Felipe Herrera has written a young-adult narrative poem concerned with ethnicity and identity. Form a book group to read *CrashBoomLove* (published in 1999 by the University of New Mexico Press). Contemplate the ways in which the structure of the poem helps to convey the poem's themes. How are the poem's characters shaped by their ethnicity? Create an oral presentation in which you share your findings on the relationship between ethnicity and identity in *CrashBoomLove* with the class. Alternatively, create an online blog in which book club members can discuss their insights and in which the rest of the class can take part via questions to book club members.

- Many of Chang's poems are inspired by nature. Select a nature poem from the collection *When the Rain Sings: Poems by Young Native Americans*, edited by Lee Francis and published by Simon and Schuster Books for Young Readers in 1999. Compare the Native American poem you have selected with "Most Satisfied by Snow." Are there similarities between the works? Consider differences in style. Chang is known for her judicious use of language; her poetry is extremely concise. How does the other poem utilize language? Prepare a comparative analysis of the poems and present it as a written paper, a Power Point presentation, or a Web page viewable by your classmates.

meaning and purpose. The title of the poem "Most Satisfied by Snow" underscores the significance of the natural world. It is while observing the snow that the poet arrives at the revelations regarding the significance of the physical world. The uncovering of such meaning results in the poet's satisfaction with having occupied her time observing the snowy day before her.

Identity

The theme of finding one's identity through personal transformation is finally explored in the

Snow viewed through a paned window (*Svetlana Larina | Shutterstock.com*)

final stanza of "Most Satisfied by Snow" after building gradually throughout the poem. While stanzas 1 and 3 of the poem contain references to the natural world, they also tie that world to the world of the poet. The fog does not just press against any windows; they are the poet's windows, as denoted by the use of a personal pronoun. The snow in the third stanza is the subject of direct observation by the first-person speaker of the poem, rather than being described by an unidentified voice. In these stanzas, Chang identifies an association between herself and the natural world.

Stanzas 2 and 4 focus more on the poet's thoughts on the nature of being. In the second stanza, the reader is included in the poet's musings, when she describes the way all of us are filled with spaces. As the poet begins to understand, in the fourth stanza, the value of such physical substances as snow and fog, an emotional and philosophical response is created. Chang begins to be aware of the way she herself matters. The structure of the poem suggests a relationship between Chang and the other types of matter already

discussed in the poem, specifically the fog and the snow. The final implication is that even Chang has a particular form and specific function. The poet's knowledge of this elicits a feeling of personal transformation or development. Knowing that she matters, that she too—like the snow and the fog and the more mysterious spaces—has purpose, the poet suggests in the final lines of the poem an evolution of her identity. She identifies herself as currently existing in a state of transformation.

STYLE

Free-verse Lyric Poetry

Chang's "Most Satisfied by Snow" is an example of a free-verse lyric poem. A lyric poem is typically short in length and is used to express a poet's personal thoughts, reflections, or emotions, rather than telling a story, as in a narrative poem. Lyric poems may take many forms but are characterized by a number of features, including their use of a subjective rather than an objective voice. Lyric poems often possess a musical or melodious quality and are sometimes more meditative in tone. "Most Satisfied by Snow" is a poem that possesses a meditative quality. As the poet contemplates the natural world, new personal revelations blossom in her consciousness.

Lyric poems can be highly structured or free verse. A free-verse poem does not contain a regular pattern of rhymed ending sounds (end rhyme), nor does it contain a consistent metrical structure. Meter is a consistent pattern of unaccented and accented syllables in a line of poetry. In the absence of rhyme schemes and metrical structures, poets use other tools, such as stanzaic divisions, line length, and punctuation, to link concepts and to shape their poetry. Chang divides her poem into five very brief stanzas. The lines in "Most Satisfied by Snow" are also quite short, and through the division of lines and stanzas, along with her use of commas, Chang creates pauses that enable the reader to linger over certain phrases. These pauses force the reader to slow down in specific sections of the poem, to contemplate the notions of fog, and space, and snow in the same fashion that the poet herself does.

Language and Internal Rhyme

Many of Chang's poems are characterized by the careful restraint she exhibits in the use of language. In "Most Satisfied by Snow," she uses only twenty-five words to express her thoughts. When attempting a matter of such precision, the poet must carefully select each word, and readers must assume that nothing was superfluous in the composition of the poem; every syllable counts. In this poem, there are several instances of internal rhyme. An internal rhyme exists when two or more words within a line rhyme. Chang also uses some end rhyme in the poem, although it lacks the consistency that would be required to identify it as a true rhyme scheme. Furthermore, in the fourth stanza, Chang employs the homonym pair of matter and matter. (Homonyms are words that are spelled the same and pronounced the same but have different meanings.) By using instances of internal rhyme, end rhyme, and homonyms, Chang forms connections between concepts in the poem, as when the first and third stanzas, those about fog and snow, are linked through rhyme. She additionally emphasizes meaning and adds to the meditative quality of the poem through the internal rhyme in the first line of the second stanza.

HISTORICAL CONTEXT

Asian American Literature in the 1970s

During the 1970s, Asian American literature was largely concerned with notions of ethnicity, identity, and otherness. Fiction and poetry written by Asian Americans during this time period typically featured Asian American characters dealing with the challenges of a dual identity. As Victoria M. Chang observes in the introduction to *Asian American Poetry: The Next Generation*, the 1970s was a time period during which "a string of anthologies of Asian American prose and poetry" was published. The authors of these works, Victoria Chang contends, laid the groundwork for the next group, or the "first generation" Asian American poets, who focused on issues of "culture, identity, family, politics, ethnicity, and place."

One of these anthologies was *Aiiieeeee! An Anthology of Asian American Writers*, published in 1974 and edited by Frank Chin, Jeffery Paul Chan, Lawson Fusao Inada, and Shawn Wong. According to Zhou Xiaojing in the 2005 *Form and Transformation in Asian American Literature*, the editors of *Aiiieeeee!* were interested in affirming the distinct Chinese and Japanese literary sources of Asian American literature, and they strongly criticized those Asian American writers who contributed to stereotypical notions of Asian Americans. In 1991, the editors of *Aiiieeeee!* published a new introduction to a revised version of the text, in which they reviewed their original aims. Specifically, the editors quote the 1974 introduction, demonstrating their original desire to protest the way Asian Americans had been "so long ignored and forcibly excluded from creative participation in American culture."

One of the editors, Frank Chin, had two years prior to the publication of the 1974 *Aiiieeeee!* attacked Diana Chang for incorporating into her work notions of white racism and for failing to address specifically Asian American themes in her works, yet an excerpt from Chang's novel, *The Frontiers of Love* (1956) appears in the 1974 *Aiiieeeee!* In an essay contained in the follow-up to *Aiiieeeee!*, published in 1991 as *The Big Aiiieeeee! An Anthology of Chinese American and Japanese American Literature*, edited by the same individuals as the first volume, Chin praises the authentic and honest way Chang depicts Asian Americans in her work.

COMPARE & CONTRAST

- **1970s:** While Asian American poetry is used to voice political concerns and express racial pride, it receives little critical attention during the 1970s. Some Asian American poets are published in such anthologies as the 1974 *Asian-American Heritage: An Anthology of Prose and Poetry*, edited by David Hsin-Fu Wand.

  Today: Asian American poetry is now readily available and widely reviewed. Contemporary Asian American poets include Timothy Liu, Cathy Park Hong, and Vandana Khanna.

- **1970s:** Environmentalism gains prominence as a serious movement. Many laws designed to protect the natural resources of the Untied States are passed. At the same time, an increased interest in developing U.S. oil production, in order to reduce the dependency on Middle Eastern oil, is generated following the oil embargo of 1973. During this time, oil-producing nations refuse to sell oil to the United States and to other countries that support Israel's military efforts.

  Today: As conflict in the Middle East continues to jeopardize U.S. access to oil, U.S. efforts to increase its own oil production are escalated. Environmentalists protest such efforts, particularly in light of environmental disasters such as the 2010 explosion of a BP oil rig in the Gulf of Mexico, an explosion that led to a massive oil leak.

- **1970s:** According to U.S. Census data, Americans of Asian or Pacific Islander descent comprise 0.8 percent of the U.S. population in 1970.

  Today: A 2002 report by the U.S. Census Bureau clarifies earlier census data on Asian Americans, noting that in the 1970 census, Americans of Asian Indian descent were classified in the "white" race category, while those of Vietnamese descent were classified in the in the "other" race category. In the 1980, 1990, and 2000 census questionnaires, respondents are given six different Asian racial categories from which to choose. According to the 2000 Census data, 4.2 percent of respondents report being of Asian descent. The 2010 Census expands the Asian and Pacific Islander category to include eleven different Asian and Pacific Islander backgrounds.

Environmentalism in the 1970s

With its focus on the natural world, "Most Satisfied by Snow" calls to mind the surge in environmentalism that occurred during the time period in which the poem was first written and published. Some scholars have called attention to the link between nature poetry and the evolution of environmentalism. Eugene Hargrove notes in the foreword to *Faces of Environmental Racism: Confronting Issues of Global Justice* that "the environmental movement arose quite naturally out of changes in attitude toward nature as a result of developments in landscape painting and photography, nature poetry, landscape gardening, and biological and botanical classification activities in the natural sciences."

During the 1970s, as many poets, including Chang, May Swenson, and Audre Lorde, focused much of their creative effort on works inspired by nature, a slew of environmental legislation was passed. Following the celebration of the first Earth Day, on April 22, 1970, the Clean Air Act was passed. Later the same year, the Environmental Protection Agency was signed into law. One of the most visible environmental groups was organized in 1971: the work of twelve activists who sought to draw attention to nuclear testing off the coast of Alaska marked the origins of the Greenpeace movement and organization. In 1973, the Endangered Species Act was passed by Congress.

The oil crisis of 1973 also helped to shape the way the United States viewed its energy

Frost on window pane (ELEN | Shutterstock.com)

consumption. Middle Eastern oil-producing nations created an oil embargo against nations, including the United States, that offered military support to Israel in its war with Egypt, Syria, and Jordan. (An embargo is an official ban established by one country against commercial trade with another country. The oil producing nations refused to sell oil to the United States and several other nations during the oil embargo.) While some effort was made to explore alternative fuel sources during this time, the embargo also resulted in a push to exploit more of the United States' own natural resources. The U.S. Congress approved the building of the Alaskan oil pipeline in 1973. Pipeline construction began in 1974 and continued through 1977, all the while being protested by environmental activists. In 1977, President Jimmy Carter created the U.S. Department of Energy. Also in 1977, the Soil and Water Conservation Act was passed. The following year, Congress also passed the National Energy Act, the Endangered American Wilderness Act, and the Antarctic Conservation Act.

CRITICAL OVERVIEW

Chang first garnered critical attention with the publication of her novel *The Frontiers of Love* in 1956. Chang "has been credited as the first American-born Chinese to write and publish a novel in the United States," Guiyou Huang observes in an essay on Chang for the *Columbia Guide to Asian American Literature Since 1945*. Chang's subsequent novels attracted more attention than her poetry. Eduardo de Almeida comments in his essay on Chang for *Asian American Poets: A Bio-Bibliographical Critical Sourcebook* that although "Chang's prose still commands vastly more critical attention than her poetry, scholars would do well to reconsider her poetry in light of its imagistic and experimental inclinations." In Almeida's estimation, Chang's poetry is characterized by "its sparseness and economy of language" and furthermore exhibits "a certain tonal and lyrical balance."

While Almeida discusses Chang's language and experimental style, other critics take a thematic approach to the analysis of Chang's poetry. Helena Grice, in an essay on Chang for the *Dictionary of Literary Biography*, notes that "nature is a common preoccupation in all of [Chang's] volumes of poetry." Chang also explores the notion of identity, as Carol Roh-Spaulding observes in an essay on Chang for *Asian American Novelists: A Bio-Bibliographical Critical Sourcebook*. Roh-Spaulding contends that in contrast to the broad approach Chang takes to identity issues in her novels, in her poetry the "complexities of issues of identity" are treated on a more personal level.

Reviewing the volume of poetry *What Matisse is After*, which was published in 1984 and includes "Most Satisfied by Snow," Janice Bishop states in the *The Forbidden Stitch: An Asian American Women's Anthology* that the work in this volume "is poetry with an economy of language as elegantly inclusive as the line and motion rendered by the French master [Matisse] himself." Bishop comments on Chang's metaphysical themes as well as the language and imagery in these poems, stating that "to read these poems exploring paradoxical perceptions is to breathe in the rhythmic interplay of word, image, idea, feeling."

CRITICISM

Catherine Dominic

Dominic is a novelist and a freelance writer and editor. In the following essay, she explores the philosophic components of "Most Satisfied by Snow." She demonstrates that the poem reveals the same metaphysical and existential concerns that Chang considers in her other poetry and novels.

While on the surface "Most Satisfied by Snow" is a simple nature poem, one in which the natural elements observed by the speaker inspire a meditative mindset, the poem's simplicity is deceptive. A close reading of the poem reveals the presence of deep philosophical contemplations and insights, consistent with Chang's sustained interest in philosophy. As Chang states in an interview with Leo Hamalian in *MELUS: The Journal of the Society for the Study of the Multi-Ethnic Literature of the United States*: "I seem preoccupied a lot with identity, with selfness." Chang also discusses the extent to which her status as a Chinese American informs her own sense of identity. She states that "being a Chinese-American woman is an elusive identity and a confusing one," that she doesn't always "write 'ethnic' work," and

WHAT DO I READ NEXT?

- Chang's novel *The Frontiers of Love*, originally published in 1956 and reprinted in 2000 by the University of Washington Press, explores the psychology of identity and ethnicity and was praised for its poetic language and insightful treatment of its characters and themes.

- Chang's volume of poetry *The Mind's Amazement: Poems Inspired by Paintings, Poetry, Music, Dance*, published in 1998 by Live Poets Society, contains experimental poems focusing on many philosophical themes such as the nature of perception and reality, as well as the connections between poetry and various art forms.

- *Behind My Eyes: Poems*, by the contemporary Chinese American poet and novelist Li-Young Lee, was published in 2008 by W. W. Norton. The acclaimed collection features poems concerned with immigration, memory, love, and loss.

- *American Born Chinese*, by Gene Luen Yang, published by First Second in 2007, is a young-adult graphic novel concerned with an alienated boy who confronts issues of race and identity. The boy's journey to self-awareness and self-acceptance is a key feature of the work and ties together several humorous plotlines. The work was a finalist for the National Book Award for Young People.

- A young-adult poetry collection, *Cool Salsa: Bilingual Poems on Growing Up Latino in the United States*, edited by Lori M. Carlson and published in 1994 by Henry Holt, explores some of the same themes that Chang's work contemplates, such as racial identity and finding one's place in American culture, but from a Hispanic rather than an Asian perspective.

- Jeffrey E. Foss's *Beyond Environmentalism: A Philosophy of Nature*, published in 2009 by Wiley, examines the relationship between the environment and humanity and outlines a philosophy of nature that transcends the limitations of contemporary notions of environmentalism.

that she views herself as a possession of her own imagination; she follows it, rather than the other way around. These statements help reveal Chang's fascination with the nature of identity, the nature of personal being, and the nature of one's relationship to the rest of the universe. "Most Satisfied by Snow" is a poem in which Chang gives voice to many of the philosophical concerns that inform her other writings; in it, one can identify the poet's ideas concerning the nature of reality and identity.

Scholars have noted the presence of existential themes in many of Chang's writings. Existentialism is a philosophical school of thought which holds that humans exist as individuals in a world devoid of universal human qualities or morals; for the existentialist, there are no universal truths. The existentialist view emphasizes the role of personal responsibility for one's identity and one's development, that is, one's own existence. Related schools of thought include nihilism and relativism. Both of these philosophies have strains of thought focused on a moral component. For the moral nihilist, there is an absence of universal moral truths, and in this absence, everything becomes meaningless. Other nihilists take a broader view of nothingness and meaninglessness, asserting that nothing in the universe has a real existence. For the moral relativist, morality is based on individual choices rather than guiding universal principles.

In an essay on Chang in *Asian American Poets: A Bio-Bibliographical Critical Sourcebook*, Eduardo de Almeida contends that Chang's work often deals with the "fragmentation of identity." Referencing Chang's comments about her own "autogenesis," or self-creation, Almeida observes the way such questions about personal identity expose Chang's "existential concerns" in some of her poetry. Furthermore, Almeida notes that in much of her later poetry, Chang grows increasingly concerned with "such disparate issues as the nature of reality, the relationship between philosophy and art, and the role of landscape in transforming consciousness."

Like Almeida, Carol Roh-Spaulding, in *Asian American Novelists: A Bio-Bibliographical Critical Sourcebook*, identifies an existential focus in Chang's writing. Roh-Spaulding maintains that a central theme of Chang's novels is the notion that "individuals have the terrifying freedom and responsibility to create their own identity." Roh-Spaulding refers to this belief as a "fundamentally existentialist idea."

With an understanding of the extent to which such concerns pervade Chang's writing, "Most Satisfied by Snow" can be approached with a fresh eye. The stanzas deal initially with the nature of the poet's perceptions of reality. (The branch of philosophy concerned with the nature of reality and the relationship between what the mind perceives and matter itself is known as metaphysics.) Tied up with Chang's observations on perception and reality are reflections on her relationship with the natural world. This leads to an assessment of the significance of the natural world. Finally, Chang addresses her understanding of her own identity. Throughout the course of "Most Satisfied by Snow," Chang explores metaphysics, nihilism, and existentialism, assessing the nature of reality and perception, of value and meaning, and of identity, in just twenty-five words.

In the first three stanzas, Chang explores metaphysical themes. Her perception of the natural world is juxtaposed with her notion of interior spaces. She insists that the reality of this inner world is just as important as the tangible world outside her window, just as meaningful as the snow and the fog. Chang's language calls attention to the various methods by which reality may be perceived. Visual perception is only one layer of perception in Chang's poem. The snow and the fog are visible, and yet the poet encounters them in other ways as well. The fog is recognized as a force with its own volition, or agency; it knows what it is supposed to do, and in its act of pressing against the windows, it signals to Chang that it exists as something greater than simply condensed moisture in the air. Similarly, the snow is something that is not only visible to one's eye but is also a substance with the power to completely engage the mind and senses of the viewer, in this case, the poet. Like the fog, the snow is acknowledged as an entity with more substance than its mere physical components.

When Chang, in the fourth stanza, contemplates the way physical matter has deep significance, she has already provided the reader with a means of comprehending the layers of meaning she has built as the poem has progressed. The substances she describes—and, by implication, other substances as well—matter as more than just objects. She questions the way physical elements are typically perceived and affords them a greater meaning, an innate power. In doing so, Chang offers the metaphysical suggestion that reality is more than that which we can perceive

Flowers looking for spring (tepic / Shutterstock.com)

with our senses. Her exploration of the notion of the interior, psychological spaces that contribute to one's sense of self underscores this idea. People, she suggests, are more than what they appear to be, in the same way that elements in nature have greater significance than their physical components would suggest.

The ostensibly simple sentiment expressed in the fourth stanza has another layer of meaning as well. To state that something matters, that anything matters, Chang directly takes a stand against nihilism, a concept often oversimplified with the statement that nothing matters. Chang argues against the notion of a universe devoid of substance, devoid of meaning, not only by insisting that things do in fact matter, but by demonstrating the ways in which seemingly simple or basic elements have a complexity and significance that transcends typical human modes of perception.

In the poem's final stanza, Chang explores the idea of personal identity. Chang depicts identity as a process of transformation, of

blossoming. Such a process is revealed to be the result of the greater awareness the poet gradually achieves throughout the course of the poem. This evolution of the self as Chang envisions it appears to be consistent with the critical assessments of the existential qualities of her other works. It exemplifies her understanding of the "freedom and responsibility" individuals have to shape their identity, as Roh-Spaulding discussed. It is the same self-invention Almeida observed in Chang's comments and in her writing. It reflects Chang's own words when she describes her intense focus on identity, on "self-ness," and her feeling that the notion of her personal identity is both "elusive" and "confusing." The existential view that identity is shaped by a person's own agency, rather than by universal, intrinsic human values, is evident in the active role Chang takes as the speaker in the poem. She watches, she perceives, she takes into herself the complexities of the reality around her and allows herself the opportunity to ascribe value and meaning where she may. She allows herself to be transformed. In doing so, she serves as the agent of her own transformation. Chang welcomes the opportunity to be responsible for the development of her own identity.

The distinct aspects of Chang's poem—each sentiment explored in each stanza—all act as separate windows through which Chang's philosophical insights may be viewed, accessed, and grasped, yet in many ways, the poem as a whole may be taken as an example of Chang's personal approach to her philosophical ideas. In "Most Satisfied by Snow," Chang demonstrates how something apparently small and uncomplicated can possess layers of meaning and complexity. Her contemplations of the natural world shape her ideas regarding reality and existence. Just as Almeida pointed out in regard to Chang's other poetry, the "landscape" sparks a consciousness-transforming process. On an individual, personal level, the poem and its meaning matter and are part of a process through which identity—Chang's and potentially the reader's—is shaped.

Source: Catherine Dominic, Critical Essay on "Most Satisfied by Snow," in *Poetry for Students*, Gale, Cengage Learning, 2011.

Leo Hamalian

In this interview, Hamalian and Chang discuss Chang's thoughts about writing, her influences, and her heritage.

Diana Chang is a native New Yorker, but she spent her early childhood in China, raised by her Eurasian mother and Chinese father. She returned to New York, where she attended high school and then Barnard College. After graduation, she worked full-time as an editor in book publishing. She lives presently in Manhattan and Water Mill, Long Island, New York.

Of herself Diana Chang says:

"I feel I'm an American writer whose background is Chinese. The source of my first and fourth novels was Chinese but exoticism can stand in the way of the universal that I strive for in my themes. Therefore, since I write fiction in English and am living my life in the United States of America, I've often subsumed aspects of my background in the interest of other truths and recognitions. I believe an abiding interest in character and emotion informs all my work, not only because the relationships, situations, and problems I write about arise out of the character of my protagonists, out of their personalities, but also because I seem preoccupied a lot with identity, with selfness."

In a poem called "Allegories," Diana Chang expresses one of the dominant themes in Asian American writing as well as in her own: the urge to relocate, to reshape the self. As a child, she says in the poem, she was translated from one culture to another, misplaced and found again. That re-discovery of the self is very important for Chinese-American writers, she believes. Reading through her work, one can see in Diana Chang an Americanization modified by memories of a distant but potent Chinese past. The tensions between these memories and her daily reality in a drastically different culture and language have created complex and rich fields of reference in Diana Chang, and perhaps have permitted her to transcend the limitations often associated with ethnic literature.

She is the author of six novels: *The Frontiers of Love*, (1956, 1994), *A Woman of Thirty* (1959), *A passion for Life* (1961), *The Only Game in Town* (1963), *Eye to Eye* (1974), and *A Perfect Love* (1978). Her three volumes of poetry are *The Horizon is Definitely Speaking* (1982), *What Matisse is After* (1984), and *Earth Water Light* (1991).

The Frontiers of Love, originally published by Random House, was reissued in the spring of 1994 by the University of Washington Press in a softcover trade edition, with a new introduction by Shirley Geok-lin Lim.

> IN POETRY I'M NOT DEALING WITH THE INTERACTIONS OF MY CHARACTERS NOR WITH MAKING THE WORK (THE CONSTRUCTION THAT IS A STORY OR A NOVEL) MOVE IN TIME. IN POEMS, IT MAY BE MYSELF I INDULGE; IN FICTION, IT'S THE SENSIBILITIES OF MY CHARACTERS I'M IN THE THRALL OF."

Most of this interview was conducted before an audience at the Hatch-Billops Archive in the Soho district of New York City.

Interviewer: Let's begin, Diana, with a general question to establish some necessary distinctions. How is being Chinese-American any different from being African American or Spanish-American?

Diana Chang: From time to time I ponder that question. It's a little hard for me to answer because, obviously, I have never been Chicano or Latino. I don't know their culture, nor have I read much about it. However, I feel very close to African Americans, and I've read everybody from Toni Morrison to Ralph Ellison to John Williams to Wesley Brown John and Wesley are friends of mine). African Americans are Americans who seem to me have contributed so much to this culture, politically and artistically, in every sphere. They've exercised the Constitution for all of us. In fighting for their own rights, they have fought for everyone else's, including mine.

Being a Chinese-American woman is an elusive identity and a confusing one, even to myself. I feel that I am a minority person, but as a writer I know that sometimes I don't write "ethnic" work, that often my imagination takes me to other situations, themes and voices. My imagination frequently doesn't seem to belong to me. Rather, I belong to it and wherever it takes me, I go.

People tend to see "Chinese-American" as a single category, but of course, like everyone else, we are different from one another. There are many kinds of Chinese-Americans—first generation, naturalized ones like my father, eighth generation ones who have never been to China, Eurasians like my mother born in this country, etc., etc. You might say that I am second generation because my father was first. On the other hand, because my mother was brought up here, I'm really third generation. So I have this kind of lopsided identity.

Interviewer: I wouldn't have asked that question had I not come across a remark of yours in a short story called "Falling Free." The story is about an elderly Chinese-American woman whose husband leaves her in order to return to China for good. You write: "All of us are Chinese some of the time." When are you Chinese?

Diana Chang: I was trying to say that all of us are human and that we are each one another. That was a way of saying it. Sometimes one doesn't remember why one says such a thing. I have a similar line in one of my poems. But when am I Chinese? How am I Chinese? My problem is not that I feel inadequate as an American, but I often do feel inadequate as a Chinese. I've written a short story apropos of this published by Calyx Books in an anthology, *The Forbidden Stitch*. It's called "The Oriental Contingent" and is about two Chinese-American women who meet, each trying to hide from the other that she feels inadequate as a Chinese, not as an American. Now this is a problem which I think hasn't been written about at all so I undertook to explore it a bit in this story.

Interviewer: If all of us are Chinese some of the time, when is Jim Hatch [co-director of the Archive] Chinese?

Diana Chang: When he is charming and sweet, of course, which is all of the time! The world, I think, is slowly turning Chinese. The more crowded it gets, the more Chinese it will become. The Chinese know how to live among masses of people. They know how to give others privacy under these conditions. The Chinese also do the opposite. Every Chinese, in a sense, is a born concierge. But the Chinese have a certain courage. As Paul Tillich, the philosopher and theologian, has said, there are two kinds of courage in this world. One is the courage to be yourself, as an individual. The West has that, but there's the other kind of courage—the courage to be part of something larger. I think the Chinese have the courage to be part of a tradition. I'm saying this in an intuitive way. I'm not a scholar so I won't attempt to back up any of this.

Interviewer: Where does that courage come from?

Diana Chang: I suppose from the family structure. Throughout the centuries, China never had a central government. If you didn't stick to the family or the clan, you had no protection against the world, no security at all. China, as you know, is a country made up of clans—perhaps accounting for the fact that there are only about a hundred surnames in China, a fact that always surprises Westerners. If you look through a Shanghai phone book, you will see pages upon pages of Changs or Chens or Wangs. It is the given name that is distinctive.

Interviewer: When you started on your career, there was no existing tradition among Chinese-Americans of women writing. Did that absence make it easier or harder for you to explore the interface of your two cultures in your first novel, The Frontiers of Love?

Diana Chang: When I wrote it, I didn't realize that I was writing a Chinese-American novel. Gropingly, I was merely trying to write something that I hoped would turn out to be a novel. Not having precedents? Well, I felt that I had many precedents. There were novels all over the world. I wrote this novel because I was full of feeling striving to become form.

I knew nothing about form. I started the novel as a linear sort of thing—the identity problem of a young woman who happened to be Eurasian rather than, say, an American from Wyoming. However, I didn't want it to be the story of a single Eurasian woman. So I explored the Eurasian problem in and through three main characters in order to get a variety of Eurasian identities and responses. The novel is set in pre-Communist Shanghai, once a "Eurasian" city that had been parceled off in a way that humiliated China. There was an International Settlement, a French Concession, etc. It seemed to me that Shanghai was a perfect metaphor for the problems of the three Eurasians in my novel.

Let me tell you about these Eurasians. When *Frontiers* came out, it was picked up by the emerging ethnic movement as a book about ethnicity in this country. Of course, that was a total misrepresentation—it wasn't—it was about people of mixed blood living in China, with conflicts in culture, emotions, values and the rest of it because of their parents.

I am so happy that Shirley Lim's introduction to the University of Washington Press's reissue of *The Frontiers of Love* straightens out this misconception and, among other things, puts my novel in its historical context.

In the case of one of my characters, Feng, his mother is English, his father a Chinese who has left the family. Feng is emotionally very torn by his dependent, somewhat disturbed mother and, in his not knowing what he is, in his amorphousness, he decides to fling himself bodily into the Communist cause which is trickling down from the north. What he is doing, perhaps unconsciously at some levels, is searching for a way to become more Chinese, to be totally Chinese, to deny the English aspect of himself, and thereby to be less conflicted.

Another Eurasian is named Mimi Lambert. Her father was an Australian adventurer, and her mother Chinese, both of whom have died before the beginning of the book. Orphaned, Mimi is being raised by her Chinese aunt, an upper-class woman, very cosmopolitan in style, but whose spirit is Chinese. To simplify and not give away the story, when her Swiss lover refuses to marry her, rejecting her because she is Eurasian, Mimi rejects herself, throwing herself away after that.

The third Eurasian, Sylvia Chen, is possibly the main character of the story. Her father, Liyi, represents Chinese liberalism, inchoate and vulnerable. Sylvia has a love relationship with Feng, whose political activities result in the murder of her young idealistic cousin. Through this painful experience she realizes who she is—not American like her mother and not Chinese like her father. She has to grow up to be Sylvia Chen. She must possess her own unique self.

Interviewer: Let's move to your fifth novel, Eye to Eye, *a first person narrative of a white male American visual artist who, though happily married, is obsessed to a disturbed degree with another woman. The burden of the novel is the psychoanalysis he undergoes to free himself. In this age of feminism, how should we interpret your choice of a white male voice to tell the story? Are you being ironic? What is behind your choice of narrator?*

Diana Chang: Let me explain myself a little. I not only write, but I also paint. My work has been shown in galleries in the Hamptons, and I am presently in an exhibition in East Hampton. I made my very first collage for this show, and amazingly, it sold. When I wrote *Eye to Eye,* I was steeping myself in the contemporary American art scene, painting almost secretly, and at that time not to show. I also know something

about the psychoanalytic process, having had some therapy myself.

One day it suddenly came to me that what in some cases an artist produces possibly reveals the artist's early emotional problems. I chose to tell this story through a man's point of view in the first person because I like to subsume myself and become my characters. In that sense, perhaps I should have been an actress, but given my face and body, I would be unconvincing as a cowboy or a guerrilla fighter in Uruguay. As a writer, I have more leeway—I can become anything, anyone. I decided that the book was going to be about creativity, about the act of seeing through art and seeing through psychoanalysis. I wanted my protagonist to be an artist but, at the same time, I wanted to make the protagonist Everyman in America. If I had made this artist Armenian...

Interviewer: (interrupting) That's what Kurt Vonnegut does in one of his novels.

Diana Chang: He does? I've got to read it then. Let's say I had made him a Lithuanian. It would have been the story of a Lithuanian artist in this country which would have brought other issues into the picture. If I had made the artist a woman, it would have been about what a woman artist has to struggle against. I decided to make him a WASP. I imagined the plot through the character of a WASP, thirty-six years old at the beginning and a year older by the end of the book.

In telling his own story in the first person, he reveals himself very gradually; he's full of defenses and subterfuges even with himself. I'll try to describe his work. He's not an assemblagist like Alfonso Ossorio, and he doesn't make accumulations the way Arman does. He makes scenes in the form of assemblages. And these scenes represent his early problems without his being aware of it. He has been forced to go into analysis because he's having emotional and physical difficulties—he's in love with a woman, an unattainable woman, who is not his wife. Despite the fact that the book is written in the first person and he is telling the story, the reader begins to realize his problem long before he does.

I didn't want his analyst to be a Viennese Jewish analyst. I wanted to get away from that cliche, so I made the analyst an American named Dr. Emerson. Emerson begins to see along with the reader. Part of the irony of the book is that Dr. Emerson recognizes about two-thirds through the novel that he should not have George Safford as his patient because of a relationship they have that he, the doctor, never suspected. He drops George like a hot potato. Having "transferred," George, of course, suffers intensely from a feeling of abandonment.

Interviewer: It is a very witty book. You wrote a piece for the American Pen *in 1970 called "Wool Gathering, Ventriloquism, and the Double Life." What are you suggesting by that title? That an artist always conceals true identity behind a mask?*

Diana Chang: When something bothers me, this botheration eventually results in a theme and gets written. That's the wool-gathering part of the title. As for ventriloquism? In *Eye to Eye*, until I heard George Safford's voice in the first person, I didn't have a way of saying what I was feeling. When his voice came to me, I knew that he should do the telling. I feel that he wrote the book. I mean that literally. That explains the ventriloquism. I wrote *Eye to Eye* in a great heat. It didn't take too long to write. The voice comes to one and takes over, and I feel that I have many, many voices.

As for the double life—when you have a novel inside you, it really feels like a double life. You are teaching or giving a party or you're at the dentist worrying about the pain he is going to cause you while this other thing is going on within you. Whenever I am preoccupied with writing a novel, I always keep scraps of paper with me. Once in a while I've even had to resort to my checkbook to jot down words or ideas for scenes or something or other that I knew belonged in the third part of the second chapter or wherever. Information surfaces and one lives in dread of forgetting it.

Now about the artist concealing true identity. In much minority literature, the authorial identity is the same as the protagonist's identity in the book. Like many of my poems and short stories, two of my novels have been written out of my Chinese-American background. But in my other novels, the identity of the characters is totally different from my own. In those cases, I don't think I am concealing anything—I am inventing something. I don't think invention is a form of dishonesty. Novels are imagined, invented lies which can be more truthful than actual life itself.

Interviewer: That was Oscar Wilde's contention. The art of lying. He said that the United States couldn't produce literature because it revered a man who boasted that he had never told a lie.

Diana Chang: He did say that? That's very interesting to me because so often I find people don't want to know that you've invented something. They keep saying, "Oh, isn't that based on your sister?" or something. It's as though they don't trust the imagination. So it turns out that's American. I'm glad that you said that just now.

Interviewer: To pursue this a bit further, your writing strikes me as almost anti-autobiographical. Do you think that term fits your work?

Diana Chang: I have not avoided using my own background as a source—two of my novels were informed by my own identity, as well as several of my short stories and many of my poems. It's true that some authors, take James T. Farrell, for instance, mine a single environment all their writing lives, and make it their own. But I am simply more restless and perhaps less self-referential. For example, as a painter, I've worked in oils, pastels, acrylics and more recently in watercolors; I've explored geometric paintings as well as representational ones and at this point find that semi-abstract landscapes come most naturally. I guess it's in my temperament to seek variety and change.

But as I've said, I follow my imagination, and how can I not relate to the humanity in themes, situations and characters whose orientation, so to speak, is not only Chinese or Chinese-American or Eurasian, female and 93 lbs fully dressed? I'm living my life among all kinds of people, and each one of them is an arena of possibilities, and almost each aspect of a single being can be the shard with which to construct a dinosaur.

When a critic or a friend's first and often last comment on something I've written is, "It's something that must have happened to you," it is the writer in me that feels up against it. I sense they are disappointed when it isn't autobiographical, though, if it is, then its achievement as a piece of writing seems discounted.

"But what about the writing!" one wants to cry out. All of us are born, experience joy or grief, love successfully or divorce painfully, so it must be in the writing that an experience is made moving or convincing.

I always told my students at Barnard, "Be loyal to the story, its requirements, its laws, its form—not to the memory. Total recall of the anthill you sat on at the picnic you are using in your story may or may not add to the tale you are weaving, though it really happened. Told poorly or out of place in the composition, the anthill episode will feel made-up and gratuitous. Effect is what you want, and not truthfulness to something that really happened; it's convincingness the writer is after."

I remember what Stella Adler, the actress and distinguished teacher of drama, said in an interview, and I'm paraphrasing hardly at all, "Don't remember, imagine!" Generations of students had been taught to remember how they felt when their grandmother died and apply the emotion to a scene of grief over the loss of a husband or a country. No, no, cut through that, she seemed to me to be saying, and imagine yourself bereft—in the skin of that particular character stricken by that particular tragedy in that particular scene of that particular play. One of her students, quoted in the same interview, said she learned more through that one instruction than she had been able to in three years of classes at another drama school.

Interviewer: Which writers have meant the most to you? From whom did you learn the most?

Diana Chang: I'll make a general statement first. I feel that I am influenced by everything. I'm influenced by Dr. Chen, who is sitting over there. I'm influenced by the way my friend Howard Sage [in the audience] is moving his hands right now. I'm influenced by the light in this room. I'm influenced by peoples' body language. They reveal themselves constantly. It's people that I'm most influenced by. My early interest in poetry was influenced by Emily Dickinson, among others. Her imagery is thrilling. More recently, I've been influenced by Theodore Roethke—by his closeness to nature and his lyricism. I've been told that my poetry has a "Zen" feeling. If it does, it is totally instinctive. I haven't studied Zen. I'm drawn to it and have read it in bits and pieces, but not systematically.

As for what I've learned about craft, let me say what I owe specifically to Ford Madox Ford's novel *The Good Soldier* for the way I wrote *Eye to Eye*. Ford's novel is narrated in the first person by one of its characters who tells the story of his relationship with his wife and another couple. He has been under the impression that they have had a glorious friendship—until he discovers that it has been a relationship full of deceit and betrayal. His wife has had an affair with the other man; the other man's wife has pimped for him. The narrator is a naive, affectless person who

can't react emotionally to anything. He accepts the social aspects of what has gone on in their lives. They meet at various watering places; they go on vacations together. The book was an eye-opener. I remember reading it and absolutely having goose bumps and saying to myself that I love the use of the first person narrator where a kind of refraction takes place. You get nobody else's point of view, but through that limited point of view, the reader understands what the narrator himself is unaware that he is revealing.

I read people who are around today. I've mentioned some of the black authors whom I have read. I'm interested right now in following Asian American authors and filmmakers...for instance, director Wayne Wang who had done two very good films I'd seen a few years ago. One of them is called *Chan is Missing*. Through the characters in this film, Wang explores different kinds of Chinese-Americans or Chinese-Chinese, some from Taiwan, for instance. They are searching for somebody, if I remember correctly, who has absconded with their money and because of this they are in and out of Chinatown, in and out of other situations which are Asian American. In the end they never do find Chan. Then Wayne Wang produced a second film, *Dim Sum*. You know, little things to eat, dumplings. It's about a relationship between a mother, a daughter whom she dominates, and a third person, a man. His dramatic rendering of Amy Tan's bestseller, *Joy Luck Club*, has been a huge box office success. Another talented director is Ang Lee, who gave us the delightful *The Wedding Banquet*.

Peter (not Wayne) Wang directed *A Great Wall*—not the Great Wall of China, but "a great wall." The wall is the wall between Chinese-Americans and real Chinese. It is the story, very amusingly and movingly done, of a Chinese-American family that takes a trip to China. It's a first rate movie I have seen twice. Then more recently there is the play and movie *M. Butterfly*, by David Henry Hwang, a Chinese-American. I find him terrifically talented.

When David was only twenty-five or six, I invited him to speak at Barnard to my class in "Imagery and Form in the Arts." I don't remember how I got hold of him but he came. At that time he had had two plays produced by Joseph Papp. The first one was called *F.O.B.* (*Fresh Off the Boat*). I caught up with his career with his second play, *The Dance and the Railroad*, a poetic play for two characters. John Lone, the Chinese-

American actor, played the lead role. Lone was brought up in Hong Kong, I believe, and studied Peking Opera there. An exquisite, handsome man, he played the Emperor in the Bertolucci movie, *The Last Emperor*, and co-stars with Jeremy Irons in *M. Butterfly*. I think there's much diversity developing among Chinese-American writers and artists, a very exciting trend.

Interviewer: The genre of Chinese-American fiction is a relatively new development in contemporary letters. In its first stages, it has been thoroughly dominated by women writers, such as Maxine Hong Kingston, Amy Tan, Fae Myenne Ng, Gish Jen, Sui Sin Far, and, of course, yourself. How do you account for this phenomenon? And what do you think of this "new wave"? How does the work of these writers differ from your own?

Diana Chang: I think it is generally accepted that women (and Chinese-American women are no exception) are more verbal than men, and more interested in exploring relationships and their dynamics on any level. A novel may be a higher form of gossiping, and gossip's function and pleasure is not mean-spirited but to help one feel in the know. A novel certainly satisfies that impulse, among others.

Sociologically-sound opinions don't come to me often, so whatever I say in answer to your question is not to be taken as gospel. (My characters have plenty of ready opinions, but I myself seem to be involved with the emotion of thought— a term of my own—that I would find hard to explain if forced to. Let's say that I believe that whatever thinking I do I do through form.)

To return to your question—we must generalize here, though it goes against my grain. Men have usually been pressured to establish themselves in professions or business or simply to hold down a job and become providers from an early age and to persevere at it until they are used up. Women, on their part, were totally submerged in homemaking, childrearing and the usually scut work of housekeeping.

However, once this condition for women was called into question and began to change, they quickly started to realize their potential and to express themselves. Also, I have observed that women, by and large, are less conformist, in some respects, than men. Having been relegated to the interstices of society for so long in almost every part of the world, they were able to be more individual as people and even, in a paradoxical way, somewhat freer.

If there is anything in what I've said, it doesn't surprise me that, as you put it, women have dominated the field of Chinese-American fiction. (But there are Steven C. Lo and David Wong Louie, too, let's not forget.) Maxine Hong Kingston, Amy Tan and Fae Myenne Ng are all exceptionally talented writers with much to say each out of her own experience and in her own style of mind. Also, with ethnicity and feminism presently at large, Chinese-American women writers could come into their own with their stories of women oppressed either in China of yore, or here; of mother/daughter relationships, etc. That the time was right for their works in no way diminishes their talent or achievements.

To avoid categorizing, which makes me uncomfortable, I've mentioned two Chinese-American men who write fiction, and I want also to emphasize again the interesting (and, in some cases, experimental) work in films being directed and produced by Asian American men.

As for how the work of these novelists differs from mine, perhaps I should put it the other way—it is rather that *The Frontiers of Love* differs from their works that have become a genre established and awaited by editors and an American reading public. At the time that *The Frontiers of Love* was published, most of the very favorable reviews seemed to take it simply as a novel, a literary effort. Can it be said that there was some merit in that? I believe so at least part of the time.

I wasn't pigeonholed by the mainstream press. In fact, misunderstood in ethnic circles that both adopted and disapproved of it, it was a novel some of them tried to force into an ideological Procrustes bed, regarding it as a novel about minority characters living in this country. I was quite baffled, truth to tell. I knew the book is set entirely in Shanghai, China, and while it is about identity, it is not about ethnicity here. I hope everyone will read Shirley Lim's introduction I mentioned earlier.

My Chinese characters are not particularly exotic, and one can wonder why. Is it because their middle-crassness frees them from characteristics the average American reader looks for in Asians, traits that perhaps they find appealingly different from their own and foreign enough to escape the humdrum, and therefore are picturesque? Everyone is eager for a change of scene, after all.

A contemporary Chinese physician, professor or lawyer in Hong Kong, Beijing or Taipei is not so different in his values, outlook and goals for himself and his children from his counterpart in New York City or Minneapolis. He is not necessarily deeply steeped only in his own traditional customs and mores, folklore, superstitions, and mindset. (They're reading Kurt Vonnegut in Taipei.) In other words, the cultural differences that readers here find intriguing may be found not so much horizontally—across the Pacific Ocean—but in the verticality of social strata and its diversity.

My work is different for a second reason: while my novel *The Only Game In Town*, an East-West spoof, also draws on my Chinese-American background, my other four novels could have been written by anyone, say, a Diana Smith. It has perplexed and bothered me that this has breached, in some eyes, proscriptions I was unaware of at first.

As David Henry Hwang put it—and I remember what he said almost word for word: In this country today, only blacks can write about blacks, only women about women, only Asian Americans about Asian Americans, but white males can write about anyone.

An interesting observation from him, and he has many. I'm happy that David has written about the sexual ambivalence of a French diplomat in his remarkable play, *M. Butterfly*, now also a film, and that Kazuo Ishiguro, whose background is Japanese and who lives in London, explored in his brilliant novel, *The Remains of the Day*, the life, misapprehensions and inhibitions of an elderly English butler—in the first person.

Supposing they had restricted themselves to Asian American themes and characters . . . what a loss it would have been. We all live in the world, an increasingly global village. Why not write about others? Why should anyone disfranchise him or herself from any human history or experience? Is anything human alien?

Interviewer: You write poetry as well as fiction. How do you decide whether your next gestating inspiration will take the form of poetry or fiction?

Diana Chang: No conscious decision seems to be involved. The theme or the idea may determine its form. I've just finished a poem titled "The Personality of Chairs." Obviously this subject would come out as a poem. (Incidentally, I find chairs haunting, not only because the Shakers hung them on their walls and the Chinese have ghost chairs set aside for their ancestors,

but also because of their innate characteristic of waiting, waiting to be filled.) A painter friend, Jennett Lam, painted only chairs in the last period of her life. Her earlier ones were illumined with an impressionist's sensuous light; the later ones were stark geometric patterns in primary colors.

I've noticed that I've written very few narrative poems—which makes some sense, since I write fiction as well. I delegate my narrative impulse to prose.

In poetry I'm not dealing with the interactions of my characters nor with making the work (the construction that is a story or a novel) move in time. In poems, it may be myself I indulge; in fiction, it's the sensibilities of my characters I'm in the thrall of.

Interviewer: Did you find that your teaching influences your writing—or vice-versa, did your writing influence your teaching?

Diana Chang: I guess my writing influenced my teaching. Being an editor, I think, influenced my teaching just as much. When I was asked to teach in the English Department at Barnard, I shook in my knee socks because I had never taught before. The chairman said he was looking for a practitioner, somebody who had written novels and poetry and somebody who had an editorial point of view as well. What happened was that (and this was very flattering) Elizabeth Hardwick, the American writer and critic, wanted to take a year off to enjoy herself and lecture after the success of her novel, *Sleepless Nights*. They invited me to take her place for a year. I accepted and found out that I loved it. If I had known that I would like teaching so much, I might have gone in for it sooner. Elizabeth Hardwick came back the following year, but Barnard wanted to retain me, which was also very flattering. So I decided to stay on.

To get back to your question. I think teaching in the English department influenced my work in this sense: before I started teaching at Barnard, I wasn't particularly interested in writing short stories. I taught short story writing, not how to write novels. Undergraduates really can't cope with novels. Writing a novel is quite different from, say, writing music. There are prodigies in music, few and far between, of course, but Mozart wrote music when he was eleven. I think to be a writer, especially of a novel, you really have to have some lived experience. You really have to know about human nature. You have to know about human life. You can't know that at fifteen, you can't know that even as a senior at Barnard.

Interviewer: Were either of your parents interested in art or in writing?

Diana Chang: My father, an architect who got his degree at Columbia University's School of Architecture, was artistic, though he didn't paint or sculpt. Among his jobs after coming to this country in his fifties to escape Communism in China, and before finding work as an architect in New York City, was the curating of a collection of Chinese art at the University of Oklahoma. He also wrote some poetry—in English, interestingly enough. My mother was always taking piano lessons, and there was always classical Western music at home. And, incidentally, the first thing I wanted to be was a dancer—perhaps ballet was what I might have pursued. My father was a very good ballroom dancer. My parents went to tea dances in Peiping and Shanghai, an aspect of pre-Communist life of Western-educated or Western influenced Chinese very few people know about. They danced to Glenn Miller and Cole Porter, which I am belatedly doing here, happy that touch dancing is finally back.

Interviewer: One last question. What advice would you give a young Chinese-American who wants to be a writer or an artist? Diana, I pose that question because we need to take into account that very often ethnic parents pressure their children in the direction of the practical. There's a skeptical attitude about the arts.

Diana Chang: To a Chinese-American student who is talented and who wants to write, I have the same advice that I have for anybody else who wants to write. First of all, you cannot "decide" to become a serious writer. You can decide to be a copywriter, you can decide to be a public relations writer, you can decide to be a medical text writer, but with creative writing, with imaginative writing, you can't say, "I am going to be the next Toni Morrison." You can't. But you can write. If you have it in you to write, you will write and you will continue to write and send things out and eventually some will be taken. After your work starts to be published, other people will say to you, "You are a writer." You cannot put that mantle on yourself is what I am saying.

The other thing is that you must find a way to make a living while you write. I worked as an editor. I discovered, however, as even a young junior editor, that I didn't have time to write because during working hours in the office my time was taken up dealing with various people in various departments. You pore over other people's texts at home, at night, on weekends; I found it very hard to be an editor and write at the same time. In those days as a junior editor, I wasn't being paid very much either. So I quit. I quit with $200 in the bank. My friends thought I was foolhardy. I didn't feel foolhardy. I guess maybe I was blind. You have to have a blind need to write. I knew I was going to collect some unemployment and I eked out an existence.

My parents weren't able to help me. They had fled China which had turned Communist, and they were having a struggle here themselves. My father was just trying to get a foothold as an architect here in New York. In a minuscule way, I was helping out my parents financially. I had also helped to get them out of China. I was very young, doing this while attending Barnard as an undergraduate on a scholarship.

At one point when I was writing my second novel, I worked for a telephone answering service at night from 11 pm to 9 am, two nights a week. Though I am a night person I didn't feel too well at nine in the morning when I got on the bus to go home. Simultaneously, I did free-lance copy editing. I remember copy editing two of Samuel Beckett's novels, *Molloy* and *Malone Dies*, for Grove Press.

People who write don't write because they have the time. They write despite having no time. You have to have that drive. If you don't have that drive, that inner need, don't do it. Life is very rich; there are many other things to get involved with. That is what I would tell any student, Chinese-American, Caucasian, Irish Catholic, or whatever.

Source: Leo Hamalian, "A *MELUS* Interview: Diana Chang," in *MELUS*, Vol. 20, No. 4, Winter 1995, pp. 29–44.

Amy Ling

In this excerpt, Ling explains how Chang reveals her own culture even when writing about the dominant culture.

Americans in the "hyphenated condition," a term Diana Chang coined in a talk at the 1976 MLA convention—and particularly non-Caucasian Americans who are most readily because most visibly distinguishable—live constantly trying to balance on an edge, now slipping over to one side of the hyphen, now climbing back only to fall down the other side. This divided or schizoid self, so well-illuminated in Marilyn Waniek's article, "The Schizoid Implied Authors of Two

IDENTITY OR 'SELF-NESS' AND LOVE ARE THE
TWO MAIN PREOCCUPATIONS IN DIANA
CHANG'S WORK."

American Jewish Novels," cannot but be apparent in the work such a person produces. Thus, even if a writer does not write of her own ethnic background, focusing instead on characters from the dominant culture, she may nonetheless reveal not necessarily her own ethnicity but the fact that she is not totally or unequivocally part of the dominant culture.

Diana Chang, author of six novels, numerous poems and articles, is Chinese-American. Born in New York City, she was taken to Peking at the age of eight months by her American-educated Chinese father, an architect, and Eurasian mother (whose mother was Irish). In China she attended American schools. She returned to New York City for high school and college and has lived there since, with a brief period in France. In her talk, "A Hyphenated Condition," Diana Chang spoke personally and frankly about the "bifocalness" of her identity:

> I have to confess tentatively, not sure what I'm really saying, that I don't really feel like a minority here. Am I turned around? In China, I know I'd be considered foreign and lost to the tribe. And they'd be right because I'm not translating myself into English. I express myself in English. I've imagined from within the points of view of white Protestant characters, as well as Chinese personae. Am I an American who sometimes writes about the Chinese in her? My imagination, based here since high school, doesn't belong to me. I belong to my imagination. It has its way with me. It's closer to lilacs blooming in doorways than to moon gates and lotus pods. I have not experienced the new China. Yet, I find myself saying, "we Chinese" quite often, which is very Chinese of me. Nice liberal Americans have no grasp of the chauvinism of the Chinese they embrace.

She has studied Walt Whitman rather than Li Po, and yet her features are decidedly Oriental, and were she living in Broken Bow, Nebraska, rather than New York City, she would have the experience of feeling like a minority. English is literally her mother-tongue (she took up the formal study of Chinese only last fall), and yet, "As long as I'm not blonde, leggy, and of Massachusetts, I choose to be myself, with this elusive, confused identity known as Chinese-American, in this country." For her, there is no other choice but the complex hyphenated condition.

In several of her poems, Chang directly explores this split. The lines, "My Chinese body/ out of its American head," come from "An Appearance of Being Chinese." In another poem, "Second Nature," she writes poignantly:

> Sometimes I dream in Chinese
> I dream my father's dreams.
>
> I wake, grown up
> And someone else.
>
> I am the thin edge I sit on.
> I begin to gray—white and black and in between.
> My hair is America.
>
> New England moonlights in me ...
> I shuttle passportless within myself,
> My eyes slant around both hemispheres,
> Gaze through walls
> And long still to be
> Accustomed,
> At home here,
>
> Strange to say.

This "strange" longing to be "at home here" in a familiar land is somewhat resolved in the affirmative stance of "Saying Yes":

> "Are you Chinese?"
> "Yes."
>
> "American?"
> "Yes."
>
> "Really Chinese?"
> "No ... not quite."
>
> "Really American?"
> "Well, actually, you see ... "
>
> But I would rather say
> yes
>
> Not neither—nor,
> not maybe,
> but both, and not only
>
> The homes I've had,
> the ways I am
>
> I'd rather say it
> twice,
> yes

But the conditional mood of the verb, "I'd rather say ... " still expresses longing for a situation contrary to fact. These poems and her first novel, *The Frontiers of Love* (New York:

Random House, 1956), are Chang's most direct expressions of her ethnic identity.

... When asked why she no longer writes of Chinese or Chinese-American characters, Diana Chang replied that "exoticism" can stand in the way of the "universal" which she strives for in her themes, and therefore she's "often subsumed aspects of her background in the interests of other truths." If she writes of white Protestant Americans in *Eye to Eye*, it is because she believes that her theme—creativity—would have been "side-tracked had she—writing and publishing here—used Chinese, Chicano or Norwegian characters."

Ethnicity, of course, does not or should not preclude "universality." Ralph Ellison's invisible man, for example, is undeniably black and suffers all the indignities of his race, but he is also a young Everyman confronted by forces beyond his control, losing his innocence through hard experience, and moving from blindness and invisibility to sight and light. In "The Art of Fiction: An Interview," (1955), Ellison discusses the relationship between "minority" and "universal" themes:

> All novels are about certain minorities: the individual is a minority. The universal in the novel—and isn't that what we're all clamoring for these days?—is reached only through the depiction of the specific man in a specific circumstance.

Though no rule binds those from ethnic minority backgrounds to writing books only about their own people and culture, nevertheless, Chinese-American writers are such rarities that the Chinese-American community looks to the few who are master-manipulators of English to speak for them, to record their history, their hopes, frustrations, and experiences; to give voice to this otherwise silent minority. The community takes pride in published works signed by Chinese names. Thus, the ambivalence of the outspoken playwright Frank Chin is understandable. In a December 1972 letter to Frank Ching, editor of *Bridge* magazine, Chin wrote:

> Now let me recommend someone to you whose work I respect and find [...] up as a thinker, a Eurasian, a Chinese-American, a mind and person, [...] up. Diana Chang. She just had another poem published in the *New York Quarterly* in which she fails to come to grips with her Chinese-American identity, but does repeat the clichés and racist stereotype with a certain style

and an occasional nice line. ... She takes a stand with white supremacy as unconsciously and unwittingly and as sincerely as any of your writers and brings it off in a tour de force of writing flash and style. She manages to have her own voice and take that white racist rhetoric about universals of art and being an individual instead of white or yellow, and mixing the best of East and West ... the whole stinking mess ... and show us accurately, how she's made it work, how she believes it. ... All that she's trained herself to ignore, the enormity of her deafness, her forced ignorance shows through absences in her work ... brilliantly. And what she writes consciously is pretty good too.

What Frank Chin ignores, however, is the fact that there is an entire spectrum of Chinese-Americans, ranging the gamut from mostly Chinese with a dash of American, to mostly American with a veneer of Chinese, or as Diana Chang put it, with "an appearance of being Chinese."

Diana Chang belongs to the latter group. Her life is set in the artistic-intellectual circles of New York City and Bridgehampton, Long Island. Out of these worlds comes *Eye to Eye*. As a painter and writer, she is concerned with perception and creativity, with the connection between initial familial relationships and later sexual adjustment, and with the relationship between neurosis and art.

... Identity or "self-ness" and love are the two main preoccupations in Diana Chang's work. The word "love" occurs in two of the titles, her first and her latest, and love is a central topic in all of her books. "By self-ness," she explains, "I mean consciousness, awareness, interiority, being. The 'I,' the 'me,' the 'myself,' and all the 'you's' and 'thou's' around. You'll find this in *Eye to Eye* and *A Perfect Love* and everything else, too, of mine."

Expression of self is indeed the artist's function. Whether this expression is direct as in autobiographies or metamorphosed by imagination into novels, the presence of the puppet master, the implied author, may be felt in the text. In final support of my sense of her subtle, slightly detached point of view, I quote from an article "Why Do Writers Write?" published by Chang in the *American Pen* some years back; in this passage she reveals her creative impulse and its relationship to her identity:

> My ego exploits my self, my experience, in order that my ego may be. With this novel, this play, this poem, this biography, these essays, I

purchase my citizenship in this land of life from which I feel estranged. Others claim their rightful place simply by virtue of being born. But I must earn it like an illegitimate child, a stateless person, and so, by some exacting game of industry and imagination, I create something in order to become all that I was meant to be.

For Diana Chang, as for her protagonist, George Safford, "I produce, therefore I am." In creating a work of art, as Blanche Gelfant has noted, the artist is creating herself. Though the need to create the self may be strongest in those who feel "estranged," "illegitimate," and "stateless," and though these adjectives may be applied to every artist, regardless of ethnic background, alienation may be said to be doubly strong for writers in the hyphenated condition.

Source: Amy Ling, "Writer in the Hyphenated Condition: Diana Chang," in *MELUS*, Vol. 7, No. 4, Winter 1980, pp. 69–83.

SOURCES

Almeida, Eduardo de, "Diana Chang," in *Asian American Poets: A Bio-Bibliographical Critical Sourcebook*, edited by Guiyou Huang, Greenwood Press, 2002, pp. 65–70.

"The Asian Population: 2000," in *U.S. Census Bureau*, http://www.census.gov/prod/2002pubs/c2kbr01-16.pdf (accessed June 1, 2010).

Bishop, Janice, Review of *What Matisse Is After*, in *The Forbidden Stitch: An Asian American Women's Anthology*, edited by Shirley Lim, Mayumi Tsutakawa, and Margarita Donnelly, Calyx, 1989, pp. 241–43.

Chan, Jeffrey Paul, Frank Chin, Lawson Fusao Inada, and Shawn Wong, eds., Introduction to *The Big Aiiieeeee! An Anthology of Chinese American and Japanese American Literature*, Meridian, 1991, pp. xi–xvi.

Chang, Diana, "Most Satisfied by Snow," in *Prentice Hall Literature: Timeless Voices, Timeless Themes: The American Experience*, Prentice Hall, 2002, p. 1101.

Chang, Victoria, ed., Introduction to *Asian American Poetry: The Next Generation*, University of Illinois Press, 2004, pp. xv–xxx.

Chin, Frank, "Come All Ye Asian American Writers of the Real and the Fake," in *The Big Aiiieeeee! An Anthology of Chinese American and Japanese American Literature*, edited by Jeffrey Paul Chan, Frank Chin, Lawson Fusao Inada, and Shawn Wong, Meridian, 1991, pp. 1–93.

"Environmental History Timeline," in *EnvironmentalHistoryTimeline*, http://www.radford.edu/wkovarik/envhist/ (accessed May 24, 2010).

"Greenpeace Ends Balcony Protest at BP Headquarters," in *BBC News*, May 20, 2010, http://news.bbc.co.uk/2/hi/uk_news/8693778.stm (accessed June 1, 2010).

Grice, Helena, "Diana Chang," in *Dictionary of Literary Biography*, Vol. 312, *Asian American Writers*, edited by Deborah L. Madsen, Thomson Gale, 2005, pp. 30–35.

"Gulf Oil Spill: U.S. Begins Criminal Investigations," in *BBC News*, June 2, 2010, http://news.bbc.co.uk/2/hi/world/us_and_canada/10211217.stm (accessed June 3, 2010).

Hamalian, Leo, "A *MELUS* Interview: Diana Chang (Maskers and Tricksters)," in *MELUS: The Journal of the Society for the Study of the Multi-Ethnic Literature of the United States*, Vol. 20, No. 4, Winter 1995, pp. 29–43.

Hargrove, Eugene, Foreword to *Faces of Environmental Racism: Confronting Issues of Global Justice*, 2nd ed., edited by Laura Westra and Bill E. Lawson, Roman & Littlefield, 2001, pp. ix–x.

"The History of Greenpeace," in *Greenpeace.org*, http://www.greenpeace.org/international/about/history (accessed May 30, 2010).

Huang, Guiyou, ed., "Introduction: The Makers of the Asian American Poetic Landscape," in *Asian American Poets: A Bio-Bibliographical Critical Sourcebook*, Greenwood Press, 2002, pp. 1–14.

———, "Diana Chang," in *The Columbia Guide to Asian American Literature since 1945*, Columbia University Press, 2006, pp. 117–18.

"Obituaries: Diana Chang Tribute," in *East Hampton Star* (East Hampton, New York), June 25, 2009, http://www.easthamptonstar.com/dnn/Obituaries/tabid/9190/Default.aspx (accessed May 24, 2010).

Patell, Cyrus R. K., "Emergent Literatures: Legacies of the Sixties," in *The Cambridge History of American Literature*, Vol. 7, *Prose Writing: 1940–1990*, edited by Sacvan Bercovitch and Cyrus R. K. Patell, Cambridge University Press, 1999.

"The Questions on the Form," in *U.S. Census Bureau*, http://2010.census.gov/2010census/how/interactive-form.php (accessed June 1, 2010).

Roh-Spaulding, Carol, "Diana Chang," in *Asian American Novelists: A Bio-Bibliographic Critical Sourcebook*, edited by Emmanuel S. Nelson, Greenwood Press, 2000, pp. 38–43.

"Table A-5: Race for the United States, Regions, Divisions, and States: 1970 (100-Percent Data)," in *U.S. Census Bureau*, http://www.census.gov/population/www/documentation/twps0056/tabA-05.pdf (accessed June 1, 2010).

"Timeline: The Alaska Pipeline Chronology," in *PBS.org*, http://www.pbs.org/wgbh/amex/pipeline/timeline/timeline2.html (accessed May 30, 2010).

Zhou, Xiaojing, "Introduction," in *Form and Transformation in Asian American Literature*, edited by Zhou Xiaojing and Samina Najmi, University of Washington Press, 2005, pp. 3–29.

FURTHER READING

Bloom, Harold, ed., *Asian-American Women Writers*, Chelsea House Publishers, 1997.

In this book, noted literary scholar and critic Bloom assembles excerpts from reviews and critical essays pertaining to the writings of Asian American women. Each set of excerpts is preceded by a brief biography of the author. The volume, which includes a chapter on Chang, provides a sampling of the critical responses the authors have received to their body of work.

Felstiner, John, *Can Poetry Save the Earth? A Field Guide to Nature Poems*, Yale University Press, 2009.

Felstiner traces the history of poems concerned with the natural world and maintains that poetry has the ability to refocus attention on the environmental crises the planet faces.

Flynn, Thomas, *Existentialism: A Very Short Introduction*, Oxford University Press, 2006.

Flynn offers an overview of existentialist thought, summarizing the arguments of the primary existentialist philosophers, including Kierkegaard, Nietzsche, Sartre, Camus, and others, and highlights the primary themes of existentialism, such as personal responsibility, individuality and identity, and free will.

Ling, Amy, ed., *Yellow Light: The Flowering of Asian American Arts*, Temple University Press, 1999.

In this work, Ling offers the responses to a set of questions presented to various Asian American artists, including visual artists, writers, musicians, performers, and filmmakers. The volume is a collection of their responses to queries concerning their views regarding their ethnicity, their conception of identity, and the impact of these notions on their work. Chang is one of the respondents included in this work.

Sturgeon, Noël, *Environmentalism in Popular Culture: Gender, Race, Sexuality, and the Politics of the Natural*, University of Arizona Press, 2008.

Sturgeon dissects the way American culture perceives what is considered natural and argues that popular culture has created an understanding of nature that inhibits the creation of equitable solutions to environmental crises.

SUGGESTED SEARCH TERMS

Diana Chang AND poetry

Diana Chang AND existentialism

Most Satisfied by Snow

Diana Chang AND Asian American literature

Diana Chang AND nature

Most Satisfied by Snow AND Diana Chang

What Matisse Is After AND Chang

philosophy AND Chang

Diana Chang AND Chinese literature

Mushrooms

MARGARET ATWOOD

1981

Margaret Atwood's "Mushrooms" is a poem that
subtly investigates both the power and limitations
of poetry and language. It also demonstrates
themes of life cycles and nature, reflecting
Atwood's environmental interests. Atwood, a
writer of worldwide acclaim known for her prose
as well as her poetry, has been a prominent political activist, feminist, and representative for
Canadian literature. All of these interests are visible in the poems that surround "Mushrooms" in
Atwood's 1981 volume *True Stories*. "Mushrooms" has also been included in Atwood collections, including *Selected Poems II: 1976–1986*,
published in 1987.

AUTHOR BIOGRAPHY

Atwood was born on November 18, 1939, in
Ottawa, Ontario, Canada. Because her father
was a forest entomologist, she spent much of
her childhood in the northern Ontario wilderness
where he worked. She enjoyed writing from a
young age and decided to pursue writing as a
career when she was sixteen. She studied English
at Victoria College, University of Toronto, and
received her B.A. in 1961. Atwood received her
A.M. in 1962 from Radcliffe College, and she
studied at Harvard University from 1962 to 1963.

In addition to novels, Atwood has published
volumes of poetry, collections of short stories,

Margaret Atwood (Francois Guillot | AFP | Getty Images)

A red mushroom (chantal de bruijne | Shutterstock.com)

In addition to writing, Atwood has worked as an editor and a journalist, and enjoys painting and photography. She has lived in England, Scotland, and France. As of 2010, Atwood lives in Toronto, Ontario, Canada.

works of nonfiction, and several children's books, and she has also written scripts for three television series. Her writing often focuses on feminist concerns in the form of social satire. Her first book, a volume of poetry titled *The Circle Game*, was published in 1966. It received two Governor General's Awards that year. Despite producing over ten volumes of poetry, including *True Stories*, which was published in 1981 and contains the poem "Mushrooms," Atwood is better known for her novels. *The Handmaid's Tale* won several awards, including the Governor General's Literary Award for Fiction, and *The Blind Assassin* won the Booker Prize for Fiction. Other well-known titles include *Alias Grace* and *Oryx and Crake*.

Atwood has received over fifty awards for her writing, sixteen honorary degrees and is a Fellow of the Royal Society of Canada. She is considered to be one of Canada's most prolific and distinguished authors. Some of her works have been adapted to film, and many have been translated into multiple languages. She has had an immense and undeniable influence on Canadian literature.

POEM SUMMARY

"Mushrooms" is a free verse poem of forty-six lines divided into four sections, which in turn are divided into stanzas. The poem is a descriptive and meditative consideration of the rapid life cycle of mushrooms. Although the entire poem evokes a sense of growth, transition, and process, each section constitutes a distinct movement of the poem.

Section 1

Though the poem could take place anywhere, it includes many definite articles that make the action of the poem seem anchored to a specific time and place. The first stanza of the first section provides the reader with a vague sense of setting: a natural place that is overcast, surrounded by water, damp, and perhaps laced with the faint sounds of storms far off. The second stanza shifts the focus to an undefined "they." Although the word mushrooms is never used in the poem, from the title and the vibrant description that follows, it is evident that the subject "they" refers to mushrooms. The second stanza supplies several similes to depict the image of the mushrooms' quiet,

MEDIA ADAPTATIONS

- Atwood recorded several of her own poems, including "Mushrooms," on a CD for the Poetry Archive: *Margaret Atwood Reading from Her Poems*, produced in 2009.

fungal, overnight growth. The third stanza provides an image of the result of this overnight growth, by describing the way the leaf mold appears in the morning after the mushrooms have sprung up. This stanza includes several different metaphors that describe the different colors and textures of the different types of mushrooms.

Section 2

The second section begins with an inquiry about how the mushrooms originate, followed by a somewhat unorthodox story of creation. The poet does not give an explanation of their growth, but instead describes the process as an underground storm, creating an image of subterranean life, movement, and activity. Atwood makes an unintuitive comparison between mushrooms and flowers, which gives the impression that mushrooms are a sort of dark parallel to something beautiful.

Section 3

The third section is made up of three sentences that have the same structure. Each describes something that the mushrooms do: feed, glow, and have taste. This section, because it emphasizes the mushroom's actions through parallel sentence structure, gives the impression that the mushrooms aren't just innocuous fungal growth, but rather have lives of their own. This section also emphasizes mushrooms' strangeness. They are made to seem bizarre and almost alien in their tendency to glow in the dark. Their taste is described with striking variety, from comparisons to flavors of spoiled food to tasty spices and solid meals. She also compares their flavor to non-food items, such as injured lips or freshly fallen snow.

Section 4

The last section presents a drastic shift in the tone and action of the poem. In the first three stanzas mushrooms have been the singular subject, but in this stanza the unnamed narrator suddenly becomes self-aware, referring to him or herself as "I" twice. The poem is no longer a simple meditation on mushrooms; it now tells a story. The narrator reveals that she hunts, and assumedly picks mushrooms for sustenance, but also for other reasons. Apparently the smell and essence of mushrooms is somehow satisfying to the narrator; she seems to have a deeper understanding of, or connection with, the mushrooms than most. To the narrator, there is an unmistakably human quality about the mushrooms.

The final stanza creates another drastic shift. It is the first stanza in which the subject is entirely ambiguous. It describes a metaphorical presentation of something by the narrator (exactly what the something is unclear), to someone, although to whom the "you" in this stanza is also unclear. It could be the reader, or anyone. One way to interpret this stanza is that it describes the narrator as metaphorically presenting a handful of mushrooms to the reader. Of course, what the narrator is actually presenting to the reader is the *poem* "Mushrooms." This interpretation draws a connection between mushrooms and poetry that the narrator makes explicit in the last line of the poem.

THEMES

Life Cycles

Much of the language and action of "Mushrooms" is centered around natural life cycles. The first section of the poem describes the mushrooms' creeping, seemingly overnight growth from the viewpoint of someone standing above ground watching them emerge from the earth. The second section similarly describes the mushrooms' development but from an underground perspective, focusing on the mushrooms' subterranean root network. In this section, rather than being described from the perspective of someone above ground, their growth is described from what could be the perspective of the mushrooms themselves, reaching up to sprout through the soil. This section describes the release of the mushrooms' reproductive spores, upon which the fruiting body of the mushroom will die. The

TOPICS FOR FURTHER STUDY

- Research Canadian literary history, and Atwood's influence upon it. Choose another country outside of North America, and research the history of literature in that country as well. Who do you think is the most influential writer of that country? Create a Web page comparing and contrasting the literary history of Canada and that of the country of your choice, including sections on Atwood and another famous writer from the second country.

- The 1960s and 1970s were an important period for feminism in Canada. Research the Canadian Human Rights Act of 1977 and the effects it had on gender equality and the rights of minority groups. Do you think the act affected one minority group more than the others? Do you think it had any significant effect at all? Write a paper explaining your opinion. Post your essay on your blog and ask your classmates to leave comments supporting or refuting your ideas.

- "Mushrooms" is a poem written in free verse. Pick a topic related to one of the themes of the poem and write your own free verse poem. Recite your poem for your classmates

or create a multimedia presentation that uses music and pictures to help express your poem.

- Atwood is a prominent political activist and feminist. Choose one of her poems that you believe conveys a strong social message. How is it similar to or different from "Mushrooms" in style, tone, and meaning? Do you think any of the themes of "Mushrooms" are present in the poem? Create a PowerPoint presentation that compares the poems.

- "Mushrooms" is a poem that uses a simple idea, the life cycle of mushrooms, as a metaphor to invoke a complex message or meaning. Pick an object that has deep significance to you. Create a collage that expresses the different ideas and feelings that you associate with that object.

- Using the young-adult nonfiction work *Women Making America* by Heidi Hemming and Julie Hemming Savage as a guide, write a paper explaining ways in which the women's liberation movement in the United States is unique from movements in other countries, including Canada.

---

third section describes the mushrooms' decay process as they decompose back into their environment. The final section describes the mushrooms being hunted, or picked, so that they may provide sustenance for other life forms. The poem is not only an idealized description of the life cycle of mushrooms themselves, but an explanation of how, like all plants and animals, mushrooms give way to new life through their own death.

Furthermore, the theme of regenerative life cycles is also manifest in the poem through specific images relating to birth, death, and fertility, particularly in the first stanza of section four. This section paradoxically compares mushrooms to the smell of death, and then immediately to the

smell of newborn babies. Line 42 ties these two comparisons together with a statement that emphasizes the cyclical, transformative nature of life and death.

Nature

Atwood's poetry frequently deals with themes of nature and environment. "Mushrooms" is certainly a poem that falls into this category. It is a nature poem insofar as the majority of the poem is centered on the life cycles of mushrooms, a very natural phenomenon, but it also contrasts nature with poetry, a product of human imagination. Throughout the poem, mushrooms are not only compared to poetry, a human product,

Mushrooms in the rain *(SergeyDV | Shutterstock.com)*

but also to human body parts such as nipples, brains, and lips. This comparison is brought to a head in the last stanza, which introduces the idea of understanding mushrooms as a metaphor for poetry. It seems that in "Mushrooms" Atwood is using the life cycle of mushrooms to say something about poetry, and the theme of nature to say something about humanity.

Light and Darkness

"Mushrooms" is heavily concentrated with images of light and dark. Darkness is suggested by the title of the poem alone, as mushrooms themselves are images of darkness, as fungi, they thrive in cool, dark shade, rather than in light like most plants. This theme is firmly established in the first section, which begins with the impression of a damp and overcast afternoon, which fades into the darkness of night and eventually gives way to morning light. Subsequently, recurrent images of darkness in the poem, such as thunder, clouds, soil, shade, and the word "darkness" itself, are

intermittently contrasted with images of light. However, the images of light, such as lightning and eye blinks, are fleeting interruptions to darkness. These intermingled images of light and dark suggest that "Mushrooms" is neither a poem of hope or despair, but a holistic consideration of the positive and negative aspects of life.

STYLE

Lyric Poem

A lyric poem is distinct from a narrative poem in that, while a narrative poem tells a story, the lyric poem is less about plot and more about feelings, images, and impressions. Although "Mushrooms" does have a loose narrative arc, the poem is not about the growth process of mushrooms as much as it is interpreting that process metaphorically in order to understand something about humanity. That is, "Mushrooms" is much more reflective than it is narrative. It also relies heavily on sensual imagery such as sights, tastes, and sounds, which can be indicative of lyric poetry.

Free Verse Poetry

The free verse style dominated contemporary English poetry from the 1950s to the 1970s. Free verse poems differ from traditional poetry in that they employ irregular meter and rhythm, and are not necessarily organized in the standard formal of lines and stanzas. However, this does not mean that the rhythm and structure of free verse poems is arbitrary. The irregular stylistic elements of good free verse poetry reflect the content of the poem.

"Mushrooms" is a free verse poem because it has no regular rhythm or rhyme scheme, and because the organization of each section, and subsequently each stanza, is based on content rather than formal elements of meter or organization. Furthermore, the poem's line breaks do not always occur in intuitive places, but sometimes occur mid-sentence or mid-clause for emphasis. The free verse movement was challenged in the 1980s, around the time Atwood published *True Stories*, by the growing popularity of new formalist poetry; however, free verse remains a popular style of poetry today.

Metaphor and Simile

"Mushrooms" includes many metaphors and similes. A metaphor is a figurative language device that compares or associates two distinct things by representing one thing as the other. For example, in line 15 Atwood uses the term "brains" to represent mushrooms. She does not literally mean that brains are coming out of the earth, rather, she is making a comparison between brains and mushrooms and pointing out that the two things have some similar qualities. A simile is like a metaphor, except similes use the connective words *like* or *as*, while metaphors do not use specific connective words. For example, the comparison of mushrooms to bubbles in line 6 is a simile because it incorporates the word *like*. Metaphors and similes often add potency or additional layers of meaning to the meaning of poems through their direct comparisons of objects.

Sound Devices and Tone

"Mushrooms" is a poem that relies heavily on sound devices in order to evoke tone. One such prominent device in the poem is consonance, or the harmonious repetition of consonant sounds,

usually in the middle or end of words. For example, the soft "s" sound is pervasive in the first section of the poem, particularly in lines 1–3 and 15–16. Additionally, the soft "th" sound is largely present in the first section (line 4 for example). The abundance of soft sounds and the void of harsh sounds such as "k"s, makes this section seem quiet, whispery, and almost dreamlike.

This mood is briefly broken by the question at the beginning of the second section, but the poem gradually slips back into a whisper. This whispery tone not only makes the poem seem dreamlike, and perhaps even a bit magical, but makes the dramatic shift that occurs in the fourth section with the introduction of "I" and "you" eerier. Suddenly the poem is not just a verbal image of the life cycle of mushrooms, but something that is being spoken to the reader by an unnamed narrator. The quietness of the tone combined with the suddenness of the transition evokes the chilling feeling of being snuck up upon.

Gothic Influence

Although "Mushrooms" does not have all of the traditional elements of a gothic poem, it features gothic influence, primarily through its dark subject matter and imagery. The gothic genre originated in the late eighteenth century as a conflation of the horror and romance genres. Gothic literature and poetry traditionally included elements of mystery, darkness, decay, high emotion, gloom, and horror. Elements of the gothic genre are manifest in much of Atwood's poetry. The quietly morose tone of the poem and grotesque imagery (lines 4, 14, 34–36, and 40–42) are markers of Atwood's use of the gothic.

HISTORICAL CONTEXT

Canadian Feminism

Several significant events concerning Canadian feminism occurred during the 1970s and early 1980s, the same time period during which Atwood's writing career was gaining substantial momentum and influence. Atwood is a noted and self-proclaimed feminist, and much of her prose and poetry deals with issues of feminism and gender inequality. Although the poem "Mushrooms" does not discuss gender issues explicitly, several of the poems in the 1981 volume *True Stories*, in which "Mushrooms" was originally published, do. Several

COMPARE
&
CONTRAST

- **1970s–1980s:** In 1970 the Don't Make A Wave Committee, one of the world's first environmental protection groups, is officially founded in Vancouver, British Columbia, Canada. The organization seeks to put an end to nuclear testing in the National Wildlife refuge in Canada. The founding of the organization was prompted by a 7,000 person protest the previous year that sought to prevent a nuclear weapons test. The protest failed. The bomb was detonated.

  Today: The Don't Make A Wave Committee has evolved into Greenpeace. The influential environmental organization has offices in over forty-two countries and focuses on worldwide environmental issues such as global warming, overfishing, and deforestation. Greenpeace has been described as the most effective environmental organization today.

- **1970s–1980s:** In 1984 the first televised debate on women's issues in Canada airs during the Canadian federal election. The debate includes the leaders of the three most prominent political parties and addresses issues such as abortion, inequality, and day care. This debate represents a huge step in promoting awareness of women's issues in Canada.

  Today: Canada is known as one of the world's frontrunners in gender equality; however, as of 2008 only 22 percent of members of parliament are women, indicating that true gender equality is yet to become a reality, at least in the government.

- **1970s–1980s:** English Canadian literature experiences a boom. After 1967 the national government increases funding for publishers, and many small presses that exhibit pronounced cultural nationalism are established. Also during these decades, several literary periodicals and journals are established including *Canadian Literature*, *Prism*, *Journal of Canadian Studies*, and *Canadian Fiction Magazine*. Because of the increased volume of published Canadian literature, new professional societies spring up, such as the League of Canadian Poets and the Writers' Union of Canada.

  Today: Many Canadian writers, such as Atwood, Alice Munro, and Douglas Coupland, are prolific and world renowned. In 1992, Michael Ondaatje is the first Canadian to win the Booker Prize for *The English Patient*. Today Canadian writers are widely anthologized.

---

poems in this volume, "Torture," "Notes Toward a Poem that Can Never Be Written," and "A Woman's Issue," depict gruesome scenes of women as victims of violence. More often than not, men are the responsible perpetrators in *True Stories*. This content is not terribly surprising considering Atwood's feminist interest and the milieu in which she was writing the collection.

In the late 1960s women's liberation movements began forming all over the country. These groups provided varied services such as day care, shelter for battered women, and abortions, as well as publishing feminist magazines and journals, putting on theater productions, and raising consciousness about women's issues. In 1967 the

Canadian federal government organized the Royal Commission on the Status of Women, to investigate the quality of life of Canadian women. The commission made 167 recommendations. However, by 1971 no changes had been made, and a feminist activist organization called the National Action Committee on the Status of Women (NAC) formed to lobby for the implementation of the 167 recommendations. The NAC eventually grew to be the largest national feminist coalition, with over 700 groups claiming affiliation. Finally, in 1977 Prime Minister Pierre E. Trudeau passed the Canadian Human Rights Act, which legally ended all discrimination based on religion, race, gender, and sexuality. It also

Mushrooms growing on a tree (*DavidEwingPhotography | Shutterstock.com*)

called for equal pay for women. However, as late as the mid-1980s there was still a huge gap between average salaries of women and men.

Environmentalism in Canada

Just before feminism became a prominent issue, environmental concern spread rapidly in Canada in the 1960s. Air pollution, water pollution, and hazardous waste became issues of social concern, and interest groups such as the Society for the Promotion of Environmental Conservation began forming. Preservation of the natural environment no longer seemed simply novel or primarily for scenic benefits, but necessary for human health. During this period there was an especially high interest in protecting unique ecosystems or natural areas as ecological reserves. Several influential environmental organizations such as Greenpeace, the Sierra Club, and World Wildlife Fund Canada were formed in Canada in the 1960s. The federal government also took action during this decade, establishing ministries for the environment, as well as passing environmental protection acts.

The 1970s witnessed not only a continued concern for the environment, but a growing concern for wildlife as well. In 1971 an act to protect endangered species was passed in Ontario, and in 1978 the Committee on the Status of Endangered Wildlife in Canada began forming a list of all species that necessitated protection. Canada was also heavily represented in the 1972 United Nations Conference on the Human Environment in Stockholm, Sweden. By the 1980s, less governmental action was being taken and non-governmental organizations (NGOs) became more heavily involved in spreading environmental awareness in Canada.

Atwood is known for her interest in the environment. She is an advocate for preservation of natural resources, as well as pollution reduction. She supports natural energy sources such as solar power and believes society could make significant environmental strides with a consumer education program that informed the public about the effects of wasteful consumerism. Atwood's concern for the environment is frequently evident in her prose and poetry.

CRITICAL OVERVIEW

Due to Atwood's status as a canonical writer, she has received ample critical attention within the past thirty years for both her prose and her poetry. The first collection of critical essays concerning her work, *The Malahat Review: Margaret Atwood: A Symposium*, was published in 1977. Since then numerous and varied anthologies have been published examining her work from many different literary perspectives.

According to Branko Gorjup in his essay "Margaret Atwood's Poetry and Poetics," published in *The Cambridge Companion to Margaret Atwood*, most of the criticism of Atwood's poetry has focused on "oppositional forces that are laid out in startling contrast" in her work. Gorjup agrees with this, but claims that "Atwood's interest in the transformative power of the imagination ... overrides the rigid boundaries of a dualistic universe." In other words, Gorjup argues that Atwood's poetry deconstructs the oppositions it presents. Gorjup also claims that Atwood's poetry is marked by a fluid and metamorphic quality.

Frank Davey, in his book *Margaret Atwood: a Feminist Poetics*, examines Atwood's work from a feminist perspective. He also explores contrasts in Atwood's poetry. Specifically he writes that her collection, *True Stories*, which includes the poem "Mushrooms," presents a world in which "torturers and oppressors are associated with masculine images of knives and technology and their victims with feminine ones of earth and flesh." He also notes that *True Stories* "questions the reliability of *story* on numerous occasions," and the poems of this collection "contain a number of references to the limitations of language and poetry." He claims that her poems often present themselves as decidedly female "gesture[s] of creativity," and that due to her biological language, "when Atwood speaks of creation there is a sense of giving birth."

In George Woodcock's essay "Metamorphosis and Survival: Notes on the Recent Poetry of Margaret Atwood," published in the anthology *Margaret Atwood: Language, Text, and System*, he, like many other critics, explores themes of change and metamorphosis in Atwood's poetry and lauds her masterful exploration of such themes. Of *True Stories* he writes that poems such as "Landcrab" and "Mushrooms" exhibit a "metamorphic process by which thoughts merge into

sensations ... yet things in a curious and compensating way become liberated into thought." An example of this is when, at the end of the poem "Mushrooms," the mushrooms become a metaphor for poetry. Woodcock notes that these poems contrast the sensual with the intellectual, or things with thoughts. Woodcock concludes that Atwood's "work—in prose and verse alike—presents a unity that reflects her dominant themes, tenacious survival and constant metamorphosis."

CRITICISM

Rachel Kathryn Porter

Porter is a freelance writer and editor who holds a bachelor of arts in English literature. In the following essay, she examines the poem's seemingly contradictory metaphors to demonstrate how the structure of "Mushrooms" mimics the life cycle of a mushroom.

Atwood's poem "Mushrooms" bears a structural semblance to the subject of its title. The poem itself creeps up on the reader in a way that is similar to the creeping, seemingly sudden appearance of mushrooms described in the poem. It reads as a fairly straightforward narrative poem until the last section, which presents a striking shift, much like the bursting of mushrooms described in the poem's second section. Atwood creates this mushroom-like effect through select images, diction, and a series of contrasting metaphors that eventually and purposefully collapse in the last stanza, as the themes of human intellectualism and nature converge.

The poem is so heavily dependent on figurative descriptions of mushrooms that some stanzas are little more than a string of such metaphors, one after another. These metaphors, which to a large degree compose and dominate the poem, become increasingly divergent throughout it. The similes of the second stanza of the first section, bubbles (line 6), balloons (line 7), and rubber glove thumbs (lines 9–10) are all vaguely round, plastic, stretchy, and artificial. All of these metaphors evoke similar images and clearly describe the same subject. Of course, bubbles and balloons are different in many ways, but in the context of this poem as comparisons for mushrooms, it is easy to understand why they would be grouped together in the same stanza. Stanza 3 of the first section turns from similes that are chiefly

WHAT DO I READ NEXT?

- *Paint Me Like I Am: Teen Poems from WritersCorps*, published in 2003, is a collection of poems written by disadvantaged youth. The poetry included in this volume explores topics ranging from race to drugs to self-image.

- *The Handmaid's Tale* by Atwood was published in 1985. This dystopian science fiction fable depicts a world where women are strictly controlled and restricted to various social classes. The novel is narrated by a woman called Offred, who explains how the strange society came to be.

- *The Collected Poems: Sylvia Plath*, published in 2008, includes poetry from the writer's collections along with several never-before published poems. This Pulitzer prize winning volume includes an introduction by Plath's late husband, Ted Hughes. Like Atwood, Plath is considered a feminist poet.

- *Complete Stories and Poems of Edgar Allan Poe*, published in 1984, is an anthology of the great writer's work. Poe's work is known for its use of the macabre and mystery. Growing up, Poe was one of Atwood's favorite writers and his influence is evident in her work.

- *Morning in the Burned House*, published in 1996, is Atwood's twelfth volume of poetry.

The poems of this volume are split into five thematic sections. They are more varied in subject matter than her earlier collections, but just as potent.

- *The New Canon: An Anthology of Canadian Poetry* was published in 2006. It includes over 200 poems by fifty modern Canadian poets, as well as an explanatory essay that denotes the poetic innovations distinguishing the different writers.

- *The English Patient*, by Michael Ondaatje, was published in 1992. Ondaatje, a Sri Lankan-born Canadian novelist, was the first Canadian to win a Booker Prize, which he won for this novel. *The English Patient* takes place in an Italian monastery at the end of World War II, and details the lives of a Hungarian burn victim and his Canadian nurse.

- *The Red Shoes: Margaret Atwood Starting Out*, published in 1998, details Atwood's early life, explaining and theorizing about the experiences that shaped her into the prolific writer she is today. Based on interviews with the writer herself as well as many of her close friends, this work is a speculative biography.

---

artificial, to metaphors that are chiefly natural and organic, such as fishgills and brains. However, as in the first stanza, these metaphors are also mainly round or orb-like, indicating that this section describes the mushrooms from the perspective of someone looking down on them. This stanza also presents the poem's first overt contradiction: mushrooms are described as being both like the sun and the moon. However, Atwood somewhat undoes the contradiction by describing the suns as dulled, and the moons as yellow. Instead of instilling an image of a bright yellow sun and a white moon, she presents two similar images of warm light.

The second section of the poem also implements images that are materially organic. Yet, as this section begins with a question about how the mushrooms originate, it also includes metaphors that describe the mushrooms' underground growth rather than how they might appear to someone looking down at them after they have sprouted.

The third section turns from an explanation of how the mushrooms look and how they originate, to what they do and how they taste. The language of this section is more direct and declaratory than the preceding sections, and the images used to describe the mushrooms in this

> THE POEM BUILDS IN COMPLEXITY AND
> INTENSITY UNTIL IT SUDDENLY BURSTS OPEN, LIKE
> A MUSHROOM RELEASING SPORES, IN THE LAST
> STANZA, THROUGH A SHIFT THAT IS
> SIMULTANEOUSLY SUDDEN AND EXPLANATORY."

section are similarly terse. The visceral description of their taste (lines 34–36) is dominated by images of damaged or decaying flesh, which recall emotions of suffering and sorrow. Surprisingly these weighty images are immediately followed by the image of light, fresh, innocent snow; a stark contrast.

The final section of the poem presents not only a jarring shift in tone and style, but also even more strikingly contrasting metaphors. In describing the mushrooms' smell the narrator compares them using two images that could hardly be more contradictory: death and the flesh of newborn babies. However, the difference between these images is, as are most of the contrasting metaphors in the poem, somewhat mitigated by Atwood's diction. In particular, the term *waxy* does not make the newborn of her poem seem warm and vivacious, but rather, motionless and silent. The final stanza in which the narrator directly addresses the reader also presents the poem's most obviously contradictory metaphors. Following the colon in line 44, the narrator lists four images, one after the next, that alternate quickly between images that are negative and those that are positive. The alteration is emphasized by parallel clause structure. The way the images are presented one after another in short clauses with commas in between makes it easy to spot their striking difference.

However, the real shock of the poem, the aforementioned jarring shift, occurs in line 38 when the seemingly omniscient narrator unexpectedly becomes a character in the poem via the pronoun "I." Subsequently, in line 44 the reader is directly addressed by the narrator by the pronoun "you." This is no longer merely a descriptive or narrative poem, but an address or a presentation from the narrator to the reader. This gives the reader a sense of immediacy and makes them feel involved in the poem. The narrator claims to present something to the reader, although exactly what is being presented is indeterminate. Because the entire poem has been about mushrooms, the word *handful* seems to imply that the narrator is metaphorically presenting a handful of mushrooms to the reader. However, what the narrator is literally presenting is the *poem* "Mushrooms" to the reader. The narrator even uses the word poetry in the last line, indicating that what is being presented must be either metaphorically or literally poetic. Thus, the last four lines of the poem fuse together the images and metaphorical descriptions of mushrooms that have been listed throughout the poem, with the image of the poem itself. In the last stanza it becomes clear that the metaphorical descriptions of mushrooms could also be applied to poetry.

Therefore, this final stanza, in which the images of the poem are most blatantly contradictory, is also the dramatic climax of the poem, the point at which what is natural, organic, and from the earth (mushrooms), is conflated with what is human, organized, and created (poetry). The entire poem has been building the collapse of this contradiction. The metaphorical images of mushrooms, which can be cataloged by several different contrasts such as internal versus external, life versus decay, human versus nonhuman, beautiful versus grotesque, or light versus dark, are not organized in any discernable pattern in the poem, but are instead mixed up throughout it. This is significant, because it indicates that they must be organized in some less obvious way. The images at the beginning of the poem are fairly traditional, noncontroversial, and easy to reconcile with one another. However, as the poem progresses the images become more complicated, contradictory, and difficult to reconcile with one another. Some of the metaphors that are listed in adjacent sentences are so indicative of opposites, such as light and dark or life and death, that it is initially difficult to understand how they can describe the same subject. The poem builds in complexity and intensity until it suddenly bursts open, like a mushroom releasing spores, in the last stanza, through a shift that is simultaneously sudden and explanatory. Although mushrooms undergo a growth process of several days, the poem describes them as though they pop up over night, probably because they go unnoticed until they are fully formed. The poem develops in a similar way. It seems to be a slow description of the life cycle of

A mushroom-shaped storm cloud (David Kay / Shutterstock.com)

than mushrooms. However, considering that this poem was first published in a volume of poetry titled *True Stories*, a volume that frequently questions the validity of language, perhaps Atwood means to interrogate the reverence that is immediately, and sometimes undeservedly bestowed upon a poem by virtue of its simply being a poem. Mushrooms, unlike flowers, are imperfect and dark. They are fungal, unattractive, and can easily be overlooked. But mushrooms are also useful in spite of their physical quality, not, like flowers, because of it. They can be used medicinally or as food. Therefore, a poetic conflation of the concept of mushrooms and the concept of poetry is a complex and sly confrontation of the nature of poetry itself.

Source: Rachel Kathryn Porter, Critical Essay on "Mushrooms," in *Poetry For Students*, Gale, Cengage Learning, 2011.

Lothar Honnighausen

In the following excerpt, Honnighausen introduces Atwood's poetry as an "irresistible, ongoing process of perception, reflection, and aesthetic organization."

On the occasion of this essay on Margaret Atwood's poetry, I take my cue both from her painter Elaine Risley, favoring "a chronological approach" for this retrospective exhibition, and from her gallerist Charna, who "wants things to go together tonally and resonate" (*Cat's Eye*). Atwood's work has been categorized and subdivided into so many styles and phases, in which she supposedly was a Canadian nationalist, literary lobbyist, liberal parodist, Amnesty International activist, or changed back and forth from poet to prose writer, from aggressive feminist harpy to soft-souled wife and mother, from progressive young woman to stone-faced sibyl, that the use of any traditional evolutionary scheme in approaching it is out of the question. Along the same lines, Atwood's poetic stance, which has been oversimplistically described as either *autobiographical* or *mythopoeic*, is probably neither or both, resulting, as with other writers, from the stylization, in changing forms, of a changing stream of experience. In any case, her sixtieth birthday seems to call not so much for yet more scholarly theorizing than for intense rereading, particularly of her poetry, which is not as well known as her fiction.

Although there are many affinities between Atwood's poetry and her fiction, her poems, in

mushrooms that anyone could easily read and understand until the last stanza, which jumps out at the reader with striking metaphors and a direct address.

Upon further examination it is evident that the diction of the poem also confuses the opposition of nature (mushrooms) and human intellectualism (poetry). The poem includes at least seven human body parts to describe different parts of the mushroom. It is almost as if in this poem Atwood has described mushrooms in terms of human anatomy, and human intellect in terms of mushrooms.

Although Atwood's intentions for the poem are of course indeterminate, there are several reasons why it may be useful to think about poetry or human thought in terms of mushrooms. Poets are often admired for their superior abilities of perception, and consequently poems are often thought of and studied as though they are perfected gems of truth. Poems are often beautiful and aesthetically pleasing, more similar to flowers contrast to her novels, stories, or essays, seem to occur like entries into a kind of artistic logbook. Writing poetry for Atwood appears to be an irresistible, ongoing process of perception, reflection, and aesthetic organization. What makes this process of poetic exploration relevant to her readers is the radicality with which she puts things to the test, and the inventive craftsmanship with which she organizes her experiences as poems: "As for the ego—I wonder if it really exists? ... One is simply a location where certain things occur, leaving trails & debris ... something in one that organizes the random bits though" (Sullivan, 220).

Furthermore, there are some other continuous traits which endear Atwood the poet to her readers: her nimble intelligence and her comic sense, her precision and scientific curiosity, her inexhaustible productivity, and her insistence on shaping rather than shouting. If her literary personae hardly ever appear in a tragic predicament, they are often plagued by doubt and revulsion, but fortunately many convey a wry sense of humor. The fascinating experience for Atwood's readers is to share with her the wide range of her artistic moods and modes of expression, as the overview of the following volumes of poetry will show: *The Circle Game* (1966), *The Animals in That Country* (1968), *The Journals of Susanna Moodie* (1970), *Procedures for Underground* (1970), *Power Politics* (1971), *You Are Happy* (1974), *Two-Headed Poems* (1978), *True Stories* (1981), *Interlunar* (1984), *Morning in the Burned House* (1995).

In a retrospective of Atwood's poetry, the title poems of her various volumes obviously constitute nodes which can serve as points of departure and foci for the proposed rereadings. Atwood's debut as a fully fledged poet, *The Circle Game*, for which she received the Governor General's Award for 1966, was as convincing as her first novel, *The Edible Woman*, dating from 1965 and published in 1969. Both the volume of poetry and the novel fuse the narcissism of an antagonistic love affair with wider thematic concerns, such as the doubtful realities of the contemporary consumer and media culture, and both these apprentice works display the same amazing assurance of tone and performance. In fact, the basic poetic techniques that Atwood adopts in her first book of poetry undergo no substantial changes, notwithstanding many subtle modifications, from her first

through her most recent volume. There are no fixed stanza forms, no rhyme, no regular meter, but a sure and continuous voice informs the poem through its remotest ramifications, and through the varying lengths of stanzas and lines. This medium proves flexible enough to accommodate widely varying topics, presenting, to somebody with the artistic ingenuity and shaping power of Atwood, every opportunity for formal precision....

Source: Lothar Honnighausen, "Margaret Atwood's Poetry: 1966–1995," in *Margaret Atwood: Works & Impact*, edited by Reingard M. Nischik, Camden House, 2000, pp. 97–99.

Valerie Broege

In the following excerpt, Broege examines the influence of the United States on Atwood's writing.

An abiding concern of Canadian literature over the years has been to articulate the range of responses Canadians have had to the American presence. Many writers of both fiction and nonfiction have tried to explore the impact of the Americans on the Canadian consciousness and way of life. Thus, such vital issues have been probed as the extent of U.S. domination of Canada's economy and culture as well as the susceptibility of Canadians to importing their standards of excellence and comparison from the United States. Particularly during the last decade and a half the output of Canadian literature dealing in some way with the U.S. has increased, reflecting the upsurge of nationalist sentiment in Canada. It is within this contemporary context that I would like to address myself to Margaret Atwood, who has been a perceptive commentator on the Canadian-American relationship. In this paper I shall examine the origin, nature, and variety of Atwood's personal attitudes concerning Americans and Canadians and the reflection of these attitudes in her poetry and fiction. Important to note is the fact that Atwood's appraisals of the U.S. run the gamut from admiration to stinging censure. As I shall demonstrate, the ambivalence displayed by Atwood is typical in general of the traditional and even stereotyped points of view Canadians have evolved of the Americans in the course of their mutual historical interactions.

I shall first consider how Atwood's exposure as a child to two key forms of American popular culture, comic books and movies, helped to shape her conceptions of the U.S., and how these conceptions were altered by her later residence and travel in the States. Atwood cites as an

**AMERICAN IGNORANCE OF THE REAL
CANADA—AS WELL AS OF THE REST OF THE
WORLD—FRIGHTENS ATWOOD."**

early formative influence in her life the voracious reading of American comic books, as well as the writing of comic books with her older brother. She especially enjoyed *Captain Marvel, Plastic Man, Batman, Blackhawk, The Human Torch,* and *Superman.* On the one hand, Atwood states that such comic books provided a kind of fantasy escape, but, on the other hand, she imputes considerably more significance to them in her remark that the truth about the universe was contained in them. She thought of them as news bulletins of the actions going on across the border which Canadians could watch, but not join. Canada was the place where the Popsicle bag offers did not apply and where everything cost ten cents extra.

It is obvious that Atwood's childhood experiences with American comic books made a lasting impression on her, since references to them are scattered throughout her poetry and fiction. In one instance, Atwood makes quite a sinister use of the U.S. comics tradition to contribute to the reader's impression of a character's paranoia. She has the unbalanced narrator in *Surfacing* ponder how the Americans became sinister figures. Originally she had seen Hitler as the exemplar of evil, courtesy of the war comic books her brother had brought home. Now Hitler was dead, but evil remained. She muses over whether it could be possible that the Americans are worse than Hitler. It can be seen that this is a complete reversal of the image of Captain America of the 1940s—the defender of truth, justice, and the American way—triumphing over the crazed and wicked Fuhrer.

The element of fantasy associated with comic books seems to define an integral part of the American psyche for Atwood. One of her poems, "Comic Books Vs. History (1949, 1969)," projects the image of the U.S. as that of "tense / needle turrets of steel / cities" and heroes who all wore capes with bullets bouncing off them, beautiful orange collisions coming from their fists. Juxtaposed to this view of America as

teeming with skyscrapers and innumerable clones of Batman and Robin is her less exalted picture of Canada. Canada " . . . held only / real-sized explorers, confined / to animal skin coats." These explorers are treated as nonentities who " . . . plodded, discovered / rivers whose names we always / forgot; in the winters / they died of scurvy." But when the poem's narrator finally visited the U.S. the crime and poverty changed her perceptions: " . . . the / red and silver / heroes had collapsed inside / their rubber suits / the riddled / buildings were decaying / magic." Upon returning to Canada the narrator began to " . . . search / for the actual, collect lost / bones, burnt logs / of campfires, pieces of fur." In this poem Atwood highlights the dangers of becoming excessively wrapped up in two-dimensional versions of reality. She seems to be saying that even though the actuality of Canada is much more mundane than the exciting fantasies defining the identity of the U.S., reality is preferable.

. . . Ironically, Atwood first thought seriously about Canada during her residence in the U.S. She has spoken of an unhappy scrambling for their own identities that occurred among Canadian students of her acquaintance in Boston. It was then that she discovered that Americans knew very little about Canada, seeing it as a sort of boring grey country, that blank area north of the U.S. from which the bad weather came. Atwood says that some Americans seemed to want to believe that her father was a Mountie and that she and her family lived in an igloo all year round. After a while, she enjoyed making them think that this was actually true. This attitude is manifested in her Canadian character, Ann, in "Dancing Girls," who is tempted to wear snowshoes and a parka to a Friends of Foreign Students party. This function is hosted by a Boston woman who requests the guests to wear their native costumes. In the same story a female student from Holland is described as the only person Ann had met in Boston who seemed to know where Canada was, since many Canadian soldiers were buried in her country. Ann felt that this fact provided her with at least a shadowy identity. Although she did not have a native costume, " . . . at least she had some heroic dead bodies with which she was connected, however remotely."

This same concern with defining the Canadian identity for Americans is reflected in "At the Tourist Centre in Boston." Examining the self-image Canadians are exporting, Atwood seems to suggest that the picture is somewhat askew. Canada appears as a practically unpopulated country with a kind of sanitized natural splendour. All blues are "of an assertive purity." "Was the sky ever that blue?" The tourists in Canada seem to be depicted in terms of a commercial, since " . . . the mother is cooking something / in immaculate slacks by a smokeless fire, / her teeth white as detergent." As in "Comic Books Vs. History (1949, 1969)," Atwood registers a plea on behalf of reality: "I seem to remember people, / at least in the cities, also slush, / machines and assorted garbage." "Who really lives there?" She seems to hark back to Canada's pioneering past of settlers and Indians when she suggests that the citizens may be gone, having run off to the forest to wait for the " . . . platoons of tourists / and plan their odd red massacres." In her query "Do you see nothing / watching you from under the water?", taken in context with the rest of the poem, Atwood seems to be an apologist for the Group of Seven sensibility. She wants the portrayal of Canada to be real, warts and all, not like the exploded fantasies of American mythology in "Comic Books Vs. History."

American ignorance of the real Canada—as well as of the rest of the world—frightens Atwood. The narrator in *Surfacing* describes two young men she mistakes for Americans: "That was their armour, bland ignorance, heads empty as weather balloons: with that they could defend themselves against anything." Elsewhere, Atwood diagnoses the national mental illness of the U.S. as megalomania. In "Two-Headed Poems iii" she describes Americans as loud and guilty of blatantly poor taste. Their knowledge of the power and importance of their country gives them the self-assurance to assert themselves. This conviction that America is where the action is has probably contributed to the mentality of the conventional American tourist, often portrayed as applying materialistic American standards to what he experiences abroad. Atwood includes two such tourists in her short story "The Resplendent Quetzal," set in Mexico. A Canadian character in the story, Sarah, regards their facetious comments about the Aztec ruins as obtuse and irreverent. One of them would rather sit in the bus and the other would prefer to go shopping, although she does not think there is much to buy.

But, even while poking fun at the foibles of Americans, many Canadians, including Atwood herself, have found their self-confidence and enthusiasm a refreshing change of pace from the colder, more suspicious reception Canadians get at home. In Canadian eyes, the American character type is what psychologist Karen Homey calls expansive; in contrast, the Canadian personality is self-effacing and undynamic. It is this contrast that causes the ambivalence in Atwood's attitude toward Americans, an attitude reflected in some of her fictional characters. Fischer, in *The Edible Woman*, says that he can always do his thesis topic in the States if it is too radical for his Canadian professors in Toronto. The Royal Porcupine with his con-create poetry in *Lady Oracle* thinks that he should take his show to the U.S. because the Canadians are so cautious and unwilling to take a chance. In his opinion, that is why Alexander Graham Bell had to go south. In *Life Before Man*, Nate wishes he lived in California or Nevada, rather than "this tight-assed churchified country" because of the complications involved in divorcing his wife, Elizabeth, to marry Lesje. It has been pointed out by Atwood that even Canadian nationalists have succumbed to the lure of being able to make more money living in the States.

Atwood also expresses the contrast between the Canadian and American character in poetic terms. In "Two-Headed Poems ii" she says that "Those south of us are lavish / with their syllables. They scatter, we / hoard." Canadian timidity is highlighted in her question—"Who was it told us / so indelibly, / those who take risks / have accidents?" "Two-Headed Poems iii" pictures the Americans as proffering friendly and envious invitations to the Canadians to visit (or is it rather to stay and become Americans too?), but, instead, the Canadians quarrel among themselves about issues of identity and finances.

For Atwood, the Americans have a much stronger sense of who they are than do the Canadians, as she discovered while studying in Boston. Atwood was struck by the fact that there were university courses in the U.S. dealing with the literature of the American Puritans, but in her experience Canadian literature was not being widely taught in Canada's schools and universities. Thus, upon her return to Canada, she felt impelled to chart the geography of the Canadian imagination both for her own sense of identity as well as that of her fellow Canadians. She believes that refusing to acknowledge where one comes from is an act of amputation. By discovering one's place, one discovers one's self. Her efforts later culminated in *Survival: A Thematic Guide to Canadian Literature*, a book that has enjoyed enormous success and has helped to draw attention to the issue of teaching Canadian literature in the nation's schools and universities. Atwood has also spent time conducting seminars for high school English teachers in order to assist them in perceiving what is characteristically Canadian in the country's literature. Her main observation in *Survival* is that Canada has a colonial mentality because of its dependent relationships with Great Britain, France, and the United States. This has resulted in a disproportionate emphasis on victims, losers, and bare survival in Canadian writing.

Despite this impression of Canadian doom and gloom, Atwood says that she prefers Canada to the U.S. for the reason that ordinary people still are able to influence politics. She cites the examples of citizen groups blocking the building of an airport in Picketing and stopping the Spadina Expressway from cutting through Toronto. In her opinion, such things are more unlikely to happen in America because the machinery of government is out of control. Canada has more of a spirit of co-operation than the U.S. does with its ethos of ruthless individualism, every man for himself. The U.S. is a tragic country, to Atwood's way of thinking, because it has a utopian vision— life, liberty, and the pursuit of happiness—that is harder to achieve than Canada's more modest goals of peace, order and good government.

Although Atwood has not spoken directly about her fascination with American movies in the same way as she has stressed the importance of American comic books in her life, it is evident from both her poetry and prose that the movies have exerted an equally strong influence on her thinking and patterns of imagery. Atwood is aware of the dangers of Canadians becoming too immersed for their own good in American popular culture, which, although exciting, is unreal, whether it be comics or movies. For example, in *Lady Oracle* Atwood explores the perils of addiction to American movies, especially of the romantic type of the 1940s and 1950s. We learn that the protagonist, Joan Foster, had been given the name Joan after Joan Crawford. Joan was always puzzled by what her mother meant in doing this. Was Joan to emulate the screen characters of her namesake or was the point to be successful? The fact of being named after a famous American movie star may have been the initial factor leading to the severe identity crisis Joan exhibits throughout the novel. At least one critic has noted the possibility of interpreting as an allegory of the Canadian condition, especially vis-a-vis the U.S., Joan's frantic desire to assume whatever identity might be required of her by other people.

The degree to which Joan has fixated on the celluloid images of the American silver screen and has been brainwashed by them illustrates perfectly what Robert Fulford has said in "Home Movies," one of the programs in the CBC series *The Great Canadian Culture Hunt*. It is his contention that American movies have been the most important force in teaching Canadians the nature of American ideology. For example, many Canadians assume from their watching of American cop shows that a Canadian policeman will read the bill of rights to a prisoner upon his arrest.

Besides her interest in romantic movies, Margaret Atwood also appears to be a devotee of American science fiction films, which she employs to good effect in articulating instructive insights into the American consciousness. Two important uses of science fiction analogies as applied to the Canadian-American relationship appear in Atwood's novel *Surfacing*. Throughout the novel the Americans are consistently portrayed as despoilers of the landscape, with the implicit contrast of the Canadians having more of a sense of kinship with nature and its creatures. Thus, at one point in the story when the narrator and her friends are sailing on the lake, they hug the shore so as to avoid the possibility of an American speedboat deliberately whizzing by them as close as it can. But the Americans vanish; "they whoosh away into nowhere like Martians in a late movie." This is not the only time that Atwood has used a Martian analogy when she wishes to imply a consciousness that is quite remote from the Canadian way of thinking. For example, her short story "The Man from Mars" deals with a young oriental man whose behaviour seems unfathomable to the Canadians with whom he comes in contact. Thus, in *Surfacing*, Atwood seems to want to express the notion that there is a great gulf between Canadian and American mentalities.

Working on this premise makes her second science fiction movie analogy all the more effective because of the shock of recognition involved. The narrator in *Surfacing* is convinced that two men who have "the candid, tanned astronaut finish valued by the magazines," and who have wantonly killed a heron, are American. Then a double irony ensues. The two men had thought that she and her friends were Americans, perhaps from Ohio, while they themselves are Canadians. One is from Sarnia and the other from Toronto. In despair, the narrator thinks that it does not matter what country they are from; they are still Americans. Everyone is turning into an American: it's like a virus taking over one's brain cells. The Americans are like the body snatchers in the late show sci-fi movies: "If you look like them and talk like them and think like them then you are them. ... " This powerful analogy is reminiscent of the popular American movie of the 1950s, *The Invasion of the Body Snatchers*. If one remembers the outcome of this movie, Atwood may be telling us that to resist the Americanization of the world is hopeless; everyone will eventually be infected by it.

Besides seeing paradigms of the Canadian-American relationship in American science fiction movies, Atwood also sees American westerns as reflections of the same relationship. One of the most beloved and enduring manifestations of American popular culture has been, of course, the Western as morality play—the good guys triumphing over the bad guys. But Americans have often been accused of espousing a black-and-white moral code that does not allow enough latitude for the various shades of grey. Robert Kroetsch has commented that Freudianism has always been popular in the U.S. because it appeals to something significant in the American experience: "the stress between the good guy and the bad guy, the id and the ego, a kind of Manichean view of the psyche." By contrast, Kroetsch regards Canada as a much more Jungian country, in that it tends to see two sides of a conflict as aspects of the same thing instead of as polar opposites. Canadians strive to keep opposites in the necessary balance all the time, but, as Kroetsch admits, this may become paralyzing. For Kroetsch the good guy in American ideology is "the frontiersman, the man in the 10-gallon hat." Atwood alludes to this kind of figure in *The Edible Woman* and in her poem "Backdrop Addresses Cowboy." In the novel, Marian, the heroine, goes to see a low-budget American western. Although she is too distracted to follow the plot closely, she knows that there "must be bad people ... trying to do something evil and good people ... trying to stop them. ... " The movie ends with "a brief shot of a waving flag and some tinny music. ... " In "Backdrop Addresses Cowboy," Atwood explores some of the darker implications of these simplified standards of fight and wrong and flag-waving Americanism.

... I think that Atwood's personal background has made her especially sensitive to the Americans' abuse of their natural surroundings, a subject that recurs numerous times in her writings. As the daughter of an entomologist, she spent much time with her parents in Northern Ontario and Quebec on nature expeditions, which she loved. She says that the moral code of her Nova Scotian ancestry has made her deplore waste in all forms.

"Polarities" affords us another good illustration of the soulless exploitation by the Americans so abhorrent to Atwood. In this short story, Morrison is an American working in Canada. Louise, his Canadian friend, sees Morrison's mind and body as alienated from each other. Morrison is able to feel sexually attracted to her only after she has suffered a breakdown, for then she was "a defeated formless creature on which he could inflict himself like shovel on earth, axe on forest, use without being used, know without being known." Note Atwood's use of similes relating to man's conquest of nature. To Morrison's credit this self-knowledge horrifies him but at least he feels some hope in recognizing that his fantasy about Louise was partly "a desire to be reunited with his own body, which he felt less and less that he actually occupied." This perception shows that Morrison is concerned about becoming whole.

The image of the Americans as despoilers and exploiters is more corrosively etched in Atwood's *Surfacing*, which, interestingly enough in terms of the author's personal background, is set in Northern Quebec. In *Surfacing*, there is less hope that the Americans will change their ways than in "Polarities."

At several points in the novel, we learn of the reactions of the narrator and her friends to various Americans whom they encounter in this resort area. Two men, whom the narrator assumes American, leave footprints which she envisions as having been produced by tractor treads which left excavations and craters in the mud path. Two businessmen from the States in a big powerboat are seen as predators. One of them—"teeth bared, friendly as a shark"—asks the group whether they have caught any fish. Animal imagery when applied to the Americans vis-a-vis Canadians inevitably features the U.S. as an animal that is big and/or strong and/or rapacious—e.g., eagle, elephant, bull, whale, gorilla (King Kong), crocodile, cat, wolf, vampire. A shark fits these categories perfectly. The narrator is disgusted by the presence of these intruders. She says that if the Americans catch one fish they will be here all night, and that this part of the lake will be swarming with Americans like ants around sugar, or lobsters. But, if they do not get a bite within fifteen minutes, they will blast off and scream around the lake, deafening all the fish. She thinks that they are the kind who will catch more than they can eat and would use dynamite if they could get away with it. The narrator recalls several stories she had heard about American greed and wastefulness, and the methods by which some had tried to smuggle large numbers of illegal fish out of the country. When bribery of a game warden was unsuccessful, they said that Canada was a lousy country and that they would not come back. For sport they enjoyed chasing loons in their motor boats until they drowned or got chopped up in the propeller blades.

Atwood perceives an essential difference in the way in which animals are regarded by Canadians and Americans. For the Americans, hunting and killing an animal is an heroic deed, confirming man's ability to "conquer" the forces of nature, from which he has become so alienated. It is almost like a coming of age ritual for men to mount their trophies on the wall. This mystique associated with the hunting and killing of animals indicates to Atwood "the general imperialism of the American cast of mind" (*Surv.*). A Canadian, by contrast, tends to identify sympathetically with the victim status of animals. As an illustration of these points, the narrator of *Surfacing* says she hates all Americans, because they had turned against the gods. She wishes that she could press a button and make the Americans vanish without disturbing anything else. That way there would be more room for the animals; they would be rescued. "It would have been different in those countries where an animal is the soul of an ancestor or the child of a god, at least they would have felt guilt." The emotionally disturbed young narrator has been seen as representative of the Canadian psyche—feminine, passive, lacking identity, and suffering a victim complex which has projected upon the Americans the role of victimizers.

Source: Valerie Broege, "Margaret Atwood's American and Canadians," in *Essays on Canadian Writing*, No. 22, Summer 1981, pp. 111–36.

Jane Lilienfeld

In the following essay, Lilienfeld uses five Atwood poems to illustrate what Atwood calls "the growth

> **"** *YOU ARE HAPPY* INCORPORATES IN ITS FOUR SEQUENCES THE PROGRESSION OF MARGARET ATWOOD'S POETRY: REFUSAL OF ANGER, ANGER, WIT, AND TRANSFORMATION."

of 'a word like an unclenching flower,' a word which is first silent, then scornful, then sings love."

In one of Margaret Atwood's earliest poems, her speaker addresses "The Director of Protocol." He is the male viewer, the male watcher, the male embodiment of the voice women in this culture have ingested with their selfhood, the voice saying No, you must not. No, you cannot, No, you are not a woman if you feel or say that.

> You would like to keep me
> from saying anything . . .
>
> Sometimes you put it more strongly,
> I can feel your thumbs
> on my windpipe . . .
>
> I can feel you nailing STOP signs
> all over my skin on the inside . . .

The direction of her whole poetic endeavor is to find a voice in which to speak to "The Director of Protocol." The speakers' fight to voice their truths is a two part struggle, for the "Director of Protocol" has a brother in the men the speakers love. Atwood's speakers have first to express their anger as they recognize their mufflings. Should they remain attached to male figures of denial? The speakers grow in strength through separation; freely speaking at last, they find the men they love have changed in nature. Discussing five poems taken from Atwood's six volumes, I will examine what Atwood calls the growth of "a word like an unclenching flower," a word which first is silent, then scornful, then sings love.

In her earliest volume of poetry, *The Circle Game* (1966). Atwood presents the stunning poem, "A Sibyl." In that poem the speaker has an analogue in the sibyl who lives in "thin green wine bottles; emptied of small dinners / ovaltine jars, orange brown / emptied of easy sleep. . . ." This enclosure is represented by the sibyl's lines being indented and sometimes placed in parentheses. The speaker is vulnerable both to her plugged up sibyl—"(every woman / should have one)"—and to her dangerous lover.

> and a man dances
> in my kitchen, moving
> like a metronome
> with hopes of staying
> for breakfast in the half-empty
> bottle in his pocket

This man seems to have pocketed the very jars which contain the sibyl, jars whose contents he has perhaps transformed, jars perhaps full of that which he has absorbed from the speaker. Immediately before she introduces him, the speaker tells us "Right now / my skin is a sack of clever tricks, five / senses ribboned like birth / day presents unravel / in a torn web around me. ..." Her connection to the man has opened her to a defenseless state, has ripped her covering apart. Part of her is speaking with the sibyl; part of her is in her lover's pocket. Where will a whole voice come from? How can she love, be open to a man, and also prophecy women's situation?

> Only the sibyl's voice is unmuffled:
>
> she calls to me with the many
> voices of the children
> not I want to die
> but You must die
> later or sooner alas
> you were born weren't you
> the minutes thunder like guns
> coupling won't help you
> or plurality
> I see it
> I prophecy

In Ovid's *Metamorphosis 32* the Cumaen Sibyl retained life but not youth; she had no lover but had a voice of prophecy. Underlining her unattractiveness, her difference from the speaker whose very body echoes with the ricochets of her lover's touch, the sibyl is frighteningly other than we like to imagine an attractive sexual woman: "wrinkled as a pickled / baby, twoheaded prodigy / at a freakfair / hairless, her sightless eyes like eggwhites." The vision of a woman whose existence is itself a prophecy of alienation, oracular commentary, and resistance to heterosexuality occurs more and more in contemporary women's poetry. Rosellen Brown's Cora Fry goes home to her husband because she does not want to become like a woman she sees in Boston, a woman bum, tattered, crazed-looking, a looter of trash cans, while the poet Irena Klepfisz fears that her childless state may ally her

to those she calls "the shopping-bag-women" who are given a wide berth by other subway travellers. Similary, in Atwood's poem the sibyl has no heterosexually attractive attributes: to the speaker, she is old, ugly, infertile, and thus a freak.

For these reasons, the speaker denies her potential relation to the sibyl. She tries to silence the apparition: "I'll / uncork you ... or I'll ignore you. ... " Her body's longings turn her once again to the man whose touch has unravelled her, yet she sees his message as clearly as she does that of the sibyl, for she says in lines indented to parallel the sibyl's:

> There are omens of
> rockets among the tricycles
> I know it
> time runs out
> in the ticking hips of the
> man whose twitching skull
> jerks on loose
> vertebrae in my kitchen
> flower
> beds predict it
>
> the city burns with an
> afterglo of explosions....

As Atwood clearly notes in other of her writings, patriarchal men do contain and unleash lethal weapons. More than the speaker's refusal to be a mother to the children who throughout *The Circle Game* play ominous games in the flower-beds, the speaker's vision of her lover's menace contains the knowledge that patriarchal modes and technology not only unravel her skin, but could detonate the city. The lover ticks away like a time bomb to a tune of his own, yet it is his voice she cannot do without. She knows his meaning, she knows his intent, yet she wants him. She splits her own life in two:

> The thing that calls itself
> I
> right now
> doesn't care
>
> I don't care
>
> I leave that to my
> necessary sibyl
> (that's what she's for)
> with her safely bottled
> anguish and her glass
> despair

The poem leaves us with the two voices sounding in different containers in the poem, as the sibyl's voice is blocked off on the page, visually in a glass column of its own. The speaker may not acknowledge her sibyl's voice as issuing from her own mouth, but the speaker is too honest and too aware to deny her sibyl's existence.

Two years later Margaret Atwood published another poem on the same theme, "The Shadow Voice" in which the vision of the patriarchal culture and its different deaths are spoken clearly by a sexless voice of vision. Once again the speaker cannot bring her own sexual needs for male partnership into alignment with this shadow voice. The voice promises a sexless life, "a life of water and clean crusts," a life of words alone. The speaker cannot accept the oracular mode, being a priestess, a virgin of that goddess. She rejects the anger which of necessity precedes a true integration of the sibyline voice with that of a woman committed to working out a life in which men are more than lethal enemies or frequent visitors who bottle us in their pockets.

The central metaphor of the next volume of poetry, *Procedures for Underground*, published in 1970, explains the way the speaker came to accept her anger and her separation from "The Director of Protocol" and his brothers. Whether this separation would be temporary, or what harm to the self might result from it, is not clear, but that it is impossible to live any longer in a bottle and silence anger and difference into parentheses bursts forth in "Interview with a Tourist." The Tourist is a man different from those men underground, for they are similar in body and need to the women underground. They have been transformed through their underground existence into beings other than Tourists or "Directors of Protocol." Underground is the country of the sibyl, of the virgin priestess sacred to the Mother goddess, of the unreachable past, of the home of poetry, beneath time as men have forced it into linear progression. Beneath time, under water, in the woman's world, the poem unfolds.

"You speed by me with your camera and your spear / and stop and ask me for directions / I answer there are none" begins the poem. The speaker is committed to the underground which is not cut up into manageable chunks; in its oneness there is no need for directions. The Tourist wants to understand the country underwater; he asks why it appears as it does; "why the light here / is always the same colour;" Like other oppressed people, the speaker has succeeded because she commands two languages. She can speak to the Tourist in his vocabulary: "I talk about the diffuse / surfaces, angles of refraction." But because these words are issuing from her mouth as she presents

the meaning of her territory, the Tourist cannot grasp what she is saying. The very fact of his being a Tourist, his weapons ridiculous and useless, makes him deaf. Because he is underground, he would need her language, and he has been cut off even from his own.

Finally in desperation he asks "why I can't love you"

> It is because you have air in your lungs
> and I am an average citizen
>
> Once when there was history
> some obliterating fact occurred.
> no solution was found
>
> Now this country is underwater;
> we can love only the drowned

Biological differences are real. He breathes air; she can filter her necessities from water. She is one of many, "an average citizen," perhaps a sister to the other citizens of the underground. But because the speaker has developed the subtleties of her vision, the word average has another meaning, for in a patriarchal culture, women are not to exceed the average, otherwise they are no longer women. Which side of the struggle caused "the obliterating fact" is unclear, but the choice of another existence is not. Though she can speak his hard metallic language of instruments and machines, the speaker has lungs which insure her survival and enable her to speak in a new way.

All the strengths the speaker gathers from sources underground modulate her voice so that she can speak anger directly and clearly. She chooses sarcasm, satire and ridicule, the weapons Virginia Woolf advised women to use in talking back to the patriarchy. Margaret Atwood has learned that language: "You fit into me / like a hook into an eye / a fish hook / an open eye." So begins *Power Politics*. Here sounds the voice of a speaker who has no illusions and many strengths. Poem after poem skewers the mock-heroic lover, names him with witty ridicule. Clearly articulate, seeing wholly, the speaker is safe from the desperation of need which earlier riddled the lives of the other speakers of the poetry. Her wit gives her distance and supports her separation from the beloved. For no matter his appearance in her fantasies as "the hinged bronze man, the fragile / man built of glass pebbles / the fanged man with his opulent cape and boots," he is her beloved. Her politics do give her power, for as she examines her poetic pictures of the mock-hero, the speaker accepts her part in supporting his patriarchal posturings, as she has clothed him in their imagery to insure her poetic fame. "Please die I said / so I can write about it." Finally she admits his reality, his desire for a relationship in which his vulnerability is as present as her withering vision, his wish for "a love without mirrors and not for / my reasons but your own." The volume ends as a man comes toward the speaker from underground. Whether she will accept him she does not prophecy, but that she has helped him into existence, into accepting the life underground, she has clearly spoken.

Anger is too simple a term for the complexity of language, metaphor, and imagery, of plot and counterplot, in *You are Happy*. Four sections integrate the theme. The unhealed wounds of a now-ended love affair of the earliest section, "You Are Happy," melds into the acerbic wit, the grace of revenge in "Songs of the Transformed," the second section, in which animals take back their power. Remorselessly honest, clear speaking with wit honed by oppression, the animals reveal that their underground existence will lead to the true heroic, as for example in "Song of the Worms." These two sections merge in "Circe/Mud Poems" in which Circe, as heroic as Odysses, sees through his patriarchal stance to his "moonmarks"—the wounds dealt him from his acceptance of his warrior role. She moves from ridicule to compassion, from laughingly demanding "Don't you ever get tired of saying Onward?" to a recognition of the price Odysses paid for his scars. Circe too has been maimed, for the Mother renounced her when she had intercourse with Odysses. She is not, then, a priestess of the Mother any longer in this sequence but neither is she the slave of Odysses. She is a self radiant with intelligence and skill in reality. Pelucid, sparkling with wit, she is a seer into the relations between men and women, she who once was a seer into the earth.

"Circe/Mud Poems" posits another island on which unfurls a future for Circe and Odysses. On it they have a fertile peace and are one another's equals. The resources, the discoveries, and the work of "Circe/Mud Poems" occur in the present in the final sequence, "There is Only One of Everything." The three final poems of that sequence are among the most perfect Atwood has written. A discussion of all three is beyond the limits of the present paper, but because the last of these, "Book of Ancestors," gathers up and brings to a new vision all the issues we have been discussing, it is to that poem I will turn for my conclusion.

The poem begins with the origins of patriarchy, the sacrifice of human life to a warrior god: "the plumed and beak- / nosed priests pressing his arms and feet down, heart slashed from his opened / flesh … The victim's posture in the sacrifice parallels that of Circe as Odysses took her for the first time, thus aligning her firmly with the victims of the priestly elite. Can the oppressed, the sacrificed, feel their lives are ceded by their own choice, asks the poem, "Whether he thinks this is / an act of will." Many women have lived lives cramped and threatened only unconsciously unwilling. The violence of the slaughter, in language as powerful as any in Atwood's poetry, culminates in the instant of insight smashed by death, singed back into the regions of art. For stanza one turns out to take place in a woven tapestry. Margaret Atwood in having designed a verbal tapestry pays tribute to centuries of women artists who celebrated warrior ritual by wearing tapestries in consecration and memorial, as for example the Bayeux Tapestry. Atwood herself wove an earlier tapestry of commentary on the patriarchal world of blood and ritual in the title poem of *The Animals in That Country*. Earlier neither speaker nor lovers had got beyond the borders of the weaving; here they do.

Odysses' battle scars, his vulnerabilities, he never exposed as openly as this lover whose body lies ready for the knife of the poet's mind. She realizes that though the "demands" of the patriarchy are "static," demanding the same round of repetitious behavior, possibly there is a way beyond that ritual of war. These lovers, too, have their "death patterns," yet says the poet, for them, "history / is over." That line recalls a time beyond history in "Interview with a Tourist." Here, too, is a history of the "obliterating fact," yet the lovers have moved so far beyond those traps that they can only see them archeologically: "These frescoes / on a crumbling temple / wall we look at now and can scarcely / piece together." Their other island, the place of Circe's wish, is an "undivided / space" rather like the oneness of underground, a space of freedom and choice, for "no necessities / hold us closed, distort / us." If this space can be imagined and set forth in poetry, can it not be brought to birth?

In that space of reality the lovers meet in winter in front of the fire. Years before Atwood had viewed a scene of intense menage in

"Midwinter, Presolstice" in which two lovers had been snowed in together by a Canadian winter. Their relation had not ended in an embrace for the "gentle husband" had put his wife's head in a bag along with his other necessities. Even "Circe/Mud Poems" has embraces resulting from aggression, anger melded into wit, and sexual pleasure sharpened by strategies of battle. But in this sequence all is the silence of intense trust.

As in *Power Politics*, the speaker is clearly the artist in control of the situation. For centuries male speakers have described their lovers longing for the poets' embraces; male painters have painted innumerable women readying themselves for their lovers. Here the woman poet creates a man stripped of weapons and pretense, as vulnerable as ever woman was, for his very eyes can be "easily bruised." As he "opens" himself to his lover, she turns to him, her language incorporating into it a coda of the first part of the poem, a history of maiming and aggression, the tapestry of violence in the name of necessity. But the language itself is transformative. What had been slaughter is here embrace, lovers touching in a sacred space of language, equal, fearful, tentative and loving:

> you open
>
> yourself to me gently, what
> they tried, we
> tried but could never do
> before, without blood, the killed
> heart to take
> that risk, to offer life and remain
>
> alive, open yourself like this and become whole

You Are Happy incorporates in its four sequences the progression of Margaret Atwood's poetry: refusal of anger, anger, wit, and transformation. The sequences move from the anger of a deserted lover, to the rage of the animals, to the balance between Odysses and Circe, to the final transformation in contemporary lovers meeting to live out the recognition that love "is a journey, not a war," that lovers need to "fight" "our way, our ways / not out but through." This final volume of Margaret Atwood's poetry contains in it the learnings of her ten years' previous work, for without the long refusal to be angry, and anger's open celebration in wit and ridicule, a movement beyond it would sound hollow indeed. The voice of sibyline prophecy does not predict the future of the lovers. They are mortal, they are human, and they will not always be so open to one another.

What the speaker will say after their embrace we must wait for the next volume of poetry to see.

Source: Jane Lilienfeld, "Silence and Scorn in a Lyric of Intimacy: The Progress of Margaret Atwood's Poetry," in *Women's Studies*, Vol. 7, 1980, pp. 185–94.

SOURCES

Atwood, Margaret, "Mushrooms," in *Selected Poems II: 1976–1986*, Houghton Mifflin, 1987, pp. 78–80.

Cooper, G. Burns, "Molecules and Crystals of Free Verse: Lines and Phrases," in *Mysterious Music: Rhythm and Free Verse*, Stanford University Press, 1998, pp. 92–115.

Davey, Frank, "The Insufficiency of Poetry," in *Margaret Atwood: a Feminist Poetics*, Talonbooks, 1984, pp. 37–56.

Eichler, Margrit, and Marie Lavigne, "Women's Movement," in *The Canadian Encyclopedia*, http://www.thecanadianencyclopedia.com/index.cfm?PgNm = TCE&Params = A1ARTA0008684 (accessed June 10, 2010).

Gorjup, Branko, "Margaret Atwood's Poetry and Poetics," in *The Cambridge Companion to Margaret Atwood*, edited by Coral Ann Howells, Cambridge University Press, 2006, pp. 130–44.

Harris, Robert, "Elements of the Gothic Novel," in *Virtual Salt*, October 11, 2008, http://www.virtualsalt.com/gothic.htm (accessed June 10, 2010).

Hengen, Shannon, "Margaret Atwood and Environmentalism," in *The Cambridge Companion to Margaret Atwood*, edited by Coral Ann Howells, Cambridge University Press, 2006, pp. 72–85.

Howells, Coral Ann, "Introduction" in *The Cambridge Companion to Margaret Atwood*, edited by Coral Ann Howells, Cambridge University Press, 2006, pp. 1–11.

Hummel, Monte, "Environmental and Conservation Movements," in *The Canadian Encyclopedia*, http://www.thecanadianencyclopedia.com/index.cfm?PgNm = TCE&Params = A1ARTA0002627 (accessed June 10, 2010).

"Margaret Atwood," in *Encyclopedia of World Biography*, http://www.notablebiographies.com/An-Ba/Atwood-Margaret.html (accessed June 10, 2010).

New, W. H., "Literature in English," in *The Canadian Encyclopedia*, http://www.thecanadianencyclopedia.com/index.cfm?PgNm = TCE&Params = A1ARTA0004709 (accessed June 21, 2010).

Oates, Joyce Carol, "Margaret Atwood's Tale," in *New York Review of Books*, November 2, 2006, http://www.ybooks.com/articles/archives/2006/nov/02/margaret-atwoods-tale/ (accessed June 10, 2010).

Staines, David, "Margaret Atwood in her Canadian Context," in *The Cambridge Companion to Margaret Atwood*, edited by Coral Ann Howells, Cambridge University Press, 2006, pp. 12–27.

"Women in National Parliaments," in *Inter-Parliamentary Union*, http://www.ipu.org/wmn-e/classif.htm (accessed July 6, 2010).

Woodcock, George, "Metamorphosis and Survival: Notes on the Recent Poetry of Margaret Atwood," in *Margaret Atwood: Language, Text, and System*, edited by Sherrill E. Grace and Lorraine Weir, University of British Columbia Press, 1983, pp. 125–42.

FURTHER READING

Hessing, Melody, Rebecca Raglon, and Catriona Sandilands, eds., *This Elusive Land: Women And the Canadian Environment*, University of Washington Press, 2005.

This nonfiction work examines how gender can affect one's relationship with the Canadian environment. It also examines how women are politically active in developing environmental policy, and how women are mediated by the environment.

Ingersoll, Earl G., ed., *Waltzing Again: New and Selected Conversations with Margaret Atwood*, Ontario Review, 2006.

This collection of twenty-one interviews with Atwood reveals her views on a variety of topics ranging from her career to feminism to Canadian nationalism.

Marchand, Philip, *Ripostes: Reflections on Canadian Literature*, Porcupine's Quill, 1998.

This collection of critical essays examines Atwood alongside many of her compatriot contemporaries in their Canadian context. Marchand examines not just the positive attributes, but also the vices of Canadian literature at large.

Murphy, Patrick D., ed., *Literature of Nature: An International Sourcebook*, Routledge, 1998.

This reference book examines literary representations of nature, as well as representations of human interactions with nature, from around the world. This collection includes a chapter on Canadian environmental literature specifically, and draws upon Atwood's work.

Nischik, Reingard M., ed., *Margaret Atwood: Works and Impact*, Camden House, 2002.

One of the most recent collections of criticism on Atwood's work, this compellation of essays by Atwood scholars provides insight on her poetry and prose from perspectives such as gender politics, ecology, popular culture, and constructivism.

SUGGESTED SEARCH TERMS

Margaret Atwood

Margaret Atwood AND poetry

Margaret Atwood AND Canadian literature

Margaret Atwood AND Mushrooms

Margaret Atwood AND True Stories

Margaret Atwood AND environmentalism

Margaret Atwood AND feminism

Atwood AND Canada

Atwood AND nature

The New Colossus

EMMA LAZARUS

1883

To commemorate the centennial of the Declaration of Independence, the people of France raised money to build the Statue of Liberty. The statue was to be a sign of friendship between France and the United States and a symbol of freedom and democracy. On this side of the Atlantic Ocean, the people of the United States raised money to build the pedestal upon which the huge statue would sit in the harbor of New York City. To help encourage people to donate to the cause, an auction was held. One of the items in that auction was Emma Lazarus's poem "The New Colossus."

The construction, shipment, and erection of the statue took longer than expected, so the centennial of the Declaration of Independence came and went before the statue was completely installed in 1886. And though Lazarus's poem was officially published at the auction in 1883, it did not become a part of the statue until 1903, after the poet's death. Without ceremony, a bronze tablet on which "The New Colossus" was engraved was finally attached to the interior wall of the pedestal.

Though the poem received little initial attention, today the words of Lazarus's poem (especially the last five lines) have become synonymous with the Statue of Liberty. It is through the power of Lazarus's "The New Colossus" that the statue stands not only for freedom and democracy but also as a welcoming beacon to immigrants who come to this country.

Emma Lazarus *(The Library of Congress)*

AUTHOR BIOGRAPHY

Lazarus is considered one of the first successful female Jewish poets in the United States. As David Lehman wrote in *Smithsonian* magazine, Lazarus was "a fascinating figure and a much more substantial poet than she has been given credit for." Though today she is primarily remembered for "The New Colossus," in the late nineteenth century she was considered an important American poet.

Lazarus was born in New York City on July 22, 1849, the fourth of seven children of Moshe and Esther Lazarus. Her parents were Sephardic Jews whose ancestors were exiled from Portugal and emigrated to New York during America's colonial period. As a child, she lived both in New York City and in Newport, Rhode Island. Lazarus was educated by private tutors. Her father, one of her biggest fans, was impressed by his daughter's early writings and supported her development as a poet. When Lazarus was seventeen, her father financed the private printing of a collection of her poems, called *Poems and*

Translations: Written between the Ages of Fourteen and Sixteen (1866). Shortly after this publication appeared, Lazarus met Ralph Waldo Emerson, the famed American poet, who would, for a time, become her mentor. Though they would eventually part ways, Emerson is credited with helping Lazarus improve and develop her writing.

When Lazarus was twenty-two, her second book, *Admetus and Other Poems* (1871) was published. Three years later, she published a novel, fictionalizing a story of the German author Johann Wolfgang von Goethe. The novel, *Alide: An Episode of Goethe's Life* (1874), was the only novel that Lazarus would write.

For the rest of her life, Lazarus focused on poetry and essays. Her poetry was often published in magazines, and the respect she earned with her writing was the reason she was sought by the committee responsible for raising funds for the pedestal upon which the Statue of Liberty would eventually stand. "The New Colossus" was engraved on a bronze plaque in 1903 and placed inside the walls of the pedestal.

Though she did not practice Judaism as an adult, Lazarus focused on the plight of Jews throughout the world during the latter part of her life, especially the challenges that Jewish immigrants faced and the anti-Semitism and persecution they faced in the late nineteenth century in Russia and Germany. It was her empathy for these European Jews that led her to become involved with immigrants, often visiting Ellis Island and talking to the new arrivals about their experiences. Her association with these immigrants influenced the overall theme of "The New Colossus."

In an effort to regain her physical and emotional strength following the death of her beloved father in the spring of 1885, Lazarus spent more than two years abroad, traveling to England, France, and Italy. Unfortunately, the years overseas did not improve her health. She returned home exhausted and died in New York on November 19, 1887.

POEM TEXT

Not like the brazen giant of Greek fame,
With conquering limbs astride from land to land;
Here at our sea-washed, sunset gates shall stand
A mighty woman with a torch, whose flame
Is the imprisoned lightning, and her name   5
Mother of Exiles. From her beacon-hand

Glows world-wide welcome; her mild eyes
   command
The air-bridged harbor that twin cities frame.
"Keep, ancient lands, your storied pomp!" cries
   she
With silent lips. "Give me your tired, your poor, 10
Your huddled masses yearning to breathe free,
The wretched refuse of your teeming shore.
Send these, the homeless, tempest-tost to me,
I lift my lamp beside the golden door!"

POEM SUMMARY

Lines 1–8

"The New Colossus," a tribute to the Statue of
Liberty, begins with an attention-getting statement that, together with the title, alludes to
another large statue, the ancient Colossus of
Rhodes. At one time, this Greek structure stood
at the entrance to the harbor of the island of
Rhodes, as the soon to be constructed Statue of
Liberty would stand at the entrance to New York
Harbor. Because of the similar roles that these two
colossal statues would play as well as their related
dimensions, the connection between the Colossus
of Rhodes and the Statue of Liberty is easily
made. In addition, the French sculptor Frédéric-
Auguste Bartholdi, who was commissioned to
create the statue, had also connected the two statues in his mind. His ideas were inspired by the
Colossus of Rhodes—by its large size, its position
of prominence in the Rhodian harbor, and its
powerful symbolism.

    Though Lazarus was aware of the connec-
tion between the ancient Colossus of Rhodes and
the Statue of Liberty, her ideas about the relationship between the two statues differed from
Bartholdi's. Lazarus does not deny that the two
colossal statues have elements in common; however, she suggests that there is a contrast between
their surface form and their deeper meaning. She
claims that the ties between the two statues exist
only if one takes a hurried look at both. The
statues may both be huge structures that grace
harbors, but the similarities stop there. So with
the first line of her poem, Lazarus makes it clear
that, in her mind, Bartholdi's statue is actually
nothing like the ancient Colossus. The poem will
develop this theme throughout the octave, or the
first eight lines, of this Italian sonnet. She will
reflect on the Colossus of Rhodes, but the poem's
main focus will be on the Statue of Liberty—the
new colossus.

MEDIA ADAPTATIONS

- American composer Irving Berlin wrote a
  song based on Lazarus's poem. Various versions of Berlin's composition "Give Me
  Your Tired and Your Poor" are performed
  on YouTube.com.

- Another version of Berlin's composition
  based on "The New Colossus" was recorded
  on the album *Miss Liberty* (1991) and an
  MP3 music download of "Give Me Your
  Tired and Your Poor" can be found at
  Amazon.com.

"The New Colossus," describes the ancient
colossus as being audacious, or boldly shameless.
The ancient colossus, after all, was a statue of
the Greek god Helios. This image implies that the
statue has supernatural powers that were meant
to frighten Rhodian enemies away from their
harbor. Whereas the Colossus of Rhodes was
more like a boastful bully, marking the statue
with a sort of arrogance that a champion of war
might display, the Statue of Liberty is something
else. Although the poem has not yet specifically
described the Statue of Liberty, readers have a
hint of what the speaker of this poem in about
to say. For example, because the speaker has
already stated that the American statue is nothing like the Colossus of Rhodes, readers can infer
that the speaker believes that the Statue of Liberty is neither bold nor arrogant.

    In the second line, before the speaker of this
poem identifies the attributes of the State of Liberty, she further describes the Rhodian statue.
Because the Colossus of Rhodes was destroyed
by an earthquake in 224 BCE, there is no authentic historical representation of the actual Greek
statue. There are only widely varying written
descriptions. Lazarus adopted a popular description of the Colossus of Rhodes that some modern-day architects believe would have been
impossible to construct. This depiction, some

believe, had the male statue bridging the sides of the harbor at Rhodes with his torso, with one of his feet on one side of the water and the other on the opposite shore. This is a more aggressive pose, one that epitomizes the power of a mighty god who has won a great battle. Though the actual pose of the Colossus of Rhodes might have not been so emboldened, Lazarus is correct in stating that the great Colossus did symbolize victory in war.

It is in line 4 of the octave that the speaker finally introduces the statue that will soon stand on the American shores and begins to add details as to how the two statues differ from one another. As opposed to the male statue in Rhodes, the American statue is a female figure. The speaker implies that in the Statue of Liberty's hands, there are no weapons of war. Rather, there is a torch, a symbol of the power of fire or light. This power is different from the powerful weapons of war because it is not destructive. The torch represents a guiding light. The sculptor Bartholdi had named the statue "Liberty Enlightening the World." This title was chosen to praise the people of the United States for their accomplishment in creating and putting into place a working democratic government. The torch, for Bartholdi, was said to stand for enlightenment (in the sense of illumination or clarification), or a light being sent out to demonstrate the knowledge of how democracy should and could work. But Lazarus interprets the Statue of Liberty and the statue's torch slightly differently. For her, the statue is the embodiment of a nurturer, a motherly figure. The torch, which represents her power, has been tamed. Unlike the ancient colossus who boasts of his war-like power, the Statue of Liberty constrains her strength and turns it into a beacon of light that not only guides shiploads of people to the shores of the United States but also welcomes them, changing the darkness of their journey into light.

In line 6 of the octave, Lazarus turns her attention to the immigrants who are coming to the American shores. She refers to them as exiles. And it is here in the sixth line that Lazarus more fully changes the symbolic image of the statue from one of celebrating democracy and freedom to one of nurturing lost souls. The statue becomes a mother figure who welcomes all the weary strangers coming to a new land. And she does so not with threats or warnings, but with outstretched arms. Her beacon is not only a guiding light that marks a safe passage; it is also a signal of full acceptance. Unlike the ancient Colossus whose fierce gaze looked upon the harbor with warnings to intruders, the Statue of Liberty has soft eyes that are watching over the new arrivals like a protective mother.

Lines 9–14

Line 9 marks the beginning of the sestet (the last six lines of an Italian sonnet) of Lazarus's poem. It is in the sestet that the speaker explains what the Statue of Liberty represents by having the statue speak for herself, albeit with stone lips. She shouts to the ancient colossus to keep his famed magnificence to himself. The Statue of Liberty, obviously, wants nothing to do with the spectacle of battled victories. She is not about glorified display. In other words, she is not, the speaker emphasizes again, like the Colossus of Rhodes.

After this declaration that reiterates one of the major themes of the poem, the speaker concentrates on the sonnet's real message, which is contained in lines 10–14. These last five lines are the most quoted from "The New Colossus." They are the lines that most people remember, as well as the lines that most effectively mark the statue as the compassionate mother of all immigrants to this country. Beginning with line 10, the Statue of Liberty continues to exclaim her intention. The Statue wants to usher the people who are suffering in their lands to America, where they will be welcomed by her open arms. It is here that the statue will guard them and give them a safe place to rest. She will offer them ways to make a living and to free them from want. She suggests that those people who have gathered in frightened groups elsewhere in the world should come to the American shores, where they will find the freedoms that have been denied them. In their homelands, these people have been defined as dispensable as garbage. But this is not how the Statue of Liberty sees them. They are not enemies of this land. They are not less than any other human beings. They are merely people who are tired of war, poverty, and disease.

In line 14, the poem returns its attention to the lamp that the Statue of Liberty holds in her hand. With that torch, the Statue of Liberty not only lights the passage across the ocean and through New York Harbor, but also illuminates a special door. The speaker of this poem suggests that that door opens onto a promised land, full of hope and dreams and the means to make them come true.

THEMES

Power

Different forms of power are either mentioned or alluded to in "The New Colossus." First there is power as exemplified by the ancient statue, the Colossus of Rhodes. Lazarus uses the Colossus to set up a contrast between the power exerted by warriors and conquerors and the power of mothers and nurturers. The Colossus of Rhodes represents the power of a victorious Greek god. This god, in statue form, celebrates the victory of the people of Rhodes over an army that attacked their city. The Rhodians held back the invaders and erected their colossal statue as a warning to future invaders.

There is another type of power, according to this poem, that is equally successful. This is the power of welcoming those who need help. This power is more maternal—a mother loving her children. The mother figure, as represented by the Statue of Liberty, guides her children to safety. She embraces them and welcomes them home. She does not force them. Her power is subtle, emotional, and loving.

Suffering

The suffering of those who have been exiled from their home countries, the only places they have known, is another theme of the poem. These people have been forced to leave their homeland, their friends, and, in some cases, their families. The reasons for their exiles vary. Natural disasters such as famine have driven some people to leave their countries. Others are forced to leave because they are being persecuted for their religious beliefs or their ethnicity. When they arrive in a new country, the suffering sometimes continues because many immigrants have no means of support. They are hungry, tired, and poor.

Through her poem, Lazarus suggests that the United States should help to ease the suffering of those who have been forced to leave their homelands. The poem encourages American citizens to use the Statue of Liberty as a symbol of empathy for all the suffering people who come to these shores. The immigrants should not have to suffer, this poem suggests. They have arrived in a country that has the means to ease their suffering.

Freedom

Freedom is another theme suggested in the poem. The poem implies that the Statue of Liberty is a symbol of the freedom represented by the United States and stands in contrast to the repression and war of the countries from which the immigrants have come. The old lands that once were home for these exiles are symbolized as creatures with arms made of weapons. In contrast, the new lands, such as the United States, should open their arms and beckon the immigrants to take deep breaths as they arrive and realize that they are now free.

The freedom that the poem suggests is not just religious or political freedom but also freedom from hunger and debt. Whether Lazarus believed that the United States truly represented freedom or whether she wrote the poem to encourage Americans to strive to become a model of freedom is not clear. However, she definitely describes the Statue of Liberty as a figure that, if she were able to speak, would tell immigrants that their dreams of freedom can be realized here.

Hope

The theme of hope is presented in many ways, beginning with the torch that the statue holds in her hand. The torch could represent a guiding light for those who are being tossed in the dark storms of war and poverty on the other side of the ocean. In this sense, the torch could stand for the hope of peace and safety. If readers take the torch to be a source of energy, the light could stand for a rebirth of spirit, giving hope to those who were so beaten down they were close to death. But here in America, they can begin to hope for new life.

Lazarus adds another element of hope to the end of the poem, when she mentions the symbol of the portal of gleaming gold. Not only is this an opening into a new world, it is a symbol of treasure or wealth, whether this richness is spiritual, physical, or psychological. This treasure lies behind the door. It is like the pot of gold at the end of the rainbow, something made of wishes. It is here in this country, the poem implies, that hope reigns supreme.

TOPICS FOR FURTHER STUDY

- Research the history of American immigration during the last half of the nineteenth century. Who were the immigrants at that time? Where did they come from? Why were they coming to the United States? How were they treated when they arrived here? Then compare these earlier immigrant issues with those of today. Where do the largest numbers of immigrants come from today? Why do immigrants come to the United States today? How are they treated? Create a display of charts and images of your findings to use in an oral presentation to your class.

- Read about the customs and practices of Sephardic Jews. Where did they live? When and why were they banished? What became of them? How do they differ from other Jews, such as the Ashkenazic from Germany and eastern Europe and the Mizrahim from the Middle East? Gather all your information on a Web page. Include images, historical backgrounds, and cultural information. Provide maps that show where each group comes from and to which countries many of them emigrated during the twentieth century. Also collect images of special clothing, hair styles, or other elements that might distinguish one group from another. Then direct your classmates to your Web page.

- To more fully understand and appreciate Lazarus's poem, read about the experiences of immigrants. Recommended books for young adults include Janet Bode's *The Colors of Freedom: Immigrant Stories* (2000), Adele Geras's *Voyage* (2007), or Amada Irma Perez's *My Diary from Here to There* (2002). Present your findings to your class, telling them some of the stories about what life is like for immigrants coming to America and adjusting to a new country and culture. Include personal stories if you or someone you know is an immigrant or a direct descendant of one.

- Imagine that the president of the United States has asked you to write a poem to welcome immigrants to the United States. What would be your message? Create a poem in any form you prefer (sonnet, free verse, or even a series of haiku) stating what you think the United States offers people who want to start their lives over in this country. Think about what immigrants should expect when they come here. What do you think their challenges would be today? What does America have to offer them? Read your poem to your class, or record it with background music using a computerized video or audio program, explaining that your poem will be placed next to Lazarus's poem inside the pedestal of the Statue of Liberty. Ask your classmates to compare the two poems.

- Videotape interviews with students at your school who either are immigrants or have immigrant parents. Ask them to share some of the best experiences they have had so far in their new country. Why did their parents want to come here? Have their views of the United States changed since they arrived? How? Produce a short video, upload it to YouTube, and share the results with your class.

- Create a clay figure of a modernized Statue of Liberty. Decide if this statue should be male or female and be prepared to explain why. Study the symbols that the original Statue of Liberty is holding and what they stand for. Then create symbols for your statue and tell your class why you chose them and what they represent. Keep in mind that the statue you create is supposed to greet immigrants to this country. What message do you think would make immigrants feel most welcome?

Immigrant family is greeted by the symbol of freedom *(FPG | Getty Images)*

STYLE

Italian Sonnet

A sonnet is a special poetic form. On a basic level, the form of a sonnet consists of fourteen lines that follow a specific rhyming scheme, depending on what type of sonnet it is. The first type of sonnet was perfected by Francesco Petrarch (1304–1374), an Italian poet who used the form to write love poetry. This type of poetic form was called the Italian or Petrarchan sonnet and was adapted in the sixteenth century by the English poet Thomas Wyatt and later by William Shakespeare. Shakespeare varied the form slightly, using a different rhyme scheme that became known as the Shakespearean, or English, sonnet.

The fourteen lines of an Italian sonnet are divided into an octave, or eight lines, and a sestet, or six lines. The octave follows the rhyming pattern of *a-b-b-a, a-b-b-a* with *a* representing the first rhyme and *b* standing for the next rhyme. This means that in an Italian sonnet, the first, fourth, fifth, and eighth lines end in matching rhymes as do the second, third, sixth, and seventh lines. In the sestet, however, the rhyming

pattern differs from that in the octave. The sestet rhyming pattern can follow one of several styles, most commonly either *c-d-e, c-d-e* or *c-d-c, d-c-d*.

In Lazarus's poem, lines 1, 4, 5, and 8 end in a rhyme with a word ending with the sound "ame." Lines 2, 3, 6, and 7 end with the words ending in the sound "and." This is the conventional form of an Italian sonnet.

In the sestet, lines 9, 11, and 13 end with words rhyming with the sound of a long *e*, and lines 10, 12, and 14 end with the sound of "or." The rhyming pattern in the sestet differs from that of the octave, providing a break not only in the form but in the thought.

Traditionally, in the first section (the octave) a question is posed. In the second section (the sestet), that question is answered. The poet might also merely make a point in the octave and then emphasize that point in the sestet.

Allusion

An allusion is a literary device that makes a reference to either a historical or a literary event, person, or object that conjures up images in the reader's imagination. The use of allusion can add deeper meaning to a poem without the use of many words.

An example of an allusion in the modern world might be the World Trade Center, often referred to as the twin towers. When a writer mentions the World Trade Center, readers are reminded of the 2001 terrorist attack and all the horrors attached to this image. This image creates an emotional state of fear, anger, or sadness. Another allusion might be astronaut Neil Armstrong's landing on the moon, which represented excitement and achievement, as well as a hint of what space exploration might be like in the future.

Poets might allude to another poet's work, borrowing a few lines from a famous poem. If a poet includes the words "the road less traveled," readers familiar with the works of the American poet Robert Frost would know that the allusion was to Frost's famous "The Road Not Taken." They would also be aware of the rest of the poem and the meaning implied by these words, which accentuate the power of adventure and individuality. Some poets also make religious allusions, taking images from the Bible (such as referring to Moses as someone who leads people to the promised land).

In "The New Colossus," the colossus is an allusion to the Colossus of Rhodes, a huge male statue that once graced the harbor of the island of Rhodes in the Aegean Sea but was later destroyed by an earthquake. By making this allusion, the poet creates an image of what was one of the Seven Wonders of the ancient world—a massive structure that celebrated the successful defense of the city. Lazarus uses the allusion to bring the image of greatness into her poem in reference to the Statue of Liberty but also to bring out the contrast between the Colossus of Rhodes as a reference to war compared to the Statue of Liberty, which Lazarus saw as a symbol of peace.

HISTORICAL CONTEXT

History of the Statue of Liberty

Inspired by stories of the Colossus of Rhodes, one of the Seven Wonders of the ancient world, French sculptor Frédéric- Auguste Bartholdi designed a statue to be given to the American people to commemorate the centennial of the Declaration of Independence. The French had helped the colonists fight the British in the American Revolution. The statue was intended to honor the friendship between France and the United States, as well as commend Americans for successfully creating a democratic government, something the French attempted to emulate in the years following the French Revolution. Alexandre-Gustave Eiffel, who designed the Eiffel Tower in Paris, constructed the framework and assisted Bartholdi in the difficult task of engineering such a huge statue.

Construction of the statue was a challenge, as was funding and transporting this great monument. The people of France were responsible for paying for the statue, while the people in the United States were asked to cover the cost of building a pedestal. Through generous donations, the money was collected and construction began. The statue was completed in 1884, and the pedestal in 1886. In order to ship the statue from France to New York Harbor, the statue had to be reduced to 350 separate pieces. It took four months to reassemble the statue onto the pedestal in the courtyard of Fort Wood on Bedloe's Island (now Liberty Island). The statue was inaugurated on October 28, 1886, (ten years after the U.S. centennial) by President Grover Cleveland, who accepted the statue on behalf of the people of the United States.

From the ground to the tip of the torch in the statue's raised right hand measures 305 feet. There are twenty-five windows from which visitors can look out from the crown of the statue. The seven rays of the statue's crown stand for the seven seas. On the tablet that the statue holds in her left hand is inscribed the date July 4, 1776, the day on which the Second Continental Congress adopted the Declaration of Independence. The date is written in Roman numerals.

The Colossus of Rhodes

Where the Aegean Sea meets the Mediterranean at the southwestern tip of present-day Turkey is the island of Rhodes. This area was an influential economic center in the fourth and fifth centuries BCE. Many people fought for control of this port island, including leaders from Persia and Greece. When Alexander the Great, conqueror of Greece, died in 323 BCE, three Greek generals, Ptolemy, Seleucus, and Antigous, fought for control of Rhodes. When Rhodes supported Ptolemy, Antigous sent forces commanded by his son Demetrius to conquer the city and take the Rhodian ships and port. After besieging Rhodes for a year, Demetrius was forced to give up and retreat. To celebrate, the people of Rhodes erected a huge statue to grace the harbor.

Demetrius's forces left behind many metal weapons and machinery. The people of Rhodes melted these weapons down and used the bronze to create the outer form of what would become the Colossus of Rhodes. As a frame, the Rhodians confiscated the huge tower that had used by Demetrius's army in their attempt to climb the protective walls that the Rhodians had built as part of the city's defense.

The Colossus of Rhodes was a representation of the god Helios, who was the city's patron. The statue took almost a dozen years to complete and stood from 100 to 120 feet tall exclusive of the height of the pedestal. Since the statue was destroyed by a powerful earthquake in 225 BCE, no one knows definitely what the statue looked like or where it stood at the harbor. Some have suggested that the statue was erected so that it straddled the harbors's entrance. Others have argued that this pose would have been all but impossible to construct. They suggest that, like the Statue of Liberty, the Colossus stood on one side of the harbor. Most agree that the Colossus

COMPARE
&
CONTRAST

- **1880s:** A new wave of immigrants from eastern Europe and Russia land on the East Coast of the United States in large numbers to escape escalating threats of religious and ethnic persecution and for the economic opportunities offered by the American Industrial Revolution.

  Today: Large populations of Hispanics from Central and South America and the Caribbean immigrate to the United States in search of jobs.

  1880s: France gives the Statue of Liberty to the United States as a way of expressing a friendship between the two countries that extends back to the time of the American Revolution. The statue is erected on Bedloe's Island, which is later renamed Liberty Island, in New York Harbor.

  Today: The Statue of Liberty is closed after the terrorist attacks on the World Trade Center on September 11, 2001. The pedestal and outdoor observation decks reopened in 2004. On July 4, 2009, the crown on the head of the statue is finally reopened to visitors.

  1880s: Lazarus is considered the most recognized Jewish female poet of her time.

  Today: After being awarded prestigious prizes that include the MacArthur Fellowship (1994), the Wallace Stevens Award (1996), and the Lifetime Achievement Award from the Lannan Foundation (1999), Adrienne Rich, one of the most noted Jewish female poets of today, is honored with the Griffin Poetry Prize (2010) in recognition of her lifetime work.

---

was a great feat of construction, earning it the prestige of being called one of the seven wonders of the ancient world.

U.S. Immigration, 1880–1920

In the early 1800s, most immigrants to the United States came from northern and western Europe. Hoping to escape hunger from massive crop failures and revolution, large populations, especially from Ireland and Germany, fled to North America. Between 1830 and 1860, immigrants to the United States numbered almost 5 million. After 1860, because of the U.S. Civil War, the number of immigrants dropped significantly except for Chinese laborers who arrived on the West Coast to help build the transcontinental railroad.

In the 1880s, the immigrant population swelled again. Between 1880 and 1920, almost 24 million new immigrants arrived in the United States. Whereas prior to the Civil War most immigrants came from western and northern Europe and China, people seeking refuge in America now

.came from southern and eastern Europe, and Russia. Lack of jobs in eastern Europe as well as the persecution of Jews were two major reasons for the mass immigration. Most immigrants settled in the major cities in the northeast and in Chicago, where they found jobs in factories that provided work but very low wages. Many of these new immigrants lived in poverty, in crowded housing called tenements that had little provision for sanitation. As a result, diseases spread throughout the communities. Poor health and poor pay led some to crime in order to survive. The general attitude of the American public toward these large numbers of immigrants was not positive. Many people blamed them for taking jobs away and for wreaking havoc on the city environment.

Listening to the public outcries against immigrants, the U.S. Congress passed new laws in 1882 that controlled the numbers and the types of immigrants allowed into the country. Criminals and those with certain diseases were not allowed to enter. In addition, taxes were imposed, forcing immigrants to hand over money, which many of

Ocean steamer passes the Statue of Liberty
(© ClassicStock / Alamy)

them did not have. Those who could not pay were forced to return to the country they had come from. Finally, in 1924, Congress passed another Immigration Act that further limited the number of immigrants entering the United States by instituting a quota system (meaning that only a limited number from each country were allowed in).

CRITICAL OVERVIEW

Esther Schor, in her biography *Emma Lazarus* writes that "The New Colossus," when chosen for the pedestal, "transformed" the Statue of Liberty from a symbol of freedom to "a new sort of colossus altogether." The poem relieved the statue "of a heavy inheritance of tyranny," which was what the Colossus of Rhodes stood for. After being placed in the pedestal, Lazarus's poem was "mentioned widely in the press," Schor says. She also quotes James Russell Lowell, an American poet, who likens Lazarus's poem to a "'noble' pedestal for the statue." Lowell writes that Lazarus used "just the right word to be said, an

achievement more arduous than that of the sculptor" of the statue.

In his review of the poem, David Lehman, writing for *Smithsonian* states: "There is no more memorable statement of . . . the American dream than the promise of safe haven," which Lazarus's poem voices. Lehman adds that the poem is not a "boast but [rather] a vow." The focus of the poem is not on a "glorification of the self but on the rescue of others." Lehman also praises Lazarus herself, writing that she was a "much more substantial poet than she has been given credit for."

In her review for *Shofar*, Wendy Zierler says that Lazarus's poem is a powerful voice, especially for female poets who are inspired not by "classical, patriarchal traditions," but by feelings for the "oppressed or marginalized people of the world."

Reviews written in Lazarus's day tend to praise her work, though they do so in a somewhat patronizing manner. A reviewer for the *Nation* says that Lazarus's poems "indicate more than common ability." Another critic, writing for *Galaxy* reports that Lazarus's poetry has qualities that "distinguish it broadly from the ordinary work of women," as well as from "the best work of most young writers."

CRITICISM

Joyce Hart

Hart is a published author and teacher of creative writing. In the following essay, she explores the underlying emotional content of "The New Colossus."

"The New Colossus," is, at its heart, a plea for help and mercy. Lazarus, well informed about the plight of immigrants to the United States at the end of the nineteenth century, was so moved by the stories of exiles that she created a poem that changed the meaning of the Statue of Liberty from a symbol of democracy to one embracing the weary immigrants who arrived on the country's shores. Lazarus presents sorrowful images from the lives of immigrants and attempts to move readers to empathize with the newcomers who have been stripped of hope and who are enduring so much suffering. To accomplish her task, the poet has to expose her emotions in her attempts to get the reader to feel the pain of the immigrants' lives on which the poem focuses. She must make readers look beyond the torn clothing

WHAT DO I READ NEXT?

- *Emma Lazarus: Selected Poems* (2005) includes many of Lazarus's poems that did not gain the widespread fame of "The New Colossus." Her poems in this collection focus on the casualties of the U.S. Civil War and on immigration to America, with a special emphasis on the lives of Jewish people. Some of the outstanding poems included in this collection are "Heroes" and "The Day of Dead Soldiers," both of which deal with war. Other poems are "On the Jewish New Year" and "In Exile," which focus on Jewish issues.

- Hannia S. Moore has written a fictional account of Lazarus's life in her novel *Liberty's Poet: Emma Lazarus* (2005). Moore creates a fictionalized version of Lazarus as a young girl born to a wealthy Jewish family in the United States in the 1800s. The story features a young poet who is befriended by none other than Ralph Waldo Emerson, the noted poet.

- Young-adult readers might enjoy *Emma Lazarus Rediscovered* (1999) by the poet Eve Merriam. This book was originally published in 1956 but was republished as a tribute to Lazarus during the celebration of the 150th anniversary of her birth. The book includes an introduction by Morris Schappes, who has done extensive studies of Lazarus's life and work.

- The American poet Ralph Waldo Emerson served as a mentor to Lazarus for many years, influencing the form and content of her writing. In *The Essential Writings of Ralph Waldo Emerson* (2000) readers gain an understanding of his style of writing as well as the underlying concepts and themes of his work.

- For a different view of immigration, read Jack Marshall's *From Baghdad to Brooklyn: Growing Up in a Jewish-Arabic Family in Mid-century America* (2005). This coming-of-age memoir received a starred review from *Publishers Weekly*. In this book, Ralph Waldo Emerson's poetry becomes a heavy influence on the young boy's life.

- Born around the time of Lazarus's death, Isaac Rosenberg, whose parents were Jewish immigrants to the United Kingdom, based much of his poetry on his experiences in World War I. He is often referred to as the best war poet of his generation. Though Lazarus wrote about war from a spectator's standpoint, Rosenberg had firsthand experiences. For a long time, the only published copies of Rosenberg's poetry were in the form of pamphlets that the poet self-published. *Selected Poems and Letters*, published in 2004, is a good source for his work.

- For young or second-language readers, Linda Glaser has written the book *Emma's Poem: The Voice of the Statue of Liberty* (2010). The story of Lazarus and her famous poem is told through words and illustrations.

---

and unkempt appearances of the immigrants, which often emboldens people to dismiss them as unwanted or unworthy foreigners—people who do not belong. Lazarus wants readers to uncover the hearts and souls of these newcomers to the United States. Even if people speak different languages, have unfamiliar social customs, and come with no money with which to feed themselves properly, she wants readers to find the common element that binds them to the exiles. Every living creature has basic needs, and those who have them satisfied have a duty to help those who do not, Lazarus implies. But how does the poet make this appeal? How does she make her readers feel what she has felt?

Lazarus expresses anger throughout her poem. First, she refers to Colossus of Rhodes as a symbol of war and destruction. Later, the

IN ESSENCE, LAZARUS IS CHALLENGING
AMERICANS TO RAISE THEIR IDEALS, TO
SEE THEMSELVES AS A NATION OF GIVERS,
NOT TAKERS."

subject of the poem cries out, condemning the countries from which many of the immigrants of Lazarus's time were fleeing. She refers to these countries as the old lands, where statues, created in the classical Greek image, pose with weapons in their hands, emblems of ancient wars and old hatreds. She means those countries whose modern battles involved the persecution of Jews in eastern Europe, especially Russia, one of the largest causes of immigration at the turn of the twentieth century. This persecution included denial of civil rights, including the right to work in certain professions, imprisonment, or even execution. Lazarus condemns these cruel actions. Her emotions reflect those of an angry crusader, one who uses words rather than swords. But her words do not draw blood. Her poem does not take lives. The anger she feels is directed verbally at the monarchies of the old world, with their arrogant displays of military power and egotistical philosophies that preach that they have the right to purge their countries of those who, in their opinion, do not fit in. Lazarus uses anger to rouse her readers against those who cause pain and suffering. Through the poem, she awakens in her readers an awareness of the life-threatening challenges that the immigrants faced. She employs anger to incite empathy for the immigrants. She pits the immigrant against state-sponsored persecution. The poem implies that the immigrants have no one to protect them. Lazarus suggests that the immigrants desperately need America's help.

By the third line, the speaker's voice has turned from anger to pride, as she proclaims the arrival of the Statue of Liberty on the U.S. shore. Through this pride, Lazarus wants American citizens to feel a similar pride not only in their country but in themselves. Here is a powerful woman, the speaker says as she points to the Statue of Liberty, but she is not strong in the same way as the military forces in Europe. This statue is free of old prejudices. She does not seek war or revenge. Her hands are free of weaponry. She is an improvement over the old colossal statue. The old statue represents the closed mind of a leader with the taste of blood in his mouth, anxious to kill. In the old country, the governments want to purge those it believes do not belong. But in this new country, with its new statue, people in power want just the opposite. The inference is that the monarchies of Europe are cruel and uncaring, whereas in the United States, the people and the government are benevolent. Even if Lazarus is not convinced of this evaluation of the government and people of the United States (and there is no sure way to confirm this from the poem), she has written the poem as if she wants to believe that Americans have open hearts and want to help the immigrants. And with this belief, the speaker's emotions in this poem turn more positive. Instead of speaking angrily of the circumstances of the past, the speaker's voice softens, first with pride and then with hope. This is a new country, with a new symbol to grace its harbor. There is hope that there is a place in this world where all people are welcome.

But with the first line of the sonnet's sestet, in line nine, Lazarus returns to the anger that she expressed in the first line of the octave. She again shouts to the old country to keep its ancient pageantry, its old customs. Readers can infer that the speaker does not want anything to do with the old ways, especially if they result in people suffering. In contrast to the pain that is inflicted on the exiles in the old countries, the speaker suggests that the Statue of Liberty has quite a different message to send out to the world. As if wanting to follow the same pattern of emotions that Lazarus created in the octave, the speaker changes her anger into a softer tone. She, through the Statue of Liberty, takes on the voice of a motherly figure. Rather than speaking in hatred and anger, the statue speaks with pure empathy and love. The voice in the poem (whether of the poet, the speaker, or the statue) implores the rest of the world to place into her welcoming hands those people that the old world does not want. In doing so, the poet is attempting to instruct her readers. She is using the Statue of Liberty as a model of what she hopes the United States will become. The speaker projects onto the American people a dream she has envisioned. Like the Statue of Liberty, the speaker hopes

The golden doors to freedom (*Alex Uralsky* / *Shutterstock.com*)

this country will be the beacon of light for immigrants searching for an end to suffering. She hopes that citizens will open their hearts to the homeless, the hungry, and the tired, and share their good fortune with those less fortunate. She hopes citizens will comfort these suffering people and celebrate freedom with them. Lazarus uses this hopeful dream as an emotional ploy to make people feel the pain of the immigrants, as one human to another. In essence, Lazarus is challenging Americans to raise their ideals, to see themselves as a nation of givers, not takers.

As with modern messages that are used to raise concern for people who are suffering through disasters in other parts of the world, or even in other parts of the United States, Lazarus appeals not to the minds but to the hearts of those who can help. Through her poem, she uses a patterned emotional tactic. She begins both the octave and the sestet of this poem with an angry cry. It is with that cry that she attempts to shame those who make others suffer. She then

uses a model of ideal love and compassion (in this case what she believes the Statue of Liberty to stand for) to set an example for how people should react to those who have been debilitated by their challenges. She suggests unending empathy for immigrants who have traveled a long way and have endured physical and psychological threats. She promises love and understanding to the strangers who arrive in this country, thereby encouraging those who already live in this country to open their hearts, to give the immigrants hope. The old emotions of anger and hatred should be replaced with the new feeling of empathy. The aggressive feeling should be replaced with love and understanding.

Source: Joyce Hart, Critical Essay on "The New Colossus," in *Poetry for Students*, Gale, Cengage Learning, 2011.

Gregory Eiselein

In this excerpt, Eiselein claims that Lazarus wrote her poems with an "orientation toward learning."

The history of Emma Lazarus's reputation as a poet is peculiar. After publishing her first volume, *Poems and Translations*, in 1866, the seventeen-year-old prodigy began a correspondence with Ralph Waldo Emerson, the most distinguished author in U.S. letters at the time. He spoke highly of her work and appointed himself her "tutor" (Rusk 4). In 1871, she published a second book, *Admetus and Other Poems*, which critics greeted with praise; The *Illustrated London News* suggested that she would "hereafter take a high place among the best poets in this age" ("New" 359). During the 1880s, "The New Colossus"—her famous Statue of Liberty sonnet in which the "mighty woman" tells the world, "Give me your tired, your poor,/Your huddled masses yearning to breathe free"—began to assume an enduring place in U.S. popular memory, even though its pro-immigration position directly opposed anti-immigration sentiment in the United States. Throughout her life, she maintained friendships with talented and famous authors, including William James and Henry James, Ivan Turgenev, Robert Browning, William Morris, and many others. At her death at the age of 38, she was one of the most critically admired women poets of her time and the most famous Jewish writer in the United States.

Despite this auspicious beginning, Lazarus's place in literary history is far from secure. She has been harshly judged by some, fondly but

> WHILE THE ORIENTATION TOWARD
> LEARNING APPEARS IN LAZARUS'S THEMES AND
> UNFAMILIAR SUBJECT MATTER, LAZARUS'S POEMS
> ALSO REVEAL THEIR PEDAGOGICAL ASPIRATIONS
> AT THE FORMAL LEVEL, IN THE STRUCTURES,
> FIGURES, AND SOUNDS OF THE VERSE ITSELF."

patronizingly admired by others, and generally forgotten by most ("The New Colossus" is the noted exception). Curiously, some rather active forgetting began with her sisters, Mary, Annie, and Josephine Lazarus. Shortly after her death, they prepared a selection of poems, for which Josephine wrote an introduction that portrays Emma as shy, unassuming, and decidedly feminine: "There was something more than modesty in her unwillingness to assert herself or claim any prerogative,—something even morbid and exaggerated, which we know not how to define, whether as over-sensitiveness or indifference. Once finished, the heat and glow of composition spent, her writings apparently ceased to interest her. [...] The explanation is not far, perhaps, to seek. Was it not the 'Ewig-Weibliche' [eternal-feminine] that allows no prestige but its own? Emma Lazarus was a true woman, too distinctly feminine to wish to be exceptional" (Josephine Lazarus 8–9). This passage implies that it might be inappropriately voyeuristic to continue on and actually read the poems of this demure woman who neither strove for artistic distinction nor sought a public audience. The essay depicts Emma as a moody sibling who wrote in emotional bursts but nonetheless felt indifferent to the reception of her work by others. Near its conclusion, the introduction contends that Emma never thought of writing poetry as a "profession" (38) but as simply one of several artistic interests she cultivated, along with music and art appreciation. While recent critics have cast a sceptical eye on Josephine's introduction (Young 13–24), it had a major, detrimental influence on twentieth-century perceptions of Emma Lazarus.

Her sisters also impeded research about her life and further publication of her writings.

Excerpts in Josephine's introduction reveal that Emma kept a detailed diary, yet that document has vanished. Emma wrote and received hundreds of letters, but the bulk of them have disappeared. Her large, extraordinary library is also missing (Jacob 206). Although it is not clear what exactly happened to her correspondence, diary, and library, one speculation is that her sisters hid, destroyed, or otherwise disposed of them. Regardless of their fate, the scarcity of important primary documents is a key reason that no one has yet written an adequate, full-length biography. With more certainty we know that another of her sisters, Annie Lazarus Johnston, who held the copyright to Emma's work, refused in 1926 to give Bernard Richards permission to prepare an edition of complete works. In her response to Richards, Johnston explains her reluctance to grant permission in terms of wanting to quietly quell the circulation of her sister's impassioned Jewish-themed writings:

> While her politico-religious poems are technically as fine as anything she ever wrote, they were nevertheless composed in a moment of emotional excitement, which would seem to make their theme of questionable appropriateness today. [...] There has been, moreover, a tendency, I think, on the part of some of her public, to overemphasize the Hebraic strain of her work, giving it thus a quality of sectarian propaganda, which I greatly deplore, for I understood this to have been merely a phase in my sister's development. [...] If my sister were here today I feel that she might prefer to be remembered by the verses in her more serene mood. (qtd. in Jacob 209–10)

In short, she sees these poems as emotional, Jewish, and ephemeral. Lazarus wrote Jewish-themed verse throughout her life, but Johnston (who married and converted to Catholicism) insists that the "politico-religious" poems are relics of an excited "phase" in her sister's otherwise tranquil life. Offering to let him reprint only a small portion of the non-Jewish poems, Johnston wanted to recall only the ostensibly less emotional and less Jewish Lazarus. Richards abandoned his editing plans, and no edition of complete writings has ever been published.

While her sisters played a key part in making Lazarus's place in literary history more obscure than it might have been, literary scholars have had a complementary role. Although Morris Schappes's editing work on Lazarus was consistently valuable and conscientious, most critics actively disparaged her poetry (Gibbs) or ignored it (the major U.S. literature anthologies do not include her work). Those who seriously studied her writing did her little good. Arthur Zeiger's study used laudable research on her reading to present an interpretation of Lazarus as an unimaginative, "sourcebound," minor poet. Even sympathetic critics did little to dispel the notion that Lazarus's poems were emotional but unremarkable. Dan Vogel, for instance, refers to Lazarus as a sentimental writer and summarizes her significance to literary history by emphasizing feeling at the expense of talent or intellect: "She belongs in that special section of the Poets' Valhalla reserved for those who are beloved more than studied. [. . .] She is the spokesman [sic] not of the head, but of the heart." In the 1990s, a few critics attempted to change the direction of this critical reception by giving Lazarus's work careful and uncondescending treatment. Shira Wolosky and Diane Lichtenstein, for example, have recently emphasized the cultural contexts of Lazarus's writing and insightfully examined the questions of ethnic, national, religious, and gender identity raised by her poems.

My essay does not focus on identity in the ways that Lichtenstein and Wolosky do. Yet, like Lichtenstein, I examine Lazarus not as a withdrawn, private poet but as a professional, publicly engaged one. Like Wolosky, I attend carefully to Lazarus's historical poems and their challenge to anti-Semitism. Convinced that ignorance about Jewish life fed anti-Semitic and anti-immigrant hostilities and weakened Jewish resistance to such hostilities, Lazarus fashioned her Jewish historical poems as attempts to counteract anti-immigrant and anti-Semitic hatred through powerfully or memorably presented lessons in Jewish history and culture. What Zeiger sees as unimaginative—her recurrent use of historical sources—I see as central to her aims. From this perspective, her project appears significantly public and intellectual, and thus I abstain from reading these poems as essentially personal texts whose meanings are closely related to Lazarus's own life, identity, or individual feelings. I do not regard the "emotional excitement" of these poems as a symptom of a personal "phase" or a sign that she should be classified with minor poets "of the heart." Instead, setting aside the opposition of feeling to intellect, my essay draws on a systems-theory approach to emotion to clarify the function of emotion within Lazarus's fundamentally intellectual and pedagogical project. Because her historical poems typically deploy affect to enhance learning, intellectual insight, and moral judgement, the limited but still-common perspective that opposes intellect to emotion is inadequate for recognizing the value and purposes of these poems. Systems theory—which sees emotion as a component within a complex process that includes cognition, feedback, adaptation, and response—offers a framework for more precisely appreciating the misunderstood role of emotion in Lazarus's work.

. . . In Lazarus's Jewish historical poetry, there are indisputably sentimental moments. In her mediaeval verse drama *The Dance to Death*, for example, as the Christians prepare to burn all the Jews in the village, Reuben asks to hold his father's hand during their execution: "May I stand by thy side, / And hold my hand in thine until the end?," thus emphasizing the emotional bond between father and son and their basic moral goodness while also highlighting the depravity of their enemies' act. One could find several other examples of sentimentality in Lazarus's work, and sentimentality is certainly a fascinating area of study for scholars interested in emotion and literature. Nevertheless, emotion tends to serve different purposes in Lazarus's historical verse; these poems usually orient affect toward learning or intermingle moral judgement with learning.

An initial reason to see an orientation toward learning is that Emma Lazarus's poems frequently read as if they are attempts to circulate information about the world. During the last decade of her career in particular, her poems retrieve disregarded historical knowledge to make it part of contemporary memory. By rendering history into verse, she hopes to give the past an affective intensity, an immediacy, and a re-memorability that would keep it from slipping again into obscurity. Her poetry of erudition is not only about history, however, but also ideas, cultures, and the arts. A survey of Lazarus's poetry can begin to resemble a Victorian museum, or those nineteenth-century texts with sweeping accounts of world history, or the bourgeois magazines in which she published, such as the *Century*, *Lippincott's*, and *Scribner's Monthly*. Readers move in her poems from object to object; some of them are obscure, some exotic, some curious, but all are presented for examination and observation. Like a museum, world history book, or edifying magazine, Lazarus's poetry offers up an array of knowledge for contemplation: the persecution of Jews in mediaeval Germany (*The Dance to Death*), the queen of Romania ("To Carmen Sylva"), legends about the French Talmudist Rashi ("Raschi in Prague"), Henry George's socialist economic theory ("Progress and Poverty"), late Muslim Spain ("Arabesque"), Schumann's piano music ("Phantasies"), a famous North African Jewish philosopher ("Moses Maimonides"), American Indian creation stories ("The Creation of Man"), Auguste Bartholdi's Liberty Enlightening the World ("The New Colossus"), the death of the French Prince Imperial in Southern Africa ("Destiny"), and so on. Even in an individual text such as "Gifts," readers embark on a broad tour of world cultures, visiting ancient Egyptian, then Greek, Roman, and, finally, Jewish culture. Like turning the corner in a museum or flipping the page in the *Century*, reading Lazarus's poetry is an experience of sudden shifts in perspective that present new, unfamiliar information. Such shifts and such novelty generate surprise-startle, that interruption of consciousness we might consider the basic emotion.

A second reason to see an orientation toward learning in Lazarus's poetry is her attitude toward the perils of ignorance, especially anti-Semitic ignorance. Several of her texts express deep concern about the widespread misunderstanding and hatred of Jewish people. For example, in "Translation of Heine and Two Imitations," a three-poem cycle set in late mediaeval Spain, Lazarus illustrates how ignorance about Judaism, Jews, and their relationships to Christians permits Christians to indulge in various forms of anti-Semitism from unintentional insults to intentional ones, to persecution, torture, and murder. In the second poem, "Don Pedrillo," the title character tells the Rabbi:

> All your tribe offend my senses,
> They're an eyesore to my vision,
> And a stench unto my nostrils.
> When I meet these unbelievers,
> With thick lips and eagle noses,
> Thus I scorn them, thus revile them,
> Thus I spit upon their garment.

Ironically, what the contemptuous young Don does not know is that the Rabbi he insults is his biological father, a fact that might change the way he thinks, speaks, and behaves. In poems like "Don Pedrillo," Lazarus partially locates anti-Semitic feeling in self-ignorance and ignorance about Jewish people, their history, and the history of anti-Jewish prejudices. Thus, one of the ways she confronts anti-Semitism is to use her poetry as a conduit for historical and cultural reformation about Jewish people and anti-Semitism.

For post-Holocaust readers, such an approach to anti-Semitism might seem naive. After Hannah Arendt's dismantling of "common sense" explanations of anti-Semitism and Zizek's demonstration of anti-Semitism's resilience in the face of reason or fact, historical information might seem a futile corrective to anti-Semitic ideology. Lazarus's emphasis in these poems is not, however, on simply correcting the factual, historical, or logical errors embodied in anti-Jewish images and stereotypes. Indeed, in "A Translation of Heine and Two Imitations," and in other poems, she creates personae like Don Pedrillo who heartily endorse hatred of Jewish people, and she allows them to spew anti-Semitic invective without direct authorial commentary. In her dramatic monologue "The Guardian of the Red Disk: Spoken by a Citizen of Malta— 1300," the anti-Semitic speaker describes with awe the Lord Bishop of Malta, the "Guardian" of the title. According to the narrator, Jewish people "so infest the isle" that some way was needed "to protect / From the degrading contact Christian folk." The Lord Bishop develops a policy of branding each Jew with a "Red Disk," a "scarlet stamp of separateness, of shame." Legislated by the Fourth Latern Council in 1215, this mark of Jewish identity allows Christians to "breathe freely now, not fearing taint." The speaker describes how it encourages children to abuse the Jews: "When one appears therewith, the urchins know / Good sport's at hand; they fling their stones and mud." The most significant function of the red disk is its humiliation of Jewish people. The poem does not directly critique anti-Semitism; instead it works ironically by simply providing the speaker's thoughts and feelings as he calls the Jewish people "vermin" and remains utterly untouched by their suffering. The emphasis is not on the suffering Jews but on the speaker: his disgust, his admiration of his leader, his anxiety about "infection," and his sadistic delight in seeing others controlled and humiliated. His emotional bonds of identification with the leader and disidentification with the marked Jews give him a sense of identity and belonging: his anti-Semitic hatred lets him know that he is a "citizen of Malta." Poems like "Don Pedrillo" and "The Guardian of the Red Disk" do not directly correct false beliefs about Jewish people but instead draw attention to anti-Semitic emotions and their social and psychic functions. In these poems, Lazarus addresses the perils of anti-Semitic ignorance by making anti-Semitic feeling itself the object for scrutiny. Such poems disclose their cognitive bias not despite but through their emotional subjects and content.

While the orientation toward learning appears in Lazarus's themes and unfamiliar subject matter, Lazarus's poems also reveal their pedagogical aspirations at the formal level, in the structures, figures, and sounds of the verse itself. Take, for example, her use of irony and ottava rima in "An Epistle from Joshua Ibn Vives of Allorqui." (In my introduction to Lazarus's *Selected Poems*, I use this example to make a similar point.) In the poem's headnote, she states that she is merely rendering a fifteenth-century letter into poetry. Yet her act of historical recovery expands and translates his prose into thirty-four eight-line stanzas of English rhymed abababcc. In this letter to a former rabbi who is now attacking Judaism, Allorqui (as he is called) asks his former teacher to explain the reasons for his conversion to Christianity. The student's tone is deferential, but the letter critiques the conversion, the motivations behind it, the false justifications of it, and the hypocrisy it signifies. To highlight the letter's irony, Lazarus turns to ottava rima. Since at least Byron's Don Juan, this stanzaic form has often used its final couplet to delight readers with an unexpected turn. In the final couplet of Stanza 26, to cite a particularly apt example, Allorqui describes the Christian "God of Love" as: "Meek-faced, dove-eyed, pure-browed, the Lord of life, / Know him and kneel, else at your throat the knife!" Coming as it does at the end of the stanza, the suggestion that the meek and merciful Christian deity has his followers terrorize non-believers is meant to surprise readers with its incongruity. Yet this ironic surprise—so different from the melodramatic sensation and tender pity that arouse readerly emotions in sentimental texts— works not only to delight readers (with a sense of humour) but also to focus their emotionally elevated attention on the document and the overlooked history it reveals. "An Epistle" is not exactly a retelling of an historical event, as in many of her historical poems. Instead, the poem is the document itself, a re-presentation in verse of a vital but neglected selection from the historical archive.

Another way Lazarus uses poetic language to interrupt consciousness and induce emotion is contradiction and paradox. "Bar Kochba," for instance, opens with sorrow in the form of a somewhat startling command: "Weep, Israel!" Yet perhaps even more disruptive is the poem's paradoxical depiction of Bar Kochba (often transliterated "Bar Kokhba") as a conquered champion, a triumphant loser. In her essay entitled "The Last National Revolt of the Jews," Lazarus returns to this paradox by referring to Bar Kochba's failure as "the last irremediable defeat of the Jews, a defeat which ultimately resulted in the highest of spiritual victories." Lazarus's poem asks Israel to pay homage to Bar Kochba, this "last Warrior Jew," to revere him and present him with his just reward, as if he were a mighty victor. Although he did have some initial success in driving the Romans out of Judea and thwarting Hadrian's attempts to culturally integrate the Jews, Bar Kochba was ultimately a disastrous failure. The Roman army re-took Jerusalem, killed Bar Kochba, and smashed the Jewish resistance. The remaining Jewish population of Judea was exiled, and Jews were thereafter prohibited from entering Jerusalem (Graetz 2:405–23). The controversial nature of Lazarus's interpretation of Bar Kochba as a hero would only add to nineteenth-century readers' feelings of incongruity, for those who knew the history of second-century Palestine widely regarded Bar Kochba to be a false messiah. In a series reprinted in The Jewish Messenger five years before Lazarus's poem was written, Ernest Renan had laid out such an interpretation. Insisting that the rebellion was "insane," he painted a picture of Bar Kochba as a "violent" troublemaker, impostor, and fanatic.

Such contradictions—the poem's central paradox and the revisionist tenor of Lazarus's interpretation—work as immunological "alarm signals" in psychic systems (Luhmann 371). They trigger an emotional focussing of attention and heightening of sensitivity to information. For readers who stay with the poem, instead of laying it aside out of confusion or disagreement, "Bar Kochba" ultimately provides a way to understand such incongruity. The contradiction in the conquered champion image resolves itself in the unity of the "victory"/"defeat" distinction— what unites these terms is the notion of struggle. For Lazarus, it is not so much Bar Kochba's victory or defeat that matters but his cause, his struggle for religious freedom and what it represents to Jewish people in the present. It is not "Victory" that "makes the hero" but the willingness to struggle "for freedom, loving all things less, / Against world-legions." Thus, while Renan's view of Bar Kochba as a doomed fake was widely accepted, Lazarus deploys paradox to arrest such expectations, re-focus perceptions, and provide readers with what she hopes is a powerful and memorable historical interpretation of Bar Kochba as a hero, a champion of "The weak, the wronged, the miserable."

Source: Gregory Eiselein, "Emotion and the Jewish Historical Poems of Emma Lazarus," in *Mosaic*, Vol. 37, No. 1, March 2004, pp. 33–49.

Daniel Marom

In this excerpt, Marom "exposes the influence and expression of Lazarus's Jewish background and literary heritage" in "The New Colossus."

. . . Despite no explicit reference to Jews or Judaic sources, the poem's profoundly Jewish character is disclosed through a close look at the context in which it emerged, its place in Lazarus's biographical and artistic development, and its actual content. "The New Colossus" would seem to give voice to local aversion to the presumptuous French gesture of bestowing Liberty upon America by rejecting its original symbolism and suggesting one that transforms the Statue into a New World heroine. However, Lazarus wrote the poem when her energies and writing were primarily devoted to championing the cause of Jewish refugees fleeing pogroms in Eastern Europe in the early 1880's. Moreover, a record of its commission clearly reveals that she was enticed to write the sonnet on the basis of this concern. Thus, in the work itself, Lazarus shrewdly stated her case for the American intake of Jewish immigrants by not referring to them directly and attempting instead to compel her audience to live up to a Hebraic definition of America as redeemer of persecuted peoples. It is claimed that Lazarus ventured this feat by drawing her image of the Statue from a Jewish tradition that viewed the biblical matriarch Rachel as "Mother of Exiles."

. . . The works of few Jewish writers among the nations have reached the canonical stares attained in Americana by the last four and a half lines of Emma Lazarus's "The New Colossus." However one might judge their literary quality, it is arguable that a majority of Americans, and perhaps an even larger group of English-speakers around the world, will almost automatically recognize these lines and associate them with America's leading symbol, the Statue of Liberty. While the majority of those who recognize these lines might not be capable of actually reciting them by

> 'I HAVE NEVER BELIEVED IN THE WANT OF A THEME—WHEREVER THERE IS HUMANITY, THERE IS A THEME FOR A GREAT POEM—& I THINK IT IS THE POET'S FAULT IF HE DO NOT KNOW HOW TO UTILIZE THE MATERIALS AND THE ACCESSORIES WHICH SURROUND HIM.'"

heart, or even of indicating the title of the sonnet in which they are found, the name of its author, or the date of its composition, they would still, in most cases, assume that these lines speak for Liberty itself.

The question remains, however, as to whether Emma Lazarus's Jewishness had anything at all to do with the actual content and widespread popularity of "The New Colossus." Indeed, the fact that the poem includes on explicit reference to Jews, Judaic sources, or events in Jewish history would seem to suggest that its substance and history go well beyond the influence and scope of something Jewish in Lazarus's life and letters. Nevertheless, in what follows, I shall argue that the poem's allusions are profoundly bound up with the Jewish biography and literary heritage of its author, and I will suggest that this Jewish influence must be taken into account as a factor in the poem's renown.

1

While one might naturally assume that "The New Colossus" would not include Jewish references, it is quite surprising to discover that the poem makes no real mention of the Statue of Liberty as well. Ironically, one could never know from the verses that are most commonly associated with the Statue that there is a giant edifice called Liberty Enlightens the World standing in the New York harbor, that it was fashioned as the Roman goddess Libertas, and that this goddess holds the American Declaration of Independence in one hand while casting the light of freedom from the uplifted torch in her other hand to countries all over the world. This striking omission, I would submit, is the appropriate point of departure for the exploration into the Jewish aspects of "The New Colossus," for Lazarus's negation of Liberty's original symbolism appears to have been the first step she took toward the introduction of an alternative symbolism for the Statue that she drew from Jewish sources.

The story of Lazarus's negative response to Liberty is an intricate one that cannot be grasped on the basis of a reading of "The New Colossus" alone, without any recollection of the events that led up to its writing in 1883. The linchpin is in Lazarus's reference to "the brazen giant of Greek fame"—the Colossus of Rhodes—as the negative contrast to her "New Colossus." Though her associative powers and mastery of classical and renaissance history and literature were undoubtedly strong enough for her to make such a comparison, it had already become common knowledge at the time, since it was repeatedly used as a fund-raising device for the erection of Liberty in America. Seeing as the proposed Statue would be physically bigger than the Rhodian Colossus, whose hitherto unequaled proportions distinguished it as one of the Seven Wonders of the World, fund-raisers made the comparison so as to convince people that their contributions would help put America on the map of world history. In fact, so prevalent was this association by that time, both in speech and in print, that, as one of the leading scholars on the Statue has put it, "Liberty was associated in everybody's mind with the Colossus of Rhodes."

Lazarus's novelty was in her reversal of the popular comparison between the two colossi so that it worked negatively. By distinguishing between the classical giant of Apollo standing at Rhodes and the "New Colossus" standing at the "sunset gates" of the New World, Lazarus was in effect attacking Liberty as it was given to America and suggesting that Americans take over the Statue as their own. Furthermore, as the negative contrast between the "New Colossus" and that of "Greek fame" is extended, the rationale for this expropriation deepens. Going well beyond the difference between the two colossi's origins, and ignoring altogether their competition over size, Lazarus ultimately cast them as two opposing approaches to international human relations. Thus, "Not like" sets up the structure of the whole of the first section and, for that matter, provides a framework for the sonnet as a whole. In what follows, we learn that whereas the inhumane "brazen giant" of antiquity unfeelingly allowed its "conquering limbs" to stride over land after land, the modern colossus with the "mild eyes" stands by the "golden door," raises her "beacon-hand" and utters impassioned words of welcome to the (literally) downtrodden of the "ancient lands."

The genuine basis for Lazarus's portrayal and critique of Liberty as a hollow icon of modern imperialism becomes more than apparent against the historical background provided by Marvin Trachtenberg's brilliant study of the Statue. Two central points emerge here. Fist, Trachtenberg reveals that Auguste Bartholdi's Liberty Enlightens the World was fashioned not so much out of deep respect for America, but rather as an expression of the sculptor's personal obsession with outdoing his classical predecessors in the erection of colossal statuary. Bartholdi had unsuccessfully tried to erect a similar statue at the Suez Canal in Egypt long before Liberty and would probably have found an alternative site for his grandiose dreams had "the American project" never gotten off the ground. When Liberty was completed in 1885, Bartholdi was already depicting it as "the largest work of its kind that has ever been completed" and boasting that "the famous Colossus of Rhodes . . . was but a miniature in comparison."

More significant, Trachtenberg shows how the French people's offering of Liberty to Americans had more to do with internal French politics than with the centennial celebration of the American Revolution. Edouard de Laboulaye, the jurist and republican statesman who initiated the whole idea in 1865, though a great admirer of America and a true scholar of American constitutional history, also belonged to a long tradition of Frenchmen, including Voltaire and Tocqueville, who focused public attention in France on the New World in order to address issues at home. Apparently, Laboulaye and the small group of French republicans who joined his initiative understood that offering the Statue to the Americans could be a vicarious way of coaxing the French people to live up to their stated commitment to liberal ideas.

Indeed, through its broad colonial schemes, prolific missionary activities, and numerous international expositions, France had for decades been involved in the act of projecting itself around the world as the picture of industrial, scientific, and cultural eminence. If, in this vein, it could be arranged for France to give Liberty to the Americans as a gracious gift from a wise old father to a youthful and inexperienced child, it might ironically "ennoble" the French into out-doing the Americans in their liberal forms of government. Under the guise of the grandiose gesture, the message would be simple: while America has been persistent and consistent in its loyalty to the liberal principle of its revolution—even at the price of civil war—France at that time had yet to embody its 1789 revolution in the form of a stable and functioning republic. Gazing upon France from afar, Liberty would, in essence, serve as a watchdog for the new republic.

The dubious nature of this initiative came to the fore once it became clear that the Americans would have to contribute funds to the project—particularly to the erection of the Statue's pedestal. Unsurprisingly, they were less than enthusiastic. Why should Americans comply with a scheme that exploited America in order to glorify France, especially when this glorification was really a veil for the vulnerability of the French republic? Still, despite this predicament, the "Bartholdi Pedestal Fund" persisted in its fund-raising efforts, using tricks like the comparison between Liberty and the Colossus of Rhodes to strengthen its appeal. It was at this point that Emma Lazarus was approached in late 1883 with a request to write a poem on Liberty for the Fund's "art auction."

Beyond her predictable disdain toward writing a poem on order, Lazarus herself was not likely to hail Liberty in verse at that time. Only months before she was approached by the Pedestal Fund, she returned somewhat disappointed from her first visit to France. While in Europe, she made a short trip there on Bastille Day, July 14 of 1883. Though, in Versailles, Lazarus was impressed by the fact that "the crowd who celebrate the birth of the republic wander freely through the halls and avenues, and into the most sacred rooms of the king," she did not experience the glory of the French Revolution on this day. "There are ruins on every side in Paris," she is reported by her sister to have commented. "Ruins of the Commune, or the Siege, or the Revolution; it is terrible—it seems as if the city were seared with fire and blood. With such impressions fresh in her mind, Lazarus would not have been too likely to be impressed with Liberty Enlightens the World back in New York. If not able to see right through the political ploys of Laboulaye and friends, she hardly could have allowed herself to be conquered by their patronizing pretentiousness or to be swayed by the flattery of their tribute to America.

On the other hand, in asking Lazarus to write about Liberty, the Pedestal Fund had paradoxically provided her with a good opportunity to make a positive statement about America in critique of the inauthentic monumentalism of the French. This coincided all too well with Lazarus's vehement commitment to the ideal of a truly indigenous American literature. In a letter that she wrote that same year, Lazarus responded to the claim that the "extremely adverse conditions" of America explain the absence of a great national poet in its literary history by proudly asserting that "I have never believed in the want of a theme—wherever there is humanity, there is a theme for a great poem—& I think it is the poet's fault if he do not know how to utilize the materials and the accessories which surround him." Now she could "utilize" the Pedestal Fund's commission to debunk the hypocrisy and hubris of Liberty's paternalism and subsequently help Americans take possession of the Statue from the French by offering an alternative and genuinely American symbolism for it—one that takes its images from beyond the context of classical or strictly European culture.

With this background in mind, we can now more fully understand Lazarus's structuring her sonnet on the basis of a negative comparison between the Colossus of Rhodes and the "New Colossus." Having overcome her initial resistance to writing poetry on request, Lazarus reversed her energies and focused them on a deliberate undertaking of what was really being asked of her—to compose a poetic work that could arouse local sympathy for the Statue of Liberty so that Americans would contribute to the Pedestal Fund.

Lazarus then engaged in what was no less than a complete reworking of the Statue's original symbolism. She began by subtly providing her audience with the experience of taking Liberty away from France by pronouncing that it was "not like" the French had originally supposed it to be. By portraying the Colossus of Rhodes as nothing but a political monster "with conquering limbs astride from land to land," she was also exposing Liberty Enlightening the World as a devious cover for French cultural and political imperialism. Behind this cover was also a record of violence and inhumanity undertaken in the name of liberty. Three years before Liberty had even been erected in America, Lazarus was in essence telling the French to "keep your storied pomp" for themselves.

Having done so, Lazarus then reversed the symbolism of the French original. Bartholdi had shrewdly chosen Bedloe's over Governor's Island as the site for Liberty, so as to avoid the insult in having her stand with her back directly facing the Americans. This way, New Yorkers could at least see Liberty gazing out beyond the seas so as to "enlighten the world." In her sonnet, Lazarus transformed Bartholdi's revealing gesture into the Statue's raison d'etre by further tilting Liberty's gaze so that it was directed primarily inward, toward America. Hence, rather than allowing France's Liberty to "enlighten" the world (i.e., further France's narcissistic imperialistic designs), she re-created the Statue as a New World colossus that shows France and the rest of the world where Liberty could really be found.

In an even more daring stroke, Lazarus omitted all mention of the name or the word "liberty" as she described Liberty Enlightening the World. Though her poem was unique in this exclusion, it would be wrong to claim that it attempted to completely disassociate the monument from the idea of liberty. Rather, in an almost educational manner, Lazarus boldly disassociated the practice of liberty from the erection of monuments in its name. As if to respond to the audacity of the attempt of Laboulaye's elite group of liberals to ennoble themselves and the French people through the symbol of Liberty, Lazarus's poem posed a definition of liberty as a mode of being rather than as a metaphysical idea. A society's adherence to the idea of liberty is judged by how it relates to each and every one of its members, no matter how lowly his or her condition. The number and the size of the icons labeled "Liberty" within its midst are immaterial. It would seem, then, that Lazarus purposely ignored Liberty's name in order to represent her as a living embodiment of this attitude. Rather than philosophically enlightening the world, her version of the Statue actually does something for somebody. Her light not only "illuminates" a political truth, but also itself acts in line with that truth. Emanating from the torch in the "Mother of Exiles"' outstretched "beacon-hand," it "glows world-wide welcome" to the "tired," "poor," and "homeless" and shows them the way to "the golden door."

The completeness of this idol-breaking reconstruction of Liberty's original symbolism becomes even more apparent when one notes that Lazarus's New World colossus addresses her words of welcome specifically to the tired, poor, and homeless of the "ancient lands" (read: Europe). By calling the downtrodden "your tired," "your poor," and so on, Lazarus suggested a causal connection between the imperialism of the "brazen giant of Greek fame," the "storied pomp" of the ancient lands, and the deplorable condition of its "huddled masses, yearning to breathe free." It is precisely because the "ancient lands" are taken with the idea of liberty and with their self-glorification through its projection abroad, the sonnet intimates, that many of their people are suffering and neglected at home. These people then become "the wretched refuse of your teeming shore."

Furthermore, beyond merely exposing this sad consequence of Old World hypocrisy, "The New Colossus" posed the New World as nobly compensating for, or even correcting, the wrongful doing by offering a political haven for the now "homeless" masses. In America, in whose tranquil "air-bridged harbor" stand "our sea-washed sunset gates," the bronze idol of Liberty is transformed into a humane "Mother of Exiles," whose silent lips command the Old World to "Give me" and "Send...to me" the "wretched refuse of your teeming shore." Her compassion leads her to cherish these forgotten undesirables, and her humanity causes her to value the opportunity to ennoble herself through their political redemption. She seeks to empower them on her territory in the faith that their lowly condition was only a function of how they had been treated and that they will thrive in the New World, where liberty is genuinely a way of life.

"I liked your sonnet about the Statue much better than I liked the Statue itself," wrote the renowned American literary critic and diplomat James Russell Lowell, in a personal letter to Lazarus. It was written only a few weeks after "The New Colossus" was read aloud at the opening of the Pedestal Fund's art loan exhibition. Since the portfolio contributed a disappointing amount of $1,500 to the auction—its committee expected to sell it for $3,000—Lazarus's effort had not been overly beneficial in achieving the immediate goal of amassing funds for the pedestal. However, as Lowell testified in the continuation of his letter, something in Lazarus's poem provided a potential basis for American identification with the Statue of Liberty that was apparently absent in Bartholdi's original: "[B]ut your sonnet gives it a raison d'etre which it wanted before quite as much as it wants a pedestal. You have set it on a noble one, saying admirably just the right word to be said, an achievement more arduous than that of the sculptor."

Source: Daniel Marom, "Who is the 'Mother of Exiles?':
Jewish Aspects of Emma Lazarus's 'The New Colossus,'"
in *Prooftexts: A Journal of Jewish Literary History*, Vol.
20, No. 3, Autumn 2000, p. 231.

Bette Roth Young

In the following essay, Young explains the relevance that the poem and the statue have to each other and to Lazarus's body of work.

Emma Lazarus, nineteenth century American poet, is best remembered for her sonnet, "The New Colossus." History needn't apologize; the poem has become an American anthem. It was written in 1883 to be auctioned at the Art Loan Fund Exhibition in Aid of the Bartholdi Pedestal Fund for the Statue of Liberty, and was the only entry read at the gala opening of that exhibit on 3 December of that year. James Russell Lowell wrote Emma that her poem had given the Statue a "raison d'être." Except for an appearance in one daily after that, however, it fell into obscurity. At the unveiling of the Statue in 1886, both Emma and her sonnet were absent. Nevertheless, she thought the piece important enough to give it first place in her notebook of poems, transcribed a year before her death.

The sonnet was rescued from oblivion in 1901, when Georgina Schuyler set in motion a successful attempt to memorialize her friend by placing the poem, inscribed on a bronze tablet, inside the pedestal of the Statue. On 6 May 1903, after two years of red tape, Schuyler was able to report to her friends that "dear Emma's poem" was in place.

The relationship between the Statue of Liberty and "The New Colossus" is taken for granted. In 1986, in honor of the tandem renovations of the Statue of Liberty and Ellis Island, liberty coins were struck on which the Statue, the immigrant, and the lines of the sonnet were inscribed. To quote Oscar Handlin, the Statue, the immigrant, and the sonnet are "connected."

"Liberty Enlightening the World" was given to the United States by the French people in honor of each country's revolution. At the unveiling ceremonies on 28 October 1886, President Grover Cleveland viewed the Statue as a goddess who had "made her home here." He said that the fires from her "chosen altar" would be kept alive by "willing votaries" and would shine "upon the shores of our sister republic in the east." Liberty's light would "pierce the darkness of man's ignorance and oppression," until Liberty enlightened the world.

Emma Lazarus gave the Statue a very different name and purpose. Calling her "Mother of Exiles," she brought America's most illustrious immigrant down to earth to welcome exiles from around the world. Her Statue could not wait for the concept of liberty to triumph in distant lands; she offered liberty now, to the globe's great unwashed. Lazarus' poem reinforced the concept of America as a haven for the homeless. It came, appropriately, at a time when this country was overwhelmed by an unending torrent of immigrants. To this day, hyphenate Americans continue to claim the Statue as their own.

Furthermore, various segments of American society, pleading for social justice, continue to use the Statue as a kind of intercessor. With an absence of awe, some have climbed her stairways and chained themselves to the railing around her crown. Many have used Emma's words as prooftext for their cause. In addition, the sonnet has become a part of America's musical repertoire. Put to music by Irving Berlin, it is sung by schoolchildren at vocal music concerts as a replacement for "America the Beautiful."

Emma Lazarus gave a goddess to a world full of strangers and called her Mother. She breathed life into that icy majesty, rescuing her from the "stuff of Fourth of July oratory." The Statue of Liberty is an American icon. So, in a sense, is Emma Lazarus. But while the Statue "lives" in a New York harbor, "battered and assaulted by wind and weather," Emma Lazarus has been put on a pedestal of sorts. She is viewed as brilliant, morbid, reclusive, and pure, an unapproachable American aristocrat. Nevertheless, she is a "patron saint" for American Jews. Seen in her time as the leading spokesperson for an East European Jewry forced to leave the barbarity of Czarist Russia, she is still honored today by such diverse groups as the Emma Lazarus Federation of Jewish Women's Clubs and the American Jewish Historical Society, for example.

The federation, founded in 1951, is an offshoot of the Jewish People's Fraternal Order. The JPFO, which grew out of the Jewish-American section of the International Workers Order, was liquidated during the McCarthy era. The Federation continues to exist. Its members are octogenarian Jewish women, for the most part, whose commitment to the principles of Karl Marx informs their group. The publication of Lazarus' poetry and prose has been an ongoing project of this national organization that sees Emma Lazarus as a "progressive," i.e., socialistic, Jew. Her one essay on William Morris as well as her "secular" humanistic Judaism inspires this view.

The American Jewish Historical Society, housed on the campus of Brandeis University, is one of two archives for American Jewish artifacts. The Emma Lazarus Foundation is one of three endowments created by the Society for the purpose of raising funds. In addition, in 1986, in honor of the Centennial of the Statue of Liberty, the Society inaugurated the Emma Lazarus Statue of Liberty Award Dinner, "the only national event during the centennial celebration of the Statue of Liberty to focus on the role American Jewish immigrants have played in the development of our nation."

Emma Lazarus was never "radical," nor was she comfortably Jewish. She was more at home in the cultured milieu of New York, Newport, Concord, and London than in the Jewish world she so ardently embraced in the last years of her life. Said to have had a "conversion" experience upon meeting East European Jewish refugees at Ward's Island, she became their spokesperson in poetry and prose. Nevertheless, her world remained as it had been, one of gentility and high culture.

Source: Bette Roth Young, "The Statue," in *Emma Lazarus in Her World: Life and Letters*, Jewish Publication Society, 1995, pp. 3–5.

SOURCES

Ambrose, Stephen E., *Nothing Like It in the World: The Men Who Built the Transcontinental Railroad, 1863–1869*, Simon & Schuster, 2000.

Byers, Ann, *The History of U.S. Immigration: Coming to America*, Enslow Publishers, 2006.

Curlee, Lynn, *The Seven Wonders of the Ancient World*, Atheneum, 2002, pp. 24–26.

Dubnow, Simon, *History of the Jews in Russia and Poland, Vol. 3 of 3: From the Earliest Times Until the Present Day*, Forgotten Books, 2010, pp.66–101.

Frost, Robert, *The Road Not Taken: A Selection of Robert Frost's Poems*, Holt Paperbacks, 2nd rev. ed., 2002, p. 270.

"Immigration, The Journey to America, The Chinese," in *Oracle ThinkQuest Education Foundation*, http://library.thinkquest.org/20619/Chinese.html (accessed May 24, 2010).

Lazarus, Emma, "The New Colossus," in *Emma Lazarus, Selected Poems*, edited by John Hollander, Library of America, 2005, p. 58.

Lehman, David, "Colossal Ode," in *Smithsonian*, Vol. 35, No. 1, April 2004, pp. 120–22.

Review of *Admetus, and Other Poems*, in *Galaxy*, Vol. 13, No. 1, January 1872, pp. 136–37.

———, in *Nation*, Vol. 14, No. 345, February 8, 1872, p. 92.

Schor, Esther, *Emma Lazarus*, Schocken Books, 2006, pp. 188, 191.

"Statue of Liberty," in *National Park Service*, http://www.nps.gov/stli/index.htm (accessed on May 25, 2010).

Zierler, Wendy, "The Making and Re-Making of Jewish-American Literary History," in *Shofar*, Vol. 27, No. 2, Winter 2009, p. 69.

FURTHER READING

Ash, Russell, *Great Wonders of the World*, DK Children, 2000.

 Ash focuses his attention in this young-adult book on many spectacular accomplishments in history. The Colossus of Rhodes is included, along with more generalized categories, such as the great accomplishments in engineering, inventions, and special phenomena in the natural world.

Bray, Ilona, J.D., *U.S. Immigration Made Easy*, 14th ed., updated by Jeptha Evans and Ruby Lieberman, NOLO, 2009.

 Using topics such as how to begin your journey toward immigration, dealing with the paperwork involved, finding a lawyer, and obtaining a green card, the authors of this book (all lawyers) provide information about how to immigrate to the United States.

Coan, Peter Morton, *Ellis Island Interviews: In Their Own Words*, Facts on File, 1997.

 Coan explores the history of Ellis Island, where immigrants, especially between 1892 and 1924, first landed in the States. Interviews with more than 130 different people from Europe and the Middle East, some of them famous, most of them not, heighten the emotional content of the reading.

Gallo, Donald, *First Crossing: Stories about Teen Immigrants*, Candlewick, 2007.

 In this young-adult collection, Gallo presents stories about the experiences of contemporary teenagers who have immigrated to the United States. The stories focus on a wide variety of teens, from those being smuggled across the border from Mexico to the culture clash experienced by a teen attempting to adjust after moving to the United States from Korea.

Hammerschmidt, Peter A., *History of American Immigration*, Mason Crest, 2009.

In this young-adult book, Hammerschmidt examines the history of immigration in the United States, demonstrating how diverse the people of this country are. Describing various cultures and customs, he explores the influence of immigrants on American life.

Khan, Yasmin Sabina, *Enlightening the World: The Creation of the Statue of Liberty*, Cornell University Press, 2010.

Khan provides an history of the Statue of Liberty, recounting the reasons behind France's creation of this gift to the United States. She describes the work of the French sculptor Auguste Bartholdi and the fundraising work of American publisher Joseph Pulitzer to pay for the pedestal, and gives details about Emma Lazarus's life.

Polacheck, Hilda Satt, *I Came a Stranger: The Story of a Hull-House Girl*, edited by Dena J. Polacheck Epstein, University of Illinois Press, 1989.

In this memoir, Polacheck recounts her immigration to Chicago from Poland. Polacheck was a young Jewish woman when she arrived.

Later in life, she wrote her story but could not find a publisher. She died without knowing that her work was finally put into book form through the efforts of her granddaughter.

SUGGESTED SEARCH TERMS

Emma Lazarus

The New Colossus

Statue of Liberty

history of U.S. immigration

Liberty Island

Lazarus and Statue of Liberty

Lazarus and Jewish literature

female Jewish poets

Ralph Waldo Emerson and Emma Lazarus

Immigration and Naturalization Service

Ellis Island

A Simile

N. SCOTT MOMADAY
1960

"A Simile" is one of Native American poet and novelist N. Scott Momaday's earliest published poems. He wrote it during his first year in the creative writing graduate program at Stanford University, and it was one of thirteen poems submitted for his masterApos;s degree in 1960. It was first published in the magazine *Sequoia* that same year. Momaday included the poem in his first poetry collection, *Angle of Geese and Other Poems*, in 1974, and he republished it two years later in *The Gourd Dancer*. Both these books are now out of print, but the poem also appears in Momaday's *In the Presence of the Sun: Stories and Poems* (1992), and in two anthologies, *Compact Literature: Reading, Reacting, Writing*, 7th ed., edited by Laurie G. Kirszner and Stephen R. Mandell (Cengage Learning, 2010) and *The McGraw-Hill Book of Poetry*, edited by Robert DiYanni (McGraw-Hill, 1993).

"A Simile" is a free-verse poem of only eight short lines in which the poet, by using a simile drawn from his observation of several deer, reflects on a change that has taken place in a close human relationship. The poem is notable both for its observation of the natural world and for its thought-provoking question about the world of human emotions and behavior.

AUTHOR BIOGRAPHY

Momaday was born on February 27, 1934, in Lawton, Oklahoma. His father, Albert, a Kiowa

N. Scott Momaday (MPI / Getty Images)

Indian, was a painter and teacher of art, and his mother, Natachee, was a teacher and writer who strongly identified with the Indian culture of her Cherokee great-grandmother. Momaday lived briefly on a family farm in Oklahoma, after which the family moved west, living from 1936 to 1943 on reservations in New Mexico and Arizona, where Momaday learned about Navajo culture. In 1943, they moved to Hobbs, New Mexico, where Momaday's father worked at Hobbs Air Force Base. It was during this three-year period at Hobbs that Momaday wrote his first poem, at the age of nine.

After World War II, Momaday's parents taught at a school in Jemez Pueblo, New Mexico. Over the next few years, Momaday acquired a strong sense of his Native American heritage, but he was also well acquainted with Anglo American culture, speaking English as his first language, so in that sense he grew up bicultural. He was an able student and particularly excelled during his final year of high school, which he spent at Augusta Military Academy in Fort Defiance, Virginia. In 1952, he enrolled at the University of New Mexico in Albuquerque. After studying law at the University of Virginia

from 1956 to 1957, Momaday returned to the University of New Mexico, graduating in 1958 with a B.A. in political science. By this time he had developed a strong interest in writing. Momaday then worked for a year as a teacher at the Dulce Independent School on the Jicarilla Reservation in New Mexico before winning a scholarship to study poetry at Stanford University. At Stanford he was supervised by the noted literary critic and teacher, Yvor Winters, who became a strong influence on Momaday's early poetry. Momaday received an M.A. from Stanford in 1960 and a Ph.D. in 1963. He began teaching at the University of California the same year.

Momaday also wrote prose, and in 1969, he became the first Native American to win the Pulitzer Prize, for his first novel, *House Made of Dawn*, which was published in 1968. In 1969, he was initiated into the Gourd Dance, or Taimpe, Society, a Kiowa tribe organization, and his collection of stories illustrated by his father, *The Way to Rainy Mountain*, was published.

From 1969 to 1973, Momaday taught at the University of California at Berkeley. In the fall of 1973 he joined the faculty of Stanford University. In 1974, his first poetry collection, *Angle of Geese and Other Poems*, which included "A Simile," was published. This was followed two years later by *The Gourd Dancer*, a volume he illustrated himself. He developing an interest in drawing, and his drawings and paintings have since been exhibited in galleries.

Other works by Momaday include his autobiography, *The Names: A Memoir* (1976); a novel, *The Ancient Child* (1989); *In the Presence of the Sun: Stories and Poems, 1961–1991* (1992); *The Man Made of Words: Essays, Stories, Passages* (1997); and *In the Bear's House* (1999).

Since 1982, Momaday has been a professor of English and comparative literature at the University of Arizona at Tucson.

POEM SUMMARY

Line 1

The first line of "A Simile" is a question, although it is not followed by a question mark. There is no punctuation at all in this one-sentence, free-verse poem of eight short lines. The speaker is reflecting on a relationship he has with someone who is, or used to be, close to him. The question is addressed

MEDIA ADAPTATIONS

- In *Momaday: Voice of the West* Momaday reads from his memoirs and other published works. This thirty-minute video was released by PBS Home Video in 1997.

to this person. The two are not identified further, described only by the plural pronoun "we." It could be a husband and wife, boyfriend and girl-friend, or a couple in some other kind of close relationship as friends or even colleagues. The speaker is beginning a reflection on something that he and the other person said to each other at some time in the past.

Line 2

Line 2 indicates by the word now that there has been a change in the relationship between these two people. Although it is not yet made explicit, the change has more distance between them. This line introduces the simile that gives the poem its title. In their relationship, the couple is now like deer. The poem thus moves from the human world to the animal world and announces through the simile that a comparison is to be made between the two.

Line 3

Line 3 begins the description of certain aspects of the deer that will be likened to the way the couple now behave and act toward each other. There is more than one deer in the visual image that begins in this line, although how many deer is not stated. The characteristic emphasized here is that the deer do not walk alongside each other but in single file, one behind the other. The comparison is with the human couple who, it is to be presumed, used to walk alongside each other but now do not. They are less close to each other, less able or perhaps less willing to communicate than they were formerly.

Lines 4–6

These three short lines, each beginning with the word *with* describe the physical posture of the deer and how it perceives its environment. Each line gives a separate visual image of a different aspect of the deer. Together, the lines suggest both the alertness and the watchfulness of the deer, its capacity to use its senses to respond quickly to whatever happens in its environment. In terms of the simile, it suggests that the human couple has also become more watchful and wary of each other, less spontaneous.

Line 7

This line, longer than the three that preceded it, also begins with the word *with* and continues the description of the way the deer behaves in a way that elaborates on the simile, in which the human couple is compared to deer. The deer treads firmly on the ground; it is sure-footed. This is part of the watchfulness and readiness that have been emphasized in lines 3 to 6. The reader must wait until the next line to gather the full purpose of the description here.

Line 8

Line 8 explains why the deer is so careful to tread firmly on the ground, and why it is ever watchful of its environment. It may need to run at any moment to escape danger from a predator or some other potential hazard. The fact that this is part of the simile that compares the deer to the unnamed human couple shows that the couple has become cautious in their interactions with each other. Whereas before they were close, now it seems that at some level they are fearful of communicating with each other. They are always on the alert, perhaps fearing that they will be hurt by the words spoken by the other person, so they are always ready to run away from the situation.

THEMES

Relationships

"A Simile" is a simple poem that uses visual images of deer to comment on a human relationship. One can imagine the speaker, who is one part of the couple, out on a walk with his companion. He spots some deer, walking characteristically in single file, one behind the other. Perhaps he and his companion are doing this very same thing. He notices how alert the deer are to danger. They are

TOPICS FOR FURTHER STUDY

- Observe the behavior of an animal. It could be a domesticated animal such as a cat or dog, or you could choose a squirrel, a mouse, a cow, or any other kind of animal. Write a simile poem in which you note some aspect of the animal's behavior and use it to reflect on or highlight a human behavior or attitude. Create a poster, using Glogster or another on-line software program, that includes images and the text of your poem.

- Research Native American legends and stories. Select a legend that you like and develop it into a short story that you can read to your class. For help in how to construct an interesting and effective short story visit www.story jumper.com and follow StoryStarter, which guides you through seven main components of a story: character, challenge, motivation, setting, obstacles, climax, and closing.

- Consult *Poetry for Young People: Animal Poems*, edited by John Hollander and published by Sterling in 2004, which contains poems about animals by noted poets including William Blake, Emily Dickinson, Robert Frost, and Theodore Roethke. Select two poems that you like, and write an essay in which you compare and contrast them with Momaday's "A Simile." Post your essays on a class blog and invite fellow students to debate your conclusions as you debate theirs.

- Research the topic of deer in your county or state. What is the estimated deer population? What strategies are in place for managing deer population? Are there any problems with deer in your area that have an effect on the human population? Information about deer in your area can usually be found on the Web site of the Department of Natural Resources for your state. Make a short class presentation on the subject that incorporates the use of charts, graphs, and tables to explain the situation.

always ready to run, and this leads the speaker to reflect on how his relationship with this person has changed. Two people formerly close are now, if not estranged, more distant from each other. Perhaps they have quarreled, maybe more than once. Perhaps they did not see eye to eye, and the argument was a painful one, not fully resolved but with the disagreement papered over and hurt remaining. Since it is a human instinct to avoid pain, whether mental or physical, these two people have become wary of communicating with each other in any deep fashion because they are frightened of their own emotions, of what might be stirred up within them by their interaction. Why this happened, and what the circumstances were, is not answered. In fact, the whole poem is formed as a question that is never answered. The speaker does not know what caused the rift between the couple. The fact that the poem is phrased in the form of a question posed by a single speaker, with no rejoinder from the person to whom the question is addressed, suggests the isolation into which they have fallen. Perhaps it also suggests the unfathomable nature of close relationships between people. It is not always possible to know what causes significant shifts such as this one in a relationship.

Trust

The poem contains an implied contrast between two ways of being in a close relationship with another person. The first way is not described directly, because is it now in the past, so the reader has to imagine for himself or herself what it might have been like. However, it can be surmised that before the quarrel between these two people, or before whatever words were exchanged that caused the difficulty between them, there was a free flow of communication from one person to the other. Affection, more than likely, was given and received.

A watchful deer on alert (Tony Campbell / Shutterstock.com)

There was trust between them, and openness. It was a relationship without walls, so to speak. But now the poem emphasizes, as if the relationship is sharply divided between the past and the present, all that has changed. Intimacy has given way to fear; trust has turned into wariness; and emotional distance has replaced a former closeness. Each person, it might be guessed, is now more careful about what he or she says to the other. The old ease and spontaneity has gone, and now they find themselves more withdrawn, anxious not to enter into emotional territory that has become problematic for them but afraid that it might invade their relationship anyway, whether they want it to or not. They are therefore fearful, ready to run from anything that might reopen emotional wounds that would be too painful for them to deal with.

STYLE

Free Verse

"A Simile" is written in free verse. Free verse is the most popular verse form used by modern poets. Free verse does not employ rhyme or traditional meter; as the term suggests, it allows the poet greater freedom in selecting the techniques he or she employs to create the desired effect. Some of the poetic effect in this poem is gained through repetition of the word *with* at the beginning of lines 4, 5, 6, and 7. The short lines 4–6, each consisting of only three words, may not only refer to the alertness of the deer's senses, but may also suggest the corresponding jerky (to the human eye) movements the deer makes as it remains on the alert for any possible danger.

Diction

Diction refers to the poet's choice of language in a poem, to the words and phrases used. Diction can be formal or colloquial, simple or elaborate, literal or figurative. The diction in this poem is simple and straightforward. All but five of the words are momosyllabic (consisting of one syllable only). They are everyday words that anyone can understand. The simplicity of the words and phrases used is a contrast to the emotional complexity that has become a part of the couple's relationship. In spite of its simplicity, the language can also be considered figurative, since the poem is made up almost entirely of a simile.

Simile

A simile is a figure of speech in which one thing is compared to another. Similes can often be recognized by the words *as* or *like* that introduce them (as in line 2 of this poem). The two things compared may be dissimilar on the surface, but the simile brings out aspects in which they resemble each other. In this poem, the posture of the deer, the fact that deer walk in single file and are always ready for flight, is likened to the distance and wariness that exists between the human couple who is similarly always ready to sense dangerous emotional situations in their relationship and quickly shy away from them. The simile takes up almost the entire poem, and the poet brings attention to the device in the poem's title.

HISTORICAL CONTEXT

Native American Literature of the 1960s and 1970s

The 1960s and 1970s was a period of enormous growth and creativity among Native American writers. As Matthias Schubnell points out in *N. Scott Momaday: The Cultural and Literary Background*, many more Native Americans of the post–World War II generation were educated in non-Indian schools and universities, gained greater proficiency in the English language, and desired to use it to create literature. Momaday, at home in both Anglo and Native American cultures and educated at Stanford University, is a case in point. His work was the first by a Native American to make its mark in mainstream American literature. *House Made of Dawn*, a novel that explores issues of cultural and ethnic identity that were part of the emerging zeitgeist of the 1960s, was published in 1968. In the novel, a Native American who is raised on an Indian reservation in New Mexico serves in the U.S. military in World War II, and then lives in Los Angeles, where he loses his Indian identity in the harsh urban environment.

It was through the work of Native American writers from this period that knowledge of Indian history, beliefs, practices, and contemporary attitudes and issues was preserved in the form of poetry and novels. The mainstream American literary culture became somewhat more accepting of such works in the 1970s. Until then, Native

American writers had access to only small presses such as Crossing Press, Elizabeth Press, and others, with circulation limited to a few hundred copies, so their work was not generally known. However, in 1972, the New York publisher Harper & Row began a Native American Publishing Program, which published Momaday's *The Gourd Dancer* in 1976. Other Native American works in that series included James Welch's novel *Winter in the Blood* (1974), which is set on an Indian reservation in Montana; *Carriers of the Dream Wheel* (1975), an anthology of Native American poetry edited by Native American poet Duane Niatum (the title is that of a poem by Momaday); and individual volumes of poetry that included *Going for the Rain* (1976) by Simon Ortiz; Niatum's *Ascending Red Cedar Moon* (1973); and Ray Young Bear's *Winter of the Salamander* (1980). Another major publisher, Viking Press, also had a Native American publishing program, which published *Voices of the Rainbow*, an anthology of Native American poetry edited by Kenneth Mark Rosen, in 1975. In 1978, the American Indian Studies Center at the University of California at Los Angeles began a publishing program and published Paula Gunn Allen's major work *Shadow Country* in 1982. Other important Native American works of the period include Leslie Marmon Silko's poetry collection *Laguna Woman* (1974) and novel *Ceremony* (1977); Joy Harjo's poetry collections *The Last Song* (1975) and *What Moon Drove Me to This?* (1978); *The Blind Lion* (1974), the first volume of poetry by Paula Gunn Allen; and *Voices from Wah'kon-tah* (1974), an anthology of Native American poetry edited by Robert K. Dodge and Joseph B. McCullough.

Native American History in the 1960s and 1970s

During the 1960s, minority groups such as African Americans, and also women, developed a much greater awareness of the need for collective action to establish their civil rights and to make economic progress. The civil rights movement resulted in the landmark Civil Rights Act of 1964, which made it illegal to discriminate against anyone based on race, religion, gender, or ethnicity. During the late 1960s, Native Americans also became more assertive in their attempts to preserve their cultural heritage and claim their rights as U.S. citizens. In 1969, for example, over 200 Native Americans from a group called Indians of all Tribes took control of Alcatraz Island, the

COMPARE
&
CONTRAST

- **1970s:** Many thousands of Indians live in dire poverty on reservations. The unemployment rate for Native Americans is ten times that of the general population, and the death rate is one-third higher.

  Today: Native Americans still constitute an impoverished minority in the United States. Some tribes have taken advantage of the 1988 Indian Gaming Regulatory Act, which permits gaming on tribal lands, and operate successful casinos. However, Native Americans continue to have higher rates of poverty, lower educational achievement, and higher rates of disease and illness than the general population.

- **1970s:** Native American poets grow in number and publish their work in a variety of outlets, including magazines, newspapers, small presses, and also several major publishers. Many are rooted in particular areas of the country, such as the Southwest (Simon Ortiz and Wendy Rose), the plains (Momaday and James Welch), and the northeast (Peter Blue Cloud and Maurice Kenny). These poets represent many different tribes, including Kiowa (Momaday), Blackfeet/Gros Ventre (Welch), Acoma (Ortiz), Hopi/Miwok (Rose), and Mohawk (Kenny and Blue Cloud).

  Today: A new generation of Native American poets makes its mark on American literature. Among the many Native American poets writing in the twenty-first century are Trevino L. Brings Plenty, Heid E. Erdrich, and LeAnne Howe. Born on a reservation in South Dakota, Brings Plenty is a Minneconjou Lakota living in Portland, Oregon. His poetry volumes include *Drinking with the Rocks* (2002) and *Removing Skin* (2005). Erdrich, the sister of the novelist Louise Erdrich, has written *Fishing for Myth* (1997) and *National Monuments* (2008). Howe's book *Evidence of Red: Prose and Poems* (2005) won the Oklahoma Book Award in 2006. Howe, a Choctaw Indian from Oklahoma, is also the author of the novel *Shell Shaker* (2001), which received an American Book Award in 2002.

- **1970s:** As individual states develop successful wildlife management systems, the population of deer begins to rise again across almost all of the United States. This follows a long decline in the deer population caused in the early 1900s by unregulated hunting.

  Today: There are estimated to be over 20 million deer in the United States, and the population is steadily increasing. Together with wildlife management and restrictions on hunting, part of the increase is the result of a shift in human population from rural to suburban areas. Combined with farmland that has been allowed to revert to forest, an environment of open and forested land in which deer can flourish has been established. The increase in the number of deer has also raised concerns in many communities about the negative effects of large numbers of deer on human society. These include damage to crops and gardens, transmission of Lyme disease, and collisions between deer and cars.

---

former federal penitentiary in San Francisco Bay. The occupation lasted for nineteen months, until June 1971. It was intended as a protest against bad conditions on Indian reservations. In 1970, unemployment among Native Americans was ten times the national average, and 40 percent of Native Americans lived below the poverty line. Average life expectancy for Indians was only forty-four years, compared to sixty-six years for the general population.

Native American militancy continued into the 1970s in the form of the American Indian Movement (AIM). In November 1972, AIM occupied the Bureau of Indian Affairs building

Single file, deer move at night *(2009fotofriends | Shutterstock.com)*

in Washington, D.C., for a week to bring attention to their cause. In 1973, 200 members of AIM, many of them armed, occupied the town of Wounded Knee, on the Pine Ridge Reservation in South Dakota. Wounded Knee was the site of a massacre of Sioux Indians by the U.S. Army in 1890.

CRITICAL OVERVIEW

In critical discussion of Momaday's poetry, "A Simile" is usually not mentioned, the focus instead being on more weighty poems such as "Angle of Geese" and "The Gourd Dancer." However, comments made by Kenneth C. Mason, in an essay on *The Gourd Dancer* in the *South Dakota Review* in 1980, might well be applied to "A Simile." After remarking that "the book presents a distinct and distinguished music in post-modern poetry and a fresh and compelling vision," Mason notes that two poems "Angle of Geese" and "Comparatives" "show that Momaday is primarily a meditative poet, working directly in the American tradition of meditative poetry. The predominant mood is

quiet reflection; the tone is sober and serious." "A Simile" is certainly a meditative poem of this type, and it is also typical of Momaday's work in the sense that it moves from observation of the natural world—frequently animals—to a reflection on human behavior or the human condition. Charles L. Woodward, in a conversation with Momaday published in *Ancestral Voice: Conversations with N. Scott Momaday*, commented on the fact that Momaday sometimes uses questions in his poems, as he does in "A Simile," and other poems such as "The Bear" and "Buteo Regalis." Momaday replied, "I'm not sure why those questions are there. Maybe because I have a sense of wonder. And the belief that there are elemental questions to be addressed."

CRITICISM

Bryan Aubrey

Aubrey holds a Ph.D. in English. In the following essay, he discusses the etching that Momaday used to illustrate "A Simile."

WHAT
DO I READ
NEXT?

- *Bestiary: An Anthology of Poems about Animals* (1996) is a multicultural anthology of animal poems compiled by Stephen Mitchell. Many ages and many cultures are represented, including poems by Chinese, Japanese, Jewish, Latin American, European, and American authors.

- *The Hidden Life of Deer: Lessons from the Natural World* (2009), by Elizabeth Marshall Thomas, contains a wealth of fascinating observations about the social life of deer. In southern New Hampshire, naturalist Thomas, who is well known for her books about the psychology and behavior of cats and dogs, observed deer in her woods and fields in all seasons for a period of twelve months.

- *Harper's Anthology of Twentieth Century Native American Poetry* (1988), edited by Duane Niatum, contains in its 432 pages selections from thirty-six Native American poets, including Jim Barnes, Thomas Welch, Simon J. Ortiz, Linda Hogan, Maurice Kenny, Ray A. Young Bear, Joy Harjo, Louise Erdrich, and Wendy Rose. Momaday is represented by ten of his poems. The anthology contains brief biographies of each poet and a bibliography.

- Momaday's *The Names: A Memoir* (1976) is an imaginative memoir of Momaday's childhood and adolescence, up to the age of about seventeen, just before he entered his last year of high school at a military academy. The memoir contains many family photographs, with captions in Momaday's handwriting, and some of Momaday's own drawings.

- Momaday's *The Ancient Child: A Novel* (1989) takes as its starting point a Kiowa myth in which a boy turns into a bear. A contemporary middle-aged Native American raised in white society feels drawn to this myth, and so begins his search for identity, aided by a young Indian medicine woman named Grey.

- *Four Arrows & Magpie: A Kiowa Story* (2006), is Momaday's telling of a traditional Kiowa legend about how the tribe first came to Oklahoma. Momaday tells the story from the perspective of two Kiowa children, and it is suitable for young-adult readers. The book is illustrated with Momaday's own sketches.

- *Rising Voices: Writings of Young Native Americans* (1993) is an anthology, compiled by Arlene Hirschfelder and Beverly Singer, of more than sixty poems and essays by Native American children and young adults, covering a period from 1887 to 1990. Some of the authors write about their attempts to hold onto their Indian identity while living in white society; others discuss their experience of prejudice against them. The book is divided into six sections: Identity, Family, Homelands, Ritual and Ceremony, Education, and Harsh Realities.

- Momaday's contemporary Joy Harjo is one of the most prominent Native American poets. *How We Became Human: New and Selected Poems 1975–2001* (2002) gives a representative sample of her work over a quarter of a century, drawn from six of her previous books. There are also thirteen new poems. Harjo's relentless search for truth, conveyed through a variety of poetic forms and including myth and traditional chants and storytelling, makes for compelling poetry.

N. Scott Momaday's short but deft, thought-provoking poem "A Simile" has received little comment from reviewers or critics. Momaday himself, in his many interviews with journalists and scholars, has seldom mentioned it. Perhaps part of the reason for this, other than the poem's sheer simplicity—Momaday has written many far more complex poems—is that Momaday is

"

IN THE POEM THERE IS FEAR ON BOTH SIDES,
AS IF EACH PERSON IS SCARED OF TRUSTING THE
OTHER ONE AGAIN. IT WOULD APPEAR THAT THE
EMOTIONAL WOUNDS THESE TWO PEOPLE HAVE
INFLICTED ON EACH OTHER ARE TOO DEEP TO
FULLY HEAL, AND NEITHER IS PREPARED TO RISK
REOPENING THEM."

known primarily as a Native American poet, and most of the questions directed to him, and the interests of literary critics, regard those aspects of his work that seem specifically to be connected to his Native American heritage. Notwithstanding the fact that the poem results in part from a close observation of the movements of deer, and that Native American culture is known for its understanding of and empathy with nonhuman life ("A deer was killed only after obtaining his ceremonial assent to the killing that enabled all life to endure in its ordered pattern," writes Frank Waters in his essay "Two Views of Nature: White and Indian"), there is nothing about "A Simile" that might be thought of as Native American in theme, tone, or structure. The poem seems to have arisen from a confluence of real or imagined circumstances: the peculiar characteristics of the deer, always alert to possible danger, are noted by a speaker who sees in those animals a reflection of the behavior pattern of two humans in some kind of close, or formerly close, relationship.

There has been comment on "A Simile," however, in a rather surprising and unexpected form. In addition to being a distinguished poet, Momaday is also a skilled artist, and when he published *In the Presence of the Sun: Stories and Poems* (1992), a collection of his work in poetry and prose stretching over three decades, he illustrated it himself. There are sixty illustrations, black and white reproductions of original artwork done in various forms—including etching, watercolor, acrylic, ink, and graphite and wash—over a period of eighteen years. It is a remarkable book that even puts in mind, in the way each illustration seems to comment on the poem it illustrates and vice versa, the work of another great poet who

illustrated his own works, the English romantic William Blake (1757–1827).

One of the poems Momaday illustrates is "A Simile." It is illustrated by an etching done in 1985 and captioned "Marriage at Heurfano." Huerfano is the name of a river and a county in Colorado that are rich with Native American history. Momaday offers no further explanation of the etching; it seems likely that it was created without any reference to "A Simile" in mind, but seven years later when he was compiling *In the Presence of the Sun: Stories and Poems*, Momaday must have realized that the etching would make a rather apt illustration for the poem that had been written thirty years earlier.

The etching shows two human figures, a man and a woman, standing close together. They are both clad in long, dark, loose clothing—the man's garment is streaked with white—and they are so close they appear almost as one body, their individual contours obscured. The woman is completely turned to the side, looking away from the man, her head pulled back and looking upward (like the heads of the deer in the poem). The man's head is close to the woman's, yet he is looking down and slightly away, and although facial features are not clearly drawn, the dark streak across his face gives the impression of anger or discontent. If this is a marriage, it does not look like a happy one, but the etching may offer visual insight into what has happened to the couple in the poem. The etching is cunningly placed opposite another poem titled, "Earth and I Gave You Turquoise," which is narrated by a widower who still grieves for the young wife with whom he shared happy times and who, it appears, died young. Happy, if tragic, love is thus contrasted with unhappy love as shown in "A Simile" and the etching.

The etching illustrates the poem in the sense that it shows a human couple estranged from each other and yet still—clearly so in the etching—bound closely to each other, for better or worse. The married individuals in the etching are unable to escape each other, whether they like it or not. But like the couple in the poem, they are no longer able to communicate with each other, or perhaps even to try. The upward thrust of the woman's head suggests pride and intransigence; for whatever reason, she has made herself unreachable to her husband, whose own posture might suggest regret and frustration as well as anger. In both cases, etching and poem, two people who should be, and have at some time been, close, enjoying each other's companionship and affection, find themselves separated by an invisible but impassable gulf. In the poem there is fear on both sides, as if each person is scared of trusting the other one again. It would appear that the emotional wounds these two people have inflicted on each other are too deep to fully heal, and neither is prepared to risk reopening them.

There is tragedy in this short poem because distance has replaced intimacy, and if the illustration is indicative, there is little hope for a reconciliation or a return to former delight. These two people guard themselves now, careful not to drop their defensive stance, unable to allow the free flow of love that once was present between them. Who can explain such a turn of events, which is so common that almost everyone must have experienced it at some point or another in their lives? Today's world is full of psychotherapists and relationship experts who devote their lives to helping people understand and overcome precisely the kind of situation that Momaday depicts in poem and etching. One of the best writers on the topic is psychologist John Welwood. In his essay "Dancing on the Razor's Edge," he explores the demands and pitfalls of romantic relationships, describing them as a "dizzying dance of polarities." The dance begins when two people are attracted to each other and begin a relationship. Each reaches out in love to the other, transcending the sense of separateness, and this is soon followed by the mutual fear that individuality is being lost. What follows is a struggle to reclaim that individuality while also enjoying a union with the other person. Welwood comments, "The dance of relationship always involves such alternations—between coming together and moving apart, taking hold and letting go, yielding and taking the lead, giving ourselves and maintaining our integrity." Welwood continues—and here is the relevance for the poem—"Many couples soon lose the rhythm and wind up deadlocked in opposing positions, knowing only how to attack or withdraw."

Welwood's job is to offer practical advice that will help people, but this is not the task that Momaday gives himself in "A Simile." Perhaps wisely, he structures the poem as a question that he makes no effort to answer. Maybe that is a way of saying that there is no answer, the devoted work of Welwood and many others

> MOMADAY HAS SOUGHT TO FUSE BOTH VERSIONS OF HIS STORY—THE RECOVERY OF ANCESTRY AND THE PROCESS OF SELF-INVENTION— THROUGH APPROPRIATING THE HEROIC ADVENTURERS OF AMERICAN FRONTIER MYTH."

notwithstanding. The coming together of two people in love, and the forces that work either to deepen that love or drive the couple apart, are essentially mysterious and perhaps unknowable processes. When things turn bad, people often become aware of what has happened in their relationship only when it is too late to do anything about it other than to run for cover and settle back into the dull safety of the single, separate self.

Source: Bryan Aubrey, Critical Essay on "A Simile," in *Poetry for Students*, Gale, Cengage Learning, 2011.

Jason W. Stevens

In this excerpt, Stevens discusses Momaday's view of ethnicity and its role in literature.

N. Scott Momaday rejects the label "Indian writer": "I don't know what that means. I am an Indian, and I am a writer, but I just don't want to say 'Indian writer' or talk about Indian literature. . . . I don't identify with it at all." Momaday further asserts that he never has and never will allow himself to become a spokesman for "the Indian," preferring instead to be seen as a mainstream writer with a distinguishing ethnic heritage. Since his debut in the late 1960s, Momaday has been received by most of his critics as an ethnic storyteller who, in deftly combining tribal mythologies and Euro-American lore, demonstrates the versatility of an imagination that can role-play the West's master discourses while maintaining the integrity of a Native American heritage. What these commentators do not consider is the extent to which Momaday's representation of his Native American identity draws from powerful frontier archetypes that have framed the way white Americans conceive ethnicity.

Werner Sollors argues that the concept of ethnicity in the United States is a semiotic intent to mark boundaries between what are actually shifting components of external (voluntary) and inherited identification. Americans honor ethnicity when it is achieved, or chosen, rather than bequeathed; in the national imagination, this choice generally involves dissent from one group representing outmoded, inherited convention and integration into another representing a new consensual order. Under the ideology of consensus, an American ethnic subject may decide what to appropriate from an ancestral heritage. For Native Americans, however, colonial deracination has left sizable gaps in a cultural history marked by the intercession of external powers intent on destroying tribal traditions. The insistently hermeneutical materials of culture are thus made more complex by a genealogical burden. Many Native Americans, moreover, believe that the articulation of their cultural identities involves reimagining as much as it does rediscovery. Despite the popular belief in a changeless Indian consciousness, Native Americans have had to "reinvent the viable conditions of being Indian," which involves acquiring knowledge of their descent and imaginatively filling the gaps in this knowledge. Questions of how to integrate traditional ideas and beliefs with the modern mainstream—without producing a monolithic, abstract notion of tradition that confines Native Americans to terms of descent—have been at the fore of discussions.

In this regard, Momaday's representation of what it means to recover Indian roots reflects a problem of identity many Native Americans face. Momaday's Kiowa identity, he claims, is considerably self-fashioned, involving the negotiation of indigenous and "external" elements, which Sollors describes as American ethnicity's basic rhetorical structure. Drawing from many sources, Momaday has reinvented the Kiowa out of his readings in ethnographic history, his memories of his grandmother's and his father's stories, his contact with Kiowa living on reservations, and, not least significant, the myths of the American frontier. While the Native side of Momaday's cultural dialogue has been discussed at length by others, only cursory attention has been granted to relevant American Western archetypes that have influenced Momaday's personal mythmaking. While these mainstream sources may be read as "external," in the sense that they are not indigenous to American Indian cultures, they must not be treated as secondary to Momaday's imaginary. To argue, as Louis Owens does,

that frontier figures like Billy the Kid in *The Ancient Child* are appropriated strictly for parody is to presume that the dimensions of Native and non-Native and of Indian and American are more clearly separated in Momaday's voice than his work manifests (*OD*, 118–122). In fact, Momaday's recovery of his Kiowa Indian ancestry has been both facilitated and frustrated by American frontier myths that have disturbed him since his youth; the resulting dialectic in his work registers his contention with the ways the U.S. mainstream has scored Indian ethnicity.

In frontier mythology, two figures stand out: the White adventurer and the Indian savage. Both are central to Momaday's construction of his past. "The savage," a colonial invention to signify the opposite of U.S. civilization, has been used to describe Indians as immutably descent-based identities and to equate them with the category Nature; the term's symbolic power, moreover, has enabled the alignment of Indians with ethnic purity. Momaday angrily confronts the savage stereotype in his early essay "The Morality of Indian Hating" (1963) and in his 1997 postscript to it: "[I]t is imperative that the Indian define himself.... that he refuses to let others define him."

Resisting the savage stereotype, Momaday has struggled throughout his career to define a tenable ethnic persona. His notion of his own ethnicity has wavered between his understanding of an authentic body of traditional knowledge on one hand and his development of a stylized, modern posture on another. Although he grew up among Navajo and Jemez influences, Momaday has tended to portray his life story as a drama of self-transformation in which he becomes Kiowa. Since the publication of *The Journey of Tai-Me* (1967) and *House Made of Dawn* (1968) in his early thirties, he has identified himself as a Kiowa after his father's lineage. He did not, however, grow up within the Kiowa tribal traditions on which his works draw, and he admits knowing very little of the Kiowa language. Reflecting on this declension, he claims to have appropriated his Kiowa ethnicity with an attitude of adventure: he is attracted to his Kiowa side because it seems "exotic" and presents "a greater challenge to understand." In his autobiography, *The Names* (1976), Momaday cites his mother as an influence on his decision to make himself over as a Kiowa Indian. As a teenager, his mother began "to see herself as an

Indian," he says. "That dim native heritage became a fascination and a cause for her. ... She imagined who she was. This act of the imagination was, I believe, among the most important events of my mother's early life, as later the same essential act was to be among the most important of my own." In an interview in 1989, Momaday suggests that his Kiowa identity is an imaginative recreation from pieces of Kiowa history and thought: "I would not like to know everything about my heritage. I want to be absolutely free to imagine parts of it. The facts are not important. The possibilities are everything." Yet Momaday makes equally strong claims for an indigenous Kiowa identity: "I think there was a time while growing up when I might have lost my sense of Kiowa heritage, but that's no longer so. ... It's so deeply entrenched in me. ... I'm Kiowa." Central to Momaday's self-narrative is the saving remembrance of his father's and grandmother's oral stories; from these, he says, he takes his voice, which "bears close relationship to Indian oral tradition. That is my deepest voice. It proceeds out of an ancient voice. It is anchored in that ancient tradition." Describing his story in this instance as one of recovered ancestry rather than self-transformation, Momaday claims that his Kiowa ethnicity is both that which defines him and that which he defines. Because Momaday cannot escape describing himself as an ethnic person, the issue raised by this and alternative versions of the formation of his identity is how much choice he has in specifying what Kiowa is and what his relationship is to that construct.

Momaday has sought to fuse both versions of his story—the recovery of ancestry and the process of self-invention—through appropriating the heroic adventurers of American frontier myth. As critics like Annette Kolodny, Richard Slotkin, and Paul Seydor have shown, frontier myth describes a return to origins in the wilderness as a means to a realization of the self. I argue that although Momaday valorizes a storyteller persona who, as an indigenous Kiowa, represents him, he depicts the Kiowa's historical experience and imaginative perception so that the storyteller bears resemblance to the popular conception of the American frontier hero as hunter and outlaw. Momaday thus tries to perform "Kiowa-ness" as an authentic version of a heroic identity that antedated the emergence of the U.S. frontiersman. Yet he does not overcome the contradiction within popular myths between the hunter-outlaw's nostalgia for union with the wilderness and his

individuating act of self-creation, for this paradox corresponds to Momaday's ambivalence toward the Kiowa heritage he imagines.

Momaday's interest in the frontier began in childhood with westerns, such as *My Darling Clementine* (1946) and Billy the Kid serials, and pulp novels, such as Walter Noble Burns's *The Saga of Billy the Kid* (1927). He grew up, he recalls, imagining himself as the cowboy shooting the Indian or as Billy the Kid's avenger shooting Pat Garrett. As an adult, Momaday regards frontier myth as a vital fund of ideas for Americans: "[T]he literature of the West still has vitality, because the frontier—in a sense—is still being opened.... [I]t deals with a recent and ongoing experience in the American imagination." Momaday is nonetheless aware that his affirmation of the frontier as a mythic space in the American mind is shadowed by fictions of the savage that attend it. In an impromptu lecture at the University of Arizona in 1992, Momaday defended a controversial passage in *The Ancient Child* in which Grey, a teenage Indian girl, is raped by a brutish cowboy. The rape is symbolic of the American experience of the frontier, he explained, because the literature of the frontier facilitated the destruction of Indians by turning them into an emblem, twinned with savage wilderness, to serve the desire for adventure in "civilized" readers. Yet in a characteristic motion, he mystified this "civilized" longing for adventure: "The Boston bank clerk who could go and read a Ned Buntline novel and just be transported into a wilderness that satisfied all his cravings ... and then even more wonderful was the fact that, by God, it was there. People could go out on the Oregon trail and find Indians ... that's the terrible, exciting feature of America."

Key adventurer types that have emerged from narratives of the American wilderness are Faustian figures and pariahs rather than integrated members of a community. The hunter-hero, whose most enduring image is perhaps James Fenimore Cooper's Leatherstocking, and the outlaw, his later counterpart exemplified in legendary figures like Billy the Kid, are both subject to the same fate—the death of their social identity after renouncing their membership in a "civilized" community. They divide, however, along important developmental lines. The hunter-hero seeks a spiritual marriage with the wild through the slaying of a beast or an Indian enemy, both of which are figures in an iconography of the wilderness legacy that the hunter has internalized. Union with the wilderness through violence promises self-regeneration, if not redemption, for his rejection of community. The outlaw figure, contrarily, may flee for refuge to the wilderness, but he does not seek a pact with it. For the outlaw, who is either unthinking or morbidly introspective—cut off from any sense of identity other than his motive for revenge or his sense of estrangement—the wilderness has no aesthetic or moral appeal. Whereas Leatherstocking chooses his exile, the outlaw is typically a victim of destiny, carried out by civilized law.

Both figures are wanderers doomed by their inner savagery. In popular dramatizations, such as the film western, these figures have become a potent image of the American individualist who either knows and mirrors the savage or refuses to relinquish his own savage side to overbearing laws. The return to wilderness supposedly brings forth the quintessential American qualities of resourcefulness and the will to self-transformation. According to the logic of the frontier narrative, however, the discovery of these qualities is possible only for the non-native. The return-to-wilderness motif presumes a hero reborn in the wild, who forswears his previous origin. Since the Indian already belongs to the wilderness as a "savage," he can find in it only the natural self he already is. The non-native, however, can partake of "the savage" to become another self.

To insert himself, along with his Kiowa influences, into the frontier myth, Momaday attempts to regenerate the frontier hero's violent individuation as a principle of transformation, which he attempts to locate in his personal story. For this purpose, he portrays Kiowa culture as embodying self-transformation: "Each time a Kiowa ponders his Kiowa-ness, he invents that whole history—and it is his invention, it is whatever he makes of it in his own mind." Momaday, moreover, patterns the Kiowa partly on the hunter and outlaw types, and he applies some of the same terms, such as *centaur* and *nomad*, to Billy the Kid in explicit comparison to his Kiowa ancestors. The Kiowa become an ethnic persona mediating Momaday's self-invention without threatening the sacrifice of his "Indian" authenticity. When I speak of authenticity here, I intend a sense of certification as much as a fiction of original, sacrosanct character. Momaday does not want to simply name himself Kiowa; he also wants to have been named for the Kiowa. Yet as I

will suggest, while he receives his name from his ancestors (literally, his Kiowa name; figuratively, his identity), he has understood that name to intend self-metamorphic power.

More than any other Native American writer of his generation, Momaday has integrated frontier myths into his self-narrative and the narrative of a tribal people. While other Native American authors also face representational problems as ethnic figures, Momaday's literary response is distinctive, and his struggle to come to terms artistically with the contradictions inherent in this effort at integrating heroic frontier stories with Kiowa myth and history is itself written into his re-imagining of these materials. Momaday's literary construction of his Kiowa identity hence becomes confessional as much as performative. With his last novel, *The Ancient Child* (1989), his attempt to graft these myths onto native elements results in irony, as he begins to magnify both the nostalgia for lost origins and the incertitude of identity, which make up the dark side of the popular return-to-wilderness motif. In *The Ancient Child*, the odyssey of Momaday's autobiographical character Locke Stetman (or Set), a contemporary, assimilated Kiowa Indian, leads back to the wilderness of his ancestors. Set's journey is placed in parallel contrast to the early demise of the Wild West's outlaw Billy the Kid. Momaday uses the legend of Billy the Kid to cast into relief the history of the Kiowa's origin in the wilderness and their declension from it; in his personal retracing of that migration, he hopes to reverse American spiritual renunciation of the wilderness and its consequent loss of heroic, transformative power. The return-to-wilderness motif, as portrayed through Set's example, thus becomes a mediation for Momaday's quest for identity, intended to contrast with Billy's fate. Set, however, collapses into inarticulacy at the close of the novel, suggesting that Momaday's Kiowa ethnicity, as imagined through frontier symbols, does not specify his identity. . . .

Source: Jason W. Stevens, "Bear, Outlaw, and Storyteller: American Frontier Mythology and the Ethnic Subjectivity of N. Scott Momaday," in *American Literature*, Vol. 73, No. 3, 2001, pp. 599–631.

Hertha D. Sweet Wong

In this excerpt, Sweet Wong uses Momaday as an example of the reconfiguration of pictographic traditions and native subjectivities.

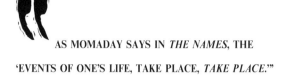

AS MOMADAY SAYS IN *THE NAMES*, THE
'EVENTS OF ONE'S LIFE, TAKE PLACE, *TAKE PLACE*.'"

N. SCOTT MOMADAY AND HACHIVI EDGAR HEAP OF BIRDS

... Neither pictography nor indigenous artists have disappeared. Even though Candace Green explains the "sudden disappearance of Cheyenne pictographic art in the mid-1890s" as due to the forced end of the warrior society, today both writers and visual artists continue to reconfigure pictographic (and other graphic) traditions and Native subjectivities. Let me briefly introduce a couple of examples: N. Scott Momaday and Hachivi Edgar Heap of Birds.

N. Scott Momaday, Pulitzer Prize winning author as well as artist, has long been interested in the "correspondence between words and pictures, those two ways of seeing." "Writing is a kind of drawing," he notes, "words on the picture plane." This "angle of vision" is evident in Momaday's *The Way to Rainy Mountain* in which the words (their layout and the images they evoke) are part of an intricate graphic structure, not surprisingly one that articulates a Kiowa subjectivity rooted in history (myth) and place. His father's (Al Momaday's) drawings, some of which hearken back to nineteenth-century pictographic conventions, contribute to the visual features of the autobiography, of course. Momaday's well known book presents a good example of one type of visual autobiography, what W. J. T. Mitchell might refer to as an "imagetext" (a "composite, synthetic work" combining "image and text"), with history and place and a collective Kiowa subjectivity at its center. This is evident in the four narrative modes (mythic, historical, personal, and visual) that merge in his ultimate call for an American Indian environmental ethic, a personal relationship to our histories, cultures, geographies. For Momaday, Native (indeed, human) subjectivity cannot be articulated except in relation to history and place.

Hachivi Edgar Heap of Birds, a Cheyenne artist trained in the Western European art tradition, has made a conscious decision to articulate his personal and community history by exploring both Native North American and European art forms. He has explained that he tries to work in a way to unify both (and to resist easy pigeonholing as an "Indian artist"). Like many Plains warriors from the late nineteenth century, Edgar Heap of Birds' great great grandfather, Many Magpie Birds, was a prisoner in Fort Marion in the 1870s. Heap of Birds, then, has a personal connection to Cheyenne history and a familiarity with Plains Indian prison ledger books (several of which he has examined). Furthermore, as "a headsman of the traditional Cheyenne Elk Warrior Society," Heap of Birds considers himself a modern "warrior" who fights to keep alive Cheyenne culture and language. "Today strong artworks with the warrior spirit, such as these from Fort Marion," he explains, "remain as a method of a more modern warfare." Like the men imprisoned in Fort Marion a century ago, Heap of Birds uses contemporary forms to communicate to a (primarily, but not only) non-Native public as a way of making visible Native people. Even though separated by over one hundred years, the artists share certain concerns: resisting social and cultural captivity and erasure, negotiating with and critiquing the dominant society, and retaining or reclaiming tribal/community values and ideals. Heap of Birds sees himself as "on the edge of battle to re-educate non-Native peoples" about Indians. For him art is both a (multi)cultural tool and a weapon. But how does any artist educate and politicize and yet resist didacticism? Or move beyond realism? "Do I make a bunch of narrative paintings of Custer killing children in the Washita River?" Heap of Birds asks on a video.

Heap of Birds answers this question by working in a variety of forms: public art (in which he asserts, simultaneously, a historical and contemporary Native presence into the local); word drawings; abstract paintings; and charcoal studies. In each of these forms, he forces us as viewers to re-envision what we thought we knew. Each of his public art projects focuses on history and place and the necessity of understanding those in order to know yourself, ourselves—as individuals and nation/s. In one of his earliest public art installations (1982), "In Our Language," Heap of Birds designed a 20 × 40-foot lightboard in New York City. Every twenty minutes for two weeks the Cheyenne "spoke" (in the Cheyenne language) about their views of the "white man"—the lightboard illuminating about one word per minute (like a drumbeat, he explained):

> Tsistsistas
> (Cheyenne)
> Vehoe
> (Spider) =
> white man.
> Both wrap up =
> clothes, fences.

Heap of Birds describes this as a kind of "translation" in which he conveys bilingually what some members of his Cheyenne community say about European Americans. The form of presentation resists, at least momentarily, easy comprehension. Because just one word is displayed per minute, a viewer could pass by without ever seeing that "Tsistsistas" translates as "Cheyenne." This emphasizes the alienation of a non-Cheyenne-speaking viewer as well as the gaps and interruptions inherent in any linguistic/cultural translation. Perhaps more significantly, the metaphor suggests that both the Native body and Native lands are "wrapped up," entrapped, contained, restrained by the dominant society.

In one 1988 public installation entitled, "Native Hosts," Heap of Birds placed six signs in lower Manhattan. As drivers commuted to their destinations, they were reminded of the genocide—the absent, indigenous nations—that lie beneath the cities and villages of what is now the United States. It is significant (and purposeful) that Heap of Birds employed the state and county producers of highway signs to make the pieces for this installation; that is, he used the dominant system of mapping and naming itself to criticize its own existence. The signs (from the modes and material of their production to their placement) look exactly like other road signs—only the message is from a radically different perspective. Rather than a sign that is overlaid upon a land (as all colonizing mapping) announcing with assurance where you are and how far it is to where you are headed, each of these is a sign that reverses the position (note the mirrored lettering of "NEW YORK" suggesting that the city is backwards, wrong). Mirrored words "disrupt legibility" as well as reflect the treacherous use of alphabetic literacy (treaties that were never kept, fraudulent land deeds, boarding school education as a policy of forced assimilation, etc.) against indigenous people. "Native Hosts" asks the question: do you know where you are? "Manhattan," Heap of Birds reminds us, was "a nation of people, not a city on an island" (video). He has

done several such versions of "Native Hosts," each referring to the specific indigenous people of *this* place (this place is wherever his installation is, the ground upon which he stands).

Whereas pictographic artists used images as narrative (and sometimes added words, often in syllabary, to translate the pictography), in his word paintings, Heap of Birds uses words as images. In a familiar postmodern move, he empties the letters and words of their referentiality, forcing us to attend to his black-and-white or multi-colored writing as shapes and marks on the canvas. Most people try to "read" his word paintings such as "Peru-South" (a pastel on paper, 90 inches × 110 inches), looking for patterns, rhymes, alliteration, thematic linkages, even color coordination, though it helps somewhat to realize that this is part of a four-part structure (an organizing device common to many Native ceremonial and storytelling practices) associated with the four directions; that, in fact, the piece is related to place—South (not just southern Oklahoma or the southern United States, but Peru).

In an 8-foot tall word painting (inspired by his research during which he found a list of the names of all the warriors imprisoned at Fort Marion), his method is purposeful. He uses the painting as a way to annotate history, using words not merely as forms of testimony or documentary, but as image. This is "a big painting," he explains, "of just the words." The red words refer to his relatives who died at Fort Marion. At times, though, in his word paintings, he distills verbal potency and constructs a visual syntax, interlinking seemingly disparate shapes and meanings. Addressing both Native and non-Native audiences, he challenges preconceived stereotypes about Native Americans and the history of this land. His aim is to reclaim his Cheyenne language, name, and nation and in so doing construct a contemporary Cheyenne subjectivity capacious enough for all the contradictions and cultural crossings of a postmodern world.

In all of his many artistic forms are embedded "coded little stories," he says. But the fragmentation (reflective of postmodern deconstruction, to be sure, but also indigenous multiplicity) is dominant. He offers only fragments, only fragmentary knowledge, and it is the viewer who has to find "all the pieces [to] put it together." Such a process forces viewers to reformulate notions of Native American history and subjectivity.

While Heap of Birds stridently criticizes the colonizers of Native bodies, histories, lands, he also offers solutions. Painful acknowledgment of history is only one step. In his more clearly auto-biographical (or personal) paintings, he returns to his relationship with the land (particularly, Oklahoma and its landforms, water, trees). "This is where my paintings come from," he says. Just as his word paintings disrupt referentiality, his land-form (I don't use the term "landscape") paintings are equally non-figurative. Both, he insists, are parts of his visual autobiographical articulation. In his "Neuf" Series of 4 (acrylic on canvas, 56 inches × 72 inches), the shapes and colors allude to natural forms—of leaves or water. This is part of a series of how he maps himself in relation to each of the four directions as well as to Oklahoma, how he positions himself in a precise geography, a particular place called "home."

In addition to his identification with nine-teenth-century Cheyenne warrior culture, Heap of Birds, is Trickster-like (that is, a culture hero, a creator, a principle of energy) in his attempt to subvert the dominant discourse of American his-tory and make possible Native subjectivities on their own terms. Like other male Native Amer-ican artists and writers (like N. Scott Momaday, Gerald Vizenor, and James Welch), he fancies himself a word warrior. Whereas pictographic artists moved from the freedom of the plains to the constraints of the reservation, Heap of Birds moves from the limitations of European/Amer-ican definitions of Indians (and art) to the free-dom of self-determination. He insists:

> People of color have the right to invent their lives. It's not about how it can relate to the white man or even just back to their own indig-enous culture. I'm very clear that what I'm doing is inventing my own life. (video)

Although this project of self-construction is fraught with the trappings of enlightenment notions of self-invention and the dangers of cul-tural and ethnic nationalism, such asserting/ reclaiming/inventing an identity is fundamental to the experience of internally colonized Native people, people whose very self-imaginings have been objectified by the dominant society and transformed into ethnic commodities. Moma-day has said that "the greatest tragedy is to go unimagined" but, I would add, it is far graver to leave yourself to the imaginings of others.

... As Momaday says in *The Names*, the "events of one's life, take place, *take place*" (Momaday's emphasis). For the Western Apache, as Keith Basso has described in detail, "wisdom sits in places"—all these places have stories and the places and stories together shape a Western Ap-ache person's subjectivity (a kind of psychic map). Here I do not wish to conflate distinct cultures and geographies, but to reiterate that there is a link between place and subjectivity in many indigenous cultures. "Our stories cannot be separated from their geographical locations, from actual physical places on the land," insists Silko, "there is a story connected with every place, every object in the landscape" (*Yellow Woman*). Of course there is a debate about whether you have to live in that particular place or if a remembered (from afar) place ("the remembered earth," as Momaday referred to it in *The Way to Rainy Mountain*) is sufficient. The very construction of the handmade editions of *Sacred Water* emphasize place, but place transported elsewhere. In *Yellow Woman*, Silko reports that the blue cover is made of Ste-phen Watson's Blue Corn paper (made in Albu-querque) and contains bits of blue corn (another limited edition was covered in Watson's white Volcanic Ash paper containing small amounts of fine ash obtained from the volcanoes just west of Albuquerque).

For contemporary Native American writers and artists, like Momaday, Silko, and Heap of Birds, to articulate their distinctive, contempo-rary, transcultural subjectivities, they must coun-ter stereotypes, they must retell history (not only the five-hundred-year history of European coloni-zation, but the thousands of years before that—reaching back into "myth"—just another word for "history"—both a collection of "stories" rooted in a particular geography and experience); and they must tell the stories of place (including displace-ment—removal, relocation), the stories of home, homeland, or homelessness. Only by situating ourselves in relation to history (time) and place (space and memory), Momaday, Heap of Birds, and Silko suggest, can lushly polyphonous Native North American subjectivities be enabled.

Source: Hertha D. Sweet Wong, "Native American Vis-ual Autobiography: Figuring Place, Subjectivity, and History," in *Iowa Review*, Vol. 30, No. 3, Winter 2000–2001, pp. 145–56.

Howard Meredith

In this review, Meredith explains how the collec-tion suggests the presence of a particular man.

In the Presence of the Sun, a collection of poetry, stories, and visual-art pieces, presents a set of individual works that define Scott Momaday's style, from his early period and to more recent times, as well as his visual expression in still lifes and figure studies. Each of the works has individual traits, but there are elemental connections among them. Included are familiar early poems from volumes such as *Gourd Dancer* and *Angle of Geese*, a series of poems focusing on Billy the Kid; new poems; a reprint of *In the Presence of the Sun: A Gathering of Shields*, originally published as a signed, limited letterpress edition by the Rydal Press earlier in 1992. Illustrations include acrylics, graphite sketches, monoprints, etchings, pen-and-ink drawings, and watercolors. Momaday writes: "The poems and stories, the drawings here, express my spirit fairly, I believe. If you look closely into these pages, it is possible to catch a glimpse of me in my original being."

Momaday brings a significant vision of his ethnic foundations and period style in American poetry and art and expresses the healing relations within the universe. He flowers in the fire of the spirit of an ancient culture. As a poet, he brings a sense of order in the form of a special case to the creative chaos of the present. In the works of art gathered here, connections are made within Anglo-American cultural imperatives, yet with a sense of reference that speaks of Native American concerns for all living beings.

The collection is excellent, although it does not pretend to possess any sense of symmetry. Dream images recur throughout but are ever more powerfully expressed in the selection of stories and drawings entitled "In the Presence of the Sun: A Gathering of Shields." The expression of dreams, visions, and natural events finds unity in the power of the special medicine of these words. Momaday explains through allegory, to those who are prepared to listen, the nature of medicine power and the miracle of the Kiowa mind-set, which extends beyond the dualism and the adversarial nature of Western dialogue to provide for personal understanding and empathy within the unity of creation. He indicates a path through which the reader can move from the individual mind and spirit to become one with the universal mind and spirit.

Three contemporary poems form a fitting conclusion to the volume. "December 29, 1890: Wounded Knee Creek" is movement within

THE PHYSICAL IMAGES CARRY THE FULL FORCE, OFTEN THROUGH DOUBLE SENSE, OF ABSTRACTION: THE SHADOW *DEFINES*; AND DEATH IS THE IMPENETRABILITY, THE INCOMPREHENSIBILITY, OF BLACK *DENSITY*."

images, including black-and-white photo reflections of the Ghost Dance bringing the spirits of all into communion. "Fort Sill: Set-angia" relates the continuing presence of no less a person than Sitting Bear. "At Risk" points to the power within images, memory, and words that require exacting performance.

In images and words the collection suggests the presence of a particular man. His art, in turn, provides a glimpse of the depths of existence that extends cultural perspectives to understand better the living universe.

Source: Howard Meredith, Review of *In the Presence of the Sun: Stories and Poems, 1961–1991*, in *World Literature Today*, Vol. 67, No. 3, Summer 1993, p. 650.

Roger Dickinson-Brown

In this excerpt, Dickinson-Brown offers a stylistic examination of several of the poems in Angle of Geese.

The Kiowa Indian N. Scott Momaday came to public attention in 1969, surprising everyone, including himself and his editors, by winning the Pulitzer Prize for his novel *House Made of Dawn*. He has before and since maintained a quiet reputation in American Indian affairs and among distinguished *literati* for his genius, his extraordinary range, his fusion of alien cultures, and his extraordinary experiments in different literary forms.

. . . It is surprising that Momaday has published so few poems. *Angle of Geese* contains only eighteen—the considered work of a great poet around the age of forty. But the poems are there, astonishing in their depth and range. "Simile," "Four Notions of Love and Marriage," "The Fear of Bo-talee," "The Story of a Well-Made Shield," and "The Horse that Died of Shame" are variously free verse (the first two, which are slight and sentimental) or prose poems.

They partake of the same discrete intensity that characterizes the storytelling in *The Way to Rainy Mountain*, and which makes them some of the few real prose poems in English.

The poems written in grammatical parallels are much better: "The Delight Song of Tsoai-talee" and "Plainview: 2." In the latter, Momaday has used a form and created emotions without precedent in English:

I saw an old Indian
At Saddle Mountain.
He drank and dreamed of drinking
And a blue-black horse.

Remember my horse running.
Remember my horse.
Remember my horse running.
Remember my horse.

Remember my horse wheeling.
Remember my horse.
Remember my horse wheeling.
Remember my horse.

Remember my horse blowing.
Remember my horse.
Remember my horse blowing.
Remember my horse.

Remember my horse standing.
Remember my horse.
Remember my horse standing.
Remember my horse.

Remember my horse hurting.
Remember my horse.
Remember my horse hurting.
Remember my horse.

Remember my horse falling.
Remember my horse.
Remember my horse falling.
Remember my horse.

Remember my horse dying.
Remember my horse.
Remember my horse dying.
Remember my horse.

A horse is one thing,
An Indian another;
An old horse is old;
An old Indian is sad.

I saw an old Indian
At Saddle Mountain.
He drank and dreamed of drinking
And a blue-black horse.

Remember my horse running.
Remember my horse.
Remember my horse wheeling.
Remember my horse.
Remember my horse blowing.
Remember my horse.
Remember my horse standing.

Remember my horse.
Remember my horse falling.
Remember my horse.
Remember my horse dying.
Remember my horse.
Remember my blue-black horse.
Remember my blue-black horse.
Remember my horse.
Remember my horse.
Remember.
Remember.

A chant or a parallel poem is necessarily bulky and especially oral. I have often recited this poem to individuals and groups, in part to test its effect upon an English-language audience. My own voice is consciously based upon the oral readings of Pound, Winters, and Native American chant, with a dash of childhood Latin Mass. I read the lines without musical intonation but with emphatic regularity and little rhetorical variation. The results are extreme: about half the listeners are bored, the other half moved, sometimes to tears. The poem is obviously derived from Momaday's experience of Indian chant, in which, as in most other cultures, small distinction is made between music and poetry. In this respect "Plainview: 2" is a part of the abandoned traditions of Homer, *The Song of Roland*, oral formulas, the Christian, Muslim, and Jewish chant, and even certain Renaissance poems. The various forms of repetition in these works are still common in the Islamic and black African and certain other worlds, but they survive in the West (where individual originality has destroyed community), only through such traditional popular genres as commercial song (which, unlike "modern intellectual" poetry and "classical" music, preserves the fusion), nursery rhymes, and among the nonwhite minorities. These are our surviving traditions of form, which is by nature repetitive.

In addition to the obvious repetitions in "Plainview: 2," the repetition of stanza 1 at stanza 10, and the two-line rehearsal of the four-line stanzas turn the poem. The whole poem is, in fact, simply a subtle variation, development, and restatement of the first stanza, with the extended, reiterated illustration of both the beauty of the horse's actions and its death. The ninth stanza occupies the poem like a kernel of gloss, but even its third and fourth lines are simply restatements of its first and second.

The form of this poem distinguishes with rare clarity what we call denotative and connotative. In a literate age of recorded language, where memory and repetition—sides of a coin— have each faded from our experience, we are inclined to regard such hammering as a waste of time—but it can, instead, be an intensification and a kind of experience we have lost. That is precisely the division of modern response to the poem.

The rest of Momaday's poetry is traditionally iambic or experimentally syllabic. Winters has called the iambic pentameter "Before an Old Painting of the Crucifixion" a great poem, and perhaps it is, in spite of a certain stiltedhess and melodrama, reminiscent of the worst aspects of *House Made of Dawn*. Yet the iambic poems are certainly among the best of their kind in Momaday's generation, and it is only the exigency of space that limit me to a few lines from "Rainy Mountain Cemetery":

> Most is your name the name of this dark stone.
> Deranged in death, the mind to be inheres
> Forever in the nominal unknown . . .

Momaday's theme here is an inheritance from Winters, though it is as old as our civilization: the tension, the gorgeous hostility between the human and the wild—a tension always finally relaxed in death. Winters did a great deal to restore and articulate that consciousness, after and in the light of Romanticism. And it was Winters too who taught Momaday one of his greatest virtues, the power and humanity of abstraction—heresy in the cant of our time: *deranged* is a pure and perfect abstraction.

And there is more Winters:

> . . . silence is the long approach of noon
> Upon the shadow that your name defines—
> And death this cold, black density of stone.

We have already seen this in *House Made of Dawn*. Winters called it post-symbolist method. The physical images carry the full force, often through double sense, of abstraction: the shadow *defines*; and death is the impenetrability, the incomprehensibility, of black *density*. Yet the images are not metaphors, for they are not subservient to the abstractions they communicate, nor are they synecdochical. They persist in the very mortal obstinacy which they mean. This style is everywhere in Momaday, but it is something which Winters could not have duplicated, for it is also profoundly Kiowa. . . .

Momaday's syllabic poetry is his best and experimentally most exciting work. Even deprived of the rest of the poem, the middle stanza of "The Bear" seems to me among the perfect stanzas in English, rhythmically exquisite in its poise between iamb and an excess of syllabic looseness, utterly comprehensive in its presentation of the motionless wild bear and its relationship to time:

> Seen, he does not come,
> move, but seems forever there,
> dimensionless, dumb,
> in the windless noon's hot glare.

"Comparatives" is a tour-de-force of alternating unrhymed three-and four-syllable lines, again with Momaday's abstract and physical fusion. Momaday succeeds in presenting such unrhymed, short lines rhythmically, in spite of a necessarily high incidence of enjambment; the faint lines convey a melancholy appropriate to the antiquity and death which are the consequence of his juxtaposition of the dead and the fossil fish:

> . . . cold, bright body
> of the fish
> upon the planks,
> the coil and
> crescent of flesh
> extending
> just into death.
>
> Even so,
> in the distant,
> inland sea,
> a shadow runs,
> radiant,
> rude in the rock:
> fossil fish,
> fissure of bone
> forever.
> It is perhaps
> the same thing,
> an agony
> twice perceived.

Momaday's greatest poem is certainly "Angle of Geese," a masterpiece of syllabic rhythm, of modulated rhyme, of post-symbolic images, and of the meaning of language in human experience. Although perhaps none of its stanzas is equal to the best stanza of "The Bear," each functions in a similar way, shifting from perfect to imperfect to no rhyme with the same supple responsiveness Dryden mastered, but with more range. Nevertheless the largest importance of this poem, even beyond its extraordinary form is its theme, which is probably the greatest of our century: the extended understanding of the significance of language and its relation to identity—an understanding increased not only by the important work done by the linguists of our century but also by the increased mixture of languages which has continued to accelerate over the last hundred years or so: French or English among Asians and Africans, often as first or only languages among nonetheless profoundly non-European people; Spanish established on an Indian continent; and, of course, English in America. These are non-native native speakers of English, as it were, further distinguishing literature in English from English literature. Their potential has much to do with their relative freedom from the disaster and degeneracy which Romantic ideas have created among their European-American counterparts: many of these new English writers still have deep connections with their communities, instead of the individualistic elitism which characterizes contemporary European-American art, music, and poetry. They are more like Shakespeare, Rembrandt, and Homer. And they often have fewer neuroses about the evils of form. Momaday, as a Kiowa, a university scholar, and a poet of major talent, is in an excellent position to take advantage of these multi-cultural possibilities. The result is "Angle of Geese":

> How shall we adorn
> Recognition with our speech?—
> Now the dead firstborn
> Will lag in the wake of words.
>
> Custom intervenes;
> We are civil, something, more:
> More than language means,
> The mute presence mulls and marks.
>
> Almost of a mind,
> We take measure of the loss;
> I am slow to find
> The mere margin of repose.
>
> And one November
> It was longer in the watch,
> As if forever,
> Of the huge ancestral goose.
>
> So much symmetry!
> Like the pale angle of time
> And eternity.
> The great shape labored and fell.
>
> Quit of hope and hurt,
> It held a motionless gaze,
> Wide of time, alert,
> On the dark distant flurry.

The poem is difficult and a little obscure, mostly because the subject is—but also because Momaday has indulged a little in the obscurantism that makes modern poetry what it is—and an explication of the poem is therefore necessary.

The first stanza presents the subject and observes that the Darwinian animal which we were, who is our ancestor, cannot be rediscovered in our language, which is what moved us away and distinguished us from the animal.

The second stanza explains the divorce: we have become civilized, but not wholly. "The mute presence" may, by syntax, seem to be the presence of language, but it is not. It is the presence of wilderness which is mute. We live in connotation, which is wild response. "Mulls" and "civil" are odd diction.

The third stanza contemplates this ambivalence, this incompleteness, and moves from the general to the particular. We are almost whole, or wholly civilized and conscious, and to precisely this extent we have lost our own wilderness. The speaker, introduced at this point, is slow to realize, outside language, what is wild in him. The language is typical of Momaday in its outright and exact abstraction: "mere" in the old sense of pure or unadulterated—here, by language and civilization; "margin" because this is where humans, with their names and mortality, overlap with wilderness, which has neither; "repose" because what is wild is forever and at every moment perfect and complete, without urgency, going nowhere, perpetuating itself beautifully for no sake at all. It is useful to remember wilderness here primarily in terms of immortal molecules and galaxies, without number or name—except those collective names imposed upon them by men who have to that extent simply perceived and thought about that which is unaltered by thought, which does not know the thinker, and which is, finally, a kind of god—not a god, as Stevens said, "but as a god might be." It is a kind of altered Romantic god, but one supported rather more by the pure sciences than by Deism and Benevolism: a nature pure and perfect, composed of sub-atomic particles and framed in an unimaginable universe with no edge. Language contradicts itself with this god, who is its enemy. It is the wilderness of our century, deprived of Romantic benevolence but retaining its old terrifying innocence and immense and nameless beauty, which ignores us and must destroy us, one by one. It is a god of mere repose. The goose, which the hunter waits for one November, is almost perfectly a part of the god (Momaday only implies the word), although a goose shares with men certain forms of individual consciousness of itself and others. Some animals have some language, and to this extent the goose knows the same clear and lonely condition we do, and is an imperfect symbol of the wilderness. The long watch, in any case, implies the eternity which is the whole of which the goose is an indiscriminate part: *as if forever*. The goose is huge because it is inseparable from the wild deity: what Emerson called the "not I," which neither names nor knows itself, which cannot die—whatever is, like the grasshopper of the ancient Greeks, immortal because the individuals have no name. That is our ancestor who does not know us, whom we hardly know.

So, in the fifth stanza, the symmetry of the angle or V of the flock of geese implies the perfection for which geometry and symmetry have always served as imaginary means. A goose is shot, and falls out of the angle, into the speaker's world.

The last stanza gives the goose a little of that hope and hurt which grants this sophisticated animal a part of what will kill the speaker: a conscious identity. But the goose is essentially wild, and it holds, like an immortal cockatrice, an inhuman gaze—motionless, outside the time in which we live and die, wildly, purely alert—fixed on the receding flurry of the flock out of which it fell, growing as dark and distant physically as it is in truth to the dying speaker who watches it too and for whom, alone, something has changed. The word "flurry" fuses with the flock all the huge vagueness which is our blind source.

It seems to me the best example both of Momaday's greatness and his importance to contemporary literature: it profoundly realizes its subject, both denotatively and connotatively, with greater art in an important new prosodic form than anyone except Bridges and Daryush. It also presents, better than any other work I know—especially in the light of what has only recently been so developed and understood—perhaps the most important subject of our age: the tragic conflict between what we have felt in wilderness and what our language means.

Source: Roger Dickinson-Brown, "The Art and Importance of N. Scott Momaday," in *Southern Review*, Vol. 16, No. 1, January 1978, pp. 30–45.

SOURCES

"Census: 4.21 Million Claim 'American Indian' Heritage," in *USA Today*, February 13, 2002, http://www.usa today.com/news/nation/census/2002-02-13-indians.htm (accessed April 29, 2010).

"General Deer Population Facts," in *Cornell University Cooperative Extension, Wildlife Control Information*, http://wildlifecontrol.info/deer/Pages/DeerPopulation Facts.aspx (accessed April 15, 2010).

"The History of Whitetail Deer," in *HuntingNet.com*, http://www.huntingnet.com/staticpages/staticpage_detail. aspx?id = 36 (accessed April 15, 2010).

Mason, Kenneth, C., "Beautyway: The Poetry of N. Scott Momaday," in *South Dakota Review*, Vol. 18, No. 2, Summer 1980, pp. 61–83.

Momaday, N. Scott, *The Gourd Dancer*, Harper & Row, 1976, p. 16.

———, "Simile," in *In the Presence of the Sun: Stories and Poems*, St. Martin's Press, 1993, p. 7.

"The Native American Power Movement," in *Digital History*, http://www.digitalhistory.uh.edu/database/ article_display.cfm?HHID = 387 (accessed April 29, 2010).

"Native American Timeline," in *Legends of America*, http://www.legendsofamerica.com/na-timeline6.html (accessed April 18, 2010).

Schubnell, Matthias, *N. Scott Momaday: The Cultural and Literary Background*, University of Oklahoma Press, 1985, pp. 13–39.

———, "M. Scott Momaday," in *Dictionary of Literary Biography*, Vol. 175, *Native American Writers of the United States*, edited by Kenneth M. Roemer, Gale Research, 1997, pp. 174–86.

Waters, Frank, "Two Views of Nature: White and Indian," in *The American Indian Speaks in Poetry, Fiction, Art, Music, Commentary*, edited by John R. Milton, University of South Dakota Press, 1969.

Welwood, John, "Dancing on the Razor's Edge," in *Challenge of the Heart: Love, Sex, and Intimacy in Changing Times*, edited by John Welwood, Shambhala, 1985, p. 253.

Wiget, Andrew, "Sending a Voice: The Emergence of Contemporary Native American Poetry," in *College English*, Vol. 46, No. 6, October 1984, pp. 598–609.

Woodward, Charles L., *Ancestral Voice: Conversations with N. Scott Momaday*, University of Nebraska Press, 1989, p. 145.

FURTHER READING

Molin, Paulette F., *American Indian Themes in Young Adult Literature*, Scarecrow Press, 2005.

This book provides an analysis of information on American Indian-themed literature, identifying the stereotypes and misinformation in this genre and lauding those authors who provide accurate portrayals of Native Americans in their literature.

Momaday, N. Scott, *The Man Made of Words: Essays, Stories, Passages*, St. Martin's Griffin, 1998.

This is a collection of Momaday's prose writings over a period of thirty years. He discusses topics such as his Indian ancestors, his travels and the places he has lived, and the differences between Indian and white culture.

Nerburn, Kent, ed., *The Wisdom of the Native American*, New World Library, 1998.

This is a collection of historical Native American writings that includes, among many other writings, the speeches of Chief Red Jacket, Chief Joseph, and Chief Seattle. The book is divided into three parts: the ways of the Native American, the soul of an Indian, and the wisdom of the great chiefs.

Schubnell, Matthias, ed., *Conversations with N. Scott Momaday*, University Press of Mississippi, 1997.

This collection contains seventeen interviews given by Momaday from 1997 to 1993. He discusses a wide range of topics, including the role of Native Americans in today's society and how his work represents a synthesis of traditional Native American oral traditions and Western literature. He also speaks of his development as a writer and comments on specific works.

SUGGESTED SEARCH TERMS

Momaday

Momaday AND Native American literature

Momaday AND poetry

Native American poetry

Momaday AND Kiowa

Native American literature

Native Americans AND 1960s

Gourd Dancer

Native American reservations AND literature

Two People I Want to Be Like

EVE MERRIAM

1983

A poet inspired as much by her passion for language as by social and political issues, Eve Merriam wrote for a wide range of audiences. Well known for fiction, plays, and poetry, Merriam composed numerous volumes of poetry for children. *If Only I Could Tell You: Poems for Young Lovers and Dreamers*, published in 1983, is one such volume. The work contains a simple poem about admiration and love, "Two People I Want to Be Like." In this free-verse poem, Merriam paints a portrait of two characters. One is a man who, despite being stuck in traffic, opts to stay calm and happy. The other is a woman who works as a clerk in a grocery store. Merriam describes the woman as she helps customers during rush hour; the clerk, like the man, remains smiling and unflustered by the hustle and bustle surrounding her. The speaker in Merriam's poem imagines the two people together, married, and then speculates that perhaps it is better they are not. Apart, they may be better able to share their harmonious natures with others. Through this poem Merriam conjures an idealized vision of two individuals and additionally projects an innocent view of love and purpose. Included in a poetry collection aimed at young readers, "Two People I Want to Be Like" captures a youthful perspective and at the same time creates a positive outlook on adulthood, and possibly marriage, for her readers.

"Two People I Want to Be Like" was originally published by Alfred Knopf in the volume *If*

Evening rush hour traffic jam (egd | Shutterstock.com)

Only I Could Tell You: Poetry for Young Lovers and Dreamers in 1983. Currently, much of Merriam's poetry, including this volume, is out of print. The poem can still be found in some textbooks, including *Glencoe Literature: Reading with Purpose, Active Learning and Note Taking Guide, Course 2*, published by McGraw-Hill in 2007.

AUTHOR BIOGRAPHY

Born in Philadelphia on July 19, 1916, to Max and Jennie Siegel Moskovitz, Merriam was the youngest of four children. Her given name was Eva Moskovitz. Merriam's parents, who owned a chain of women's dress stores, were Russian immigrants who had been living in Pennsylvania since their own childhood. A love of poetry as a child led Merriam to compose poems for a high school magazine and for the school's weekly newspaper. Merriam studied at Cornell University and later at the University of Pennsylvania, from which she received a bachelor of arts degree in 1937. She pursued graduate studies at the University of Wisconsin and at Columbia University. In 1939, she married Erwin Spitzer; they later divorced.

Abandoning her graduate studies, Merriam settled upon the idea of securing a position in advertising, as one of her favorite poets, Carl Sandburg, had done. Merriam continued to write poetry while she worked for various magazines. Following the 1946 publication of her first volume of poetry, *Family Circle*, for which Merriam was awarded the Yale Younger Poets Prize, Merriam worked as a fashion copy editor for *Glamour* magazine from 1947 to 1948. In 1947, Merriam married Martin Michel, and the couple had two sons. This marriage also ended in divorce.

Merriam continued to write poetry for adults, in addition to nonfiction pieces and essays related to political and social issues, such as women's rights and civil rights. In 1952 her first children's book, *The Real Book about Franklin Delano Roosevelt*, was published. She continued to write poetry, fiction, and plays for both adults and children. Her activism was promoted in poetry such as the 1969 collection *The Inner City Mother Goose*, in which Merriam uses the rhythm and language of the nursery rhyme structure to explore racism. In 1981, Merriam was awarded a National Council of Teachers of English award.

In poetry addressed to an adult audience, in the volume *The Double Bed from the Feminine Side* (1958), and in poetry geared toward a youthful audience, such as that contained in the 1983 volume *If Only I Could Tell You: Poems for Young Lovers and Dreamers*, Merriam explores the relationships between men and women. With a third failed marriage, to Leonard Lewin in 1963, behind her, Merriam wed Waldo Salt in 1983. She continued to write prolifically in a variety of genres until her death from cancer on August 11, 1992.

POEM SUMMARY

Stanza 1

"Two People I Want to Be Like" is divided into four short stanzas. A stanza is a unit of poetry in which lines are grouped by the poet in a particular fashion, usually to emphasize specific themes, ideas, or images. Stanzas divide poetry in the same way that paragraphs divide prose. In the first stanza, Merriam describes a character, a man who is stuck in traffic. The nine lines of the stanza include details designed to highlight aspects of the man's character. Although caught in a traffic jam, the man does not act out angrily by hitting his steering wheel or by attempting to squeeze into the next lane of traffic. The poet depicts the man as smiling, as though he is contemplating all the times he has not been stuck in traffic. The details, word choice, and slow, steady rhythm of the lines work together to convey to the reader a sense of the man's friendliness, his easy patience, and his peaceful mindset.

Stanza 2

In the second stanza, Merriam paints a portrait of a female supermarket clerk. The poem's language conveys a busy rush hour scene and captures the hurrying and clattering involved in the ringing up and bagging of customers' groceries. The details and pace stand in sharp contrast to the unmoving nature of the traffic jam endured by the man in the previous stanza. Around the man, traffic is stalled. Around the woman, people race through their errands, yet the woman, like the man, manages to smile through an activity that would fluster many people. They are both portrayed as calm and peaceful centers. The man is the center of a storm of frustration, while the woman is the steady, rooted point in a sea of hurried commotion.

Stanza 3

The third stanza is comprised of one short line in which the Merriam emphasizes the presence of a first-person narrator in the poem. (A first-person narrator is a figure who refers to him- or herself as "I" and who relates the details of a story or poem. This narrator, or speaker, may or may not be associated with the poet.) Merriam's speaker is first revealed in the "I" used in the poem's title. The speaker conveys a wish that the two people just discussed, the man and the woman, were married to one another. Because this one sentiment is the only thought expressed in this stanza, the reader is forced to pause and consider the wish and why the narrator might wish it. By employing a first-person speaker in this line, Merriam draws the reader's attention back to the title of the poem, in effect linking the two wishes: the wish to be like the people in the poem and the wish that they were married. In doing so, the poet/speaker suggests that it is because the people are admirable (she wants to be like them) that she wishes them to marry.

Stanza 4

In the final stanza, the speaker's personal desire recedes into the background. The "I" has disappeared, but another speculation is presented. Perhaps, the poet states, it is better if the people are not married. The peace and harmony that the two people appear to possess individually might be more easily distributed to others, the poet suggests, if the people are not married. Whether or not this sentiment is the poet's or the speaker's (or both, if in fact they are intended to be taken as the same person) is unclear. The conflict between the wish expressed in the third stanza and the thoughts conveyed in the fourth stanza is apparent. Marriage may offer happiness to the individuals, but a greater good may be achieved through the people retaining their status as single individuals rather than merging to form a couple. In the first line of this final stanza, the poet undercuts the sense of peacefulness that has been building in the poem by stating flatly that it may be better that the man and woman are not married. Such a statement forces the reader to wonder for whom this situation might be better. Is it better for the man and woman to not be married to one another? Or is it better for society in general for the man and woman to not marry? The last two lines suggest the latter, that more people could benefit from the peaceful nature of the man and the woman if they remain apart, yet the sense of conflict remains. The question—what impediment to peacefulness does marriage imply—lingers.

<hr>

THEMES

Peace

Throughout the course of the first two stanzas of "Two People I Want to Be Like," or eighteen of the poem's total twenty-two lines, Merriam constructs an idealized portrait of two characters, characters used by Merriam to expound on inner peace and paths to its cultivation. Through the details Merriam employs, the inner sense of peace the two individuals appear to possess becomes apparent. The man in the first stanza is initially characterized by what he does not do, by his inaction rather than by his actions. Sitting in traffic, he does not give in to frustration or impatience. Rather, he cultivates a sense of tranquility by consciously smiling and using his inertia to recall better times. Merriam's descriptions offer the reader images of the irritation and anger that other drivers are feeling; presumably they are doing the things the man is not, such as pounding their fists on their steering wheels or attempting to maneuver into other lanes. In the

TOPICS FOR FURTHER STUDY

- When the speaker in "Two People I Want to Be Like" wishes that the man and the woman in the poem were married, she touches on the notion of love and relationships. Initially her perspective seems to be an innocent youthful one, when she wishes for the marriage. As the poem progresses and the speaker sees futility in such a union, a more pessimistic tone is used. Poems in Hispanic American Gary Soto's young-adult volume of poetry, *Partly Cloudy: Poems of Love and Longing* (2009), similarly explore the nature of such relationships. Select a poem from Soto's volume and compare it with "Two People I Want to Be Like." Do the poems include a similar tonal shift or a combination of positive and negative ideas or themes? How successfully do adult writers like Merriam and Soto capture and express for a youthful audience ideas about relationships? Create a Venn diagram or concept web/map that compares the two poems.

- The speaker in "Two People I Want to Be Like" describes two individuals with admirable qualities. She offers specific details regarding the man and the woman, details that provide deep insights regarding their character. Write your own free-verse poem about two people you want to be like. Consider the techniques Merriam employs in her poem. For example, she does not offer a list of features or characteristics but rather describes each character in a particular scene. Reflect on the qualities you admire and then about how these qualities may be personified in characters you create. Think about line length, word choice, and imagery and how they can work together to convey the meaning you intend. Share your poem with the class, or create a Web page where your poetry may be viewed and com-mented on by your classmates. Challenge them to guess about whom you are writing.

- Merriam's feminist tendencies are apparent throughout much of her work. Betty Friedan played a prominent role in the evolution of the feminist movement during Merriam's lifetime. Research Friedan's life and works. Consider how her work, such as 1963's *The Feminine Mystique*, influenced the feminist movement. Present your findings in a biographical essay, in a Power Point presentation, or on a Web page that can be accessed by members of your class.

- With its reflections on the limitations of marriage, Merriam's poem offers an opportunity for further exploration of society's attitudes toward marriage and divorce. Research and analyze the way Americans' ideas and habits have changed with regard to marriage and divorce from the 1980s to today. How have divorce rates changed since the 1980s? How have attitudes toward marriage and divorce shifted over the past two decades? The University of Virginia's National Marriage Project (http://www.virginia.edu/marriage project) offers many articles and statistics regarding American society and marriage. For example, a 2000 article by Barbara Dafoe Whitehead and David Popenoe, "Changes in Teen Attitudes Toward Marriage, Cohabitation and Children: 1975–1995," explores the evolution of youthful attitudes regarding marriage. Compile a detailed report published on a Web page with links to the sources you used for your research. List your print resources as well. Alternatively, create your report as a print document with charts and graphs inserted into the text.

middle of this frustrated mix sits the man. Merriam describes the way a slow grin unfurls itself across the man's face. He is depicted as stable, even-keeled, and happy. He has good times to remember and he keeps those in mind as he waits patiently in the traffic. Peacefulness is a path that the man consciously chooses.

The woman likewise makes a concerted effort to remain peaceful during a chaotic time. In the hectic rush, she opts to smile at her customers. Notably, she does not peer at them and smile in a shy manner; she quite directly engages people and shoots a smile at them. Merriam's word choice emphasizes the conscious effort involved the woman's actions.

Almost as quickly as her narrator makes the wish for the two people to be together, Merriam suggests that this might not be the best course of action. It is possible, as the next two lines connote, that the individuals may be better able to use their peaceful natures as a means of creating greater harmony in the world if they remain apart. The implication is that there is a larger purpose to be served—one of spreading peace—that is more important than the possible happiness the man and woman might discover in marriage to one another.

Marriage

The conflict and ambiguity at the poem's conclusion centers on the prospect of a marriage between the two people in the poem. Merriam initially projects a childlike innocence regarding the individuals in the poem and the notions of love and marriage. As the poem's title indicates, the narrator states that she wants to be like the man and woman described in the poem. The people are depicted in overwhelmingly positive terms. Two such like-minded people, the narrator observes, should be together; they should marry. The narrator's wish is youthfully sweet and also naïve, in the sense that these two people do not even know each other. They are wished together because of a similar character trait the narrator admires, yet in the final stanza, this wish is revoked. In the speaker's (or possibly Merriam's) view, a marriage between the two people would prevent them from sharing their sense of peace and harmony with others.

This final sentiment shares a sense of hopefulness that the harmonious nature of the man and woman will spread to others. At the same time, this stanza presents a rather limiting view of the institution of marriage. Merriam suggests in this final stanza that marriage would limit rather than enhance the ability of the man and

A happily married couple share their joy (Iia Dukhnovska / Shutterstock.com)

woman to be agents of positive change in their community. Merriam's poem presents three instances of a nagging negativity that threatens the sense of peace that the rest of the poem encourages. The first is the frustration of the commuters in the first stanza—a feeling the man avoids. The second is the sense of exasperation suggested by the hustle and bustle that surrounds the woman, by which she manages to remain unaffected. The third is this rather pessimistic view of marriage, and it is this third instance that may be regarded as the most unsettling aspect of the poem. In the first two instances, the man and the woman stand out as positive aspects of negative situations, but in the final instance, marriage—something generally taken to be a positive goal, an affirmation of love—is presented as the negative element, one that the man and woman are to avoid if they are to successfully pursue their calling as agents of peace.

STYLE

Free Verse

"Two People I Want to Be Like" is a free-verse poem. Free-verse poems do not contain any regular rhyme pattern or metrical structure. Meter is a consistent pattern of unaccented and accented syllables in a line of poetry. In the absence of such structure, poets utilize other tools in order to convey the particular meaning they want to express. Merriam structures her poem into four distinct stanzas, drawing the reader's attention first to the man, then to the woman, then to one possible view of marriage—the coming together of like-minded individuals, and finally to the parting notion with which she leaves her readers—the idea of marriage as an institution likely to be more harmful than beneficial.

The language Merriam uses in the free-verse poem is another method by which she controls the pace of the poem and the reader's perceptions. In the first stanza, the details suggest stasis, or inactivity, and two distinct responses to being stuck—frustration or patience. The second stanza depicts an active or even an overly active scene. Merriam uses words and images that suggest the fast pace of rush-hour shoppers and the woman's response to them. Her actions are, unlike the man's, not slow and steady, but physical and hurried, yet like the man she smiles in spite of it all. The transition from the lack of movement in the first stanza to the frenzied movement of the second is supported by words and line length that force the reader to slow down or rush along accordingly. In such a way, Merriam uses words, images, and the structure of her stanzas to shape a poem that is unfettered by metrical patterns or rhyme schemes.

Lyric Poetry

A lyric poem is one in which the poet, rather than telling a story, shares his or her responses to ideas or events. Lyric poems are often brief, and are characterized by the poet's personal feelings. "Two People I Want to Be Like" may be described as a lyric poem because it reflects Merriam's admiration for the two people she describes in her poem. It additionally offers her meditation on the idea of marriage. The descriptions of the two individuals in the poem are detailed images that embody particular qualities—peacefulness, patience—that the poet admires. These ideas support the larger theme of marriage and its potential to restrict rather than empower a couple. Merriam's emotional reaction to the people in the poem and their possible futures together or apart forms the core of this lyric poem. While Merriam creates vivid characters, the poem does not tell a story. Merriam provides glimpses into the lives of two individuals and shares her responses to them rather than telling the reader the story of their lives or what happened to them before or after the scenes described in the first two stanzas.

HISTORICAL CONTEXT

Poetry in the 1980s

By the 1980s, poetry had been influenced for decades by a movement in which free-verse poetry—poetry that eschewed traditional forms and structures—prevailed. Free-verse poetry was initially a rejection of formal modes and later simply an open method by which individuality and emotional responses could be freely expressed. As Christopher Beach observes in the introduction to *The Cambridge Introduction to American Poetry*, poets writing during the 1970s and 1980s benefited from a "burgeoning network of journals, presses, and academic creative-writing programs."

New movements, including language poetry and new formalism, aided in the continued growth and development of American poetry in the 1980s. The language poetry movement and the new formalist movement were in some ways reactions to free-verse poetry's rejection of formalist techniques. While new formalist poets embraced the metrical constructions and often-complex rhyme schemes of pre-twentieth-century poetry, language poets focused on the particular technical element of language. The nontraditional, or avant-garde, poems of the language poets were experiments with words and sound and were highly focused on the reader or speaker as an active participant in the poem.

Just as Beach observes the prevalence of language poetry and new formalism in the 1970s and 1980s, he also pinpoints the continued popularity of an earlier mode of poetry, the confessional mode. During this time period, poems that revealed personal and private meditations on "relationships, sex, marriage, and domestic life," were regarded as post-confessional (in that poems in this category were technically a resurgence of the earlier confessional mode) and had

COMPARE
&
CONTRAST

- **1980s:** In 1980, 92 percent of forty-year-old white female college graduates are married, as are 96 percent of white female high school graduates.

  Today: In 2008, only 86 percent of those forty-year-old white female college graduates are married. The marriage rate for white female high school graduates drops to 88 percent.

- **1980s:** In 1981, *A Visit to William Blake's Inn* by Nancy Willard, becomes the first book of poetry to win the John Newbery Award (it also is a Caldecott Honor book). It is seen by some critics as a foundation for a renaissance in children's poetry, according to Shelley J. Crisp in an essay for *Children's Literature in Education.*

  Today: Over seventy-five new poetry or poetry-related books for young people are scheduled to be published in 2010, including books by distinguished writers such as Pat Mora, Naomi Shihab Nye, and Jane Yolen.

- **1980s:** By the end of the 1980s, the average commute time by automobile is 22.4 minutes.

  Today: By the 2008, the average commute time by automobile has increased to just over 29 minutes.

- **1980s:** First used at Marsh's Supermarket in 1974 in Troy, Ohio, the bar code scanner becomes common equipment in grocery store checkout lines.

  Today: Customers can scan their own items at self-service checkout aisles since bar codes are used on every product in the grocery store, even fresh fruit and vegetable labels.

---

become so popular they "soon came to constitute the new mainstream of American poetry."

While children's poetry cannot be described as a trend, a number of poets composed poetry directed at children during the 1980s as well. Merriam wrote numerous volumes of poetry for children and took a unique approach. According to Glenna Sloan in a 1981 issue of *Language Arts* magazine, Merriam was "astonished when an anthologist once told her that she was the only poet who wrote poetry for children on social issues." Earlier in her career, she took on racism, for example, in the 1969 *The Inner City Mother Goose.* In other poems, she contemplated gender roles, as she does in "Elizabeth Blackwell," a poem about the first female doctor; it was published in Merriam's 1968 volume, *Independent Voices.* In later collections, including the 1983 *If Only I could Tell You: Poems for Young Lovers and Dreamers*, Merriam also questions traditional notions of the value of marriage, as she does in "Two People I Want to Be Like."

Feminism in the 1980s

Much of Merriam's work—especially that which is targeted at adults, including poetry, plays, and nonfiction—is characterized by her politics, in particular, her feminism. Merriam was in her forties and fifties during the onset and early years of the feminist movement in the 1960s and 1970s. The efforts of women to assert their rightful place in American society can be traced back to the first settlers of the American colonies. However, the first major movements toward women's rights began in the late-nineteenth and early-twentieth centuries, as women fought for the right to vote. This privilege was granted in 1920 with the ratification of the Nineteenth Amendment.

In post-World War II America, the dissatisfaction perceived by many American women was given a voice with the 1963 publication of Betty Friedan's *The Feminine Mystique.* This sparked what was known as the second wave of American feminism, the first having been the

A smiling grocery store clerk (SFC | *Shutterstock.com*)

suffrage movement. In the 1980s, after women had lobbied for two decades for such rights as equal opportunities in education and in the work force, the feminist movement, according to some observers, stalled. As Astrid Henry comments in the 2004 *Not My Mother's Sister: Generational Conflict and Third Wave Feminism*, "the 1980s have routinely been characterized as a time when feminism was no longer necessary." The decade was commonly regarded as post-feminist. This term, Henry explains, describes both the perceived successes and failures of the movement.

Henry contends that the perception that feminism died out during the 1980s was intensified by the "popular-press coverage of the women's movement" during that time, coverage claiming that feminism had failed "to transform women's lives, to make woman happy, to effect social and political change." However, Henry also insists that many women continued to fervently support feminist ideals during the 1980s. Organizations such as the National Organization for Women, organized in 1966 under

Friedan's leadership, fought in the 1980s for equal pay for women in the workforce, civil rights for lesbians, and additional reproductive rights for women.

CRITICAL OVERVIEW

While "Two People I Want to Be Like" is rarely the subject of critical analyses, Merriam's poetry in general, and often her earlier poetry, has received a greater share of critical attention. In particular, critics often observe the way in which she plays with language in her poetry. Also analyzed is Merriam's treatment of social issues in her nonfiction work, plays, and poetry. Jeffrey S. Copeland, in a 1993 collection of interviews, *Speaking of Poets: Interviews with Poets Who Write for Children and Young Adults*, comments on both Merriam's advocacy for equal rights, as well as on her use of a narrator, or first-person speaker, in her poetry. He states that the "typical speaker" in Merriam's poetry "is a young, inquisitive, full-of-joy human being." Furthermore, Copeland observes, this person "is also not designated as male or female; rather, the speaker is a human being first, a member of the world," and that additionally "this is a nonsexist world." Such a description could be applied to the speaker in "Two People I Want to Be Like."

Other critics have made note of Merriam's social activism. In a 1992 article for the *New York Times*, Bruce Lambert describes the way the 1969 collection of poetry *The Inner City Mother Goose* was attacked by those who claimed "it glamorized crime and denigrated people." Lambert further observes the way Merriam's "word play and social commentary often displayed incisive wit." In an article published in a 1981 issue of *Language Arts* magazine, Glenna Sloan recounts an interview with Merriam. Sloan describes Merriam as a "versatile writer" who is keenly focused on "bringing children and poetry together." Additionally Sloan praises Merriam's "wit in word play," a feature of her style that has been lauded by other critics as well. Sylvia M. Vardell, in the 2007 book *Poetry People: A Practical Guide to Children's Poets*, observes that Merriam's work "is characterized as smart, playful, and lively and often explores the sounds and origins of words."

As Laura M. Zaidman maintained in a chapter on Merriam for in the 1987 *Dictionary of Literary Biography* volume *American Writers for Children Since 1960: Poets, Illustrators, and Nonfiction Authors*, "Merriam's many books of children's poetry prove her strong belief that poems are as essential to everyday lives as daily bread is to diets." Like Sloan, Zaidman identifies Merriam's commitment to exposing children to the vitality and necessity of poetry. Zaidman further notes that Merriam's poetry often focuses on "the inner emotional conflicts and stark realities of the world facing children." Merriam's poetry for children, as these critics have recognized, is respectful of the insight and emotional and intellectual range that children possess.

CRITICISM

Catherine Dominic

Dominic is a novelist, freelance writer, and editor. In the following essay, she explores, within the context of the evolution of the feminist movement in the 1980s, the views on marriage and personal fulfillment that Merriam expresses in the poem "Two People I Want to Be Like."

In many ways, "Two People I Want to Be Like" is a poem about potential fulfilled and potential thwarted. While the work is not overtly feminist, Merriam's views on marriage and its limitations, as expressed within the short verse, are consistent with feminist attitudes on marriage prevalent during the 1980s. A close examination of the poem reveals that the speaker in the poem regards marriage as a potentially limiting force that could prevent the individuals described earlier in the poem from maximizing their particular gifts or talents. Although Merriam, a self-described lifelong feminist, attempts to portray these views in a positive light through her turn of phrase and through the poem's otherwise optimistic tone, the pessimistic connotations expressed cannot be entirely ignored.

A stanza-by-stanza analysis of "Two People I Want to Be Like," when viewed within the context of prevailing feminist views contemporary with the poem's publication, reveals both the poet's sense of idealism as well as a distinct cynicism hidden beneath an outpouring of optimistic attitudes. In the first two stanzas of the poem, Merriam draws two portraits, one of a man, another of a woman. They possess similar natures, such as a tendency toward patience in frustrating situations and the ability to smile gracefully under pressure. Presumably it is because of these qualities that the speaker

in the poem wants to be like these two people; they are admirable and worthy of emulation in her eyes.

One could argue that the speaker's regard for the two individuals is extremely idealistic. Having glimpsed only one aspect of their personalities—the sense of peacefulness they seem to exude—the speaker longs to be like them. Witnessing a glimmer of goodness in their natures, the speaker expresses a desire to emulate the individuals, knowing nothing else about them. The speaker further builds on this sense of idealism by wishing these two apparently like-minded individuals could be married to one another. One positive personality trait is all that links the two people together and, in the speaker's mind, yokes them to her as well. She creates a fantasy in which the two people are together and places them on a pedestal so that she can admire them and mirror their behavior.

It is in the fourth and final stanza of "Two People I Want to Be Like" that Merriam further amplifies the significance of the three previous stanzas. After envisioning one possible future for the laudable people she has just described so carefully, a future in which the individuals have formed a wedded couple, Merriam swiftly and jarringly, in the first line of the fourth stanza, undercuts the optimism and idealism she has been building thus far in the poem. Here she suggests that perhaps the people should not be together after all, and in the last two lines of the poem, Merriam explains why they should not marry. If they do not find one another and wed they will be able to share with those around them their peaceful amicability. The subtle and rather pessimistic inference is that they would be unable to share such peace with others if they were married. Merriam seems to suggest that marriage would either make the people less peaceful, or, that marriage would somehow limit the two individuals' ability to maximize their full potential in other areas of their lives, outside of the marriage.

This view that Merriam expresses in the poem's last stanza regarding the confining nature of marriage is not incongruent with feminist attitudes toward marriage in the 1980s. During what became known as the second wave of feminism in America, feminists increasingly regarded marriage as an obstacle toward achieving professional success and personal fulfillment. As reported by Stephanie Coontz in a

WHAT DO I READ NEXT?

- Merriam edited and introduced the volume *Growing Up Female in America: Ten Lives*, which was published in 1971 by Doubleday. The volume uses primary documents (original writings such as letters and journals by the women featured) to explore the lives of ten early American women. Merriam's selection of the women was based on their interest in the issue of women's rights in the decades of American history that preceded the women's suffrage movement. Her introduction reveals her interest both in the rights of women, as well as in the notions of identity that children develop throughout their youth.

- Merriam's award-winning play, *The Club: A Musical Diversion*, is a satirical examination of gender roles in early twentieth-century America. It was produced in 1976 and published the following year by Samuel French.

- *The Defiant Muse: Hispanic Feminist Poems from the Middle Ages to the Present*, edited by Angel Flores and Kate Flores, is a bilingual anthology of feminist poetry by Hispanic poets. The editors offer an introduction, providing historical, cultural, and aesthetic context for understanding the poems. The volume, which was published in 1993 by the Feminist Press at CUNY (City University of New York), further provides biographical sketches on each poet.

- David Levithan's young-adult poetry collection *The Realm of Possibility*, published in 2004 by Knopf Books for Young Readers, is a series of poems in which Levithan creates a set of characters, who, as a circle of friends, speak about their lives and relationships through interconnected free-verse poems. Students of Merriam's "Two People I Want to Be Like," in which the poet inhabits a youthful perspective and contemplates adult relationships, will be exposed to the interpretation of young-adult relationships from the perspective of a twenty-first century poet.

- Dawn Currie, Deirdre M. Kelly, and Shauna Pomerantz contemplate the notions of gender identity in girls who have grown up in a culture in which girls were encouraged to view themselves as females empowered to achieve whatever they set their minds to. *Girl Power: Girls Reinventing Girlhood*, published in 2009 by Peter Lang, studies the notion of girl power as an idea inspired by earlier phases in the feminist movement and traces the influence of this idea on the emotional development of girls.

- The book-length young-adult poem *Harlem: A Poem*, by African American poet Walter Dean Myers, celebrates Harlem and its people. Like the poetry of Merriam, Myers's poem revels in details that powerfully convey the sights, sounds, and multisensory texture of an urban community. The book was published in 1997 by Scholastic.

2006 article for the United Kingdom's daily online news magazine, the *First Post*, while views on marriage have since changed, the prevailing sentiment in the 1970s and 1980s was that as more women joined the workforce "the feminist movement raised their discontent with the traditional division of labor at home," leading to a "surge of divorce and harsh criticism of marriage that appeared in Western Europe and North America."

The conflicted nature of feminists' views regarding marriage, family, and career choices is reflected in Betty Friedan's *The Second Stage*, published in 1981. Rosemarie Putnam Tong summarizes and explores Friedan's views in the 1998 work *Feminist Thought: A More Comprehensive*

Relaxing in the car (Galina Barskaya / Shutterstock.com)

Introduction. Tong states that Friedan recognized "the difficulty of combining marriage, motherhood, and career," and believed that "1980s feminists needed to stop trying to 'do it all' and 'be it all.'"

Although a poet's personal life is not always relevant to every poem he or she writes, there are instances where understanding a poet's personal background can aid the reader in understanding the views expressed in the poem. In "Two People I Want to Be Like," the overall meaning of the poem hinges on the ideas expressed in the final stanza. One of those ideas is that marriage has the potential to obstruct rather than aid the people involved with one another in realizing their dreams for themselves. The man and the woman may not be able to share their gifts and values with others if they marry, according to Merriam. Merriam's personal history with marriage may not be completely irrelevant to the poem, when one considers the particulars of her past. While candid in interviews about her philosophic beliefs, Merriam did not often discuss her relationship history, which included

four marriages and three divorces. Merriam married her fourth husband, Waldo Salt, in 1983, the same year that "Two People I Want to Be Like" was published in the volume *If Only I could Tell You: Poems for Young Lovers and Dreamers*. It is impossible to say to what extent her own experience with marriage influenced her views as expressed in "Two People I Want to Be Like," but it is not unreasonable to suggest that her past shaped the notions she expressed on the subject within the poem.

Both Merriam and Friedan expressed views indicating that while marriage has the potential to harm the ability to realize one's full potential as a human being, both women and men are equally deserving of the opportunity to seek such fulfillment. Tong explains that Friedan's perspective in the 1980s was one in which men and women could work together "to develop the kind of social values, leadership styles, and institutional structures that will permit both genders to achieve fulfillment in both the public and private worlds." Similarly, in his essay on her in *Speaking of Poets: Interviews with Poets Who*

Write for Children and Young Adults, Jeffrey S. Copeland quotes Merriam as stating "I believe first and foremost in equality of the sexes, equality of everybody on earth." Merriam, in the interview with Copeland, went on to assert: "I am particularly involved in trying to do non-sexist work in literature for the young." While "Two People I Want to Be Like" may present a view of marriage as an obstacle toward the full development of one's individual gifts, the poem nevertheless expresses the desire that both the man and the woman be allowed a real opportunity to exploit their personal gifts of patience and peace for the greater good of the world in which they live.

Source: Catherine Dominic, Critical Essay on "Two People I Want to Be Like," in *Poetry for Students*, Gale, Cengage Learning, 2011.

Eve Merriam

In this essay, Merriam discusses the effects of aging on an author.

I'm seventy-four, and people are always amazed when they hear that. They say, "Oh, you look so young." But that is one of those jokes. You could be in your coffin and they'd say you don't look it. But the fact is, one does take it as a compliment. My hair, for example, is not entirely gray yet, and I like it when people say, "What lovely hair. You're so vigorous and your body is just in great shape." It pleases me, yes it does.

Eve Merriam was born and raised in Philadelphia, the youngest child of Russian-born parents who owned a chain of women's dress shops. Books and reading were an important part of her youth, and the written word has captivated her ever since. Over the years, she has found several avenues of expression as a writer, most notably as a poet and playwright. She has written over fifty books of prose and poetry for both adults and children, including Fresh Paint, Mommies at Work, *and* The Inner City Mother Goose.

I can't really praise age. That would be unfair, because all of us would like to be immortal and live forever. We always think that aging, as well as death, is what happens to other people. I think what has come upon me is a very slight degree of tranquility toward the future, a sort of "*Que sera, sera,*" what will happen in the future will happen. I no longer feel I can control all the destiny that there is. So age tends to make

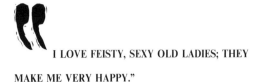

" I LOVE FEISTY, SEXY OLD LADIES; THEY MAKE ME VERY HAPPY."

me a little more humble toward the universe. Remember the great story about Margaret Fuller when she exclaimed, "I accept the universe!" and Ralph Waldo Emerson responded, "Madam, you damn well better."

So I think one comes to accept aging. Yet there's a shyness that I find that I never had before in life. A certain shyness about, "Oh, dear, I'm an old lady now, my hair has turned gray, will young people want to be with me?" Even though I've spent all my life with younger people because the bulk of my work is in the theater and poetry. There is that certain shyness that I find. I don't know whether this pertains to other older people too. I don't know whether I still belong in the magic circle of immortality or not. And I want to be part of the dance.

I think I'm sort of inclined to agree with Lillian Hellman that one gets older but not necessarily wiser. Perhaps one of the few good things about getting older is that life becomes so precious on a day-to-day basis. I think I've always had a certain amount of daily joy, but now I find it even more so—the sight of a clear sky in New York, which doesn't come all that often, or being out in the country, or right now in the spring, in April, where the trees are just the greenest they've ever been, and even the colors that people wear. I feel the senses become heightened. I know that some scientists think that our senses become dimmed with age, but I think it's just the reverse.

I think that a love for the ordinary is what is most important as one ages, not for the extraordinary. There are always trips to Bali or Yokohama or Paris, but to get the joy out of the dailyness, that's what struck me when I hit my sixties. I thought, Good heavens, I'm getting so much pleasure out of my breakfast. I didn't know grapefruit juice could taste so good. This is really amazing. It's as though some kind of slight film over the world has been stripped away and there is now a clarity that one didn't have before. I'm a big walker—I love to walk—and the rhythm of my body walking just seems to give me more pleasure now. And I feel that the visual sense is heightened, despite using glasses for reading. I think the sense of smell, even though I've heard that it dims, is for me sharper and clearer. Smell is the most evocative of memories, and we have more memories as we age, naturally. The sense of touch becomes very, very significant. I've always had a lot of plants in my apartment, but I think the pleasure that I get now out of pruning them and trimming them is even more. So I'm deliberately talking about ordinary things, and that is something that I want very much to pass on to younger people and to children. In fact, I did a book for children called *Unhurry Harry*, in which the main character is very slow because he's always savoring all of his five senses.

I have finally learned to pare away things that don't interest me that much. There's no question that time is more precious now and I really hate to waste it. I used to be the kid who would go to three parties every night—heaven forbid that I would miss something. Now I don't do that. I pick and choose very carefully. And I feel the same way with seeing people. I really only want to see people I can get something out of. I'm looking for a meeting of minds, not that we necessarily have to feel the same way about politics or the social order, but so that I can get something out of the experience.

I suppose you'd say it's a cleaning out time for me. I'm even cleaning out the clothes closets. I used to be a fashion editor, so I know pretty much the sort of things that are becoming to me, and now I'm clearing out clothes and trying to clear out clutter from my desk—papers that I don't really need. There is a very good feeling about cleaning up debris.

But, you know, there's a lot of debris you can never fully get rid of. I never quite believe those people who say, "I regret nothing." I can't imagine that there wouldn't be regrets unless one is the sort of person who's never done anything. And all my life I've been very impulsive. I once got married after I knew somebody for three weeks; it was not a marriage that lasted forever. I will give things away on impulse. I will write on impulse. I've always done that, so I've made many errors of judgment in the course of my life. When I look back there are many things that I would have done differently. I wish that I had my children earlier and wish that I had more

of them. I was thirty-five when my first son was born, and then I wanted to have children quick, so the second was born just ten and a half months later. I wish that my last marriage, which was the happiest marriage of my life, had come earlier. I wish a lot of things, I regret a lot of things. But on the other hand, there are so many highs that I've had.

I had my most passionate marriage when I turned sixty, so I think that older women have the ability to be passionate forever and ever. It's easier for women than for men, because I think we find sensuality, as well as sexuality, in different areas. I think that the fact that we deal with children, that we deal with the domestic as well, lends an extra edge to the sexual and the sensual. But our society really doesn't like to think of older ladies as sexy. Nobody wants to think that there are women out there howling like banshees and having relationships with younger men, which is always threatening. We're a very conservative society, and always have been, so we put things in slots. You know, there's young love, there's adolescence, then you get married, then you raise your family, and then you sort of turn into a walking television box and just sit there like Darby and Joan. It's possible that Darby and Joan had a terrific sex life. I'm sure William Blake and his wife did. I knew Dr. W. E. B. Du Bois, the great African-American scholar, and when he was ninety-six he would kiss you and you knew you had been kissed. And certainly somebody like Louise Nevelson exuded sexuality until she was very, very far along in her life. Or what about Martha Graham? I loved her vanity of wearing little white gloves so that you wouldn't notice the veins on her hand. I think she was a very sexual person. I love feisty, sexy old ladies; they make me very happy.

Source: Eve Merriam, "Eve Merriam," in *The Ageless Spirit: Reflections on Living Life to the Fullest in Midlife and the Years Beyond*, edited by Connie Goldman, Fairview Press, 2004, pp. 195–200.

Rebecca Lukens

In this essay, Lukens discusses the sensory awareness in Merriam's poetry.

> Eve Merriam:
> To paint without a palette,
> To dance without music

The three senses implied in these lines—and more—are teased in the poetry of Eve Merriam. The poems even taste good. In "How to Eat a

Poem," she gives permission to be voracious, to gobble each last nibble of sound. "Inside a Poem" encourages us to "hear with/our/heels," to inhale, to "swerve in a curve," and to feel with our eyes "what they never touched before." Reading Merriam through, end to end, awakens all our senses to sharpness, but touches our intellects, too. The unexpected juxtapositions, the keen contrasts, the onomatopoeic series, even the clichés freshened to surprise—all are parts of Merriam's own pleasure, and now of ours.

Taking the everyday not for granted but for novelty, Merrian alerts us to a "Thumbprint," "My signature,/thumbing the pages of my time./ My universe key," and thus shows that each person is startlingly singular. Or take socks. In "The Hole Story" we find we needn't worry about mending that hole. No need to say, "'Oh, darn,'/For I'm spinning you a yarn." The hole's at the top. Merriam's words play with us, surprising us with double meanings—three in two short lines.

Further delight in words shows in her contrasts. "Argument" is a series of one term oppositions like a confrontation between two obstinate speakers shouting "Over./ Under./ Cloudless./ Thunder" and concluding "By way... ?/ MY WAY!" Even clichés are fresh as the visual poem "Euphemistic" forms a page pattern including every known phrase for what has happened to great-great-great-great Uncle Clyde, then ends abruptly with the single line "*died.*"

Merriam loves the sensory opposition, the surprising synergy of image and metaphor. Her series of sensory appeals in "What Makes a Poem?" is filled with surprises as she speaks of the "secrets of rain," and opposes "the touch of grass/ Or an icy glass," the "shout of noon" and "the silent moon." In "A Matter of Taste" she asks, "What does your tongue like the most?" Contrast sharpens our tastebuds to appreciate anew chewy meat and crunchy toast, "soft marshmallow or a hard lime drop," "hot pancakes or a sherbet freeze."

In addition to this sharply honed sensory awareness, a continuous sense of play spurs us to savor words and explore new meanings. Merriam does not stop with words we know; she creates more. In "Mean Song," which rings of "Jabberwocky," she builds a series of mean wishes, begins with short sounds (snickles and podes,/ Ribble and grodes"), crescendoes to "A nox in the groot,/ A root in the stoot," and

reduces us to shudders with the threat of "one flack snack in the bave." In "One, Two, Three— Gough!" her rhymes are proof of the irrationality of English; rhyming dough/sough, through/ blough. With equal wit she introduces us to the absurd bird called "Gazinta"; Two gazinta four two times..."

Merriam is highly skilled in use of sound. Her onomatopoeia in describing a rusty spigot in "Onomapotoeia" for example, the internal rhyme in "What in the World," and her frequent yet not cloying assonance and consonance make her poems exactly the stuff for reading aloud. We hear the spondees and sprung rhythm. But the *look* of the poem matters too. *Out Loud*, for example, seems inadequately titled; out loud is not enough, not nearly. Without the book before us, we miss the engaging visual form of short lines and long, broken words and portmanteaux.

The conclusion to draw from a close look at Merriam's poetry remains delight—delight in its freshness and its deceptive spontaneity worked with high craftsmanship. Merriam's own definitions of poetry describe what she creates: acute sensory awareness and the joy of words and wit.

Source: Rebecca Lukens, "The Place of Poetry," in *Children's Literature Association Quarterly*, Vol. 5, No. 4, Winter 1981, p. 45.

SOURCES

"ACS, Census, Average Commute Time by Place of Residence in 2008, USA, 2010," in *American Communities Survey of Census*, http://factfinder.census.gov/ (accessed October 2, 2010).

Beach, Christopher, "Introduction," "The New Criticism and Poetic Formalism," and "The Confessional Mode," in *The Cambridge Introduction to Twentieth-Century American Poetry*, Cambridge University Press, 2003, pp. 1–6, 137–53, 154–72.

"Business Cycle Dating Committee, National Bureau of Economic Research: NBER Committee Confers: No Trough Announced," in *National Bureau of Economic Research*, http://www.nber.org/cycles/april2010.html (accessed May 3, 2010).

"Business Cycle Expansions and Contractions," in *National Bureau of Economic Research*, http://www.nber .org/cycles.html (accessed May 3, 2010).

Carr, Brian, "Average Gas Mileage Relatively Flat between 1980 and 2004," in *Daily Fuel Economy Tip*, October 19, 2006, http://www.dailyfueleconomytip .com/miscellaneous/average-gas-mileage-relatively-flat-between-1980-and-2004/ (accessed October 2, 2010).

"Chronology of the Equal Rights Amendment, 1923–1996," in *National Organization for Women*, http://www.now.org/issues/economic/cea/history.html (accessed May 1, 2010).

Coontz, Stephanie, "How Feminism Saved Marriage," in *First Post*, December 22, 2006, http://www.thefirstpost.co.uk/5431,news-comment,news-politics,why-feminism-is-good-for-marriage (accessed May 1, 2010).

Copeland, Jeffrey S., "Eve Merriam," in *Speaking of Poets: Interviews with Poets Who Write for Children and Young Adults*, National Council of Teachers of English, 1993, pp. 119–25.

Crisp, Shelley J., "Children's Poetry in the United States: The Best of the 1980s," in *Children's Literature in Education*, Vol. 22, No. 3, 1991.

"Economic News Release," in *Bureau of Labor Statistics*, April 2, 2010, http://www.bls.gov/news.release/empsit.nr0.htm (accessed May 1, 2010).

Green, Carol Hurd, "Eve Merriam: 1916–1992," in *Jewish Women: A Comprehensive Encyclopedia*, http://jwa.org/encyclopedia/article/merriam-eve (accessed May 1, 2010).

Henry, Astrid, "Daughterhood Is Powerful: The Emergence of Feminism's Third Wave," in *Not My Mother's Sister: Generational Conflict and Third-Wave Feminism*, Indiana University Press, 2004, pp. 16–51.

"Highlights from NOW's Forty Fearless Years," in *National Organization for Women*, http://www.now.org/history/timeline.html (accessed May 3, 2010).

Hopkins, Lee Bennett, "Eve Merriam," in *Books Are by People: Interviews with 104 Authors and Illustrators of Books for Young Children*, Citation Press, 1969, pp. 180–82.

"Labor Force Statistics from the Current Population Survey," in *Bureau of Labor Statistics*, http://www.bls.gov/cps/prev_yrs.htm (accessed May 1, 2010).

Lambert, Bruce, "Eve Merriam, 75, Poet and Author Who Wrote for Children, Is Dead," in *New York Times*, April 13, 1992, http://www.nytimes.com/1992/04/13/nyregion/eve-merriam-75-poet-and-author-who-wrote-for-children-is-dead.html?st=cse&sq=eve+merriam&scp (accessed May 1, 2010).

Merriam, Eve, "Two People I Want To Be Like," in *If Only I Could Tell You: Poetry for Young Lovers and Dreamers*, Alfred A. Knopf, 1983, p. 50.

"The Paycheck Fairness Act," in *American Association of University Women*, http://www.aauw.org/act/issue_advocacy/actionpages/paycheckfairness.cfm (accessed May 2, 2010).

Parker-Pope, Tara, "Marriage and Women Over 40," in *New York Times*, October 2, 2010, http://well.blogs.nytimes.com/2010/01/26/marriage-and-women-over-40/ (accessed October 2, 2010).

Saad, Lydia, "By Age 24, Marriage Wins Out," in *Gallup*, August 11, 2008, http://www.gallup.com/poll/109402/Age-24-Marriage-Wins.aspx (accessed May 1, 2010).

Sloan, Glenna, "Profile: Eve Merriam," in *Language Arts*, Vol. 58, No. 8, November/December 1981, pp. 957–62.

Tong, Rosemarie Putnam, "Liberal Feminism," in *Feminist Thought: A More Comprehensive Introduction*, Westview Press, 1998, pp. 10–44.

Vardell, Sylvia M., "Eve Merriam," in *Poetry People: A Practical Guide to Children's Poets*, Libraries Unlimited, 2007, pp. 89–91.

———, "Poetry 2010 Sneak Peek List," in *Poetry for Children: about Finding and Sharing Poetry with Young People*, http://poetryforchildren.blogspot.com/2010/01/poetry-2010-sneak-peek-list.html (accessed October 2, 2010).

Whitehead, Barbara Dafoe, and David Popenoe, "Changes in Teen Attitudes Toward Marriage, Cohabitation and Children: 1975–1995," in *National Marriage Project*, 2000, http://www.virginia.edu/marriageproject/pdfs/print_teenattitudes.pdf (accessed May 1, 2010).

Zaidman, Laura M., "Eve Merriam," in *Dictionary of Literary Biography*, Vol. 61, *American Writers for Children Since 1960: Poets, Illustrators, and Nonfiction Authors*, edited by Glenn E. Estes, Gale Research, 1987, pp. 224–33.

FURTHER READING

Collins, Robert M., *Transforming America: Politics and Culture in the Reagan Years*, Columbia University Press, 2006.

> Collins offers a detailed historical analysis of the political atmosphere and popular culture of 1980s America, during the years of Ronald Reagan's presidency. Collins discusses the way Reagan's policies shaped American lives. The historian discusses, for example, Reagan's handling of the cold war and his funding for AIDS research.

Duffy, Carol Ann, ed., *I Wouldn't Thank You for a Valentine: Poems for Young Feminists*, illustrated by Trisha Rafferty, Henry Holt, 1997.

> In Duffy's collection of feminist poetry from scores of poets, including Nikki Giovanni and Alice Walker, issues of race, identity, and equality feature prominently. The anthology is targeted at a teen audience.

Friedan, Betty, *The Second Stage: With a New Introduction*, Harvard University Press, 1998.

> Friedan's 1981 exploration of the evolution of the feminist movement, *The Second Stage*, was reissued in 1998 with the inclusion of an updated introduction to the volume by Friedan. The author emphasizes her interest not just in equal rights and freedoms for women, but for all humans.

Merriam, Eve, *The Voice of Liberty: The Story of Emma Lazarus*, illustrated by Charles W. Walker, Farrar, Straus and Cudahy, 1959.

> Merriam's biography of Emma Lazarus, the Jewish American poet known for composing "The New Colossus" (which appears on the pedestal of the Statue of Liberty), is geared toward a young-adult audience. The volume emphasizes Lazarus's status as both a poet and a champion of Jewish refugees in America. Merriam's choice of subject matter reflects her own background as a fellow Jewish American poet, as well as her interest in social activism and in showcasing strong female historical figures to young-adult readers.

Snyder, Gail, *Marriage & Family Issues*, Mason Crest Publishers, 2007.

> A part of the "Gallup Major Trends and Events: The Pulse of Our Nation 1900 to the Present" series, this volume explores the way the American family has been shaped by trends in divorce rates and attitudes toward marriage. Snyder's book is targeted at a young-adult audience.

SUGGESTED SEARCH TERMS

Eve Merriam AND poetry

Eve Merriam AND feminism

Eve Merriam AND children

Eve Merriam AND Friedan

Eve Merriam AND Jewish writers

Eve Merriam AND Two People I Want to Be Like

Eve Merriam AND children's poetry

Eve Merriam AND anthologies

Eve Merriam AND activism

When I Consider (Sonnet XIX)

JOHN MILTON

C. 1652

John Milton's poem, "When I Consider," also known variously as "Sonnet XIX" and "On His Blindness," is thought to have been written in the early 1650s. Most scholars select 1652 as probable, since Milton was completely blind by this date. Other scholars favor 1655, basing this choice on a chronological sequencing of Milton's sonnets. "When I Consider" is a fourteen-line Italian sonnet. Milton adapts the form of the sonnet by employing an enjambment technique to carry his thoughts through multiple lines while retaining the traditional rhyme scheme. "When I Consider" is Milton's first reference in his poetry to his blindness. In the opening lines he questions God, while the concluding lines introduce a new voice that counsels patience. Although the loss of his sight is a blow, the poet finds solace in being reminded that the future is not empty of God's promise: his talents are not lost with his sight. As a result, "When I Consider" should be read as a testament to the poet's faith.

"When I Consider" was first published in a compilation of Milton's poetry, *Poems*, published in 1673. In this collection, the poem is listed as Sonnet XVI. However, "When I Consider" is generally titled as Sonnet XIX, based on an earlier numbering system used by Milton. This poem is one of Milton's most famous works and is reprinted in many anthologies of British literature, as well as in all collections of Milton's poetry. "When I Consider" can be found in *John Milton: Complete Poems and Major Prose*, edited

John Milton (*The Library of Congress*)

by Merritt Y. Hughes (1957). Additional sources include *John Milton: The Major Works*, reissued by Oxford in 2008, and *The Norton Anthology of English Literature*, Volume 1, 8th edition, published by W. W. Norton in 2006.

AUTHOR BIOGRAPHY

Milton was born in London, England, on December 9, 1608, one of three children born to John Milton Sr. and Sara Jeffrey Milton. His father was a scrivener (worked as a notary and performed secretarial/administrative duties for the government) who also earned money through short-term loans and by buying and selling real estate. The family was wealthy enough that Milton was initially taught at home by private tutors. In 1620, when he was twelve years old, Milton was enrolled at St. Paul's School in London, which he attended for the next four years. In 1625 Milton was admitted to Christ's College, Cambridge, but he was suspended a year later after an argument with his tutor. However, Milton was soon back at Cambridge, where he

completed both bachelor of arts (1629) and master of arts degrees (1632). Milton was probably intended to study for the clergy, but after seven years at Cambridge, he left without the degree of doctor of divinity. It is likely that Milton was too Calvinist in his religious beliefs for Cambridge, which held more strictly to views of the Church of England than to the Puritan-Calvinist view that Milton embraced.

While at Cambridge, Milton began to write poetry. Many of the elegies and sonnets from this early period were first published in a collection of his poems in 1645. Also not published until 1645 was "On the Morning of Christ's Nativity," one of the most notable of Milton's early poems, written in 1629. After he left the university, Milton returned to his father's London home to live. The sonnet, "On Shakespeare," written in 1630, became Milton's first published poem in 1632 when it was included anonymously in a second folio edition of Shakespeare's plays. Milton also began writing a masque, a common form of theatrical entertainment among the nobility, in which a play and accompanying music were staged with elaborate costumes and stage decor. *A Mask Presented at Ludlow Castle*, known as *Comus*, was first performed in 1634 and was published anonymously in 1637 by Henry Lawes, who wrote the music for the drama. The pastoral elegy "Lycidas," which Milton wrote to commemorate the death of Edward King, a former Cambridge classmate, was included in a memorial volume of poetry published by Cambridge in 1638. Milton began a tour of Europe, which was common for young, educated English males, in the fall of 1638, but his tour of the continent ended when rumors of civil war in England reached him, and he returned to London in July 1639.

Because his father was very wealthy, he was able to support his son's vocation as a poet for most of his life. After his return to London, Milton tutored his two nephews as well as the sons of several wealthy families and began publishing pamphlets about his religious and political ideology. The most famous of these early pamphlets is his 1642 *The Reason of Church-Government Urged against Prelaty*.

Also in 1642, Milton married Mary Powell, whom he met when he went to collect a debt from her father. At age seventeen, Mary was half Milton's age, and within weeks of the marriage, she returned to her father's home. Milton soon published several tracts in favor of divorce, including *The Doctrine and Discipline of Divorce* (1643, revised and enlarged in 1644). Also in 1644, Milton published *Areopagitica: A Speech for the Liberty of Unlicensed Printing*, a tract opposing government censorship that is still quoted more than 350 years later. Mary returned to Milton in 1645 after three years of separation, and the couple reconciled. Although the marriage had initially gotten off to a rocky start, the couple eventually had four children before Mary's death in childbirth in May 1652. Only a month after the death of his wife, Milton's only son died at the age of one year. In 1656 Milton married Katherine Woodcock but within two years, both she and their infant daughter died.

Milton supported the English Revolution, the deposition and execution of King Charles I in 1649, and the establishment of Oliver Cromwell as Lord Protector. In March 1649, Milton became Cromwell's secretary of foreign tongues, a largely diplomatic position in which he wrote defenses of the revolution and the abolition of the monarchy. The most famous of these tracts is *The Tenure of Kings and Magistrates* (1649), in which Milton defended regicide (the killing of kings) in the interest of the national good. Milton used poetry as a personal response to the events in his life, whether political or familial.

By the time Cromwell died in 1658, it seemed clear to most observers that the monarchy would soon be restored. Cromwell had become too much of a military autocrat. In addition, Puritan rule resulted in a life with so little joy that both Cromwell and Puritanism had gradually become every bit as unpopular as the rule of Charles I had been two decades earlier. The Commonwealth officially ended in 1660 when Parliament offered to restore Charles II to the throne upon his promise of greater religious tolerance. Parliament also asked for a general amnesty for those involved in the civil war. Charles II returned to England in May 1660 as king. The amnesty did not include the people who had been directly responsible for the execution of the king's father, Charles I. Charles II's promise of religious tolerance was rescinded a year after the king returned.

In the fall of 1659 Milton was jailed for his propagandist writings and his support of Cromwell's Commonwealth. Milton's former secretary, the poet Andrew Marvell, was influential in securing his release from prison in December 1659. In 1663 Milton married Elizabeth Minshull and retired from public life; he returned to tutoring students and began writing his great epic, *Paradise Lost, Poem in Ten Books*, which was published in 1667. *Paradise Regain'd* and *Samson Agonistes* were published in 1673. Milton reissued *Paradise Lost* in twelve books in 1674. He died on November 8, 1674, probably of gout, and is buried at St. Giles-without-Cripplegate Church, in London, England.

POEM TEXT

When I consider how my light is spent,
Ere halt my days, in this dark world and wide,
And that one Talent which is death to hide,
Lodg'd with me useless, though my Soul more bent
To serve therewith my Maker, and present   5
My true account, lest he returning chide;
"Doth God exact day-labor, light denied,"
I fondly ask; But patience to prevent
That murmur, soon replies, "God doth not need
Either man's work or his own gifts; who best   10
Bear his mild yoke, they serve him best; his State
Is Kingly. Thousands at his bidding speed
And post o'er Land and Ocean without rest:
They also serve who only stand and wait."

POEM SUMMARY

Lines 1–2

"When I Consider" begins with a phrase familiar to readers who know Shakespeare's sonnets. Milton borrowed the opening phrase from Shakespeare's 1609 "Sonnet XV," in which he notes the transient quality of life. "When I Consider" is a reference to Shakespeare's sonnet with a reminder that age brings the failings of the human body. In the first line, the poet considers his light or his sight, which has diminished. The passing of years has brought him to a time in his life in which his sight, which had guided him, is gone. The opening line acknowledges not only the loss of his physical sight but also the loss of the perfection of youth, as line 2 makes clear.

The opening lines of "When I Consider" contain a plaintive recognition that the poet has half of his adult life remaining and is now blind. The reference to half his days suggests two possible explanations. If the sonnet was written in 1652, half of his days would be forty-four,

MEDIA ADAPTATIONS

- *Milton the Puritan: Portrait of a Mind* (1977) is an audiobook of the biography by A. L. Rowse. The book is read by Stuart B. Courtney. An audiocassette was published by Books on Tape.

- Derek Jacobi narrates a selection of Milton's poems on *Great Poets: John Milton*, released by Naxos AudioBooks in 2008. Several of the poems have been set to music.

- *Penguin English Verse: Volume 2, The Seventeenth Century, Donne to Rochester*, a 1999 recording of several of Milton's poems, also includes poetry by several of his contemporaries.

- Milton's epic poem *Paradise Lost* has been recorded multiple times. A 2007 recording by Blackstone Audio contains some paraphrasing of sections of the poem.

- A 1995 Naxos recording of *Paradise Lost*, narrated by Anton Lesser, is a slightly abridged reading.

- An unabridged reading of *Paradise Lost*, narrated by Fredrick Davidson, was recorded by Blackstone in 1994 and is available in used copies.

Milton's age that year. That would suggest that he expected to live until age eighty-eight, but the life span of a man in the mid-seventeenth century was generally about seventy years. Milton's father lived into his mid-80s, but it remains unlikely that Milton was speaking so literally about half his life having passed. Another possibility is that Milton was writing about his adult life. If he is suggesting that he was an adult upon completing his B.A. at Cambridge in 1629, half his adult life would be in 1654, when Milton was 46. Exactness about age and dates is a modern attribute. In Milton's lifetime, people were much more casual about age. Milton could easily conflate two or three years for poetic necessity. Hence, it is likely that

in 1652, Milton laments that half his professional life has passed. The last half of his professional life will be spent in the dark, his sight now extinguished.

Lines 3–4

In line 3, Milton speaks of his talent as a poet, which recalls the parable of the talents, found in Matthew 25:14–30. Jesus tells of a man who is given a talent; instead of using the talent, he buries it and is then punished by his master. Milton has a creative skill, which he fears has thus far been wasted. Thus when Milton writes in line 3 that he has but one talent, which has remained hidden, he is expressing concern that he has not yet written the great epic that he had always intended to write. This is a concern that Milton also wrote of in Sonnet VII, "How Soon Hath Time," and in *The Reason for Church Government*.

In line 4, Milton continues his lament for his wasted talent. The talent that he has long cherished and nourished remains within but is stagnant with disuse. However, Milton counters the lament for his unproductive talent with an expression of faith. He explains that while his talent lies fallow and unused, his soul is even more directed toward serving his God. The poet uses the word *bent*—he has an artistic bent, a creative proclivity, which although it remains untested, still reflects his desire to use his abilities.

Lines 5–6

Line 5 begins with a continuation of Milton's claim that his soul is directed to serve God. His use of the word *more* establishes that his blindness has made him even more determined to serve God, his maker, the master of the biblical Parable of the Talents. His heart is even more turned toward honoring God than in the past.

With the second phrase of line 5, Milton begins an explanation that continues in line 6. The poet will present God with an honest accounting of himself and wants to remove any doubt that he has been letting his talent lie fallow. His plans for the future are now complicated by his blindness, but they still remain within him. When Milton began losing his sight, his detractors claimed that his blindness was God's punishment for his support of Cromwell and of the deposing and beheading of Charles I. Milton had always planned on writing a great English epic, and while he certainly would not have given credence to the notion that God was punishing him, he is mindful of the need to justify his use of this talent, in case God, the "Maker" of line 5, returns and admonishes him, demanding an accounting.

Lines 7–8

In line 7, Milton imagines what he might say when God returns to ask about his use of his talent. *Exact* also means to require, and thus he is asking if God would require a full day's labor from a man who is now blind. This line recalls another parable, found in Matthew 20:1–16, in which a vineyard owner hires men to work for him and pays all the men the same day's wages regardless of how long they worked. The men complain and the owner responds that he treats all who serve him the same way. This parable is a reminder that God is generous to all who serve him, including those who have served only a short time. Milton is asking what is expected of him now that his circumstances have changed. The use of *day-labour* reminds readers that he is now blind and that work traditionally performed during the day, when it is light, must now be performed in the dark, given that his days are all nights now that he is blind.

Line 8 is the final line of the octave, the first eight-line section of a sonnet, the section that poses a problem or question. The word *fondly* meant *foolishly* in the seventeenth century. Milton acknowledges that his questioning of God in the previous line is foolish. The voice of patience answers the poet. Patience is the voice of Milton's inner being, the voice of God, which the poet imagines responding to his question. Traditionally, the octave ends at line 8 with a period, but Milton modifies the format of the sonnet to continue the thought in line 9. This forces the reader to continue reading without stopping, hastening on to the next point, which is Milton's intent. He wants readers to know that patience has forestalled the complaint.

Lines 9–10

Line 9 of "When I Consider" continues the voice of patience begun on line 8. "Murmur" in this line means complaint; the voice of patience quells the complaint before it can be given voice and reminds the poet that God has no need of man's labor or his gifts. The poet hopes to honor God with the talent given to him by God, but God has no need of these gifts.

Lines 11–12

The final two words from line 10 carry the reader to line 11, where patience reminds the poet that what pleases God most is man's service. In Matthew 11:30, Jesus says that the yoke of belief is an easy burden to bear and will relieve his followers of the heavier burden they carry. The heavier burden is the lack of salvation without God. Milton was devoutly religious, and his turning to God and to Matthew for answers is in keeping with his own deep belief that God offers solace and reassurance to those who ask. Since Milton spent the first 8 lines of this sonnet asking for help, the response in these lines reflects his deep belief that God will comfort him and answer his prayers. The ideas expressed in these lines are intended to carry the reader to this point, which is an important one: service to God is all that is required of man.

In line 12, Milton refers to God as "kingly." This again reminds readers that God has no need of man's work or gifts. The first 11 lines of the poem have all been one sentence, which concludes with the period following the second word in line 12. The phrase at the end of this sentence makes a very quick point that provides the culmination of this first sentence—God is everything. He owns everything and needs nothing because he alone is king over everything. The reference to "thousands" in line 12 recalls the thousands of chariots and of angels who hasten to do God's bidding in Psalms 68:17 and reinforces the earlier notion that God does not need work or gifts from man.

Lines 13–14

Thousands serve God and they do his bidding swiftly throughout the world. The word "post" in line 13 continues the idea of "speed" from line 12. These heavenly servants of God work without rest to fulfill God's requests.

Line 14 is one of the most famous lines of poetry ever written. It is quoted often, even by those who have never heard of Milton and have no knowledge of his sonnet. The voice of patience reminds the poet that there are ways in which he can still serve God: his duty is to wait until he is called to serve. This echoes the words of Jesus in Matthew 24 and 25 where he tells his followers that they must watch and wait because they do not know when the Lord will come. This final line of "When I Consider" reminds the poet that no action is required of him; instead, a

TOPICS FOR FURTHER STUDY

- Milton's poem is really a journey from questioning to knowledge. Write an essay that explores a personal journey that you have made from questioning a choice to the acknowledgment of understanding that your choice was the correct one for you.

- Milton is only one of many notable seventeenth-century poets. Andrew Marvell, George Herbert, Robert Herrick, and Henry Vaughan were also important English poets and contemporaries of Milton. Choose one of these poets to research and create a Web page in which you discuss the poet, his work, and his legacy as a poet. Invite discussion from your classmates and teacher.

- Milton was a Calvinist at the beginning of his adult life, but his later poetry suggests that he was drifting toward Arminianism later in his life. Understanding these different religious beliefs is crucial to understanding his poetry. Research John Calvin and Jacobus Arminius and their respective theological ideas. Then create a poster presentation using Glogster (or a similar online poster program) in which you compare these two different Protestant viewpoints.

- Jorge Luis Borges was a twentieth-century Argentine poet who composed several poems about his blindness. One poem in particular provides a good comparison to "When I Consider." Compare Milton's seventeenth-century sonnet with Borges's sonnet "On His Blindness." Write an essay in which you compare the structure, tone, and themes of the two sonnets.

- Arnold Adoff writes poems for young adults. In *Slow Dance Heartbreak Blues*, he focuses on poetry about teenagers and their concerns. Read "Listen to the Voice in Your Head," in which Adoff deals with disappointment and the realization that the poem's speaker will never achieve what he hopes. Consider how Adoff's poem differs in tone and content from Milton's poem. Prepare an evaluation of the differences that you noted and present your findings to your classmates.

- Milton's poem is about his fear that his blindness might prevent him from being able to achieve all that his talents had promised. Write your own poem that explores a concern that you have about your future plans. Use the same opening phrase that Milton uses in "When I Consider." When you have completed your poem, write a brief evaluation of your work, comparing it to Milton's poem. In your written critique of your poem, consider what you learned about the difficulty of writing poetry about life's disappointments.

- Many contemporary poets create audio recordings of themselves reading their poems. Milton's life predated the kinds of technology that would have allowed him to record his poetry. As a consequence, it is not possible to really hear the poem as the poet intended it to be heard. Create your own audio recording of Milton's poetry. Choose at least two or three of Milton's sonnets and record them aloud. Ask at least two of your classmates to read the same poems and record their readings as well. Then listen carefully to the recordings that have been made and write a short reaction paper in which you discuss the differences that you noted in these readings. Consider whether the different readers emphasized particular words, whether each reader paused at different words or lines, and whether the tone of the poems has changed with each reading and each reader's interpretation.

- William Blake used art to interpret many of Milton's poems. Use whatever artistic medium fits your talents and create your own interpretation of this poem on the questioning of destiny and faith. After you have completed your art project, write a short reflective paper in which you discuss what you learned about Milton's poem when you interpreted it artistically.

willingness to serve if asked to do so is all that is needed. Additionally, the fact that the poet "stands" might indicate that he has not fallen to Satan. For Milton this sonnet is more than a poem. It is a reflective meditation in which he works through his purpose in life, now that he is blind. The sestet (the last six lines of a sonnet) provides a contemplative resolution to the question posed in the octave.

THEMES

Faith

Milton sets up a dialogue with God in "When I Consider" in which he wonders about his ability to serve God. Half his life is over and he thinks he has not fulfilled all that his talent had predicted. Now he is blind, and in his dismay at the loss of his sight, Milton questions how he can complete the work that he was sure God had always intended him to accomplish. He discusses the most difficult moment of his life and wonders if he will still be able to write the national epic he had always planned to write, and if not, in what way will he be able to serve God. The first part of the sonnet, the octave, is focused on Milton's questioning of how best to serve God if he is blind; the sestet, the last six lines of the poem, is the voice of patience, of God, who provides the answer. Milton is told that those believers who wait patiently for the time when they are called upon to serve God are also serving God by simply waiting. By standing, of course, the poet has not fallen to sin and to Satan. In patience, rather than in despair, God provides the answer and reassurance the poet seeks. Thus Milton's faith in God provides the comfort he needs to continue serving God in spite of the loss of his sight.

Patient Suffering

During much of Christian history, and certainly throughout the period in which Milton was writing, patience was an important facet of Christian life. Patient suffering was regarded as a virtue that would lead to greater faith in God: if people could endure their suffering on Earth, they would be rewarded by a better life in heaven with God. This need to embrace the idea of a heavenly reward reflects the difficulty of living during a time when plague, poverty, and high infant mortality rates kill many people. The Book of Job is the ultimate model of patient suffering, in which the sufferer endures much but is ultimately rewarded for his enduring faith in God. In the concluding lines of "When I Consider," Milton embraces the concept of patient suffering. His blindness is difficult to endure, but the reward is in serving God.

Regret

In line 3, Milton refers to his talent as a poet. Milton worries that he will be damned for not having used the talent he was given. Line 3 recalls the Parable of the Talents in Matthew 25:14–30, in which Jesus tells the story of a man who is given a talent that he does not use. Milton has a creative skill, which thus far he fears has been wasted. Thus when Milton writes in line 3 that he has but one talent, which has remained hidden, he acknowledges the responsibility that accompanies the endowment of a talent given by God. The pattern of Milton's concern about having wasted talent is one of clear progression. In a sonnet written at age twenty-four ("How Soon Hath Time," also known at Sonnet VII), he was concerned that he had not yet fulfilled his talent. Ten years later, at thirty-four, Milton expresses the same concern in a tract on church government (*The Reason for Church-Government Urged against Prelaty*). Finally at age forty-four, Milton turns once again to the theme of wasted talent in "When I Consider." Knowing that Milton keeps returning to this theme reminds readers that the fear that he has been wasting his talents is a very important issue for the poet.

STYLE

Sonnet

A sonnet is a fourteen-line poem. There are basically two different kinds of sonnets. The Petrarchan or Italian sonnet is named for the fourteenth-century Italian poet Petrarch, who was the earliest major poet to use the form, with which he wrote love poems. The Italian sonnet is divided into an octave of eight lines, in which a proposition or problem is presented, and a sestet of six lines, in which there is a resolution or answer. The rhyming pattern, called the rhyme scheme, of the octave is *abba abba*. The rhyme scheme of the sestet varies; one of the most common patterns, *cde cde*, is the one used by Milton in "When I Consider." Although Milton often varies the usual Italian formula for

Hands folded in prayer (Supri Suharjoto / Shutterstock.com)

the final six lines that make up the sestet, in writing "When I Consider," he uses the Italian form without change to the rhyme.

The English sonnet is called the Shakespearean sonnet because Shakespeare was the greatest writer to use this form. He altered the Italian sonnet to reflect his own needs and objectives. The rhyme scheme of the octave of the Shakespearean sonnet is *abab cdcd*. As in the Italian sonnet, there is a break in the thought after the octave, and the sestet continues with the rhyme scheme *efef gg*. There is another thought break after line 12, and the final two lines forming what is called a rhyming couplet.

Although Milton composed sonnets in the seventeenth century, his sonnets reflect both the style and content, though modified, of the typical sixteenth-century sonnet. Shakespeare and other English poets altered the sonnet, and Milton altered it again to reflect the needs of his poetry. Milton took what he wished from the Italian sonnet, largely the octave's rhyme, and created a sestet that reflected his own themes. Content, too, is open to modification. Where

Shakespeare used the sonnet to explore a variety of secular ideas, the poets who followed in the early seventeenth century turned to religion, creating a dialogue with God in their sonnets. The pinnacle of this adaption of the traditional sonnet is reached with Milton, who found the sonnet a useful vehicle for exploring time, politics, and his own personal pain, as well as reaffirming his belief that God had not abandoned him.

Enjambment

Enjambment occurs when a line of poetry continues onto the following line. Milton makes frequent use of this run-on line technique in "When I Consider." For example, line 3 extends into line 4, with a continuation of the complaint that the poet's talent is lodged within him unable to be used. An even more dramatic instance is at line 8, which one would expect to end with a period, but in this sonnet there is no period and the poet's thoughts continue without interruption through the following line. This also gives the sonnet a more unified feel, rather than the two-part structure of octave and sestet. Milton's purpose is to move the reader along rapidly from one thought to the next.

Meditative Poetry

Meditative poetry connects meditation to the metaphysical poetry of the sixteenth and seventeenth centuries. Meditative poetry allows the poet the opportunity to reflect upon his inner life and come to an understanding of his relationship with God. Since metaphysical poetry is essentially the psychological analysis of emotions explored in verse form, it is easy to see how such analysis can be wedded to meditation. Puritan belief emphasized examination of the self, which is what Milton is doing in "When I Consider" as he explores his response to his blindness and his continuing relationship with God.

Parable

A parable is a story that teaches a lesson. It is a brief allegory, which in turn is an extended metaphor, in which objects or persons in a story are equated with meanings outside the story. Parables differ from allegory or metaphor in that they most often refer to matters of spiritual belief, which are made clearer through a story. Milton refers to parables frequently in "When I Consider." The Gospel of Matthew is rich in parables and Milton uses several in this poem, most notably the Parable of the Talents.

Paradox

In the final line of his sonnet, Milton creates a paradox. A paradox is a statement that initially appears contradictory but upon closer examination is understood to be true. Paradox is closely associated with philosophy and theology, where it is understood that language is conceptual, rather than literal. Milton's final line in "When I Consider" claims that the poet will serve even when he does nothing. However, the deeper meaning is that the poet also serves God when he stands and does not fall to Satan's temptation.

HISTORICAL CONTEXT

Political Turmoil

Milton's writings reflect seventeenth-century political, religious, and environmental influences. Milton was born into a traditional Royalist family during the reign of James I (1603–1625). Yet he supported the revolution, the execution

of Charles I in 1649, and the role taken by Oliver Cromwell, who controlled government from 1649 to 1658. The first battle of the civil war in 1642 capped years of tension and conflict between King Charles I and Parliament. Parliament had tried for several years to control finances and limit the king's lavish spending. Charles was supported by the nobility and wealthy landowners, as well as by the Anglican Church, or the Church of England. Parliament had more support in towns and cities. In 1643, Cromwell, who had been a member of Parliament, took control of the army that represented Parliament and the Scots, and in 1646, defeated the Royalist army and King Charles. Rather than surrender to Parliament, Charles surrendered to the Scots, who sold the king to Parliament for a monetary reward. The army did not set out to topple or execute a king. The arrogance and inflexibility of Charles I and his inability to compromise led to his beheading. After he briefly escaped in 1648, civil war broke out again. At that point it became clear that Charles would have to die before peace would be lasting. The execution of Charles I in January 1649 raised new questions about the divine rights of kings, upon which English government had long rested. Milton attempted to answer concerns about the execution of Charles I with his prose work *The Tenure of Kings and Magistrates*, written just weeks after the death of Charles. In this text, Milton justifies the execution of a bad king as necessary for the well-being of the citizens.

What happened to lead to the execution of a king? Part of the reason was the rise of the middle class. Banking investments created money and gave the middle class some power over the aristocracy. The middle class lent money to the nobility and royalty. The sons of the middle class were educated at Cambridge and Oxford. Education brought more power, which in turn created questions about the political and social separation of the middle class from the nobility. The increase in taxes and the corruption of the Stuart kings angered the middle class, who were resentful of the art collections and the theater of royalty. For many years the king had petitioned the dramatist, Ben Jonson, to write masques for performance. These were exorbitantly expensive to stage and the king and the nobility increased taxes to cover the costs. Ultimately this conflict over money, combined with the disbanding of Parliament and unfair taxation, proved to be more powerful than concept of the divine right

COMPARE & CONTRAST

- **Mid-1600s:** In 1642, the great Elizabethan and Jacobean theaters of Shakespearean fame are closed by the Puritans, who claim the theaters offend God.

  Today: Theater life in London thrives. Shakespeare's Globe theater was rebuilt in 1997 on the site of the original Globe. London is also home to the Royal Shakespeare Company, as well as to many West End theaters and proudly calls itself the theater capital of the world.

- **Mid-1600s:** In 1649, Charles I of England is beheaded. The monarchy is abolished and England is declared a commonwealth and free state under the rule of Parliament. In 1653 Oliver Cromwell is installed as Lord Protector of the Commonwealth.

  Today: England is governed by Parliament but retains the monarchy. The Parliament has two chambers, upper and lower. The upper is the House of Lords, composed equally of senior bishops from the Church of England (called the Lords Spiritual) and hereditary or life peers (called the Lords Temporal). The lower chamber is the House of Commons, elected by the people.

- **Mid-1600s:** In 1651, the English philosopher Thomas Hobbes publishes *Leviathan*, in which he argues that citizens must be willing to give up their individual rights and submit to a sovereign, who will provide complete protection without challenge or questioning.

  Today: Individual rights are often analogous to human rights. The Human Rights Watch (www.hrw.org) posts dozens of human rights violations around the world, including recent incidents of torture by British security services in Pakistan, who claim they are protecting British citizens.

- **Mid-1600s:** The first coffee house opens in London. Initially, coffee houses are meeting places for merchants to gather, but their popularity makes them popular gathering spots for men to discuss politics and share opinions. Within fifty years, there will be more than 1,000 coffee shops in London.

  Today: Coffee house are ubiquitous. In addition to the many national chains, local coffee shops are popular sites for gathering to read the newspaper, meet friends, or make use of free WiFi service.

---

of kings. Milton was a young man in the period leading to civil war when he began writing political tracts in support of Parliament and the rights of men. He was also the educated son of a middle-class father who was transformed from royalist to revolutionary by the political turmoil of the mid-seventeenth century.

Religious Turmoil

It was not just the divine right of kings that was questioned by the newly wealthy middle class. The authority of the church was also questioned. The new middle class could read the Bible and understand it and they revolted against the Anglican Church, the official church of England's monarchy. A more radical religious element, Puritan Calvinism, was in direct conflict with the ceremony and corruption of the Anglican Church and the Roman Catholic influence of King Charles's Spanish queen. Every aspect of religion was debated and became cause for greater conflict. The controversies included ritual practices and ecclesiastical appointments of bishops. There were also basic conflicts about predestination, a Calvinist doctrine, and free will, a Catholic belief. The king, who was the official head of the Church of England, allowed theater and sports on Sundays, which deeply offended the Puritans, who thought that the Sabbath should be devoted to prayer. While the Anglicans

---

Clouds and moon, representing darkness and light *(Shukaylov Roman | Shutterstock.com)*

wanted to retain their traditions, ceremonies, and church hierarchy, the Puritans wanted to "purify" the church and eliminate everything not directly contained within the Bible.

Both James I and his son Charles I were hostile to Puritan demands for religious reform, and Charles I tried to prevent Puritan preaching and the publication of Puritan religious texts. Ultimately this religious conflict was one of the causes of the English Civil War and played a role in the Puritan settlement of North America. Before Charles I was executed in 1649, the largely Calvinist Parliament abolished the Anglican Church, and the Puritans passed many laws eliminating Sunday entertainment and placing many restrictions on behavior. Much of this religious turmoil is reflected in Milton's poetry and in his prose treatises; many of Milton's poems attack the Anglican and Catholic churches. Milton was a Calvinist and was a deeply religious man who firmly believed in God and salvation. His Calvinism is evident in "When I Consider," in Milton's patient acceptance of God's ultimate plan for the poet, who is still able to serve, even if blind.

CRITICAL OVERVIEW

While there are no contemporary reviews of "When I Consider," the importance of Milton's work and the legacy of his poetic talents are well established. In a chapter written for *A Concise Companion to Milton*, John T. Shawcross lists many of the ways that Milton influenced the arts in the 400 years since his birth. For example, British poets Andrew Marvell and John Dryden were influenced by Milton. William Wordsworth, whose poem to Milton, "London, 1802," makes the claim that Milton's voice was as "pure as the naked heavens, majestic, free."

Milton's influence is also found in drama, such as Samuel Becket's dialectical borrowings in *Waiting for Godot*, in which debate and discussion are an essential way to understand truth. The English romantic poet and artist William Blake illustrated many of Milton's works, as did the French painter Gustave Doré. According to Shawcross, the twentieth-century Argentine poet Jorge Luis Borges, who was also blind, was inspired by "When I Consider," to write several poems about his blindness. These are, according to Shawcross, only a few examples of the importance of Milton's legacy.

In the period leading up to the 400th anniversary of Milton's birth, there were several celebrations in recognition of the poet's legacy. Milton's admirers celebrated with multiple readings of all twelve books of *Paradise Lost*. In addition, the Bodleian Library at Oxford University staged an exhibit of Milton's many books and pamphlets, and his birthday was celebrated with lectures and biographical programming. At the same time, many newspapers ran columns praising Milton and his influence on the British literary tradition. In "Milton's Life: Some Aspects Lost and Found in 2 Accounts," *Washington Times* columnist Martin Rubin notes the importance of Milton's literary legacy. Rubin writes that "no other poet but Shakespeare even approaches Milton's presence in English literary and national consciousness." As Rubin reminds readers, Milton was not a dramatist whose plays could be staged and filmed and thus remain familiar fixtures in popular culture. Instead, Milton created work that "is austere, opaque, demanding, ornate, hung about with biblical and classical allusions, steeped in learning." Milton, claims Rubin, "set a standard of achievement at once daunting and inspiring." He also reminds readers that Milton inspired the writers and thinkers who came after him.

In a column for the London *Daily Telegraph*, Simon Heffer writes of how important Milton was not only to poets but to political thinkers. In "If Ever There Were an Hour When We Needed Milton, This Is It," Heffer writes that Milton should be remembered as a journalist who was "driven by his conscience, impelled by an iron grip on logic and powered by a facility with words that sparked fear and anger in his opponents." As Heffer notes, "Milton's influence on our world has been immense. We use his words every day. We quote him, often unknowingly." Heffer, Rubin, and Shawcross all emphasize Milton's enduring legacy and his importance in literary, artistic, and political studies. It is worth remembering that one of the greatest gifts given by Milton is not often recognized and acknowledged by his readers. In *Areopagitica*, Milton argues against state censorship of books and other writings. The importance of that text and Milton's argument against censorship are still evident today in a much cherished freedom to read books and newspapers, regardless of political or religious content. This is perhaps Milton's most important legacy.

CRITICISM

Sheri Metzger Karmiol

Karmiol teaches literature and drama at the University of New Mexico, where she is a lecturer in the University Honors Program. In the following essay, she discusses the importance of the role of patience and the Book of Job in "When I Consider."

"When I Consider," is a testament to Milton's faith in God. In the opening octave of the sonnet, Milton questions God; the concluding sestet, introducing a calmer voice, counsels patience. This reliance upon patience to endure suffering is an important part of seventeenth-century religious thought. In many ways, this sonnet is a reflection of the Book of Job, which embodied the seventeenth-century belief that patient suffering was a test of religious faith. The Book of Job is also founded on faith, the faith that, in the end, God will somehow set right all the suffering of righteous men—if only they are patient. Milton's acceptance of the loss of his sight and his determination to continue with his work, and thus be rewarded by God with a glory comparable to Job's, is an important aspect of "When I Consider." Milton's sonnet reflects not only the poet's response to his blindness, but also his belief that God will reward those believers who suffer patiently for the Lord. For Milton, Job's patient acceptance of his suffering exemplifies the model given by God on which Milton and his contemporaries should pattern their lives.

Patient suffering was a fundamental part of seventeenth-century life. Within this context, the Book of Job was not just a part of the larger biblical text, but a part of every man's life. Job's trials were thought to be an actual historical account, recorded by Moses and designed by God to facilitate the acceptance of suffering as a necessity for the reward believers will receive when God welcomes them to heaven. Samuel Masters, a seventeenth-century clergyman, explains the reality of Job's story in his 1689 text, *The Duty of Submission to Divine Providence*, in which he claims that, "Job lived in the time of the Patriarchs, being a Nephew of Abraham, descended from Esau." Thus the story of Job is not simply a biblical story or legend. It is real, and as such, provides important lessons for mankind. Masters claims that Moses wrote about Job in the Bible and that "he presented this Book to them, to teach them Patience under their Afflictions from Job's Example, and to confirm their Faith and Hope in

WHAT DO I READ NEXT?

- *John Milton: The Major Works*, published in a new edition by Oxford University Press in 2008, is a complete edition of Milton's poetry and many of his prose works, with extensive textual notes.

- Milton's epic poem *Paradise Lost* is available in a 2004 annotated edition published by W. W. Norton. This edition contains sources and background information about the poem, including excerpts from Milton's prose writings, as well as multiple critical essays about the poem.

- Milton was a great admirer of the sixteenth-century poet Edmund Spenser. Spenser's epic poem, *The Faerie Queene*, available in a 1979 Penguin edition, inspired Milton's desire to write a great epic and was an important influence on Milton's epic poem, *Paradise Lost*.

- *A Preface to Milton*, by Lois Potter, published by Longman in a revised edition in 2000, is a slim book that provides background information on Milton and the period in which he lived.

- *Sir Thomas Browne: The Major Works*, published by Penguin Classics in 1977, is a good resource for understanding the theological and philosophical milieu of Milton's world. Browne was a contemporary of Milton and is best known for his essays and treatises that explore religion and melancholy, important issues in seventeenth-century thought.

- *George Herbert and the Seventeenth-Century Religious Poets*, a Norton Critical Edition (1978), contains poems by Milton's contemporaries. This text also includes critical essays on these poets.

- *Out of Sight* (2006), by Robert Rayner, is a novel about a young Chinese girl who is determined to help a friend who is slowly losing his sight. This is a sports novel with fast-moving action and is especially suited for young-adult readers.

- *Aloha Crossing* (2008), by Pamela Bauer Mueller, is the story of a teenager who raises a puppy to be a canine-assist dog for a blind companion. This book explores the difficulties and strength of character that is required in raising a dog and giving him to another person as an assist dog. This book is also well suited for young-adult readers.

---

the Divine." Masters continues his description of Job's usefulness as a "Pattern of Patience, to instruct and support us under the many Troubles to which we are always obnoxious." Masters's purpose in writing of Job was to comfort a bereaved friend with a reminder of the rewards to come from God after the end of earthly suffering. Masters's view of Moses as the author of Job was consistent with Milton's own knowledge of the biblical story.

Certainly Milton was thinking of the promise of heavenly reward when he wrote *The Christian Doctrine*. This treatise articulates Milton's thoughts on patience as a virtue leading to greater faith in God. Milton defines patience as "that whereby we acquiesce in the promises of God, through a confident reliance on his divine providence, power, and goodness, and bear inevitable evils with equanimity, as the dispensation of the supreme Father, and sent for our good." Milton's definition of patience seems to echo that of St. Augustine of Hippo, who wrote in *De Patientia* that "the patience of man, which is right and laudable and worthy of the name of virtue, is understood to be that by which we tolerate evil things with an even mind, that we may not with a mind uneven desert good things, through which we may arrive at better." According to St. Augustine, men should have the patience to endure evil with equanimity so as

> FOR MILTON, JOB'S PATIENT ACCEPTANCE OF
> HIS SUFFERING EXEMPLIFIES THE MODEL GIVEN BY
> GOD ON WHICH MILTON AND HIS CONTEMPORARIES
> SHOULD PATTERN THEIR LIVES."

not to abandon the good through which mankind arrives at a better life. Milton also gives voice to these ideas in his epic poem *Paradise Lost*. In Book XII, as Adam and Eve are preparing to leave paradise, they are told by the Archangel Michael that the secret of happiness lies within themselves if they live lives defined by virtues such as faith and patience.

"When I Consider," with its reliance on the voice of patience to calm and reassure the questioning voice of the octave, reflects the seventeenth-century trust that God will ultimately compensate believers for their suffering. For Milton, at least, this sonnet reflects his own person belief about the importance of patience as a way to endure suffering. Paul Baumgartner notes in his essay "Milton and Patience" that Milton's later writings "manifest a new and real conviction in the Christian virtue of patience and in its corollaries, dependence on and submission to, the will of God." Baumgartner also states that Milton was not born with this patient attitude but rather that his "blindness and the Restoration are partly responsible for a change in Milton." Patience, then, is born of the loss of his sight and the loss of the republic that he had embraced under Oliver Cromwell's leadership. Baumgartner also professes that Milton always had a "nominal" belief in these virtues but that the events of the 1650s forced him to "realize them in terms of experience." Baumgartner continues with a discussion of "When I Consider," in which he mentions that prior to the composition of this sonnet, there are only two references to patience in Milton's poems, while there are seventeen references after he writes this sonnet on his blindness. Noting that Milton was resigned to his blindness, Baumgartner defines patience for Milton as "resignation to the Divine decrees and the acceptance of results, whether immediately good or bad, as belonging to the ultimately

beneficent Providence of God." Baumgartner also feels that Milton's resignation is obvious in the final line of the sonnet and that Milton "is not renouncing action, but rather stating that, like the Angels in Revelation who serve before the throne and wait upon the command of God, man also serves by simply waiting upon the Divine Will." The resolution in "When I Consider" reveals a speaker who is accepting and patient. In adopting a strategy of patient waiting, Milton is modeling himself after a familiar biblical figure who exemplified the idea of patient suffering—Job.

In 1652, Milton's wife died in childbirth, his one-year old son died, and he lost his sight. This was a year of great suffering. The poet was able to find a model of patient suffering in the biblical story of Job, whose story Milton quotes with great frequency in *The Christian Doctrine*. Job has also suffered disappointment and darkness and laments, "when I looked for good, evil came; / and when I waited for light, darkness came." Both Job and Milton ask what it is that God wants of them. However, Job's questioning is an impatient pleading for answers: "Why hast thou made me thy mark? / Why have I become a burden to thee? / Why dost thou not pardon my transgression and take away my iniquity?" In contrast to Job's pleading, Milton's initial question, in which he considers how his light has been diminished, takes on the appearance of reflection. Job and Milton begin their lament in different ways, and both men feel compelled to continue to question God as the reason for their suffering. Job's suffering increases with his willingness to suffer; and, still, he only responds, "Shall we receive good at the hand of God, and shall we not receive evil?" Even when Job can bear his suffering no longer he still refuses to curse God. Instead he curses the day of his birth.

Job's patience with his loss and pain is tremendous, but eventually he begins to question why he must suffer. In anger he says, "I will give free utterance to my complaint; / I will speak in the bitterness of my soul." In considering the problem of impatience in *The Christian Doctrine*, Milton observes that sometimes Job is impatient with God's failure to respond. When Job is finally answered, it is not the voice of patience that replies, but the voice of God telling him to "gird up his loans like a man." Surely, it is human nature to question the reason men must

Man standing by water, waiting (kwest | Shutterstock.com)

suffer. Job's loss of family, wealth, and health have provoked his questioning of God. Likewise, Milton has lost a wife and a son and now his sight. Unlike Job, Milton does not ask why. He only asks how. How can he continue to serve when he is blind? Both men feel that God need not answer their questions; yet both receive answers, though of different kinds. Job is chastised by God and reminded of God's glory: "Where were you when I laid the foundation of the earth?" But patience's answer to Milton is a gentle reminder that God does not need man's labor or his gifts. Both men are made heroes through their faith. Job continues to believe in a faith that offers a heavenly reward for earthly suffering, though he does get a bit testy when God does not promptly provide the requested answers. In like fashion, Milton still seeks to fulfill his obligation to God though he is now blind. Neither man asks for a reward, and yet each trusts in God's implied promise that he will be rewarded for his faith. Milton has no need to

question why God has made man or why God chooses to permit man's suffering. The New Testament and the sacrifice of Christ are the ultimate models of suffering and judgment for Milton. Still, Job does provide a model of misery, undeserving of such pain, and as Samuel Masters has already related, man still needs the Book of Job as a reminder that suffering will eventually lead to greater faith and reward with God.

In writing "When I Consider," Milton is composing an acceptable theological response to his blindness. The nature of the rhetorical use of "when" in the first line moves the text into a reflective mode. Milton is not demanding an answer, he is pondering the problem. But his pondering is akin to a suggestion. Milton would still like an answer. The loss of his sight is a terrible tragedy. The most accepting man still hopes for some word from God; some answer or reason for this loss. In his essay "Outrageous Noise and the Sovereign Voice: Satan, Sin, and

Poetry for Students, Volume 37

Syntax in Sonnet XIX and Book VI of *Paradise Lost*," Stephen Wigler notes that the octave, filled with references to a great loss, is heavy with personal pronouns. Wigler notes that the first-person pronouns "I, me, and my" occur eight times. "When I Consider" is Milton's story, consumed with his own personal sense of loss. The reply, as supplied by patience, moves away from the first-person pronoun and promises an answer applicable to all men, not just to the author of the text. God has no need of Milton's gift, or of Job's piety; rather, he requires that man stand and wait until God needs him.

Like Job, Milton eventually begins to reflect on his loss. Where Job becomes angry because God does not answer, Milton only asks how is he to serve. His response is to find strength in the loss of his sight. In the final lines of his sonnet, Milton accepts his blindness as a gift from God, enabling him to suffer and sacrifice for his faith. As a student of the Bible, Milton knows Job's story well. Masters has already established the familiarity that the average man had with Job, and Milton's level of literacy was certainly far above that of the average man. The Milton in "When I Consider" is a reflective man and not a man in the grip of suffering such as that which befell Job. In his essay "When I Consider: Milton's Sonnet XIX," Thomas Stroup describes Milton's sonnet on his blindness as "a spiritual exercise, an interior drama, an examination of conscience, a contemplation, and a consideration." Milton is reflecting upon his loss of sight and asking God how he can best serve Him. Milton knows he is blameless before God. Thus, his lament in the octave in one of genuine reflection. It is only the query from a man who asks how his work will now be completed. The answer of patience is intended for all men, from Job to Milton.

John Milton lost his sight with half his professional life still remaining. How he felt about the loss is expressed in "When I Consider." The rhetorical question in the sonnet's opening lines seeks no answer. As with Job, God comes through in the end when patience evokes understanding. Job was admired and revered in the seventeenth century as a religious hero who suffered greatly, and yet he was also a man made glorious by God. Milton is always aware of the model set forth by Job. The reflective man, willing to suffer, reminded by patience of the reward from God, finds an expression of his glory in his text. Milton does triumph, before God and before man.

Source: Sheri Metzger Karmiol, Critical Essay on "When I Consider," in *Poetry for Students*, Gale, Cengage Learning, 2011.

Dixon Fiske

In the following excerpt, Fiske offers an interpretation of the opening lines of "Sonnet XIX."

Scholars have struggled for many years now with the implications of the opening lines of Milton's sonnet XIX. I will quote the entire poem for the reader's convenience:

> When I consider how my light is spent,
> Ere half my days, in this dark world and wide,
> And that one Talent which is death to hide,
> Lodg'd with me useless, though my Soul more bent
> To serve therewith my Maker, and present
> My true account, lest he returning chide;
> "Doth God exact day-labor, light denied,"
> I fondly ask; But patience to prevent
> That murmur, soon replies, "God doth not need
> Either man's work or his own gifts; who best
> Bear his mild yoke, they serve him best; his State
> Is Kingly. Thousands at his bidding speed
> And post o'er Land and Ocean without rest:
> They also serve who only stand and wait."

Milton tells us that he is doing his considering "Ere half" his days are spent, and scholars have given various estimates as to what Milton expected his total years to be. But, as Evelyn J. Hinz observes, Milton unequivocally accepts in *De Doctrina* the Psalmist's view (Ps. 90:10) that the natural human life span is seventy to eighty years. This suggests a date of composition between 1642 and 1647, but contradicts the evidence of the Trinity Manuscript that Milton numbered his sonnets chronologically. If he did, sonnet XIX could not have been written before the occasion of sonnet XVIII, the massacre in Piedmont, which was not reported in England until May, 1655. The earlier dating strongly affects our interpretation of the sonnet, for it precludes any reference to Milton's blindness, since that was not complete until 1652, when he was forty-three. Yet the interpretations of most commentators require the later dating, for when Milton refers to his "spent" light, most understand a reference to his blindness, one comparable to many others in his prose and poetry, and one important to the meaning of the poem.

WHEN MILTON WRITES IN SONNET XIX OF HIS GREAT TRIAL 'ERE HALF' HIS DAYS HE SIGNALS HIS CRITICAL AND TRADITIONAL CONFUSION IN THE MIDDLE OF LIFE."

Lysander Kemp and others do suggest an interpretation consistent with the earlier dating. They argue that the spent light solely represents absent inspiration and grace. But in the sonnet Milton says nothing about any specific poetic frustrations or spiritual failures that have forced him to conclude that his inspiration is spent and his talent, therefore, useless. He does, on the other hand, combine the reference to his spent light with a significant allusion (ll. 7–8) to Christ's healing of the blind man in John 9. But this contrary evidence is weakened by the fact that long before he was blind Milton used the same allusion in the letter that he wrote to accompany sonnet VII; and he combined it with an allusion to the parable of the talents, just as he does in sonnet XIX. Of course, he does not in the letter speak in terms of light and dark as he does in the sonnet.

But why in the first place does Milton find it at all significant to refer to the number of his days? He is too great a poet to do it merely for the sake of information. An obvious answer is that he is emphasizing the pathos of his situation. He is blind so young, "Ere half" his days. But I wish to suggest the further probability that he is making use of then familiar scriptural and literary symbolism. The symbolism, I think, importantly sets the stage for the spiritual conflict that Milton dramatizes in the sonnet. Knowledge of it eases at least some of the difficulties that have been so troubling. And, I think, it justifies an important re-interpretation both of the sonnet's later allusions to scripture and of its leading ideas.

Three scholars in passing have already noted the similarity between Milton's opening and the opening of the *Commedia*. But we have had no discussion of how Milton would have understood Dante's situation and so of how recognizing an allusion would really enhance our understanding of sonnet XIX. Dante tells us that in the middle, or half-way point of the road of our life, he found himself lost in a dark wood obviously resembling Milton's "dark world and wide."

> Nel mezzo del cammin di nostra vita
> mi ritrovai per una selva oscura
> che la diretta via era smarrita.

For Milton Dante's lines perhaps represented the most impressive use of the symbolism to which I have referred. But Milton would have known it as well in the works of many later poets. Above all he would have been intimately familiar with the scriptural passages and commentary from which the literary symbolism itself derived.

Milton could have learned directly about Dante's meaning in at least three great Renaissance editions and commentaries on the *Commedia*. Those of Christiphoro Landino and Allesandro Vellutello were frequently published, and Milton probably owned the rarer one by Bernardino Daniello. All three begin their interpretation of Dante's opening lines by referring to a passage in the *Convivio* where Dante argues that both the natural middle and perfection of human life potentially occur in the thirty-fifth year. But this year is itself in the middle of the stage of life called youth ("gioventute"), between childhood, which runs up to the twenty-fifth year, and age, which runs from the forty-sixth to the seventieth year.

This whole twenty year stage of life is the middle of life, and in it Dante and his commentators recognize certain properties that make it the natural time for Dante's vision to have occurred. It is the critical time, they say, when reason can fully awaken, assert itself, conquer appetite, and be perfected. Or it may terribly fail. Daniello explains (p. 1) that the young are too dominated by appetite to change and the old who have not changed are too habituated to vice. So "il divino poeta nostro Dante Alighieri, il quale accorgendosi essere nella profonda, & oscura valle d'error', et cieca ignoranzia nel mezo dell'età sua, si indrizza al monte luminoso della virtù." Turning to virtue, he leaves the blind ignorance of the dark wood, which is, of course, identified with the familiar wood of error.

Petrarch uses the same symbolism several times in the *Rime*. In an early madrigal, for example, he describes finding himself in morally perilous byways, lured into his own wood of error, but making his escape at the critical noon of life:

> vidi assai periglioso il mio viaggio;
> et tornai indietro quasi a mezzo 'l giorno.

Daniello and Vellutello, who wrote commentaries on Petrarch as well as Dante, agree in associating the symbolism of Petrarch's "mezzo 'l giorno" here with Dante's. Just as the critical middle of life may be compared to the middle of a journey, it may be compared to the middle of the day. Another instance of this form of the symbolism seems to occur in *The Tempest*, when Prospero begins his work of conversion just "past the mid season" (I.ii. 239). Ariosto is probably also using the symbolism without comparisons when he says in *Orlando Furioso* that the eighty year old hermit who converts Ruggero was himself converted to his Christian way of life when he was nearly forty, that is, at almost half the *maximum* life allotted to man. The passage and its implications, at least, seem to have recalled the beginning of the *Commedia* to Harington, whose translation of the *Orlando* Milton possessed. And in the sonnets of one Henry Lok, we have the symbolism at length, though without much elegance:

> Into thy vineyard Lord unworthie I,
> Desire to come, to travell out the day,
> Thou calledst me thereto, and didst espie
> Me loytring idle, by the worldes high way:
> At first to come my follies did me stay,
> Whom colde and hunger now to worke compell,
> Though half my dayes be spent, say me not nay,
> The other halfe to the, employed well.

The scriptural allusions in Lok's poem and in the sermon that Ariosto's hermit delivers to Ruggero, incidentally, have much in common with those in Milton's sonnet.

... For understanding Milton's opening lines, undoubtedly the most remarkable scriptural passage is one pointed out in Daniello's commentary on the *Commedia*, the one that Milton probably owned. Dante begins, Daniello says (p. 1) by directly imitating the beginning of Hezekiah's psalm after his sickness (Is. 38:10). In the vulgate quoted, it reads: "In dimidio dierum meorum vadam ad portas inferi." This may be translated: "In the middle of my days, I will go to the gates of hell." The verse and its context show so many connections with Milton and his sonnet that I cite it, even though it is translated differently in Milton's usual texts (Tremellius, Geneva, and King James). For in *De Doctrina* Milton refers to Hezekiah's psalm to illustrate the very argument that patience echoes in the sestet of the sonnet. Hezekiah, we are told, recognizes that merit cannot be the basis for salvation: "although Hezekiah asserts his uprightness in the sight of God," Milton says, "he is so far from considering this as constituting any claim to reward, that he acknowledges himself indebted to the free mercy of God for the pardon of his sins." Thus, in the critical middle of life, Hezekiah suffers a trial of faith. He descends into deadly confusion, to hell in the vulgate, but he triumphs when he recognizes the inadequate merit of his "perfect heart" (Is. 38:31), and relies faithfully upon God. That is also the pattern of sonnet XIX.

The tradition behind Milton's reference to half his days allows us, I think, to interpret more loosely those arithmetical implications that have created so many difficulties in the dating of sonnet XIX. Milton could not have avoided invoking the symbolism whose extensive background we have traced, and the symbolism encouraged poets to see far more significance in the general period than in the precise arithmetical half of life between thirty-five and forty. By Dante's figures, admittedly, even the middle period of Milton's life ended before 1655, the year of composition suggested by the manuscript evidence. Readers may prefer Parker's dating of 1651 or 1652, though no longer, I hope, because they would agree with his theory that Milton is alluding to half the life span he expects as result of his father living to the age of eighty-four. Yet the manuscript evidence for the chronological arrangement of the sonnets is both very strong and too little studied. As I have said, that suggests composition after May, 1655, and I would urge dating the poem in the latter part of that year. In 1655 Milton was forty-six, while Dante says that the middle period ends at forty-five. But that seems close enough. Milton's blindness became complete in 1652, within the period, and Milton still had every reason three years later to see it as the culminating trial of his middle years. We certainly do not have a good reason any longer for accepting a dating much before 1652, when blindness could not furnish the otherwise lacking motivation for the impatient outburst described in the sonnet.

The symbolic implications of Milton's opening lines are meant to characterize his situation far more sharply and severely than has been realized. Most discussions of sonnet XIX, including two recent ones by Hinz and Joseph Pequigney, do not take the speaker's initial confusion very seriously. (The speaker is Milton's impatient self.) Hinz, like Kemp, believes that the octave documents a loss of the poetic "light" of inspiration and argues that this would not be sinful, though she seems to recognize a movement from impatience (surely sinful) to patience. Pequigney also agrees with Kemp, suggesting that the octave shows more despondency and self-concern than rebellion. Only the latest commentator, Thomas B. Stroup, emphasizes the speaker's great pride and distrust of God in the octave. But though Stroup presents an excellent account of Milton's general ideas in the poem, Stroup and most commentators have been misled by some of the speaker's vital deviations from those ideas.

Milton's opening symbolism is meant to prepare us for critical spiritual confusion in the octave, for an argument of insidious intent leading to the foolish and rebellious question that patience prevents. It is also meant to prepare us for the speaker's unknowing abuse of the very scriptures and scriptural symbolism that would otherwise enable him to understand his situation. The irony is common in medieval and Renaissance poetry. In the beginning, he surely perceives only the pathetic implications that I have already noted. Not only is he blind, but blind so young, "Ere half" his days. Under the stress of his great loss, he is blind to the deeper implications of his words, to the terrible dangers of spiritual failure in the middle of life. He does not even remember the context of the Psalmist's allusion to our three-score years and ten: "Teach us to number our days," the Psalmist prays only two verses afterwards, "that we may apply our hearts unto wisdom" (90:12).

The confusion continues when the speaker complains about his useless talent. Students of the sonnet have generally believed that Milton is referring to his poetic talent, though there have been other suggestions. Blindness (or lack of inspiration) seems at least at times to have rendered his poetic (or political or spiritual) talent useless. But we must recognize that whatever Milton's speaker believes that talent

to be, he must, given his assumptions, be wrong. He asserts that the talent is "useless," a condition for which God must be responsible, since He supposedly "denied" the speaker light. (Note the increasing bitterness: the light is only "spent" in the first line.) But the speaker's fear inconsistently arises from the fact that it is "death to hide" the talent, an act that logically only the speaker himself could commit, and he proceeds to deny ever wanting to commit it when he claims that his soul is "more bent / To serve." And then the speaker's notion of the parable leads him to jump to the untenable conclusion that God is in effect malevolent, having committed the incredible injustice of rendering useless the very talent whose use is supposedly essential to the speaker's salvation.

The speaker of the octave very probably does consider his poetic talent the spiritually vital talent for him, but is not his doing so at this point really a precise measure of his confusion and pride? The speaker's assertion that his "Soul" is "bent / To serve ... and present" his "True account" may suggest humility, but such humility must be false, for its immediate result is that "fondly" asked question, that loud "murmur" of disbelief in God's justice. The murmurer presumes to know more and to judge better than God. Concealed in his determination to serve, then, must be a presumptuous expectation that he may set the terms for his service, very probably for that poetic service that we know Milton had long dreamed of performing. But, as Foxell suggests (p. 22), might not poetic service be a more glamorous and exalted service than God might allot? That is the possibility that Milton must have faced and to which he is ultimately reconciled in the sonnet.

... We must not, I think, believe that patience is urging a single-minded wait *for* any specific opportunity for active service, certainly not for the glorious service upon which the speaker seems to have insisted, the chance to use the poetic talent. To do so would be to return to the confusion in the middle of life that has been so carefully dramatized in the octave, a confusion that most discussions of the sonnet seem to have repeated. Knowing of Milton's high ambitions, commentators have fallen victim to the speaker's reasoning in the octave, failing to recognize that Milton might subject even those powerful inward promptings to religious scrutiny. Pyle, for example, makes Milton's salvation depend upon his waiting for creative power to return, and remaining "bent" to write *Paradise Lost* "in God's good time" (p. 383). And Stroup identifies Milton's waiting with the contemplative life of the scholar and poet (p. 255). They do not recognize the full implications of patience's distinction. Poetry for Milton is above all an active, educative service (hardly the service of cloistered virtue). Waiting is altogether distinct. Our waiting must be upon God, not upon our ambitions, which may or may not be appropriate. *De Doctrina* defines it as the expression of faithful trust in God, ("fiducia"), which is in turn defined as "an effect of Love … whereby we wholly repose on" Him. Patience is not agreeing that active service is impossible, but saying that if it is, waiting is enough. Her parallelism even suggests that waiting may be equivalent.

When Milton writes in sonnet XIX of his great trial "Ere half" his days he signals his critical and traditional confusion in the middle of life. He prepares us for his moral and intellectual descent into a hell of error before he emerges triumphant through patience. Milton is not content with the righteous stance of the second *Defensio*. Rather, he recognizes and dramatizes in his own person what he later does most strikingly in the characters of Satan and Samson. In his trial he has his own sense of injured merit, itself the product of a deep and irascible impulse in man to usurp God's prerogatives faithlessly. As Hinz suggests (p. 7), the sonnet portrays what Milton calls a "good temptation" in *De Doctrina*. But, as I hope that I have shown, we are to recognize that the temptation described in the octave is critical, the human failing in the middle of life dangerously severe. That is what makes the recovery in the sestet so magnificent.

Source: Dixon Fiske, "Milton in the Middle of Life: Sonnet XIX," in *ELH*, Vol. 41, No. 1, Spring 1974, pp. 37–49.

Gilbert K. Chesterton

In the following excerpt, Chesterton studies the apparent contrast between Milton the man and Milton the poet and considers Milton's place among his contemporaries.

All the mass of acute and valuable matter written or compiled about Milton leaves eternally an unanswered question; a difficulty felt by all, if expressed by few, of his readers. That

> HE WAS NOT SUPREMELY CLASSICAL; BUT HE WAS CLASSICAL IN A TIME WHEN CLASSICISM WAS ALMOST FORGOTTEN."

difficulty is a contrast between the man and his poems. There exists in the world a group of persons who perpetually try to prove that Shakespeare was a clown and could not have written about princes, or that he was a drunkard and could not have written about virtue. I think there is a slight fallacy in the argument. But I wonder that they have not tried the much more tempting sport of separating the author of "L'Allegro" from the author of the *Defensus Populi Anglicani*. For the contrast between the man Milton and the poet Milton is very much greater than is commonly realized. I fear that the shortest and clearest way of stating it is that when all is said and done, he is a poet whom we cannot help liking, and a man whom we cannot like. I find it far easier to believe that an intoxicated Shakespeare wrote the marble parts of Shakespeare than that a marble Milton wrote the intoxicated, or, rather, intoxicating, parts of Milton. Milton's character was cold; he was one of those men who had every virtue except the one virtue needful. While other poets may have been polygamists from passion, he was polygamous on principle. While other artists were merely selfish, he was egoistic.

The public has a quick eye for portraits, a very keen nose for personality; and across two centuries the traditional picture of Milton dictating to his daughters till they were nearly dead has kept the truth about Milton; it has not taken the chill off. But though the mass of men feel the fact Milton after two hundred years, they seldom read the poetry of Milton at all. And so, because Milton the man was cold, they have got over the difficulty by saying that the poet Milton is cold too; cold, classical, marmoreal. But the poetry of Milton is not cold. He did in his later years, and in a fit of bad temper, write a classical drama, which is the only one of his works which is really difficult to read. But taken as a whole he is a particularly poetical poet, as fond of symbols and witchery as Coleridge, as fond of colored pleasures as Keats. He is sometimes sufficiently amorous to be called tender; he is frequently sufficiently amorous to be called sensual. Even his religion is not always heathen in his poetry. If you heard for the first time the line,

> By the dear might of Him that walked the waves.

you would only fancy that some heart of true religious heat and humility, like Crashaw or George Herbert, had for a moment achieved a technical triumph and found a faultless line. If you read for the first time,

> But come, thou Goddess fair and free.
> In heaven yclept Euphrosyne,

you would think that the most irresponsible of the Elizabethans had uttered it as he went dancing down the street, believing himself in Arcady. If you read

> Blossoms and fruits at once of golden hue
> Appeared, with gay enamelled colors mixed,

or

> Silence was pleased. Now glowed the firmament
> With living sapphires,

you would think that all the rich dyes of the Orient and the Middle Ages had met, as they do in some quite modern poet, such as Keats or even Swinburne. If you read the account of the ale and the elf and the Christmas sports in "L'Allegro," you might think them written by the most rollicking of rustic poets; if you read some lines about Eve in *Paradise Lost*, you might think them written at once by the most passionate and the most chivalrous of lovers. *Paradise Lost* is not dull; it is not even frigid. Anyone who can remember reading the first few books as a boy will know what I mean; it is a romance, and even a fantastic romance. There is something in it of *Thalabe the Destroyer*; something wild and magical about the image of the empire in the abyss scaling the turrets of the magician who is king of the cosmos. There is something Oriental in its design and its strange colors. One cannot imagine Flaxman illustrating Milton as he illustrated Homer. Nor is it even true that the rich glimpse of tropical terrors are conveyed in a clear outline of language. No one took more liberties with English, with metre, and even with common sense than Milton; an instance, of course, is the well-known superlative about Adam and his children.

Milton was not a simple epic poet like Homer, nor was he even a specially clear epic poet like Virgil. If these two gentlemen had studied his verse, they would have certainly acknowledged its power; but they would have shrunk from its inversions, its abrupt ellipses, its sentences that sometimes come tail foremost. I might even say that Homer reading Milton might have much the same feelings as Milton reading Browning. He would have found

> Or of the eternal coeternal beam

a trifle obscure, and

> nor sometimes forget,
> Those other two, equalled with me in fate, etc., etc.,

almost entirely unintelligible. In this sense it is absurd to set up Milton as a superlatively clear and classic poet. In the art of turning his sentences inside out he never had an equal; and the only answer is to say that the result is perfect; though it is inside out, yet somehow it is right side out.

Nevertheless, the tradition which puts Milton with Virgil and the large and lucid poets, must possess and does possess some poetic significance. It lies, I think, in this: the startling contrast between Milton and the century in which he lived. He was not supremely classical; but he was classical in a time when classicism was almost forgotten. He was not specially lucid; but he was moderately intelligible in an age when nearly all poets were proud of being unintelligible; an age of one hundred Brownings gone mad. The seventeenth century was a most extraordinary time, which still awaits its adequate explanation. It was something coming after the Renaissance which developed and yet darkened and confused it, just as a tree might be more tangled for growing. The puns that had been in Shakespeare few and bad became numberless and ingenious. The schisms of thought which under Wickliffe and Luther had at least the virtue of heartiness, and were yet full of a human hesitation, became harsh, incessant, exclusive; every morning one heard that a new mad sect had excommunicated humanity. The grammars of Greek and Latin, which the young princes of the Renaissance had read as if they were romances, were now being complicated by bald-headed pedants until no one on earth could read them. Theology, which could always in light moments be given the zest of an amusement, became a disease with the Puritans. War, which had been the sport of gentlemen, was now rapidly becoming the ill-smelling science for engineers it still remains. The air was full of anger; and not a young sort of anger; exasperation on points of detail perpetually renewed. If the Renaissance was like a splendid wine, the seventeenth century might be compared to the second fermentation into vinegar. But whatever metaphor we use the main fact is certain; the age was horribly complex; it was learned, it was crabbed, and in nearly all its art and utterance, it was crooked.

Remember the wonderfully witty poets of Charles I; those wonderfully witty poets who were incomprehensible at the first reading and dull even when one could comprehend them. Think of the scurrilous war of pamphlets, in which Milton himself engaged; pages full of elaborate logic which no one can follow, and elaborate scandals which everyone has forgotten. Think of the tortured legalities of Crown and Parliament, quoting against each other precedents of an utterly different age; think of the thick darkness of diplomacy that covers the meaning (if it had any) of the Thirty Years' War. The seventeenth century was a labyrinth; it was full of corners and crotchets. And against this sort of background Milton stands up as simple and splendid as Apollo. His style, which must always have been splendid, appeared more pure and translucent than it really was in contrast with all the mad mystification and darkness.

Source: Gilbert K. Chesterton, "Milton: Man and Poet," in *Catholic World*, Vol. 104, No. 622, January 1917, pp. 463–70.

David Masson

In this essay, Masson explains the background of "Sonnet XIX."

... The Piedmontese Sonnet certainly, and probably also the preceding Sonnets to Cromwell and Vane, had been written by Milton after he had lost his sight. His blindness, which had been coming on slowly for ten years, and had been hastened by his labour in writing his *Defensio Prima pro Populo Anglicano* in answer to Salmasius (1651), appears to have been complete before the middle of 1652, when he was only forty-four years of age. This appears from a statement of his nephew Phillips in his *Life of Milton*; from one of Milton's own *Familiar Epistles*, giving an exact account of his blindness and of its first symptoms (dated Sept. 28, 1654, and addressed *Leonardo Philara, Atheniensi*); from passages in Milton's prose pamphlets; and from the second of the two subsequent Sonnets to Cyriack Skinner. The fact is corroborated by a minute of the Council of State, of date March 11, 1651–2, appointing Mr. Weckherlin to be assistant to Milton in his Foreign Secretaryship to the Council. At this last date Milton was not quite blind, for there are signatures of his to nearly as late a date; but his blindness was then such at least as to require assistance to him in his official duties. April, May and June 1652 appear to have finished the disaster. Milton, therefore, we are to imagine, after having been Secretary to the Council of State for a year or two with his sight failing, continued to act as Secretary through Cromwell's Protectorate (1653–58) with his sight totally gone. Almost all that he had written after the close of 1651, if not for a while before that, had been written by the method of dictation; and hence his Sonnets to Cromwell and Vane do not appear in his own hand among the Cambridge MSS. It is positively certain, however, that the Sonnet on the Piedmontese Massacre, and all the State Letters for Cromwell or his son Richard, and all the contemporary pamphlets, were produced by dictation. The blindness that had thus fallen upon Milton in the prime of his manhood, and that shrouded the last two-and-twenty years of his life in darkness, was felt as the greatest of calamities by himself, and was pointed to with coarse exultation by his enemies, at home and abroad, as a divine judgment on him for his defences of the execution of Charles I, and for the part he had otherwise taken in the English Revolution. Again and again in Milton's later writings, in prose and in verse, there are passages of the most touching sorrow over his darkened and desolate condition, with yet a tone of the most pious resignation, and now and then an outbreak of a proud conviction that God, in blinding his bodily eyes, had meant to enlarge and clear his inner vision, and make him one of the world's truest seers and prophets. The present Sonnet is one of the first of these confidences of Milton on the subject of his blindness. It may have been written any time between 1652 and 1655; but it follows the Sonnet on the Piedmontese Massacre in Milton's own volume of 1673.

Source: David Masson, "Sonnet XIX: On His Blindness," in *The Poetical Works of John Milton,* edited by David Masson, 1890, pp. 231–32.

SOURCES

Augustine of Hippo, St., *De Patientia*, in http://www
.episcopalnet.org, http://www.episcopalnet.org/READ
INGS/Hippo/Patience.html (accessed May 12, 2010).

Baumgartner, Paul R., "Milton and Patience," in *Studies
in Philology*, Vol. 60, 1963, pp. 204–08.

Brandon, David, *Life in a 17th Century Coffee Shop*,
Sutton, 2007, p. 2.

"Civil War of Ideas," in *The Norton Anthology of English
Literature: Norton Topics Online*, http://www.wwnorton
.com/college/english/nael/17century/topic_3/welcome.htm
(accessed May 27, 2010).

Harmon, William, and Hugh Holman, *A Handbook to
Literature*, 11th ed., Pearson Prentice Hall, 2009, pp. 11,
199, 336–37, 342, 397–98.

Heffer, Simon, "If Ever There Were an Hour When We
Needed Milton, This Is It," in *Daily Telegraph* (London,
England), December 10, 2008, p. 22.

Holy Bible, Revised Standard Version, Thomas Nelson &
Sons, 1952, pp. 30–33, 526, 530, 550, 557, 560.

Hooker, Richard, "The European Enlightenment, the
Case of England," in *World Civilizations Home Page*,
http://www.wsu.edu/~dee/ENLIGHT/ENGLAND.HTM
(accessed May 27, 2010).

Johansson, Daniel, "London's Vibrant West End Theatre
Scene," in *TheatreHistory.com*, http://www.theatrehistory
.com/british/londons_vibrant_west_end.html (accessed
May 27, 2010).

Jokinen, Anniina, "Life of John Milton," in *Luminarium
.org*, http://www.luminarium.org/sevenlit/milton/
miltonbio.htm (accessed May 20, 2010).

Masters, Samuel, *The Duty of Submission to Divine Providence*, London, 1689, pp. 14–15.

Milton, John, "The Christine Doctrine," in *The Works of
John Milton*, Vol. 17, translated by Charles R. Sumner,
Columbia University Press, 1934, p. 67.

———, "How Soon Hath Time," in *Complete Poems and
Major Prose*, edited by Merritt Y. Hughes, Odyssey
Press, 1957, p. 76.

———, *Paradise Lost*, in *Complete Poems and Major
Prose*, edited by Merritt Y. Hughes, Odyssey Press,
1957, p. 467.

———, *The Reason of Church Government Urged Against
Prelaty*, in *The Norton Anthology of English Literature*, Vol.
1, 8th ed., edited by Stephen Greenblatt, W. W. Norton,
2006, pp. 1812–15.

———, "When I Consider," in *Complete Poems and
Major Prose*, edited by Merritt Y. Hughes, Odyssey
Press, 1957, p. 168.

"Parliament and Crown," http://www.parliament.uk/
about/how/role/parliament-crown// (accessed May 27,
2010).

Rubin, Martin, "Some Aspects Lost and Found in 2
Accounts," in *Washington Times*, July 27, 1997, p. B8.

Shakespeare, William, "Sonnet 15," in *Shakespeare's
Sonnets*, edited by Katherine Duncan-Jones, Arden
Shakespeare, reprinted 2005, p. 141.

Shawcross, John T., "The Life of Milton," in *The Cambridge Companion to Milton*, edited by Dennis Danielson,
Cambridge University Press, 1989, pp. 1–219.

———, "'Shedding Sweet Influence,': The Legacy of
John Milton," in *A Concise Companion to Milton*, edited
by Angelica Duran, Wiley-Blackwell, 2006, pp. 28–42.

Stroup, Thomas B., "'When I Consider': Milton's Sonnet
XIX," in *Studies in Philology*, Vol. 69, 1972, pp. 242–58.

Tracer, James, *The People's Chronology*, Henry Holt,
1992, pp. 239–45.

"The Two House System," http://www.parliament.uk/
about/how/role/system/ (accessed May 27, 2010).

"UK: Torture Inquiry Decisions Important First Step,"
in *Human Rights Watch*, http://www.hrw.org/en/news/
2010/05/21/uk-torture-inquiry-decision-important-first-
step (accessed May 27, 2010).

Wigler, Stephen, "Outrageous Noise and the Sovereign
Voice: Satan, Sin, and Syntax in Sonnet XIX and Book
VI of *Paradise Lost*," in *Milton Studies*, Vol. 10, 1977,
pp. 155–65.

Wordsworth, William, "London, 1802," in *English
Romantic Writers*, edited by David Perkins, Harcourt
Brace Jovanovich, 1967, p. 288.

FURTHER READING

Bradford, Richard, *The Complete Critical Guide to John
Milton*, Routledge, 2001.

> This guide to Milton's work provides a discus-
> sion of his life and the period in which he was
> writing, while making connections to the texts.

Danielson, Dennis, ed., *The Cambridge Companion to
Milton*, 2nd ed., Cambridge University Press, 1999.

> This book contains a selection of critical essays
> about Milton's works. In addition to an over-
> view of the poet's work, the essays provide
> social and historical context.

Fish, Stanley, *How Milton Works*, Belknap Press of Harvard University Press, 2001.

> Fish provides a comprehensive look at Mil-
> ton's work, focusing on Milton's use of lan-
> guage and a close reading of the text and
> ignoring the more common cultural and histor-
> ically based readings of the poet's work.

Lake, Peter, with Michael C. Questier, *The Anti-Christ's
Lewd Hat: Protestants, Papists and Players in Post-
Reformation England*, Yale University Press, 2002.

> This book looks at the production of pamphlets
> in early sixteenth- and seventeenth-century

England and shows how the competing religious communities used those pamphlets to further their own agendas.

Lewalski, Barbara Kiefer, *The Life of John Milton: A Critical Biography*, Blackwell, 2000.
    Lewalski uses Milton's works and a meticulous study of the period to create a comprehensive guide to the poet's life and works.

Smith, David L., *Oliver Cromwell: Politics and Religion in the English Revolution 1640–1658*, Cambridge University Press, 1991.
    Milton was a great admirer of Oliver Cromwell and believed in the goals of the English Revolution. This book, designed for high school readers, provides a good history of Cromwell and of the English Civil War and gives important background information and context for Milton's poetry.

SUGGESTED SEARCH TERMS

When I Consider

When I Consider AND Sonnet XIX

John Milton AND blindness

John Milton AND Sonnet XIX

John Milton AND When I Consider

17th century British poets

John Milton AND English Civil War

John Milton AND Calvinism

John Milton AND patient suffering

John Milton AND Oliver Cromwell

When I Consider AND On His Blindness

The World as Will and Representation

ROBERT HASS

2007

Robert Hass's poem "The World as Will and Representation" is a direct reference to the philosopher Arthur Schopenhauer, who published his most important work, *The World as Will and Representation*, in 1818. Schopenhauer posited that it is through art that human beings are capable of glimpsing the universal truth that resides in the particulars of human experience, and that aesthetic experience can also silence the endlessly desiring nature of the will so that we can glimpse the universal. The silencing of the will, or of desire, is one of the central tenets of Buddhism, a belief system that influenced both writers.

"The World as Will and Representation" is narrative and confessional in nature, and is written in a conversational tone, a style characteristic of much of Hass's work. Hass is a poet who often explores the ways that vernacular language expresses truths of which the speaker might be unaware. Hass is also a poet for whom universal truths are nearly always glimpsed through the mundane details of everyday life; that is, rather than seeking the sublime in elevated language or romantic imagery, Hass seeks to illuminate the ways in which even ordinary moments can be emblematic of larger and more universal truths.

Hass has been a major voice in American poetry since the 1970s, and is particularly representative of a West Coast poetic voice, one that values a conversational tone, a deep attention to

Robert Hass (AP Images)

the natural world, and an appreciation of domestic life. The publication of *Time and Materials: Poems 1997–2005*, the collection in which "The World as Will and Representation" appears, garnered Hass both the National Book Award and the Pulitzer Prize for Poetry, and further solidified his place in the American poetic canon.

AUTHOR BIOGRAPHY

Hass was born on March 1, 1941, in San Francisco, California. He grew up in Marin County, just north of the city, and attended St. Mary's College in nearby Moraga, California, where he majored in biology. He earned both an M.A. and a Ph.D. in English at Stanford University, and he taught at St. Mary's from 1971 to 1989; since 1989 he has taught at the University of California at Berkeley, where he currently holds the Distinguished Chair in Poetry and Poetics. The landscape and culture of the San Francisco Bay area and the northern Sierra Nevada

Mountains, where he has lived for most of his life, form one of the central themes of his work. Hass has three children by his first marriage, Leif, Kristen and Luke, and he is currently married to the poet Brenda Hillman. As of 2010, they lived in Berkeley, California.

Hass's career was launched in 1973 when he won the prestigious Yale Younger Poets prize for his first book of poetry, *Field Guide*. His next volume, *Praise*, which contains his most-anthologized poem "Meditations at Lagunitas," won the William Carlos Williams award in 1979. In 1984 Hass won a MacArthur Fellowship, also known as a "genius grant" because it cannot be applied for, and is granted to those who are doing cutting-edge work in their fields. The MacArthur grant freed him to write *Human Wishes*, which was published in 1989. After the MacArthur grant, he left St. Mary's College and began teaching at the University of California at Berkeley; his next book, *Sun under Wood*, won the National Book Critics Circle Award for Poetry in 1996. In 2007 *Time and Materials: Poems 1997–2005* was published and won the National Book Award in 2007 and the Pulitzer Prize for Poetry in 2008. *The Apple Trees at Olema: New and Selected Poems* was published in 2010. Hass has also worked as a translator on seven volumes of poetry with the Nobel Laureate, Polish poet Czeslaw Milosz. His collaboration with Milosz was a deep influence on his own poetry. Hass has also published works on Robinson Jeffers, the Swedish poet Tomas Tranströmer, and on the haiku of the Japanese poets Basho, Buson, and Issa. He has written two books of essays, *Twentieth Century Pleasures*, for which he won the 1984 National Book Critics Circle Award for Criticism, and *What Light Can Do: Essays on Art Imagination and the Natural World*, published in 2010.

From 1995 to 1997 Hass served two consecutive terms as Poet Laureate of the United States. Because the position is based out of the Library of Congress, Hass moved to Washington, D.C., where he revitalized what had previously been a largely ceremonial position. He wrote a popular weekly poetry column, "Poet's Choice," that was syndicated in many newspapers nationwide. He also cofounded the River of Words project for the purpose of, as the project's Web site states, "connecting kids to their watersheds and imaginations through poetry and art." Hass, a longtime environmental activist, studied biology as an undergraduate and has long believed that learning to observe and understand the natural world is crucial to our understanding of the world as well as to our ability to make art.

POEM SUMMARY

While "The World as Will and Representation" is not written in stanzas, the poem can be divided into units that are loosely defined by elements of imagery and narrative.

Lines 1–3

These lines serve to set the tone and the scene of the poem. The poem opens in a conversational tone with a narrator who seems to be telling a story about an event from his childhood. Like many reminiscences, it starts with an assertion of repetition, that the same thing happened every morning. This assertion is followed in line 2 by the more measured voice of the adult narrator correcting himself, no, he says, not every morning, but most mornings, during a specific period of time when he was about ten years old. What happened during this time was that his father gave his mother a drug that was designed to stop her from drinking alcohol. The first few lines set up the situation. The boy is remembering his father trying to stop his mother from drinking. Readers are plunged into a family drama.

Lines 4–7

In this section of the poem the narrator, staying very close to the point of view of the boy he had once been, explains to the reader, as his father must have explained to him, what the pills are called, and how to administer them to the mother. The narrator also relates the crucial detail that his father does not trust his mother to take the pills, that she must be monitored in a way that renders her childlike, and unparental.

Lines 8–15

In these lines the narrator reflects upon the era of his childhood. It was the mid-twentieth century, and the father he recalls was a man of his time, a time when men wore suits, and went off to work, leaving the women and children at home. The father makes light of the project of these mornings, and of the mother's reluctance to take the drug. The father uses phrases from gangster movies in order to ally the boy to his cause, while seeming to make light of the seriousness of the situation. This language posits that the boy and the man are the authorities, that, to quote another source from popular culture "Father Knows Best." This use of slang from gangster movies further infantilizes the mother. Her attempts to evade taking the medication are posited as mere willfulness, the sort of refusal a toddler makes when attempting to get out of swallowing a bitter medicine.

This section of the poem is not narrated by the boy who experienced it, but by the adult man who is writing the poem. The narrator points out sociological details that would have been invisible to the boy at the time, noting that certain social expectations and gender relations were the norm then, although they no longer are. The narrator, who is now an adult, can also see looking back into the past that perhaps his father's exaggerated winks and his use of the jocular language of the movies were an attempt to make light of the situation for the young boy involved. As the poem continues, the severity of the mother's alcoholism becomes clear, as it must have been to the father, and to some extent to the boy, and yet, the family drama into which we have been invited by the poem is one in which all figures are desperate to play down its severity. This section of the poem is about representation, how we represent ourselves to the outside world, to one another, and to ourselves. The narrator, even as a boy, was uncomfortable with the jocular representation of the father-son morning ritual, but went along with it. As an adult, the sound of those phrases from the 1940s and 1950s, even in old movies, makes him uncomfortable, and his attention wanders as he seeks to distance himself from them.

Lines 16–23

The jocular tone of lines 8 through 15 dissipates as the narrator explains the conflict that lies at the heart of the morning ritual. The pills must be ground up so that his mother does not hide them under her tongue and spit them out later. The father must administer the medication to the mother with enough time so that he can monitor her, making sure she does not vomit it up before he leaves for the day. The implication is given here, without the frivolity of the previous section with which the father tried to cover it up for the boy, that the mother is untrustworthy. The voice of the narrator in this section becomes quite clinical, taking no one's side, but attempting to describe what the boy had been told, and what he knew to be true. In line 17, he describes the danger that the pills could be hidden in the passive voice, not that the mother would hide them, but that they could be hidden, while even in line 21, which is the first time that what the mother wants is directly addressed, where she is seen to have volition of her own, that what she might want is to vomit up the medication. Implied in this statement is the assertion of the mother's will. She does not want the medication. She wants to drink. She wants to drink badly enough that the father is forced to act as a sort of parent to his wife, or as a sort of jailer. The son also admits during this section of the poem that he knows that the reasons his father has given for the procedure and timing of the morning medication ritual are true, that he had not only been told that his mother would do these things, but he had seen her evade the medication. What is implied but not spoken here is that he has seen the effect of his mother's evasion of the medication, the kind of drunkenness that has resulted in his father's monitoring his mother in this way. One might say that this section of the poem is about will, the imposition of the father's will upon the mother, the willful resistance by the mother, and the boy who is caught between them.

Lines 23–28

A shift occurs in the middle of line 23, from the point of view of the boy watching the morning ritual play out, to the adult narrator looking back upon the scene. The narrator wants to portray the weight of the ritual, and as is typical for Hass, he does it through minute examination of the things involved. The father grinds two yellow pills in a glass, reduces them to powder, and then fills the glass with water. He hands it to the mother and watches her drink. The language is interesting here. All the actions are performed by the father. Even the act of drinking on the mother's part is described as something the father watches, not something she actively participates in. The father is wearing a gray suit, the symbol of mid-century patriarchy, and a shirt that the mother has ironed. While the tone of the entire poem is rueful, and even gentle, the actions described are quite brutal. The father, the man in the suit, is forcing the mother to take the medication he administers, and he is monitoring her intake, and ensuring that the drug has taken effect before he leaves her there in the house to iron his shirts. The narrator declares at the outset of this section

that he wants to describe the inexorable feeling of this ritual. However, what the adult narrator describes is the kind of nonconsensual act that is familiar to children, but that is turned upside down by the fact that it is the father who imposes upon his mother, instead of the more normal situation where a parent forces the taking of medication upon the child. This reversal is confusing to the boy, and is perhaps why the boy narrator cannot entirely name the problem. Children are often made to take medication, finish their dinners, or do their homework and are usually monitored by adults as they do so. It is a different thing altogether when one adult imposes upon another adult in this way. It is a difficult scene and one that seems more difficult with the benefit of hindsight. The 1940s and 1950s were a time when both men and women were confined to roles. The father is confined to his suit, with the ironed shirt, the mother is confined to the house, and the boy is confined to childhood.

Lines 29–37

In this section of the poem, the boy narrator seeks refuge from the brutality of the scene, a brutality he does not entirely understand, in the world of popular culture. He retreats to the comics, seeking to mediate the disturbing morning ritual by encasing it in the language of the comics much as the father used the language of detective movies in lines 8–15. The boy narrator retreats to the domestic world of the *Blondie* comic, a world in which a hapless, yet well-meaning father is invisibly managed by his beautiful and competent wife Blondie. The humor in that strip was generated by the ironic distance between Dagwood's language, which sought to position him as the man of the house, the patriarch, the person in charge, and the actions of his kind bombshell of a wife, who always managed to fix his bungles before they caused trouble, all the while reinforcing his image of himself as the one in charge. The domestic happiness of the cartoon, where all problems are resolved as mere misunderstandings in four frames or less, is a far cry from the troubled domestic world Hass portrays in this poem. It is not until lines 35–37 that readers discover the reason the boy narrator is retreating to the comics: there are some mornings when he is left to administer the drugs on his own, times when his father must leave early for work. The father again retreats to the false language of films, using the language of cowboy films to remind the boy that he is in charge now that the father must leave, and that he must put on the mantle of the patriarch in his father's absence.

Lines 38–44

The memory of being left to administer the medication to his mother is so traumatic that even the adult narrator breaks off here, changes the subject the way one does when trying to tell a story, uncertain whether one is getting one's point across. Suddenly the narrator asks the listener to remember a passage in the *Aeneid*, the passage about when all hope has been lost, the great city of Troy is burning, the prophet is shouting from the ramparts, and Aeneas flees, carrying his father and leading his son by the hand, his wife lost in the chaos of disaster. The narrator refers to this image without putting it in context at all. This is one of the great images of lost hope and ruin in all of literature, and Hass places it here in juxtaposition to the moment when the young boy is left in the house with his mother, a woman incapable of caring for him. If the family is like a civilization, this is the moment when the civilization of the boy's family crumbles for him. All hope is lost. He is left alone with the task of preventing his ruined mother from causing herself further damage. The city that is his family is on fire, the hero has fled, and the blind prophet, to whom no one listened, is left shouting from the inner recesses of the chaos. Because the boy is only a boy, he is incapable of expressing this terror, a terror so encompassing that even the adult narrator of the poem, a person of whom it can be believed has survived the wreckage of the childhood he describes, can only express it by importing wholesale one of the great images of ancient literature.

Lines 45–49

Unlike the comics, unlike the movies of the 1940s and 1950s, and unlike the great epics of ancient times, this story has no triumphant or happy ending. In these last few lines of the poem, the boy narrator has been abandoned in the house by his father, left with his mother, whose will to drink is so strong that even after swallowing the drug, even after seeming to capitulate to the will of her husband, and by extension, to the will of society and the medical establishment, the boy watches his mother begin drinking alcohol in her bathrobe at the kitchen table. She drinks, and gags as the medication attempts to work, but her will to drink is stronger than the

medication, and she drinks right through it. The battle over, the boy sits at the kitchen table while the adult narrator looks back on the lesson he learned, a lesson about power and gender, and about what is fair and moral in the world. However, Hass, as a poet, is more interested in asking questions than answering them, and so he is not explicit about the lesson. Rather, he speculates that all of us learn these lessons, but from where? Do we learn these lessons from the dramas we witness at the kitchen table, or from movies, or from the comics, or even from the great dramas of literature? Or do we learn them from the kinds of effort we see at work throughout this poem in which both the boy and the father seek to impose meaning on the central mystery of their family: Why is the mother's will to drink stronger than all else?

THEMES

Fatherhood

While the mother's inability to stop drinking is the drama that drives this narrative poem, much of the content of the poem concerns fatherhood and what it means to be a father. In the 1940s and 1950s, the dominant social model for the family was a unit led by a father who went out into the world to work, while the mother stayed at home to take care of the house and raise the children. This model was reinforced when, after the end of World War II, many women who had been called into the workplace were told that it was now their patriotic duty to quit their jobs so that men could have them, and that they should go home, marry, and raise children. While the family in the Hass poem seems to fit this model of the nuclear family, consisting of a mother, father, and children living in semi-isolation in the suburbs, there are signs throughout the poem that none of these figures is entirely comfortable with his or her role. The father in the poem dresses the part, he even wears a gray suit, which echoes the title of a popular satirical novel of the 1950s that exposed the inner emptiness of this family model, *The Man in the Gray Flannel Suit*. However, the manner in which the father retreats into catchphrases illustrates his anxiety about the role into which he has been cast. As the father, he is supposed to be the "king of his castle" and yet, he cannot control his wife's destructive drinking, not even with the help of

TOPICS FOR FURTHER STUDY

- In "The World as Will and Representation," Hass uses quotations from popular culture of the 1940s and 1950s as an ironic counterpoint to the situation in which the boy narrator is placed. This technique of sampling has been used extensively in contemporary music. Find a song you like, and using YouTube and the video archives of the television networks, find five to seven clips from television sitcoms that you can use to illustrate the song you chose in the ironic manner in which Hass uses phrases from popular culture of the 1940s and 1950s. Then, using a video editing program like iMovie, create a music video in which you sample video clips to enhance or comment upon the lyrics of the song.

- In "The World as Will and Representation," Hass makes reference to Aeneas, hero of the *Aeneid*. Research the *Aeneid*, and the story to which the poem refers. Create a presentation that explains the story to which Hass refers in the poem and explain why you think he used this particular image. How does the story in the *Aeneid* relate to the story in Hass's poem? Then research illustrations of this episode from the *Aeneid* and present your report as a PowerPoint or iPhoto slideshow in which you use visual aids to reinforce your explication of the epic poem.

- Every family is a small culture unto itself, and most families have catchphrases of the sort that the narrator's father uses throughout the poem. Collect catchphrases from older members of your own family and make a list of them. They do not have to be in English; if there are members of your family who speak other languages, be sure to collect their sayings as well. Once you have ten to fifteen phrases, write them down on separate slips of paper and then use them as the starting point for a poem. Play with the placement of the slips of paper until a poem suggests itself to you. What do these phrases mean to the person who uses them? What do they mean to you? How do they illustrate something about your family or culture? Make sure the poem expresses this feeling.

- Read Sherman Alexie's young-adult novel *The Absolutely True Diary of a Part-time Indian*. While Alexie's book is set in a different place and time than "The World as Will and Representation," both works concern young boys who are forced by circumstance to navigate adult situations before their time, and who survive by taking refuge in their imaginations. Compare the two works, and write a short story or poem in which the protagonists of the two works encounter one another at school. Feel free to add comics, as in the Alexie book, if you so choose, using ToonDoo or another computer cartoon-creator program.

- Alcoholism is not a problem confined to the 1940s and 1950s, the time during which "The World as Will and Representation" is set. Using your cross-disciplinary skills, research the history of the treatment of alcoholism. Was the treatment Hass describes typical of the time? Is it typical of our time? What special problems apply to mothers who suffer from alcoholism? Write a paper that examines treatments of alcoholism across the past half-century, and compare the fates of the mother in the Hass poem with a contemporary mother in terms of their treatment options.

modern medicine. However, the father's appropriation of the language of movie heroes and tough guys is always addressed to his young son and serves to align the boy with the father's purpose, which is to overcome, through coercion if necessary, his wife's attempts to evade taking the drug that will serve as a sort of babysitter for the day, a drug that will make her physically reject the alcohol she craves. The father and son are uneasy partners in this project, the father retreating into empty language and the son seeking refuge in the newspaper comics. This drama occurred every morning, or some mornings, and even more mornings where the father, on his way to work early, abandoned his duty to the son, and fled the house. The social construction of fatherhood into which the father in this poem is trying to fit does not suit him much better than the role of mother fits his wife. Both parties seem to have failed somehow to fulfill their roles, and the poem ends in an image of ruin, with the mother sorry and willing to do as she is told, nonetheless drinking through the medication and gagging at the kitchen table in her bathrobe.

Popular Culture

In this poem the catchphrases of popular culture become important touchstones to both the father and the son, and in some cases provide a means by which they attempt to communicate with one another. The father, who seems uncomfortable with the morning ritual even while he is determined to complete it every morning, resorts to mannerisms and catchphrases from the popular culture of his time. Even his wink, notes the narrator, was a wink specific to its time, a slightly exaggerated gesture meant to be taken both seriously and with an ironic twist. The 1940s and 1950s were a time when movies were full of stories of wily criminals and the upright lawmen who chased and eventually caught them. These narratives provided reassurance that the forces of social order would always prevail against the chaotic and rebellious criminal element. The father in this poem uses the language of these movies to reinforce his position as the patriarch, the one who enforces the law within the family, the one who seeks to restore social and familial order. The son too looks to popular culture for reassurance and as a means of glimpsing how the outside world works. He is just a young boy, so the world of adults, especially the world his father inhabits when working, is a mystery to him. That he looks to *Blondie* for his cues is an ironic choice on the part of the author, for *Blondie* is a comic strip that drew its comedic energy from the difference between the esteem in which the patriarchal characters of Dagwood and Mr. Dithers held themselves, and the bumbling manner in which they actually made their way in the world. In the world of the comic strip, it was always Blondie herself, a woman drawn like a pin-up

character, who quietly set things to rights, and ensured that the male characters would suffer no damage to their overblown egos. Of course, this is not the fate that awaits the male characters in the poem. The wife and mother is not going to set things to rights, she is not going to play the role of the "little woman" who clears the dishes, goes out shopping with her neighbor, then greets her husband at the door with dinner on the table. The standards of popular culture serve as a crutch for the male characters in this poem, both of whom long for a world in which the forces of social order always prevail the way they do in the movies and in the comics.

Moral Ambiguity

Moral ambiguity is a hallmark of Hass's poetry, for he is a poet who prefers to highlight the complications to which human beings are exposed than to make pronouncements. Writing in the *American Poetry Review*, the poet Tony Hoagland notes that Hass has "a deep postmodern distrust of the easy manners of wisdom . . . [and] an ongoing and related dissatisfaction with closure." For Hass, the complications of moral life are always more interesting than any easy pronouncements. In "The World as Will and Representation" Hass portrays a father who is acting toward the mother in a manner that we would currently denounce as coercive. However, this portrait is made ambiguous by the father's discomfort with the act. He tries to cover up the imposition of power the boy is witnessing each morning by turning it into a sort of joke out of popular culture. Women, the father seems to imply, are wily and untrustworthy, but, he blusters, they cannot put one over on us men. But even the boy recognizes it as bluster, because neither the father nor the son is quite able to muster his way past the reality of the situation, which is that the minute the father leaves the house, the mother is going to start drinking, antabuse or no antabuse. The father imposes his will, but it is an impotent will, and hence, even the imposition is ambiguous. Throughout the poem, the mother is portrayed as a passive character, someone to whom actions are done, not someone who acts on her own. Even her attempts to hide the drugs under her tongue are rendered in the passive voice, pills can be hidden under the tongue, but no one is actively hiding them. She seems a passive presence, acted upon and infantilized in such a way that we might be tempted to see her as a victim of the repressive and

Fathers go to work *(© David Hancock | Alamy)*

patriarchal society in which she lived. That would be the sort of easy wisdom to which Hoagland refers. The ambiguity comes in when, at the end of the poem, the mother comes to life, drinking and gagging in her bathrobe at the kitchen table; she is finally an actor in her own drama. Even at the poem's end, what looks like a declaration that lessons were learned about moral ideas is left open ended when the poet declares that these lessons must be learned, but then questions the source from which they are learned. Is it the family drama? The lessons of popular culture? Those gleaned from classical texts like the *Aeneid*? The poet does not say but leaves the answer ambiguous, for the reader to decide.

STYLE

Narrative Poetry

While a lyric poem might seek to illuminate a single moment or insight, a narrative poem tells a story of some sort. "The World as Will and Representation" tells a story from the narrator's childhood. The story is also about how he was sometimes caught between his parents when his father left him in charge of administering the drug. A narrative poem can be relatively short, as is this one, or an epic like the *Aeneid* to which Hass refers in this poem. Narrative poetry that tells a personal story like this one is also known as confessional poetry and came to prominence in the late 1950s and 1960s through the work of authors like Robert Lowell, Sylvia Plath, and Anne Sexton. The inclusion of personal details, particularly personal details that do not reflect well on the poet, like discussions of alcoholism or scandalous behavior, shocked many readers and inspired countless arguments about what exactly constitutes the proper subject matter of poetry. Hass often uses the narrative form, and many of his poems include details from his life, and yet the poems are not merely stories about personal events. In poetry, the elements of style must serve the larger allegorical and metaphorical meaning of the work, which in this case is a meditation on nature of Schopenhauer's theories about will and representation, and how they play out in the world Hass inhabits.

Colloquialism

Colloquialism is the use of ordinary language rather than elevated or formal rhetorical figures in literature. A literary work written in the colloquial style is meant to sound as though ordinary people are speaking the words. Colloquial speech—both the language used by the narrator and of the catchphrases of popular culture that the father resorts to during the morning ritual of the medication—is crucial to "The World as Will and Representation." The father resorts to the slang of the 1940s and 1950s when he is uncomfortable, using it as a means of escaping the moral ambiguities of the situation in which he is engaged, the forcible administration of medication to another adult, and the manner in which he co-opts his son in this effort. In order to escape the complication of the situation, the father uses phrases out of gangster and cowboy movies, while the son seeks answers in the language of domesticity as reflected in newspaper comics. Because neither character can fully comprehend the ramifications of the drama in which they are engaged, they both retreat to the easy sureties of the debased language of popular culture. In this way, colloquial language becomes the subject of the poem as well as the tool with which it is written.

Point of View

The point of view of this poem is the first person, that is, it uses the personal pronouns "I" and "me." While the poem is consistently written from the first-person point of view, it shifts between reflecting the level of knowledge and understanding the narrator had as a child, and the level of knowledge and understanding he has as an adult. For instance, the description of the effect of antabuse on those to whom it has been administered is the language of a child, while lines 8 through 15 are the recollections of an adult looking back on childhood. The poem shifts back and forth between these narrative stances: the description of the *Blondie* cartoons is the language of a child trying to interpret the larger world, while the recollection of the *Aeneid* is the sort of narrative interruption that a person makes when telling a story, and asks a person, do you know, or do you remember? By choosing this point of view, which stays in the same person, but shifts between the knowledge possessed by that person in different periods of life, the poet achieves a sort of telescopic effect. By shifting in this manner, Hass manages to portray the naïve understanding and perception of the child while allowing the more nuanced perception of the adult to shape the poem without violating the child's point of view.

HISTORICAL CONTEXT

9/11 and Its Aftermath

"The World as Will and Representation" was published in Hass's collection, *Time and Materials: Poems 1997–2005*, a period of time that spanned the attacks of September 11, 2001, and the U.S. invasion of Iraq. It was also during this time that Czeslaw Milosz, the Nobel Laureate with whom Hass collaborated on translations of seven books, and who was a major figure in his life, died in Kraków, Poland. Each of these events informs the poetry in this collection. As a lifelong activist for peace, justice, and environmental causes, Hass was deeply disturbed by the direction the nation took after the attacks of September 11, 2001. As he told Anna Ross in an interview with *Guernica: A Magazine of Arts and Politics*, "I wouldn't feel guilty about not writing about Baghdad if I

didn't have any good ideas about how to write about it. . . . I find myself reading Brecht, Milosz, writers who tried to put politics and the political responsibility of poetry . . . at the center of their thought."

On September 11, 2001, the United States was attacked by nineteen Al Qaeda terrorists who took control of four commercial airliners, flying two of them into the World Trade Center towers in New York City, one into the Pentagon in Arlington, Virginia, near Washington, D.C., and crashed a fourth plane in rural Pennsylvania. As a result, President George W. Bush declared a "war on terror." Aspects of this effort included the invasion of Afghanistan, whose Taliban government had given safe haven to Al Qaeda, and the passage of the Patriot Act, which granted the government increased powers of surveillance and search (several of which were later struck down by the courts). Although the attacks of September 11, 2001, were not the first attacks by a foreign power on American soil, the spectacular and unexpected nature of the event shocked the nation. While historians and pundits continue to wrestle over the ultimate meaning of the events, it is safe to say that they brought a new sense of physical vulnerability to much of the population.

In March 2003 the United States and an international force invaded Iraq. Some members of the U.S. government believed that Iraq was manufacturing and hiding weapons of mass destruction, and that the government of Iraq, led by Saddam Hussein, was harboring terrorists and oppressing their own people. While Saddam and his government were toppled with relative ease, securing peace has proved more difficult. Turmoil continues in the region even as the United States seeks to stabilize the government. The invasion of Iraq was opposed by many on the left, including Robert Hass, and his anger at this military incursion appears in several poems in *Time and Materials*. In the interview with Ross, Hass explained that his objection to the U.S. invasion was due in part to the callous disregard for the civilian deaths the military had calculated would occur. Hass's political roots lie in the 1960s. He told Ross: "When I began writing poems . . . the literary and cultural atmosphere was very much affected by what was going on in the world." During that period, Hass noted that the war in Vietnam "seemed to a lot of us like a catastrophe from the very beginning,

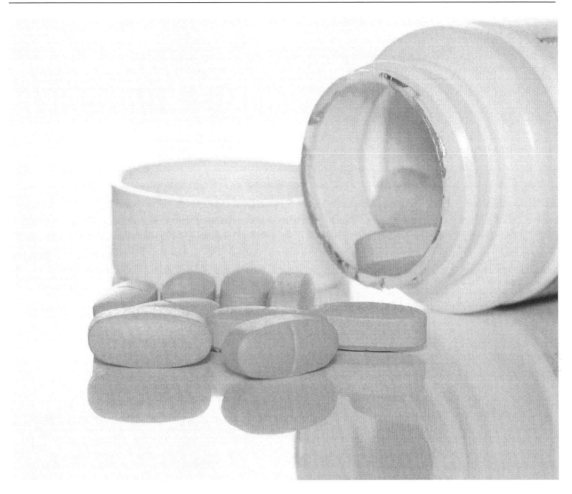

Pills spill from bottle (*vnlit | Shutterstock.com*)

inflicting immense and needless suffering on not only the American soldiers but on a lot of innocent peasants." It was this experience that informed Hass's objection to the invasion of Iraq, because he felt that the president should have been made to take personal responsibility for the civilian deaths he authorized by declaring war. As Hass noted in the *Guernica* interview, "I just wanted to say someplace in plain English, that those people didn't get to vote on their deaths."

Death of Czeslaw Milosz

Czeslaw Milosz died at the age of 93 on August 14, 2004, at his home in Kraków, Poland. Born on June 30, 1911, in Lithuania to a distinguished and literary family, his childhood in the Lithuanian countryside left him with an enduring love of the particulars of the natural world. Milosz was in Warsaw during the Nazi occupation of Poland, and wrote "A Poor Christian Looks at the Ghetto" even as the Nazis destroyed the nearby Jewish ghetto and its inhabitants. He harbored a lifelong hatred of totalitarianism, and although he served as a diplomat for the Polish government in the early years of the Communist regime, his increasing dissent led to news in 1951 that he was to be arrested for dissent against the government upon his return from Paris. He sought political refuge in France, where he lived until 1960, when he accepted a professorship in Slavic Studies at the University of California at Berkeley. There he and Robert Hass began to collaborate on translations, for even though he was fluent in English and French, Milosz believed that poetry must be written in one's mother tongue. In 1980, he was awarded the Nobel Prize for Literature. Upon his death, Leon Wieseltier noted in an essay for the *New York Times Book Review* that Milosz "was a hero of the history of his time and a hero of the literature of his time. For friends and for strangers, for lovers of liberty and for lovers of beauty, he was, for more than half a century, an indispensable man." In the interview in *Guernica*, Hass noted that for Milosz, "political responsibility was part of the deal. He wasn't happy about it. He had a sort of ironic attitude," and when he came to America, he considered becoming "an American poet; . . . a pedagogue of pears" but that ultimately, he could not forsake his true subjects, "history and the nature of evil and the nature of violence and what's in the human heart."

CRITICAL OVERVIEW

Hass has been acclaimed since winning the Yale Younger Poets Prize for his first book, *Field Guide*. Since then, he has won nearly every prize possible for a poet, including the National Book Award, the Pulitzer Prize, two National Book Critics Circle Awards, and a MacArthur "genius" Fellowship. He has served two terms as the Poet Laureate of the United States, and has been a chancellor of the Academy of American Poets. He teaches at the University of California at Berkeley, where he holds a distinguished Chair in Poetry that will carry his name after his retirement. David Orr notes in a *New York Times* review of *The Apple Trees at Olema: New and Selected Poems*, that "as poetic résumés go, Hass's is about as gold-plated as it gets."

Hass's poems have come, over the years, to rely on an increasingly loose style in which long lines are interspersed with short sections. Often these echo the haiku he often translates. He has also experimented with prose poems. However, a close look at these prose poems reveals a careful attention to scansion and internal rhyme and rhythm that leave them straddling, or investigating the line between prose and poetry. As Dan Chiasson notes in his essay "Late and Soon: Mark Strand and Robert Hass, Collected in Tranquility," published in the *New Yorker*, Hass's work has come to rely on "a technique he has called variously 'cutting' and 'gathering,' where salvage sits beside prized personal details." Chiasson continues by noting that "the zero-sum fluctuations of Hass's material, some intellect followed by some feeling, coolness here, warmth there, at

times become a formula," but that when he is at his most successful, Hass's technique "yields work that, exquisitely receptive to actual happiness, has opened up new territory for the personal poem."

Hass has been deeply influenced both by Buddhist thought and, through his long collaboration with the Polish poet, Czeslaw Milosz, by the skepticism of those who lived through the political cataclysms of twentieth-century European history. The result is a poetic voice that seeks not so much to assert its authority through the poem, as to test and interrogate the nature of poetry to affect meaning at all. This has left Hass open to criticism by other poets that he can be both sentimental and evasive. In "The Three Tenors: Glück, Hass, Pinsky and the Deployment of Talent," an essay in *American Poetry Review*, Hoagland quotes the poet Louise Glück, who claims that this tendency in Hass's work leads to "a flight from self." She claims that his poems lack "a sense of the restrictions of self, of singleness, in which perception necessitates acts of judgment, decision, assertion of priorities. His poems repudiate self." Hoagland, a poet himself, claims that this is an asset and that Hass "has learned to inhabit another kind of poem than the self-dramatic, one which is de-centered and non-linear, but rhythmic and intuitive." This sort of poetry, Hoagland notes, "can incorporate and digest its own doubts and feelings as it goes along without requiring that they be brought to crisis."

Each poet must reinvent poetry in his or her own work, and what Hass has brought to the canon is a uniquely American voice, specifically a voice located in the landscape and sensibility of late twentieth-century northern California. Hass's is a poetry in which the universal is illuminated by the details of particularity, a poetics in which the very nature of the material world is held up to the scrutiny of individual sensibility.

CRITICISM

Charlotte McGuinn Freeman

Freeman is a freelance writer and former academic who lives in Montana. In the following essay, she examines the ways in which Hass incorporates elements from Schopenhauer's philosophy in "The World as Will and Representation," which he named after the philosopher's great work.

> ❝ HASS IS NOT SIMPLY WRITING A TREATISE.
> NOR IS HE WRITING AN EXPLICATION OF
> SCHOPENHAUER'S IDEAS. RATHER, HE IS STARTING
> WITH THE IDEAS POSED BY SCHOPENHAUER, AND BY
> DRAMATIZING AND WORKING THEM OUT IN
> METAPHOR AND IMAGE, USING THEM AS A STARTING
> POINT FOR HIS OWN MEDITATION ON THEIR
> NATURE.❞

While the subject matter of "The World as Will and Representation" appears to be a rather straightforward confessional narrative, the title is a direct reference to the treatise by the same name published by the nineteenth-century German philosopher Arthur Schopenhauer. In this treatise, which is central to Schopenhauer's work and reputation, he outlined the major theses of his philosophical system regarding the nature of human motivation, and the ability of art to quell the insatiable desires that drive people. While Schopenhauer was responding most immediately to his predecessors Immanuel Kant and Georg Wilhelm Friedrich Hegel, he was also deeply influenced by his study of Eastern religions, something he and Hass have in common. Because of Hass's interest in Asian poetry and the many references to Buddhism in his poetry, as well as his association with the northern California poetry scene, critics sometimes overlook how deeply Hass has also been influenced by the great European thinkers. Like Schopenhauer, Hass incorporates Eastern and Western thought in his work, rather than rejecting one at the expense of the other.

As Robert Wicks explains in his entry on Schopenhauer for the *Stanford Encyclopedia of Philosophy*,

> Schopenhauer regards the world . . . as having two sides: the world is Will and the world is representation. The world as Will . . . is the world as it is in itself, and the world as representation is the world of appearances, of our ideas, or of objects.

However, what Schopenhauer means by *will* is not necessarily will as we might use the term in every day conversation to mean internal fortitude, or stubborn rebelliousness. For Schopenhauer, the universe is meaningless, and as Wicks explains, "Schopenhauer's particular characterization of the world as Will . . . is an endless striving and blind impulse with no end in view, devoid of knowledge, lawless, absolutely free, entirely self-determining and almighty." Human beings, seeking to create meaning out of this chaos, resort to representation. However in Schopenhauer's view, the world of appearances that we create through this process of representation, because it is fragmented and particular, separates us from the wholeness of the universal and unleashes a destructive energy that, according to Wicks, "turns upon itself, consumes itself, and does violence to itself." Human relationships are thus predicated on strife and conflict, and the only respite human beings can hope for is to be found in aesthetic experiences and art. According to Schopenhauer, art focuses the mind on universal principles and allows the spectator to lose his or her individuated subjectivity and become, as Wicks explains, "a clear mirror of the object."

We see these principles at work in "The World as Will and Representation" in several ways. The subject matter of the poem is a family group who is locked in a battle that can never be won. The father wants the mother to be something other than what she is, and he is determined to impose his will on her one way or another. The mother is determined to resist the imposition of the father's will, and the son is caught in the middle. Hass portrays the father in this poem as a conventional person, one who wears a gray suit to work, who uses jocularity to try to ameliorate the tension of the situation, and who seeks to co-opt his son to his cause. He seems to represent the forces of normality, stability, social acceptance. He is described as a person of his social world, and a person specifically situated in the 1940s and 1950s, a time period when the nation as a whole was trying to restore a sense of stability and normality after the upheavals of the Great Depression and World War II. The father seems to see it as his responsibility to ensure that his wife has taken the drugs that should prevent her from drinking while he is at work for the day. His job is to see that order is maintained in the house, that the destructive energy of drunkenness and dissipation is held at bay while he is gone. That he seems uncomfortable with this role, as evidenced by his ongoing effort to downplay the seriousness of

WHAT DO I READ NEXT?

- *The Apple Trees at Olema: New and Selected Poems* (2010) collects poems from each of Hass's previous collections along with poems written since 2005. This volume traces the trajectory of Hass's career from his early master works like "Meditations at Lagunitas" to the longer narrative poems of his later works. It is a splendid overview of the work of this poet.

- Although Hass published *Twentieth-Century Pleasures: Prose on Poetry* in 1984, his essays on the nature of poetry, and on poets such as James Wright, Tomas Tranströmer, and Czeslaw Milosz remain relevant. This collection also contains Hass's indispensable essay on prosody, "One Body: Some Notes on Form," in which he discusses the ways that ordinary speech is full of rhythms we generally think of as poetic.

- In the young-adult novel *The Opposite of Music* (2008) by Janet Ruth Young, fifteen-year old Billy and his family struggle as their father slips into a debilitating depression. As in "The World as Will and Representation," the central character of this novel struggles with a parent's inability to care for him and tries everything in his power to help.

- *California Poetry: From the Gold Rush to the Present* (2003) edited by Dana Gioia, Chryss Yost, and Jack Hicks, is a comprehensive collection of the works of 101 poets organized into four chronological sections, "Early Poets," "California Modernists," "Mid-Century Rebels and Traditionalists," and a final section covering contemporary poets. Each selection is accompanied by a detailed biographical profile of the poet, who must have been born in California or have lived there for more than half a lifetime to be included. This collection is an excellent introduction to a rich and varied poetic tradition.

- *Rosie* (1997) by Anne Lamott is the story of a teenage girl coming of age. Set in Marin County California, where Hass grew up, this novel also addresses a mother who struggles with alcohol addiction. This is a funny, wry portrait of a mother and daughter who are both struggling to grow up in a part of the country where wealth and privilege are supposed to insulate from such troubles.

- Gene Luen Yang's prizewinning graphic novel for young adults, *American Born Chinese* (2008) is the story of Jin Wang, a lonely Taiwanese American boy navigating the challenges of middle school in San Francisco. The novel filters Jin Wang's feelings of being born in the wrong body through the story of the Chinese folk hero, the Monkey King, and through the figure of Chin-kee, an amalgamation of every ugly Chinese American stereotype. This lively and emotionally affecting book was the first graphic novel nominated for the American Book Award.

- John Felstiner's anthology *Can Poetry Save the Earth? A Field Guide to Nature Poems* (2009) explores, in forty concise chapters, the manner in which poets have taken nature as their subject over the centuries. The book ranges from biblical poetry through the romantics through the American canon from Walt Whitman and Emily Dickinson to Elizabeth Bishop and Gary Snyder. It provides a good overview of a subject that is central to the work of Robert Hass.

---

the situation to his son by taking refuge in the empty language of gangster and cowboy movies, only reinforces Schopenhauer's essential point, that our struggles and desires are impossible to fulfill, and seeking to fulfill them, especially by the imposition of one person's will upon another, only leads to further individuation and alienation from one another. Such a course of action can, according to this thinking, only lead to unhappiness.

The dramatic situation of the poem exists as both a specific incident and an ongoing situation. The narrator, looking back on childhood, notes that this drama played out each morning during a time period of undisclosed duration when he was about ten years old. While the poem contains the narration of a single morning, when his father crushed the yellow pills while wearing his gray suit and watched her ingest the drugs before leaving for work, it also expands to include all the mornings that this ritual occurred, as well as those mornings when the boy was left to administer the drug himself. Both the specific instance, and the ongoing recollection end the same way though, with the boy's mother sitting at the kitchen table, drinking through the medication, despite the gag reaction it induced in her.

The mother in this poem could perhaps be seen as a personification of Schopenhauer's concept of the will. Her alcoholism is not enrobed in meaning as it might be in our own more therapeutically oriented time. The mother's presence in this poem is almost entirely limited to her drinking. For most of the poem, her presence is passive. She is referred to in the passive voice and remains someone who does not act but is acted upon. Her drinking is not explained away by her circumstances, it simply exists as a force that cannot be stopped, and one that has no intrinsic meaning. The mother drinks. The mother will continue to drink. The mother's drinking cannot be stopped by any external force. It is the destructive force that turns upon itself and destroys itself. If Schopenhauer, like the mystics of most religious traditions, identifies desire as the root of what separates us from one another and from the universal, then one could not find a better metaphor for that blind desire than a late-stage alcoholic. The mother is entirely ruled by the blind desire to drink. It is this desire and her relentless determination to try to assuage that desire with alcohol that leads to her separation from her husband and son, her isolation, and her unhappiness. She is an example of what becomes of someone who seeks only to fulfill cravings and desires; she has become those cravings and desires, and the energy with which she seeks to assuage that desire is the same energy that is eating her alive and causing her self-destruction.

There are also several examples in this poem of the ways that aesthetic experience and art provide a refuge from the conflict and strife caused by the inevitable collision of individuals seeking to fulfill their desires. While on the one hand, the father's continued use of the empty language of gangster and cowboy films is emblematic of his conventionality, on the other hand it can be seen as an attempt to flee the individual conflict in which he is engaged and to take refuge in a less individuated and less painful universal reality. The movie cowboy and the movie cop are not individuals striving to impose their will on others, but figures whose positions within those movies are fixed and immutable. They cannot be subject to the painful world in which people seek to impose themselves upon others because they are not actually people, they are simply figures. Although they are hardly the Platonic ideas that Schopenhauer had in mind, because they are types, they reflect an aspect of universal not individual truth, and therefore can be seen as a sort of aesthetic ideal. The boy in the poem resorts to contemplation of an aesthetic experience as solace for the individual battle in which he is mired. While one can hardly imagine Schopenhauer considering the *Blondie* cartoon as an example of high art, it is typical of Hass's aesthetic that this sort of homey reference can function as such. The comic nature of *Blondie* depended on the portrait it drew of the sort of stable, middle-class, white, mid-century American nuclear family that the boy recognizes as a kind of ideal. In trying to make sense of the family drama around him, he looks to an artistic representation of the kind of family to which he senses he is supposed to belong. While he finds no lasting answers in the comic, it is contemplating a universal rather than individual ideal of family life that gives him the opportunity to step out of his individual circumstances for six lines and provides exactly the kind of temporary respite from the world of strife that Schopenhauer believed in. Finally, even the adult narrator takes refuge in art from the unbearable nature of the strife and desire portrayed in the poem when in line 38 he abruptly introduces a scene from the *Aeneid*. The *Aeneid* is precisely the sort of classical work that Schopenhauer would have identified as universal. The narrator introduces this interruption with a direct address to a listener, someone of comparable education and background who can be expected to remember the scene the narrator invokes. Since this interjection occurs just as the narrator, who appears to be the adult version

Boy is worried about his mother *(Andrey Shadrin /
Shutterstock.com)*

of the boy in the poem, relates watching his
father leave him to the task of administering the
medication to his mother, the scene functions as
a dramatization of the function of art as Schopenhauer describes it. The situation has become
too painful even for the narrator, so he pauses
and introduces a dramatic scene from the *Aeneid*,
a scene that universalizes and externalizes the
sense of ruin and shame and terror inspired by
the memory of this period in his childhood.

Hass is not simply writing a treatise. Nor is he
writing an explication of Schopenhauer's ideas.
Rather, he is starting with the ideas posed by
Schopenhauer, and by dramatizing and working
them out in metaphor and image, using them as a
starting point for his own meditation on their
nature. Where the great philosophers seek to capture meaning, to make declarative statements
about the nature of reality, the human mind,
and the workings of the universe, the task of the
poet is a different one, particularly for a poet like

Hass, who is known for exactly the sort of open
ending with which he finishes this poem. Hass
does not end the poem by telling the reader
what he learned from this experience, but rather
asks the reader to contemplate the situation, to
ask him or herself from whence we get our ideas
about morality and the world. Do we formulate
them from personal experience? Do we find them
in philosophy? Are they waiting for us like secret
messages embedded in works of art or even in
popular culture? Do we hunt and gather from all
of these sources? Is it even possible that there is a
singular answer to this? Hass distrusts statements
of meaning that close a poem, and his refusal to
make one in "The World as Will and Representation" is typical of his work. It ends with those
questions with which it has wrestled throughout:
What is the nature of morality, where does come
from, and how does one apply it?

Source: Charlotte McGuinn Freeman, Critical Essay on
"The World as Will and Representation," in *Poetry for
Students*, Gale, Cengage Learning, 2011.

Tess Taylor

*In the following review, Taylor debates whether
Hass's collection* Time and Materials *is or is not
"old thinking."*

During the three and a half decades since his
celebrated first book, *Field Guide*, won the Yale
Series of Younger Poets Prize in 1973, Robert
Hass has been variously a poet of nature, of
naming, of Northern California landscape, and
of diagnosing the particular kind of loss that
emerges through the use of language. His anthology piece "Meditation at Lagunitas," published
in his second book *Praise*, is arguably one of
most beloved American poems of the past quarter century. It begins "All the new thinking is
about loss /in this it resembles the old thinking."
In it Hass, then in his mid-thirties, used elements
he's deployed throughout his career: Food, light
and a setting in or around Marin County; a
rhetorical leap off a sexy-sounding philosophical
claim; a fascination with time; a desire to explore
the limits of language; a hunger to weigh the
present against the past. "Meditation at Lagunitas" builds through a penultimate crescendo,
"longing we say, because desire is full of endless
distances," to an ultimate one, "the word is elegy
to what it signifies." The poem then doles out
several word-sized elegies: "Pine, hair, woman,

you and J." The loss is tragic but also pleasurable. The violins play, and they are sexy violins.

Time and Materials is and is not like the old thinking. It shows Hass's debt to his years translating haiku and Czeslaw Milosz, and perhaps also to his relationship with the poet Brenda Hillman. It does retrace a foggy, tangerine-lit Northern California, although now that Hass is at Iowa, there are Iowa poems too. Hass still likes to think about the relationship of language to place, finding wonder and pleasure in naming the site-specific regional plants of his California garden and hills—oxalis, hazel, toyon—which he balances against old English rediscoveries like "soughing" and "slim." He continues to be a poet of love relationships: this book is full of he and she, making love, making curry, using wry little sentences like "Tender little Buddha, she said,/Of my least Buddha-like member." He goes on diagnosing the uneasy reciprocal relationship between language and knowledge, engrossed by the former even as he distrusts its grasp of the latter, noting, "No. There are limits to saying,/In language, what the tree did." Lest we get too complacent in the land of organic cheese and fresh oysters, Hass, who once wrote a poem about buggers, reminds us: "It is a good thing sometimes for poetry to disenchant us." Lest we feel too disenchanted, his next line is, "Dance with me, dancer. Oh, I will."

But if some of the new poems resemble some of the old poems, the concerns are also differently hewn. *Time and Materials* is less about loss and more about wounds. Its posture is not one of elegy, and a great deal of it is not as much a representation of a real world (of, say, fish and food and cheese) but a representation of the represented one (of, say, paintings and paint.) The book has two central poems about paintings—one about Vermeer and one about Richter—and several poems so conscious of planes and surfaces that it is hard not to feel them as verbal paintings. A book about art-making, it veers from and then returns to the questions: in what way does art make time feel material? In what way is time art's material? In what way is art time's material? As if playing one of those pea-cup games at the county fair, the poems try different arrangements of the constellation, moving the stellae around. In between, the poet sneaks in two new stars: constructive force and destructive force. As Hass, the consummate Berkeley Buddhist, also notices, the two are often one.

The book is full of many miniature and not so miniature constructive-destructions, some wrought by art, others by time, others by art imitating time. Time wounds people. People look down and realize that they don't have hands. In dreams they realize that they have no wives, never had wives. In one poem, a man "has an Adam's apple/So protuberant it's conducting a flirtation/ With deformity." Much of the book conducts this flirtation—flirtation because Hass is nothing if not fascinated with seduction. But it is destruction, not elegy, that seduces him here. Deformity inserts itself into these poems: time deforms; art deforms; and deformed material is the stuff of time and art. One of the primary ways this book casts art is as a celebration of time's abrasion, indeed, the book's crescendo is in the last line of the title poem, an ekphrastic piece in parts describing a Gerhard Richter painting, where red layers have been applied, then gouged with a palate knife. The poem does not merely describe the painting, but mimics its layering on and slicing back, aiming "To make layers,/As if they were a steadiness of days," and calling attention to the act whereby the poem steals the world to make a world of its own.

Indeed, the abrasions Hass explores in *Time and Materials* are also acts of generation. And wounding is not the only thing the poems hope for. They also explore "a dream of restoration" which "tells the story backward" as in "Fate of the Planet," a poem about the very wounded state of nature these days. But acts of creative destruction animate the book, and oddly seem the most hopeful. And this is a book in which no sentiment is unalloyed: For Hass even bliss is blurred, "what you glimpse/From the corner of your eye, as you drive past/Running errands." The best poems get this blur exactly right. One of the most haunting and memorable poems in the collection—perhaps Hass's best in many years—"Then Time," tells the story of ex-lovers meeting after long absence. What the poem does, finally, is distill the curious realizations one can have when time itself blurs, folds, compresses. The poem, a suspended thought dialogue between he and she, distorts observation into a then-now compression. The moment seems to skew, torque, enlarge. Both of the subjects experience a double take of feeling—I never lived here, and who is the self that lives here still? Rather than regarding a terrain of loss, the poem captures dense moments of consciousness where hindsight and recognition fuse. The experience is at once brutally foreshortened and vast. The poem tracks the moment in both its constructive and destructive realities. The leap into this blur is far from immaterial. It is, perhaps, the work of thirty years.

Source: Tess Taylor, Review of *Time and Materials: Poems 1997–2007*, in *Harvard Review*, Vol. 34, June 2008, pp. 209–12.

Bruce Bond

In the following excerpt, Bond states that the generosity of Hass's work lies in how he turns the everpresence of lack, both as reflected and created by language, into not only a testament of loss, but also as an occasion for praise.

> Often enough, when a thing is seen clearly, there is a sense of absence about it—it is true of impressionist painting—as if, the more palpable it is, the more some immense subterranean displacement seems to be working in it; as if at the point of truest observation the visible and the invisible exerted enormous counterpressure.

(Hass, *Twentieth Century Pleasures*)

The word "clarity" is often unclear. If by "clear" we mean "under the clarifying light of reason," placed with quieting control in a world promoted as stable, without contradiction, then Robert Hass's poetry is repeatedly unclear. But if by "clear" we mean "lit by an immanent light," creating a persuasive model of consciousness in all its disjunctions, wonder and loss, paradox and uncertainty, then Hass's poetry has a clarity which puts its language under immense pressure. Through Hass's clarifying lens, we see words as gestures of longing rather than vestiges of truth, as motivated by a sense of their own failure, a sense of lack that no discourse can finally fill. As though always on the threshold of saying what it cannot, Hass's language is both haunted and invigorated by an "immense subterranean" absence, an absence which we imagine nevertheless as a kind of presence, a "counter-pressure" akin to a displaced unconscious. If his view toward language as both the product and producer of desire, as driven by a sense of lack at the core of its being, appears strikingly Lacanian, it may come as small surprise that Hass recalls, in his essay on Robert Creeley, the arrival of Jacques Lacan's *Ecrits* on the Anglo-American shore as revolutionary, full of both astonishing and troubling notions that struck the contemporary nerve (*TCP*).

> THROUGHOUT HASS'S WORK, FEELINGS OF 'CONNECTEDNESS,' OF INTIMACY BETWEEN THE PAST AND PRESENT, SIGNIFIER AND SIGNIFIED, SELF AND OTHER, WORD AND FLESH, RECUR AS EPHEMERAL BLESSINGS, MATTERS OF LUCK—AS WHEN MOMENTARILY THE BODY SEEMS 'NUMINOUS AS WORDS' OR WHEN WORDS APPEAR AS 'DAYS WHICH ARE THE GOOD FLESH CONTINUING.'"

The distinguishing generosity of Hass's work lies in how he turns the everpresence of lack, both as reflected and created by language, into not only a testament of loss, but also an occasion for praise-that which endears the ephemera of our lives. By way of language, absence eroticizes the world. Despite how we may feel troubled in Hass's poetry by what language cannot accommodate, his is not the austere, archetypal, syntactically pared-down universe we often find in so-called poetry of silence—much of W. S. Merwin's verse, for instance. Hass's world is abundant, expansive, richly textured with unexpected detail, philosophical and intimate, unmistakably anchored in daily life yet appealing to our lust for wonder, astonishing us with, what Hass calls in his description of Yosa Buson's poetry, "the fullness and emptiness of things" (*TCP*).

Thus language in its failure to tell the whole truth appears in Hass's poetry as nevertheless redemptive, since such failure animates the imagination and inspires its continual revisions. In Hass's later work, we feel the imaginative urge to renew let loose with particular abandon and an especially disjunctive logic. But although desire may cause disjunctions in consciousness, bringing to mind always the next needful thing, there are complicating moments in Hass's verse where desire appears briefly, paradoxically, as a connecting medium, a bridge made of the distance to be bridged. It joins what cannot logically be joined: self and other, past and present, word and the signified world.

Hass's view of words as gestures of longing, as both empty and full, animated by loss, is perhaps most familiar to his readers by way of his second collection of poems, *Praise*—in particular, the much anthologized poem "Meditation at Lagunitas" with its potently aphoristic claims that yield to an affectionately particularizing language, language which, as Hass makes explicit, can never be particular enough to bridge the gap between word and world:

> All the new thinking is about loss.
> In this it resembles all the old thinking.
> The idea, for example, that each particular erases
> the luminous clarity of a general idea. That the
>   clown-faced
> woodpecker probing the dead sculpted trunk
> of that black birch is, by his presence,
> some tragic falling off from a first world
> of undivided light. Or the other notion that,
> because there is in this world no one thing
> to which the bramble of blackberry corresponds,
> a word is elegy to what it signifies.

The word's longing to cross that impermeable Saussurian bar, to embrace the signified world on the other side, resembles a desire to retrieve a lost past, as though that past harbored an original unity of self and other—a paradise lost, "a first world of undivided light."

The paradox of desire characterizes the paradox of language in that each presupposes a distance between opposites—self and other, past and present, signifier and signified—while creating the very basis for their intimacy. In the life of words, a greeting is always a farewell, an elegy. As Lacan clams, "the being of language is the non-being of objects" ("The direction of the treatment ... ," Ecrits 263). And this non-being strangely discloses itself as a presence, a yearning, the very conveyance of the abundance of the world:

> Longing, we say, because desire is full
> of endless distances. I must have been the same
>   to her.
> But I remember so much, the way her hands
>   dismantled
> bread,
> the thing her father said that hurt her, what
> she dreamed. There are moments when the body
>   is as
> numinous
> as words, days that are the good flesh continuing.
> Such tenderness, those afternoons and evenings,
> saying blackberry, blackberry, blackberry. (*Praise*)

Desire is full, freighted with the stuff of memory, that which seems both immanent and distant. In reciting a text of remembered things, we are thus made up of a world we lack.

The phrase "numinous as words" recalls the Latin word numen ("the spiritual"). Since the numinous world is by definition contradistinguished from the physical, to call the body "numinous as words" is to blur the very concept of numinosity, to confuse so-called inner and outer domains. Such "crossbreeding" is in keeping with a typically Romantic conception of the imagination, that which invests the world with consciousness and consciousness with the world. By way of the image as the point of fusion, the word is made flesh. In his essay "Images," Hass writes, "that confusion of art and life, inner and outer, is the very territory of the image; it is what an image is. And the word was made flesh and dwelt among us" (*TCP*). Bound up inextricably in its lost presence, the word blackberry is itself sweet and palpable.

The notion of the body as numinous derives the power to astonish from its illogic—the fact that Hass in one stroke asserts and denies a distinction. Even the most intimate relation between inner and outer, present and past, self and nature, signifier and signified presupposes a distance—a difference. And it is this difference which drives the imagination forward. In his essay "One Body: Some Notes on Form," Hass claims that he doesn't share Wordsworth's belief that a childlike alliance with nature represents "the first / Poetic spirit of our human life." According to Hass, the urge to create grows rather out of a broken alliance. Hass states, "I have none of [Wordsworth's] assurance, either about the sources of the order of nature or about the absolute continuity between that first nurturing and the form-making activity of the mind. It seems to me, rather, that we make our forms because there is no absolute continuity, because those first assurances are broken. The mind, in the act of recovery, creates" (*TCP*).

"Meditation at Lagunitas" pays tribute to memory as such an act, a creative and affectionate response to a fall from the first world of undivided light. Hass's poem "Natural Theology" from his third collection of poems, *Human Wishes*, offers a similar tribute, though exploring in more detail the evolutionary pattern of a consciousness:

> White daisies against the burnt orange of the
>   windowframe,
> lusterless redwood in the nickel gray of winter,
> in the distance turbulence of water—the green
>   regions

of the morning reflect whatever can be gained,
      normally,
by light, then give way to the blue regions of the
   afternoon
which do not reflect so much as they remember,
as if the light, one will all morning, yielded to a
   doubleness
in things—

In this first world, "the green regions / of the morning," the images, with their precision of coloristic detail, appear designed to dazzle us, not with their symbolic weight, but with their mere presence, their visual sweets. They have a primary potency to them. In his essay "Images," Hass explains:

> It seems to me that we all live our lives in the light of primary acts of imagination, images or sets of images that get us up in the morning and move us about our days. I do not think anybody can live without one, for very long, without suffering intensely from deadness or futility. (*TCP*)

In "Natural Theology," Hass's way of describing the mode of this world's first appearance works to circumvent the perceiver/perceived distinction associated with "the second world," the world of language and the broken alliances that language presupposes. Not a perceiver, but the green regions themselves "reflect," and the degree to which this reflection implies transformation in the process of emergence is ambiguous. The regions, according to Hass, simply "reflect whatever can be gained, normally, by light." What is clear is that, as time passes, this light and its green regions yield to an increasingly associative consciousness. Once again, Hass's essay enlarges our reading of the poem:

> I think that, for most of us, those images are not only essential but dangerous because no one of them feels like the whole truth and they do not last. Either they die of themselves, dry up, are shed; or, if we are lucky they are invisibly transformed into the next needful thing. (*TCP*)

Secondary acts of the imagination, being more transformative, are more obviously metaphorical, and thus we find ourselves more obviously in the realm of language.

Although Hass does not explicitly associate the "green regions" with infantile experience, such a world resembles the imaginary order which Lacan claims precedes a child's "mirror stage." The mirror stage marks not only the advent of language, but also the emergence of selfhood, made precarious since images of the self are always "out there," mirrored back from the world. In Lacan's words, the "I" "is objectified in the dialectic of identification with the other" ("The Mirror Stage," *Ecrits 2*). Hass's poem dramatizes a similar mirror stage, a point at which the dynamics of memory make possible the perception of similitude and difference and thus the tension between the two as language. With an associative consciousness, identification becomes possible, and the narcissistic imagination perceives a mirroring sheen on the surface of the other:

> images not quite left behind rising as an undertow
> of endless transformation against the blurring world
> outside the window where, after the morning
>   clarities,
> the faint reflection of a face appears; among the
>   images
> a road, repetitively, with meadow rue and yarrow
> whitening its edges, and pines shadowing the
>   cranberry
> brush,
> and the fluting of one bird where the road curves and
> disappears,
> becoming that gap or lack which is the oldest
> imagination
> of need, defined more sharply by the silver-gray
>   region
> just before the sun goes down ... (*Human Wishes*)

Though one's literally reflected physical bearing provides a metaphor for the self as discrete, that independence is threatened by the otherness of the reflective surface. In Hass's poem, we feel the dissonance implicit in the emergence of selfhood as the reflected face floats tentatively over a restless flux of images.

Like the self, the other too is characterized by lack—in Hass's poem, that place out there where the road curves and disappears. As Lacan states in his typically elliptical style, "the subject has to find the constituting structure of his desire in the same gap opened up by the effect of the signifiers in those who come to represent the Other for him, insofar as his demand is subject to them" ("The direction of the treatment. ... "). For Lacan, demand includes more than mere physical need. That margin of demand which stretches beyond need is what he calls desire, and desire is infinite. Those who are subject to one's desire are always perceived as lacking.

The bird at the threshold of lack—what Hass calls, "the oldest imagination of need"—invites a cultural memory of birds that serve as correlatives to the poetic imagination. Keats and Whitman most obviously come to mind, but also Stevens, in part by parallel contrast. In Hass's essay "What Furies," he describes Wallace Stevens's bird in the poem "On Mere Being" as "both an alien being and the one true resident; it sings its song without human meaning at the edge of space, its feathers shining." What is remarkably similar between Hass's and Stevens's birds is how they are both situated spatially at the limits of consciousness, positioned to imagine what no imagination successfully can. Paradoxically, extreme artifice, in the guise of a gilded bird, provides a vocabulary for the real, that which, as a nonhuman realm, spells the death of artifice:

> The palm at the end of the mind
> Beyond the last thought, rises
> In the bronze distance,
>
> A gold-feathered bird
> Sings in the palm, without human meaning,
> Without human feeling, a foreign song.
>
> You know then that it is not the reason
> That makes us happy or unhappy.
> The bird sings. The feathers shine. (*Opus Posthumous*)

On its spare, remote threshold, Stevens's bird sits posed like an undying piece of formal glamor. The lines are short; the poem, full of silence. By contrast, Hass's bird appears but briefly, swept into the afternoon's "undertow of endless transformation." In contrast to the quiet posture of Stevens's lines, Hass's poem leads breathlessly down forty-one largely heptameter, cataloging lines before pausing at a period. Hass's expansiveness offers us a hymn to possibility, but possibility as grounded in the thing-ness of everyday life:

> ... dance is defined
> by the body's possibilities arranged, this dance
> belongs to the composures and the running down of things
> in the used sugars of five-thirty: a woman straightening
> a desk turns her calendar to another day, signaling
> that it is another day where the desk is concerned
> and that there is in her days what doesn't belong to the
> desk;
> a kid turns on TV, flops on the couch to the tinny sound
> of little cartoon parents quarreling; a man in a bar
> orders a drink, watches ice bob in the blond fluid,
> he sighs and looks around; sad at the corners, nagged by
> wind,
> others with packages; others dreaming, picking their

> noses
> dreamily while they listen to the radio ... (*Human Wishes*)

Whereas Stevens's poem tends toward paring away the meaningfully charged details of the everyday world, Hass's tends toward including them all. Since neither absolute elimination nor inclusion of such detail is possible in language, both poems create a sense of irresolution.

As in "Meditations at Lagunitas," "Natural Theology" imagines the failure of images to tell the whole truth as potentially redemptive, since such failure sparks the urge to renew. But in "Natural Theology," as in much of Hass's newer work, we feel that urge working forcefully on the syntax itself. Hass's new poems have a particularly disjunctive logic, broad canvas, and rich texture of detail. In "Natural Theology," the poem's syntactic momentum and associative skips create the sense of an unseen pressure causing the verbal ground to shift:

> The religion
> or region of the dark makes soup and lights a fire,
> plays backgammon with children on the teeth or the stilettos
> of the board, reads books, does dishes, listens
> to the wind, listens to the stars imagined to be singing
> invisibly, goes out to be regarded by the moon, walks
> dogs, feeds cats, makes love in postures so various,
> with such varying attention and intensity and hope,
> it enacts the dispersion of tongues among the people
> of the earth—compris? versteh'—and sleeps with sticky
> genitals (*Human Wishes*)

Images rapidly displace one another, unpredictable though not entirely unguided, as though we had been dipped into the lively workings of a symbolic unconscious.

In such a world, Hass tells us, it is "the dark" which "enacts the dispersion of tongues." Thus language enjoys a degree of autonomy from conscious control. It is as though language were speaking itself into existence. The autonomous nature of language, its emergence as an alien self, is yet another Lacanian theme which, as Haas points out, finds its poetic dramatization in the verse of Robert Creeley:

> The system of analogies derived from Levi-Strauss and Lacan and Derrida seems to assert that consciousness carries with it its own displaced and completely symbolic unconscious, that is, the structures of language by which consciousness is constituted. ... This is what

Creeley's mode and the attractiveness of his mode have to do with, at least much of the time; it is a poetics which addresses the tension between speaking and being spoken through language. (*TCP*)

In Lacanian terms, this tension is the tension between the "je" and the "moi," the self that speaks and the self that is spoken, "the object of the other." Most obviously in our dreams, we feel ourselves "being spoken" by an uncontrollable other, the forms of consciousness enjoying a level of abandon but nevertheless informed by some kind of organizing syntax and symbolic logic.

An element of abandon in the forms of consciousness makes possible their seductive play. In Hass's poem, the French question compris? stands posed with a semantic yearning answered by its parallel contrast in German, versteh'. The semantic resolution, albeit temporary, of parallel opposites corresponds to a sexual consummation, a metaphor made explicit as the poem then turns to an image of love's aftermath. It is comically appropriate that the question, like a seductive envoy, is in French whereas the response, offering reassuring closure, is in German:

> —compris? versteh'—and sleeps with sticky genitals
> the erasures and the peace of sleep: exactly the
> half-moon
> holds, and the city twinkles in particular windows,
> throbs
> in its accumulated glow which is also and more
> blindingly
> the imagination of need from which the sun keeps
>   rising
> into morning light,
> because desires do not split themselves up, there is
>   one
> desire
> touching many things, and it is continuous. (*Human
>   Wishes*)

Just as erotic desire rises again, so does the craving for understanding since no understanding is complete. The whole truth is always deferred, inhabiting an imaginary realm "out there."

Appropriately, Hass's closure in "Natural Theology" offers us an image dramatizing the permanent revisionism of consciousness: as the ephemeral sense of sexual and semantic resolution, the erasures and the peace of sleep, give way once again to the climbing light of morning, we are reminded that the cycle of desire is infinite. The sun's movement, slow, inevitable, mirrors

an inevitable yearning, rising, as Hass states, from "the imagination of need." Much of the power of Hass's final image lies in the tension it creates between closure and irresolution. The rising sun marks the end of a cycle, a completion which signifies the impossibility of completion. We end with a beginning.

Hass's idea that there is one desire that is "continuous" makes explicit the notion that desire is everpresent—continual. But also there is a way in which desire, being singular and touching many things, provides an associative continuity among the contents of a consciousness. In Hass's final lines, desire is credited with creating a sense not only of variety and disjunctiveness but also of coherence and belonging. In its everpresence, desire appears as a connecting medium, a subtle, undying force of contact between signs and what they bring to mind. Desire joins, albeit loosely, the many into a long and singular chain of signs and their displacing transformations, each yielding to and yet to some degree setting into motion "the next needful thing."

As we have seen, Hass's essay "Images" claims that primary acts of the imagination are transformed into "the next needful thing" only "if we are lucky." Throughout Hass's work, feelings of "connectedness," of intimacy between the past and present, signifier and signified, self and other, word and flesh, recur as ephemeral blessings, matters of luck—as when momentarily the body seems "numinous as words" or when words appear as "days which are the good flesh continuing." Naturally, the good flesh dies, as do words, as does the sensation that our words are made flesh. The explicit failure of Hass's claims to tell the whole truth humbles them to being. They gesture affectionately toward the inscrutable nature of things charged by language and thus by our desire to see them always more clearly, to retrieve them, to understand. His opulent catalogs are likewise devotional in tone, expressing an immense affection for the world, a longing to name it all. With a kind of devotional alchemy, Hass's poetry excels at creating out of humility, out of uncertainty and loss, a recovering sense of reverence and reverie.

Source: Bruce Bond, "An Abundance of Lack: The Fullness of Desire in the Poetry of Robert Hass," in *Kenyon Review*, Vol. 12, No. 4, Fall 1990, pp. 46–53.

SOURCES

Anderson, Raymond H., "Czeslaw Milosz, Poet and Nobelist Who Wrote of Modern Cruelties, Dies at 93," in *New York Times*, August 15, 2004, http://www.nytimes.com/2004/08/15/obituaries/15milosz.html?scp=1&sq=Milosz&st=cse (accessed May 29 2010).

Chiasson, Dan, "Late and Soon: Mark Strand and David Hass, Collected in Tranquillity," in *New Yorker*, November 19, 2007, http://www.newyorker.com/arts/critics/books/2007/11/19/071119crbo_books_chiasson?currentPage=all (accessed May 29, 2010).

Hoagland, Tony, "Three Tenors: Gluck, Hass, Pinsky and the Deployment of Talent," in *American Poetry Review*, July/August 2003, pp. 37–42.

Miller, Claire, "For Robert Hass, Poetry is Part of the Eco-Arsenal," in *Grist*, October 13, 2005, http://www.grist.org/article/hass/ (accessed May 6, 2010).

Olson, Leisl, "Robert Hass's Guilt or The Weight of Wallace Stevens," in *American Poetry Review*, September/October 2007, pp. 37.

Orr, David, "Robert Hass's Empathy and Desire," in *New York Times*, May 6, 2010, http://www.nytimes.com/2010/05/16/books/review/Orr-t.html?pagewanted=all (accessed May 22, 2010).

Rix, Kate, "Distinguished Chair in Poetry and Poetics to Honor Hass, Stronach," in *College of Letters and Science, University of California Berkeley*, http://ls.berkeley.edu/?q=arts-ideas/archive/distinguished-chair-poetry-and-poetics-honor-hass-stronach (accessed May 6, 2010).

Ross, Anna, "The Consequences," in *Guernica: A Magazine of Arts and Politics*, January 2008, http://www.guernicamag.com/interviews/429/the_consequences_an_interview/ (accessed May 29, 2010).

Wicks, Robert, "Arthur Schopenhauer," in *Stanford Encyclopedia of Philosophy*, November 17, 2007, http://plato.stanford.edu/entries/schopenhauer/ (accessed June 1, 2010).

Wieseltier, Leon, "Czeslaw Milosz, 1911-2004," in *New York Times*, September 12, 2004, http://www.nytimes.com/2004/09/12/books/review/12WIESELTIER.html?pagewanted=print&position= (accessed May 29, 2010).

FURTHER READING

Glotfelty, Cheryl, and Harold Fromm, eds., *The Ecocriticism Reader: Landmarks in Literary Ecology*, University of Georgia Press, 1996.

> The natural world and ecology are central to Hass's work. Glotfelty and Fromm's reader introduces the curious reader to the concept of ecocriticism, the examination of works of literature in light of the emerging theories of ecology, evolution, and the interrelatedness of all beings. This volume includes both pioneers in the field such as Lynn White and Frederick Turner, as well as newer voices like Scott Slovic and Michael Branch who are solidifying ecocriticism as a discipline of literary study. This is a good starting point for readers interested in this aspect of Hass's poetics.

Hass, Robert, *Now and Then: The Poet's Choice Columns, 1997–2000*, Counterpoint, 2008.

> While he served as Poet Laureate, Hass revived the nineteenth-century tradition of including poetry in newspapers. In a weekly column for the *Washington Post Book World*, Hass chose a poem and then explicated it for the general reader. Columns in this collection range from canonical favorites like Emily Dickinson, Walt Whitman, and William Carlos Williams to contemporary poets like Linda Pastan and Mark Doty, as well as poets in translation, including Eugenio Montale, Vasko Popa, and of course, Milosz. This is a very accessible introduction to a wide variety of modern and canonical poetry.

Hass, Robert, ed., *The Essential Haiku: Versions of Basho, Buson & Issa*, Ecco Press, 1994.

> Hass has long been fascinated by the aesthetic expressed in Japanese haiku, and in this volume he presents his versions of about one hundred haiku by each of Japan's three central masters of the form. There is an extensive introduction that serves to set the poets, their work, and their aesthetic projects into context for English-speaking readers who might only know the form as a set of syllabic rules.

Hass, Robert and Stephen Mitchell, eds., *Into the Garden: A Wedding Anthology; Poetry and Prose on Love and Marriage*, Harper Perennial, 1993.

> Although billed as an anthology from which one might select works suitable for weddings, this anthology of poetry and prose on the subjects of love and marriage also serves as an excellent introduction to the long history of love poetry. Including poets as varied as the author of the "Song of Songs," Rumi, Emily Dickinson, John Donne, and Phillip Larkin, the book spans a wide range of cultures, styles and types of love poetry. It is a great resource for readers who might be interested in poetry, but who are unsure where they would like to begin reading.

Hillman, Brenda, *Death Tractates*, Wesleyan University Press, 1992.

> Hillman is married to Hass, and while their aesthetic projects are quite different, comparison of their works illuminates points of contact, as well as divergence. In this collection Hillman takes on the impossible distances that grief and loss impose, as well as the philosophical and religious edifices human beings have built in order to encompass this fundamental aspect of existence.

Hillman, Brenda, *Bright Existence*, Wesleyan University Press, 1993.

> In this companion collection to *Death Tractates*, Hillman uses both particle physics and the dualism of Gnosticism as jumping-off places for an examination of the thrilling dazzle of both human and more-than-human existence. These two collections cemented Hillman's reputation as one of the most exciting poets of her generation.

Milosz, Czeslaw, *New and Collected Poems (1931–2001)*, Ecco Press, 2001.

> Winner of the 1980 Nobel Prize for Literature, Milosz was a giant of post-war Polish and European poetry. This collection spans the length and breadth of his career, which included both simple celebrations of the natural world like "Song" from his early life, to the heroic "Treatise on Poetry" in which, as an old man, he wrestled with the age-old question of how poetry can encompass the political concerns of an age. Many of these poems were translated into the English during his decades-long collaboration with Hass, upon whom he was a major influence.

Snyder, Gary, *The Gary Snyder Reader: Prose, Poetry, and Translations, 1952–1998*, Counterpoint, 1999.

> Snyder is about half a generation older than Hass, and like Hass, he is deeply concerned with the environment and the natural world and is influenced by the poets of Asia. Snyder is central to the modern history of California and West Coast poetry, as well as to the development of much of the modern environmental movement. This volume collects poems from each of Snyder's collections, as well as letters, interviews, and prose essays. It is an excellent compendium of the work of this major American poet.

SUGGESTED SEARCH TERMS

Robert Hass

Robert Hass AND poetry

Robert Hass AND interview

Robert Hass AND poet laureate

Robert Hass AND Czeslaw Milosz

Robert Hass AND California Poetry

Robert Hass AND environmentalism

Robert Hass AND haiku

Robert Hass AND Brenda Hillman

Glossary of Literary Terms

A

Abstract: Used as a noun, the term refers to a short summary or outline of a longer work. As an adjective applied to writing or literary works, abstract refers to words or phrases that name things not knowable through the five senses.

Accent: The emphasis or stress placed on a syllable in poetry. Traditional poetry commonly uses patterns of accented and unaccented syllables (known as feet) that create distinct rhythms. Much modern poetry uses less formal arrangements that create a sense of freedom and spontaneity.

Aestheticism: A literary and artistic movement of the nineteenth century. Followers of the movement believed that art should not be mixed with social, political, or moral teaching. The statement "art for art's sake" is a good summary of aestheticism. The movement had its roots in France, but it gained widespread importance in England in the last half of the nineteenth century, where it helped change the Victorian practice of including moral lessons in literature.

Affective Fallacy: An error in judging the merits or faults of a work of literature. The "error" results from stressing the importance of the work's effect upon the reader—that is, how it makes a reader "feel" emotionally, what it does as a literary work—instead of stressing its inner qualities as a created object, or what it "is."

Age of Johnson: The period in English literature between 1750 and 1798, named after the most prominent literary figure of the age, Samuel Johnson. Works written during this time are noted for their emphasis on "sensibility," or emotional quality. These works formed a transition between the rational works of the Age of Reason, or Neoclassical period, and the emphasis on individual feelings and responses of the Romantic period.

Age of Reason: See *Neoclassicism*

Age of Sensibility: See *Age of Johnson*

Agrarians: A group of Southern American writers of the 1930s and 1940s who fostered an economic and cultural program for the South based on agriculture, in opposition to the industrial society of the North. The term can refer to any group that promotes the value of farm life and agricultural society.

Alexandrine Meter: See *Meter*

Allegory: A narrative technique in which characters representing things or abstract ideas are used to convey a message or teach a lesson. Allegory is typically used to teach moral, ethical, or religious lessons but is sometimes used for satiric or political purposes.

Alliteration: A poetic device where the first consonant sounds or any vowel sounds in words or syllables are repeated.

Allusion: A reference to a familiar literary or historical person or event, used to make an idea more easily understood.

Amerind Literature: The writing and oral traditions of Native Americans. Native American literature was originally passed on by word of mouth, so it consisted largely of stories and events that were easily memorized. Amerind prose is often rhythmic like poetry because it was recited to the beat of a ceremonial drum.

Analogy: A comparison of two things made to explain something unfamiliar through its similarities to something familiar, or to prove one point based on the acceptedness of another. Similes and metaphors are types of analogies.

Anapest: See *Foot*

Angry Young Men: A group of British writers of the 1950s whose work expressed bitterness and disillusionment with society. Common to their work is an anti-hero who rebels against a corrupt social order and strives for personal integrity.

Anthropomorphism: The presentation of animals or objects in human shape or with human characteristics. The term is derived from the Greek word for "human form."

Antimasque: See *Masque*

Antithesis: The antithesis of something is its direct opposite. In literature, the use of antithesis as a figure of speech results in two statements that show a contrast through the balancing of two opposite ideas. Technically, it is the second portion of the statement that is defined as the "antithesis"; the first portion is the "thesis."

Apocrypha: Writings tentatively attributed to an author but not proven or universally accepted to be their works. The term was originally applied to certain books of the Bible that were not considered inspired and so were not included in the "sacred canon."

Apollonian and Dionysian: The two impulses believed to guide authors of dramatic tragedy. The Apollonian impulse is named after Apollo, the Greek god of light and beauty and the symbol of intellectual order. The Dionysian impulse is named after Dionysus, the Greek god of wine and the symbol of the unrestrained forces of nature. The Apollonian impulse is to create a rational, harmonious world, while the Dionysian is to express the irrational forces of personality.

Apostrophe: A statement, question, or request addressed to an inanimate object or concept or to a nonexistent or absent person.

Archetype: The word archetype is commonly used to describe an original pattern or model from which all other things of the same kind are made. This term was introduced to literary criticism from the psychology of Carl Jung. It expresses Jung's theory that behind every person's "unconscious," or repressed memories of the past, lies the "collective unconscious" of the human race: memories of the countless typical experiences of our ancestors. These memories are said to prompt illogical associations that trigger powerful emotions in the reader. Often, the emotional process is primitive, even primordial. Archetypes are the literary images that grow out of the "collective unconscious." They appear in literature as incidents and plots that repeat basic patterns of life. They may also appear as stereotyped characters.

Argument: The argument of a work is the author's subject matter or principal idea.

Art for Art's Sake: See *Aestheticism*

Assonance: The repetition of similar vowel sounds in poetry.

Audience: The people for whom a piece of literature is written. Authors usually write with a certain audience in mind, for example, children, members of a religious or ethnic group, or colleagues in a professional field. The term "audience" also applies to the people who gather to see or hear any performance, including plays, poetry readings, speeches, and concerts.

Automatic Writing: Writing carried out without a preconceived plan in an effort to capture every random thought. Authors who engage in automatic writing typically do not revise their work, preferring instead to preserve the revealed truth and beauty of spontaneous expression.

Avant-garde: A French term meaning "vanguard." It is used in literary criticism to describe new writing that rejects traditional approaches to literature in favor of innovations in style or content.

B

Ballad: A short poem that tells a simple story and has a repeated refrain. Ballads were originally intended to be sung. Early ballads, known as folk ballads, were passed down through generations, so their authors are often unknown. Later ballads composed by known authors are called literary ballads.

Baroque: A term used in literary criticism to describe literature that is complex or ornate in style or diction. Baroque works typically express tension, anxiety, and violent emotion. The term "Baroque Age" designates a period in Western European literature beginning in the late sixteenth century and ending about one hundred years later. Works of this period often mirror the qualities of works more generally associated with the label "baroque" and sometimes feature elaborate conceits.

Baroque Age: See *Baroque*

Baroque Period: See *Baroque*

Beat Generation: See *Beat Movement*

Beat Movement: A period featuring a group of American poets and novelists of the 1950s and 1960s—including Jack Kerouac, Allen Ginsberg, Gregory Corso, William S. Burroughs, and Lawrence Ferlinghetti—who rejected established social and literary values. Using such techniques as stream of consciousness writing and jazz-influenced free verse and focusing on unusual or abnormal states of mind—generated by religious ecstasy or the use of drugs—the Beat writers aimed to create works that were unconventional in both form and subject matter.

Beat Poets: See *Beat Movement*

Beats, The: See *Beat Movement*

Belles-lettres: A French term meaning "fine letters" or "beautiful writing." It is often used as a synonym for literature, typically referring to imaginative and artistic rather than scientific or expository writing. Current usage sometimes restricts the meaning to light or humorous writing and appreciative essays about literature.

Black Aesthetic Movement: A period of artistic and literary development among African Americans in the 1960s and early 1970s. This was the first major African-American artistic movement since the Harlem Renaissance and was closely paralleled by the civil rights and black power movements. The black aesthetic writers attempted to produce works of art that would be meaningful to the black masses. Key figures in black aesthetics included one of its founders, poet and playwright Amiri Baraka, formerly known as LeRoi Jones; poet and essayist Haki R. Madhubuti, formerly Don L. Lee; poet and playwright Sonia Sanchez; and dramatist Ed Bullins.

Black Arts Movement: See *Black Aesthetic Movement*

Black Comedy: See *Black Humor*

Black Humor: Writing that places grotesque elements side by side with humorous ones in an attempt to shock the reader, forcing him or her to laugh at the horrifying reality of a disordered world.

Black Mountain School: Black Mountain College and three of its instructors—Robert Creeley, Robert Duncan, and Charles Olson—were all influential in projective verse, so poets working in projective verse are now referred as members of the Black Mountain school.

Blank Verse: Loosely, any unrhymed poetry, but more generally, unrhymed iambic pentameter verse (composed of lines of five two-syllable feet with the first syllable accented, the second unaccented). Blank verse has been used by poets since the Renaissance for its flexibility and its graceful, dignified tone.

Bloomsbury Group: A group of English writers, artists, and intellectuals who held informal artistic and philosophical discussions in Bloomsbury, a district of London, from around 1907 to the early 1930s. The Bloomsbury Group held no uniform philosophical beliefs but did commonly express an aversion to moral prudery and a desire for greater social tolerance.

Bon Mot: A French term meaning "good word." A *bon mot* is a witty remark or clever observation.

Breath Verse: See *Projective Verse*

Burlesque: Any literary work that uses exaggeration to make its subject appear ridiculous, either by treating a trivial subject with profound seriousness or by treating a dignified subject frivolously. The word "burlesque" may also be used as an adjective, as in "burlesque show," to mean "striptease act."

C

Cadence: The natural rhythm of language caused by the alternation of accented and unaccented syllables. Much modern poetry—notably free verse—deliberately manipulates cadence to create complex rhythmic effects.

Caesura: A pause in a line of poetry, usually occurring near the middle. It typically corresponds to a break in the natural rhythm or sense of the line but is sometimes shifted to create special meanings or rhythmic effects.

Canzone: A short Italian or Provencal lyric poem, commonly about love and often set to music. The *canzone* has no set form but typically contains five or six stanzas made up of seven to twenty lines of eleven syllables each. A shorter, five- to ten-line "envoy," or concluding stanza, completes the poem.

Carpe Diem: A Latin term meaning "seize the day." This is a traditional theme of poetry, especially lyrics. A *carpe diem* poem advises the reader or the person it addresses to live for today and enjoy the pleasures of the moment.

Catharsis: The release or purging of unwanted emotions—specifically fear and pity—brought about by exposure to art. The term was first used by the Greek philosopher Aristotle in his *Poetics* to refer to the desired effect of tragedy on spectators.

Celtic Renaissance: A period of Irish literary and cultural history at the end of the nineteenth century. Followers of the movement aimed to create a romantic vision of Celtic myth and legend. The most significant works of the Celtic Renaissance typically present a dreamy, unreal world, usually in reaction against the reality of contemporary problems.

Celtic Twilight: See *Celtic Renaissance*

Character: Broadly speaking, a person in a literary work. The actions of characters are what constitute the plot of a story, novel, or poem. There are numerous types of characters, ranging from simple, stereotypical figures to intricate, multifaceted ones. In the techniques of anthropomorphism and personification, animals—and even places or things—can assume aspects of character. "Characterization" is the process by which an author creates vivid, believable characters in a work of art. This may be done in a variety of ways, including (1) direct description of the character by the narrator; (2) the direct presentation of the speech, thoughts, or actions of the character; and (3) the responses of other characters to the character. The term "character" also refers to a form originated by the ancient Greek writer Theophrastus that later became popular in the seventeenth and eighteenth centuries. It is a short essay or sketch of a person who prominently displays a specific attribute or quality, such as miserliness or ambition.

Characterization: See *Character*

Classical: In its strictest definition in literary criticism, classicism refers to works of ancient Greek or Roman literature. The term may also be used to describe a literary work of recognized importance (a "classic") from any time period or literature that exhibits the traits of classicism.

Classicism: A term used in literary criticism to describe critical doctrines that have their roots in ancient Greek and Roman literature, philosophy, and art. Works associated with classicism typically exhibit restraint on the part of the author, unity of design and purpose, clarity, simplicity, logical organization, and respect for tradition.

Colloquialism: A word, phrase, or form of pronunciation that is acceptable in casual conversation but not in formal, written communication. It is considered more acceptable than slang.

Complaint: A lyric poem, popular in the Renaissance, in which the speaker expresses sorrow about his or her condition. Typically, the speaker's sadness is caused by an unresponsive lover, but some complaints cite other sources of unhappiness, such as poverty or fate.

Conceit: A clever and fanciful metaphor, usually expressed through elaborate and extended comparison, that presents a striking parallel between two seemingly dissimilar things—for example, elaborately comparing a beautiful woman to an object like a garden or the sun. The conceit was a popular device throughout the Elizabethan Age and Baroque Age and was the principal technique of the seventeenth-century English metaphysical poets. This usage of the word conceit is unrelated to the best-known definition of conceit as an arrogant attitude or behavior.

Concrete: Concrete is the opposite of abstract, and refers to a thing that actually exists or a description that allows the reader to experience an object or concept with the senses.

Concrete Poetry: Poetry in which visual elements play a large part in the poetic effect. Punctuation marks, letters, or words are arranged on a page to form a visual design: a cross, for example, or a bumblebee.

Confessional Poetry: A form of poetry in which the poet reveals very personal, intimate, sometimes shocking information about himself or herself.

Connotation: The impression that a word gives beyond its defined meaning. Connotations may be universally understood or may be significant only to a certain group.

Consonance: Consonance occurs in poetry when words appearing at the ends of two or more verses have similar final consonant sounds but have final vowel sounds that differ, as with "stuff" and "off."

Convention: Any widely accepted literary device, style, or form.

Corrido: A Mexican ballad.

Couplet: Two lines of poetry with the same rhyme and meter, often expressing a complete and self-contained thought.

Criticism: The systematic study and evaluation of literary works, usually based on a specific method or set of principles. An important part of literary studies since ancient times, the practice of criticism has given rise to numerous theories, methods, and "schools," sometimes producing conflicting, even contradictory, interpretations of literature in general as well as of individual works. Even such basic issues as what constitutes a poem or a novel have been the subject of much criticism over the centuries.

D

Dactyl: See *Foot*

Dadaism: A protest movement in art and literature founded by Tristan Tzara in 1916. Followers of the movement expressed their outrage at the destruction brought about by World War I by revolting against numerous forms of social convention. The Dadaists presented works marked by calculated madness and flamboyant nonsense. They stressed total freedom of expression, commonly through primitive displays of emotion and illogical, often senseless, poetry. The movement ended shortly after the war, when it was replaced by surrealism.

Decadent: See *Decadents*

Decadents: The followers of a nineteenth-century literary movement that had its beginnings in French aestheticism. Decadent literature displays a fascination with perverse and morbid states; a search for novelty and sensation—the "new thrill"; a preoccupation with mysticism; and a belief in the senselessness of human existence. The movement is closely associated with the doctrine Art for Art's Sake. The term "decadence" is sometimes used to denote a decline in the quality of art or literature following a period of greatness.

Deconstruction: A method of literary criticism developed by Jacques Derrida and characterized by multiple conflicting interpretations of a given work. Deconstructionists consider the impact of the language of a work and suggest that the true meaning of the work is not necessarily the meaning that the author intended.

Deduction: The process of reaching a conclusion through reasoning from general premises to a specific premise.

Denotation: The definition of a word, apart from the impressions or feelings it creates in the reader.

Diction: The selection and arrangement of words in a literary work. Either or both may vary depending on the desired effect. There are four general types of diction: "formal," used in scholarly or lofty writing; "informal," used in relaxed but educated conversation; "colloquial," used in everyday speech; and "slang," containing newly coined words and other terms not accepted in formal usage.

Didactic: A term used to describe works of literature that aim to teach some moral, religious, political, or practical lesson. Although didactic elements are often found in artistically pleasing works, the term "didactic" usually refers to literature in which the message is more important than the form. The term may also be used to criticize a work that the critic finds "overly didactic," that is, heavy-handed in its delivery of a lesson.

Dimeter: See *Meter*

Dionysian: See *Apollonian and Dionysian*

Discordia concours: A Latin phrase meaning "discord in harmony." The term was coined by the eighteenth-century English writer Samuel Johnson to describe "a combination of dissimilar images or discovery of occult resemblances in things apparently unlike." Johnson created the expression by reversing a phrase by the Latin poet Horace.

Dissonance: A combination of harsh or jarring sounds, especially in poetry. Although such combinations may be accidental, poets sometimes intentionally make them to achieve particular effects. Dissonance is also sometimes used to refer to close but not identical rhymes. When this is the case, the word functions as a synonym for consonance.

Double Entendre: A corruption of a French phrase meaning "double meaning." The term is used to indicate a word or phrase that is deliberately ambiguous, especially when one of the meanings is risque or improper.

Draft: Any preliminary version of a written work. An author may write dozens of drafts which are revised to form the final work, or he or she may write only one, with few or no revisions.

Dramatic Monologue: See *Monologue*

Dramatic Poetry: Any lyric work that employs elements of drama such as dialogue, conflict, or characterization, but excluding works that are intended for stage presentation.

Dream Allegory: See *Dream Vision*

Dream Vision: A literary convention, chiefly of the Middle Ages. In a dream vision a story is presented as a literal dream of the narrator. This device was commonly used to teach moral and religious lessons.

E

Eclogue: In classical literature, a poem featuring rural themes and structured as a dialogue among shepherds. Eclogues often took specific poetic forms, such as elegies or love poems. Some were written as the soliloquy of a shepherd. In later centuries, "eclogue" came to refer to any poem that was in the pastoral tradition or that had a dialogue or monologue structure.

Edwardian: Describes cultural conventions identified with the period of the reign of Edward VII of England (1901-1910). Writers of the Edwardian Age typically displayed a strong reaction against the propriety and conservatism of the Victorian Age. Their work often exhibits distrust of authority in religion, politics, and art and expresses strong doubts about the soundness of conventional values.

Edwardian Age: See *Edwardian*

Electra Complex: A daughter's amorous obsession with her father.

Elegy: A lyric poem that laments the death of a person or the eventual death of all people. In a conventional elegy, set in a classical world, the poet and subject are spoken of as shepherds. In modern criticism, the word elegy is often used to refer to a poem that is melancholy or mournfully contemplative.

Elizabethan Age: A period of great economic growth, religious controversy, and nationalism closely associated with the reign of Elizabeth I of England (1558-1603). The Elizabethan Age is considered a part of the general renaissance—that is, the flowering of arts and literature—that took place in Europe during the fourteenth through sixteenth centuries. The era is considered the golden age of English literature. The most important dramas in English and a great deal of lyric poetry were produced during this period, and modern English criticism began around this time.

Empathy: A sense of shared experience, including emotional and physical feelings, with someone or something other than oneself. Empathy is often used to describe the response of a reader to a literary character.

English Sonnet: See *Sonnet*

Enjambment: The running over of the sense and structure of a line of verse or a couplet into the following verse or couplet.

Enlightenment, The: An eighteenth-century philosophical movement. It began in France but had a wide impact throughout Europe and America. Thinkers of the Enlightenment valued reason and believed that both the individual and society could achieve a state of perfection. Corresponding to this essentially humanist vision was a resistance to religious authority.

Epic: A long narrative poem about the adventures of a hero of great historic or legendary importance. The setting is vast and the action is often given cosmic significance through the intervention of supernatural forces such as gods, angels, or demons. Epics are typically written in a classical style of grand simplicity with elaborate metaphors and allusions that enhance the symbolic importance of a hero's adventures.

Epic Simile: See *Homeric Simile*

Epigram: A saying that makes the speaker's point quickly and concisely.

Epilogue: A concluding statement or section of a literary work. In dramas, particularly those of the seventeenth and eighteenth centuries, the epilogue is a closing speech, often in verse, delivered by an actor at the end of a play and spoken directly to the audience.

Epiphany: A sudden revelation of truth inspired by a seemingly trivial incident.

Epitaph: An inscription on a tomb or tombstone, or a verse written on the occasion of a person's death. Epitaphs may be serious or humorous.

Epithalamion: A song or poem written to honor and commemorate a marriage ceremony.

Epithalamium: See *Epithalamion*

Epithet: A word or phrase, often disparaging or abusive, that expresses a character trait of someone or something.

Erziehungsroman: See *Bildungsroman*

Essay: A prose composition with a focused subject of discussion. The term was coined by Michel de Montaigne to describe his 1580 collection of brief, informal reflections on himself and on various topics relating to human nature. An essay can also be a long, systematic discourse.

Existentialism: A predominantly twentieth-century philosophy concerned with the nature and perception of human existence. There are two major strains of existentialist thought: atheistic and Christian. Followers of atheistic existentialism believe that the individual is alone in a godless universe and that the basic human condition is one of suffering and loneliness. Nevertheless, because there are no fixed values, individuals can create their own characters—indeed, they can shape themselves—through the exercise of free will. The atheistic strain culminates in and is popularly associated with the works of Jean-Paul Sartre. The Christian existentialists, on the other hand,

believe that only in God may people find freedom from life's anguish. The two strains hold certain beliefs in common: that existence cannot be fully understood or described through empirical effort; that anguish is a universal element of life; that individuals must bear responsibility for their actions; and that there is no common standard of behavior or perception for religious and ethical matters.

Expatriates: See *Expatriatism*

Expatriatism: The practice of leaving one's country to live for an extended period in another country.

Exposition: Writing intended to explain the nature of an idea, thing, or theme. Expository writing is often combined with description, narration, or argument. In dramatic writing, the exposition is the introductory material which presents the characters, setting, and tone of the play.

Expressionism: An indistinct literary term, originally used to describe an early twentieth-century school of German painting. The term applies to almost any mode of unconventional, highly subjective writing that distorts reality in some way.

Extended Monologue: See *Monologue*

F

Feet: See *Foot*

Feminine Rhyme: See *Rhyme*

Fiction: Any story that is the product of imagination rather than a documentation of fact. Characters and events in such narratives may be based in real life but their ultimate form and configuration is a creation of the author.

Figurative Language: A technique in writing in which the author temporarily interrupts the order, construction, or meaning of the writing for a particular effect. This interruption takes the form of one or more figures of speech such as hyperbole, irony, or simile. Figurative language is the opposite of literal language, in which every word is truthful, accurate, and free of exaggeration or embellishment.

Figures of Speech: Writing that differs from customary conventions for construction, meaning, order, or significance for the purpose of a special meaning or effect. There are two major types of figures of speech: rhetorical figures, which do not make changes in the meaning of the words, and tropes, which do.

Fin de siecle: A French term meaning "end of the century." The term is used to denote the last decade of the nineteenth century, a transition period when writers and other artists abandoned old conventions and looked for new techniques and objectives.

First Person: See *Point of View*

Folk Ballad: See *Ballad*

Folklore: Traditions and myths preserved in a culture or group of people. Typically, these are passed on by word of mouth in various forms—such as legends, songs, and proverbs—or preserved in customs and ceremonies. This term was first used by W. J. Thoms in 1846.

Folktale: A story originating in oral tradition. Folktales fall into a variety of categories, including legends, ghost stories, fairy tales, fables, and anecdotes based on historical figures and events.

Foot: The smallest unit of rhythm in a line of poetry. In English-language poetry, a foot is typically one accented syllable combined with one or two unaccented syllables.

Form: The pattern or construction of a work which identifies its genre and distinguishes it from other genres.

Formalism: In literary criticism, the belief that literature should follow prescribed rules of construction, such as those that govern the sonnet form.

Fourteener Meter: See *Meter*

Free Verse: Poetry that lacks regular metrical and rhyme patterns but that tries to capture the cadences of everyday speech. The form allows a poet to exploit a variety of rhythmical effects within a single poem.

Futurism: A flamboyant literary and artistic movement that developed in France, Italy, and Russia from 1908 through the 1920s. Futurist theater and poetry abandoned traditional literary forms. In their place, followers of the movement attempted to achieve total freedom of expression through bizarre imagery and deformed or newly invented words. The Futurists were self-consciously modern artists who attempted to incorporate the appearances and sounds of modern life into their work.

G

Genre: A category of literary work. In critical theory, genre may refer to both the content of a given work—tragedy, comedy, pastoral—and to its form, such as poetry, novel, or drama.

Genteel Tradition: A term coined by critic George Santayana to describe the literary practice of certain late nineteenth-century American writers, especially New Englanders. Followers of the Genteel Tradition emphasized conventionality in social, religious, moral, and literary standards.

Georgian Age: See *Georgian Poets*

Georgian Period: See *Georgian Poets*

Georgian Poets: A loose grouping of English poets during the years 1912-1922. The Georgians reacted against certain literary schools and practices, especially Victorian wordiness, turn-of-the-century aestheticism, and contemporary urban realism. In their place, the Georgians embraced the nineteenth-century poetic practices of William Wordsworth and the other Lake Poets.

Georgic: A poem about farming and the farmer's way of life, named from Virgil's *Georgics*.

Gilded Age: A period in American history during the 1870s characterized by political corruption and materialism. A number of important novels of social and political criticism were written during this time.

Gothic: See *Gothicism*

Gothicism: In literary criticism, works characterized by a taste for the medieval or morbidly attractive. A gothic novel prominently features elements of horror, the supernatural, gloom, and violence: clanking chains, terror, charnel houses, ghosts, medieval castles, and mysteriously slamming doors. The term "gothic novel" is also applied to novels that lack elements of the traditional Gothic setting but that create a similar atmosphere of terror or dread.

Graveyard School: A group of eighteenth-century English poets who wrote long, picturesque meditations on death. Their works were designed to cause the reader to ponder immortality.

Great Chain of Being: The belief that all things and creatures in nature are organized in a hierarchy from inanimate objects at the bottom to God at the top. This system of belief was popular in the seventeenth and eighteenth centuries.

Grotesque: In literary criticism, the subject matter of a work or a style of expression characterized by exaggeration, deformity, freakishness, and disorder. The grotesque often includes an element of comic absurdity.

H

Haiku: The shortest form of Japanese poetry, constructed in three lines of five, seven, and five syllables respectively. The message of a *haiku* poem usually centers on some aspect of spirituality and provokes an emotional response in the reader.

Half Rhyme: See *Consonance*

Harlem Renaissance: The Harlem Renaissance of the 1920s is generally considered the first significant movement of black writers and artists in the United States. During this period, new and established black writers published more fiction and poetry than ever before, the first influential black literary journals were established, and black authors and artists received their first widespread recognition and serious critical appraisal. Among the major writers associated with this period are Claude McKay, Jean Toomer, Countee Cullen, Langston Hughes, Arna Bontemps, Nella Larsen, and Zora Neale Hurston.

Hellenism: Imitation of ancient Greek thought or styles. Also, an approach to life that focuses on the growth and development of the intellect. "Hellenism" is sometimes used to refer to the belief that reason can be applied to examine all human experience.

Heptameter: See *Meter*

Hero/Heroine: The principal sympathetic character (male or female) in a literary work. Heroes and heroines typically exhibit admirable traits: idealism, courage, and integrity, for example.

Heroic Couplet: A rhyming couplet written in iambic pentameter (a verse with five iambic feet).

Heroic Line: The meter and length of a line of verse in epic or heroic poetry. This varies by language and time period.

Heroine: See *Hero/Heroine*

Hexameter: See *Meter*

Historical Criticism: The study of a work based on its impact on the world of the time period in which it was written.

Hokku: See *Haiku*

Holocaust: See *Holocaust Literature*

Holocaust Literature: Literature influenced by or written about the Holocaust of World War II. Such literature includes true stories of survival in concentration camps, escape, and life after the war, as well as fictional works and poetry.

Homeric Simile: An elaborate, detailed comparison written as a simile many lines in length.

Horatian Satire: See *Satire*

Humanism: A philosophy that places faith in the dignity of humankind and rejects the medieval perception of the individual as a weak, fallen creature. "Humanists" typically believe in the perfectibility of human nature and view reason and education as the means to that end.

Humors: Mentions of the humors refer to the ancient Greek theory that a person's health and personality were determined by the balance of four basic fluids in the body: blood, phlegm, yellow bile, and black bile. A dominance of any fluid would cause extremes in behavior. An excess of blood created a sanguine person who was joyful, aggressive, and passionate; a phlegmatic person was shy, fearful, and sluggish; too much yellow bile led to a choleric temperament characterized by impatience, anger, bitterness, and stubbornness; and excessive black bile created melancholy, a state of laziness, gluttony, and lack of motivation.

Humours: See *Humors*

Hyperbole: In literary criticism, deliberate exaggeration used to achieve an effect.

I

Iamb: See *Foot*

Idiom: A word construction or verbal expression closely associated with a given language.

Image: A concrete representation of an object or sensory experience. Typically, such a representation helps evoke the feelings associated with the object or experience itself. Images are either "literal" or "figurative." Literal images are especially concrete and involve little or no extension of the obvious meaning of the words used to express them. Figurative images do not follow the literal meaning of the words exactly. Images in literature are usually visual, but the term "image" can also refer to the representation of any sensory experience.

Imagery: The array of images in a literary work. Also, figurative language.

Imagism: An English and American poetry movement that flourished between 1908 and 1917. The Imagists used precise, clearly presented images in their works. They also used common, everyday speech and aimed for conciseness, concrete imagery, and the creation of new rhythms.

In medias res: A Latin term meaning "in the middle of things." It refers to the technique of beginning a story at its midpoint and then using various flashback devices to reveal previous action.

Induction: The process of reaching a conclusion by reasoning from specific premises to form a general premise. Also, an introductory portion of a work of literature, especially a play.

Intentional Fallacy: The belief that judgments of a literary work based solely on an author's stated or implied intentions are false and misleading. Critics who believe in the concept of the intentional fallacy typically argue that the work itself is sufficient matter for interpretation, even though they may concede that an author's statement of purpose can be useful.

Interior Monologue: A narrative technique in which characters' thoughts are revealed in a way that appears to be uncontrolled by the author. The interior monologue typically aims to reveal the inner self of a character. It portrays emotional experiences as they occur at both a conscious and unconscious level. Images are often used to represent sensations or emotions.

Internal Rhyme: Rhyme that occurs within a single line of verse.

Irish Literary Renaissance: A late nineteenth- and early twentieth-century movement in Irish literature. Members of the movement aimed to reduce the influence of British culture in Ireland and create an Irish national literature.

Irony: In literary criticism, the effect of language in which the intended meaning is the opposite of what is stated.

Italian Sonnet: See *Sonnet*

J

Jacobean Age: The period of the reign of James I of England (1603-1625). The early literature of this period reflected the worldview of the Elizabethan Age, but a darker, more cynical attitude steadily grew in the art and literature of the Jacobean Age. This was an important time for English drama and poetry.

Jargon: Language that is used or understood only by a select group of people. Jargon may refer to terminology used in a certain profession, such as computer jargon, or it may refer to any nonsensical language that is not understood by most people.

Journalism: Writing intended for publication in a newspaper or magazine, or for broadcast on a radio or television program featuring news, sports, entertainment, or other timely material.

K

Knickerbocker Group: A somewhat indistinct group of New York writers of the first half of the nineteenth century. Members of the group were linked only by location and a common theme: New York life.

Kunstlerroman: See *Bildungsroman*

L

Lais: See *Lay*

Lake Poets: See *Lake School*

Lake School: These poets all lived in the Lake District of England at the turn of the nineteenth century. As a group, they followed no single "school" of thought or literary practice, although their works were uniformly disparaged by the *Edinburgh Review*.

Lay: A song or simple narrative poem. The form originated in medieval France. Early French *lais* were often based on the Celtic legends and other tales sung by Breton minstrels—thus the name of the "Breton lay." In fourteenth-century England, the term "lay" was used to describe short narratives written in imitation of the Breton lays.

Leitmotiv: See *Motif*

Literal Language: An author uses literal language when he or she writes without exaggerating or embellishing the subject matter and without any tools of figurative language.

Literary Ballad: See *Ballad*

Literature: Literature is broadly defined as any written or spoken material, but the term most often refers to creative works.

Lost Generation: A term first used by Gertrude Stein to describe the post-World War I generation of American writers: men and women haunted by a sense of betrayal and emptiness brought about by the destructiveness of the war.

Lyric Poetry: A poem expressing the subjective feelings and personal emotions of the poet. Such poetry is melodic, since it was originally accompanied by a lyre in recitals. Most Western poetry in the twentieth century may be classified as lyrical.

M

Mannerism: Exaggerated, artificial adherence to a literary manner or style. Also, a popular style of the visual arts of late sixteenth-century Europe that was marked by elongation of the human form and by intentional spatial distortion. Literary works that are self-consciously high-toned and artistic are often said to be "mannered."

Masculine Rhyme: See *Rhyme*

Measure: The foot, verse, or time sequence used in a literary work, especially a poem. Measure is often used somewhat incorrectly as a synonym for meter.

Metaphor: A figure of speech that expresses an idea through the image of another object. Metaphors suggest the essence of the first object by identifying it with certain qualities of the second object.

Metaphysical Conceit: See *Conceit*

Metaphysical Poetry: The body of poetry produced by a group of seventeenth-century English writers called the "Metaphysical Poets." The group includes John Donne and Andrew Marvell. The Metaphysical Poets made use of everyday speech, intellectual analysis, and unique imagery. They aimed to portray the ordinary conflicts and contradictions of life. Their poems often took the form of an argument, and many of them emphasize physical and religious love as well as the fleeting nature of life. Elaborate conceits are typical in metaphysical poetry.

Metaphysical Poets: See *Metaphysical Poetry*

Meter: In literary criticism, the repetition of sound patterns that creates a rhythm in poetry. The patterns are based on the number of syllables and the presence and absence of accents. The unit of rhythm in a line is called a foot. Types of meter are classified according to the number of feet in a line. These are the standard English lines: Monometer, one foot; Dimeter, two feet; Trimeter, three feet; Tetrameter, four feet; Pentameter, five feet; Hexameter, six feet (also called the Alexandrine); Heptameter, seven feet (also called the "Fourteener" when the feet are iambic).

Modernism: Modern literary practices. Also, the principles of a literary school that lasted from roughly the beginning of the twentieth century until the end of World War II. Modernism is defined by its rejection of the literary conventions of the nineteenth century and by its opposition to conventional morality, taste, traditions, and economic values.

Monologue: A composition, written or oral, by a single individual. More specifically, a speech given by a single individual in a drama or other public entertainment. It has no set length, although it is usually several or more lines long.

Monometer: See *Meter*

Mood: The prevailing emotions of a work or of the author in his or her creation of the work. The mood of a work is not always what might be expected based on its subject matter.

Motif: A theme, character type, image, metaphor, or other verbal element that recurs throughout a single work of literature or occurs in a number of different works over a period of time.

Motiv: See *Motif*

Muckrakers: An early twentieth-century group of American writers. Typically, their works exposed the wrongdoings of big business and government in the United States.

Muses: Nine Greek mythological goddesses, the daughters of Zeus and Mnemosyne

(Memory). Each muse patronized a specific area of the liberal arts and sciences. Calliope presided over epic poetry, Clio over history, Erato over love poetry, Euterpe over music or lyric poetry, Melpomene over tragedy, Polyhymnia over hymns to the gods, Terpsichore over dance, Thalia over comedy, and Urania over astronomy. Poets and writers traditionally made appeals to the Muses for inspiration in their work.

Myth: An anonymous tale emerging from the traditional beliefs of a culture or social unit. Myths use supernatural explanations for natural phenomena. They may also explain cosmic issues like creation and death. Collections of myths, known as mythologies, are common to all cultures and nations, but the best-known myths belong to the Norse, Roman, and Greek mythologies.

N

Narration: The telling of a series of events, real or invented. A narration may be either a simple narrative, in which the events are recounted chronologically, or a narrative with a plot, in which the account is given in a style reflecting the author's artistic concept of the story. Narration is sometimes used as a synonym for "storyline."

Narrative: A verse or prose accounting of an event or sequence of events, real or invented. The term is also used as an adjective in the sense "method of narration." For example, in literary criticism, the expression "narrative technique" usually refers to the way the author structures and presents his or her story.

Narrative Poetry: A nondramatic poem in which the author tells a story. Such poems may be of any length or level of complexity.

Narrator: The teller of a story. The narrator may be the author or a character in the story through whom the author speaks.

Naturalism: A literary movement of the late nineteenth and early twentieth centuries. The movement's major theorist, French novelist Emile Zola, envisioned a type of fiction that would examine human life with the objectivity of scientific inquiry. The Naturalists typically viewed human beings as either the products of "biological determinism," ruled by hereditary instincts and

engaged in an endless struggle for survival, or as the products of "socioeconomic determinism," ruled by social and economic forces beyond their control. In their works, the Naturalists generally ignored the highest levels of society and focused on degradation: poverty, alcoholism, prostitution, insanity, and disease.

Negritude: A literary movement based on the concept of a shared cultural bond on the part of black Africans, wherever they may be in the world. It traces its origins to the former French colonies of Africa and the Caribbean. Negritude poets, novelists, and essayists generally stress four points in their writings: One, black alienation from traditional African culture can lead to feelings of inferiority. Two, European colonialism and Western education should be resisted. Three, black Africans should seek to affirm and define their own identity. Four, African culture can and should be reclaimed. Many Negritude writers also claim that blacks can make unique contributions to the world, based on a heightened appreciation of nature, rhythm, and human emotions—aspects of life they say are not so highly valued in the materialistic and rationalistic West.

Negro Renaissance: See *Harlem Renaissance*

Neoclassical Period: See *Neoclassicism*

Neoclassicism: In literary criticism, this term refers to the revival of the attitudes and styles of expression of classical literature. It is generally used to describe a period in European history beginning in the late seventeenth century and lasting until about 1800. In its purest form, Neoclassicism marked a return to order, proportion, restraint, logic, accuracy, and decorum. In England, where Neoclassicism perhaps was most popular, it reflected the influence of seventeenth- century French writers, especially dramatists. Neoclassical writers typically reacted against the intensity and enthusiasm of the Renaissance period. They wrote works that appealed to the intellect, using elevated language and classical literary forms such as satire and the ode. Neoclassical works were often governed by the classical goal of instruction.

Neoclassicists: See *Neoclassicism*

New Criticism: A movement in literary criticism, dating from the late 1920s, that stressed close textual analysis in the interpretation of works of literature. The New Critics saw little merit in historical and biographical analysis. Rather, they aimed to examine the text alone, free from the question of how external events—biographical or otherwise—may have helped shape it.

New Journalism: A type of writing in which the journalist presents factual information in a form usually used in fiction. New journalism emphasizes description, narration, and character development to bring readers closer to the human element of the story, and is often used in personality profiles and in-depth feature articles. It is not compatible with "straight" or "hard" newswriting, which is generally composed in a brief, fact-based style.

New Journalists: See *New Journalism*

New Negro Movement: See *Harlem Renaissance*

Noble Savage: The idea that primitive man is noble and good but becomes evil and corrupted as he becomes civilized. The concept of the noble savage originated in the Renaissance period but is more closely identified with such later writers as Jean-Jacques Rousseau and Aphra Behn.

O

Objective Correlative: An outward set of objects, a situation, or a chain of events corresponding to an inward experience and evoking this experience in the reader. The term frequently appears in modern criticism in discussions of authors' intended effects on the emotional responses of readers.

Objectivity: A quality in writing characterized by the absence of the author's opinion or feeling about the subject matter. Objectivity is an important factor in criticism.

Occasional Verse: poetry written on the occasion of a significant historical or personal event. *Vers de societe* is sometimes called occasional verse although it is of a less serious nature.

Octave: A poem or stanza composed of eight lines. The term octave most often represents the first eight lines of a Petrarchan sonnet.

Ode: Name given to an extended lyric poem characterized by exalted emotion and dignified style. An ode usually concerns a single, serious theme. Most odes, but not all, are addressed to an object or individual. Odes are distinguished from other lyric poetic forms by their complex rhythmic and stanzaic patterns.

Oedipus Complex: A son's amorous obsession with his mother. The phrase is derived from the story of the ancient Theban hero Oedipus, who unknowingly killed his father and married his mother.

Omniscience: See *Point of View*

Onomatopoeia: The use of words whose sounds express or suggest their meaning. In its simplest sense, onomatopoeia may be represented by words that mimic the sounds they denote such as "hiss" or "meow." At a more subtle level, the pattern and rhythm of sounds and rhymes of a line or poem may be onomatopoeic.

Oral Tradition: See *Oral Transmission*

Oral Transmission: A process by which songs, ballads, folklore, and other material are transmitted by word of mouth. The tradition of oral transmission predates the written record systems of literate society. Oral transmission preserves material sometimes over generations, although often with variations. Memory plays a large part in the recitation and preservation of orally transmitted material.

Ottava Rima: An eight-line stanza of poetry composed in iambic pentameter (a five-foot line in which each foot consists of an unaccented syllable followed by an accented syllable), following the abababcc rhyme scheme.

Oxymoron: A phrase combining two contradictory terms. Oxymorons may be intentional or unintentional.

P

Pantheism: The idea that all things are both a manifestation or revelation of God and a part of God at the same time. Pantheism was a common attitude in the early societies of Egypt, India, and Greece—the term derives from the Greek *pan* meaning "all" and *theos* meaning "deity." It later became a significant part of the Christian faith.

Parable: A story intended to teach a moral lesson or answer an ethical question.

Paradox: A statement that appears illogical or contradictory at first, but may actually point to an underlying truth.

Parallelism: A method of comparison of two ideas in which each is developed in the same grammatical structure.

Parnassianism: A mid nineteenth-century movement in French literature. Followers of the movement stressed adherence to well-defined artistic forms as a reaction against the often chaotic expression of the artist's ego that dominated the work of the Romantics. The Parnassians also rejected the moral, ethical, and social themes exhibited in the works of French Romantics such as Victor Hugo. The aesthetic doctrines of the Parnassians strongly influenced the later symbolist and decadent movements.

Parody: In literary criticism, this term refers to an imitation of a serious literary work or the signature style of a particular author in a ridiculous manner. A typical parody adopts the style of the original and applies it to an inappropriate subject for humorous effect. Parody is a form of satire and could be considered the literary equivalent of a caricature or cartoon.

Pastoral: A term derived from the Latin word "pastor," meaning shepherd. A pastoral is a literary composition on a rural theme. The conventions of the pastoral were originated by the third-century Greek poet Theocritus, who wrote about the experiences, love affairs, and pastimes of Sicilian shepherds. In a pastoral, characters and language of a courtly nature are often placed in a simple setting. The term pastoral is also used to classify dramas, elegies, and lyrics that exhibit the use of country settings and shepherd characters.

Pathetic Fallacy: A term coined by English critic John Ruskin to identify writing that falsely endows nonhuman things with human intentions and feelings, such as "angry clouds" and "sad trees."

Pen Name: See *Pseudonym*

Pentameter: See *Meter*

Persona: A Latin term meaning "mask." *Personae* are the characters in a fictional work of literature. The *persona* generally functions as a mask through which the author tells a story in a voice other than his or her own. A *persona* is usually either a character in a story who acts as a narrator or an "implied author," a voice created by the author to act as the narrator for himself or herself.

Personae: See *Persona*

Personal Point of View: See *Point of View*

Personification: A figure of speech that gives human qualities to abstract ideas, animals, and inanimate objects.

Petrarchan Sonnet: See *Sonnet*

Phenomenology: A method of literary criticism based on the belief that things have no existence outside of human consciousness or awareness. Proponents of this theory believe that art is a process that takes place in the mind of the observer as he or she contemplates an object rather than a quality of the object itself.

Plagiarism: Claiming another person's written material as one's own. Plagiarism can take the form of direct, word-for-word copying or the theft of the substance or idea of the work.

Platonic Criticism: A form of criticism that stresses an artistic work's usefulness as an agent of social engineering rather than any quality or value of the work itself.

Platonism: The embracing of the doctrines of the philosopher Plato, popular among the poets of the Renaissance and the Romantic period. Platonism is more flexible than Aristotelian Criticism and places more emphasis on the supernatural and unknown aspects of life.

Plot: In literary criticism, this term refers to the pattern of events in a narrative or drama. In its simplest sense, the plot guides the author in composing the work and helps the reader follow the work. Typically, plots exhibit causality and unity and have a beginning, a middle, and an end. Sometimes, however, a plot may consist of a series of disconnected events, in which case it is known as an "episodic plot."

Poem: In its broadest sense, a composition utilizing rhyme, meter, concrete detail, and expressive language to create a literary experience with emotional and aesthetic appeal.

Poet: An author who writes poetry or verse. The term is also used to refer to an artist or writer who has an exceptional gift for expression, imagination, and energy in the making of art in any form.

Poete maudit: A term derived from Paul Verlaine's *Les poetes maudits* (*The Accursed Poets*), a collection of essays on the French symbolist writers Stephane Mallarme, Arthur Rimbaud, and Tristan Corbiere. In the sense intended by Verlaine, the poet is "accursed" for choosing to explore extremes of human experience outside of middle-class society.

Poetic Fallacy: See *Pathetic Fallacy*

Poetic Justice: An outcome in a literary work, not necessarily a poem, in which the good are rewarded and the evil are punished, especially in ways that particularly fit their virtues or crimes.

Poetic License: Distortions of fact and literary convention made by a writer—not always a poet—for the sake of the effect gained. Poetic license is closely related to the concept of "artistic freedom."

Poetics: This term has two closely related meanings. It denotes (1) an aesthetic theory in literary criticism about the essence of poetry or (2) rules prescribing the proper methods, content, style, or diction of poetry. The term poetics may also refer to theories about literature in general, not just poetry.

Poetry: In its broadest sense, writing that aims to present ideas and evoke an emotional experience in the reader through the use of meter, imagery, connotative and concrete words, and a carefully constructed structure based on rhythmic patterns. Poetry typically relies on words and expressions that have several layers of meaning. It also makes use of the effects of regular rhythm on the ear and may make a strong appeal to the senses through the use of imagery.

Point of View: The narrative perspective from which a literary work is presented to the reader. There are four traditional points of view. The "third person omniscient" gives the reader a "godlike" perspective, unrestricted by time or place, from which to see actions and look into the minds of characters. This allows the author to comment openly on characters and events in the work. The "third person" point of view presents the events of the story from outside of any single character's perception, much like the omniscient point of view, but the reader must understand the action as it takes place and without any special insight into characters' minds or motivations. The "first person" or "personal" point of view relates events as they are perceived by a single character. The main character "tells" the story and may offer opinions about the action and characters which differ from those of the author. Much less common than omniscient, third person, and first person is the "second person" point of view, wherein the author tells the story as if it is happening to the reader.

Polemic: A work in which the author takes a stand on a controversial subject, such as abortion or religion. Such works are often extremely argumentative or provocative.

Pornography: Writing intended to provoke feelings of lust in the reader. Such works are often condemned by critics and teachers, but those which can be shown to have literary value are viewed less harshly.

Post-Aesthetic Movement: An artistic response made by African Americans to the black aesthetic movement of the 1960s and early '70s. Writers since that time have adopted a somewhat different tone in their work, with less emphasis placed on the disparity between black and white in the United States. In the words of post-aesthetic authors such as Toni Morrison, John Edgar Wideman, and Kristin Hunter, African Americans are portrayed as looking inward for answers to their own questions, rather than always looking to the outside world.

Postmodernism: Writing from the 1960s forward characterized by experimentation and continuing to apply some of the fundamentals of modernism, which included existentialism and alienation. Postmodernists have gone a step further in the rejection of tradition begun with the modernists by also rejecting traditional forms, preferring the anti-novel over the novel and the anti-hero over the hero.

Pre-Raphaelites: A circle of writers and artists in mid nineteenth-century England. Valuing the pre-Renaissance artistic qualities of religious symbolism, lavish pictorialism, and natural sensuousness, the Pre-Raphaelites cultivated a sense of mystery and melancholy that influenced later writers associated with the Symbolist and Decadent movements.

Primitivism: The belief that primitive peoples were nobler and less flawed than civilized peoples because they had not been subjected to the tainting influence of society.

Projective Verse: A form of free verse in which the poet's breathing pattern determines the lines of the poem. Poets who advocate projective verse are against all formal structures in writing, including meter and form.

Prologue: An introductory section of a literary work. It often contains information establishing the situation of the characters or presents information about the setting, time period, or action. In drama, the prologue is spoken by a chorus or by one of the principal characters.

Prose: A literary medium that attempts to mirror the language of everyday speech. It is distinguished from poetry by its use of unmetered, unrhymed language consisting of logically related sentences. Prose is usually grouped into paragraphs that form a cohesive whole such as an essay or a novel.

Prosopopoeia: See *Personification*

Protagonist: The central character of a story who serves as a focus for its themes and incidents and as the principal rationale for its development. The protagonist is sometimes referred to in discussions of modern literature as the hero or anti-hero.

Proverb: A brief, sage saying that expresses a truth about life in a striking manner.

Pseudonym: A name assumed by a writer, most often intended to prevent his or her identification as the author of a work. Two or more authors may work together under one pseudonym, or an author may use a different name for each genre he or she publishes in. Some publishing companies maintain "house pseudonyms," under which any number of authors may write installations in a series. Some authors also choose a pseudonym over their real names the way an actor may use a stage name.

Pun: A play on words that have similar sounds but different meanings.

Pure Poetry: poetry written without instructional intent or moral purpose that aims only to please a reader by its imagery or musical flow. The term pure poetry is used as the antonym of the term "didacticism."

Q

Quatrain: A four-line stanza of a poem or an entire poem consisting of four lines.

R

Realism: A nineteenth-century European literary movement that sought to portray familiar characters, situations, and settings in a realistic manner. This was done primarily by using an objective narrative point of view and through the buildup of accurate detail. The standard for success of any realistic work depends on how faithfully it transfers common experience into fictional forms. The realistic method may be altered or extended, as in stream of consciousness writing, to record highly subjective experience.

Refrain: A phrase repeated at intervals throughout a poem. A refrain may appear at the end of each stanza or at less regular intervals. It may be altered slightly at each appearance.

Renaissance: The period in European history that marked the end of the Middle Ages. It began in Italy in the late fourteenth century. In broad terms, it is usually seen as spanning the fourteenth, fifteenth, and sixteenth centuries, although it did not reach Great Britain, for example, until the 1480s or so. The Renaissance saw an awakening in almost every sphere of human activity, especially science, philosophy, and the arts. The period is best defined by the emergence of a general philosophy that emphasized the importance of the intellect, the individual, and world affairs. It contrasts strongly with the medieval worldview, characterized by the dominant concerns of faith, the social collective, and spiritual salvation.

Repartee: Conversation featuring snappy retorts and witticisms.

Restoration: See *Restoration Age*

Restoration Age: A period in English literature beginning with the crowning of Charles II in 1660 and running to about 1700. The era, which was characterized by a reaction against Puritanism, was the first great age of the comedy of manners. The finest literature of the era is typically witty and urbane, and often lewd.

Rhetoric: In literary criticism, this term denotes the art of ethical persuasion. In its strictest sense, rhetoric adheres to various principles developed since classical times for arranging facts and ideas in a clear, persuasive, appealing manner. The term is also used to refer to effective prose in general and theories of or methods for composing effective prose.

Rhetorical Question: A question intended to provoke thought, but not an expressed answer, in the reader. It is most commonly used in oratory and other persuasive genres.

Rhyme: When used as a noun in literary criticism, this term generally refers to a poem in which words sound identical or very similar and appear in parallel positions in two or more lines. Rhymes are classified into different types according to where they fall in a line or stanza or according to the degree of similarity they exhibit in their spellings and sounds. Some major types of rhyme are "masculine" rhyme, "feminine" rhyme, and "triple" rhyme. In a masculine rhyme, the rhyming sound falls in a single accented syllable, as with "heat" and "eat." Feminine rhyme is a rhyme of two syllables, one stressed and one unstressed, as with "merry" and "tarry." Triple rhyme matches the sound of the accented syllable and the two unaccented syllables that follow: "narrative" and "declarative."

Rhyme Royal: A stanza of seven lines composed in iambic pentameter and rhymed *ababbcc*. The name is said to be a tribute to King James I of Scotland, who made much use of the form in his poetry.

Rhyme Scheme: See *Rhyme*

Rhythm: A regular pattern of sound, time intervals, or events occurring in writing, most often and most discernably in poetry. Regular, reliable rhythm is known to be soothing to humans, while interrupted, unpredictable, or rapidly changing rhythm is disturbing. These effects are known to authors, who use them to produce a desired reaction in the reader.

Rococo: A style of European architecture that flourished in the eighteenth century, especially in France. The most notable features of *rococo* are its extensive use of ornamentation and its themes of lightness, gaiety, and intimacy. In literary criticism, the term is often used disparagingly to refer to a decadent or over-ornamental style.

Romance: A broad term, usually denoting a narrative with exotic, exaggerated, often idealized characters, scenes, and themes.

Romantic Age: See *Romanticism*

Romanticism: This term has two widely accepted meanings. In historical criticism, it refers to a European intellectual and artistic movement of the late eighteenth and early nineteenth centuries that sought greater freedom of personal expression than that allowed by the strict rules of literary form and logic of the eighteenth-century neoclassicists. The Romantics preferred emotional and imaginative expression to rational analysis. They considered the individual to be at the center of all experience and so placed him or her at the center of their art. The Romantics believed that the creative imagination reveals nobler truths—unique feelings and attitudes—than those that could be discovered by logic or by scientific examination. Both the natural world and the state of childhood were important sources for revelations of "eternal truths." "Romanticism" is also used as a general term to refer to a type of sensibility found in all periods of literary history and usually considered to be in opposition to the principles of classicism. In this sense, Romanticism signifies any work or philosophy in which the exotic or dreamlike figure strongly, or that is devoted to individualistic expression, self-analysis, or a pursuit of a higher realm of knowledge than can be discovered by human reason.

Romantics: See *Romanticism*

Russian Symbolism: A Russian poetic movement, derived from French symbolism, that flourished between 1894 and 1910. While some Russian Symbolists continued in the French tradition, stressing aestheticism and the importance of suggestion above didactic intent, others saw their craft as a form of mystical worship, and themselves as mediators between the supernatural and the mundane.

S

Satire: A work that uses ridicule, humor, and wit to criticize and provoke change in human nature and institutions. There are two major types of satire: "formal" or "direct" satire speaks directly to the reader or to a character in the work; "indirect" satire relies upon the ridiculous behavior of its characters to make its point. Formal satire is further divided into two manners: the "Horatian," which ridicules gently, and the "Juvenalian," which derides its subjects harshly and bitterly.

Scansion: The analysis or "scanning" of a poem to determine its meter and often its rhyme scheme. The most common system of scansion uses accents (slanted lines drawn above syllables) to show stressed syllables, breves (curved lines drawn above syllables) to show unstressed syllables, and vertical lines to separate each foot.

Second Person: See *Point of View*

Semiotics: The study of how literary forms and conventions affect the meaning of language.

Sestet: Any six-line poem or stanza.

Setting: The time, place, and culture in which the action of a narrative takes place. The elements of setting may include geographic location, characters' physical and mental environments, prevailing cultural attitudes, or the historical time in which the action takes place.

Shakespearean Sonnet: See *Sonnet*

Signifying Monkey: A popular trickster figure in black folklore, with hundreds of tales about this character documented since the 19th century.

Simile: A comparison, usually using "like" or "as," of two essentially dissimilar things, as in "coffee as cold as ice" or "He sounded like a broken record."

Slang: A type of informal verbal communication that is generally unacceptable for formal writing. Slang words and phrases are often colorful exaggerations used to emphasize the speaker's point; they may also be shortened versions of an often-used word or phrase.

Slant Rhyme: See *Consonance*

Slave Narrative: Autobiographical accounts of American slave life as told by escaped slaves. These works first appeared during the abolition movement of the 1830s through the 1850s.

Social Realism: See *Socialist Realism*

Socialist Realism: The Socialist Realism school of literary theory was proposed by Maxim Gorky and established as a dogma by the first Soviet Congress of Writers. It demanded adherence to a communist worldview in works of literature. Its doctrines required an objective viewpoint comprehensible to the working classes and themes of social struggle featuring strong proletarian heroes.

Soliloquy: A monologue in a drama used to give the audience information and to develop the speaker's character. It is typically a projection of the speaker's innermost thoughts. Usually delivered while the speaker is alone on stage, a soliloquy is intended to present an illusion of unspoken reflection.

Sonnet: A fourteen-line poem, usually composed in iambic pentameter, employing one of several rhyme schemes. There are three major types of sonnets, upon which all other variations of the form are based: the "Petrarchan" or "Italian" sonnet, the "Shakespearean" or "English" sonnet, and the "Spenserian" sonnet. A Petrarchan sonnet consists of an octave rhymed *abbaabba* and a "sestet" rhymed either *cdecde, cdccdc,* or *cdedce.* The octave poses a question or problem, relates a narrative, or puts forth a proposition; the sestet presents a solution to the problem, comments upon the narrative, or applies the proposition put forth in the octave. The Shakespearean sonnet is divided into three quatrains and a couplet rhymed *abab cdcd efef gg.* The couplet provides an epigrammatic comment on the narrative or problem put forth in the quatrains. The Spenserian sonnet uses three quatrains and a couplet like the Shakespearean, but links their three rhyme schemes in this way: *abab bcbc cdcd ee.* The Spenserian sonnet develops its theme in two parts like the Petrarchan, its final six lines resolving a problem, analyzing a narrative, or applying a proposition put forth in its first eight lines.

Spenserian Sonnet: See *Sonnet*

Spenserian Stanza: A nine-line stanza having eight verses in iambic pentameter, its ninth verse in iambic hexameter, and the rhyme scheme ababbcbcc.

Spondee: In poetry meter, a foot consisting of two long or stressed syllables occurring together. This form is quite rare in English verse, and is usually composed of two monosyllabic words.

Sprung Rhythm: Versification using a specific number of accented syllables per line but disregarding the number of unaccented syllables that fall in each line, producing an irregular rhythm in the poem.

Stanza: A subdivision of a poem consisting of lines grouped together, often in recurring patterns of rhyme, line length, and meter. Stanzas may also serve as units of thought in a poem much like paragraphs in prose.

Stereotype: A stereotype was originally the name for a duplication made during the printing process; this led to its modern definition as a person or thing that is (or is assumed to be) the same as all others of its type.

Stream of Consciousness: A narrative technique for rendering the inward experience of a character. This technique is designed to give the impression of an ever-changing series of thoughts, emotions, images, and memories in the spontaneous and seemingly illogical order that they occur in life.

Structuralism: A twentieth-century movement in literary criticism that examines how literary texts arrive at their meanings, rather than the meanings themselves. There are two major types of structuralist analysis: one examines the way patterns of linguistic structures unify a specific text and emphasize certain elements of that text, and the other interprets the way literary forms and conventions affect the meaning of language itself.

Structure: The form taken by a piece of literature. The structure may be made obvious for ease of understanding, as in nonfiction works, or may obscured for artistic purposes, as in some poetry or seemingly "unstructured" prose.

Sturm und Drang: A German term meaning "storm and stress." It refers to a German literary movement of the 1770s and 1780s that reacted against the order and rationalism of the enlightenment, focusing instead on the intense experience of extraordinary individuals.

Style: A writer's distinctive manner of arranging words to suit his or her ideas and purpose in writing. The unique imprint of the author's personality upon his or her writing, style is the product of an author's way of arranging ideas and his or her use of diction, different sentence structures, rhythm, figures of speech, rhetorical principles, and other elements of composition.

Subject: The person, event, or theme at the center of a work of literature. A work may have one or more subjects of each type, with shorter works tending to have fewer and longer works tending to have more.

Subjectivity: Writing that expresses the author's personal feelings about his subject, and which may or may not include factual information about the subject.

Surrealism: A term introduced to criticism by Guillaume Apollinaire and later adopted by Andre Breton. It refers to a French literary and artistic movement founded in the 1920s. The Surrealists sought to express unconscious thoughts and feelings in their works. The best-known technique used for achieving this aim was automatic writing—transcriptions of spontaneous outpourings from the unconscious. The Surrealists proposed to unify the contrary levels of conscious and unconscious, dream and reality, objectivity and subjectivity into a new level of "super-realism."

Suspense: A literary device in which the author maintains the audience's attention through the buildup of events, the outcome of which will soon be revealed.

Syllogism: A method of presenting a logical argument. In its most basic form, the syllogism consists of a major premise, a minor premise, and a conclusion.

Symbol: Something that suggests or stands for something else without losing its original identity. In literature, symbols combine their literal meaning with the suggestion of an abstract concept. Literary symbols are of two types: those that carry complex associations of meaning no matter what their contexts, and those that derive their suggestive meaning from their functions in specific literary works.

Symbolism: This term has two widely accepted meanings. In historical criticism, it denotes an early modernist literary movement initiated in France during the nineteenth century that reacted against the prevailing standards of realism. Writers in this movement aimed to evoke, indirectly and symbolically, an order of being beyond the material world of the five senses. Poetic expression of personal emotion figured strongly in the movement, typically by means of a private set of symbols uniquely identifiable with the individual poet. The principal aim of the Symbolists was to express in words the highly complex feelings that grew out of everyday contact with the world. In a broader sense, the term "symbolism" refers to the use of one object to represent another.

Symbolist: See *Symbolism*

Symbolist Movement: See *Symbolism*

Sympathetic Fallacy: See *Affective Fallacy*

T

Tanka: A form of Japanese poetry similar to *haiku*. A *tanka* is five lines long, with the lines containing five, seven, five, seven, and seven syllables respectively.

Terza Rima: A three-line stanza form in poetry in which the rhymes are made on the last word of each line in the following manner: the first and third lines of the first stanza, then the second line of the first stanza and the first and third lines of the second stanza, and so on with the middle line of any stanza rhyming with the first and third lines of the following stanza.

Tetrameter: See *Meter*

Textual Criticism: A branch of literary criticism that seeks to establish the authoritative text of a literary work. Textual critics typically compare all known manuscripts or printings of a single work in order to assess the meanings of differences and revisions. This procedure allows them to arrive at a definitive version that (supposedly) corresponds to the author's original intention.

Theme: The main point of a work of literature. The term is used interchangeably with thesis.

Thesis: A thesis is both an essay and the point argued in the essay. Thesis novels and thesis plays share the quality of containing a thesis which is supported through the action of the story.

Third Person: See *Point of View*

Tone: The author's attitude toward his or her audience may be deduced from the tone of the work. A formal tone may create distance or convey politeness, while an informal tone may encourage a friendly, intimate, or intrusive feeling in the reader. The author's attitude toward his or her subject matter may also be deduced from the tone of the words he or she uses in discussing it.

Tragedy: A drama in prose or poetry about a noble, courageous hero of excellent character who, because of some tragic character flaw or *hamartia*, brings ruin upon him- or herself. Tragedy treats its subjects in a dignified and serious manner, using poetic language to help evoke pity and fear and bring about catharsis, a purging of these emotions. The tragic form was practiced extensively by the ancient Greeks. In the Middle Ages, when classical works were virtually unknown, tragedy came to denote any works about the fall of persons from exalted to low conditions due to any reason: fate, vice, weakness, etc. According to the classical definition of tragedy, such works present the "pathetic"—that which evokes pity—rather than the tragic. The classical form of tragedy was revived in the sixteenth century; it flourished especially on the Elizabethan stage. In modern times, dramatists have attempted to adapt the form to the needs of modern society by drawing their heroes from the ranks of ordinary men and women and defining the nobility of these heroes in terms of spirit rather than exalted social standing.

Tragic Flaw: In a tragedy, the quality within the hero or heroine which leads to his or her downfall.

Transcendentalism: An American philosophical and religious movement, based in New England from around 1835 until the Civil War. Transcendentalism was a form of American romanticism that had its roots abroad in the works of Thomas Carlyle, Samuel Coleridge, and Johann Wolfgang von Goethe. The Transcendentalists stressed the importance of intuition and subjective experience in communication with God. They rejected religious dogma and texts in favor of mysticism and scientific naturalism. They pursued truths that lie beyond the "colorless" realms perceived by reason and the senses and were active social reformers in public education, women's rights, and the abolition of slavery.

Trickster: A character or figure common in Native American and African literature who uses his ingenuity to defeat enemies and escape difficult situations. Tricksters are most often animals, such as the spider, hare, or coyote, although they may take the form of humans as well.

Trimeter: See *Meter*

Triple Rhyme: See *Rhyme*

Trochee: See *Foot*

U

Understatement: See *Irony*

Unities: Strict rules of dramatic structure, formulated by Italian and French critics of the Renaissance and based loosely on the principles of drama discussed by Aristotle in his *Poetics*. Foremost among these rules were the three unities of action, time, and place that compelled a dramatist to: (1) construct a single plot with a beginning, middle, and end that details the causal relationships of action and character; (2) restrict the action to the events of a single day; and (3) limit the scene to a single place or city. The unities were observed faithfully by continental European writers until the Romantic Age, but they were never regularly observed in English drama. Modern dramatists are typically more concerned with a unity of impression or emotional effect than with any of the classical unities.

Urban Realism: A branch of realist writing that attempts to accurately reflect the often harsh facts of modern urban existence.

Utopia: A fictional perfect place, such as "paradise" or "heaven."

Utopian: See *Utopia*

Utopianism: See *Utopia*

V

Verisimilitude: Literally, the appearance of truth. In literary criticism, the term refers to aspects of a work of literature that seem true to the reader.

Vers de societe: See *Occasional Verse*

Vers libre: See *Free Verse*

Verse: A line of metered language, a line of a poem, or any work written in verse.

Versification: The writing of verse. Versification may also refer to the meter, rhyme, and other mechanical components of a poem.

Victorian: Refers broadly to the reign of Queen Victoria of England (1837-1901) and to anything with qualities typical of that era. For example, the qualities of smug narrow-mindedness, bourgeois materialism, faith in social progress, and priggish morality are often considered Victorian. This stereotype is contradicted by such dramatic intellectual developments as the theories of Charles Darwin, Karl Marx, and Sigmund Freud (which stirred strong debates in England) and the critical attitudes of serious Victorian writers like Charles Dickens and George Eliot. In literature, the Victorian Period was the great age of the English novel, and the latter part of the era saw the rise of movements such as decadence and symbolism.

Victorian Age: See *Victorian*

Victorian Period: See *Victorian*

W

Weltanschauung: A German term referring to a person's worldview or philosophy.

Weltschmerz: A German term meaning "world pain." It describes a sense of anguish about the nature of existence, usually associated with a melancholy, pessimistic attitude.

Z

Zarzuela: A type of Spanish operetta.

Zeitgeist: A German term meaning "spirit of the time." It refers to the moral and intellectual trends of a given era.

Cumulative Author/Title Index

Cumulative Nationality/Ethnicity Index

Subject/Theme Index

Cumulative Index of First Lines

Had we but world enough, and time
(To His Coy Mistress) V5:276

Hail to thee, blithe Spirit! (To a
Sky-Lark) V32:251

Half a league, half a league (The
Charge of the Light Brigade)
V1:2

Having a Coke with You (Having a
Coke with You) V12:105

He clasps the crag with crooked
hands (The Eagle) V11:30

He was found by the Bureau of
Statistics to be (The Unknown
Citizen) V3:302

He was seen, surrounded by rifles,
(The Crime Was in Granada)
V23:55–56

Hear the sledges with the bells—
(The Bells) V3:46

Heart, you bully, you punk, I'm
wrecked, I'm shocked (One Is
One) V24:158

Her body is not so white as (Queen-
Ann's-Lace) V6:179

Her eyes the glow-worm lend thee;
(The Night Piece: To Julia)
V29:206

Her eyes were coins of porter and her
West (A Farewell to English)
V10:126

Here, above, (The Man-Moth)
V27:135

Here they are. The soft eyes open
(The Heaven of Animals) V6:75

His Grace! impossible! what dead!
(A Satirical Elegy on the Death
of a Late Famous General)
V27:216

His speed and strength, which is the
strength of ten (His Speed and
Strength) V19:96

Hog Butcher for the World
(Chicago) V3:61

Hold fast to dreams (Dream
Variations) V15:42

Hope is a tattered flag and a dream
out of time. (Hope is a Tattered
Flag) V12:120

"Hope" is the thing with feathers—
("Hope" Is the Thing with
Feathers) V3:123

How do I love thee? Let me count the
ways (Sonnet 43) V2:236

How is your life with the other one,
(An Attempt at Jealousy)
V29:23

How shall we adorn (Angle of Geese)
V2:2

How soon hath Time, the subtle thief
of youth, (On His Having
Arrived at the Age of Twenty-
Three) V17:159

How would it be if you took yourself
off (Landscape with Tractor)
V10:182

Hunger crawls into you (Hunger in
New York City) V4:79

I

I am fourteen (Hanging Fire)
V32:93

I am not a painter, I am a poet
(Why I Am Not a Painter)
V8:258

I am not with those who abandoned
their land (I Am Not One of
Those Who Left the Land)
V36:91

I am silver and exact. I have no
preconceptions (Mirror)
V1:116

I am the Smoke King (The Song of
the Smoke) V13:196

I am trying to pry open your casket
(Dear Reader) V10:85

I became a creature of light
(The Mystery) V15:137

I Built My Hut beside a Traveled
Road (I Built My Hut beside a
Traveled Road) V36:119

I cannot love the Brothers Wright
(Reactionary Essay on Applied
Science) V9:199

I caught a tremendous fish
(The Fish) V31:44

I died for Beauty—but was scarce
(I Died for Beauty) V28:174

I don't mean to make you cry.
(Monologue for an Onion)
V24:120–121

I don't want my daughter (Fear)
V37:71

I do not know what it means that
(The Lorelei) V37:145

I felt a Funeral, in my Brain, (I felt a
Funeral in my Brain) V13:137

I gave birth to life. (Maternity)
V21:142–143

I have been one acquainted with the
night. (Acquainted with the
Night) V35:3

I have eaten (This Is Just to Say)
V34:240

I have just come down from my
father (The Hospital Window)
V11:58

I have met them at close of day
(Easter 1916) V5:91

I have sown beside all waters in my
day. (A Black Man Talks of
Reaping) V32:20

I haven't the heart to say (To an
Unknown Poet) V18:221

I hear America singing, the varied
carols I hear (I Hear America
Singing) V3:152

I heard a Fly buzz—when I died—
(I Heard a Fly Buzz— When I
Died—) V5:140

I know that I shall meet my fate
(An Irish Airman Foresees His
Death) V1:76

I know what the caged bird feels,
alas! (Sympathy) V33:203

I leant upon a coppice gate
(The Darkling Thrush) V18:74

I lie down on my side in the moist
grass (Omen) v22:107

I looked in my heart while the wild
swans went over. (Wild Swans)
V17:221

I love to go out in late September
(Blackberry Eating) V35:23

I met a traveller from an antique land
(Ozymandias) V27:173

I prove a theorem and the house
expands: (Geometry) V15:68

I saw that a star had broken its rope
(Witness) V26:285

I see them standing at the formal
gates of their colleges, (I go
Back to May 1937) V17:112

I shall die, but that is all that I shall
do for Death. (Conscientious
Objector) V34:46

I shook your hand before I went.
(Mastectomy) V26:122

I sit in one of the dives (September 1,
1939) V27:234

I sit in the top of the wood, my eyes
closed (Hawk Roosting) V4:55

I thought, as I wiped my eyes on the
corner of my apron: (An
Ancient Gesture) V31:3

I thought wearing an evergreen dress
(Pine) V23:223–224

I, too, sing America. (I, Too) V30:99

I wandered lonely as a cloud
(I Wandered Lonely as a Cloud)
V33:71

I was angry with my friend;
(A Poison Tree) V24:195–196

I was born in the congo (Ego-
Tripping) V28:112

I was born too late and I am much too
old, (Death Sentences) V22:23

I was born under the mudbank
(Seeing You) V24:244–245

I was sitting in mcsorley's. outside it
was New York and beautifully
snowing. (i was sitting in
mcsorley's) V13:151

I WENT to the dances at
Chandlerville, (Lucinda
Matlock) V37:171

Pilgrimage, Canto IV, stanzas 178–184) V35:46

There is no way not to be excited (Paradiso) V20:190–191

There is the one song everyone (Siren Song) V7:196

There will come soft rains and the smell of the ground, (There Will Come Soft Rains) V14:301

There you are, in all your innocence, (Perfect Light) V19:187

There's a Certain Slant of Light (There's a Certain Slant of Light) V6:211

There's no way out. (In the Suburbs) V14:201

These open years, the river (For Jennifer, 6, on the Teton) V17:86

These unprepossessing sunsets (Art Thou the Thing I Wanted) V25:2–3

They eat beans mostly, this old yellow pair (The Bean Eaters) V2:16

They said, "Wait." Well, I waited. (Alabama Centennial) V10:2

They say a child with two mouths is no good. (Pantoun for Chinese Women) V29:241

they were just meant as covers (My Mother Pieced Quilts) V12:169

This girlchild was: born as usual (Barbie Doll) V9:33

This is a litany of lost things, (The Litany) V24:101–102

This is my letter to the World (This Is My Letter to the World) V4:233

This is the Arsenal. From floor to ceiling, (The Arsenal at Springfield) V17:2

This is the black sea-brute bulling through wave-wrack (Leviathan) V5:203

This is the ship of pearl, which, poets feign, (The Chambered Nautilus) V24:52–53

This poem is concerned with language on a very plain level (Paradoxes and Oxymorons) V11:162

This tale is true, and mine. It tells (The Seafarer) V8:177

Thou still unravish'd bride of quietness (Ode on a Grecian Urn) V1:179

Three days Natasha'd been astray, (The Bridegroom) V34:26

Three times my life has opened. (Three Times My Life Has Opened) V16:213

Time in school drags along with so much worry, (Childhood) V19:29

to fold the clothes. No matter who lives (I Stop Writing the Poem) V16:58

To him who in the love of Nature holds (Thanatopsis) V30:232–233

To replay errors (Daughter-Mother-Maya-Seeta) V25:83

To weep unbidden, to wake (Practice) V23:240

Toni Morrison despises (The Toni Morrison Dreams) V22:202–203

Tonight I can write the saddest lines (Tonight I Can Write) V11:187

tonite, *thriller* was (Beware: Do Not Read This Poem) V6:3

Truth be told, I do not want to forget (Native Guard) V29:183

Turning and turning in the widening gyre (The Second Coming) V7:179

'Twas brillig, and the slithy toves (Jabberwocky) V11:91

'Twas mercy brought me from my pagan land, (On Being Brought from Africa to America) V29:223

Two roads diverged in a yellow wood (The Road Not Taken) V2:195

Tyger! Tyger! burning bright (The Tyger) V2:263

W

wade (The Fish) V14:171

Wailing of a flute, a little drum (In Music) V35:105

Wanting to say things, (My Father's Song) V16:102

We are saying goodbye (Station) V21:226–227

We came from our own country in a red room (Originally) V25:146–147

We cannot know his legendary head (Archaic Torso of Apollo) V27:3

We could be here. This is the valley (Small Town with One Road) V7:207

We met the British in the dead of winter (Meeting the British) V7:138

We real cool. We (We Real Cool) V6:242

We tied branches to our helmets. (Camouflaging the Chimera) V37:21

Well, son, I'll tell you (Mother to Son) V3:178

What dire offense from amorous causes springs, (The Rape of the Lock) V12:202

What happens to a dream deferred? (Harlem) V1:63

What I expected was (What I expected) V36:313–314

What of the neighborhood homes awash (The Continuous Life) V18:51

What passing-bells for these who die as cattle? (Anthem for Doomed Youth) V37:3

What thoughts I have of you tonight, Walt Whitman, for I walked down the sidestreets under the trees with a headache self-conscious looking at the full moon (A Supermarket in California) V5:261

Whatever it is, it must have (American Poetry) V7:2

When Abraham Lincoln was shoveled into the tombs, he forgot the copperheads, and the assassin . . . in the dust, in the cool tombs (Cool Tombs) V6:45

When despair for the world grows in me (The Peace of Wild Things) V30:159

When he spoke of where he came from, (Grudnow) V32:73

When I consider how my light is spent ([On His Blindness] Sonnet 16) V3:262

When I consider how my light is spent (When I Consider (Sonnet XIX) V37:302

When I die, I want your hands on my eyes: (Sonnet LXXXIX) V35:259

When I go away from you (The Taxi) V30:211–212

When I have fears that I may cease to be (When I Have Fears that I May Cease to Be) V2:295

When I heard the learn'd astronomer, (When I Heard the Learn'd Astronomer) V22:244

When I see a couple of kids (High Windows) V3:108

When I see birches bend to left and right (Birches) V13:14

When I was a child (Autobiographia Literaria) V34:2

When I was born, you waited (Having it Out with Melancholy) V17:98

When I was one-and-twenty (When I Was One-and-Twenty) V4:268

When I watch you (Miss Rosie) V1:133

Cumulative Index of Last Lines

I am not brave at all (Strong Men, Riding Horses) V4:209

I could not see to see— (I Heard a Fly Buzz—When I Died—) V5:140

I cremated Sam McGee (The Cremation of Sam McGee) V10:76

I didn't want to put them down. (And What If I Spoke of Despair) V19:2

I have been one acquainted with the night. (Acquainted with the Night) V35:3

I have just come down from my father (The Hospital Window) V11:58

I hear it in the deep heart's core. (The Lake Isle of Innisfree) V15:121

I know why the caged bird sings! (Sympathy) V33:203

I lift my lamp beside the golden door!" (The New Colossus) V37:239

I never writ, nor no man ever loved (Sonnet 116) V3:288

I rest in the grace of the world, and am free. (The Peace of Wild Things) V30:159

I romp with joy in the bookish dark (Eating Poetry) V9:61

I see Mike's painting, called SARDINES (Why I Am Not a Painter) V8:259

I shall but love thee better after death (Sonnet 43) V2:236

I should be glad of another death (Journey of the Magi) V7:110

I stand up (Miss Rosie) V1:133

I stood there, fifteen (Fifteen) V2:78

I take it you are he? (Incident in a Rose Garden) V14:191

I, too, am America. (I, Too) V30:99

I turned aside and bowed my head and wept (The Tropics in New York) V4:255

I would like to tell, but lack the words. (I Built My Hut beside a Traveled Road) V36:119

If Winter comes, can Spring be far behind? (Ode to the West Wind) V2:163

I'll be gone from here. (The Cobweb) V17:51

I'll dig with it (Digging) V5:71

Imagine! (Autobiographia Literaria) V34:2

In a convulsive misery (The Milkfish Gatherers) V11:112

In balance with this life, this death (An Irish Airman Foresees His Death) V1:76

in earth's gasp, ocean's yawn. (Lake) V23:158

In Flanders fields (In Flanders Fields) V5:155

In ghostlier demarcations, keener sounds. (The Idea of Order at Key West) V13:164

In hearts at peace, under an English heaven (The Soldier) V7:218

In her tomb by the side of the sea (Annabel Lee) V9:14

in the family of things. (Wild Geese) V15:208

in the grit gray light of day. (Daylights) V13:102

In the rear-view mirrors of the passing cars (The War Against the Trees) V11:216

In these Chicago avenues. (A Thirst Against) V20:205

in this bastion of culture. (To an Unknown Poet) V18:221

in your unsteady, opening hand. (What the Poets Could Have Been) V26:262

iness (l(a) V1:85

Into blossom (A Blessing) V7:24

Is Come, my love is come to me. (A Birthday) V10:34

is love—that's all. (Two Poems for T.) V20:218

is safe is what you said. (Practice) V23:240

is still warm (Lament for the Dorsets) V5:191

It asked a crumb—of Me ("Hope" Is the Thing with Feathers) V3:123

It had no mirrors. I no longer needed mirrors. (I, I, I) V26:97

It is our god. (Fiddler Crab) V23:111–112

it is the bell to awaken God that we've heard ringing. (The Garden Shukkei-en) V18:107

it over my face and mouth. (An Anthem) V26:34

It rains as I write this. Mad heart, be brave. (The Country Without a Post Office) V18:64

It takes life to love life. (Lucinda Matlock) V37:172

It was your resting place." (Ah, Are You Digging on My Grave?) V4:2

it's always ourselves we find in the sea (maggie & milly & molly & may) V12:150

its bright, unequivocal eye. (Having it Out with Melancholy) V17:99

It's the fall through wind lifting white leaves. (Rapture) V21:181

its youth. The sea grows old in it. (The Fish) V14:172

J

Judge tenderly—of Me (This Is My Letter to the World) V4:233

Just imagine it (Inventors) V7:97

K

kisses you (Grandmother) V34:95

L

Laughing the stormy, husky, brawling laughter of Youth, half-naked, sweating, proud to be Hog Butcher, Tool Maker, Stacker of Wheat, Player with Railroads and Freight Handler to the Nation (Chicago) V3:61

Learn to labor and to wait (A Psalm of Life) V7:165

Leashed in my throat (Midnight) V2:131

Leaving thine outgrown shell by life's un-resting sea (The Chambered Nautilus) V24:52–53

Let my people go (Go Down, Moses) V11:43

Let the water come. (America, America) V29:4

life, our life and its forgetting. (For a New Citizen of These United States) V15:55

Life to Victory (Always) V24:15

like a bird in the sky ... (Ego-Tripping) V28:113

like a shadow or a friend. *Colombia.* (Kindness) V24:84–85

Like Stone— (The Soul Selects Her Own Society) V1:259

Little Lamb, God bless thee. (The Lamb) V12:135

Look'd up in perfect silence at the stars. (When I Heard the Learn'd Astronomer) V22:244

love (The Toni Morrison Dreams) V22:202–203

Loved I not Honour more. (To Lucasta, Going to the Wars) V32:291

Luck was rid of its clover. (Yet we insist that life is full of happy chance) V27:292

M

'Make a wish, Tom, make a wish.' (Drifters) V10: 98

make it seem to change (The Moon Glows the Same) V7:152

The self-same Power that brought me there brought you. (The Rhodora) V17:191

The shaft we raise to them and thee (Concord Hymn) V4:30

the skin of another, what I have made is a curse. (Curse) V26:75

The sky became a still and woven blue. (Merlin Enthralled) V16:73

The song of the Lorelei. (The Lorelei) V37:146

The spirit of this place (To a Child Running With Outstretched Arms in Canyon de Chelly) V11:173

The town again, trailing your legs and crying! (Wild Swans) V17:221

the unremitting space of your rebellion (Lost Sister) V5:217

The woman won (Oysters) V4:91

The world should listen then—as I am listening now. (To a Sky-Lark) V32:252

their dinnerware. (Portrait of a Couple at Century's End) V24:214–215

their guts or their brains? (Southbound on the Freeway) V16:158

Then chiefly lives. (Virtue) V25:263

There are blows in life, so hard ... I just don't know! (The Black Heralds) V26:47

There is the trap that catches noblest spirits, that caught— they say— God, when he walked on earth (Shine, Perishing Republic) V4:162

there was light (Vancouver Lights) V8:246

They also serve who only stand and wait." ([On His Blindness] Sonnet 16) V3:262

They also serve who only stand and wait." (When I Consider (Sonnet XIX)) V37:302

They are going to some point true and unproven. (Geometry) V15:68

They have not sown, and feed on bitter fruit. (A Black Man Talks of Reaping) V32:21

They rise, they walk again (The Heaven of Animals) V6:76

They say a child with two mouths is no good. (Pantoun for Chinese Women) V29:242

They think I lost. I think I won (Harlem Hopscotch) V2:93

They'd eaten every one." (The Walrus and the Carpenter) V30:258–259

This is my page for English B (Theme for English B) V6:194

This Love (In Memory of Radio) V9:145

Tho' it were ten thousand mile! (A Red, Red Rose) V8:152

Though I sang in my chains like the sea (Fern Hill) V3:92

Till human voices wake us, and we drown (The Love Song of J. Alfred Prufrock) V1:99

Till Love and Fame to nothingness do sink (When I Have Fears that I May Cease to Be) V2:295

Till the gossamer thread you fling catch somewhere, O my soul. (A Noiseless Patient Spider) V31:190–91

To an admiring Bog! (I'm Nobody! Who Are You?) V35:83

To be a queen! (Fear) V37:71

To every woman a happy ending (Barbie Doll) V9:33

to float in the space between. (The Idea of Ancestry) V36:138

to glow at midnight. (The Blue Rim of Memory) V17:39

to its owner or what horror has befallen the other shoe (A Piéd) V3:16

To live with thee and be thy love. (The Nymph's Reply to the Shepherd) V14:241

To mock the riddled corpses round Bapaume. ("Blighters") V28:3

To strengthen whilst one stands." (Goblin Market) V27:96

To strive, to seek, to find, and not to yield (Ulysses) V2:279

To the moaning and the groaning of the bells (The Bells) V3:47

To the temple, singing. (In the Suburbs) V14:201

To wound myself upon the sharp edges of the night? (The Taxi) V30:211–212

too. (Birdfoot's Grampa) V36:21

torn from a wedding brocade. (My Mother Combs My Hair) V34:133

Turned to that dirt from whence he sprung. (A Satirical Elegy on the Death of a Late Famous General) V27:216

U

Undeniable selves, into your days, and beyond. (The Continuous Life) V18:51

under each man's eyelid. (Camouflaging the Chimera) V37:21

until at last I lift you up and wrap you within me. (It's like This) V23:138–139

Until Eternity. (The Bustle in a House) V10:62

unusual conservation (Chocolates) V11:17

Uttering cries that are almost human (American Poetry) V7:2

W

War is kind (War Is Kind) V9:253

watching to see how it's done. (I Stop Writing the Poem) V16:58

water. (Poem in Which My Legs Are Accepted) V29:262

We are satisfied, if you are; but why did I die? (Losses) V31:167–68

we tread upon, forgetting. Truth be told. (Native Guard) V29:185

Went home and put a bullet through his head (Richard Cory) V4:117

Were not the one dead, turned to their affairs. (Out, Out—) V10:213

Were toward Eternity— (Because I Could Not Stop for Death) V2:27

What will survive of us is love. (An Arundel Tomb) V12:18

When I died they washed me out of the turret with a hose (The Death of the Ball Turret Gunner) V2:41

when they untie them in the evening. (Early in the Morning) V17:75

when you are at a party. (Social Life) V19:251

When you have both (Toads) V4:244

Where deep in the night I hear a voice (Butcher Shop) V7:43

Where ignorant armies clash by night (Dover Beach) V2:52

Which Claus of Innsbruck cast in bronze for me! (My Last Duchess) V1:166

Which for all you know is the life you've chosen. (The God Who Loves You) V20:88

which is not going to go wasted on me which is why I'm telling you about it (Having a Coke with You) V12:106

which only looks like an *l*, and is silent. (Trompe l'Oeil) V22:216

whirring into her raw skin like stars (Uncoiling) V35:277

white ash amid funereal cypresses (Helen) V6:92

Who are you and what is your purpose? (The Mystery) V15:138

Why am I not as they? (Lineage) V31:145–46

Wi' the Scots lords at his feit (Sir Patrick Spens) V4:177

Will always be ready to bless the day (Morning Walk) V21:167

will be easy, my rancor less bitter . . . (On the Threshold) V22:128

Will hear of as a god." (How we Heard the Name) V10:167

Wind, like the dodo's (Bedtime Story) V8:33

windowpanes. (View) V25:246–247

With courage to endure! (Old Stoic) V33:144

With gold unfading, WASHINGTON! be thine. (To His Excellency General Washington) V13:213

with my eyes closed. (We Live by What We See at Night) V13:240

With silence and tears. (When We Two Parted) V29:297

with the door closed. (Hanging Fire) V32:93

With the slow smokeless burning of decay (The Wood-Pile) V6:252

With what they had to go on. (The Conquerors) V13:67

Without cease or doubt sew the sweet sad earth. (The Satyr's Heart) V22:187

Would scarcely know that we were gone. (There Will Come Soft Rains) V14:301

Wrapped in a larger. (Words are the Diminution of All Things) V35:316

Y

Ye know on earth, and all ye need to know (Ode on a Grecian Urn) V1:180

Yea, beds for all who come. (Up-Hill) V34:280

You live in this, and dwell in lovers' eyes (Sonnet 55) V5:246

You may for ever tarry. (To the Virgins, to Make Much of Time) V13:226

you who raised me? (The Gold Lily) V5:127

You're all that I can call my own. (Woman Work) V33:289

you'll have understood by then what these Ithakas mean. (Ithaka) V19:114